THE PSYCHOLOGY OF WOMEN

THE PSYCHOLOGY OF WOMEN

SIXTH EDITION

Margaret W. Matlin
SUNY Geneseo

THOMSON
WADSWORTH

Australia • Brazil • Canada • Mexico • Singapore
Spain • United Kingdom • United States

The Psychology of Women, Sixth Edition
Margaret W. Matlin

Publisher: *Michele Sordi*
Assistant Editor: *Dan Moneypenny*
Editorial Assistant: *Rachel Guzman*
Technology Project Manager: *Bessie Weiss*
Marketing Manager: *Kimberly Russell*
Marketing Assistant: *Natasha Coats*
Marketing Communications Manager: *Linda Yip*
Project Manager, Editorial Production: *Marti Paul*
Creative Director: *Rob Hugel*
Art Director: *Vernon Boes*

Print Buyer: *Doreen Suruki*
Permissions Editor: *Bob Kauser*
Production Service: *Scratchgravel Publishing Services*
Photo Researcher: *Nicole Root*
Copy Editors: *Pat Tompkins, Carol Lombardi*
Illustrator: *Lotus Art, Greg Draus*
Cover Designer: *Katherine Minerva*
Cover Image: *Elyse Lewin/Getty Images*
Text and Cover Printer: *Thomson West*
Compositor: *ICC Macmillan Inc.*

Printed in the United States of America
1 2 3 4 5 6 7 11 10 09 08 07

Library of Congress Control Number: 2007920374

Student Edition:
ISBN-13: 978-0-495-09154-7
ISBN-10: 0-495-09154-5

International Student Edition:
ISBN-13: 978-0-495-10495-7 (Not for sale in the United States)
ISBN-10: 0-495-10495-7

Thomson Higher Education
10 Davis Drive
Belmont, CA 94002-3098
USA

For more information about our products, contact us at:
Thomson Learning Academic Resource Center
1-800-423-0563
For permission to use material from this text or product, submit a request online at
http://www.thomsonrights.com
Any additional questions about permissions can be submitted by e-mail to
thomsonrights@thomson.com

To the students in my Psychology of Women classes

Brief Contents

CONTENTS

PREFACE

People who trust the popular media would probably conclude that the women's movement is virtually invisible in the current era. Newspapers and magazines seldom discuss the gap between men's and women's salaries. Instead, the articles on the workplace tell us (incorrectly) that thousands of frustrated women are quitting their high-powered jobs so that they can return to their domestic activities.

It is true that the current political climate in the United States is more conservative than when I began teaching a course on the psychology of women during the mid-1970s. However, my own students—and most students who are reading this preface—still react with anger when people are treated unfairly because of their gender, their ethnicity, or some other social category.

My students also demonstrate the same empathy and compassion as those from previous eras. For example, during the week when I was writing this preface, I received emails from three students who had recently taken my psychology of women class. Each of them described how a concern for gender issues and social justice was a central part of their lives. One woman wrote about her challenging job, in which she presented programs about HIV prevention at schools, homeless shelters, and drug-treatment facilities. A second student described her first semester as a graduate student in a public health program. She had written two papers, one on the Women's Health Initiative and another that compared maternal–child health in Finland and in the United States. A third woman wrote about a close friend who had been sexually assaulted. Her experience in helping this friend motivated her to become a volunteer counselor at a rape crisis center.

Fortunately, the subject of the psychology of women is just as exciting and just as rewarding as it was more than three decades ago. One reason is that students now have access to more information. For instance, a course about international or multicultural issues is a requirement for many contemporary students. Furthermore, students can easily locate relevant information through the Internet. As a result, students in the twenty-first century may be better informed, especially about people living in countries outside North America. Ten years ago, when I asked students in my psychology of women class how many had heard about the sweatshop problem, about 20% would raise their hands. When I asked this same question during spring semester in 2006, all the students in my class raised their hands.

Another component of the psychology of women has improved dramatically over the years. When the first edition of this textbook was published in 1987, we had only limited research on many aspects of women's lives. In addition, it was difficult to find women's own descriptions about their experiences. During the 1980s, I couldn't locate much information about women of color. Cross-cultural studies were even less common. In the twenty-first century, it's a unique challenge to keep up with the hundreds of books and thousands of articles published on this subject each year, with many resources addressing the diversity of women.

This sixth edition of *The Psychology of Women* provides a synthesis that guides readers through important facets of women's lives. I have made a special effort to include significant topics that are omitted or abbreviated in most other textbooks: children's gender development, women and work, love relationships, pregnancy and motherhood, women with disabilities, and women in later adulthood.

The resources cited in the reference section represent only a fraction of the literature I examined in preparing this book. In the first edition of *The Psychology of Women,* I commented that many writers would be reluctant to write a textbook about this topic because of the limited research. The explosion of research during recent decades has made the task rewarding, but authors now face a different challenge: The knowledge base about psychology of women could easily fill a multivolume encyclopedia!

TEXT FEATURES AND ORGANIZATION

The sixth edition of *The Psychology of Women* combines both developmental and topical approaches. In the introductory chapter, I present general concepts and several important cautions about research methods and biases. In Chapter 2, we explore some stereotypes that help shape gender-related expectations and behavior. In Chapters 3 and 4, we examine female development throughout infancy, childhood, and adolescence.

In the next nine topical chapters (Chapters 5–13), we consider important components of women's lives. These include cognitive and social gender comparisons (Chapters 5 and 6), work experiences (Chapter 7), love relationships

(Chapter 8), sexuality (Chapter 9), childbirth (Chapter 10), physical and psychological health (Chapters 11 and 12), and violence against women (Chapter 13).

Some of the material in Chapters 5 through 13 also foreshadows the experiences of older women, whose lives are examined in Chapter 14. For example, we consider the long-term romantic relationships of older women in Chapter 8, sexuality and aging in Chapter 9, and health issues in Chapter 11. Following these nine topical chapters, in Chapter 14 we focus specifically on middle-aged and elderly women. In the concluding chapter of this textbook, we assess the current status of women, women's studies, and gender relations as we move through the early twenty-first century.

Organization is an important component of both my teaching and my textbooks. For example, the combination of life-span and topical approaches provides a cohesive framework that my own students appreciate. However, every chapter is self-contained. Instructors who prefer a different approach can easily rearrange the sequence of topics. The three to five sections within each chapter all have their own summaries, to allow further flexibility.

A second organizational feature is the four general themes about the psychology of women (see pages 28–30). These themes can be traced through many components of women's lives. In addition, the themes help provide continuity for a subject that might otherwise seem overwhelming to both instructors and students.

I have also retained the following special features that professors and students praised in the five previous editions of *The Psychology of Women:*

- **Topical outlines** provide students with an overall structure at the beginning of each chapter.
- **True-false statements** near the beginning of each chapter encourage student interest; they also foreshadow many of the key issues that we will examine.
- The **writing style** is clear and interesting; I try to engage readers by including many examples and quotations in which women describe their own experiences.
- All of the **key terms** appear in boldface type, and they are defined within the same sentence. Some professors choose to assign chapters in a nonlinear order. To accommodate this preference, I define a key term in each chapter where it appears. For example, the term *social construc-tionism* is defined in Chapter 1, but also in several subsequent chapters. In addition, I provide a pronunciation guide for terms with potentially ambiguous pronunciations.
- Informal **demonstrations** encourage active involvement and clarify the procedures for crucial research studies.
- **Section summaries** help students review the primary concepts in a section of a chapter before they begin the next section. Each chapter includes three to five section summaries.

- The **end-of-chapter review questions** encourage students to clarify and synthesize concepts. Some instructors have told me that they also use these questions as either discussion topics or writing assignments.
- A **list of key terms** at the end of each chapter invites students to test themselves on important concepts.
- Finally, the **recommended readings** suggest extra resources for students who want to explore in greater detail the topics in each chapter. I have annotated each reference to clarify its scope.

This book is intended for students from a variety of backgrounds. I have included extensive learning aids to make it readable for students who have taken only an introductory course in psychology. However, *The Psychology of Women* should also be useful for advanced-level students, because the coverage of topics is complete and the references are extensive. This textbook is primarily designed for courses in the psychology of women, psychology of gender, psychology of gender comparisons, and psychology of gender roles. Instructors who focus on the psychology of gender may wish to supplement the book with one of several textbooks currently available on the psychology of men.

FEATURES OF THE SIXTH EDITION

The sixth edition of *The Psychology of Women* continues to emphasize the special features and writing style that students and professors admired in the earlier editions. Professors who reviewed the fifth edition were pleased with its overall structure. Accordingly, I retained the same topic sequence for the sixth edition. However, readers should note the following features:

- Whenever possible, I have expanded coverage on women of color who live in the United States and Canada.
- I now include more information on cross-cultural perspectives, reflecting the current research in this area. This material provides a broader view of women's lives in many parts of the globe.
- "Women's voices" are more widely included. I searched numerous resources to locate quotations that could enrich and supplement the quantitative research about girls and women.
- This sixth edition is a thoroughly revised textbook. It features a total of 2,864 references; 1,415 of these references are new to this edition. Furthermore, 1,925 of all the references were published in 2000 or later. This new revision reflects changes in women's lives, changes in their views of themselves, and changes in society's attitudes toward women's issues.

NEW COVERAGE IN SPECIFIC CHAPTERS

For professors familiar with the fifth edition, here is a brief guide to some of the major changes in this new textbook:

- **Chapter 1** includes new information about social class, racism, and U.S.-centered nationalism.

- **Chapter 2** has been reorganized, and it contains new material on women in religion, implicit gender stereotypes, and cross-cultural issues.
- **Chapter 3** contains updated information about female infanticide, intersexed individuals, and international perspectives on education.
- **Chapter 4** includes new information about cultural attitudes toward menstruation, the development of ethnic identity, and the experiences of young lesbians.
- **Chapter 5** discusses Harvard President Lawrence Summers's statements about women in science; this chapter also includes new cross-cultural research and expanded information about stereotype threat.
- **Chapter 6** examines new research on gender comparisons in heroism, close friendships, and leadership styles.
- **Chapter 7** includes current information on salary discrimination, treatment discrimination, and couples' division of household tasks.
- **Chapter 8** contains updated information about cohabitation, the legal status of lesbian relationships in other countries as well as in North America, and the experiences of single women.
- **Chapter 9** presents new information about the double standard of sexuality, sex education in the schools, and the cross-cultural use of contraceptives.
- **Chapter 10** includes more information about ethnic-group comparisons during pregnancy, cross-cultural perspectives on childbirth, and post-partum disturbances.
- **Chapter 11** has updated information about the prevalence of various health problems, as well as new information about social class and more detail about human papillomavirus.
- **Chapter 12** features more than 200 references published in the current decade. It also examines two new topics: the criticism about the *Diagnostic and Statistical Manual of Mental Disorders* and the research on psychotherapy and social class.
- **Chapter 13** has been extensively updated, with many new examples of violence against women, current information on prevalence rates, and cross-cultural perspectives.
- **Chapter 14** discusses a new meta-analysis on the double standard of aging, as well as new information about retirement and economic issues and lesbians grieving the loss of a life partner.
- **Chapter 15** includes updated information about the number of women in psychology and an expanded discussion of women of color and feminism; the last part of the chapter has also been reorganized.

ACKNOWLEDGMENTS

I especially enjoy writing the acknowledgments section of a book because it gives me the opportunity to thank the people who have provided ideas, references, perspectives, and encouragement. Lucinda DeWitt, a long-time co-author on my textbook ancillaries, read every chapter carefully and noted unclear passages, inconsistencies, and topics that are challenging to students.

Twenty-one psychologists reviewed the manuscript for the sixth edition of *The Psychology of Women*. I especially appreciated the useful suggestions, as well as insights about content, current research, organization, and presentation, from these reviewers: Cheryl Anagnopoulos, Black Hills State University; Janine Buckner, Seton Hall University; Joyce Carbonel, Florida State University; Wendy C. Chambers, University of Georgia; Darlene DeFour, Hunter College; Mary Ellen Dello Stritto, Western Oregon University; Sandy R. Fiske, Onondaga Community College; Beverly Goodwin, Indiana University of Pennsylvania; Gloria Hamilton, Middle Tennessee State University; Patricia Kaminski, University of North Texas; Beth Lux, University of Massachusetts, Amherst; Kim MacLean, St. Francis Xavier University; Melanie Maggard, Mt. San Jacinto Community College; Peggy Moody, St. Louis Community College, Florissant Valley; Nina Nabors, Eastern Michigan University; Mary O'Neil, Rollins College; Wendy M. Pullin, Concordia University College of Alberta; Zoa Rockstein, St. Cloud State University; Natalie Smoak, University of Connecticut; Jennifer Taylor, Humboldt State University; Wendy Wallin, Solano Community College.

My continuing thanks go to the reviewers of the first five editions: Alice Alexander, Harriet Amster, Linda Anderson, Julianne Arbuckle, Illeana Arias, Carole Beal, Cheryl Bereziuk, Nancy Betts, Beverly Birns, Krisanne Bursik, Joan Chrisler, Gloria Cowan, Mary Crawford, Kay Deaux, Lucinda DeWitt, Sheri Chapman De Bro, Nancy DeCourville, Amanda Diekman, Claire Etaugh, Joan Fimbel DiGiovanni, Elaine Donelson, Gilla Family, Susan K. Fuhr, Grace Galliano, Margaret Gittis, Sharon Golub, Beverly Goodwin, Michele Hoffnung, Chris Jazwinski, Linda Lavine, Liz Leonard, Laura Madson, Wendy Martyna, Nina Nabors, Agnes O'Connell, Maureen O'Neill, Michele A. Paludi, Letitia Anne Peplau, Jean Poppei, Rebecca Reviere, Carla Reyes, Janis Sanchez-Hucles, Barbara Sholley, Linda Skinner, Myra Okazaki Smith, Susan Snelling, Hannah Steinward, Noreen Stuckless, Beverly Tatum, Lori Van Wallendael, Barbara S. Wallston, Dolores Weiss, Yvonne V. Wells, Barbara J. Yanico, and Cecilia K. Yoder.

I also want to acknowledge the contributions of Mary Roth Walsh, who died in February 1998. During a period of nearly 20 years, Mary generously shared with me her perspectives, resources, and insights on the psychology of women. I continue to miss our conversations.

I'm delighted that Lucinda DeWitt could continue to co-author the *Instructor's Manual/Test Bank* for this sixth edition! Lucinda has written or contributed to the test item file or instructor's manual for five previous textbooks. I am consistently impressed with her organizational skills and her expertise in the psychology of women, as well as her ability to track down information for the ancillary section called "Women's Issues Web Sites."

I would also like to thank friends, relatives, and colleagues for suggesting many important references: Susan Arellano, Christine Beard, Charles Brewer, Lawrence Casler, Cheryl Chevalier, Jacques Chevalier, Johanna Connelly, Joanna Cotton, Ganie DeHart, Lisa Elliot, Hugh Foley, Joanne Goodrich (from the About Canada Project), Jennifer Gullo, Diane Halpern, Marion

Hoctor, Andrea James, Patricia Kaminski, Jamie Kerr, Arnold Matlin, Beth Matlin, Sally Matlin, Kathy McGowan, Stuart J. McKelvie, Murray Moman, Patricia Murphy, Josephine Naidoo, Tracy Napper, Thaddeus Naprawa, Lisa Naylor, George Rebok, Daniel Repinksi, Monica Schneider, Philip Smith, Eth Weimer, Susan Whitbourne, Helen S. White, and Diony Young.

Many students provided valuable suggestions and feedback on this book: Kate Bailey, Marcia Barclay, Caitlin Bennett, Laurie Ciccarelli, Lindsay M. Cole, Kelly Crane, Patty Curry, Kathryn Delaney, Michael Derrick, Jennifer Donlon, Stephanie Doyle, Amy Jo Eldred, Susan Flood, Lori Gardinier, Charlie Gilreath, Myung Han, Ivy Ingber, Erik Jacobsen, Lisa Kaplan, Karen Kreuter, Kari Kufel, Heidi Lang, Christine Lauer, Laura Leon, Yau Ping Leung, Amy Liner, Zorayda Lopez, Tracy Marchese, Kathleen Matkoski, Erin Mulcock, Torye Mullins, Cory Mulvaney, Cathleen Quinn, Ralph Risolo, Marriane Rizzo, Bridget Roberts, Stephanie Roberts, Lindsay Rokos, Kristen Setter, Sarah Teres Sifling, Jennifer Swan, Emily Taylor, Marcie Trout, Jessica Weimer, Megan Weinpres, Kristen Wheeler, Amanda Williams, Katharine Wilkowski, Sui Ling Xu, and Cindy Zanni.

Constance Ellis and Carolyn Emmert provided numerous services that permitted me to devote more energy to writing. I also want to acknowledge the superb student assistants who were especially helpful in locating references and organizing material related to the sixth edition of *The Psychology of Women*: Stephanie Doyle, Kristina Condidorio, Alexandra Cope, Allison Katter, Catherine Burke, Lisa Lazio, Jessica Mooney, Abigail Hammond, and Karen Beaulac.

The members of the Milne Library staff at SUNY Geneseo demonstrated their professional expertise in tracking down elusive references, documents, and information. My thanks go especially to Harriet Sleggs and her assistants in Milne's Information Delivery System, as well as to Diane Johnson and Louise Zipp.

At Thomson Wadsworth, I am pleased to work once again with three wonderful editors who have guided many of my previous textbooks. Special thanks to Susan Badger (CEO), Sean Wakely (President), and Eve Howard (Vice President/Editor-in-Chief). Michele Sordi (Publisher) was especially helpful in guiding the final phases of the manuscript.

Other Thomson Wadsworth staff who deserve my thanks include Rachel Guzman, psychology editorial assistant, who efficiently managed many details in preparing this textbook for production. Managing assistant editor, Dan Moneypenny was especially helpful in working with Lucinda DeWitt and me on the *Instructor's Manual*. I also appreciate the talents of several especially skilled marketing staff members: Kimberly Russell, Natasha Coats, and Linda Yip. Additional thanks go to the cover designer, Katherine Minerva.

All textbook authors know that their book's production team is absolutely essential to their mental health during the final stages of writing a book. I was very fortunate to have Marti Paul, Content Project Manager, serve as the Thomson Wadsworth staff member in charge of production.

Anne Draus, of Scratchgravel Publishing Services, coordinated the flow of edited manuscript and page proofs. She was also exemplary in keeping me well informed about new developments, even in the midst of power outages and other challenges! Carol Lombardi efficiently checked the text citations and the reference section of this book. Pat Tompkins edited the manuscript, suggesting alternate wordings, noting inconsistencies, and providing updated information. Special thanks also go to Linda Webster, who prepared the indexes for this book. Linda and I have now worked together on 10 textbooks, and I continue to value her skill in producing detailed, thoughtful resources!

Throughout my academic training, I was fortunate to be guided by three inspirational individuals. Harry K. Wong was my first mentor; in high school, he encouraged me to try my first research project. During my undergraduate years at Stanford University, Leonard M. Horowitz inspired me with his superb classroom lectures. He also kindled my enthusiasm for psychology research. Robert B. Zajonc, my dissertation advisor at the University of Michigan, provided an ideal role model because of his impressive breadth of knowledge throughout social and cognitive psychology.

Finally, I thank the most important people in my life for their help, suggestions, love, and enthusiasm. My parents—a photo of whom you will see on page 248—provided an ideal home for raising three strong daughters. My mother, Helen Severance White, taught me to value learning and to love the English language. My father, Donald E. White, provided a model of a scientist who cared deeply about his profession in geochemistry research. Dad also taught me the phrase *terminal velocity*, clearly a useful concept for a textbook author! I was preparing the final draft of the fifth edition of *The Psychology of Women* when Dad died on November 20, 2002. How different the world would be if all women could have such supportive parents!

I was fortunate to marry a feminist before "feminism" was a word in my daily vocabulary; Arnie Matlin and I have been married for 40 years. Arnie's suggestions, encouragement, and optimism continue to support and inspire me when I encounter roadblocks. Our daughters now live on opposite coasts of the United States. Beth Matlin-Heiger, her husband Neil Matlin-Heiger, and their son Jacob Matlin-Heiger live in Boston, Massachusetts. (The photo on page 322 shows Beth with Jacob, several weeks after he was born.) Sally Matlin currently lives in Oakland, California, where she has worked as the bilingual staff member for organizations that focus on preventing domestic violence; she is now a first-year law student. My family members' appreciation and pride in my work continue to make writing textbooks a joyous occupation!

Margaret W. Matlin
Geneseo, New York

THE PSYCHOLOGY
OF WOMEN

© Paul J. Richards/Getty Images

1 | INTRODUCTION

True or False?

_____ 1. If a corporation refuses to consider hiring a male for a receptionist position, then this corporation is practicing sexism.

_____ 2. If you believe that women should be highly regarded as human beings, then you are a feminist.

_____ 3. Feminists disagree among themselves about whether men and women are very different from each other or whether the two genders are fairly similar.

_____ 4. Ironically, the most prominent female psychologists in the early 1900s conducted research designed to demonstrate that men are more intellectually competent than women.

_____ 5. Research on the psychology of women grew especially rapidly in the 1950s in both the United States and Canada because so many women were earning Ph.D. degrees in psychology.

_____ 6. If a box of crayons has one crayon labeled "flesh" and that color is light pink, this is an example of the White-as-normative concept.

_____ 7. Asian American women are much more likely than European American women to graduate from college.

_____ 8. Native Americans in the United States have more than 250 different tribal languages.

_____ 9. An important problem in research on gender is that researchers' expectations can influence the results of the study.

_____ 10. Gender differences are larger when researchers observe people in real-life situations, rather than in a laboratory setting.

During the week when I began to write this chapter, three articles in the media caught my attention. Not one of these articles was especially alarming. However, each illustrated that females are treated differently from males, even in the current era:

- Wal-Mart, the largest employer in the United States, is being sued for discriminating against its female employees. Although approximately 70% of its employees are women, only 14% of the managers are female. Men also earn higher salaries than the women, at all levels. For instance, the average male store manager earns $105,700, whereas the average female store manager earns $89,000. Men also earn more money at the low-level jobs. For instance, the average male cashier earns $14,500, compared to $13,800 for the average female cashier (Burk, 2004).

- In 2004, the U.S. Senate confirmed President George W. Bush's appointment of J. Leon Holmes to a U.S. District Court in Arkansas. In a newspaper article that Holmes had written several years earlier, he stated, "The wife is to subordinate herself to her husband" and "The woman is to place herself under the authority of the man." However, the Senate confirmed this controversial appointment, by a vote of 51 to 46 (Chatterjee, 2004).

- Japan's Crown Prince Naruhito and his wife, Princess Masako, were married in 1993. They have a young daughter, Aika, but the Japanese law specifies that only males can inherit the throne. Princess Masako has suffered from stress-related illnesses because of the pressure to produce a male heir. Her education, career, and personal character count for nothing.

The young daughter also has no value, because a "Crown Princess" is unacceptable ("Princess or Prisoner?" 2004). It now appears that Aiko's male cousin, Hisahito, is in line for the throne.

These three examples illustrate a pattern that we will encounter throughout this book. Even in the twenty-first century, women are frequently treated in a biased fashion. This biased treatment is often relatively subtle, but it can also be life threatening.

Furthermore, the popular media and the academic community frequently neglect women and issues important to them. For example, I searched for topics related to women in the index of a recent introductory psychology textbook. Pregnancy isn't mentioned, even though pregnancy is an important part of most women's lives. The topic of rape is also missing from the index. However, the listings under the letter *R* do include receptor sensitivity curves, as well as multiple references to reflexes and to rapid eye movements.

The reason we need to study the psychology of women is to explore a variety of psychological issues that concern women specifically. Women have unique experiences; these include menstruation, pregnancy, childbirth, and menopause. Other experiences are inflicted almost exclusively on women, such as rape, domestic violence, and sexual harassment. In addition, when we study the psychology of women, we can focus on women's experiences in areas that are usually approached from the male point of view, such as achievement, work, sexuality, and retirement.

Still other important topics compare females and males. Are boys and girls *treated* differently? Do women and men differ substantially in their intellectual abilities or their social interactions? These topics, which are neglected in most psychology courses, will be our central focus throughout this book.

Our exploration of the psychology of women begins with some key concepts in the discipline. Next, we'll briefly consider the history of the psychology of women. The third section of this chapter provides a background on women of color, to give you a context for the discussion of ethnicity in later chapters. Then we'll explore some of the problems and biases that researchers face when they study the psychology of women. In the final section, we'll describe the themes of this book, as well as several features that can help you learn more effectively.

CENTRAL CONCEPTS IN THE PSYCHOLOGY OF WOMEN

Let's first consider two related terms, *sex* and *gender,* that are crucial to the psychology of women. Other central concepts that we'll examine include several forms of bias, various approaches to feminism, and two psychological viewpoints on gender similarities and differences.

SEX AND GENDER

The terms *sex* and *gender* have provoked considerable controversy (e.g., Kimball, 2003; LaFrance et al., 2004; Pryzgoda & Chrisler, 2000). **Sex** is a relatively narrow term that typically refers only to those inborn biological characteristics relating to reproduction, such as *sex chromosomes* or *sex organs* (Kimball, 2003).

In contrast, *gender* is a broader term. **Gender** refers to psychological characteristics and social categories that human culture creates. For example, a friend showed me a photo of her 7-month-old son, whom the photographer had posed with a football. This photographer is providing gender messages for the infant, his mother, and everyone who sees the photo. In this textbook we focus on psychology, rather than on biology. As a result, you'll see the word *gender* more often than the word *sex*. For example, you'll read about gender comparisons, gender roles, and gender stereotypes.

Unfortunately, the distinction between sex and gender is not maintained consistently in psychology articles and books (Kimball, 2003). For instance, a highly regarded scholarly journal is called *Sex Roles*, although a more appropriate title would be *Gender Roles*.

A useful related phrase is *doing gender* (Golden, 2004; C. West & Zimmerman, 1998a). According to the concept of **doing gender**, we express our gender when we interact with other people; we also perceive gender in these other people. For example, you provide gender messages to other people by your appearance, your tone of voice, and your conversational style. At the same time, you perceive the gender of your conversational partner, and you are likely to respond differently to a male than to a female. The phrase *doing gender* emphasizes that gender is an active, dynamic process rather than something that is stable and rigid.

THE SCOPE OF SOCIAL BIASES

An important term throughout this book is *sexism* (which probably should be renamed *genderism*). **Sexism** is bias against people on the basis of their gender. A person who believes that women cannot be competent lawyers is sexist. A person who believes that men cannot be competent nursery school teachers is also sexist. Sexism can reveal itself in many forms, such as social behavior, media representations of women and men, and job discrimination. Sexism can be blatant. For example, a student in my psychology of women course last year was attending a recruitment session for prospective high school teachers. She was dressed in a suit that was similar to the suit of a male student standing behind her in line. The interviewer greeted her by saying, "Hi, kid, how are you doin'?" The same interviewer greeted the young man by saying, "Hi, good to meet you," and then he extended his arm for a handshake. However, sexism can also be more subtle, as in using the word *girl* to refer to an adult woman.

Because this book focuses on women, we will emphasize sexism. However, numerous other biases permeate our social relationships. In each case, one social category is considered "normal," and the other categories are considered deficient (Canetto et al., 2003). For example, **racism** is bias against people on the basis of racial or ethnic groups. Research suggests that White preschoolers tend to choose other White children as their friends, even when the classroom includes many Black children (Katz, 2003). As we'll see throughout this book, sexism and racism combine in complex ways. For instance, the experiences of women of color may be quite different from the experiences of European American men (Brabeck & Ting, 2000; Kirk & Okazawa-Rey, 2001).

This book focuses on women, and so we will emphasize sexism. However, we'll also examine several other social biases in which a person's category membership can influence his or her social position. Another example is **classism**, or bias based on social class, defined by such factors as income, occupation, and education. As with sexism and racism, classism provides special privileges to some humans, based on their social category. Unfortunately, psychologists have paid little attention to social class, even though this factor has a major impact on people's psychological experiences (Fine & Burns, 2003; B. Lott, 2002; Ocampo et al., 2003; Saris & Johnston-Robledo, 2000). In the United States, for instance, the chief executive officers of corporations earn approximately 475 times as much as their lowest-paid employees (Belle, 2004). Executives and entry-level employees certainly have different experiences, as we will see in Chapter 7. However, psychologists typically assume that social class should be left to sociologists (Ostrove & Cole, 2003). We'll also see in Chapter 11 that social class has a profound effect on people's health and expected life span.

An additional bias is **ableism**, or bias against people with disabilities (Olkin, 2004; Weinstock, 2003). Just as psychologists ignore social class, they also ignore disability issues—even though disabilities have a major impact on people's lives (Asch & McCarthy, 2003). In Chapter 11, we'll see how ableism can create inequalities for people with disabilities, both in the workplace and in personal relationships.

Another important problem is **heterosexism**, or bias against lesbians, gay males, and bisexuals, three groups of people who are not exclusively heterosexual. Heterosexism appears in the behaviors of individuals and in the policies of institutions, such as the legal system (Garnets, 2004a; Herek, 2000). Heterosexism encourages people to believe that male-female romantic relationships should be considered normal, and therefore people in same-gender relationships do not have the same rights and privileges. In Chapters 2 and 8, we will explore heterosexism in detail, and in Chapters 4, 9, 10, and 12, we will also discuss psychological aspects of lesbians' lives.

We will emphasize **ageism**, or bias based on chronological age, in Chapter 14. Ageism is typically directed toward elderly people (Schneider, 2004; Whitbourne, 2005). Individuals can reveal ageism in terms of biased beliefs, attitudes, and behaviors. For example, a teenager may avoid sitting next to an elderly person. Institutions can also exhibit ageism, for instance, in their hiring policies.

FEMINIST APPROACHES

A central term throughout this book is *feminism*, the principle that women should be highly regarded as human beings. **Feminism** is a belief system in which women's experiences and ideas are valued; feminists emphasize that women and men should be socially, economically, and legally equal (Pollitt, 2004). As Rozee and her colleagues (2004) point out, "Feminism is a life philosophy, a worldview, a blueprint for justice" (p. xii).

We must emphasize several additional points about feminists. First, reread the definition of feminism and notice that it does not exclude men. Indeed, men as well as women can be feminists. Many current books and articles discuss feminist males (e.g., Enns & Sinacore, 2001; Goldrick-Jones, 2002; A. J. Lott, 2003). Think about it: You probably know some men who advocate feminist principles more than some of the women you know. We'll discuss male feminists and the growing discipline of men's studies in the final chapter of this book.

Second, many of your friends would qualify as feminists, even though they may be reluctant to call themselves feminists (Dube, 2004; Liss et al., 2000; Pollitt, 2004). You have probably heard someone say, "I'm not a feminist, but I think men and women should be treated the same." This person may mistakenly assume that a feminist must be a person who hates men or a person who believes that females should replace all males in positions of power. However, remember that the defining feature of feminism is a high regard for women, not antagonism toward men.

Third, feminism encompasses a variety of ideas and perspectives, not just one feminist viewpoint (Dube, 2004). Let's consider four different theoretical approaches to feminism: liberal feminism, cultural feminism, radical feminism, and women-of-color feminism.

1. **Liberal feminism** focuses on the goal of gender equality, giving women and men the same rights and opportunities. Liberal feminists argue that this goal can be achieved by passing laws that guarantee equal rights for women and men (Chrisler & Smith, 2004; Enns & Sinacore, 2001). Liberal feminists emphasize that gender differences are relatively small; these differences would be even smaller if women had the same opportunities as men (Enns, 2004a). Women and men who are liberal feminists believe that everyone benefits if we reduce our culture's rigid gender roles (Goldrick-Jones, 2002).

2. **Cultural feminism** emphasizes the positive qualities that are presumed to be stronger in women than in men—qualities such as nurturing and caretaking. Cultural feminism therefore focuses on gender differences that value women rather than on the gender similarities of liberal feminism (Chrisler & Smith, 2004; Enns, 2004a; Henley et al., 1998). Cultural feminists often argue that society should be restructured to emphasize cooperation rather than aggression (Enns & Sinacore, 2001; Kimball, 1995).

3. **Radical feminism** argues that the basic cause of women's oppression lies deep in the entire sex and gender system rather than in some superficial laws and policies. Radical feminists emphasize that sexism permeates our society, from the personal level in male-female relationships to the national and international level (Chrisler & Smith, 2004; Tong, 1998). Radical

feminists often argue that our society needs to dramatically change its policies on sexuality and on violence against women (Enns, 2004a). They maintain that the oppression of women is so pervasive that massive social changes are necessary to correct the problem (Enns & Sinacore, 2001; Goldrick-Jones, 2002).

4. **Women-of-color feminism** points out that the other three types of feminism overemphasize gender while ignoring other human dimensions such as ethnicity and social class (Baca Zinn et al., 2001; Chrisler & Smith, 2004). According to this perspective, a genuinely feminist approach cannot be accomplished with a few minor adjustments to liberal feminism, cultural feminism, or radical feminism (Enns, 2004a). For example, the life of a lesbian woman of color is substantially different from the life of a lesbian woman who is European American (Lorde, 2001). If we want to understand the experiences of a Black lesbian, we must begin with her perspective, rather than focusing on European American lesbians and then "adding difference and stirring" (Baca Zinn et al., 2001).

In Chapter 15, we'll further explore perspectives on feminism and women's studies. A central point, however, is that feminism isn't simply one unified point of view. Instead, feminists have created a variety of perspectives on gender relationships and on the ideal pathways for achieving better lives for women. To clarify the four feminist approaches discussed in this section, try Demonstration 1.1 on page 8.

PSYCHOLOGICAL APPROACHES TO GENDER SIMILARITY AND DIFFERENCE

When psychologists examine gender issues, they usually favor either a similarities perspective or a differences perspective. Let's explore these two approaches.

THE SIMILARITIES PERSPECTIVE.   Those who emphasize the **similarities perspective** believe that men and women are generally similar in their intellectual and social skills. These psychologists argue that social forces may create some temporary differences. For example, women may be more submissive than men in the workplace because women typically hold less power in that setting (Kimball, 1995; B. Lott, 1996). Supporters of the similarities perspective also tend to favor liberal feminism. By reducing gender roles and increasing equal rights laws, they say, the gender similarities will increase still further.

If the similarities perspective is correct, then why do women and men often *seem* so different? One explanation for the perceived differences focuses on the social constructionist perspective. First, however, read the following passage:

> Chris was really angry today! Enough was enough. Chris put on the gray suit, marched into work, and went into the main boss's office and yelled: "I've brought in more money for this company than anybody else and everybody gets promoted but me!" . . . The boss saw Chris's fist slam down on the desk. There was an angry look on Chris's face. They tried to talk but it was useless. Chris just stormed out of the office in anger. (Beall, 1993, p. 127)

Demonstration 1.1

Imagine that, in a discussion group, each of these eight individuals makes a statement about feminism. Read each statement and write down whether the approach represents liberal feminism, cultural feminism, radical feminism, or women-of-color feminism. The answers are on page 34.

1. Cora: "The way marriage is currently designed, women are basically servants who spend most of their energy improving the lives of other people." _____
2. Marta: "Too many feminists think that White women are at the center of feminism, and the rest of us are out at the edges of the feminist circle." _____
3. Nereyda: "Laws must be made to guarantee women the right to be educated the same as men; women need to reach their full potential, just like men do." _____
4. Sylvia: "My goal as a feminist is to value the kind of strengths that have traditionally been assigned to women, so that women can help society learn to be more cooperative." _____
5. María: "Society needs to change in a major way so that we can get rid of the oppression of women." _____
6. Michelle: "I consider myself a feminist. However, I think that many feminists just don't pay enough attention to factors such as social class and ethnicity." _____
7. Stuart: "I think women should be given exactly the same opportunities as men with respect to promotion in the workplace." _____
8. Terry: "Because women are naturally more peaceful than men, I think women need to organize and work together to build a peaceful society." _____

Source: Based on Enns (2004a).

Most people conclude that Chris is a man, although Chris's gender is not stated. Instead, readers construct a gender, based on their cultural knowledge about gender.

According to **social constructionism**, individuals and cultures construct or invent their own versions of reality, based on prior experiences, social interactions, and beliefs (Gergen & Gergen, 2004; Kimball, 2003; Lonner, 2003; Marecek et al., 2004). A young woman develops a female identity, for example, by learning about gender through her social interactions and other experiences in her culture.

Social constructionists argue that we can never objectively discover reality because our observations will always be influenced by our beliefs (Marecek et al., 2004; Yoder & Kahn, 2003). In the current era in North America, our culture considers women to be very different from men. As a result, we tend to perceive, remember, and think about gender in a way that exaggerates the differences between women and men. The views in this textbook (and most other current psychology of women textbooks) support both the similarities perspective and the social constructionist view.

THE DIFFERENCES PERSPECTIVE. In contrast, other psychologists interested in women's studies emphasize the **differences perspective**, which argues that men and women are generally different in their intellectual and social skills. Feminist psychologists who support the differences perspective usually emphasize women's positive characteristics that have been undervalued, primarily because they are associated with women. These psychologists might emphasize that women are more likely than men to be concerned about human relationships and caregiving. As you might imagine, those who favor the differences perspective also tend to be cultural feminists. Critics of this perspective point out a potential problem: If we emphasize gender differences, we will simply strengthen people's stereotypes about gender (Clinchy & Norem, 1998).

People who endorse the differences perspective often believe that essentialism can explain gender differences. **Essentialism** argues that gender is a basic, unchangeable characteristic that resides *within* an individual. According to the essentialist perspective, all women share the same psychological characteristics, which are very different from the psychological characteristics that all men share. Essentialism also emphasizes that women's psychological characteristics are universal and occur in every culture—a proposal that is not consistent with cross-cultural research (Chrisler & Smith, 2004; Lonner, 2003; Wade & Tavris, 1999). The essentialists emphasize that women are more concerned than men about caregiving because of their own internal nature, not because society currently assigns women the task of taking care of children (Hare-Mustin & Marecek, 1994; Kimball, 1995). We'll explore essentialist views on caregiving in more detail in Chapter 6.

Section Summary

Central Concepts in the Psychology of Women

1. *Sex* refers only to biological characteristics related to reproduction (e.g., sex chromosomes); in contrast, *gender* refers to psychological characteristics (e.g., gender roles). The term *doing gender* means that we display gender in our social interactions and that we perceive gender in other people during those interactions.

2. The social biases to be discussed in this book include sexism, racism, classism, ableism, heterosexism, and ageism.

3. Feminism emphasizes that women and men should be socially, economically, and legally equal. Women and men who hold these beliefs are feminists; however, many people endorse feminist principles, even if they do not identify themselves as feminists.

4. Four feminist perspectives discussed in this section are liberal feminism, cultural feminism, radical feminism, and women-of-color feminism.

5. Psychologists typically favor either a gender similarities perspective (often combined with social constructionism) or a gender differences perspective (often combined with essentialism).

A BRIEF HISTORY OF THE PSYCHOLOGY OF WOMEN

Psychology's early views about women were generally negative (Kimball, 2003). Consider the perspective of G. Stanley Hall, who founded the American Psychological Association and pioneered the field of adolescent psychology. Unfortunately, Hall opposed college education for young women because he believed that academic work would "be developed at the expense of reproductive power" (G. S. Hall, 1906, p. 592; Minton, 2000). As you might imagine, views like Hall's helped to encourage biased research about gender. Let's briefly examine some of this early work, then trace the emergence of the psychology of women, and finally outline the discipline's current status.

Early Studies of Gender Comparisons

Most of the early researchers in psychology were men, although a few women made valiant attempts to contribute to the discipline of psychology (Furumoto, 2003; Pyke, 1998; Scarborough & Furumoto, 1987). The early research on gender typically focused on gender comparisons, and it was often influenced by sexist biases (Milar, 2000; Morawski, 1994).

Psychologist Helen Thompson Woolley (1910), claimed that this early research was permeated with "flagrant personal bias, . . . unfounded assertions, and even sentimental rot and drivel" (p. 340). For example, many early researchers believed that the highest mental capacities were located in the frontal lobes of the brain. Not surprisingly, early researchers reported that men had larger frontal lobes than women (Shields, 1975). Furthermore, researchers often revised their earlier statements to match whatever brain theory was currently fashionable.

During the early 1900s, however, two female psychologists reached different conclusions. Helen Thompson Woolley demonstrated that men and women had similar intellectual abilities. Furthermore, women actually earned higher scores on some memory and thinking tasks (E. M. James, 1994; H. B. Thompson, 1903). Leta Stetter Hollingworth (1914) also studied gender bias, and she demonstrated that women's menstrual cycles had little effect on their intellectual abilities (Benjamin & Shields, 1990; Klein, 2002). This first generation of female psychologists used their research findings to argue that women and men should have equal access to a college education (LaFrance et al., 2004; Milar, 2000).

The Emergence of the Psychology of Women as a Discipline

Most psychologists paid little attention to research on gender in the early years of psychology. During the 1930s, women constituted roughly one-third of the members of the American Psychological Association (M. R. Walsh, 1987). However, women were seldom hired for faculty positions at research universities where they could conduct psychological research or construct theories (Chrisler & Smith, 2004; Furumoto, 1996; Scarborough, 1992). As a result, the psychology of women did not move forward substantially during the first half of the twentieth century (Marecek et al., 2003; Morawski & Agronick, 1991).

In the 1970s, however, the number of women in psychology had begun to increase. Feminism and the women's movement had gained recognition on college campuses, and colleges added numerous courses in women's studies (Howe, 2001a; Marecek et al., 2003; Rosen, 2000). This rapidly growing interest in women had an impact on the field of psychology. For example, the Association for Women in Psychology was founded in 1969. In 1973, a group of American psychologists established an organization that is now called the Society for the Psychology of Women; it is currently one of the largest divisions within the American Psychological Association (Chrisler & Smith, 2004).

In 1972, a group of Canadian psychologists submitted a proposal for a symposium—called "On Women, By Women"—to the Canadian Psychological Association. When they learned that the organization had rejected their proposal, they cleverly decided to hold this symposium at a nearby hotel. Shortly afterward, these leaders formed the Canadian Psychological Association Task Force on the Status of Women in Canadian Psychology (Pyke, 2001).

In both the United States and Canada, the psychology of women was increasingly likely to be a standard course on college campuses (Marecek et al., 2003). Many psychologists found themselves asking questions about gender that had never occurred to them before. For example, I recall suddenly realizing in 1970 that I had completed my undergraduate degree in psychology at Stanford University and my Ph.D. in psychology at the University of Michigan with only one female professor during my entire academic training! I wondered why these universities hadn't hired more women professors and why so little of my training had focused on either women or gender.

During the 1970s, the field of the psychology of women expanded dramatically. Researchers eagerly explored topics such as women's achievement motivation, domestic violence, sexual harassment, and other topics that had previously been ignored (Kimball, 2003; LaFrance et al., 2004; A. J. Stewart, 1998).

Looking back on the 1970s from the perspective of the twenty-first century, many people have remarked on that decade's sense of excitement and discovery. However, the work done in the 1970s typically had two problems. First, we did not realize that the issue of gender was extremely complicated. For example, most of us optimistically thought that just a handful of factors could explain why so few women held top management positions. Now we realize that the explanation encompasses numerous factors, as you'll see in Chapter 7.

A second problem with the 1970s framework is that women were sometimes blamed for their own low status. In trying to determine why women were scarce in management positions, researchers from this era typically constructed two answers: (1) Women were not assertive enough, and (2) they were afraid of success. Researchers ignored an alternative idea—that the *situation* might be faulty (Henley, 1985; LaFrance et al., 2004; Marecek et al., 2003). Researchers and the popular media often emphasized that the fault could be traced to women's personalities rather than to stereotypes and biased institutional policies. Gradually, however, many researchers shifted their focus from gender differences to gender discrimination and sexism (Unger, 1997).

THE CURRENT STATUS OF THE PSYCHOLOGY OF WOMEN

Today, we emphasize that questions about the psychology of women are likely to generate complex answers. Furthermore, research in this area continues to increase rapidly. For example, a search of a library resource called PsycINFO for January 2000 to June 2006 revealed that 138,054 scholarly articles mention the topics of women, gender, or feminism. Four journals that are especially likely to publish relevant articles are *Psychology of Women Quarterly, Sex Roles, Feminism & Psychology,* and *Canadian Woman Studies/Les cahiers de la femme.*

A related development is that psychologists are increasingly aware of how factors such as ethnicity, social class, and sexual orientation interact in complex ways with gender. As you'll see throughout this book, we typically cannot make statements that apply to *all* women. Contrary to the essentialist approach, women are definitely not a homogeneous group! As we'll note in Chapter 12, for example, the incidence of eating disorders seems to depend on factors such as ethnic group and sexual orientation.

The current field of the psychology of women is also interdisciplinary. In preparing all six editions of this book, I have consulted resources in areas as varied as biology, medicine, sociology, anthropology, history, philosophy, religion, media studies, political science, economics, business, education, and linguistics. For this current edition, I accumulated a stack of reprints that was literally more than 8 feet tall, in addition to more than 600 relevant books—all published in the past 4 years! Current research in the psychology of women is especially lively because women now earn the majority of psychology Ph.D. degrees—for example, 72% in 2002 (Bailey, 2004).

Still, research on the psychology of women is relatively young, and several important issues are not yet clear. At many points throughout this textbook, you will read a sentence such as, "We don't have enough information to draw conclusions." My students tell me that these disclaimers irritate them: "Why can't you just tell us what the answer is?" In reality, however, the conflicting research findings typically cannot be summarized in a clear-cut statement (Unger, 1997).

Another issue is that our knowledge base continues to change rapidly. New research often requires us to revise a previous generalization. As a result, this current edition of your textbook is substantially different from the five earlier editions. For example, the coverage of gender comparisons in cognitive abilities bears little resemblance to the material on that topic in the first edition. Other areas that have changed dramatically include adolescence, women and work, and women and physical health. The field of psychology of women is especially challenging because both women and men continue to change as we move further into the current century. You'll see, for example, that the number of women working outside the home has changed dramatically. On many different dimensions, women in 2006 are psychologically different from women in 1956. It is fascinating to contemplate the future of the psychology of women toward the end of the twenty-first century.

Section Summary

A Brief History of the Psychology of Women

1. Most early research on gender examined gender differences and emphasized female inferiority; however, Helen Thompson Woolley and Leta Stetter Hollingsworth conducted gender-fair research.

2. Gender research was largely ignored until the 1970s, when the psychology of women became an emerging field in both the United States and Canada. However, researchers in that era underestimated the complexity of the issues; in addition, women were often blamed for their own low status.

3. Current research on gender is widespread and interdisciplinary; the knowledge base continues to change as a result of this research.

WOMEN AND ETHNICITY

Earlier in this chapter, we introduced the term *racism*, or bias against certain ethnic groups. In this section, we'll specifically focus on ethnicity to provide a framework for future discussions. When we consider the psychology of women, we need to examine ethnic diversity so that we can establish an accurate picture of women's lives, rather than simply White women's lives. We also need to appreciate how women construct or make sense of their own ethnic identity (Madden & Hyde, 1998). Let's begin by exploring a concept called "White as normative" and then consider some information about ethnic groups. Our final topic is U.S.-centered nationalism, a kind of bias in which U.S. residents believe that the United States holds a special status that is superior to other countries.

THE WHITE-AS-NORMATIVE CONCEPT

According to Peggy McIntosh (2001), our culture in the United States and Canada is based on the hidden assumption that being White is normative or "normal." According to the **White-as-normative concept**, White people have certain privileges that they often take for granted. For example, if a White woman is late for a meeting, people do not conclude, "She is late because she's White." A White woman can use a credit card and not arouse suspicions that she had stolen the card. However, White people seldom realize the advantages of having white skin (Corcoran & Thompson, 2004). Our school systems also assume that Whites or European Americans are normative.

At present, our terminology for this ethnic group is in flux. I will use the terms *Whites* and *European Americans* to refer to individuals who do *not* consider themselves to be Latina/Latino, Asian American, or Native American.

Consider this example of the White-as-normative concept: McIntosh reports that, as a White woman, she knows that her children will be taught material that focuses on their ethnic group. In contrast, a child from any other ethnic background has no such guarantee. For instance, Aurora Orozco (1999) was born in Mexico and came to California as a child. She recalls a song the students sang in her new U.S. school:

> The Pilgrims came from overseas
> To make a home for you and me.
> Thanksgiving Day, Thanksgiving Day.
> We clap our hands, we are so glad. (p. 110)

Orozco felt as though her own ethnic heritage was invisible in a classroom where children were supposed to clap their hands in celebration of their Pilgrim ancestors.

Another component of the White-as-normative concept is that White individuals often think that Blacks, Latinas/os, Asian Americans, and Native Americans belong to ethnic groups—but that European Americans do not (Peplau, Veniegas et al., 1999; Weedon, 1999). In fact, each of us has an ethnic heritage. Can you think of other hidden assumptions that are customary in our White-as-normative culture?

WOMEN OF COLOR

Figure 1.1 shows the estimated number of U.S. residents in the major ethnic groups, as of 2004. Figure 1.2 indicates the ethnic origins of people who live in Canada. Let's briefly consider each of four groups, so that you have a context for future discussions about ethnicity.

LATINA WOMEN.   As Figure 1.1 reveals, Latinas/Latinos are currently the second-largest ethnic group in the United States. At present, most individuals in this ethnic group prefer this term rather than *Hispanic*, the term often used by governmental agencies (Fears, 2003). The problem is that *Hispanic* focuses on Spanish origins rather than on Latin American identity. Unfortunately, though, the term *Latinos* has an *-os* ending that renders women invisible when speaking about both males and females. I will follow the current policy of using *Latinas* to refer to women of Latin American origin and *Latinas/os* to refer to both genders. (Latin American feminists have recently created a nonsexist alternative that incorporates both the *-as* and the *-os* endings; it is written *Latin@s*.)

Mexican Americans currently constitute about 60% of the Latina/o population in the United States (Pulera, 2002). Incidentally, Mexican Americans often refer to themselves as *Chicanas* or *Chicanos*, especially if they feel a strong political commitment to their Mexican heritage (D. Castañeda, 2004).

Any exploration of ethnicity must emphasize the wide diversity of characteristics and experiences within every ethnic group (D. Castañeda, 2004). For example, Latinas/os share a language and many similar values and customs. However, a Chicana growing up in a farming community in central California has different experiences from a Puerto Rican girl living in Manhattan. Furthermore, a Latina whose family has lived in Iowa for three generations has different experiences from a Latina who recently left her Central

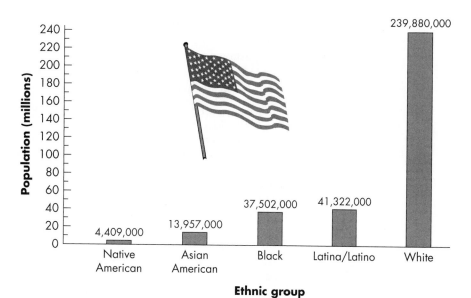

FIGURE 1.1 | U.S. POPULATION IN 2004, BY ETHNIC GROUPS.

Note: Some individuals listed two or more races, and so they are tallied for each applicable category.

Source: U.S. Census Bureau (2006).

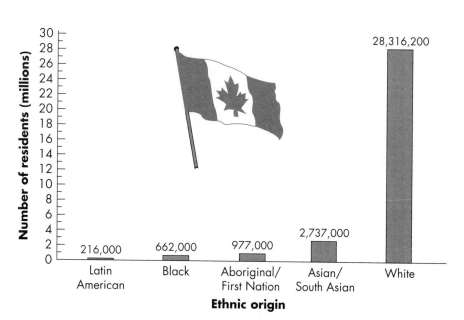

FIGURE 1.2 | SELF-REPORTED ETHNIC ORIGINS OF CANADIAN RESIDENTS.

Source: Statistics Canada (2006).

American birthplace because her family had been receiving death threats (Martin, 2004).

Donna Castañeda (2000b) described how she and other Latinas must navigate two cultures, frequently crossing borders between their Latina heritage and the European American culture in which they now live. As she writes:

> The notion of border crossing has a deep resonance for me each time I go home to visit my family. In a family of seven children, I have been the only person to go to college, and on top of that I went on to get a Ph.D. As the eldest daughter in a family that places great value on children . . . not only do I not have any children, but I am also unmarried! Each homecoming is like moving from one world into another, from one self to another. The transitions are now much smoother for me than in earlier years, but only after a process of coming to understand that at any point in time I am more than one person, one dimension. (p. 205)

BLACK WOMEN.   If you re-examine the U.S. data in Figure 1.1, you'll see that Blacks constitute the third-largest ethnic group in the United States. Some Blacks may have arrived recently from Africa or the Caribbean, whereas the families of others may have lived in North America since the 1700s. In Canada, Blacks are likely to have emigrated from the Caribbean, Africa, or Great Britain. However, about half of Black residents were born in Canada (Knight, 2004).

Every non-White ethnic group has encountered racism, and this book will provide many examples of racial bias. In the United States, however, Black people's experiences with racism have been especially well documented (Schneider, 2004). For example, Bernestine Singley (2004) is a Black lawyer in her 50s who dresses conservatively. Still, as she writes, every time she flies out of the Dallas–Fort Worth Airport, "A security agent pulls me aside, removes my carry on bags, searches them and me, then hooks up my bags to a monitor and chemically analyzes them to ensure I don't board the plane with illegal drugs or bombs. This is all done in full public view" (p. 13).

The terms *Black* and *African American* are often used interchangeably. In general, I'll use the term *Black* because it is more inclusive (Boot, 1999). *African American* seems to ignore many U.S. residents who feel a strong connection to their Caribbean roots (e.g., in Jamaica, Trinidad, or Haiti) as well as Blacks who live in Canada. As the Black poet Gwendolyn Brooks, former U.S. Poet laureate, said in an interview, she likes to think of Blacks as family who happen to live in countries throughout the world. *Black* is a welcoming term, like an open umbrella (B. D. Hawkins, 1994).

ASIAN AMERICAN WOMEN.   As with Latinas/os, Asian Americans come from many different countries. Asian Americans include Chinese, Filipinos, Japanese, Vietnamese, Koreans, South Asians (for example, people from India, Pakistan, and Bangladesh), and about 25 other ethnic-cultural groups (Chan, 2004). Consider a Laotian woman who is one of the 10,000 refugees belonging to the Hmong tribe and now living in Minnesota. She may have little in common with a Taiwanese woman living in Toronto's Chinatown or a South Asian woman who is a physician in New Jersey (Chan, 2004). Although many Asian

American women have professional careers, women who are Filipino, Korean, and Chinese garment workers experience some of the most stressful labor conditions in North America (Kato, 1999; Võ & Scichitano, 2004).

Asian Americans are often stereotyped as the ideal minority group, and in fact they are often academically successful (Daseler, 2000; Schneider, 2004). For example, 46% of Asian American women in the United States have earned at least a bachelor's degree, in contrast to 27% of European American women ("The Nation: Students," 2004).

However, we'll see throughout this book that women from an Asian background face many roadblocks. For instance, Dr. Madhulika Khandelwal describes her experiences as a professor at the University of Massachusetts, Boston: "Stereotypically [Asians] are presumed to have had limited access to English before arriving in America. They are considered followers rather than leaders. And the women are seen as either downtrodden or sexual 'exotics.'" She recalls being praised once after a lecture because she "spoke so well." In fact, India was colonized by the British, and Dr. Khandelwal had grown up speaking English as her first language (Collison, 2000, p. 21).

NATIVE AMERICAN AND FIRST NATIONS WOMEN.   Native Americans and First Nations people[1] may share a common geographic origin and a common history of being invaded, dispossessed, and regulated by White North Americans. However, their languages, values, and current lifestyles may have little in common (Hall & Barongan, 2002; McLeod, 2003). In the United States, for example, Native Americans have more than 250 different tribal languages and more than 550 separate native backgrounds (Daly, 2001; Trimble, 2003).

Many Native American women struggle as they try to integrate their own aspirations with the values of their culture. For example, a Native American teenager explained this conflict: "As a young woman, I should have been starting a family. When Grandma told them I was going to college, they'd look away. But in my eyes, going to college wasn't going to make me less Indian or forget where I came from" (Garrod et al., 1992, p. 86).

We have seen that each ethnic group consists of many different subgroups. Even if we focus on one specific subgroup—perhaps Chinese Americans—the variability *within* that one subgroup is always large (American Psychological Association, 2003; Kowalski, 2000). Whenever we examine how the various ethnic groups differ from one another, keep in mind the difficulty of drawing any generalizations that also reflect this within-group diversity. As noted at the beginning of this section, we must re-examine the perspective that routinely considers European Americans to be normative. In the United States and Canada, most European American students have learned a perspective in which

---

[1]In referring to people whose ancestors lived in Canada before the arrival of European Americans, most Canadians use either of two terms, *First Nations* and *Aboriginal*. The two terms are used somewhat interchangeably, although some people limit the term *First Nations* to descendents of the original inhabitants of Saskatchewan and Manitoba (McLeod, 2003).

the "normal human" is White, middle class, and North American (Cushner, 2003).

Most current research about the psychology of women still describes the experience of White middle-class people, but the focus of the discipline is broadening. For example, groups such as the Society for the Psychology of Women and the Association for Women in Psychology sponsor numerous conferences and presentations on women of color. Whenever possible in this book, we will examine the diversity of experiences for all women.

U.S.-CENTERED NATIONALISM

Earlier in this section, we emphasized the White-as-normative concept. Now let's focus on a related bias, in which U.S. residents consider the United States to be normative.

According to the principle of **U.S.-centered nationalism**, the United States dominates over all other countries in the world, which are believed to have lower status. U.S.-centered nationalism reveals itself in many ways that may be invisible to U.S. residents (Hase, 2001). For example, my colleagues in Canada have e-mail addresses that end in "ca." The e-mail address for Japanese residents ends in "jp," and those in Greece end in "gr." In contrast, residents of the United States do not need to add any extra letters to their e-mail addresses because our country occupies a position of privilege. We are "normal," whereas the other countries have "second-class status." (If you are a U.S. resident, and this point doesn't seem accurate, how would you feel if Japan were the normative country, and every U.S. e-mail address required the "us" ending?)

To illustrate U.S.-centered nationalism, suppose that you looked at a newspaper tomorrow and discovered that soldiers in another country (say, Italy or France) had been torturing political prisoners who are citizens of the United States. Some of these prisoners have been held for more than a year in solitary confinement, without any trial. Others have been stripped naked and forced to sodomize one another. Still others have been beaten and had their heads forced down a toilet. All of these tortures have been forbidden by the international laws specified by the Geneva Conventions. How would you respond? Would you be outraged that anyone would treat U.S. citizens so cruelly?

Now, switch countries, so that U.S. soldiers are the torturers, and the people from the other nation are being tortured. Does the torture seem more justified, because of U.S.-centered nationalism? During the summer of 2004, the world learned that U.S. soldiers had in fact been using these specific kinds of torture on citizens from Iraq and from several European countries who were being held in prisons in Iraq and Cuba.

U.S.-centered nationalism is a challenging topic to discuss in the United States (Hase, 2001). It's difficult for students to hear their own country criticized. This attitude is often strengthened by students' educational experiences.

If you grew up in the United States, for example, students at your high school were probably encouraged to respect and value people from ethnic groups other than their own. However, were you taught to value other countries equally—or did everyone simply assume that the United States had a special, privileged status compared with the rest of the world? Throughout this book, we will explore biases such as sexism, racism, and ageism—situations in which one group has a more powerful position than other groups. We need to keep in mind that U.S.-centered nationalism creates similar problems of inequality on an international level rather than on the interpersonal or intergroup level.

Section Summary

Women and Ethnicity

1. In North American culture, being White is normative; as a result, White individuals may mistakenly believe that they do not belong to any ethnic group.

2. Latinas/os share a language as well as many values and customs, but their other characteristics vary tremendously. Latinas often comment that they must frequently cross boundaries between Latina culture and European American culture.

3. Blacks constitute the third-largest ethnic group in the United States. Blacks differ from one another with respect to their residential community and their family's history.

4. Asian Americans also come from diverse backgrounds. Although they are considered the ideal minority, they often experience discrimination and stressful work conditions.

5. Even though Native Americans and Canadian Aboriginals share a common geographic origin and history, they represent numerous different native backgrounds.

6. The variability within any ethnic group—or subgroup—is always large.

7. Another form of bias that is related to ethnic bias is U.S.-centered nationalism, in which U.S. residents believe that their country has higher status than other countries; for example, the U.S. government believes our country should be allowed to break international laws.

PROBLEMS AND BIASES IN CURRENT RESEARCH

Earlier in this chapter, we mentioned the biased research that characterized the early history of the psychology of women. Let's now explore the kinds of problems that sometimes arise when contemporary researchers conduct studies on the psychology of women and gender.

Anyone conducting research in psychology faces the problem of potential biases. However, biases are a particular problem in research on the psychology of women because researchers are likely to have strong pre-existing emotions, values, and opinions about the topics being investigated (LaFrance et al., 2004). In contrast, consider people who conduct research in the area of visual shape perception. As they were growing up, they probably did not acquire strong emotional reactions to topics such as the retina and the visual cortex! Pre-existing reactions to gender issues may be especially strong in connection with research on women who do not conform to the traditional feminine stereotypes, such as unmarried women or lesbian mothers.

Figure 1.3 shows how biases and inappropriate procedures can influence each step of research. Psychologists are trained to carefully consider each phase of research to eliminate these problems. Although most current studies avoid obvious flaws, students must learn how to evaluate psychological research. Let's look at each phase of this research in more detail, and then we'll consider the more general issue of critical thinking in psychology.

FORMULATING THE HYPOTHESIS

Researchers are often strongly committed to a certain psychological theory. If this theory is biased against women, then the researchers may be predisposed to biased findings before they even begin to conduct their study (Caplan & Caplan, 1999; McHugh & Cosgrove, 1998). For example, Sigmund Freud argued that women actually enjoy suffering. Notice that psychologists who endorse this concept would be biased when they conduct research about women who have experienced domestic violence.

A second problem is that psychologists may formulate a hypothesis based on previous research that is unrelated to the topic they want to study. Several decades ago, for example, researchers wanted to determine whether children were psychologically harmed when their mothers worked outside the home. Psychologists' own biases against employed mothers led them to locate studies showing that children raised in low-quality orphanages often developed psychological problems. The life of a child whose mother works outside the home for 40 hours a week is very different from the life of a child raised in an institution without a mother or father. Still, these early researchers argued that the children of employed mothers would develop similar psychological disorders.

The final way that biases can influence hypothesis formulation concerns the nature of researchers' questions. For example, researchers studying Native American women typically examine issues such as alcoholism or suicide (Hall & Barongan, 2002). If researchers have a biased attitude that these women are somehow deficient, they will not ask questions that can reveal the strengths of these women. For example, do women with extensive tribal experience have more positive attitudes about growing old?

So far, we have reviewed several ways in which biases can operate in the early stages of hypothesis formulation. Specifically, biases can influence the

I. Formulating the hypothesis

    A. Using a biased theory
    B. Formulating a hypothesis on the basis of unrelated research
    C. Asking questions only from certain content areas

II. Designing the study

    A. Selecting the operational definitions
    B. Choosing the participants
    C. Choosing the researcher
    D. Including confounding variables

III. Performing the study

    A. Influencing the outcome through researcher expectancy
    B. Influencing the outcome through participants' expectancies

IV. Interpreting the data

    A. Emphasizing statistical significance rather than practical significance
    B. Ignoring alternate explanations
    C. Making inappropriate generalizations

V. Communicating the findings

    A. Leaving out analyses that show gender similarities
    B. Choosing a title that focuses on gender differences
    C. Journal editors rejecting studies that show gender similarities
    D. Secondary sources emphasizing gender differences instead of gender similarities

FIGURE 1.3 | HOW BIAS CAN INFLUENCE RESEARCH DURING FIVE DIFFERENT STAGES.

psychologists' theoretical orientation, the previous research they consider relevant, and the topics they investigate.

DESIGNING THE STUDY

An important early step in designing a research study is selecting the operational definitions. An **operational definition** tells exactly how researchers will measure a **variable** (or characteristic) in a study. Consider a study investigating gender comparisons in **empathy** (that is, your ability to experience the same emotion that someone else is feeling). For our operational definition, we might decide to use people's answers to a question such as "When your best friend is feeling sad, do you also feel sad?" In other words, we will measure empathy in terms of self-report.

This operational definition of empathy may look perfectly innocent until we realize that it contains a potential bias. Women and men may really be equal in their personal thoughts about empathy, but men may be more hesitant to *report* that they feel empathic. Gender stereotypes emphasize that men should not be overly sensitive. Suppose that we had used another measure, such as observing people's facial expression as they watch a sad movie. Then we might have reached a different conclusion about gender comparisons in empathy. Ideally, researchers should test a hypothesis with several different operational definitions to provide a richer perspective on the research question.

The second source of bias in research design is the choice of participants. Psychologists typically conduct research with participants who are European American middle-class individuals—most often, college students. As a result, we know relatively little about people of color and people who are economically poor (S. Graham, 1997; B. Lott, 2002; Saris & Johnston-Robledo, 2000). The choice of research topics also influences the choice of participants. Studies on low-income mothers or on female criminal behavior have typically focused on Black and Latina women. In contrast, studies on body image or salary equity have usually been limited to European Americans.

A third source of bias in designing a study is the choice of the person who will actually conduct the study. For example, the gender of the researcher may make a difference (e.g., F. Levine & Le De Simone, 1991). Let's imagine that a researcher wants to compare women's and men's interest in babies by interviewing the participants. If the researcher is a man, male participants may be embarrassed to demonstrate a strong interest in babies; gender differences may be large. The same study conducted by a female researcher could produce minimal gender differences.

A final source of bias is the inclusion of confounding variables. A **confounding variable** is any characteristic, other than the central variable being studied, that is not equivalent under all conditions; this confounding variable has the potential to influence the study's results. In studies that compare women and men, a confounding variable is some variable other than gender that is different for the two groups of participants. For example, if we want to compare the spatial ability of college men and women, a potential confounding variable is the amount of time they have spent on video games and other activities that emphasize spatial ability. College men are likely to have more experience with these activities. Therefore, any gender difference in spatial ability might be traceable to the discrepancy in the amount of spatial experience, rather than to a true difference in the actual spatial ability of college women and men.

The reason we must be concerned about confounding variables is that we need to compare two groups that are as similar as possible in all characteristics except the central variable we are studying. Careless researchers may fail to take appropriate precautions. For example, suppose that researchers want to study whether sexual orientation influences psychological adjustment, and they decide to compare married heterosexual women with women who are lesbians. The two groups would not be a fair comparison. For example, some of the lesbians may not currently be in a committed relationship. Depending on the goals of the researchers, a more appropriate study might compare single heterosexual women in a committed relationship and single lesbians in a committed relationship.

Each of these problems in designing a study may lead us to draw inadequate or inappropriate conclusions. The choice of participants in some research means that we do not know much about the behavior of certain groups of people. Furthermore, the operational definitions, the gender of the researcher, and confounding variables may all influence the nature of the conclusions.

Conducting the Study

Further complications arise when the psychologists actually perform the study. One source of bias at this point is called researcher expectancy (Rosenthal, 1993). According to the concept of **researcher expectancy,** the biases that researchers bring to the study can influence the outcome. If researchers expect males to perform better than females on a test of mathematics ability, they may somehow treat the two groups differently. Males and females may therefore respond differently (Halpern, 2000). Any researcher—male or female—who has different expectations for males and females can produce these expectancy effects.

Other areas of psychology also encounter the problem of researcher expectancy. In gender research, the investigators can't help noticing which participants are female and which are male. Suppose that researchers are rating female and male adolescents on their degree of independence in working on a difficult task. These ratings may reflect the researchers' expectations and stereotypes about female and male behavior. These researchers may rate male adolescents higher than female adolescents on a scale of independence, even though a more objective frequency tally of their actual behavior would reveal no gender differences.

Participants, as well as researchers, have typically absorbed expectations and stereotypes about their own behavior (Jaffee et al., 1999). For example, many women have learned that they are expected to be moody and irritable just before their menstrual periods. If a woman is told that she is participating in a study on how the menstrual cycle affects mood, then she may supply more negative ratings during the premenstrual phase of the cycle. If she had been unaware of the purpose of the study, her responses might have been different. When you read about a study that uses self-report, keep this potential problem in mind.

In summary, the expectations of both the researchers and the participants may bias the results and distort the conclusions.

INTERPRETING THE DATA

The data from studies on gender and the psychology of women can be misinterpreted in many ways. For example, some researchers confuse statistical significance and practical significance. As we'll discuss in Chapter 5, a difference between male and female performance on a math test may be *statistically* significant. **Statistical significance** means that the results are not likely to occur by chance alone. The mathematical formulas used in calculating statistical significance are influenced by sample size. For example, almost any gender difference is likely to be statistically significant if a study has tested 10,000 males and 10,000 females.

Suppose that a standardized geometry test was given to 10,000 males and 10,000 females. A statistical analysis of the data reveals that the males scored significantly higher than the females. However, a close inspection reveals that the males received an average score of 40.5, in contrast to the females' average score of 40.0. Even though the difference was statistically significant, this difference has little *practical* significance. **Practical significance,** as the name implies, means that the results have some meaningful and useful implications for the real world (Halpern, 2000). A half-point difference in these hypothetical geometry scores would have no imaginable implications for how males and females should be treated with respect to teaching geometry. Unfortunately, researchers often discuss only statistical significance, when they should also discuss whether a gender difference has practical significance.

When researchers interpret the data they have gathered, another potential problem is that they may ignore alternative explanations. For example, suppose researchers claim that males' superior performance on a test of spatial ability is due to their superior inborn spatial ability. The researcher may be ignoring an alternative explanation that we mentioned earlier: Compared to females, males often have more experience with spatial tasks. Consider another example. Suppose that females score higher on a test measuring anxiety. This difference might really be caused by males' reluctance to *report* anxiety that they feel, rather than by any gender differences in true anxiety. In interpreting this study, researchers must consider alternative explanations.

An additional problem occurs when researchers make inappropriate generalizations. For example, researchers may sample unusual populations and draw conclusions from them about the psychological characteristics of more typical populations. Suppose that you are investigating infants who had been exposed to abnormally high levels of male hormones before they were born. Unfortunately, researchers may overgeneralize and draw conclusions about the way that male hormones influence normal infants (Halpern, 2000). Other researchers might examine a sample of European American female and male college students and then assume that their findings apply to all people, including people of color and people who have not attended college (Reid & Kelly, 1994).

In summary, the interpretation phase of research contains several additional possibilities for distorting reality. Researchers have been known to ignore practical significance, bypass alternative explanations, and overgeneralize their findings.

COMMUNICATING THE FINDINGS

After researchers conduct their studies and perform the related analyses, they usually want to report their findings in writing. Other sources of bias may now enter. Psychologists continue to be preoccupied with gender differences, and a gender similarity is seldom considered startling psychological news (Bohan, 2002; Caplan & Caplan, 1999; LaFrance et al., 2004). Therefore, when researchers summarize the results of a study, they may leave out a particular analysis showing that females and males had similar scores. However, they are likely to report any *gender difference* that was discovered. As you can imagine, this kind of selective reporting underrepresents the gender similarities found in research and overrepresents the gender differences.

Biases are even likely to influence the choice of a title for a research report. Until recently, titles of studies focusing on the psychological characteristics of men and women were likely to include the phrase *gender differences*. Thus, a study examining aggression might be titled "Gender Differences in Aggression," even if it reported one statistically significant gender difference and five comparisons that showed gender similarities. The term *gender differences* focuses on dissimilarities, and it suggests that we should search for differences. Accordingly, I prefer to use the more neutral term *gender comparisons*.

After researchers have written a report of their findings, they send their report to journal editors, who must decide whether it deserves publication. Journal editors, along with the researchers themselves, may be more excited about gender differences than about gender similarities (Clinchy & Norem, 1998; Halpern, 2000). This selective-publication bias therefore overrepresents gender differences still further, so that gender similarities receive relatively little attention.

Even further distortion occurs when the published journal articles are discussed by secondary sources, such as textbooks, newspapers, and magazines. For example, an introductory psychology textbook might discuss one study in which men are found to be more aggressive than women and ignore several other studies that report gender similarities in aggression.

The distortion of results is typically even more blatant when research on gender is reported in the popular press. For example, an article on dreaming in *Newsweek* includes a section called "Different Dreamers: Age and Gender." This section doesn't actually discuss any gender comparisons. A table elsewhere in the article lists the most common dreams for men and women, but no description of the relevant study (Kantrowitz & Springen, 2004). Furthermore, men and women differ by an average of only 7%, a gender difference without practical significance. Similarly, a newsletter intended for college

Demonstration 1.2

ANALYZING
MEDIA REPORTS
ABOUT GENDER
COMPARISONS

Locate a magazine or a newspaper that you normally read. Look for any reports on gender comparisons or the psychology of women. Check Figure 1.3 as you read each article. Can you discover any potential biases?

In addition, can you find any areas in which the summary does not include enough information to make a judgment (e.g., the operational definition for the relevant variables)?

educators featured the headline "Gender Affects Educational Learning Styles, Researchers Confirm" (1995), even though the original research did *not* find a statistically significant gender difference (Philbin et al., 1995).

In an attempt to entice their audience, the media may even misrepresent the species population. For example, a magazine article on stress during pregnancy emphasized the research conducted with rats (Dingfelder, 2004). However, the article included a large photo of a distressed-looking pregnant woman. Many readers might conclude that stress clearly causes disorders in human babies. When you have the opportunity, try Demonstration 1.2 to see whether you find similar media biases.

CRITICAL THINKING AND THE PSYCHOLOGY OF WOMEN

As we have discussed, people must be cautious when they encounter information about gender. They need to carefully inspect published material for a variety of potential biases. This vigilance is part of a more general approach called critical thinking. **Critical thinking** consists of the following three components:

1. Ask thoughtful questions about what you see or hear.
2. Determine whether the conclusions are supported by the evidence that has been presented.
3. Suggest alternative interpretations of the evidence.

One of the most important skills you can acquire in a course on the psychology of women and gender is the ability to think critically about the issues. As Elizabeth Loftus (2004) emphasizes, "Science is not just a giant bowl of facts to remember, but rather a way of thinking. . . . An idea may *seem* to be true, but this has nothing to do with whether it actually *is* true" (p. 8). Unfortunately, the popular culture does not encourage critical thinking (Halpern, 2004b). We are often asked to believe what we see or hear without asking thoughtful questions, determining whether the evidence supports the conclusions, or suggesting other interpretations.

Consider, for example, a scenario described by psychologist Sandra Scarr (1997). She had been invited to discuss—on National Public Radio—the topic of mothers' employment. She therefore described eight recent research studies, all showing that maternal employment had no impact on infants' emotional security. The other female guest on the show was a psychotherapist, the author of a new book arguing that mothers should stay home. The source of her evidence was her own clients, who reported that they had been emotionally harmed during their childhood by having a caretaker other than their mother. The psychotherapist argued that she must speak for young infants, because she knows their pain and they are too young to express their distress.

Scarr reported that both the talk-show host and the listeners who called the show seemed to consider her own research-based evidence and the other guest's intuition-based remarks to be equally persuasive. Critical thinkers, however, would ask good questions, examine the evidence, and think of other interpretations. For example, they might ask whether we should generalize from the retrospective reports of a small number of therapy clients to draw conclusions about infants whose mothers are currently employed. They might also ask whether the psychotherapist ever directly measured distress in the young infants she claimed to represent. Naturally, critical thinkers would also examine Scarr's more research-based findings for evidence of potential bias.

Because accuracy is an important aim of research, we must identify and eliminate the sources of bias that can distort accuracy and misrepresent women. We must also use critical thinking skills to examine the research evidence (Halpern, 2004b). Only then can we have a clear understanding about women and gender.

Section Summary

Problems and Biases in Current Research

1. When researchers formulate their hypotheses, biases can influence their theoretical orientation, the research they consider relevant, and the topics they choose to investigate.

2. When researchers design their studies, biases can influence how they choose their operational definitions, participants, and the people who conduct the research; another bias is the inclusion of confounding variables.

3. When researchers perform their studies, biases may include researcher expectancy as well as the participants' expectations.

4. When researchers interpret their results, biases may include ignoring practical significance, overlooking alternative explanations, and overgeneralizing the findings.

5. When researchers communicate their findings, gender differences may be overreported; the title of the paper may emphasize gender differences; articles that demonstrate gender difference may receive preference; and the popular media may distort the research.

6. An important part of critical thinking is being alert for biases; critical thinking requires you to ask thoughtful questions, determine whether the evidence supports the conclusions, and propose alternative interpretations for the evidence.

ABOUT THIS TEXTBOOK

I designed this book to help you understand and remember concepts about the psychology of women. Let's first consider the four themes of the book, and then we'll examine some features that can help you learn more effectively.

THEMES OF THE BOOK

The subject of the psychology of women is impressively complex. Furthermore, the discipline is so young that we cannot identify a large number of general principles that summarize this diverse field. Nevertheless, you'll find several important themes woven throughout this textbook. Let's discuss them now, to provide a framework for a variety of topics you will encounter.

THEME 1: Psychological Gender Differences Are Typically Small and Inconsistent.   The earlier section on research biases noted that published studies may represent gender differences as being larger than they really are. However, even the published literature on men's and women's abilities and personalities shows that gender similarities are usually more impressive than gender differences. In terms of permanent, internal psychological characteristics, women and men simply are not that different (Basow, 2001; Bem, 2004; Hyde & Plant, 1995). In gender research, one study may demonstrate a gender difference, but a second study— apparently similar to the first—may demonstrate a gender similarity. Gender differences often have a "now you see them, now you don't" quality (Unger, 1998; Yoder & Kahn, 2003).

You'll recognize that Theme 1 is consistent with the similarities perspective discussed on page 7. Theme 1 also specifically rejects the notion of essentialism. As we noted earlier, essentialism argues that gender is a basic, stable characteristic that resides within an individual.

Let's clarify two points, however. First, I am arguing that men and women are *psychologically* similar; obviously, their sex organs make them anatomically different. Second, men and women acquire some different skills and characteristics in our current culture because they occupy different social roles (Eagly, 2001; Yoder & Kahn, 2003). Men are more likely than women to be chief executives, and women are more likely than men to be receptionists. However, if men and women could have similar social roles in a culture, those gender differences would be almost nonexistent.

Throughout this book, we will see that gender differences may appear in some social contexts, but not in others. Gender differences are most likely to occur in these three contexts (Basow, 2001; Unger, 1998; Yoder & Kahn, 2003):

1. When people evaluate themselves, rather than when a researcher records behavior objectively.
2. When people are observed in real-life situations (where men typically have more power), rather than in a laboratory setting (where men and women are fairly similar in power).
3. When people are aware that they are being evaluated by others.

In these three kinds of situations, people drift toward stereotypical behavior. Women tend to respond the way they think women are supposed to respond; men tend to respond the way they think men are supposed to respond.

Theme 1 focuses on **gender as a subject variable,** or a characteristic within a person that influences the way she or he acts. We will see that the gender of the participant or subject (that is, the person who is being studied) typically has little impact on behavior.

THEME 2: *People React Differently to Men and Women.*   We just pointed out that gender as a subject variable is usually not important. In contrast, gender as a *stimulus variable* is important (Bem, 2004). When we refer to **gender as a stimulus variable,** we mean a characteristic of a person to which other people react. When psychologists study gender as a stimulus variable, they might ask, "Do people react differently to individuals who are female than to people who are male?"

Gender is an extremely important social category. In fact, gender is probably the most important social category in North American culture (Bem, 1993). To illustrate this point, try ignoring the gender of the next person you see!

Throughout the book, we will see that gender is an important stimulus variable. In general, we will see that males are more valued than females. For example, many parents prefer a boy rather than a girl for their firstborn child. In Chapter 2, we will also discuss how males are represented more positively in religion and mythology as well as in current language and the media. In addition, men are typically more valued in the workplace.

If people react differently to men and women, they are demonstrating that they believe in gender differences. We could call this phenomenon "the illusion of gender differences." As you will see, both men and women tend to exaggerate these gender differences.

THEME 3: *Women Are Less Visible Than Men in Many Important Areas.*   Men are typically featured more prominently than women in areas that our culture considers important. A quick skim through your daily newspaper will convince you that males and "masculine" topics receive more emphasis (Berkman, 2004). In Chapter 2, we will discuss the research on all forms of media, confirming that men are seen and heard more than women are. Another example is the relative invisibility of girls and women in the classroom, which arises because teachers tend to ignore females (Sadker & Sadker, 1994). Females may also be relatively invisible in the English language. In many respects, our language has traditionally been **androcentric:** The male experience is treated as the norm (Basow, 2001; Bem, 1993, 2004). Instead of *humans* and *humankind,* many people still use words such as *man* and *mankind* to refer to both women and men.

Psychologists have helped to keep some important topics invisible. For example, psychology researchers seldom study major biological events in women's lives, such as menstruation, pregnancy, childbirth, and breast feeding.

Women *are* visible in areas such as women's magazines, the costume committee for the school play, and low-paying jobs. However, these are all areas that our culture does not consider important or prestigious.

As we noted in a previous section, women of color are even less visible than White women. In Chapter 2, we will emphasize how women of color are absent in the media. Psychologists have only recently paid attention to this invisible group (Guthrie, 1998; Holliday & Holmes, 2003; Winston, 2003). When was the last time you saw a newspaper article or movie about women who are Asian American, Latina, or Native American? Low-income women also rarely appear in television and film.

THEME 4: Women Vary Widely from One Another.   In this textbook, we explore how women differ from one another in their psychological characteristics, their life choices, and their responses to biological events. In fact, individual women show so much variability that we often cannot draw any conclusions about women in general (Kimball, 2003). Notice that Theme 4 contradicts the essentialism perspective, which argues that all women share the same psychological characteristics that differentiate them from men.

Think about the variability among women you know. They probably differ dramatically in their aggressiveness or in their sensitivity to other people's emotions. Women also vary widely in their choices in terms of careers, marital status, sexual orientation, desire to have children, and so forth. Furthermore, women differ in their responses to biological events. Some women have problems with menstruation, pregnancy, childbirth, and menopause; others find these experiences neutral or even positive.

In the previous section, we discussed ethnicity, and we noted that the diversity within each ethnic group is remarkable. Throughout this book, when we examine the lives of women in countries outside North America, we will gather further evidence that women vary widely from one another.

We have emphasized that women show wide variation. As you might imagine, men show a similarly wide variation among themselves. These within-gender variabilities bring us full circle to Theme 1 of this book. Whenever variability *within* each of two groups is large, we probably will not find a statistically significant difference *between* those two groups. In the case of gender, we are unlikely to find a large difference between the average score for females and the average score for males. In Chapter 5, we will discuss this statistical issue in more detail. The important point to remember now is that women show wide within-group variability, and men also show wide within-group variability.

HOW TO USE THIS BOOK EFFECTIVELY

This textbook is designed to provide many features that will help you learn the material more effectively. Read this section carefully to make the best use of these features.

Each chapter begins with an outline. When you start a new chapter, be sure to read through the outline to acquaint yourself with the scope of the chapter.

The second feature in each chapter is a box with 10 true-false statements. The answers appear at the end of each chapter together with the page number where each item is discussed. These quizzes will encourage you to think about some of the controversial and surprising findings you'll encounter in the chapter.

The chapters contain a number of demonstrations, such as Demonstrations 1.1 (page 8) and 1.2 (page 26). Try them yourself, or invite your friends to try them. Each demonstration is simple and requires little or no equipment. The purpose of the demonstrations is to make the material more concrete and personal. According to research about human memory, material is easier to remember if it is concrete and is related to personal experience (Matlin, 2005; T. B. Rogers et al., 1977).

In the text, key terms appear in boldface type (e.g., **gender**) and are defined in the same sentence. I have also included some phonetic pronunciations, with the accented syllable in italics. (My students say they feel more comfortable about using a word in discussion if they know their pronunciation is correct.) Concentrate on these definitions. An important part of any discipline is its terminology.

Many textbooks include summaries at the end of each chapter, but I prefer summaries at the end of each major section. For example, Chapter 1 has five section summaries. This feature helps you review the material more frequently, so that you can feel confident about small, manageable portions of the textbook before you move on to new material. At the end of each section, you can test yourself to see whether you can recall the important points. Then check the section summary to see whether you were accurate. Incidentally, some students have mentioned that they learn the material more effectively if they read one section at a time, then take a break, and review that section summary before reading the next portion.

Chapter review questions appear at the end of each chapter. Some questions test your specific recall, some ask you to draw on information from several parts of the chapter, and some ask you to apply your knowledge to everyday situations.

At the end of each chapter is a list of the key (boldface) terms, in the order in which they appear in the chapter. You should test yourself to see whether you can define each term. This list of terms also includes page numbers, so that you can check on the terms you find difficult. Each term also appears in the subject index at the end of the book.

A final feature, also at the end of each chapter, is a list of several recommended readings. These are important articles, books, or special issues of journals that are particularly relevant to that chapter. These readings should be useful if you are writing a paper on one of the relevant topics or if you find an area that is personally interesting to you. I hope you'll want to go beyond the information in the textbook and learn on your own about the psychology of women.

Section Summary

About This Textbook

1. Theme 1 states that psychological gender differences are typically small and inconsistent; gender differences are more likely (a) when people evaluate themselves, (b) in real-life situations, and (c) when people are aware that they are being evaluated by other people.

2. Theme 2 states that people react differently to men and women; for example, males are typically more valued.

3. Theme 3 states that women are less visible than men in many important areas; for instance, our language is androcentric.

4. Theme 4 states that women vary widely from one another; for example, they vary in their psychological characteristics, life choices, and responses to biological processes.

5. Features of this book that can help you learn more effectively include chapter outlines, true-false statements, demonstrations, boldfaced key terms, section summaries, chapter review questions, lists of key terms, and recommended readings.

CHAPTER REVIEW QUESTIONS

1. The terms *sex* and *gender* have somewhat different meanings, although they are sometimes used interchangeably. Define each term, and then decide which of the two terms you should use in discussing each of the following topics: (a) how boys learn "masculine" body postures and girls learn "feminine" body postures; (b) how hormones influence female and male fetuses prior to birth; (c) a comparison of self-confidence in elderly males and females; (d) the development during puberty of body characteristics such as pubic hair and breasts in females; (e) people's beliefs about the personality characteristics of women and men.

2. Apply the two terms *feminism* and *sexism* to your own experience. Do you consider yourself a feminist? Can you identify examples of sexism you have observed during the past week? How do the terms *feminism* and *sexism*, as used in this chapter, differ from the popular use in the media? Also, define and give an example for each of the following terms: racism, classism, heterosexism, ableism, ageism, U.S.-centered nationalism, and the White-as-normative concept.

3. Describe the four kinds of feminism discussed in this chapter. How are the similarities perspective and the differences perspective (with respect to gender comparisons) related to those four kinds of feminism? How are social constructionism and essentialism related to these two perspectives?

4. Describe the early research related to gender and the psychology of women. In the section on problems in research, we discuss biases that arise in formulating hypotheses. How might these problems be relevant in explaining some of this early research?

5. Briefly trace the development of the psychology of women from its early beginnings to the current state of the discipline.

6. Turn back to Figures 1.1 and 1.2. Does the information about the diversity of racial and ethnic groups match the diversity at your own college or university? If not, what are

the differences? How does the information on ethnicity relate to two of the themes of this book?

7. Imagine that you would like to examine gender comparisons in leadership ability. Describe how a number of biases might influence your research.

8. Suppose that you read an article in a news magazine that concludes, "Women are more emotional than men." From a critical-thinking perspective, what questions would you ask to uncover potential biases and problems with the study? (Check Figure 1.3 to see whether your answers to Questions 7 and 8 are complete.)

9. Describe each of the four themes of this book, providing an example for each theme. Do any of the themes contradict your previous ideas about women and gender? If so, how?

10. What is the difference between gender as a subject variable and gender as a stimulus variable? Suppose that you read a study comparing the aggressiveness of men and women. Is gender a subject variable or a stimulus variable? Suppose that another study examines how people judge aggressive men versus aggressive women. Is gender a subject variable or a stimulus variable?

KEY TERMS

*sex (3)

*gender (4)

doing gender (4)

*sexism (4)

*racism (4)

classism (5)

*ableism (5)

*heterosexism (5)

*ageism (5)

*feminism (5)

*liberal feminism (6)

cultural feminism (6)

*radical feminism (6)

women-of-color feminism (7)

*similarities perspective (7)

*social constructionism (8)

*differences perspective (8)

*essentialism (9)

White-as-normative concept (13)

U.S.-centered nationalism (18)

*operational definition (21)

*variable (21)

*empathy (22)

*confounding variable (22)

researcher expectancy (23)

*statistical significance (24)

*practical significance (24)

*critical thinking (26)

gender as a subject variable (29)

gender as a stimulus variable (29)

*androcentric (29)

 Note: The terms asterisked in the Key Terms section serve as good search terms for InfoTrac@ College Edition. Go to http://infotrac.thomsonlearning.com and try these added search terms.

RECOMMENDED READINGS

Bernal, G., Trimble, J. E., Burlew, A. K., & Leong, F. T. L. (Eds.). (2003). *Handbook of racial and ethnic minority psychology.* Thousand Oaks, CA: Sage. This volume is a comprehensive guide to ethnicity. The 32 chapters address topics such as depression in ethnic minorities, psychological perspectives on ethnic identity, and cross-cultural career counseling.

Caplan, P. J., & Caplan, J. B. (1999). *Thinking critically about research on sex and gender* (2nd ed.). New York: Longman. Paula Caplan is a well-known psychologist whose work on the psychology of women is discussed throughout this textbook. She and her son Jeremy wrote this excellent book on applying critical-thinking principles to the research on gender.

Chrisler, J. C., Golden, C., & Rozee, P. D. (Eds.). (2004). *Lectures on the psychology of women* (3rd ed.). Boston: McGraw-Hill. This excellent book features 23 chapters written by prominent researchers in the psychology of women; the topics include poverty, body weight, and sexual harassment.

Eagly, A. H., Beall, A. E., & Sternberg, R. J. (Eds.). (2004). *The psychology of gender* (2nd ed.). New York: Guilford. Of the resources listed in this "Recommended Readings" feature, this book by Eagly and her coauthors provides the most information about theory and about biological factors.

Enns, C. Z. (2004). *Feminist theories and feminist psychotherapies* (2nd ed.). New York: Haworth. I strongly recommend this book, especially because of its clear descriptions of different approaches to feminism and its excellent overview of feminist therapy, a topic we'll discuss in Chapter 12.

Scarborough, E., & Furumoto, L. (1987). *Untold lives: The first generation of American women psychologists*. New York: Columbia University Press. If you are searching for interesting women in the early history of psychology, this book is ideal. It focuses not only on these important women but also on the forces that shaped their lives.

ANSWERS TO THE DEMONSTRATIONS

Demonstration 1.1: 1. radical feminism; 2. women-of-color feminism; 3. liberal feminism; 4. cultural feminism; 5. radical feminism; 6. women-of-color feminism; 7. liberal feminism; 8. cultural feminism.

ANSWERS TO THE TRUE-FALSE STATEMENTS

1. True (p. 4); 2. True (p. 5); 3. True (pp. 7–9); 4. False (p. 10); 5. False (p. 11); 6. True (p. 13); 7. True (p. 17); 8. True (p. 17); 9. True (p. 23); 10. True (p. 28).

2 | GENDER STEREOTYPES AND OTHER GENDER BIASES

True or False?

_____ 1. Historians and archeologists have typically paid great attention to men's lives, whereas they often ignore contributions made by women.

_____ 2. Before about 1900, all the prominent philosophers maintained that women were clearly inferior to men.

_____ 3. When people hear a sentence such as "Each student took his pencil," they typically think of a male student, rather than a female student.

_____ 4. Today, women constitute about 40% of all TV sportscasters.

_____ 5. Black women and men are fairly well represented on television, but Latinas and Latinos account for fewer than 5% of all characters on prime-time television.

_____ 6. When people complete a standard written questionnaire about stereotypes, their gender stereotypes are stronger than when the stereotypes are measured without their awareness.

_____ 7. People are especially likely to be biased against women's competence when women are acting in a stereotypically masculine fashion.

_____ 8. According to surveys, about half of high-school lesbians and gay males report that they have been verbally harassed about their sexual orientation.

_____ 9. When parents are asked to explain why their daughter gets high grades in mathematics, they tend to attribute her success to hard work. In contrast, parents tend to attribute their son's high grades to his mathematical ability.

_____ 10. Current research suggests that Japanese college students, Mexican American college students, and European American college students are equally likely to internalize the traditional gender stereotypes.

On the morning when I began to write this chapter, I was also waiting for two movers who were coming to our home to pick up a desk that would be taken to an office in another location. As the series of everyday events began to unfold, I suddenly realized that I was experiencing an elaborate sequence of gender stereotypes. First, Jim from the other office called to say that two men, Bob and Jake, would be arriving in a white van, and Jim double-checked on the directions to our house. (Automatically, I thought, "Most men wouldn't be so conscientious about calling ahead and also clarifying the directions, but most women would.") When Bob and Jake arrived, Bob took one look at the desk and joked with Jake that the desk was so small that Jake could move it single-handedly. (Automatically, I thought, "Hmmm . . . just like most men; they don't want a woman to think that they are weaklings.") I asked if they would like coffee and cookies. (Automatically, I thought, "These delicate little cookies aren't appropriate, but I don't have any 'guy cookies.' ") They welcomed the coffee but didn't touch the cookies. Jake was a college student. So the three of us began to talk about occupations, grandparenting, and children whose parents are divorced. (With some effort, I thought, "I could have almost the same conversation with two women whom I had just met.")

Stereotypes are the beliefs that we associate with particular groups of people. **Gender stereotypes** are therefore the beliefs that we associate with

TABLE 2.1 | COMPARING THREE KINDS OF GENDER BIAS ABOUT WOMEN

Term	Brief Definition	Example
Stereotype	Belief about women's characteristics	Chris believes that women aren't very smart.
Prejudice	Negative attitude or emotions toward women	Chris doesn't like female lawyers.
Discrimination	Biased behavior toward women	Chris won't hire women for a particular job.

females and males (Fiske, 2004; D. J. Schneider, 2004). In other words, stereotypes refer to thoughts about a social group, which may not correspond to reality (Whitley & Kite, 2006).

Some gender stereotypes may be partly accurate; for example, men may be less likely than women to ask for directions to a destination. However, this stereotype does not apply to every man; after all, Jim had asked me to clarify the directions to our home. Furthermore, I know some women who would wander for an hour, rather than ask for directions. Theme 4 emphasizes that people differ widely from one another, no matter which psychological characteristic you are considering. No stereotype can accurately describe every woman, or every man. However, we all hold gender stereotypes—even psychologists who study stereotypes (Salinas, 2003; D. J. Schneider, 2004).

Several additional terms are related to stereotypes. **Prejudice** is a negative attitude or emotional reaction toward a particular group of people (Crandall & Eshleman, 2003; Whitley & Kite, 2006). **Discrimination** refers to biased treatment of a particular group of people (Fiske, 2004; Ostenson, 2004; Whitley & Kite, 2006). For example, the chief executive of a corporation may have prejudiced attitudes about women and can discriminate against them by refusing to promote them to the executive level. Table 2.1 contrasts these three terms. The most general term, **gender bias**, includes all three issues: gender stereotypes, gender prejudice, and gender discrimination.

Let's begin our examination of gender stereotypes by noting how women have been represented in history, philosophy, and religion and how they are currently represented in language and the media. In the second section of this chapter, we focus on the content of contemporary stereotypes: What are the current stereotypes? The third section explores how these stereotypes can have an impact on our thinking, our behavior, and even our identity.

BIASED REPRESENTATIONS OF WOMEN AND MEN

A systematic pattern emerges when we look at the way women and men are portrayed. As we'll see in this section, women are the "second sex" (de Beauvoir, 1961). Consistent with Theme 2, women are often represented as being inferior to men. In addition, consistent with Theme 3, women are frequently invisible. As you read about gender biases in history, language, and the media, think about how they may have shaped your own beliefs about women and men.

GENDER BIASES THROUGHOUT HISTORY

A few pages of background discussion cannot do justice to a topic as broad as our legacy of gender bias. However, we need to summarize several topics to appreciate the origin of current views about women.

THE INVISIBILITY OF WOMEN IN HISTORICAL ACCOUNTS.   In recent decades, scholars have begun to realize that we know little about how half of humanity has fared throughout history (Erler & Kowaleski, 2003; Stephenson, 2000). Archeologists interested in prehistoric humans typically focused their research attention on tools associated with hunting, which was most often men's activity. They ignored the fact that women provided most of the diet by gathering vegetables and grains. Women also built and repaired the huts (Hunter College Women's Studies Collective, 1995; Stephenson, 2000). In Europe during the 1600s, women often raised crops, cared for the farm animals, and brought products to the market (Wiesner, 2000).

However, women have been left out of many history books because their work was typically confined to home and family. Women artists often expressed themselves in music, dance, embroidered tapestries, and quilting. These relatively fragile and anonymous art forms were less likely to be preserved than men's artistic efforts in painting, sculpture, and architecture. Women rarely had the opportunity or encouragement to become artists (Wiesner, 2000). However, in recent years, feminist historians have begun to examine women's contributions beyond the home and family (Erler & Kowaleski, 2003; Wiesner, 2000). In Italy, for instance, Lavinia Fontana painted portraits during sixteenth-century Bolgona (C. P. Murphy, 2003), and Artemesia Gentileschi was an active artist who lived in Rome and Florence during the seventeenth century; Gentileschi's life has inspired a movie, a historical novel (Vreeland, 2002), and a recent exhibit of her paintings (e.g., "Orazio and Artemisia," 2002).

In addition, many of women's accomplishments have been forgotten. Did you know that women often presided over monasteries before the ninth century (Hafter, 1979)? Did your history book tell you that the Continental Congress chose Mary Katherine Goddard to print the official copy of the Declaration of Independence in 1776? Traditional historians, whether consciously or unconsciously, have ensured women's invisibility in most history books. Scholars interested in women's history, however, are uncovering information about women's numerous accomplishments. Many college history and art courses now focus on women's experiences, making women central rather than peripheral.

PHILOSOPHERS' REPRESENTATION OF WOMEN.   Philosophers throughout the centuries have typically depicted women as inferior to men. For example, the Greek philosopher Aristotle (384–322 B.C.) believed that women could not develop fully as rational beings. Aristotle also believed that women are more likely than men to be envious and to tell lies (Dean-Jones, 1994; Stephenson, 2000).

More recent philosophers have often adopted the same framework. For instance, Jean-Jacques Rousseau (1712–1778) argued that the function of women was to please men and to be useful to them (Hunter College Women's Studies Collective, 1995). In other words, this prominent Enlightenment philosopher was definitely not enlightened about the roles of women! Rousseau's views were echoed by political figures. For example, the French emperor Napoléon Bonaparte (1769–1821) wrote: "Nature intended women to be our slaves. . . . They are our property. . . . Women are nothing but machines for producing children" (cited in Mackie, 1991, p. 26).

Before the twentieth century, perhaps the only well-known philosopher whose views would be acceptable to current feminists was John Stuart Mill (1806–1873). Mill was a British philosopher whose viewpoint was strongly influenced by his wife, Harriet Taylor Mill (1807–1858). John Stuart Mill argued that women should have equal rights and equal opportunities. They should be able to own property, to vote, to be educated, and to choose a profession. John Stuart Mill is prominently featured in philosophy textbooks, but his views on women were omitted until recently (Hunter College Women's Studies Collective, 1995).

GENDER BIASES IN RELIGION AND MYTHOLOGY

We've seen that history and philosophy have not been kind to women. In addition, women are often treated differently from men in traditional religion and mythology. Although women are often less visible than men, women may be portrayed with positive characteristics as well as negative ones.

Consider the difference between Adam and Eve in the story shared by Jews and Christians. First, God created man "in His own image." Later, God made Eve, constructing her from Adam's rib. In other words, women are made from men, and women are therefore secondary in the great scheme of things. In addition, Eve gives in to temptation and leads Adam into sin. When Adam and Eve are expelled from Paradise, Adam's curse is that he must work for food and survival. Eve's much harsher curse is that she must endure the pain of bearing children, and she must also obey her husband.

In Judaism, further evidence of the position of women appears in the traditional prayer for men, "Blessed art Thou, O Lord our God, King of the Universe, that I was not born a woman." Furthermore, the Torah specifies 613 religious rules, but only 3 of them apply to women. In these important Jewish traditions, women are relatively invisible (Ruth, 2001; R. J. Siegel et al., 1995).

For Christians, many parts of the New Testament treat men and women differently (Sawyer, 1996). For example, a letter of St. Paul notes that "the women should keep silence in the churches. For they are not permitted to speak, but should be subordinate, as even the law says" (1 Corinthians 14:34, Revised Standard Version).

As we move into the twenty-first century, Jewish women have become rabbis and scholars, and many ceremonies designed for males have been adapted for females (P. D. Young, 2005). Women have also assumed leadership responsibilities in Protestant religions. For instance, the Episcopal Church USA recently elected a woman—Katharine Jefferts Schori—as its national presiding bishop. Within the Catholic church, some women serve as lay leaders, although women cannot hold higher positions within the church (P. D. Young, 2005).

Other religions have also promoted negative views of women. Consider the yin and yang in traditional Chinese beliefs. The feminine yin represents darkness, ignorance, and evil. The yang, the masculine side, represents light, intellect, and goodness (Levering, 1994; Pauwels, 1998).

The Islam religion is based on the teachings of Muhammad as written in the Qur'an (Koran). Scholars point out that Muhammad was concerned about equal treatment of women and men (Sechzer, 2004; Useem, 2005). However, Muhammad's successors devised more restrictions. In the current era, Islamic cultures vary widely in their treatment of women (El-Safty, 2004).

In Hinduism, a woman is defined in terms of her husband. As a consequence, an unmarried woman or a widow has no personal identity (Siegel et al., 1995). Kali is an especially powerful Hindu goddess, a monster with fangs, crossed eyes, and bloodstained tongue, face, and breasts. Hindus believe that she emerges from the bodies of admirable deities, destroys her enemies, and drinks their blood (Wangu, 2003).

When we combine views of women from various religions and from traditional Greco-Roman mythology, we can derive several conflicting views of women:

1. *Women are evil.* Women can bring harm to men, as Eve did to Adam. Women may even be bloodthirsty, like the goddess Kali.

2. *Women are terrifying sorceresses.* Women can cast spells, like the wicked witches and evil stepmothers in fairy tales. Scylla, in Greek mythology, was a six-headed sea monster who squeezed men's bones together and ate them.

3. *Women are virtuous.* Women can also be virtuous and saintly, especially when they nurture men and small children. For example, the Virgin Mary represents the essence of caring and self-sacrifice. Mary also demonstrates that women must never demand anything for themselves. In addition, mythology sometimes represents women as "earth mothers" who are fertile and close to nature (Mackie, 1991; Sered, 1998).

Notice that these images are sometimes negative and sometimes positive. However, each image emphasizes how women are *different* from men. These traditions illustrate **androcentrism** or the **normative-male problem:** Men are normal; women are "the second sex."

GENDER BIASES IN LANGUAGE

Language, as with religion, frequently encourages a second-class status for women. Specifically, people often use subordinate or negative terms to refer to women. In addition, women are often invisible in language—for example, when the term *he* is used in reference to both men and women (Weatherall, 2002). Incidentally, we'll consider a related topic in Chapter 6 when we compare how men and women use language.

TERMS USED FOR WOMEN.   In many situations, people use different terms to refer to men and women, and the two terms are not parallel (Adams & Ware, 2000; Gibbon, 1999). For example, John Jones, M.D., will be called a *doctor,* whereas Jane Jones, M.D., may be called a *lady doctor.* This usage implies that being a male doctor is normal and that a female doctor is an exception.

Sometimes, the female member of a pair of words has a much more negative, sexualized, or trivial connotation than the male member does. Think about the positive connotations of the word *bachelor:* a happy-go-lucky person, perhaps with many romantic partners. How about *spinster?* Here the connotation is much more negative; no man wanted to marry her. Similarly, compare *master* with *mistress, major* with *majorette, sculptor* with *sculptress,* and *wizard* with *witch* (Adams & Ware, 2000; Gibbon, 1999; Weatherall, 2002). Language may also infantilize women. For example, people often refer to women as *girls* or *gals* in situations where men would not be called *boy.* When a newspaper article uses these biased terms to refer to a woman, people judge her to be less competent than when she is referred to in gender-neutral terms (Dayhoff, 1983).

THE MASCULINE GENERIC.   A cognitive psychology textbook with a 1998 copyright begins with this introduction: "Who and what are we? What is the mind and how does it function? . . . Such questions certainly have been with us as long as man has existed." As I read these sentences, I wondered whether women were really included in the author's term *man?* Women have surely pondered these same questions. The example of *man* illustrates a problem called the masculine generic. The **masculine generic** (sometimes called the **androcentric generic**) is the use of masculine nouns and pronouns to refer to all human beings—both males and females—instead of males alone (Wodak, 2005). Table 2.2 shows some of these masculine generic terms. A teacher may

TABLE 2.2 | EXAMPLES OF MASCULINE GENERIC TERMS

businessman	patronize
manpower	he/his/him (to refer to both genders)
chairman	salesman
master of ceremonies	mankind
forefather	workmanship
Neanderthal man	man-made
fraternal twins	

Sources: American Psychological Association (2001) and Doyle (1995).

Demonstration 2.1

Ask a friend to listen as you read sentence 1 aloud. Then ask the friend to describe any image that comes to mind. Repeat the process with the remaining sentences. For each of the target (T) sentences, note whether your friend's image represents a male, a female, or some other answer.

1. Fire hydrants should be opened on hot days.
(T)   2. The average American believes he watches too much TV.
3. The tropical rain forests of Brazil are a natural wonder.
(T)   4. Pedestrians must be careful when they cross the street.
5. The apartment building was always a mess.
(T)   6. After a patient eats, he needs to rest.
7. In the corner sat a box of worn-out shoes.
(T)   8. Teenagers often daydream while they do chores.

Did your friend supply more male images for sentences 2 and 6 than for sentences 4 and 8? To obtain a broader sample of replies, have several friends respond to this demonstration, or combine data with other classmates.

---

have told you that *his* really includes *her* in the sentence, "Each student took his pencil." Essentially, you were supposed to consider *his* in this sentence as gender neutral, even though any female content is invisible (Adams & Ware, 2000; Romaine, 1999; Wayne, 2005; Weatherall, 2002).

We have clear research evidence that these masculine generic terms are not actually gender neutral. Approximately 50 studies have demonstrated that terms such as *man* and *he* produce thoughts about males rather than thoughts about both genders (e.g., M. Crawford, 2001; Lambdin et al., 2003; Romaine, 1999; Weatherall, 2002). The issue is no longer simply a grammatical one; it has become both political and practical.

Demonstration 2.1 illustrates part of a classic study, conducted by John Gastil (1990). Gastil presented a number of sentences that used a masculine generic pronoun (e.g., "The average American believes he watches too much TV"). Other sentences used a gender-neutral pronoun (e.g., "Pedestrians must be careful when they cross the street"). Gastil asked participants to describe the mental image that each sentence evoked.

As Figure 2.1 shows, female participants reported four times as many male images as female images when they responded to sentences containing *he*. In contrast, females reported an equal number of male and female images (i.e., a 1:1 ratio) when they responded to sentences containing *they*. Figure 2.1 also shows that males, in responding to the *he* sentences, reported an astonishing 13 times as many male images as female images, but only a 4:1 ratio in response to the *they* sentences. In short, masculine generic terms produce more thoughts about males than do gender-neutral terms.

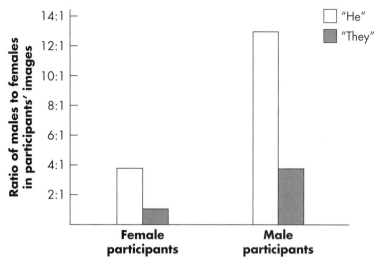

FIGURE 2.1 RATIO OF MALE IMAGES TO FEMALE IMAGES, AS A FUNCTION OF THE PRONOUN CONDITION AND THE GENDER OF THE PARTICIPANT.

Source: Based on Gastil (1990).

Other research has shown that the masculine generic issue has important implications for people's career choices. For example, Briere and Lanktree (1983) presented students with different versions of a paragraph describing careers in psychology. Students who had seen the gender-neutral version rated psychology as a more appealing career for women than did those who had seen the masculine generic version. M. E. Johnson and Dowling-Guyer (1996) reported a related finding: College students rate psychology counselors more positively if the counselors use gender-neutral language rather than masculine-generic language.

The use of gender-biased language has clearly decreased in recent years. For example, most writers now use the term *people* rather than the masculine generic term *man*. Furthermore, most college students tend to prefer nonsexist language (Parks & Roberton, 1998a, 1998b, 2000). People who have low scores on a test of gender bias are especially likely to avoid sexist language (Swim et al., 2004). Parks and Roberton (1998a) also report that some male students make positive comments about gender-neutral terms. For example, a male college student reported:

> Being a male myself, it's easy to think that people are making mountains out of molehills. . . . But I think that if the roles were reversed, I would want change. . . . It wouldn't be fair if I was part of womankind, so it shouldn't be fair for women to be part of mankind. We should all be part of humankind. (p. 451)

Organizations such as the American Psychological Association (2001) strongly caution against gender-biased language. In addition, many books and

TABLE 2.3 | SUGGESTIONS FOR NONSEXIST LANGUAGE

1. Use the plural form. "Students can monitor their progress" can replace "A student can monitor his progress."

2. Use "you." The sentence "Suppose that you have difficulty recalling your Social Security number" is less sexist—and also more engaging—than "Suppose that a person has difficulty recalling his Social Security number."

3. Use "his or her" or "her or his," as in the sentence "A student can monitor her or his progress." The order of these pronouns may sound awkward, but females do not always need to appear second.

4. Eliminate the pronoun. "The student is typically the best judge of the program" can replace "The student is usually the best judge of his program."

Source: Based on American Psychological Association (2001).

articles provide helpful suggestions about substitutions for gender-biased terms (e.g., Foertsch & Gernsbacher, 1997; Gibbon, 1999; Pauwels, 1998; Russo, 1999). Table 2.3 offers some suggestions.

Language change does require some effort, and we may find ourselves slipping back into the masculine generic. For example, a truck driver once passed my car when the visibility was poor, and I shouted, "What in the world does he think he is doing?" My daughter, then 9 years old, gently reminded me, "Or *she*, Mom."

GENDER BIASES IN THE MEDIA

An advertisement for perfume in an upscale magazine shows a woman reclining with her eyes closed, adorned by flowers, as if it were her funeral. Another ad shows a woman about age 20 applying antiwrinkle cream; the text says to use this cream *before* your first wrinkle. Can you imagine switching the genders—using a corpselike male model to advertise men's cologne or running an ad to encourage 20-year-old men to purchase an antiwrinkle cream? If you want to see whether an advertisement is sexist, here's a test that is usually helpful: switch the genders and note whether the revision seems bizarre.

In Chapter 3, we'll consider media directed toward children. Here, let's first examine gender stereotypes found in media directed toward adults, and then we'll discuss the effects of these stereotyped representations.

STEREOTYPED REPRESENTATIONS.   Hundreds of studies have examined how women are represented in the media. You may find an occasional example of nurturant dads and intellectual moms. However, the research generally demonstrates the following eight conclusions, which support both Theme 2 (differential treatment of women) and Theme 3 (invisibility of women).

1. Women are relatively invisible.   The research shows that women are underrepresented in the media. For example, women are relatively invisible in the news. Studies of the front pages of newspapers in the United States and Canada show that the articles refer to women only 15–25% of the time (Bridge, 1994; United Nations, 1995; C. Wheeler, 1994). On television, women report only about 20% of the news stories about economic, political, or international issues (Grieco, 1999; Hoynes, 1999). Furthermore, only 20% of sportscasters are female (R. L. Hall, 2004). In five major U.S. newspapers and magazines, women constitute just 10% to 28% of the opinion columnists (Ashkinaze, 2005).

In addition, men dominate entertainment. For example, about 60 to 70% of the actors in prime-time television are male (Lauzen & Dozier, 2002; Perse, 2001). Also consider film, specifically the main character in films that have won an Oscar for best motion picture. Between 1965 and 2001, only three winning films focused on a woman—and all these women were European American (A. G. Johnson, 2001). An analysis of characters on TV shows found 2.4 times as many males as females (Gerbner, 1997). In addition, we rarely see women athletes on TV. Television coverage of women's sports is only 9% of the total sports coverage (R. L. Hall, 2004).

In current prime-time television advertisements, 54% of the central characters are male and 46% are female. These are exactly the same percentages reported in 1988 (Bretl & Cantor, 1988; Ganahl et al., 2003). Even new technology emphasizes males. For instance, 65% of computer clip-art images are male (Milburn et al., 2001). In addition, women are seldom the heroes of video games, partly because fewer than 10% of video-game designers are female ("Online," 2004).

2. Women are relatively inaudible.   Women are not seen much, and they are *heard* even less. For instance, only 5% of radio talk-show hosts are women (Flanders, 1997). Women are also inaudible in television advertisements (Perse, 2001). Try to recall a typical TV ad. Whose voice of authority is praising the product's virtues? Usually, it is a man's voice. The percentage of males in these voice-overs has remained reasonably constant in recent years. Studies in the United States report that 70–90% of voice-overs are male; similar data are reported in Great Britain, Portugal, France, Denmark, Australia, Turkey, and Japan (Arima, 2003; Bartsch et al., 2000; Furnham & Mak, 1999; Furnham & Skae, 1997; Hurtz & Durkin, 1997; Neto & Pinto, 1998; Uray & Burnaz, 2003).

3. Women are seldom shown working outside the home.   For example, television advertisements and popular magazines are much more likely to show men rather than women in an employment setting (Arima, 2003; Morrison & Shaffer, 2003; D. J. Schneider, 2004). In addition, women on television programs may mention their professions, but they are seldom shown actually *working* on the job.

In Chapter 4, we'll see that adolescent girls may have ambitious career plans. However, they frequently abandon these plans as they work on cultivating romantic relationships. Several analyses of magazines such as *Seventeen* have revealed a similar emphasis (Peirce, 1990; Schlenker et al., 1998; Willemsen, 1998). The articles on physical appearance and finding a boyfriend consistently outweigh the articles about career planning and independence. In magazines intended for adult women, the articles on love relationships, food, cosmetics, and home products far outnumber the articles on careers and other serious topics (S. H. Alexander, 1999; French, 1992).

4. Women are shown doing housework.   Here, unfortunately, the percentages probably capture reality accurately. Television and radio commercials seldom show men taking care of children or performing household chores, whether the sample is gathered in North America, Europe, Asia, or Africa (Arima, 2003; Bartsch et al., 2000; Furnham & Mak, 1999; Furnham & Thomson, 1999; Furnham et al., 2000; G. Kaufman, 1999; Mwangi, 1996; Perse, 2001; Vigorito & Curry, 1998).

5. Women and men are represented differently.   The media are likely to treat men more seriously than women. For example, when a woman runs for elected office, it's difficult to find a newspaper article that does not mention her hairstyle, her "figure flaws," or her clothing choices (Pozner, 2001). Interestingly, the only categories of TV ads in which women appear more often than men are for beauty products and clothing (Ganahl et al., 2003). In addition, sports commentators refer to male athletes as "men," whereas the female athletes are called "girls," consistent with the biased language we discussed earlier in this section (R. L. Hall, 2004). The media also portray women and men as having different personalities. The women are relatively powerless and passive, and the men are often aggressive and macho, both on television and in the movies (Haskell, 1997; Scharrer, 1998).

6. Women's bodies are used differently from men's bodies.   Magazines and television rarely show images of overweight women (G. Fouts & Burggraf, 1999; Greenwood & Pietromonaco, 2004; Lin, 1998). In action comic books, the women have exaggerated bodies, with enormous breasts and tiny waists. They also wear short skirts or clinging bodysuits, and they are often partially nude (Fraser, 1997; Kilbourne, 2003; Massoth, 1997). Furthermore, if you glance through magazine advertisements, you'll notice that the women are more likely than the men to serve a decorative function. Women recline in seductive clothes, caressing a liquor bottle, or they drape themselves coyly on the nearest male. In contrast, the men are strong and muscular, and they typically adopt a rigid, dignified body posture (Millard & Grant, 2001).

Physical attractiveness is definitely more important for women than for men. On prime-time television, for instance 65% of the compliments about appearance are directed toward women, even though only 40% of the actors are female (Lauzen & Dozier, 2002).

7. Women of color are underrepresented, and they are often shown in a particularly biased way.   On television, people of color appear primarily in situation comedies (C. C. Wilson & Gutiérrez, 1995). For example, Blacks are seldom shown in romantic relationships (Perse, 2001).

Blacks are now represented in a reasonable number of TV programs and advertisements. However, other ethnic groups are virtually invisible (Boston et al., 2001; Coltrane & Messineo, 2000; Perse, 2001). For example, Latinas/os are the fastest-growing ethnic group in the United States, and they now represent about 12% of the U.S. population. However, they account for only about 2% of all characters on prime-time television shows and people in magazine advertisements (Espinosa, 1997; Kilbourne, 1999). Most often, these Latinas/os appear only in minor supporting roles (Cortés, 1997; Rodríguez, 1997). Native American women are especially rare in the media (S. E. Bird, 1999; Perse, 2001).

In the earlier discussion of women and religion, we noted that religions represent women as either saints or sinners. The same polarized representation is often true for women of color in the media. Most women of color are either "good girls" or "bad girls"—either asexual or sexpots. The characters are seldom well enough developed to reveal the interesting combination of traits depicted in the media for European American individuals (Coltrane & Messineo, 2000; Espinosa, 1997; Rodríguez, 1997; Vargas, 1999). In summary, women of color are both underrepresented and misrepresented by the media.

8. *Lower-social-class women are underrepresented, and they are often shown in a particularly biased way.*   Surprisingly, media researchers have paid remarkably little attention to social class. In fact, several books about television and other media do not even list the term *social class* in the index (Bucy & Newhagen, 2004; Cortese, 1999; Kilbourne, 1999; Shanahan & Morgan, 1999).

However, the research shows that prime-time television and other media primarily feature middle-class or wealthy individuals (Mantsios, 2001). If you are looking for low-income women on television, you'll need to watch the talk shows, such as *The Jerry Springer Show*. After all, it's considered acceptable to include low-income women if they are promiscuous or if they come from dysfunctional families (Mantsios, 2001). In newspapers or magazines, you'll rarely find any article about low-income women unless it describes a mother receiving public assistance. These articles seldom capture the difficulty of raising a family under these conditions (Bullock et al., 2001). Furthermore, about half of the lower-income women featured in magazine articles are Black—a much higher percentage than in the real world (D. J. Schneider, 2004).

Now that you are familiar with some of the ways in which women are represented in the media, try Demonstration 2.2. You can also analyze magazine advertisements to assess stereotyped representations. Pay particular attention to any nontraditional advertisements. Is the female lawyer arguing the case looking both confident and competent? How about the father changing the baby's diaper?

Demonstration 2.2

THE REPRESENTATION OF WOMEN AND MEN ON TELEVISION

Keep a pad of paper next to you during the next five television programs you watch so that you can monitor how women and men are represented. Use one column for women and one for men, and record the activity of each individual who appears on screen for more than a few seconds. Use simple codes to indicate what each person is doing, such as working at a job (W), doing housework (H), or performing some activity for other family members (F). In addition, record the number of female and male voice-overs in the advertisements. Can you detect any other patterns in the representations of women and men, aside from those mentioned in the text?

How are social class and ethnicity represented on these shows? Can you identify any nonstereotypical examples?

You may want to share your views with the advertisers, using addresses from the World Wide Web. Sponsors are often responsive to public opinion. For example, I once wrote to the chief executive of a hotel after seeing its extremely sexist ad in *Toronto Life*. He replied that the advertisement had already been discontinued as a result of complaints from the public. You should also compliment companies about nonstereotyped ads.

THE EFFECTS OF STEREOTYPED REPRESENTATIONS.   Does the biased representation of women in the media simply *reflect* reality, or does it actually *influence* reality? Although the topic has not been extensively studied, we have evidence for both options (D. J. Schneider, 2004). The media reflect the reality that women are often unseen and unheard and that they are more likely than men to do housework. The media also reflect the reality that women are too frequently believed to be decorative. However, the ads certainly do *not* reflect reality in other respects. For example, do you have any female friends who obsess about a nearly invisible age spot or who invite neighbors in to smell their toilet bowl?

Research evidence also suggests that the media can influence reality by changing some people's behaviors and beliefs. In one classic study, researchers found that college women who had seen a nontraditional version of a TV advertisement were much more self-confident than college women who had seen a traditional version (Jennings et al., 1980).

Advertisements can also influence gender-role attitudes. For example, men who are initially nontraditional are likely to become even more nontraditional after looking at nonstereotyped ads. In contrast, men who look at stereotyped ads become more traditional (Garst & Bodenhausen, 1997). Other research shows that both men and women hold a less feminist attitude after viewing stereotyped ads (MacKay & Covell, 1997).

The media can also influence how we judge other people. For example, J. L. Knight and Giuliano (2001) asked students to read an article about a female athlete and rate her on a number of dimensions. If the article emphasized her athletic skills rather than her attractiveness, the students rated her higher in talent, aggressiveness, and heroism. Even subtle differences in the representation of women and men can have an important effect on people's stereotypes (M. J. Levesque & Lowe, 1999). The media could have the power to help people adopt nontraditional gender roles, although we certainly haven't yet seen many inspiring examples.

Section Summary

Biased Representations of Women and Men

1. "Gender stereotype" refers to the characteristics we associate with females and males. Prejudice refers to negative attitudes, and discrimination indicates biased behavior.

2. We have little information about women's activities throughout history. In general, philosophers emphasized women's inferiority.

3. Judaism and Christianity both perpetuate women's inferiority; traditional Chinese beliefs and Hinduism also portray negative images of women. Various religions and ancient myths have represented women as evil people, sorceresses, and virtuous mothers.

4. The terms used for women often emphasize their secondary status, or these terms may also be negative or infantilizing.

5. Numerous studies have demonstrated that the masculine generic encourages people to think about males more often than females; gender-neutral terms can be easily substituted.

6. The media represent women in a stereotyped fashion. Women are seen and heard less than men are. They are seldom shown working outside the home; more often, they appear doing housework. The media treat men more seriously; women's bodies are also represented differently.

7. Women of color and low-income women are particularly likely to be underrepresented or to be represented in a stereotypical fashion.

8. The media's stereotyped representations of women can promote stereotyped behaviors, self-images, and attitudes. In addition, people judge women to be less competent if they have been portrayed in a gender-stereotyped fashion.

PEOPLE'S BELIEFS ABOUT WOMEN AND MEN

In the first section of this chapter, we looked at how women and men are represented in history, philosophy, religion, mythology, language, and the media. These representations certainly help to shape people's beliefs about gender. Let's now turn to the man and woman on the street—or, more likely, on the college campus. What is the nature of their gender stereotypes? Why is sexism such a complex topic? What kinds of thinking produce these stereotypes and keep them powerful? How can gender stereotypes influence people's behavior? Finally, do people adopt these stereotypes, so that women tend to describe themselves with "feminine" terms, whereas men prefer "masculine" terms?

THE CONTENT OF STEREOTYPES

Gender stereotypes are so pervasive that they extend to a wide range of human behaviors (Barnett & Rivers, 2004; P. Kaminski, personal communication, 2004). For example, most people believe that males earn higher grades than females in math classes, although we'll see in Chapter 5 that females' grades are usually better. Most people also assume that male leaders are more effective than female leaders, although we'll refute that stereotype in Chapter 6. In addition, most people believe that men are more likely than women to have a heart attack, yet we'll see in Chapter 11 that this stereotype is inaccurate.

In this section, however, we'll focus primarily on people's stereotypes about women's and men's personality characteristics. Before you read any further, look at Demonstration 2.3 below. Rather than assess your own stereotypes or beliefs about men and women, try to guess what *most people* think. You will probably find that your answers are accurate.

If you check the list of personality characteristics associated with women and with men, you'll see that those two lists are somewhat different. According

Demonstration 2.3

STEREOTYPES
ABOUT WOMEN
AND MEN

For this demonstration, you will guess what most people think about women and men. Put a W in front of those characteristics that you believe most people associate with women more than with men. Put an M in front of those characteristics associated with men more than with women.

_____ self-confident		_____ emotional	
_____ fickle		_____ talkative	
_____ gentle		_____ loud	
_____ greedy		_____ show-off	
_____ kind		_____ compassionate	
_____ warm		_____ patient	
_____ competitive		_____ modest	
_____ nervous		_____ courageous	
_____ active		_____ inventive	
_____ capable		_____ powerful	

The answers at the end of the chapter are based on responses that researchers have obtained (Cota et al., 1991; Street, Kimmel, & Kromrey, 1995; J. E. Williams & Best, 1990; J. E. Williams et al., 1999).

to theorists, the term **agency** describes a concern with your own self-interests. Terms associated with agency (such as *self-confident* and *competitive*) are usually stereotypically masculine. In contrast, **communion** emphasizes a concern for your relationship with other people. Terms associated with communion (such as *gentle* and *warm*) are usually stereotypically feminine (Eagly, 2001). In general, higher-status characteristics are those associated with men (Ridgeway & Bourg, 2004).

Let's now look at the stereotypes about men and women from various ethnic groups. Then we'll consider how several subject variables influence our stereotypes.

STEREOTYPES ABOUT WOMEN AND MEN FROM DIFFERENT ETHNIC GROUPS.   In addition to simple stereotypes about women's and men's personality, people also create stereotypes about women and men from different ethnic groups (Deaux, 1995; D. J. Schneider, 2004). For example, Yolanda Niemann and her colleagues (1994) asked college students from four ethnic groups to list the first 10 adjectives that came to mind when they thought of particular categories of people. These target categories included males and females from four different ethnic groups, so that each rater provided adjectives for a total of eight groups. Table 2.4 combines the data from all participants and shows the three most commonly listed terms for each group. As you can see, people do not have one unified gender stereotype that holds true for all four ethnic groups. Instead, gender and ethnicity combine to produce a variety of gender stereotypes.

In reality, however, we probably create subtypes within each of these gender-ethnicity categories. For example, the stereotypes often distinguish between the "good women" and the "bad women" in each ethnic group. Ethnic studies scholars note that Black women are stereotyped as either warm but sexless "Mammies"—a stereotype preserved since the slavery era—or sexually promiscuous females (C. M. West, 2004). Latinas are portrayed, with similar polarization, as either chaste, self-sacrificing virgins or sexually promiscuous women (Baldwin & DeSouza, 2001; Peña, 1998). Asian American females are seen as either shy and submissive young women or as threatening and manipulative "dragon ladies" (LeEspiritu, 2001; Matsumoto & Juang, 2004).

Interestingly, we don't know much about people's stereotypes about Native American women (Russell-Brown, 2004). Niemann and her colleagues (1994) did not study Native Americans, so Table 2.4 does not list them. When most people hear the term *Native American* or *Indian,* they think of a male, or they may think of Pocahontas or Sacagawea. In any event, residents in most regions of North America do not have clear stereotypes about this least visible group of women of color (Comas-Díaz & Greene, 1994).

The research on ethnic subtypes within gender stereotypes illustrates the complexity of these stereotypes. No simple, unified stereotype represents all women. Instead, we've created subtypes to reflect ethnicity, social class, and other characteristics of the group we are judging (Lott & Saxon, 2002).

TABLE 2.4 | THE THREE MOST FREQUENTLY SUPPLIED ADJECTIVES FOR FEMALES AND MALES FROM FOUR DIFFERENT ETHNIC GROUPS

European American Females	European American Males
Attractive	Intelligent
Intelligent	Egotistical
Egotistical	Upper-class

African American Females	African American Males
Speak loudly	Athletic
Dark skin	Antagonistic
Antagonistic	Dark skin

Asian American Females	Asian American Males
Intelligent	Intelligent
Speak softly	Short
Pleasant/friendly	Achievement-oriented

Mexican American Females	Mexican American Males
Black/brown/dark hair	Lower-class
Attractive	Hard workers
Pleasant/friendly	Antagonistic

Source: Based on Niemann et al. (1994).

FACTORS INFLUENCING STEREOTYPES.   We've just seen that various characteristics of the target—the person we are judging—can influence our stereotypes. For example, ethnicity as a *stimulus* variable can affect these stereotypes. Now let's switch topics and examine characteristics of the *subject*—the person who holds these stereotypes. Subject variables are sometimes important in research about gender. (You may want to review the distinction between stimulus variables and subject variables on page 29.)

Are stereotypes influenced by subject variables such as gender, ethnicity, and the culture in which we are raised? Alternatively, do we all share the same gender stereotypes, no matter what our own background may be? The answer seems to be somewhere between these two possibilities.

Consider the influence of the respondents' gender. Typically, men and women hold similar gender stereotypes, but men's stereotypes are somewhat more traditional (e.g., Bryant, 2003; Frieze et al., 2003; Levant & Majors, 1997; D. J. Schneider, 2004; Twenge, 1997). Within each gender, however, there are substantial individual differences in the strength of these stereotypes

(Monteith & Voils, 2001). Consistent with Theme 4, some women hold strong gender stereotypes; other women believe that men and women are quite similar.

In contrast, the respondents' ethnicity does not have a consistent influence on gender stereotypes (R. J. Harris & Firestone, 1998; Levant et al., 1998). Gender stereotypes are definitely more complicated than we originally thought (Deaux, 1999; D. J. Schneider, 2004).

Do people in other countries differ from North Americans in their stereotypes? Cross-cultural research is challenging because some of the English terms used in North America cannot be easily translated into the language of other cultures (Best & Thomas, 2004; Gibbons et al., 1997).

Deborah Best and John Williams have conducted the most extensive cross-cultural research on gender stereotypes (Best & Thomas, 2004; J. E. Williams & Best, 1990; J. E. Williams et al., 1999). They assessed gender stereotypes for 100 university students (50 females and 50 males) in each of 25 countries. In general, the research shows that people in many different cultures share similar gender stereotypes. For instance, men are typically believed to be more outgoing and ambitious, whereas women are believed to be more dependent and agreeable (Best & Thomas, 2004; Matsumoto & Juang, 2004).

In summary, factors such as gender, ethnicity, and culture have complex influences on people's gender stereotypes. Overall, however, the consistency of the gender stereotypes is more prominent than any differences among the groups. Now try Demonstration 2.4 before you read further.

IMPLICIT GENDER STEREOTYPES

So far, we have focused on **explicit gender stereotypes,** the kind you supply when you are aware that you are being tested. For instance, suppose that a researcher asks you, "Do you believe that math is more strongly associated with males than with females?" Most socially aware students answer "No." An explicit question like this implies that it's not appropriate to hold rigid stereotypes. As a result, you supply a socially desirable response, rather than an honest

Demonstration 2.4

USING THE IMPLICIT ASSOCIATION TEST TO ASSESS IMPLICIT ATTITUDES TOWARD SOCIAL GROUPS

Log onto the Internet and visit a site called "Project Implicit": <https://implicit.harvard.edu/implicit/demo/>. You can examine your own attitudes about gender, ethnicity, sexual orientation, people with disability, and the elderly. Be certain to follow the caution to make your responses as quickly as possible. More leisurely responses might assess explicit attitudes, rather than implicit attitudes.

"Yes" (Fazio & Olson, 2003). Notice, then, that these traditional explicit measures may underestimate the strength of people's gender stereotypes.

Since the late 1990s, psychologists have conducted numerous studies using a different technique. **Implicit gender stereotypes** are the stereotypes you reveal when you are not aware that your gender stereotypes are being assessed. This research typically uses the Implicit Association Test (IAT), which you tried in Demonstration 2.4. The IAT is based on the principle that people can mentally pair words together very rapidly if they are related. However, they take significantly more time to pair unrelated words (Greenwald & Nosek, 2001; Greenwald et al., 1998; Whitley & Kite, 2006).

Consider the research that Nosek and his colleagues (2002) conducted, using the Implicit Association Test (IAT). The participant sits in front of a computer screen that presents a series of words. On a typical trial—in which the pairings were *consistent* with gender stereotypes—the participant would be told to press the key on the left if the word was related to math (e.g., *calculus* or *numbers*) and also if the word was related to males (e.g., *uncle* or *son*). This same participant would press the key on the right if the word was related to the arts (e.g., *poetry* or *dance*) and also if the word was related to females (e.g., *aunt* or *daughter)*. Notice that these pairings should be easy if people hold a stereotype that math terms are related to males and the art terms are related to females.

Then the instructions shifted so that the pairings were *inconsistent* with gender stereotypes. Now, on a typical trial, the participant should press the left key for a word related to math and also for a word related to females. This same participant should press the right key for a word related to the arts and also for a word related to males. In all cases, participants were urged to respond as quickly as possible, so that they would not consciously consider their responses.

The results showed that the participants responded significantly faster to the stereotype-consistent pairings than to the stereotype-inconsistent pairings. In other words, math and males seem to go together, whereas the arts and females seem to go together. This study therefore suggests that people reveal strong gender stereotypes using an implicit measure, although they might deny these stereotypes if they were concerned about providing socially desirable responses on an explicit measure (Hewstone et al., 2002).

THE COMPLEXITY OF CONTEMPORARY SEXISM

At the beginning of this chapter, we introduced three intertwined concepts: stereotypes, prejudice, and discrimination. In the previous discussion, we focused on stereotypes. Now we'll consider prejudice (biased attitudes), and we'll also explore the complexity of sexism today.

In 1989, a Texas state senator remarked, "Do you know why God created women? Because sheep can't type" (Armbrister, cited in Starr, 1991, p. 41). That quotation is clearly sexist—no doubt about it. In contrast, present-day sexism is typically less obvious and more subtle, elusive, and complex (Brant et al., 1999). Let's examine three components of prejudice: (1) attitudes toward women's competence, (2) attitudes toward women's "pleasantness," and (3) a related topic, a recent scale designed to test the complicated ambivalent sexism that is now fairly common. Finally, we'll consider several studies that focus on discrimination against women in interpersonal interactions.

ATTITUDES TOWARD WOMEN'S COMPETENCE.   Numerous studies in the past 40 years have focused on people's attitudes about women's competence (e.g., Beyer, 1999b; Goldberg, 1968; Swim et al., 1989). In some studies, students are asked to make judgments—under well-controlled circumstances—about either a male or a female. For example, Haley (2001) asked White undergraduate students to examine a fictitious application for a college scholarship. This application included a completed application form and a two-page essay. As part of this study, some students received an application that specified the student was a male; other students received an identical application, only it specified the student was a female. The students were instructed to indicate how much money should be awarded to the person described in the application. Haley's results showed that the White males awarded about $1,900 more to the male applicant than to the female applicant. In contrast, the females awarded only about $300 more for the female applicant than for the male applicant.

Other research by Susan Fiske and her coauthors (2002) and Peter Glick and his coauthors (2004) asked students and nonstudents from 16 different countries to rate categories of people, such as men and women. The participants rated men as being significantly more likely than women to be associated with status and power.

We should note that some research does not demonstrate negative attitudes about women's competence. Researchers have tried to identify the circumstances in which women's competence is likely to be devalued. Here are some of their conclusions:

1. Males are more likely than females to downgrade women (Eagly & Mladinic, 1994; Frieze et al., 2003; Haley, 2001).
2. People are more likely to rate women less favorably than men when they don't have much information about the person's qualifications (Swim et al., 1989).
3. Evaluators who have expertise in an occupation are especially likely to downgrade women; this trend is stronger if the evaluators are male. According to this perspective, students would not be very biased—and much of the research examines students' attitudes (e.g., Haley, 2001). In real-life occupational settings, women are more likely to be evaluated by "experts," who may be quite biased.
4. Bias against women may be strongest when a woman is acting in a stereotypically masculine fashion (Eagly et al., 1992; Eagly & Mladinic, 1994; Fiske & Stevens, 1993; Fiske et al., 1993). Consider a classic case of gender discrimination that accountant Ann Hopkins brought to court

(Fiske et al., 1991; Fiske & Stevens, 1993). She was being considered for promotion to partner, the only woman among 88 candidates that year. However, the company did not promote her, even though she had brought in more business to the company than any of the 87 male candidates. The firm claimed that Hopkins lacked interpersonal skills, and they branded her "macho" because of her hard-driving managerial style.

Notice that this bias against strong, competent women presents a double bind for women. On the one hand, if these women act stereotypically feminine, then they are not likely to be persuasive. Would Ann Hopkins have brought in $25 million in business if she had acted feminine and submissive? On the other hand, if women act masculine and assertive, then their superiors often give them negative evaluations. Fortunately, however, Hopkins won the legal case when it was brought to the U.S. Supreme Court (Clinchy & Norem, 1998).

ATTITUDES TOWARD WOMEN'S PLEASANTNESS.   People don't think that women are especially competent, but they *do* think that women are generally pleasant and nice. A series of studies was conducted by Alice Eagly, whose work on gender comparisons forms the core of Chapter 6. In this research, college students were asked to rate the category "men" and the category "women" on scales with labels such as "pleasant-unpleasant," "good-bad," and "nice-awful" (Eagly, 2001, 2004; Eagly & Mladinic, 1994; Eagly et al., 1991). Compared to men, women typically receive more positive ratings on these scales. For example, the subtype "macho men" receives the lowest rating; these men are rated as much less pleasant than the somewhat comparable female subtype "sexy women." Additional studies confirm that people give women more positive ratings than they give men, and they also consider women to be warmer than men (Fiske et al., 2002; Glick et al., 2004; Whitley & Kite, 2006).

We also know that people are not equally positive about all kinds of women. For example, W. D. Pierce and his colleagues (2003) asked Canadian university students to rate their attitude toward three types of people: "man," "woman," and "feminist." Figure 2.2 shows their responses on a scale where –2 was the most negative rating, 0 was neutral, and +2 was the most positive rating. As you can see, people gave much higher ratings to "woman" than to "man." However, they gave the lowest ratings to "feminist." Similar results have been reported with students at a different Canadian university, as well as U.S. students (Haddock & Zanna, 1994; Kite & Branscombe, 1998). Before you read any further, look at Demonstration 2.5 on page 58.

AMBIVALENT SEXISM.   We have seen that contemporary sexism is complicated. Women may not be judged to be very competent, but they *are* judged to be fairly nice—unless they happen to be feminists.

Peter Glick and Susan Fiske (1996, 2001a, 2001b) have tried to capture the complexity of sexism with a scale they call the Ambivalent Sexism Inventory.

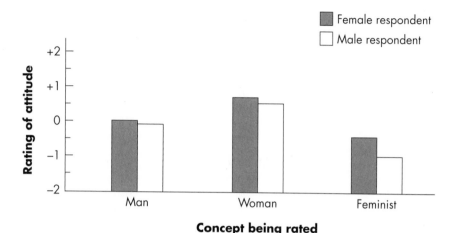

FIGURE 2.2   ATTITUDES TOWARD THE CONCEPTS "MAN," "WOMAN,"
AND "FEMINIST," AS A FUNCTION OF RESPONDENTS'
GENDER. (NOTE: +2 = EXTREMELY FAVORABLE;
−2 = EXTREMELY UNFAVORABLE.)

Source: Based on Pierce et al. (2003).

They argue that sexism is a prejudice based on a deep ambivalence toward women rather than on a uniform dislike of women. This scale contains items that tap two kinds of sexism: hostile sexism and benevolent sexism.

Hostile sexism, the more blatant kind of sexism, is based on the idea that women should be subservient to men and should "know their place." Hostile sexism is primarily directed toward nontraditional women, such as female professionals and feminists. **Benevolent sexism** is a more subtle kind of sexism that argues for women's special niceness and purity. Benevolent sexism is primarily directed toward traditional women, such as homemakers (Fiske, 2004; Fiske et al., 2002). However, it still emphasizes that women are *different* from men and that they are also weaker.

Notice that these two different kinds of sexism are consistent with the two different representations of women in religion and mythology (pp. 39–40) as well as with the mixture of negative and positive attitudes we have just discussed (pp. 55–56). All of these general tendencies reflect an ambivalence toward women. Now try a short version of Glick and Fiske's (1996) Ambivalent Sexism Inventory in Demonstration 2.5. In the United States, many studies with this inventory have shown that male participants typically score somewhat higher than female participants on the benevolent sexism subscale. However, males score much higher than females on the hostile sexism subscale (Glick & Fiske, 1996, 2001b).

The Ambivalent Sexism Inventory has also been tested with 15,000 men and women in 19 countries throughout the world (Glick et al., 2000).

Demonstration 2.5

The following items are selected from Glick and Fiske's (1996) Ambivalent Sexism Inventory. For each item, indicate the degree to which you agree or disagree with each statement, using the following scale:

0	1	2	3	4	5
disagree strongly	disagree somewhat	disagree slightly	agree slightly	agree somewhat	agree strongly

_____ 1. Many women are actually seeking special favors, such as hiring policies that favor them over men, under the guise of asking for equality.

_____ 2. Women should be cherished and protected by men.

_____ 3. Most women fail to appreciate fully all that men do for them.

_____ 4. Many women have a quality of purity that few men possess.

_____ 5. A good woman should be set on a pedestal by her man.

_____ 6. Most women interpret innocent remarks or acts as being sexist.

_____ 7. Once a woman gets a man to commit to her, she usually tries to put him on a tight leash.

_____ 8. In a disaster, women should be rescued before men.

_____ 9. Women seek to gain power by getting control over men.

_____10. No matter how accomplished he is, a man is not truly complete as a person unless he has the love of a woman.

When you have finished this test, check the scoring instructions at the end of the chapter on page 74. You may also want to ask friends to take the test to see whether you obtain the same gender differences that Glick and Fiske did.

Note: The complete test includes 22 items, some of which are worded so that a highly sexist person would disagree with them. This textbook's shortened version of the Ambivalent Sexism Inventory has not been validated. Anyone who is interested in using the scale for research or assessment purposes should refer to Glick and Fiske (1996).

Source: From Glick and Fiske, Ambivalent Sexism Inventory. Copyright © 1995 by Peter Glick and Susan T. Fiske.

Researchers have found both hostile sexism and benevolent sexism in all these countries. The studies also confirmed that gender differences are larger on the hostile sexism subscale than on the benevolent sexism subscale. In addition, Glick and his colleagues obtained data from the United Nations about gender equality in each of these 19 countries. Gender equality was based on measures such as women's share of the earned income and the percentage of high governmental positions held by women.

Let's consider the results for countries with low gender equality. These respondents tended to be high in both hostile sexism and benevolent sexism. This finding is easy to understand for hostile sexism: When people believe that women should be subservient to men, women will probably receive low salaries and hold few government positions. The relationship between gender equality and benevolent sexism is more puzzling. However, benevolent sexism also helps to justify gender inequality. It assumes women are pleasant, helpless people whom men must protect from having too much responsibility in the workplace (Glick & Fiske, 2001a, 2001b).

In short, the research on the Ambivalent Sexism Inventory highlights both the subtlety and the complexity of contemporary sexism. It also illustrates that the two different kinds of sexism are widespread throughout the world.

GENDER DISCRIMINATION IN INTERPERSONAL INTERACTIONS

So far in this section, we've looked at the nature of stereotypes and prejudice. We'll now explore gender discrimination. As you'll see, people in North America behave differently toward men and women, both in laboratory research and in real life. In some other countries, gender discrimination may even have life-threatening consequences.

DISCRIMINATION IN NORTH AMERICA.   Bernice Lott conducted the classic laboratory research in the United States; she observed pairs of unacquainted students from behind a one-way mirror while they worked together to build a structure (Lott, 1987; Lott & Maluso, 1995). This research showed that women seldom responded negatively to their partners (either male or female). However, the men made many more negative comments to their female partners than to their male partners.

The conclusions from these laboratory studies are echoed in research on real-life gender discrimination (e.g., Anthis, 2002; Landrine & Klonoff, 1997; Swim et al., 2001). For example, Janet Swim and her colleagues (2001) conducted a series of studies in which undergraduate women were asked to keep track of the number of nontrivial sexist remarks and behaviors they encountered during 2 weeks. They reported that these events occurred an average of once or twice a week. One category of sexist remarks emphasized traditional gender-stereotyped remarks (e.g.,"You're a woman, so fold my laundry"). Another category involved demeaning comments and behaviors (e.g., a woman who was talking with friends was told by a man, "Yo, bitch, get me some beer!"). A third category included sexual comments and behaviors. Another study conducted in a Northern California community documented that 61% reported that they heard sexually suggestive comments (e.g., "Nice ass") either on a daily basis or often (Nielsen, 2002).

In Chapter 7, we will explore other forms of interpersonal discrimination when we look at sexism in the workplace. In Chapter 12, we'll see that interpersonal discrimination may contribute to the relatively high rate of depression in women (Schmitt et al., 2002; Swim et al., 2001). The interpersonal discrimination that women experience does not evaporate quickly. Instead, these gender-biased experiences often reduce the overall quality of women's lives.

This section provides abundant evidence for Theme 2: Women are often treated differently from the way men are treated.

DISCRIMINATION IN OTHER CULTURES.   Most of the research discussed in this textbook focuses on the United States, Canada, and other English-speaking cultures. In many countries, however, the kind of discrimination we've discussed—such as inappropriate remarks to a female coworker—would be considered relatively minor. In recent years, Afghanistan is one the country that has practiced exteme discrimination against women. In the course of a turbulent history, an extremist Muslim group called the Taliban took control of this country in 1994. The Taliban's rules prohibited women from working outside the home. As a result, unmarried women who had previously worked as teachers, doctors, and nurses were often forced to beg in the streets to feed themselves or they became prostitutes (W. Anderson, 2001; Physicians for Human Rights, 1998; Vollmann, 2000). Girls and women were also forbidden to receive health care and to attend school (Latifa, 2001; Lipson, 2003). The literacy rate for Afghan women is only 4%, in contrast to 30% for men (Amiri et al., 2004). This contrast is larger than in most other developing countries (United Nations, 2006).

When out in public, Afghan women were required to wear a burqa, a garment that covers the entire body, with only a small mesh portion in front of the eyes that allows the wearer to see (see Photo 2.1). Women were often beaten

© AP Images/Kathy Gannon

These Afghan women were begging for money for food because the Taliban prohibited women from paid employment outside the home. (Note that the women are wearing burqas, which allow only a limited view of the world.)

if part of their body was exposed. For example, a Taliban militia member flogged an elderly woman when her ankle was accidentally exposed. He beat her with a metal cable, breaking her leg in the process. As you can imagine, these restrictions had serious consequences for the mental and physical health of Afghan women.

As you probably know, the United States destroyed much of the Taliban leadership during the war that followed the tragedies of September 11, 2001. You may not know that the United States sent billions of dollars to the Taliban during the 1990s, to help them fight troops from Russia. Unfortunately, the U.S. government ignored the Taliban's mistreatment of women during that era. Unfortunately, too, the Taliban has regained some of its power. For instance, it destroyed 30 girls' schools and threatened the teachers in these schools (A. Williams, 2003/2004). Furthermore, an increasing number of girls and women have been sexually assaulted (Kristof, 2004). Most women are still forced to wear the burqa, and most girls are married before the age of 16 (Huggler, 2006).

On the other end of the spectrum, women in Scandinavian countries experience less discrimination than women in the United States. For example, the percentage of women in Parliament (the highest government assembly in these countries) ranges from 24% in Iceland to 39% in Finland and Norway (Solheim, 2000). The current percentage of women in the U.S. Senate is only 16%. The U.S.-normative perspective encourages U.S. citizens to assume that women are especially well treated in our society. In many cases, this perspective is true. Sadly, however, this textbook will identify many exceptions to this assumption.

HETEROSEXISM

In the previous discussion of contemporary sexism, we saw that people make a major distinction between men and women. People may be hostile toward women or they may be benevolent toward women, but an important conclusion is that they think women are psychologically *different* from men. As we also emphasized in our discussion of Theme 2, people react differently to men and women. We'll see throughout this chapter that people divide the world into two categories, male and female.

Our culture's emphasis on gender categorization has an important implication for love relationships. Specifically, gender categorization encourages people to believe that a person from the category "male" must fall in love with a person from the category "female." Many people are troubled by same-gender love relationships.

A **lesbian** is a woman who is psychologically, emotionally, and sexually attracted to other women. A **gay male** is a man who is psychologically, emotionally, and sexually attracted to other men. A **bisexual** is someone who is psychologically, emotionally, and sexually attracted to both women and men. Chapter 4 examines how adolescent women begin to explore their sexual orientation. In Chapter 8, we will discuss potential explanations for sexual orientation as well as the love relationships of women who are lesbians and bisexuals.

Chapter 9 focuses on sexuality issues for lesbians, Chapter 11 discusses lesbian mothers, and Chapter 14 looks at the relationships among elderly lesbians.

In this section, however, let's focus on heterosexism. As Chapter 1 notes, **heterosexism** is a belief system that devalues lesbians, gay males, and bisexuals—or any group that is not exclusively heterosexual (Whitley & Kite, 2006). A related term, **sexual prejudice**, is a negative attitude that individuals hold against someone because of her or his sexual orientation (Garnets, 2004; Herek, 2004). Let's consider some examples of heterosexism and then see what factors are correlated with it. We have emphasized that sexism places men in the center and women on the periphery. Similarly, heterosexism places heterosexuals in the center and everybody else on the periphery.

EXAMPLES OF HETEROSEXISM.   Many different types of heterosexism reveal that our culture values people who love someone from the other gender category, rather than someone from the same gender category. For instance, many lesbians and gay males report that their partners are not welcome at family celebrations. Furthermore, more than half of high school lesbians and gay males have been verbally harassed about their sexual orientation (D'Augelli et al., 2002). For example, Carla was the president of her senior class when she told her classmates she was gay. The next day, someone had spray-painted "Carla will die" in big red letters across one of the walls of the school building (Owens, 1998).

Surveys also indicate that approximately one-third of lesbians and gay males have been chased or followed. Approximately one-third have also been assaulted (Herek et al., 1997; Herek et al., 2002; Pilkington & D'Augelli, 1995). For instance, one woman described how she and some women friends were walking in a public park when three men threatened them. Even though the women said they did not want to fight, the men attacked them. One woman had her nose broken, another was knocked unconscious, another had a gash on her cheek, and another was severely bruised (Herek et al., 2002).

We've seen that gays and lesbians frequently experience interpersonal discrimination—heterosexist biases, verbal harassment, and physical assault—because of their sexual orientation. They also face institutional discrimination; that is, the government, corporations, and other institutions discriminate against gays, lesbians, and bisexuals. For example, most insurance companies deny benefits to same-gender partners. I recall a friend discussing with irony that her insurance benefits could not cover her lesbian partner, with whom she had lived for 20 years. In contrast, a male colleague's wife could receive benefits even though the couple had been married less than 3 years and were now separated.

FACTORS CORRELATED WITH HETEROSEXISM.   Attitudes toward lesbians, gays, and bisexuals are complex. In general, men are more negative than women in their attitudes toward gays and lesbians (Herek, 2002a; Whitley & Kite, 2006). Men are also much more likely than women to commit anti-gay hate crimes (Herek et al., 2002). Furthermore, people generally have more negative

Demonstration 2.6

**ATTITUDES
TOWARD
LESBIANS AND
GAY MEN**

Answer each of the following items either yes or no. (Please note that the original questionnaire was designed for heterosexuals, so some items may seem inappropriate for lesbian, bisexual, and gay male respondents.)

1. I would not mind having gay friends.
2. I would look for a new place to live if I found out that my roommate was gay.
3. I would vote for a gay person in an election for a public office.
4. Two adults of the same gender holding hands in public is disgusting.
5. Homosexuality, as far as I'm concerned, is not sinful.
6. I would mind being employed by a gay person.
7. I would decline membership in an organization if it had gay members.
8. I would not be afraid for my child to have a gay teacher.
9. Gay people are more likely than heterosexuals to commit deviant sexual acts, such as child molestation.
10. I see the gay movement as a positive thing.

To obtain a rough idea about your attitudes, add the number of yes answers you provided for items 1, 3, 5, 8, and 10. Next, add together the number of no answers you gave for items 2, 4, 6, 7, and 9. Then, combine these two subtotals; scores close to 10 indicate positive attitudes toward gay people.

Source: Based on Kite and Deaux (1986).

attitudes toward gay men than toward lesbian women (Herek, 2002a; Schellenberg et al., 1999).

In addition, people with traditional gender roles are more likely than nontraditional people to express sexual prejudice (Basow & Johnson, 2000; Whitley & Ægisdóttir, 2000; Whitley & Kite, 2006). Also, people with heterosexist attitudes tend to be politically conservative, religiously conservative, and racist (Horvath & Ryan, 2003; Kite & Whitley, 1998, 2002). However, students often become more tolerant and less heterosexist as they go through college (Hewitt & Moore, 2002; Schellenberg et al., 1999). To assess your own attitudes toward lesbians and gay men, try Demonstration 2.6.

Section Summary

**People's Beliefs
About Women
and Men**

1. People believe that men and women differ substantially on a number of personality characteristics. They consider men to be higher in agency, and women to be higher in communion. These stereotypes have remained fairly consistent throughout recent decades.

2. People have different stereotypes about women and men from different ethnic groups; in most cases, however, the stereotypes about women include both ''good women'' and ''bad women'' within each ethnic group.

3. The strength of your gender stereotype may be influenced by such factors as your gender and culture. However, the overall consistency of stereotypes is impressive.

4. Psychologists have developed the Implicit Association Test, which assesses the strength of stereotypes in terms of response speed, rather than a rating-scale measure for which people might provide socially appropriate answers.

5. Women's competence is likely to be downgraded when (a) evaluators are male, rather than female, (b) little other information is available, (c) evaluators are experts, and (d) women act in a stereotypically masculine fashion.

6. People typically rate women higher than men on scales assessing pleasantness; however, feminists receive relatively low ratings.

7. Men score higher than women on both the benevolent sexism and the hostile sexism subscales of the Ambivalent Sexism Inventory.

8. Research shows evidence of gender discrimination in interpersonal interactions (e.g., negative statements about women and sexist comments). Sexism in cultures such as Afghanistan has more serious consequences than it does in North America.

9. Heterosexism is encouraged by strict gender categorization; lesbians and gay males frequently experience harassment, and many are physically assaulted. Men often show more sexual prejudice than women, and people with traditional gender roles are also likely to show more sexual prejudice.

THE PERSONAL CONSEQUENCES OF GENDER STEREOTYPES

So far, we have examined many stereotypes related to gender, and we have discussed gender prejudice and gender discrimination. However, gender stereotypes can also have an important effect on our own cognitive processes, behavior, and gender identity. In fact, stereotypes can powerfully affect our lives (Schaller & Conway, 2001).

GENDER STEREOTYPES AND COGNITIVE ERRORS

One personal consequence of gender stereotypes is that they encourage us to make cognitive errors—that is, errors in our thought processes. The social cognitive approach explains how these errors arise. This approach also provides a useful theoretical explanation for gender stereotypes, heterosexist stereotypes, and stereotypes based on categories such as ethnicity, sexual orientation, social class, disability status, and age. According to the **social cognitive approach,** stereotypes are belief systems that guide the way we process information, including information about gender (Schaller & Conway, 2001; Sherman, 2001).

One cognitive process that seems nearly inevitable is our tendency to divide the people we meet into social groups (Brehm et al., 2005; Macrae & Bodenhausen, 2000; D. J. Schneider, 2004). We categorize people as females or males, White people or people of color, people with high occupational status or people with low occupational status, and so forth.

The social cognitive approach argues that stereotypes help us simplify and organize the world by creating categories. The major way we categorize people is on the basis of their gender (Harper & Schoeman, 2003; Kunda, 1999; D. J. Schneider, 2004). This process of categorizing others on the basis of gender is habitual and automatic. The problem, however, is that this process of categorizing and stereotyping often encourages us to make errors in our thinking. These errors, in turn, produce further errors. Specifically, because we have a stereotype, we tend to perceive women and men differently, and this perception adds further "evidence" to our stereotype. A strengthened stereotype leads to an even greater tendency to perceive the two genders differently. As a result, stereotypes are especially resistant to change (Barone et al., 1997; Macrae & Bodenhausen, 2000).

Let's look at several ways that gender stereotypes encourage cognitive errors:

1. People tend to exaggerate the contrast between women and men.
2. People tend to see the male as normative and the female as nonstandard.
3. People often make biased judgments on the basis of stereotypes.
4. People often selectively remember information that is consistent with gender stereotypes.

EXAGGERATING THE CONTRAST BETWEEN WOMEN AND MEN.   We tend to exaggerate the similarities within a group and exaggerate the contrast between groups (T. L. Stewart et al., 2000; Van Rooy et al., 2003). When we divide the world into two groups—male and female—we tend to see all males as being similar, all females as being similar, and the two gender categories as being different from each other; this tendency is called **gender polarization** (Bem, 1993). Gender polarization encourages people to condemn individuals who deviate from this rigid role definition. For example, we saw on page 56 that many people have a negative attitude toward feminists, although they have a positive attitude toward women in general.

As we will emphasize throughout this textbook, the characteristics of women and men tend to overlap. Unfortunately, however, gender polarization often creates an artificial gap between women and men. People tend to believe that gender differences in psychological characteristics are larger than they really are (J. A. Hall & Carter, 1999; C. L. Martin, 1987). Human cognitive processes seem to favor clear-cut distinctions, not the blurry differences that are more common in everyday life (Van Rooy et al., 2003).We especially emphasize distinctions based on gender.

THE NORMATIVE MALE.   As we discussed earlier in this chapter, the normative male concept (or androcentrism) means that the male experience is considered the norm—that is, the neutral standard for the species as a whole. In contrast, the female experience is a deviation from that supposedly universal standard (Basow, 2001; Bem, 1993, 2004). One example of the normative male principle is that when we hear the word *person,* we tend to believe that this individual is a male rather than a female (M. C. Hamilton, 1991; Merritt & Kok, 1995). Similarly, D. T. Miller and his colleagues (1991) asked people to visualize a "typical American voter"; 72% of their participants described a male. Furthermore, both adults and children usually refer to a stuffed animal as "he," unless this toy has clearly feminine clothing (Lambdin et al., 2003).

The normative male principle also reveals itself when people discuss gender differences (Tavris, 1992). As you'll learn in Chapter 5, men and women sometimes differ in their self-confidence. However, the research typically assumes that males have the "normal" amount of self-confidence and that females are somehow defective. In other words, men are serving as the standard of comparison. However, the truth may be that females actually have the appropriate amount of self-confidence; they may judge the quality of their performance fairly accurately. From that perspective, males would be over-confident and overly self-serving.

We have already seen evidence of androcentrism in Chapter 1; the early history of the psychology of gender assumed that the male is normative. Our discussions of masculine generic language and the representation of gender in the media also reflect androcentrism. In addition, androcentrism is apparent in the workplace, family life, and medical care (Basow, 2001), as we will see in later chapters of this book.

MAKING BIASED JUDGMENTS ABOUT FEMALES AND MALES.   Many stereotypes are based on grains of truth, so these stereotypes may be at least partly accurate (Schaller & Conway, 2001). However, our stereotypes may also lead us to interpret certain behaviors in a biased manner (Blair, 2001). For example, people display stereotyped interpretations when they judge men's and women's emotional reactions (M. D. Robinson & Johnson, 1997).

Chingching Chang and Jacqueline Hitchon (2004) conducted a representative study about biased judgments. They gave U.S. undergraduate students an advertisement, either for a male political candidate or for a female political candidate. Let's focus on the condition in which the ads did not mention the candidate's knowledge about certain gender-stereotyped areas of expertise. After reading the advertisement, the students were instructed to rate the candidate's competence in these areas. Even though the students had no relevant information, they judged that female candidates would be more competent than the males in "women's issues," such as children and health care. Furthermore, they judged that the male candidates would be more competent than the females in "men's issues," such as the economy and national security. When we make judgments—and we lack relevant information—we fall back on gender stereotypes.

Naturally, several variables influence our tendency to make stereotyped judgments. Specific information about individuals can sometimes be so persuasive that it overrides a stereotype (Kunda & Sherman-Williams, 1993). A woman may be so well qualified for a job that her strengths outweigh the "problem" that she is female. However, we are especially likely to use a stereotype if we are busy working on another task at the same time (Macrae & Bodenhausen, 2000; D. J. Schneider, 2004).

Many studies have been conducted on a particular kind of judgment called attributions. **Attributions** are explanations about the causes of a person's behavior. Chapter 5 discusses how people make attributions about their *own* behavior. In this current chapter, we'll discuss how people make stereotypical attributions about the behavior of *other individuals*.

The research on attributions is both extensive and complex. It shows that people often think a woman's success on a particular task can be explained by effort—she tried hard (D. J. Schneider, 2004; Swim & Sanna, 1996). For example, researchers have examined parents' attributions for their children's success in mathematics. When a daughter does well in math, parents attribute her success to hard work. In contrast, they attribute their son's success to his high ability (Eccles, 1987). Notice the implications of this research: People think that females need to try harder to achieve the same level of success as males.

People may use the same "effort and hard work" explanation when trying to account for the success of other groups that are commonly believed to be inferior. For example, people were asked to judge why a White male in a scenario had become a successful banker; they attributed his success to his high ability (Yarkin et al., 1982). However, they showed a different attributional pattern when judging a White female, a Black male, or a Black female. For those three individuals, hard work and luck were judged to be the most important reasons for success. People had trouble believing that these three had succeeded because they were competent.

Let's review what we know so far about the social cognitive approach to gender stereotypes. We know that stereotypes simplify and bias the way we think about people who belong to the social categories "female" and "male." Because of gender stereotypes, we exaggerate the contrast between women and men. We also consider the male experience to be normal, whereas the female experience is the exception that requires an explanation. In addition, we make biased judgments about females and males, for instance, when we assess their expertise about stereotypically masculine or feminine political topics. Research in social cognition also emphasizes one final component of stereotypes: people's memory for stereotyped characteristics.

MEMORY FOR PERSONAL CHARACTERISTICS.   People sometimes, but not always, recall gender-consistent information more accurately than gender-inconsistent information (e.g., Cann, 1993; D. F. Halpern, 1985; T. L. Stewart & Vassar, 2000). For instance, Dunning and Sherman (1997) asked participants to read a sentence such as "The women at the office liked to talk around the water cooler." During a later memory test, the researchers presented a series of sentences and asked the participants to decide whether each sentence was old (that is, seen in exactly the same form on the initial presentation) or new.

The most interesting results in this study concerned people's judgments about new sentences that were consistent with the gender stereotype implied by a sentence presented earlier (e.g., "The women at the office liked to gossip around the water cooler"). People erroneously judged that 29% of these sentences were old. In contrast, when they saw new sentences that were inconsistent with a gender stereotype (e.g., "The women at the office liked to talk sports around the water cooler"), they erroneously judged that only 18% of these sentences were old. Apparently, when people saw the original sentence about women talking around the water cooler, they sometimes made gender-consistent inferences (e.g., that the women must be gossiping). As a result, when they later saw a sentence that explicitly mentioned gossiping, that sentence looked familiar.

The research in social cognition shows that we are especially likely to recall stereotype-consistent material when we have other tasks to do at the same time, such as remembering other information, and when we have a strong, well-developed stereotype (Hilton & von Hippel, 1996; Sherman, 2001). When we are undistracted and when stereotypes are weak, we may sometimes remember material inconsistent with our stereotypes.

GENDER STEREOTYPES AND BEHAVIOR

We began the previous section by discussing the content of gender stereotypes and the complex nature of contemporary sexism. We've just examined the social cognitive approach, which helps us to understand how errors in our thinking can arise. However, if we focus entirely on our thought processes, we may forget an extremely important point: Stereotypes can influence people's behavior. That is, stereotypes can affect actions and choices, in other people and in ourselves.

Stereotypes can influence behavior through a **self-fulfilling prophecy**: Your expectations about someone may lead him or her to act in ways that confirm your original expectation (Rosenthal, 1993; Skrypnek & Snyder, 1982). For example, if parents expect that their daughter will not do well in mathematics, she may become pessimistic about her ability in that area. As a result, her math performance may drop (Eccles et al., 1990; Jussim et al., 2000).

A related problem is called stereotype threat. Imagine you belong to a group that is hampered by a negative stereotype, and someone reminds you about your group membership. In this situation, you may experience **stereotype threat**; you may become anxious, and your performance may suffer (K. L. Dion, 2003; Jussim et al., 2000; C. M. Steele et al., 2002).

Consider some research by Shih and her colleagues (1999), in which all the participants were Asian American college women. In North America, one stereotype is that Asian Americans are "good at math" (compared to other ethnic groups). In contrast, another stereotype is that women are "bad at math" (compared to men). One group of participants in this study were asked to indicate their ethnicity and then answer several questions about their ethnic identity; afterward, they took a challenging math test. These women answered 54% of the questions correctly. A second group of participants did not answer any questions beforehand; they simply took the same math test. The women in this control group answered 49% of the questions correctly. A third group began by indicating their gender and then answering several questions about their gender identity; afterward, they took the same math test. These women answered only 43% of the questions correctly.

Apparently, when Asian American women are reminded of their ethnicity, they perform relatively well. However, when Asian American women are reminded of their gender, they experience stereotype threat and they perform relatively poorly. This study has been replicated with Asian American girls in elementary and middle school (Ambady et al., 2001). Other research suggests that Latina college women are more vulnerable to stereotype threat than European American college women are (Gonzalez et al., 2002).

However, people are not always at the mercy of gender stereotypes (Fiske, 1993; Jussim et al., 2000). We are not marionettes, with other people pulling our strings. Our own self-concepts and abilities are usually stronger determinants of behavior than are the expectations of other people. Furthermore, the three groups of students in the math study did not have extremely different math scores (Shih et al., 1999). Still, we should be concerned about the potentially powerful effects of gender stereotypes. As Jussim and his colleagues (2000) emphasize, these stereotypes help to maintain important gender inequities.

INTERNALIZING GENDER STEREOTYPES

In this chapter we have explored these topics: (1) the representation of gender stereotypes in religion, language, and the media; (2) the nature of people's current gender stereotypes; and (3) the influence of gender stereotypes on our thinking and our behavior. However, stereotypes not only describe our perceptions about the characteristics of women and men. They also describe how women and men *ought* to behave (Clinchy & Norem, 1998; Eagly, 2001). According to the traditional view, women should try to be "feminine" and men should try to be "masculine." Do people actually adopt these stereotypes, so that women and men have extremely different standards about the ideal person they should be?

ASSESSING SELF-CONCEPTS ABOUT GENDER.   Researchers have developed several different scales to assess people's ideas about their own gender-related characteristics. For example, Sandra Bem (1974, 1977) designed the Bem Sex-Role Inventory (BSRI), a test in which people rate themselves on a variety of psychological characteristics.

The BSRI provides one score on a femininity scale and one score on a masculinity scale. A person who scores high on both scales would be classified as **androgynous** (pronounced an-*draw*-jih-nuss). In the 1970s, psychologists often urged both women and men to develop more androgynous characteristics.

Hundreds of studies have been conducted to try to discover whether androgynous individuals might possess any unusual advantages; several resources provide reviews of the research (e.g., Auster & Ohm, 2000; Matlin, 2000; C. J. Smith et al., 1999; Stake, 2000; C. A. Ward, 2000). You will still hear about the concept of androgyny, especially in the popular press.

In contrast to the media, however, contemporary psychologists have become disenchanted with androgyny. They argue that the concept of androgyny has several problems. For example, the research shows that androgynous people are *not* more psychologically healthy than other people. Also, according to critics, androgyny tempts us to believe that the solution to gender bias lies in changing the individual. However, we should try instead to reduce institutional sexism and discrimination against women. In 1983, Sandra Bem herself argued against the concept of androgyny, and she urged psychologists to turn their attention to a different question explored throughout this textbook: Why does our culture place such a strong emphasis on gender?

Do People Internalize Gender Stereotypes?   Although the specific concept of androgyny is no longer popular with psychologists, many researchers continue to explore whether people incorporate gender stereotypes into their own concepts about themselves. In the workplace, for example, many people develop some skills that are considered traditionally masculine and some that are considered traditionally feminine (J. A. Harvey & Hansen, 1999; Stake, 1997).

Many people do internalize gender stereotypes into their own self-concepts. However, social context clearly matters. For instance, many women say that they would act stereotypically feminine if they were in a social situation where most people were strangers (C. J. Smith et al., 1999).

Cross-cultural research suggests that people in some ethnic groups may not adopt the gender stereotypes held by European Americans. For example, Sugihara and Warner (1999) administered the BSRI to Mexican American college students. Only 22% of the female students could be classified as stereotypically feminine, and only 22% of the male students could be classified as stereotypically masculine. Furthermore, Sugihara and Katsurada (1999, 2000) studied gender self-concepts among college students in Japan. The male students scored significantly higher than the female students on the masculine scale of the BSRI, but males and females had similar scores on the feminine scale of the BSRI. In addition, both males and females scored significantly higher on the femininity scale than on the masculinity scale. Another explanation may be that some gender-related terms cannot be successfully translated into another language (Best & Thomas, 2004).

Are Gender Stereotypes Personally Important?   So far, we've seen that people show some tendency to incorporate gender stereotypes into their own self-concepts. But do they believe that these gender stereotypes are crucial aspects of their own personality? Auster and Ohm (2000) asked U.S. undergraduates to complete the BSRI by rating each characteristic according to how important

TABLE 2.5 | TOP 10 TRAITS THAT FEMALE AND MALE U.S. STUDENTS CONSIDER MOST IMPORTANT FOR THEMSELVES

Female Students	Male Students
1. Loyal	1. Loyal
2. Independent	2. Defends own beliefs
3. Individualistic	3. Willing to take a stand
4. Defends own beliefs	4. Understanding
5. Self-sufficient	5. Independent
6. Understanding	6. Ambitious
7. Ambitious	7. Willing to take risks
8. Self-reliant	8. Self-reliant
9. Sensitive to the needs of others	9. Self-sufficient
10. Compassionate	10. Has leadership abilities

Source: Auster & Ohm (2000).

they felt it would be to have this characteristic. Table 2.5 lists the 10 characteristics that each gender judged to be most important. As you can see, the lists are remarkably similar. In fact, seven items appear on both the women's and the men's lists.

CONCLUSIONS ABOUT INTERNALIZING GENDER STEREOTYPES.   In this discussion, we've seen that people often adopt flexible self-concepts about gender. However, studies suggest that many European Americans do adopt gender-stereotypical characteristics, especially among males and especially in some social settings. The current evidence also suggests that females and males in some other cultures may be similar in many gender-related characteristics. Furthermore, U.S. female and male students are remarkably similar in the characteristics that they consider personally important.

We should not oversimplify the conclusions in our current discussion about internalized gender stereotypes. However, women and men often have similar views about their gender-related characteristics. Consistent with Theme 1, gender differences in psychological characteristics are usually small. As we'll emphasize throughout this textbook, women and men do not live on different psychological planets with respect to their beliefs, abilities, and personal characteristics.

Furthermore, you may discover specific information about your own stereotypes. As a student in one of my classes wrote:

> Our stereotypes are deeply ingrained in our thinking and passed from generation to generation. It will take introspection and conscious effort for us to change these stereotypes. Only by analyzing our own beliefs, ideas, and culture will our society be able to understand the inequalities. It is difficult to question what we know, but it is ultimately valuable. (Coryat, 2006)

Section Summary

The Personal Consequences of Gender Stereotypes

1. One consequence of gender stereotypes is that we make errors in our cognitive processes; these errors are relevant for the social cognitive approach to stereotypes.

2. According to the social cognitive approach to stereotypes, people tend to (a) exaggerate the contrast between women and men, (b) consider the male experience to be normative, (c) make biased judgments about females and males, and (d) remember gender-consistent information more accurately than gender-inconsistent information.

3. Stereotypes can influence behavior through self-fulfilling prophecies, according to research on topics such as parents' expectations for their children's mathematical abilities. Also, the research on stereotype threat shows that people's own gender stereotypes can undermine task performance on tests, when their gender is emphasized.

4. In specific settings, many people adopt flexible self-concepts about gender, rather than internalizing rigid gender stereotypes. Studies also indicate that European Americans may be more likely than other cultural groups to internalize gender stereotypes. In addition, women and men in U.S. colleges tend to rate themselves similarly on important gender-related traits.

CHAPTER REVIEW QUESTIONS

1. How would you define the term *gender stereotype*? Based on the information in this chapter, would you suppose that the stereotype of a female can accurately represent a specific woman whom you know? Why or why not?

2. In this chapter, we examined how women have been left out of history. Discuss the kinds of topics related to women that scholars have previously ignored. Mention several reasons why women have not received much attention in history books.

3. We discussed in this chapter how women often seem invisible; for example, men are normative, whereas women are secondary. Summarize the information about women's invisibility, mentioning history, religion, mythology, language, and the media. What does the social cognitive research on androcentrism demonstrate?

4. In this chapter, we pointed out that people often hold more positive views about men than about women. Discuss this statement, citing support from philosophers, religion, mythology, language, and the media. Then point out why the issue is more complicated when we consider current research on ambivalent sexism.

5. What does the research show about people's stereotypes regarding women from various ethnic groups (i.e., ethnicity as a stimulus variable)? Similarly, what does the research show about how a person's ethnicity influences his or her gender stereotypes (i.e., ethnicity as subject variable)? Finally, how is ethnicity relevant in people's tendency to internalize gender stereotypes?

6. What is heterosexism, and how are gender stereotypes related to heterosexism? The social cognitive approach proposes that our

normal cognitive processes would encourage people to develop stereotypes about lesbians and gay males. Describe how the four cognitive biases (listed on page 65) would encourage these stereotypes.

7. The social cognitive approach proposes that stereotypes arise from normal cognitive processes, beginning with the two categories "men" and "women." Describe some of the cognitive biases that would encourage people to believe that women are more talkative than men (a stereotype that actually is not correct).

8. What is a self-fulfilling prophecy? Why is it relevant when we examine how stereotypes

can influence behavior? Identify one of your own behaviors that is more gender stereotyped than you might wish, and point out how a self-fulfilling prophecy might be relevant.

9. Women and men are represented differently in the media and in people's gender stereotypes, yet people may not incorporate these stereotypes into their own self-concepts. Discuss this statement, using material from throughout the entire chapter.

10. Throughout this chapter, we discussed cross-cultural research. How do gender biases operate in cultures outside North America? When are gender differences substantial in other cultures, and when are they relatively small?

KEY TERMS

*stereotypes (36)

*gender stereotypes (36)

*prejudice (37)

*discrimination (37)

*gender bias (37)

*androcentrism (40)

normative-male problem (40)

*masculine generic (41)

androcentric generic (41)

*agency (51)

*communion (51)

explicit gender stereotypes (53)

implicit gender stereotypes (54)

hostile sexism (57)

benevolent sexism (57)

*lesbian (61)

*gay male (61)

*bisexual (61)

*heterosexism (62)

*sexual prejudice (62)

*social cognitive approach (64)

*gender polarization (65)

*attributions (67)

*self-fulfilling prophecy (68)

*stereotype threat (68)

androgynous (69)

 Note: The terms asterisked in the Key Terms section serve as good search terms for InfoTrac College Edition. Go to http://infotrac.thomsonlearning.com and try these added search terms.

RECOMMENDED READINGS

Barnett, R., & Rivers, C. (2004). *Same difference: How gender myths are hurting our relationships, our children, and our jobs.* New York: Basic Books. When authors write about gender for the general public, they typically perpetuate the well-known stereotypes. In contrast, this well-written book explains how these stereotypes are harmful for both women and men. I strongly recommend it.

Moskowitz, G. B. (Ed.). (2001). *Cognitive social psychology.* Mahwah, NJ: Erlbaum. This book

includes 23 chapters, most of which are related to stereotypes, either directly or indirectly.

Schneider, D. J. (2004). *The psychology of stereotyping.* New York: Guilford Press. I recommend this clear and well-organized book. The author explores the content of certain stereotypes, and he also examines how children develop stereotypes about race and gender.

Whitley, B. E., Jr., & Kite, M. E. (2006). *The psychology of prejudice and discrimination.*

Belmont, CA; Wadsworth. Bernard Whitley and Mary Kite are well known for their studies about sexism, ageism, and heterosexism. This excellent textbook includes interesting quotations and media reports about biases, as well as a clear discussion of the relevant research.

ANSWERS TO THE DEMONSTRATIONS

Demonstration 2.3: Most people believe that the following items are characteristics of women (W): fickle, gentle, kind, warm, nervous, emotional, talkative, compassionate, patient, modest. They also believe these items are characteristic of men (M): self-confident, greedy, competitive, active, capable, loud, show-off, courageous, inventive, powerful.

Demonstration 2.5: Add together the total number of points from the following items: 1, 3, 6, 7, 9. These items represent the hostile sexism subscale. Then add together the total number of points from items 2, 4, 5, 8, and 10. These items represent the benevolent sexism subscale. Adding these two subscale scores together provides an index of overall sexism.

ANSWERS TO THE TRUE-FALSE STATEMENTS

1. True (p. 38); 2. False (p. 39); 3. True (pp. 41–42); 4. False (p. 45); 5. True (p. 47); 6. False (pp. 53–54); 7. True (p. 55); 8. True (p. 62); 9. True (p. 67); 10. False (p. 70).

© Arnold Matlin, M.D.

3 | INFANCY AND CHILDHOOD

True or False?

_____ 1. During the first few weeks of prenatal development, females and males have similar sex glands and external genitals.

_____ 2. People living in the United States and Canada have strong preferences about the gender of their firstborn child; more than two-thirds would prefer a son rather than a daughter.

_____ 3. When adults think they are interacting with a baby boy, they typically hand this baby a football; if the same baby is introduced as a baby girl, people typically hand this baby a doll.

_____ 4. We can explain children's gender development almost entirely by the fact that parents reward gender-consistent behavior and punish gender-inconsistent behavior.

_____ 5. Parents consistently criticize aggressive girls more than they criticize aggressive boys.

_____ 6. At least a dozen studies have demonstrated that European American parents are more likely than other parents to send strong gender messages to their children.

_____ 7. Teachers typically give more educational feedback to boys than to girls.

_____ 8. Research conducted during the past 10 years shows that boys and girls are now almost equally represented in children's television programs and that children rarely act in gender-stereotyped ways in these programs.

_____ 9. By the age of 6 months, infants can perceive that a female face belongs in a different category from a series of male faces.

_____ 10. In general, girls are more likely than boys to reject an occupation that is considered nontraditional for their gender.

One hot summer day, a little girl was attending the birthday party of another preschooler. The children managed to stay cool by taking off their clothes and wading in the backyard pool. The little girl's mother picked her up from the party, and the two began discussing the afternoon's events. The mother asked how many boys and how many girls had attended the party. "I don't know," the child replied. "They weren't wearing any clothes" (C. L. Brewer, personal communication, 1998). As we'll see in this chapter, children's conceptions of gender are often surprisingly different from adult perspectives. However, we'll also see that children can be quite knowledgeable. For example, even preschoolers are well informed about our culture's gender stereotypes.

In this chapter, we will discuss a process called gender typing. **Gender typing** includes how children acquire their knowledge about gender and how they develop their personality characteristics, preferences, skills, behaviors, and self-concepts (Eckes & Trautner, 2000b; Liben & Bigler, 2002). We'll start by considering the early phases of development, during the prenatal period and infancy, and then we'll discuss some theoretical explanations of gender typing. Next, we'll examine factors that contribute to children's gender typing. These factors—such as the school system and the media—virtually guarantee that children growing up in North America will be well informed about the importance of gender in our culture. Finally, we'll focus on children's knowledge and stereotypes about gender; as we'll see, even infants can tell the difference between female and male faces.

BACKGROUND ON GENDER DEVELOPMENT

Some important biological components of gender—such as the sex organs—develop during the **prenatal period,** the time before birth. Our culture then conveys many messages about gender during **infancy,** the period between birth and 18 months of life. An adequate theory about gender development must be sufficiently complex to explain the societal forces that encourage children's gender typing. The theory must also emphasize that children contribute to their own gender typing by actively working to master their lessons about gender.

Prenatal Sex Development

At conception, an egg with 23 chromosomes combines with a sperm, which also has 23 chromosomes. Together, they form a single cell that contains 23 chromosome pairs. The 23rd pair is called the **sex chromosomes**—that is, the chromosomes that determine whether the embryo will be genetically female or male. The other 22 chromosome pairs determine numerous additional physiological and psychological characteristics.

The egg from the mother always supplies an X sex chromosome. The father's sperm, which fertilizes the egg, contains either an X chromosome or a Y chromosome. If an X chromosome fertilizes the egg, then XX represents the chromosome pair, and the child will be a genetic female. If a Y chromosome fertilizes the egg, then XY represents the chromosome pair, and the child will be a genetic male. The situation is ironic. Our culture emphasizes the importance of gender—whether someone is an XX person or an XY person (Beall et al., 2004). However, this outcome is determined simply by whether a sperm bearing an X chromosome or a sperm bearing a Y chromosome penetrates the egg cell first!

TYPICAL PRENATAL DEVELOPMENT.   Female and male embryos differ in their chromosomes. However, until about 6 weeks after conception, female and male embryos are virtually identical in all other characteristics (M. Hines, 2004). For instance, each human fetus has two sets of primitive internal reproductive systems. The internal female system, called müllerian ducts, will eventually develop into a uterus, egg ducts, and part of the vagina in females. The internal male system, called wolffian ducts, will eventually develop into the male internal reproductive system, which includes structures such as the prostate gland and the vesicles for semen (Federman, 2004).

The sex glands (or **gonads**) of males and females also look identical during the first weeks after conception. If the embryo has an XY chromosome pair, a tiny segment of the Y chromosome guides the gonads to develop into male testes, beginning about 6 weeks after conception. In contrast, if the embryo has an XX chromosome pair, the gonads begin to develop into female ovaries, beginning about 10 weeks after conception (Fausto-Sterling, 2000; M. Hines, 2004).

In about the third month after conception, the fetus's hormones encourage further sex differentiation, including the development of the external genitals.

In males, the testes secrete two substances. One of these, the müllerian regression hormone, shrinks the (female) müllerian ducts. The testes also secrete **androgen,** one of the male sex hormones. High levels of androgen encourage the growth and development of the wolffian ducts (Crooks & Baur, 2005). Androgen also encourages the growth of the external genitals. (See Figure 3.1.) The genital tubercle becomes the penis in males.

At about the same time, the ovaries in females begin to make **estrogen**, one of the female sex hormones. Consistent with the "invisible female" theme, we know much less about prenatal development in females than in males (Crooks & Baur, 2005; Fitch et al., 1998). For instance, a recent article in the prestigious *New England Journal of Medicine* shows an elaborate figure labeled "Factors Involved in the Determination of Male Sex"—but no comparable figure for the female sex (Federman, 2004). For example, the genital tubercle develops into the clitoris in females. (See Figure 3.1.) However, it isn't clear whether this developmental process requires a specific hormone or whether a clitoris simply develops when androgen is absent.

In summary, typical sexual development follows a complex sequence before birth. The first event is conception, when genetic sex is determined. Female and male embryos are anatomically identical for the first weeks after conception. As we have seen, four further processes then begin the differentiation of females and males: (1) the development of the internal reproductive system, (2) the development of the gonads, (3) the production of hormones, and (4) the development of the external genitals.

ATYPICAL PRENATAL DEVELOPMENT.   The scenario we've just examined is the typical one. However, this elaborate developmental sequence sometimes takes a different pathway. The result is an intersexed infant whose biological sex is not clearly female or male. An **intersexed individual** has genitals that are not clearly female or clearly male. An intersexed person also does not have a matching chromosomal pattern, internal reproductive system, gonads, hormones, and external genitals. In other words, the world does not have just two sex categories, female and male (Golden, 2004; S. J. Kessler, 1998; Marecek et al., 2004). In fact, Fausto-Sterling (2000) estimated that intersexed individuals represent about 2% of the general population.

One atypical pattern is called **androgen-insensitivity syndrome,** a condition in which genetic males (XY) produce normal amounts of androgen, but a genetic defect makes their bodies not respond to androgen (Fausto-Sterling, 2000; M. Hines, 2004; L. Rogers, 2001). As a result, the genital tubercle does not grow into a penis; the external genitals look female. These children are usually labeled girls because they lack a penis. However, they have a shallow cavity instead of a complete vagina, and they have no uterus. This syndrome is usually discovered when they do not begin to menstruate at the normal time of puberty (M. Hines, 2004).

A second atypical pattern is called **congenital adrenal hyperplasia,** a condition in which genetic females (XX) receive as much androgen as males do during prenatal development. The excess androgen causes their genitals to look

Undifferentiated before sixth week

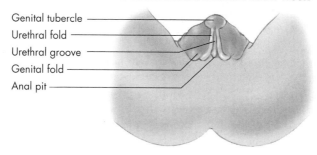

Genital tubercle
Urethral fold
Urethral groove
Genital fold
Anal pit

Seventh to eighth week

Male   Female

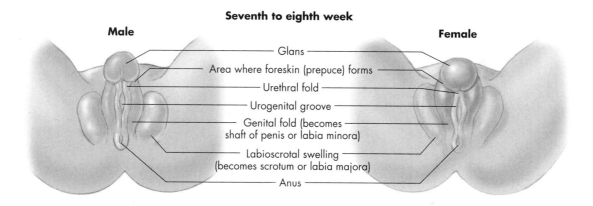

Glans
Area where foreskin (prepuce) forms
Urethral fold
Urogenital groove
Genital fold (becomes
shaft of penis or labia minora)
Labioscrotal swelling
(becomes scrotum or labia majora)
Anus

Fully developed by twelfth week

Male   Female

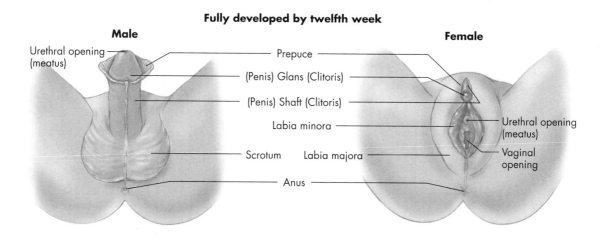

Urethral opening
(meatus)

Prepuce
(Penis) Glans (Clitoris)
(Penis) Shaft (Clitoris)
Labia minora

Scrotum   Labia majora

Anus

Urethral opening
(meatus)
Vaginal
opening

FIGURE 3.1 | PRENATAL DEVELOPMENT OF THE EXTERNAL GENITALS.

Source: Based on Crooks & Baur (2005).

somewhat masculine at birth. The traditional medical treatment is surgery, so that the genitals can appear more feminine (Chase & Hegarty, 2000; M. Hines, 2004; MacLaughlin & Donahoe, 2004).

To me, the most interesting aspect of atypical prenatal development focuses on some important questions: Why does our culture force all infants into either the female category or the male category (Blizzard, 2002; Golden, 2004; S. J. Kessler, 1998)? Why can't we accept that some people are inter-sexed, neither female nor male? Why do physicians typically recommend surgery for intersexed individuals, so that the external genitals can appear to be either clearly feminine or clearly masculine? Many intersexed adults now argue that such children should not be forced to adopt one gender just because it is socially acceptable (Colapinto, 2000; M. Diamond & Sigmundson, 1999; Fausto-Sterling, 2000; Navarro, 2004). As one intersexed adult writes:

> I was born whole and beautiful, but different. The error was not in my body, nor in my sex organs, but in the determination of the culture. . . . Our path to healing lies in embracing our intersexual selves, not in labeling our bodies as having committed some "error." (M. Diamond, 1996, p. 144)

We pointed out in the previous two chapters that gender polarization forces us to see the two genders as being very different from one another. As Carla Golden (2004) writes, "Feminist psychology is about seeing things differently" (p. 99). From this new viewpoint, can we overcome gender polarization and acknowledge that we humans are not limited to just two options?

PEOPLE'S RESPONSES TO INFANT GIRLS AND BOYS

We consider a person's gender—the label "female" or "male"—to be very important, as noted in previous chapters and in the discussion of intersexed individuals. You probably know many women who chose, during their pregnancy, to learn the gender of their baby several months before childbirth. Interestingly, when a woman chooses *not* to know the baby's gender, she is likely to find that her friends and relatives may become insistent: "Couldn't you just do me a favor and ask? I want to crochet some booties for your baby, and I need to know what color to make them!"

PARENTAL PREFERENCES ABOUT SEX OF CHILDREN.   Several decades ago, researchers in the United States and Canada found that most men and women preferred a boy for their firstborn child. More recent research shows no clear-cut pattern of infant-sex preferences (Marleau & Saucier, 2002; McDougall et al., 1999). Try Demonstration 3.1, which focuses on gender preferences.

In some other cultures, however, parents do have strong preferences for boys. Favoritism toward boys is so strong in India and Korea that many women seek prenatal sex determinations. If the fetus is female, the mother often requests an abortion (Bellamy, 2000; Carmichael, 2004). Selective abortion and female infanticide are also common in China, where the discrepancy in the female population has important social consequences. In some regions of

Demonstration 3.1

You've just read that most North Americans no longer have clear-cut preferences for the sex of their offspring. However, some individuals you know may have strong opinions on the topic. To try this demonstration, locate 10 women and 10 men who do not have children, and ask them whether they would prefer a boy or a girl as their firstborn child. Be sure to select people with whom you are comfortable asking this question, and interview them one at a time. After noting each person's response, ask for a brief rationale for the answer. Do your male and female respondents differ in their preferences? Do you think their responses would have been different if they had filled out an anonymous survey?

China, for instance, the preference is so strong that about 120 infant boys are born for every 100 infant girls. This pattern of selective abortion means that many Chinese men of marrying age will not be able to find a spouse (Beach, 2001; Glenn, 2004; Hudson & den Boer, 2004; Pomfret, 2001). This bias against female babies is an important example of Theme 2 of this book: People often respond differently to females and males. Unfortunately, this information about prenatal preferences demonstrates that the bias begins even before the child is born (Croll, 2000; Rajvanshi, 2005).

The bias against female babies also appears in other cultures, even those that do not practice selective abortion (Croll, 2000). For example, C. Delaney (2000) reported that residents of Turkish villages consider girls to be temporary guests in the family home because they leave when they marry. In contrast, boys remain in the house after marriage, and they eventually inherit the property. A common saying in this region is "A boy is the flame of the hearth, a girl its ashes" (p. 124).

The bias against female babies may also have important health consequences. For example, I know a student, now in her mid-20s, who had been born in Korea, in a premature delivery. Many years later, her father told her that the family had decided not to put her in a hospital incubator because she was a girl. However, they would have chosen the incubator option if she had been a boy. Fortunately, she survived anyway.

PEOPLE'S STEREOTYPES ABOUT INFANT GIRLS AND BOYS.   Do people think baby girls are different from baby boys? In a classic study, Katherine Karraker and her colleagues (1995) investigated 40 mother-father pairs, 2 days after their infant son or daughter had been born. The researchers made certain that the sons were objectively similar to the daughters in terms of size and health. All the parents were asked to rate their newborn infant on a number of scales.

As you can see in Figure 3.2, parents of girls rated their daughters as being relatively weak, whereas parents of boys rated their sons as being relatively strong. Notice that the parents also thought that the girls were more fine-featured, delicate, and feminine, in comparison to the sons. Other research shows that parents treat daughters and sons differently by choosing

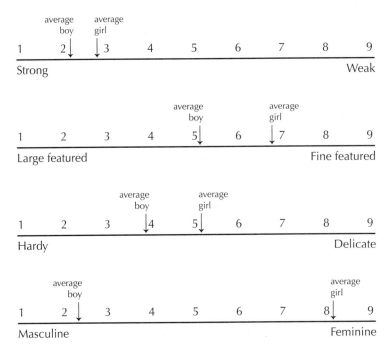

FIGURE 3.2 | AVERAGE RATINGS FOR NEWBORN GIRLS AND BOYS ON FOUR
                DIMENSIONS.

Source: Based on Karraker et al. (1995).

"gender appropriate" room decorations and toys (A. Pomerleau et al.,
1990).

Strangers also show this same tendency to make distinctions based on
gender. For instance, have you ever assumed an infant was a boy, and then
learned it was a girl? Most of us find this experience puzzling. We try to
maintain a nonsexist perspective, yet we find ourselves immediately justifying
this gender transformation: "Oh, of course, I didn't notice her long eyelashes,"
or "Yes, her hands are so delicate." In general, the research evidence confirms
that people judge infants differently when they are perceived to be female
rather than male (e.g., Archer & Lloyd, 2002; Condry & Condry, 1976; Delk
et al., 1986; Demarest & Glinos, 1992; C. Lewis et al., 1992).

We should emphasize, however, that some adults do not view infants
through gender-stereotyped lenses. For example, Plant and her colleagues
(2000) asked women and men to watch a short video. The video showed a
9-month-old infant who looked gender neutral, crying in response to the
removal of a toy. Before watching the video, half of the participants were told
that they would see a girl named Karen, and half were told that they would see a
boy named Brian. (Otherwise, both the "Karen" group and the "Brian" group
were the same.) After seeing the video, everyone rated the infant's emotions.

Anger is considered to be a stereotypically masculine emotion. Would the participants judge "Brian" to be angrier than "Karen"?

Plant and her colleagues found that male participants who had strong gender stereotypes typically provided higher anger ratings for the "boy" than for the "girl." However, the remaining participants provided similar ratings in the two gender conditions. We must note that the participants live in Madison, Wisconsin, one of the most liberal communities in the United States. The general North American population would probably reveal much stronger gender stereotypes.

So far, we've just looked at adults' judgments about infants. Do they actually interact differently with girls and boys? Some research has demonstrated that people hand different toys to infants based on their perception of the infants' gender. In one study, college students who thought they were playing with a baby girl handed "her" a doll 80% of the time and a football 14% of the time. Students who thought they were playing with a baby boy handed "him" a doll 20% of the time and a football 64% of the time (Sidorowicz & Lunney, 1980). Unfortunately, if children play only with stereotyped toys, they will limit their interests and abilities.

Marilyn Stern and Katherine Karraker (1989) reviewed the research in which infants had been given male or female labels. More than two-thirds of the studies showed at least one gender-label effect; that is, the gender label "boy" or "girl" had a significant influence on people's ratings of the infant. In general, the differences were largest when people judge infants' activities and physical characteristics. The differences were smallest when people judge developmental achievements and personality characteristics (Golombok & Fivush, 1994).

In addition, relatives and friends may convey gender stereotypes through their choice of greeting cards. Figure 3.3 illustrates a typical contrast between cards intended for parents of newborn girls and those intended for parents of newborn boys. In general, cards for boys show physical activity and action toys, whereas the cards for girls emphasize the baby's sweetness. In addition, cards for boys are more likely to mention how happy the parents must be (Bridges, 1993). Parents therefore receive a strong gender message as soon as they open the envelopes.

Notice that these studies on adults' treatment of infants tend to support a social constructionist approach. As we discussed in Chapter 1, **social constructionism** argues that we tend to construct or invent our own versions of reality based on our prior experiences and beliefs. For example, when we are told that an infant is female, we tend to see delicate, feminine behavior. When we are told that the same infant is male, we tend to see sturdy, masculine behavior. That is, we create our own versions of reality, based on our prior beliefs about gender.

This discussion suggests we can explain gender typing at least partly by the way people respond to infant girls and boys: Both parents and strangers make some gender distinctions. However, differential treatment by adults is not the complete answer. As we'll see later in this chapter, part of the explanation

FIGURE 3.3 | REPRESENTATIVE CARDS FOR PARENTS OF A BABY BOY OR A BABY GIRL.

Note: The original card for the girl is pink, and the card for the boy is blue.

comes from girls' and boys' own ideas about the importance of gender. Children acquire these ideas initially from adults, other children, the school system, and the media, and they exaggerate these ideas still further through their own patterns of thought.

THEORIES OF GENDER DEVELOPMENT

How can we account for the development of gender? What theories explain how children acquire their knowledge about gender, as well as their gender-related personality characteristics, preferences, self-concepts, skills, and behaviors?

One early explanation of gender development was Sigmund Freud's elaborate psychoanalytic theory. However, research has not supported that theory, and it is seldom discussed in contemporary explanations for the development of gender (e.g., Bussey & Bandura, 2004; Liben & Bigler, 2002; C. L. Martin et al., 2002). If you are interested in the topic, you can consult other resources (e.g., L. C. Bell, 2004b; Callan, 2001). In this discussion of gender development, we will focus instead on two contemporary perspectives. These perspectives emphasize two different processes that operate during child development: the social learning approach and the cognitive developmental approach. Two decades ago, these two approaches were considered rival theories. We now must conclude that gender development is such a complex process that neither explanation is sufficient by itself. Instead, children apparently acquire their information about gender by both of these important methods (Bem, 1981, 1993; Bussey & Bandura, 2004; Powlishta et al., 2001):

1. In the social learning approach, children learn gender-related *behaviors* from other people.
2. In the cognitive developmental approach, children actively synthesize and create their own *thoughts* about gender.

THE SOCIAL LEARNING APPROACH.   The social learning approach argues that traditional learning principles explain an important part of gender development (Bandura & Bussey, 2004; Bussey & Bandura, 2004; B. Lott & Maluso, 2001; W. Mischel, 1966). More specifically, the **social learning approach** proposes two major mechanisms for explaining how girls learn to act "feminine" and how boys learn to act "masculine":

1. Children are rewarded for "gender-appropriate" behavior, and they are punished for "gender-inappropriate" behavior.
2. Children watch and imitate the behavior of other people of their own gender.

Let's first see how rewards and punishments might operate through direct learning experiences. Jimmy, age 2, races his toy truck, producing an impressive rumbling-motor sound. His doting parents smile, thereby rewarding Jimmy's "masculine" behavior. If Jimmy had donned his sister's pink tutu and waltzed around the dining room, his parents would probably actively try to discourage him. Now imagine how Sarah, also age 2, might win smiles for the pink tutu act but possible frowns for the rumbling-truck performance. According to this first component of the social learning approach, children directly learn many gender-related behaviors, based on positive and negative responses from other people. As we'll soon see, adults and other children may respond differently to a girl's behavior than to a boy's behavior (Fabes & Martin, 2000).

According to the second of the two social learning components, children also learn by watching others and imitating them, a process called **modeling.** Children are especially likely to imitate a person of their own gender or a person who has been praised for a behavior (Bussey & Bandura, 2004; Carli & Bukatko, 2000; Leaper, 2000; B. Lott & Maluso, 2001). For example, a little girl would be particularly likely to imitate her mother, especially if someone praised her mother for her actions. Also, children frequently imitate characters from books, films, and television, as well as real people (Bussey & Bandura, 2004).

Direct learning, by means of rewards and punishments, is an important way that very young children learn "gender-appropriate" behavior. As children grow older, the second component (modeling) becomes active. Children can now observe the behavior of others, internalize that information, and imitate that behavior later (Bussey & Bandura, 1999, 2004; B. Lott & Maluso, 2001; Trautner & Eckes, 2000). Now let's see how our gender schemas and other cognitive processes contribute to a lifetime of learning about gender.

THE COGNITIVE DEVELOPMENTAL APPROACH.   Whereas the social learning approach focuses on *behaviors,* the cognitive developmental approach focuses on *thoughts.* More specifically, the **cognitive developmental approach** argues that children are active thinkers who seek information from their environment; children also try to make sense of this information and organize it in a coherent fashion (Liben & Bigler, 2002; C. L. Martin et al., 2002).

One important concept in the cognitive developmental approach is called a *schema.* A **schema** (pronounced *skee*-mah) is a general concept that we use to organize our thoughts about a topic. As we saw in Chapter 2 (page 65), we humans seem to automatically sort people into groups.

At a relatively early age, children develop powerful **gender schemas;** they organize information into two conceptual categories, female and male. These gender schemas encourage children to think and act in gender-stereotyped ways that are consistent with their gender schemas (C. L. Martin & Halverson, 1981; C. L. Martin & Ruble, 2004; C. L. Martin et al., 2002, 2004). A child's gender schema may include relatively important information, such as the fact that the kindergarten teacher instructs children to form a boys' line and a girls' line (Bem, 1981, 1993). The schemas may also include trivial information, such as the idea that females have more prominent eyelashes than males do. As children grow older, their gender schemas become more complex and also more flexible (C. L. Martin & Ruble, 2004).

According to the cognitive developmental approach to gender development, children actively work to make sense of their own gender (Kohlberg, 1966). One of the first major steps in gender development is **gender identity,** or a girl's realization that she is a girl and a boy's realization that he is a boy. Most children are accurate in labeling themselves by the time they are 1 1/2 to 2 1/2 years old (C. L. Martin et al., 2004).

Soon after children label themselves accurately, they learn how to classify other males and females. At this point, they begin to prefer people, activities, and things that are consistent with their own gender identity (Kohlberg, 1966; C. L. Martin et al., 2002; Powlishta et al., 2001). A child who realizes that she is a girl, for example, likes feminine objects and activities. A woman in one of my classes provided a useful example of these preference patterns. Her 4-year-old daughter asked about the sex of every dog she met. If it was a "girl dog," she would run up and pat it lovingly. If it was a "boy dog," she would cast a scornful glance and walk in the opposite direction. Girls prefer stereotypically feminine activities because these activities are consistent with their female gender identity, according to the cognitive developmental approach.

GENERAL COMMENTS ABOUT THEORIES OF GENDER DEVELOPMENT.   We have explored two major theoretical approaches to development; both of these theories are necessary to account for children's gender typing. Together, they suggest the following:

1. Children's behaviors are important, as proposed by social learning theory.
   a. Children are rewarded and punished for gender-related behavior.
   b. Children model their behavior after same-gender individuals.

2. Children's thoughts are important, as proposed by cognitive developmental theory.
   a. Children develop powerful gender schemas.
   b. Children use gender schemas to evaluate themselves, other people, and other things.

Both the social learning and the cognitive developmental approaches work together to account for children's development of gender typing (e.g., Bussey & Bandura, 1999, 2004; C. L. Martin et al., 2002, 2004). To some extent, children *behave* before they *think*. In other words, the two components of social learning theory may begin to operate before children have clear gender schemas or other thoughts about gender (Warin, 2000). As children's cognitive development grows more sophisticated, however, their ideas about gender schemas enhance their ability to learn gender-typed behavior, through direct learning and modeling.

For the remainder of this chapter, we turn our attention to the research about children's gender development. We'll first consider the external forces that encourage gender typing, including the parents and teachers who reward and punish children's gender-related behavior and the media that provide models of gender-stereotyped behavior. Then we'll consider how children's thoughts about gender develop from infancy to late childhood.

Section Summary

Background on Gender Development

1. During typical prenatal development, male and female embryos initially look identical; male testes begin to develop at 6 weeks, and female ovaries begin to develop at 10 weeks.

2. An embryo's neutral external genitals usually grow into either female or male genitals during prenatal development.

3. In atypical prenatal development, an intersexed infant is born; this child is neither clearly male nor clearly female. For example, genetic males with androgen-insensitivity syndrome may have external genitals that look female. Also, genetic females with congenital adrenal hyperplasia (too much androgen) have external genitals that look masculine.

4. The research demonstrates that our culture is uncomfortable with intersexed infants because they do not fit into one of the two "acceptable" gender categories.

5. Most parents no longer have a strong preference for male offspring in the United States and Canada; gender preferences are so strong in some other countries (e.g., India, Korea, and China) that female fetuses may be aborted.

6. Parents tend to make different judgments about their newborn infant as a function of the infant's gender.

7. Strangers often judge babies differently, depending on whether they believe a baby is a boy or a girl; they also interact differently with infants, depending on the infant's perceived gender.

8. We can best explain gender typing by combining two approaches: (a) the social learning approach (children are rewarded for "gender-appropriate" behavior and punished for "gender-inappropriate" behavior, and children imitate the behavior of same-gender individuals) and (b) the cognitive developmental approach (children's active thinking encourages gender typing, and children use gender schemes for evaluation).

FACTORS THAT SHAPE GENDER TYPING

In the previous section, we discussed two general explanations for gender typing. The social learning approach emphasizes that parents often reward gender-typed behavior more than "gender-inappropriate" behavior; also, parents and the media typically provide models of gender-typed behavior. The cognitive developmental approach emphasizes that children actively construct their gender schemas based on messages they learn from parents and other sources. Let's look in closer detail at several important factors that shape gender typing, beginning with parents and then moving on to peers, schools, and the media. As you'll see, each factor contributes to children's development of gender roles.

PARENTS

We saw earlier that parents react somewhat differently to male and female infants. Those reactions tend to be stereotyped because parents do not yet know their infants' unique characteristics (Jacklin & Maccoby, 1983). By the time children become toddlers, however, the parents know much more about each child's individual personality (B. Lott & Maluso, 1993). Therefore, parents often react to toddlers on the basis of each child's personality characteristics rather than on the basis of his or her gender.

In this section, we'll see that parents sometimes encourage gender-typed activities and conversational patterns. They also treat sons and daughters somewhat differently with respect to two social characteristics: aggression and independence. However, parents often do not make as strong a distinction between boys and girls as you might expect (R. C. Barnett & Rivers, 2004; Fagot, 1995; Leaper, 2002; Ruble & Martin, 1998). We'll also consider the factors related to parents' gender-typing tendencies.

GENDER-TYPED ACTIVITIES.   Parents encourage gender-typed activities when they assign chores to their children. As you might expect, girls are more likely to be assigned domestic chores, such as washing the dishes or taking care of children, whereas boys are typically assigned outdoor work, such as mowing the lawn or taking out the garbage (Antill et al., 1996; Coltrane & Adams, 1997; Leaper, 2002). Research in Asia shows that girls typically perform more time-consuming chores than boys do, whereas boys are allowed more time for schoolwork (Croll, 2000). Furthermore, in nonindustrialized cultures, boys have roughly twice as much free time as girls do (McHale et al., 2002).

According to the research, parents often encourage their children to develop gender-typed interests by providing different kinds of toys for daughters than for sons (Caldera & Sciaraffa, 1998; Coltrane & Adams, 1997; Leaper, 2002). However, an observational study showed that parents have relatively little stereotypical behavior when the child is actively playing with toys (Idle et al., 1993). In other words, if parents notice that 3-year-old Tanya likes playing with the Fisher-Price gas station, they won't interfere by handing her a doll. In general, however, girls have greater flexibility in the toys they play with, whereas boys typically avoid feminine toys (E. Wood et al., 2002).

Perhaps an even stronger force than encouragement of gender-typed activity is parents' *discouragement* of activities they think are inappropriate. They are particularly likely to discourage sons, rather than daughters, from playing with "gender-inappropriate" toys. That is, parents are much more worried about boys being sissies than about girls being tomboys (Campenni, 1999; Sandnabba & Ahlberg, 1999). One possible explanation is that adults tend to interpret feminine behavior in a boy as a sign of gay tendencies, but they are less likely to view masculine behavior in a girl as a sign of lesbian tendencies (Sandnabba & Ahlberg, 1999).

We have seen that male children are more likely than female children to *receive* strong messages about "gender-appropriate" behavior. Similarly, the research shows that male adults are more likely than female adults to *give* these messages (Bussey & Bandura, 1999; Coltrane & Adams, 1997; Leaper, 2002). For example, fathers are more likely than mothers to encourage their daughters to play with stereotypically feminine items, such as tea sets and baby dolls, and to encourage their sons to play with stereotypically masculine items, such as footballs and boxing gloves.

In summary, parents do seem to promote some gender-typed activities in their children. As we'll soon see, however, many parents conscientiously try to treat their sons and daughters similarly.

CONVERSATIONS ABOUT EMOTIONS.   Another kind of gender-typed activity focuses on conversations. Parents are more likely to talk with their daughters than with their sons about other people and about emotions (Bronstein, 2006; Fivush et al., 2000; Shields, 2002).

Perhaps the most interesting aspect of parent-child conversations is that parents typically discuss different emotions with their children, depending on the child's gender (Chance & Fiese, 1999; Fivush & Buckner, 2000; Leaper, 2002). In the section on infancy, we saw that some adults tend to judge that a crying baby boy is more likely than a crying baby girl to be angry. Related research examined mothers' conversations with children between the ages of 2 1/2 and 3 years. During a session that lasted about half an hour, 21% of mothers discussed anger with their sons, whereas 0% of mothers discussed anger with their daughters. Instead, they talked with their daughters about fear and sadness (Fivush, 1989). Mothers are especially likely to discuss sadness in detail with their daughters to discover exactly why their daughters had been sad on a particular occasion (Fivush & Buckner, 2000). Also, mothers speak in a more emotional fashion when interacting with their daughters, rather than their sons (Fivush & Nelson, 2004).

Fathers, as well as mothers, are much more likely to discuss sadness with their daughters than with their sons (S. Adams et al., 1995; Fivush & Buckner, 2000; Fivush et al., 2000). Not surprisingly, then, studies of 3- and 4-year-olds show that girls are more likely than boys to spontaneously talk about sad experiences (Denham, 1998; Fivush & Buckner, 2000). In Chapter 12, we'll see that when women are sad, they may spend time trying to figure out the precise nature of their sadness, an activity that may lead to higher rates of depression in women than in men (Nolen-Hoeksema, 1990, 2003). Early family interactions may encourage these gender differences during adulthood.

ATTITUDES ABOUT AGGRESSION.   In popularized accounts of gender-role development, you may read that parents discourage aggression in their daughters but tolerate or even encourage aggression in their sons. This description may be intuitively appealing. However, the research findings are inconsistent. Some studies show that parents are more likely to discourage aggression in their daughters than in their sons, but other studies show little differences (Lytton & Romney, 1991; Powlishta et al., 2001; Ruble & Martin, 1998). Try Demonstration 3.2 when you have a chance. What do your own observations suggest about parents' responses to aggressive daughters and aggressive sons?

Demonstration 3.2

TOLERANCE FOR
AGGRESSION IN
SONS AND
DAUGHTERS

For this demonstration, you will need to find a location where parents are likely to bring their children. Some possibilities include grocery stores, toy stores, and fast-food restaurants. Observe several families with more than one child. Be alert for both verbal and physical aggression from the children, directed toward either a parent or a sibling. What is the parent's response to this aggression? Does the parent respond differently to aggression, depending on a child's gender?

In Chapter 6, we'll discuss how adult males tend to be more aggressive than adult females in some kinds of interpersonal interactions. Apparently, we cannot explain most of this difference in terms of parents' rewarding and punishing boys differently from girls.

However, parents can provide information about aggression and power in other ways. As the second component of social learning theory emphasizes, some boys may learn to be aggressive by imitating their aggressive fathers. Furthermore, the structure of the family provides information for children's schemas about proper "masculine" and "feminine" behavior, as emphasized by cognitive developmental theory. Children notice in their own families that fathers make decisions and announce which television show will be watched. Fathers may also use physical intimidation to assert power. By watching their parents, children often learn that physical aggression and power are "boy things," not "girl things."

ATTITUDES ABOUT INDEPENDENCE.   According to popularized accounts of gender-role development, parents encourage their sons to explore and pursue activities on their own, but they overprotect and overhelp their daughters. Once again, the evidence is not as clear-cut as the media suggest.

In some situations, parents do encourage more independence in boys than in girls. In research on toddlers, boys are more often left alone in a room, whereas girls are more likely to be supervised (Bronstein, 2006; Fagot, 1978; Grusec & Lytton, 1988). Also, a study of mothers showed that they allowed their sons more independence than their daughters in a variety of everyday activities (Pomerantz & Ruble, 1998).

Some research indicates that parents give the same kind of verbal directions to their sons and their daughters (Bellinger & Gleason, 1982; Leaper et al., 1998). However, other research shows that mothers are more likely to provide cautions to their daughters, rather than their sons, perhaps because they believe that daughters are more likely to listen to these cautions (Leaper, 2002; Morrongiello & Hogg, 2004). Clearly, gender differences in this area are far from consistent (Leaper, 2002; Powlishta et al., 2001; Zemore et al., 2000).

INDIVIDUAL DIFFERENCES IN PARENTS' GENDER TYPING.   We have seen that parents may encourage gender-typed activities. They often spend more time talking about sadness with their daughters than with their sons. However, they do not consistently encourage aggression or independence in their sons more than in their daughters (Leaper, 2002; Powlishta et al., 2001; Ruble & Martin, 1998).

Consistent with Theme 4 (individual differences), parents vary widely in the kinds of gender messages they provide to their children. Some parents treat their sons and daughters very differently, whereas others actively try to avoid gender bias. For example, Tenenbaum and Leaper (1997) studied Mexican American fathers interacting with their preschool children in a feminine setting: playing with toy foods. Fathers who had traditional attitudes toward gender did not talk much with their children in this setting. In contrast, nontraditional fathers asked their children questions such as "What is on this sandwich?" and

"Should we cook this egg?" By asking these questions, the fathers are sending a message to their children that men can feel comfortable with traditionally feminine tasks.

Relatively few studies have focused specifically on ethnic differences in parents' treatment of sons and daughters (Hill, 2002; Raffaelli & Ontai, 2004). As might be expected when the variability is so great within each ethnic group, the results are often complex or contradictory (L. W. Hoffman & Kloska, 1995; P. A. Katz, 1987). For example, a study by Flannagan and Perese (1998) reported that mothers' conversations with their daughters and sons depended on both the family's ethnicity and their social class. The only consistency I detected in the research about parents' ethnicity is that African American mothers tend to raise their children in a less gender-stereotyped fashion if they are well educated (Flannagan & Perese, 1998; Hill, 2002).

Another source of individual differences in parents' gender typing is more clear cut. You won't be surprised to learn that parents' personal ideas about gender can have a significant effect on the kind of messages they give their sons and daughters. For example, Fiese and Skillman (2000) studied a group of parents, most of whom were European American. Each parent was instructed to tell a story to her or his 4-year-old child, focusing on the parent's own childhood experience. Mothers who had stereotypically feminine personal characteristics and fathers who had stereotypically masculine personal characteristics tended to interact with their children in a gender-stereotypical fashion. That is, they told about three times as many stories about achievement to their sons as they did to their daughters. However, parents who had a mixture of stereotypically feminine and masculine personal characteristics tended to interact in a nonstereotypical fashion. Specifically, they told about the same number of achievement-related stories to their daughters and to their sons.

Some parents make impressive efforts to treat their children in a gender-fair manner. We discussed the theories developed by Sandra Bem in connection with the topic of androgyny in Chapter 2, and we explored her perspective on gender schemas in this chapter. Bem (1998) described how she and Daryl Bem had raised their daughter and son:

> For example, we took turns cooking the meals, driving the car, bathing the baby, and so on, so that our own parental example would not teach a correlation between sex and behavior. This was easy for us because we already had such well-developed habits of egalitarian turn-taking. In addition, we tried to arrange for both our children to have traditionally male and traditionally female experiences—including, for example, playing with both dolls and trucks, wearing both pink and blue clothing, and having both male and female playmates. This turned out to be easy, too, perhaps because of our kids' temperaments. Insofar as possible, we also arranged for them to see nontraditional gender models outside the home. (p. 104)

This discussion about individual differences in parents' gender typing demonstrates that ethnicity does not have a clear-cut influence on parents' treatment of daughters and sons. However, parents who endorse nontraditional gender beliefs in their own lives may indeed treat their sons and daughters in a gender-fair fashion.

Before we move on, let's review the general conclusions about parents. By their reactions to their children's "masculine" and "feminine" activities, parents often encourage gender typing They also discuss emotions, especially sadness, more with their daughters than with their sons. In contrast, they often treat their daughters and sons similarly with respect to aggression and independence. When we take everything into account, parents are not as consistent about encouraging gender typing as articles in the popular media would suggest. We need to consider additional forces that are responsible for gender typing, including three factors that reveal greater gender bias: peers, schools, and the media.

PEERS

Once children in the United States and Canada begin school, a major source of information about gender is their **peer group**—that is, other children of approximately their own age. A child may have been raised by relatively nonsexist parents. However, on the first day of class, if Jennifer wears her hiking boots and Johnny brings in a new baby doll, their peers may respond negatively. According to the research, peers seem to be more influential than parents in emphasizing gender typing (Maccoby, 2002).

Peers encourage gender typing in four major ways: (1) They reject children who act in a nonstereotypical fashion; (2) they encourage gender segregation; (3) they are prejudiced against children of the other gender; and (4) they treat boys and girls differently. As you read this discussion, consider how social learning theory and gender schema theory would explain each topic's contribution to children's gender typing.

REJECTION OF NONTRADITIONAL BEHAVIOR.   In general, children tend to reject peers who act in a fashion that is more characteristic of the other gender (C. P. Edwards et al., 2001). For example, children tend to think that girls should not play aggressive, "fighting" electronic games (Funk & Buchman, 1996). Also, girls who dominate discussions are downgraded as being too bossy (Zucker et al., 1995). Women who had been tomboys as children often report that their peers were influential in convincing them to act more feminine (B. L. Morgan, 1998). As we saw in the discussion of social learning theory, children are rewarded for "gender-appropriate" behavior, and they are punished for "gender-inappropriate" behavior (Bussey & Bandura, 2004).

Nontraditional boys usually experience even stronger rejection (Bussey & Bandura, 2004; Fagot et al., 2000). For example, Judith Blakemore (2003) asked children between the ages of 3 and 11 to judge whether they would like to be friends with a child who violated traditional stereotypes. The children were especially likely to say that they would dislike a boy who wore a girl's hairstyle or a girl's clothing, who played with a Barbie doll, or who wanted to be a nurse. In contrast, they judged girls significantly less harshly for comparable role violations. Peers contribute to an unwritten boys' code, a set of rigid rules about how boys should speak and behave (Pollack, 1998). This code explicitly forbids boys from talking about anxieties, fear, and other "sensitive" emotions. As we saw in the discussion of the cognitive developmental approach, children's gender schemas are often extremely rigid.

GENDER SEGREGATION.   The tendency to associate with other children of the same gender is called **gender segregation.** Children in the United States and Canada begin to prefer playing with same-gender children by age 3 or 4 years, and this tendency increases until early adolescence (C. P. Edwards et al., 2001; Gardiner et al., 1998; Maccoby, 1998, 2002). In one study, for instance, more than 80% of 3- to 6-year-old children clearly preferred to play with another child of the same gender (C. L. Martin & Fabes, 2001).

One problem with gender segregation is that these single-gender groups encourage children to learn—and practice—gender-stereotyped behavior (Fabes et al., 2003; Golombok & Hines, 2002; Maccoby, 1998, 2002). Boys learn that they are supposed to be physically aggressive and not admit that they are sometimes afraid. Girls learn to focus their attention on clothing and glamour rather than on competence. These different activities, in turn, strengthen children's gender schemas, so that the "boy" category seems distinctly different from the "girl" category (Fabes et al., 2003).

Both girls and boys also learn that the boys' group has greater power. This inequality encourages a sense of **entitlement** among the boys; the boys will feel that they *deserve* greater power simply because they are male rather than female (McGann & Steil, 2006; L. M. Ward, 1999). Another major problem with gender segregation is that children who grow up playing with only same-gender peers will not learn the broad range of skills they need to work well with both females and males (Fagot et al., 2000; Shields, 2002).

This preference for playing with children of the same gender continues to increase until about the age of 11 (Maccoby, 1998). As romantic relationships develop in early adolescence, boys and girls then increase their time together.

GENDER PREJUDICE.   A third way in which peers encourage gender typing is with prejudice against members of the other gender (Carver et al., 2003; Narter, 2006). As we discussed in connection with gender schema theory, children develop a preference for their own gender. For example, Powlishta (1995) showed 9- and 10-year-old children a series of brief videotaped interactions between children and adults. After viewing each video, the children rated the child in the video, using a 10-point scale of liking that ranged from "not at all" to "very, very much."

As you can see in Figure 3.4, girls liked the girl targets in the videos better than the boy targets, and boys preferred the boy targets to the girl targets. Similarly, in a study with Brazilian 3- to 10-year-olds, children gave positive ratings to same-gender children and negative ratings to children of the other gender (de Guzman et al., 2004). This kind of prejudice arises from children's clear-cut gender schemas, and it reinforces children's beliefs that females and males are very different kinds of people.

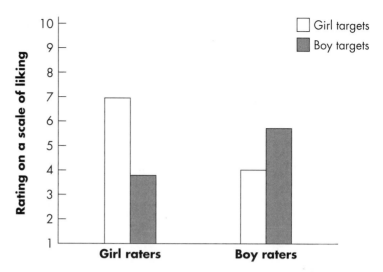

FIGURE 3.4 | RATINGS SUPPLIED BY FEMALE AND MALE CHILDREN FOR THE GIRLS AND BOYS IN VIDEOS. THE DATA SHOW PREJUDICE AGAINST THE OTHER GENDER.

Source: From Powlishta, K. (1995). Intergroup processes in childhood. *Developmental Psychology, 31,* 781–788. © 1995 by the American Psychological Association. Reprinted with permission.

DIFFERENTIAL TREATMENT.   A fourth way in which peers promote gender typing is that they use different standards in their interactions with boys than with girls. One of the most interesting examples of differential treatment is that children respond to girls on the basis of their physical attractiveness, but attractiveness is largely irrelevant for boys. In a classic study, Gregory Smith (1985) observed middle-class European American preschoolers for 5-minute sessions in a classroom setting on 5 separate days. He recorded how other children treated each child. Were the other children prosocial—helping, patting, and praising the child? Or were the other children physically aggressive—hitting, pushing, or kicking the target child?

Smith then calculated how each child's attractiveness was related to both the prosocial and aggressive behavior that the child received. The results showed that attractiveness (as previously rated by college students) was correlated with the way the girls were treated. Specifically, attractive girls were much more likely to receive prosocial treatment. Figure 3.5 shows a strong positive correlation. In other words, the "cutest" girls were most likely to be helped, patted, and praised. In contrast, the less attractive girls received few of these positive responses. However, Smith found no correlation between attractiveness and prosocial treatment of boys; attractive and less attractive boys received a similar number of prosocial actions.

Gregory Smith (1985) also found a comparable pattern for physical aggression scores. That is, the less attractive girls were more likely to be hit, pushed, and kicked, whereas the cutest girls rarely received this treatment.

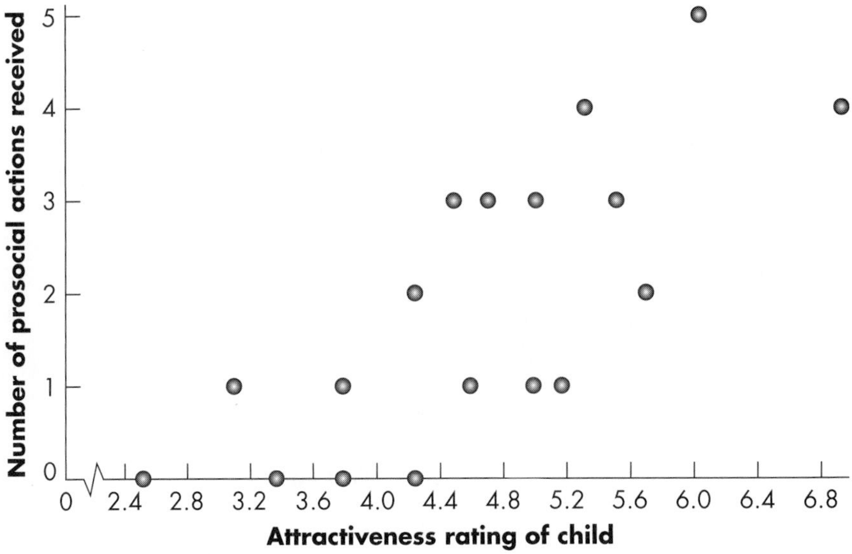

FIGURE 3.5 | POSITIVE CORRELATION BETWEEN ATTRACTIVENESS AND PROSOCIAL TREATMENT OF GIRLS ($r = +.73$).

Source: G. J. Smith (1985).

However, attractiveness was not related to the aggression directed toward boys. Young girls learn a lesson from their peers that will be repeated throughout their lives: Physical attractiveness is important for females, and pretty girls and women will receive better treatment. Boys learn that physical attractiveness is not really relevant to their lives.

Researchers have not examined the influence of peers on gender typing as thoroughly as the influence of parents (Maccoby, 2002). However, we have seen that, in several ways, children can influence others who are their own age. Specifically, they can reject nontraditional behavior in their peers. They can encourage gender segregation, so that boys and girls have minimal contact with one another. They can also express prejudice against children of the other gender. Finally, they can respond differently to girls than to boys, for example, by emphasizing attractiveness for girls but not for boys.

School

The typical child in elementary school in North America spends more waking hours in school with teachers than at home with family members. As a result, teachers and schools have numerous opportunities to influence gender typing (Maher & Ward, 2002).

Even the structure of a school provides evidence that males are treated differently and valued more than females (Theme 2). Specifically, most principals and other high-prestige officials are male, whereas about 80% of those who teach "the little kids" are female (Maher & Ward, 2002; Meece & Scantlebury, 2006). Let's investigate how teachers' behavior may favor boys. Then we'll consider how gender-fair programs can encourage children to become less gender stereotyped. Finally, we'll consider a serious problem in some developing countries, where girls are much less likely than boys to receive a good education.

TEACHERS' BEHAVIOR.   In the early 1990s, the media began to publicize an important problem: Girls do not receive equal treatment in the classroom (Grayson, 2001; Rensenbrink, 2001; Sadker & Sadker, 1994). The publicized reports highlighted the invisibility of girls in the educational system, a point that is clearly consistent with Theme 3 of this textbook. According to the reports, classroom activities are often selected to appeal to boys, teachers typically pay more attention to boys in the classroom, and females are absent or misrepresented in the textbooks and other teaching materials (Maher & Ward, 2002; Meece & Scantlebury, 2006).

More specifically, the research suggests that boys generally receive more positive feedback in the classroom. They are also more likely to be recognized for their creativity, called on in class, and included in class discussions (Basow, 2004; DeZolt & Hull, 2001; B. Lott & Maluso, 2001). Sadker and Sadker (1994) discussed a typical example: The teacher asks, "What is an adjective? Maria?" Maria answers appropriately, "A word that describes something." Simultaneously, Tim calls out, "Adjectives describe nouns." The teacher responds, "Good, Tim" (p. 74). Notice how the teacher reinforces Tim, ignoring Maria's correct answer. Teachers also tend to offer more specific suggestions to boys than to girls (American Institutes for Research, 1998). Incidentally, both female and male teachers typically pay more attention to boys (Basow, 2004).

Female students of color are especially likely to be ignored in the classroom. In early school years, Black girls speak up in the classroom. However, their assertiveness may be discouraged. By fourth grade, they may become more passive and quiet (Basow, 2004). In addition, teachers do not typically encourage Black girls to take on academic responsibilities, such as tutoring or showing a new student how to prepare an assignment (Grant, 1994).

Social class is another factor that influences teachers' behavior (Maher & Ward, 2002). Teachers may encourage a child from a middle-class family to learn independently. In contrast, they typically emphasize simple memorization for a girl from a lower-class family (B. Lott, 2003; Rist, 2000).

Teachers also emphasize gender roles through a variety of messages. For example, a friend showed me an invitation to a Mother's Day Tea Party, which her 5-year-old son had brought home from school. Mothers were urged to wear "tea party dresses," with a fancy hat, if possible. The event was described as a good way to teach children about proper etiquette. The following month, fathers were invited to a Father's Day celebration. However, nothing in the invitation mentioned clothing and proper manners. Think about the message that this contrast provided to the children in the class . . . and also to the children's parents!

In short, several factors in the school system may operate so that girls are shortchanged. Luckily, most of us have known several inspirational teachers who value girls and boys equally. However, in many cases, girls may be ignored, they may not be given appropriate feedback, and they may not be encouraged to be academically competent. In addition, the school system may convey important messages about the roles of women and men.

ENCOURAGING CHANGE IN NORTH AMERICAN SCHOOLS.   So far, our exploration of gender and education has emphasized that school structure and teachers' behavior often favor boys over girls. Fortunately, however, many North American colleges and universities that train teachers now require courses about gender and ethnic diversity. Media coverage of the "silenced female" problem has also alerted teachers about the need for more equal attention to girls and boys (Maher & Ward, 2002). As a result, an increasing number of schoolteachers are intensely concerned about gender-fair education (Rensenbrink, 2001).

Some programs have been designed to change children's stereotypes (Bigler, 1999a; Maher & Ward, 2002; Wickett, 2001). For instance, Bigler (1995) assigned 6- to 9-year-old children either to control classrooms or to gender-emphasized classrooms during a 4-week summer school program. Teachers in the control classrooms were instructed not to emphasize gender in their remarks or in their treatment of the children. Meanwhile, teachers in the gender-emphasized classrooms used gender-segregated seating, with girls' and boys' desks on opposite sides of the classroom. The teachers also displayed girls' and boys' artwork on different bulletin boards, and they frequently instructed boys and girls to perform different activities.

The most interesting results concerned those children who did not have strong gender schemas before the program began. Those enrolled in gender-emphasized classrooms were 50% more likely than those in the control classrooms to make stereotyped judgments about which jobs males and females could hold. In contrast, children who initially had strong gender schemas were not influenced by the nature of the program.

Unfortunately, we cannot expect that years of learning gender stereotypes can be erased with one simple, brief intervention. Many programs have been unsuccessful (Bigler, 1999a). In general, children change their stereotypes more dramatically when they work together on an issue, rather than when an adult tries to persuade them to change perspectives (Aboud & Fenwick, 1999; Bigler, 1999b). The approach to gender and education must be more sophisticated, keeping in mind that children actively construct their gender schemas. Children do not simply acquire information by means of the more passive social learning approach (Bigler, 1999a). Educators must also emphasize a more comprehensive approach toward gender, so that teachers from kindergarten onward are encouraged to pay equal attention to girls and to reduce inappropriate stereotypes about gender.

GENDER AND EDUCATION IN NONINDUSTRIALIZED COUNTRIES.   At the international level, we often encounter a more extreme problem about education for young girls. In many countries, boys are much more likely than girls to be enrolled in school. For instance, in 45 out of the 55 countries in Africa, boys have higher elementary-school enrollments than girls do (United Nations, 2006).

United Nations data also show that there are about 800 million illiterate adults in the world, and about two-thirds of them are women (UNESCO, 2004). Where food and other essentials are limited, the education of females is considered a luxury. Literacy rates for women in nonindustrialized countries vary greatly. For example, 97% of women in Cuba can read, in contrast to 50% in nearby Haiti (UNESCO, 2007). Some countries have recently begun literacy campaigns (Gold, 2001; M. Nussbaum, 2000). In rural Iran, for instance, girls' enrollment in primary schools rose from 60% to 80% in just 5 years (Bellamy, 2000).

Unfortunately, girls who have not been educated will experience a lifelong handicap. As adults, they will not be able to read newspapers, write checks, sign contracts, or perform numerous other activities that can help them to become independent and economically self-sufficient (M. Nussbaum, 2000). In addition, educated women are more likely to obtain employment. Educated women typically postpone marriage, and they have much lower birthrates than uneducated women. Infant mortality is also lower. Their children are usually healthier, and these children are more likely to obtain an education (W. Chambers, 2005). In other words, women's education has widespread effects on the health and well-being of people in nonindustrialized countries.

The gap between nonindustrialized countries and wealthy countries continues to widen (Bellamy, 2000). In addition, the governments of wealthy countries—such as the United States—rarely subsidize literacy programs or other socially responsible projects that could make a real difference in the lives of women in the less wealthy countries. For example, the United States has spent billions of dollars in Afghanistan, yet less than 1% of this money is spent on the health and education of Afghan people (Lipson, 2003).

One woman living in the Canary Islands, off the coast of North Africa, described why she regrets that she never learned to read:

> The greatest treasure that exists in life is to read and understand what one is reading. This is the most beautiful gift there is. All my life I have wished to learn to read and write, because, to me, knowing how to do so meant freedom. (Sweetman, 1998, p. 2)

THE MEDIA

So far, we have considered how parents, peers, and schools often treat girls and boys differently. Children also receive gender messages from many other sources. For example, the educational software designed for preschoolers has twice as many male main characters as female characters (Sheldon, 2004). Older children learn about gender through video games, but females are entirely absent from about 40% of the games with human characters (Cassell & Jenkins, 1998; Dietz, 1998). "Barbie Fashion Designer" has been one of the most successful interactive games designed for girls (Subrahmanyam et al., 2002), and this game sends a clear gender message.

Occasionally, we'll see a creative alternative, such as the program *The Adventures of Josie True,* featuring an 11-year-old Chinese American girl detective (Donovan, 2000; the website is http://www.josietrue.com). In general, though, the large number of masculine video games encourages boys to use these games more often than girls do. The games also help boys develop more extensive computer skills (Subrahmanyam et al., 2002).

Even Halloween costumes convey messages about gender: Girls can be beauty queens, princesses, or cuddly animals, whereas boys can be warriors, superheroes, or monsters (A. Nelson, 2000). Most of the research on gender and the media examines how males and females are represented in books and television, so we'll explore these two areas in more detail.

BOOKS. Most of the main characters in children's picture books are males, usually by a ratio of about 2 to 1 (R. Clark et al., 2003; M. C. Hamilton et al., 2006; Tepper & Cassidy, 1999). I did locate one study, however, in which the sample showed an equal number of males and females (Gooden & Gooden, 2001). But in general, males also appear more often in the books' illustrations (R. Clark et al., 1993; Gooden & Gooden, 2001; Tepper & Cassidy, 1999).

What are the males and females doing in these books designed for young children? Males are portrayed in a wider variety of occupations compared to females (Crabb & Bielawski, 1994; Gooden & Gooden, 2001). Also, boys help others, solve problems independently, and play actively. In contrast, girls need help in solving their problems, and they play quietly indoors (D. A. Anderson & Hamilton, 2005; R. Clark et al., 2003; L. Evans & Davies, 2000; M. C. Hamilton et al., 2006).

Some authors are clearly trying to write nonsexist books that portray strong female characters who are active and independent. Unfortunately, however, most of these authors still portray males in stereotypically masculine roles (Diekman & Murnen, 2004). Furthermore, in a study of 200 best-selling children's books, many more mothers were shown than fathers. Mothers also interacted much more frequently with their children, compared to fathers. Sadly, not one book showed a father kissing or feeding a baby (D. A. Anderson & Hamilton, 2005). Regrettably, in the twenty-first century, children's books are not showing gender equality!

As you've been learning about the traditional gender stereotypes in children's literature, perhaps you felt uneasy. Should we really worry about what children read? As it turns out, these biases do have important consequences for children. For example, Ochman (1996) designed a study in which children watched videotapes of an actor reading a series of stories. Each story required the main character to solve a problem, which then enhanced this character's self-esteem. The same stories were presented to classrooms of 7- to 10-year-olds; however, a boy was the main character for half of the classes and a girl was the main character for the remaining classes.

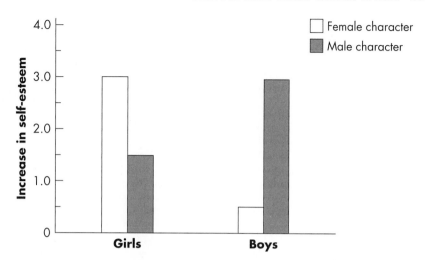

FIGURE 3.6 | IMPROVEMENT IN GIRLS' AND BOYS' SELF-ESTEEM (COMPARED TO BASELINE) AFTER HEARING STORIES ABOUT A FEMALE CHARACTER OR A MALE CHARACTER.

Source: Based on Ochman (1996).

The researchers administered a standard measure of self-esteem at the beginning of the study. Then the children saw the videotaped stories over a period of about 6 weeks, and the researchers measured self-esteem a second time. Finally, the researchers calculated the change in the children's self-esteem. As Figure 3.6 shows, girls had a greater increase in self-esteem if they heard the stories about an achieving girl rather than an achieving boy. The boys showed a comparable pattern; their self-esteem increased after they heard stories about an achieving boy rather than an achieving girl.

Think about the implications of Ochman's research. If children hear stories about strong, competent boys, but not girls, the boys are likely to experience a boost in self-esteem. Meanwhile, the girls' self-esteem will not be improved.

Conscientious parents and teachers should review the books that children will see, to make sure that competent females and nurturant males are well represented (Bem, 1998). They can also be alert for new resources. For example, a feminist magazine called *New Moon* is edited by girls and young women (see Figure 3.7).

TELEVISION.   The average U.S. home has 2.4 televisions (Giles, 2003). Furthermore, preschoolers average more than 20 hours of television per week (Paik, 2001). By the time teenagers graduate from high school, they have spent about 18,000 hours in front of the TV set, in contrast to about 12,000 hours in classroom instruction (D. G. Singer & Singer, 2001). In Chapter 2, we examined stereotyping in programs intended for adult audiences. Now let's consider the television programs and advertisements aimed at children. As we'll see, 18,000 hours of television can provide a strong education in gender stereotypes.

FIGURE 3.7 | *New Moon,* A MAGAZINE FOR GIRLS AND YOUNG WOMEN, DISCUSSES ISSUES SUCH AS GENDER, RACISM, AND ECOLOGY.

Reprinted, with permission, from New Moon: The Magazine for Girls and Their Dreams; Copyright New Moon Publishing, 2 West First Street, #101, Duluth, MN 55802. Subscriptions $34.95/ 6 issues. Call 1-800-381-4743 or visit http://www.newmoon.org.

Males appear much more frequently than females in children's television programs and advertisements (R. F. Fox, 2000; Huntemann & Morgan, 2001; Perse, 2001). For instance, a sample of television advertisements aimed at children showed 183 boys and only 118 girls (M. S. Larson, 2003).

Males and females also perform different activities on television. For example, males are more likely to be shown in the workplace, whereas females are shown as caregivers (T. L. Thompson & Zerbinos, 1995; Van Evra, 2004). Just as we saw in the analysis of children's books, males are more likely to show leadership and ingenuity. Males in television programs are frequently violent, using guns, lasers, and karate kicks to destroy other people. Clearly these programs contribute to children's gender schemas that males are often aggressive (Gunter et al., 2003; Kundanis, 2003; M. S. Larson, 2003; Perse, 2001). In contrast, females are more likely to be affectionate and helpless (T. L. Thompson & Zerbinos, 1995).

An occasional television program looks promising at first. For example, "The Powerpuff Girls" features three young females. However, their names are Blossom, Buttercup, and Bubbles. These three cute, tough cartoon characters fight against each other physically, compete for the attention of a powerful man, and seldom solve problems on their own (Corcoran & Parker, 2004).

But do children learn gender-role stereotypes by watching television? Let's consider a well-controlled study conducted by Signorielli and Lears (1992). These researchers studied 530 fourth- and fifth-graders, using a sample of ethnic groups that resembled the distribution in the United States. Each child completed a test of gender stereotyping. A typical question on this test asked whether a chore, such as washing dishes, should be done by girls only, boys only, or either girls or boys. Signorielli and Lears found that the children who watched many hours of television were significantly more likely than other children to be highly gender stereotyped.

If you recall some of the potential research problems raised in Chapter 1, you might wonder whether confounding variables might explain those results. For example, maybe well-educated parents limit their children's television viewing and also discourage gender stereotypes. However, Signorielli and Lears (1992) conducted a second analysis in which they statistically controlled for potential confounding variables such as gender, ethnic group, reading level, and parents' education. The correlation between TV viewing and gender stereotyping still remained statistically significant, although it was not very strong. In general, the research tends to show modest correlations between television viewing and gender stereotypes (e.g., C. P. Edwards et al., 2001; Huntemann & Morgan, 2001; Perse, 2001).

Cautious parents who want to raise nonstereotyped children should limit television viewing. Parents should also encourage their children to watch programs in which women are shown as competent people and men are shown in nurturant roles. In addition, parents can select educational and entertaining videos that avoid stereotypes and feature competent females. Furthermore, parents can occasionally stop these videos at appropriate intervals to discuss gender-related issues with their children (Gunter & McAleer, 1997). Television and videos have the potential to present admirable models of female and male behavior, and they could even make children less stereotyped. So far, unfortunately, the media have not lived up to that potential.

Section Summary

Factors That Shape Gender Typing

1. Parents tend to encourage gender-typed activities (e.g., toy choice and chore assignment), and they discuss different emotions with daughters than with sons; they also treat sons and daughters somewhat differently with respect to children's aggression and independence, but the differential treatment is not consistent.

2. Parents vary widely in their differential treatment of girls and boys, but ethnicity does not have a consistent effect on parents' gender typing. Parents can devise creative ways to treat their children in a gender-fair fashion.

3. Peers react negatively to another child's nonstereotypical behavior; peers also encourage gender segregation; they are prejudiced against children of the other gender; and they use different standards (e.g., attractiveness) when interacting with girls rather than boys.

4. North American schools encourage gender typing through the distribution of men's and women's occupations in the school system. Boys also receive more attention and useful feedback in the classroom compared to girls.

5. Some schools have developed programs to help children reduce stereotypes, but these programs must be both comprehensive and sophisticated to have an important impact. In many nonindustrialized countries, boys are more likely than girls to attend school and to learn to read.

6. Children's books and television continue to underrepresent females and to show males and females in stereotyped activities. According to research, reading books and watching television can influence children's ideas about gender.

CHILDREN'S KNOWLEDGE ABOUT GENDER

We've just outlined several important ways in which children receive gender messages from the surrounding culture. Now let's see how well children learn their gender lessons: What do they know about gender, and what kind of stereotypes do they hold? In Chapter 2, we explored adults' stereotypes. As you'll see, many of these ideas about gender are well established before children begin kindergarten. Keep in mind a point we emphasized in connection with the cognitive developmental explanation of gender typing: Children actively work to create gender schemas, and these schemas encourage them to act in a manner that is consistent with their gender.

Interestingly, even 6-month-old infants know something about gender; they can place males and females in different categories (Golombok & Hines, 2002; C. L. Martin & Dinella, 2001; Ruble et al., 2004). In a typical study, P. A. Katz and Kofkin (1997) showed each infant a series of slides of the heads and shoulders of different women. (The slides showed a variety of clothing, hairstyles, facial expressions, and so forth.) After a number of slides, the infant lost interest in these female stimuli. Then the researchers presented a new slide, showing either a male or a female. Katz and Kofkin found, for example, that 6-month-olds looked significantly longer at the slide of a male than at the slide of a female. This looking pattern tells us that young infants recognize that the new slide belongs to a different category than the slides previously shown. Infants also looked longer at a slide of a female after seeing a series of slides showing males.

Additional research shows that 8-month-old infants know that a female voice should come from a female face, and a male voice should come from a male face (Bussey & Bandura, 2004; M. L. Patterson & Werker, 2002). This series of studies shows us that infants divide people into two categories on the basis of gender. Furthermore, they know this information long before they are able to say their first word or take their first step.

As you can imagine, gender knowledge is much easier to test in children who are old enough to talk. For instance, almost all 3-year-olds can correctly identify whether they are a girl or a boy (P. A. Katz, 1996; Narter, 2006). However, as illustrated in the birthday-party anecdote at the beginning of this chapter, children's ideas about gender often differ from adults' perspectives. Young children believe that clothing is the most accurate way to determine a person's gender. Children typically cannot explain the differences between males and females until they are 6 or 7 years old (Ruble et al., 2004).

Let's begin by examining children's knowledge about gender-stereotyped activities and occupations. Then we'll discuss their knowledge about gender-stereotyped personality characteristics, a more abstract distinction. We'll also examine some factors that influence the strength of children's stereotypes.

CHILDREN'S STEREOTYPES ABOUT ACTIVITIES AND OCCUPATIONS

At an early age, children have clear ideas about activities that are gender consistent. As the cognitive developmental approach argues, children actively construct gender schemas. For instance, when 4- and 5-year-olds choose a picture to color, 75% of boys select a picture of a car, a baseball player, or some other masculine scene, whereas 67% of girls select a picture of a cat, a ballet dancer, or some other feminine scene (Boyatzis & Eades, 1999). Also, 4-year-olds know that boys are "supposed to" like toy tools, whereas girls are "supposed to" like toy dishes (Raag, 1999). Furthermore, adults have difficulty persuading children to play with toys considered appropriate for the other gender (Fisher-Thompson & Burke, 1998). By the age of 5, most children show strong preferences for "gender-appropriate" toys (C. F. Miller et al., 2006).

In addition, children remember a greater number of gender-stereotypical activities, compared to neutral or nonstereotypical activities (F. M. Hughes & Seta, 2003; Susskind, 2003). Children's gender schemas also extend to occupations (G. D. Levy et al., 2000; Liben et al., 2002). For instance, Gary Levy and his colleagues (2000) interviewed younger children (ages 3 to 4) and older children (ages 5 to 7), using questions such as those in Demonstration 3.3.

Demonstration 3.3

With a parent's permission, enlist the help of a child who is between the ages of 4 and 7 years. Then ask the child each of the following four questions. After listening to each answer, ask the child, "Why do you suppose that a (man/woman) would be best for that job?"

1. An airplane pilot is a person who flies an airplane for other people. Who do you think would do the best job as an airplane pilot, a woman or a man?
2. A clothes designer is a person who draws up and makes clothes for other people. Who do you think would do the best job as a clothes designer, a woman or a man?
3. A car mechanic is a person who fixes cars for other people. Who do you think would do the best job as a car mechanic, a woman or a man?
4. A secretary is a person who types up letters and mails things for other people. Who do you think would do the best job as a secretary, a woman or a man?

After asking all four questions, ask the child which job she or he would like best and which one would be worst. (For younger children, you may need to remind them what each employee does.)

Source: Based on G. D. Levy et al. (2000).

TABLE 3.1 | CHILDREN'S JUDGMENTS ABOUT THE RELATIVE COMPETENCE OF WOMEN AND MEN IN FOUR GENDER-STEREOTYPED OCCUPATIONS

	Child's Age Group	
	Younger (3- to 4-year-olds)	Older (5- to 7-year-olds)
"Feminine" occupations		
Percentage who judged women more competent	75%	78%
Percentage who judged men more competent	25%	22%
"Masculine" occupations		
Percentage who judged women more competent	32%	7%
Percentage who judged men more competent	68%	93%

Source: G. D. Levy et al. (2000).

As in this demonstration, the study required a choice; researchers told children to respond either "a woman" or "a man." As you can see from Table 3.1, even the younger children have well-developed gender stereotypes about occupations.

Sadly, children also show strong stereotypes when thinking about their own future occupations. For example, in another part of the study, Levy and his colleagues (2000) asked children to choose which emotion they would feel if they grew up to have each of the four occupations described in Demonstration 3.3. Girls were likely to say that they would be happy with a stereotypically feminine occupation and angry or disgusted with a stereotypically masculine occupation.

Furthermore, boys preferred stereotypically masculine occupations, and they were extremely angry and disgusted with a stereotypically feminine profession. We have seen throughout this chapter that gender roles constrict boys more than they constrict girls. Other research confirms this tendency with respect to future occupations (Etaugh & Liss, 1992; Helwig, 1998). For instance, Etaugh and Liss (1992) found that not one single boy in their study of kindergartners through eighth-graders named a "feminine" career choice.

CHILDREN'S STEREOTYPES ABOUT PERSONALITY

Children's stereotypes about personality are somewhat slower to develop than their stereotypes about activities, perhaps because personality characteristics are more abstract than activities and occupations (Powlishta et al., 2001). Even so, children between the ages of 2 1/2 and 4 show some tendency to believe that strength and aggression are associated with males and that softness and gentleness are associated with females (G. Cowan & Hoffman, 1986; Heyman, 2001; J. E. Williams & Best, 1990). By the age of 5, children are also developing stereotypes about girls' and boys' responses to emotional events (Widen & Russell, 2002).

In a representative study focusing on children's stereotypes, 8- to 10-year-old children looked at a series of photographs of women, men, girls, and boys (Powlishta, 2000). The children rated each photo on several gender-related personality characteristics, such as "gentle" and "strong." Consistent with previous research, the children rated female photos significantly higher than male photos on the stereotypically feminine characteristics, and they rated male photos significantly higher than the female photos on the stereotypically masculine characteristics.

FACTORS RELATED TO CHILDREN'S GENDER STEREOTYPES

Several factors influence the strength of children's stereotypes. We mentioned earlier that boys have stronger stereotypes about career choices than girls do. Ethnicity and social class probably have a complex relationship with children's gender stereotypes. Unfortunately, we do not have large-scale studies that examine the stereotypes of children from different ethnic groups and different social classes. In general, however, cross-cultural research shows that children in different countries are similar to North American children in their views of the personality characteristics associated with males and females (Best & Thomas, 2004; Gibbons, 2000). Another cross-cultural finding is that children usually have stronger stereotypes about males than about females. Once again, masculine stereotypes are relatively rigid.

Are children's gender ideas influenced by their family's views? Parents who have strong gender stereotypes about child rearing are likely to have children with stronger gender stereotypes (Ex & Janssens, 1998; O'Brien et al., 2000; Powlishta et al., 2001).

As you might expect, children's age influences their stereotypes (Durkin & Nugent, 1998; Lobel et al., 2000; Powlishta et al., 2001). Some studies assess children's knowledge about culturally accepted gender stereotypes. The older children clearly know more than the younger children. After all, the older children have had more opportunities to learn their culture's traditional notions about gender. However, other studies have assessed the flexibility of children's stereotypes. A typical question might be: "Who can bake a cake? Can a woman do it, can a man do it, or can they both do it?" Older children were generally more likely to reply, "Both can do it." In other words, older children are typically more flexible than younger children. We can conclude that older children know more about gender stereotypes, but they are also aware that people do not need to be bound by them (Blakemore, 2003; Trautner et al., 2005).

Finally, children vary widely in their beliefs about gender, consistent with Theme 4. Their own unique interests often lead them to specific experiences with stereotypical and nonstereotypical activities (Liben & Bigler, 2002). These experiences, in turn, shape their beliefs and their knowledge about gender.

Section Summary

Children's Knowledge About Gender

1. Even 6-month-old infants show some ability to distinguish between males and females.

2. Children have well-developed stereotypes about women's and men's activities, occupations, and personality characteristics.

3. Children's stereotypes are fairly consistent across cultures; parents who have traditional ideas about gender usually have children with stronger gender stereotypes. Furthermore, older children know more about stereotypes, but they have more flexible beliefs.

CHAPTER REVIEW QUESTIONS

1. Early in prenatal development, infant boys and girls are similar. By the time they are born, they differ in their gonads, internal reproductive systems, and external genitals. How do these three kinds of differences emerge during normal prenatal development? Also explain how an infant may not be clearly female or clearly male.

2. According to a well-known proverb, "Beauty is in the eye of the beholder." Similarly, the masculinity or femininity of an infant is also in the eye of the beholder. In what ways do both parents and strangers provide evidence for the perceived differences between male and female infants?

3. Five-year-old Darlene is playing with a doll. How do current psychological theories explain her behavior? Be sure to mention the two mechanisms proposed by social learning theory as well as the central ideas of the cognitive developmental approach.

4. Imagine that a family has twins, a girl named Susan and a boy named Jim. Based on the information on families and gender typing, how would you predict that their parents would treat Susan and Jim? Discuss four areas in which parents might respond differently to boys and girls: (a) gender-typed activity, (b) discussion of emotion, (c) aggression, and (d) independence.

5. Discuss four ways in which peers encourage gender typing. How might skillful teachers minimize gender typing? What other precautions should these teachers take to make certain that females and males are treated fairly in the classroom?

6. Describe in detail how books and television convey gender stereotypes. How can these media influence children's toy preferences and other activities?

7. Suppose that you are working at a day care center where you interact with children between the ages of 6 months and 5 years. How do researchers know that the 6-month-olds already have some information about gender? Also describe what the older children of different ages will know about gender and gender stereotypes.

8. As children grow older, they know more about gender stereotypes, but these stereotypes are also more flexible. Describe the research that supports this statement. What implications does this statement have for the influence of peers on gender typing?

9. Children actively work to construct their ideas about gender. Discuss several ways in which they create gender schemas. With respect to the four topics examined in the discussion about peers, how could these gender schemas encourage them to treat their peers differently?

10. Are gender stereotypes more restrictive for boys than for girls and are fathers more likely than mothers to encourage these stereotypes? Discuss this issue, being sure to mention parents' reactions to their children's gender-related activities, children's ideas about occupations, and any other topics you consider relevant.

KEY TERMS

*gender typing (76)

*prenatal period (77)

*infancy (77)

*sex chromosomes (77)

*gonads (77)

*androgen (78)

*estrogen (78)

*intersexed individual (78)

*androgen-insensitivity syndrome (78)

*congenital adrenal hyperplasia (78)

*social constructionism (83)

*social learning approach (85)

*modeling (85)

*cognitive developmental approach (86)

*schema (86)

*gender schemas (86)

*gender identity (86)

*peer group (93)

*gender segregation (94)

entitlement (94)

 Note: The terms asterisked in the Key Terms section serve as good search terms for InfoTrac@College Edition. Go to http://infotrac.thomsonlearning.com and try these added search terms.

RECOMMENDED READINGS

Eagly, A. H., Beall, A. E., & Sternberg, R. J. (Eds.). (2004). *The psychology of gender* (2nd ed.). New York: Guilford. This excellent book contains several chapters about gender issues during childhood, including the biological basis of prenatal development, theories of children's gender typing, and cultural issues.

Eckes, T., & Trautner, H. M. (Eds.). (2000). *The developmental social psychology of gender*. Mahwah, NJ: Erlbaum. I strongly recommend this handbook, which features such topics as gender socialization, theories of gender development, children's gender stereotypes, and cross-cultural research.

Rensenbrink, C. W. (2001). *All in our places: Feminist challenges in elementary school classrooms*. Lanham, MD: Rowman & Littlefield. The title refers to the song many students sing in early elementary school, "We're all in our places with bright shiny faces." The book provides a different message: Feminist teachers can create classrooms that are relatively free of gender bias.

Van Evra, J. P. (2004). *Television and child development* (3rd ed.). Mahwah, NJ: Erlbaum. If you were interested in this textbook's discussion of media and children's gender typing, Van Evra's book provides additional information about topics such as violence, cultural diversity, and advertising.

ANSWERS TO THE TRUE-FALSE STATEMENTS

1. True (p. 77); 2. False (p. 80); 3. True (p. 83); 4. False (pp. 85–86); 5. False (p. 90); 6. False (p. 92); 7. True (p. 97); 8. False (pp. 102–103); 9. True (pp. 104–105); 10. False (pp. 106–107).

© Ronnie Kaufman/Corbis

4 | ADOLESCENCE

111

True or False?

_____ 1. Researchers believe that there is no physical explanation for menstrual pain.

_____ 2. A clear-cut cluster of symptoms, often called premenstrual syndrome (PMS), typically affects between 35% and 50% of adolescent females in the United States and Canada.

_____ 3. According to surveys in North America, White adolescents are more concerned about their ethnic identity than adolescents of color are.

_____ 4. Recent research confirms that females are much lower than males in their self-esteem, beginning in childhood and continuing through middle age.

_____ 5. During the current decade, schools, teachers, and peers offer strong support for young women who want to pursue careers in math and science.

_____ 6. For all major ethnic groups in the United States, women are more likely than men to attend college.

_____ 7. Adolescent males and females are interested in pursuing careers that are similar in level of prestige.

_____ 8. According to research, most adolescents get along fairly well with their parents.

_____ 9. Researchers have found that the friendships of adolescent women are consistently more intimate than the friendships of adolescent men.

_____ 10. Young lesbians are more likely to "come out" to their mothers than to their fathers.

A young African-American woman described why she decided to leave her inner-city home to pursue a college education:

> I just decided that I wanted to go to college. . . . I didn't want to be poor. I didn't want to live in the projects. I wanted to have a home and drive a nice car. But now I'm a big girl, and I understand that education is more than getting a paycheck. . . . It's a continual exploration. It's a continual wealth of knowledge, even after you get your degree, there's still so much that you don't know. Education is a process. You live the experience and graduate. You get your credentials, then, the next week, you turn on the television and learn that something brand new happened in the field that you graduated from. It's like an ongoing evolution of knowledge. It's pretty neat. (Ross, 2003, p. 70)

This young woman's narrative shows us how girls and young women today can construct a thoughtful life for themselves—one that is not constrained by stereotypical views of gender. In this chapter, we'll explore physical and psychological changes during adolescence, focusing on the changes where gender plays a particularly important role. In human development, **adolescence** is defined as a transition phase between childhood and adulthood. Adolescence begins at **puberty,** the age at which a young person becomes physically capable of sexual reproduction (DeHart et al., 2004). For females, a major biological milestone of puberty is **menarche** (pronounced meh-*nar*-key), or the beginning of menstruation.

In contrast, no specific event marks the end of adolescence and the beginning of adulthood. We usually associate the beginning of adulthood with milestones such as living separately from our parents, completing college, holding a job, and finding a romantic partner. However, none of these characteristics is essential for adulthood.

Adolescents often find themselves caught between childhood and adulthood. Adults may sometimes treat adolescents as children—a mixed blessing that eases their responsibility but limits their independence and their sense of competence (Zebrowitz & Montepare, 2000). Adults also give adolescents mixed messages about issues of sexuality and the transition into adulthood. Parents tell them not to grow up too quickly. On the other hand, their role models tend to be adolescents who have grown up too quickly: sexy teenage television and movie stars, teens in ads, and maybe even the girl next door (Cope-Farrar & Kunkel, 2002; Gleeson & Frith, 2004).

In this chapter, we will examine four important topics for adolescent females: (1) puberty and menstruation, (2) self-concepts, (3) education and career planning, and (4) interpersonal relationships. We'll mention other relevant topics (such as cognitive abilities, sexuality, and eating disorders), but later chapters will discuss them more completely.

PUBERTY AND MENSTRUATION

Let's begin by discussing the physical changes that girls experience as they enter adolescence. We'll briefly consider puberty before we look at menstruation in greater detail.

PUBERTY

Most girls enter puberty between the ages of 10 and 15; the average age at menarche is 12 (Chumlea et al., 2003; Ellis, 2004; Wu et al., 2002). In general, Black and Latina girls in the United States reach menarche somewhat earlier than European American girls, and Asian American girls reach menarche somewhat later than other ethnic groups (S. E. Anderson et al., 2003; Chumlea et al., 2003; Ellis, 2004; Hayward, 2003). Unfortunately, data are not currently available for Native American girls. Researchers do not have a satisfactory explanation for ethnic differences, but body weight is one important factor (Adair & Gordon-Larsen, 2001; K. K. Davison et al., 2003).

Menarche is seldom depicted in television programs or films. When the popular media do focus on menarche, most of the messages are negative (Kissling, 2002, 2005). In real life, young women's emotional reactions to menarche vary widely. Young women who can communicate with a trusted adult may feel comfortable about menstruation (Piran & Ross, 2006). However, young women report largely negative reactions from family members (Costos et al., 2002). For instance, one woman recalled that her mother "just handed me a Tampax and said, 'You know, you're a woman now and you have to be careful.'. . . I don't know what I was supposed to be careful of" (p. 54). In short, the varied emotional messages about menarche provide evidence for the individual differences theme of this textbook.

During puberty, young women experience the most dramatic physical changes they have undergone since infancy. Specifically, at around 10 to 11 years of age, they experience a transformation in their **secondary sex characteristics,** which are features of the body related to reproduction but not directly involved in it. These characteristics include breast development and pubic hair (Ellis, 2004; Fechner, 2003; Summers-Effler, 2004). During puberty, young women also accumulate body fat through the hips and thighs—often a source of resentment in a culture that emphasizes slender bodies (La Greca et al., 2006; Piran & Ross, 2006; Stice, 2003).

BIOLOGICAL ASPECTS OF THE MENSTRUAL CYCLE

Let's briefly discuss the biological components of menstruation and the sequence of events in the menstrual cycle. The average woman menstruates about 450 times during her life. Naturally, then, this discussion on the menstrual cycle is relevant for most adult females for several decades after menarche. However, we'll discuss menstruation in the current chapter rather than postponing the topic to a later chapter.

STRUCTURES AND HORMONES RESPONSIBLE FOR MENSTRUATION.   The hypothalamus, a structure in the brain, is crucial in menstruation because it monitors the body's level of estrogen during the monthly cycle. When estrogen levels are low, the hypothalamus signals the pituitary gland, another brain structure. The pituitary gland produces two important hormones: follicle-stimulating hormone and luteinizing hormone.

In all, four hormones contribute to the menstrual cycle (L. L. Alexander et al., 2004; Crooks & Baur, 2005; Federman, 2006):

1. Follicle-stimulating hormone acts on the follicles (or egg holders) within the ovaries, making them produce estrogen and progesterone.
2. Luteinizing hormone is necessary for the development of an ovum (or egg).
3. Estrogen, primarily produced by the ovaries, stimulates the development of the uterine lining.
4. Progesterone, also primarily produced by the ovaries, regulates the system; when the level of luteinizing hormone is high enough, progesterone stops the release of that hormone.

Figure 4.1 illustrates several major structures in menstruation together with other important organs in the female reproductive system. The two **ovaries**, which are about the size of walnuts, contain the follicles that hold the **ova**, or eggs, and produce estrogen and progesterone. Midway through the menstrual cycle, one of the eggs breaks out of its follicle. It moves from an ovary into a fallopian tube and then into the **uterus**, the organ in which a fetus develops. The lining of the uterus, called the endometrium, can serve as a nourishing location for a fertilized egg to mature during pregnancy. If a fertilized egg is not implanted, the endometrium is shed as menstrual flow, and the egg disintegrates on its way out of the uterus.

THE EVENTS IN THE MENSTRUAL CYCLE.   Now that you know some of the major components of the menstrual cycle, let's see how they interact. The most

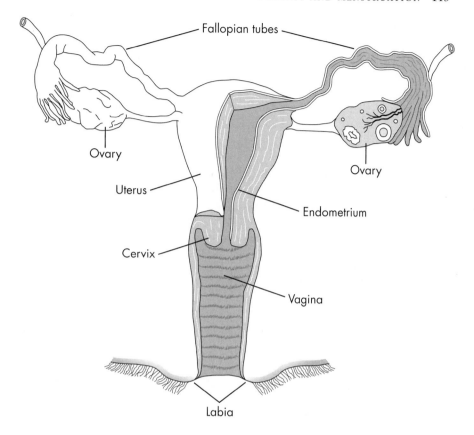

FIGURE 4.1 | FEMALE INTERNAL REPRODUCTIVE ORGANS.

Note: The right-hand side of the diagram shows the interior of the ovaries, the fallopian tube, and the uterus.

important concept to remember is that brain structures, hormones, and internal reproductive organs are carefully coordinated to regulate the menstrual cycle. They operate according to a **feedback loop**: When the level of a particular hormone is too low, a structure in the brain is signaled, and the chain of events that follows produces more of that hormone. Later on, when the level of a hormone is too high, a signal to a structure in the brain begins a chain of events that decreases that hormone. Here are the major activities during this monthly cycle:

1. In response to a low estrogen level, the hypothalamus signals the pituitary gland.
2. The pituitary gland responds by releasing follicle-stimulating hormone, which stimulates the follicles to become more mature; this hormone also signals the ovaries to increase their production of estrogen.
3. The increased level of estrogen stimulates the development of the endometrium (essentially preparing for possible pregnancy every month).

It also signals the pituitary gland to stop producing follicle-stimulating hormone.

4. The pituitary gland stops producing follicle-stimulating hormone and starts producing luteinizing hormone.

5. Luteinizing hormone usually suppresses growth in all follicles except one; therefore, only one egg typically reaches maturity.

6. The follicle then releases the ovum, or egg, on approximately the 14th day of the menstrual cycle, a process called **ovulation** (pronounced ov-you-*lay*-shun).

7. The empty follicle matures into a round structure called the corpus luteum, which secretes progesterone and estrogen. The levels of both of these hormones rise after ovulation.

8. The high level of progesterone inhibits the production of additional luteinizing hormone. As a result, the corpus luteum decomposes.

9. When the corpus luteum decomposes, the production of both progesterone and estrogen falls rapidly. With such low levels of hormones, the endometrium can no longer be maintained in the style to which it has grown accustomed. The endometrium is sloughed off, and it passes out of the vagina as menstrual flow.

10. The low level of estrogen signals the hypothalamus, causing a new cycle to begin.

Notice the checks and balances that are required to orchestrate the menstrual cycle (L. L. Alexander et al., 2004). This complex set of interactions first encourages the production of an egg, next leads to menstrual flow if no fertilized egg is implanted, and then begins another cycle. Let's now discuss the menstrual pain that often accompanies menstruation.

Menstrual Pain

Menstrual pain, or **dysmenorrhea** (pronounced diss-men-or-*ree*-ah), typically refers to painful cramps in the abdomen. It may also include headache, nausea, dizziness, fatigue, and pain in the lower back (Crooks & Baur, 2005; Hyde & DeLamater, 2003). Dysmenorrhea is not the same as premenstrual syndrome, or PMS, which we will discuss in the next section.

How common is menstrual pain? Estimates range from 50% to 75% for high school- and college-age women (Golub, 1992; A. E. Walker, 1998). Consistent with Theme 4 of this book, women's reactions to life events, such as menstruation, vary widely. Pain during menstruation is certainly common, but it is not inevitable.

In our culture, women expect that menstruation will be painful, but menstrual pain is clearly not "all in the head." The contractions of the uterus that cause menstrual pain are encouraged by prostaglandins (pronounced pross-tuh-*glan*-dins). **Prostaglandins** are substances that the body produces in high concentrations just before menstruation, and they can cause severe cramps.

Researchers have discovered that highly anxious women report having more menstrual pain than less anxious women. Perhaps anxious women focus more attention on their cramps, which could increase their intensity (Sigmon, Rohan et al., 2000). However, we must think critically about correlational results such as these. Another possibility may be that women who experience relatively strong menstrual pain (and perhaps other forms of pain) become more anxious as a consequence of these unpleasant experiences. Given the evidence, menstrual pain is probably caused by a combination of physiological and psychological factors.

Many different treatments have been used to reduce menstrual pain. Some drugs are helpful, including those that inhibit the synthesis of prostaglandins (e.g., ibuprofen). Exercise, a heating pad, muscle relaxation, adequate sleep, and dietary changes often produce additional relief (Golub, 1992; Hyde & DeLamater, 2003).

THE CONTROVERSIAL PREMENSTRUAL SYNDROME

Menstrual pain is well accepted as being part of the menstrual cycle. In contrast, premenstrual syndrome is controversial among both professionals and laypeople (Chrisler, 2004b). **Premenstrual syndrome (PMS)** is the name given to a variety of symptoms that may occur a few days before menstruating. The list of symptoms often includes headaches, breast soreness, swelling, nausea, increased sensitivity to pain, and acne—as well as various psychological reactions. These psychological reactions typically include depression, irritability, anxiety, and low energy (Chrisler, 2004b; Gottheil et al., 1999).

One reason that PMS is controversial is that researchers do not agree on its definition (Chrisler, 2004b; Figert, 1996). Read the previous list of symptoms once more, and add other symptoms that you've heard about in popular accounts of PMS. Some critics have discovered as many as 200 different symptoms presumably connected with PMS (Gottheil et al., 1999). Think of the problem created by this confusion. One researcher may be studying women whose primary symptom is anxiety; another may be studying women with depression. How can researchers study PMS systematically when we don't even have a clear-cut operational definition for the problem? Furthermore, no blood test or other biochemical test can assess whether a woman is experiencing PMS (Chrisler, 2004b; Gottheil et al., 1999).

Another reason PMS is so controversial is that some experts claim that virtually all menstruating women experience it (see Chrisler, 2004b). This claim is unfair because it suggests that all women are at the mercy of their "raging hormones" (Chrisler, 2002). An alternative view argues that PMS is entirely a myth that our culture created. This view, if taken too far, would be equally unfair because some women do experience genuine symptoms more often premenstrually than at other times in their cycle.

Our discussion of PMS takes an intermediate position between the two extremes of the biologically driven explanation and the psychological-cultural explanation. Apparently, a small percentage of women (maybe 2% to 5%) have significant symptoms that are related to their menstrual cycle (Hardie,

1997; Jensvold & Dan, 2001). Other women do not. This situation is an example of this textbook's theme of large individual differences among women. We cannot make a statement that holds true for all women.

Let's examine the aspect of PMS that has received the most attention: the presumably dramatic mood swings during the menstrual cycle. We'll also consider methods of coping with PMS and a different perspective, called menstrual joy.

Mood Swings.   Much of the research that supposedly supports the concept of PMS is plagued by biases. For example, many researchers ask women to recall what their moods had been during various times throughout previous weeks of the menstrual cycle. You can anticipate some problems with this kind of retrospective study. For example, the popular press often discusses PMS and negative moods. As a result, women may recall their moods as being more negative premenstrually than they actually were (Chrisler & Caplan, 2002).

Most of the carefully controlled research has produced results that should make us skeptical about the mood-swings component of PMS (e.g., Chrisler, 2002, 2004b; Chrisler & Caplan, 2002; Offman & Kleinplatz, 2004). For example, Klebanov and Jemmott (1992) examined the effects of expectations on PMS symptoms. They gave women a fictitious medical test, which misinformed the women that they were either midcycle or premenstrual. Then the women took a standard scale called the Menstrual Distress Questionnaire. Those who believed that they were premenstrual, even if they were not, reported more symptoms than did those who thought they were midcycle.

Let's consider another study that is critical of the PMS concept. Hardie (1997) asked 83 menstruating women who were university employees to keep records in a booklet titled *Daily Stress & Health Diary*. Each day, for 10 weeks, they recorded their emotional state, stress level, general health, exercise, laughter, crying, menstrual bleeding, and so forth. At the end of the 10 weeks, the women completed a questionnaire about women's health issues. Included in this questionnaire was a crucial item: "I think I have PMS."

To assess PMS, Hardie used an operational definition that several others have used: A woman's mood during the premenstrual phase needs to be more depressed and emotional than during other parts of her menstrual cycle. Not one of the 83 women met this criterion for two menstrual cycles during the 70-day study. In addition, the women who believed they had PMS did *not* have more negative emotions premenstrually than did the women who reported no PMS. In other words, both groups actually reported similar cyclic changes.

The psychological-cultural explanation for PMS argues that our current culture clearly accepts PMS as an established fact, even though it cannot be systematically documented. With this kind of cultural endorsement, women believe that PMS is normal. If a woman is feeling tense and she is premenstrual, she blames her emotions on PMS (Cosgrove & Riddle, 2001a; Hardie, 1997). For example, one woman explained how she often interprets her emotions: "I feel irritable for some reason and then I'll think about why I am irritable and then I'll think, oh, well, it's the week before my period and sometimes I'll say, well, maybe that's what it is" (Cosgrove & Riddle, 2001a, p. 19).

Demonstration 4.1

POSITIVE
SYMPTOMS OF
MENSTRUATION

If you are a female who has menstrual cycles, complete the following questionnaire, which is based on the Menstrual Joy Questionnaire (Chrisler et al., 1994; J. Delaney et al., 1988). If you do not have menstrual cycles, ask a friend if she would be willing to fill out the questionnaire.

Instructions: Rate each of the following items on a 6-point scale. Rate an item 1 if you do not experience the feeling at all when you are menstruating; rate it 6 if you experience the feeling intensely.

_____ high spirits

_____ affection

_____ sexual desire

_____ self-confidence

_____ vibrant activity

_____ creativity

_____ revolutionary zeal

_____ power

_____ intense concentration

Did you or your friend provide a positive rating for one or more of these characteristics?

Unfortunately, the concept of PMS encourages women to view themselves as having a cyclical illness. Men who endorse the PMS concept may hesitate before they support a female candidate for a job (Chrisler, 2004b). After all, she may be out of control for several days every month! (Incidentally, try Demonstration 4.1 before you read further.)

Hormonal factors may indeed cause premenstrual problems in a small percentage of women. However, two other factors—which we will soon discuss—are probably more important:

1. Psychological factors, such as anxiety and strong endorsement of traditionally feminine gender roles (Sigmon, Dorhofer et al., 2000; Sigmon, Rohan et al., 2000).
2. Cultural factors, such as our culture's belief that PMS is a well-established fact and its emphasis on biological explanations (Chrisler, 2004b; Cosgrove & Riddle, 2001b).

COPING WITH PREMENSTRUAL SYNDROME.   It's difficult to talk about coping with or treating PMS when we have no clear-cut definition of the problem and no comprehensive theory about its origins (Golub, 1992; A. E. Walker, 1998). Another issue is that women who frequently experience depression or anxiety are more likely than other women to report that they have PMS (Sigmon et al., 2004). This research suggests that women should monitor their emotional reactions throughout the menstrual cycle to determine whether tension or anxiety is just as likely to occur during phases that are *not* premenstrual. The best strategy may be to figure out how to reduce the problems that create those emotions during *all* phases of the menstrual cycle. When the problems are severe, psychotherapy may be helpful for developing these strategies.

When health professionals believe that PMS is a genuine, biologically driven problem, they often recommend physical exercise as therapy. They also suggest avoiding salt, sugar, and caffeine (Grady-Weliky, 2003). None of these remedies can hurt, although their value has not been established. Some physicians recommend antidepressants that drug companies are now marketing for women who presumably experience PMS (P. J. Caplan, 2004; Chrisler & Caplan, 2002). These drugs can cause side effects, and they are not necessary for most women. As Chrisler and Caplan (2002) conclude:

> Taking medication may provide apparent serenity to individual women, but it does nothing to alleviate the oppresive conditions that contributed to the stress and tension that caused them to report severe PMS. PMS is a form of social control and victim blame that masquerades as value-free. (p. 301)

MENSTRUAL JOY

Go ahead; read the title of this section again. Yes, menstrual joy. Joan Chrisler and her colleagues noticed that the menstruation questionnaires focused only on negative aspects of menstruation. Furthermore, the popular press had generated hundreds of articles on the negative—and often exaggerated—aspects of changes associated with the menstrual cycle (Chrisler, 2004b; Chrisler & Levy, 1990; Chrisler et al., 1994). Surely some women must have some positive reactions to menstruation! Therefore, Chrisler and colleagues (1994) administered the Menstrual Joy Questionnaire (J. Delaney et al., 1988), which is similar to Demonstration 4.1. Interestingly, women who first completed the Menstrual Joy Questionnaire were likely to rate their level of arousal more positively when they later completed a different questionnaire about menstrual symptoms. Compared to women who had not been encouraged to think about the positive side of menstruation, these women were more likely to report feelings of well-being and excitement and bursts of energy (Chrisler et al., 1994).

Research in the United States and Canada confirms that many women have some positive responses to menstruation, such as increased energy, creativity, and psychological strength (Aubeeluck & Maguire, 2002; Chrisler & Caplan, 2002; S. Lee, 2002). For example, one woman wrote:

> I think it's a wondrous event, how the body can collect nutrition for a potentially growing egg and then just let it go. . . . I find it a time for introspection and reflection and being more in touch with my own body. I feel positive about it. (S. Lee, 2002, p. 30)

Some women feel that menstruation reaffirms their positive feelings of being female. As one woman wrote, "It's a part of being a woman . . . it's what I am . . . so I love it" (S. Lee, 2002, p. 30). A friend of mine mentioned another positive image: Menstruation connects her with women everywhere. When she is menstruating, she is reminded that women all over the world, of different ethnicities, shapes, and ages, are menstruating as well. Less poetically but nonetheless significantly, many women greet a menstrual period with joy because it means they are not pregnant.

We need to emphasize that menstrual cramps and other problems will not disappear if you simply adopt a more positive attitude. However, the issues may be easier to deal with if you know their cause and remind yourself that other women share similar experiences. Chrisler and her colleagues do not anticipate that they can convince the world that menstruation is truly joyous, rather than unpleasant. However, isn't it interesting that so little research has been conducted on the potentially positive side of menstruation?

CULTURAL ATTITUDES TOWARD MENSTRUATION

Throughout this book, you'll often see a contrast between people's beliefs about women and women's actual experiences. For example, people's stereotypes about women (Chapter 2) often differ from women's actual cognitive skills (Chapter 5) and women's social characteristics (Chapter 6). Similarly, we will see in this discussion that cultural attitudes about menstruation often differ from women's actual experiences.

Some cultures have a taboo against contact with menstruating women. For example, contemporary Creek Indians in Oklahoma do not allow menstruating women to use the same plates or utensils as other tribe members (A. R. Bell, 1990). Many similar menstrual practices reflect a belief in female pollution and the devaluation of women (J. L. Goldenberg & Roberts, 2004; T. Roberts & Waters, 2004; A. E. Walker, 1998). These attitudes toward menstruation are consistent with Theme 2 of this book: The cultural community may have negative attitudes about something associated with women—in this instance, their menstrual periods (Chrisler, 2004b).

Most European Americans also have negative attitudes toward menstruating women. In one study, both women and men rated a "menstruating woman" as being more irritable, sad, and angry compared to an "average woman" (Forbes et al., 2003). In other research, students were told that they would be working on a problem-solving task with a female student (T. Roberts et al., 2002). In reality, this other student was a confederate. (A **confederate** is a person whom the researchers had instructed to act in a certain way, although the "real participants" believe that she is simply another participant.) At one point, the confederate opened her handbag. By "mistake" either a hair clip or a wrapped tampon fell out of her bag. Later in the session, the real participants were instructed to evaluate this woman. Both males and females rated the confederate as being less competent and less likeable if her handbag had contained a tampon, rather than a hair clip.

In most of North America, the topic of menstruation is not only negative but also relatively invisible, consistent with Theme 3 of this book. We usually do not speak openly about menstruation (Kissling, 2003). Instead, we enlist euphemisms, or more pleasant ways of saying the same thing. For example, you'll rarely hear the word *menstruation* on television. An ad referring to "that time of the month" probably does not mean the date the car payment is due. In Aída Hurtado's (2003) study of Latina adolescents, 55% of the young women had never talked with either parent about menstruation. Many of adolescents emphasized the secrecy of disposing of sanitary napkins, which one woman noted was "more complicated than making tamales" (p. 52).

Young girls' attitudes may be shaped by advertisements in media directed at North American teenagers (Erchull et al., 2002; Merskin, 1999). Jessica Oksman (2002) examined a total of 36 issues of *Seventeen* and *Mademoiselle* magazines. She found that 46 advertisements emphasized that menstruation is something secretive, and it must be concealed. For example, a typical ad pointed out that "nobody needs to know." In contrast, she found only 1 positive message about menstruation: "It is a symbol of strength, beauty, spirit. It is woman. It is you." Imagine how much more positive young women would feel about menstruation if they encountered 46 messages like this and only 1 that encouraged secrecy.

Section Summary

Puberty and Menstruation

1. Adolescence begins at puberty; for females, menarche is the crucial milestone of puberty.

2. The menstrual cycle requires a complex coordination of brain structures, hormones, and internal reproductive organs.

3. Dysmenorrhea, or menstrual pain, is common in young women. Dysmenorrhea is partly caused by prostaglandins, but psychological factors also play an important role.

4. Premenstrual syndrome (PMS) is a controversial set of symptoms that presumably includes headaches, breast soreness, depression, and irritability. PMS is challenging to study because it cannot be clearly defined. PMS-related mood swings seem to be relatively rare.

5. The psychological-cultural explanation of PMS suggests that psychological factors play a role and that cultural expectations encourage women to use PMS as an explanation for negative moods that occur on the days before their menstrual period.

6. Because of the controversy about the origins and nature of PMS, it's difficult to make recommendations about treating it.

7. Some women report increased energy and other positive reactions to menstruation.

8. Menstrual myths and other negative attitudes are found in many cultures. European Americans judge menstruating women to be less competent and less likeable, compared to other women. In addition, U.S. media directed at adolescent females suggest that menstruation should be kept secret.

SELF-CONCEPT AND IDENTITY DURING ADOLESCENCE

We have seen that adolescent females are aware of the changes in their bodies during puberty and that they experience a major transition when they reach menarche. Adolescents have the cognitive capacity to think abstractly, so they can begin to ask complex questions such as "Who am I?" (Steinberg & Morris, 2001). **Identity** refers to an individual's self-rating of personal characteristics along with biological, psychological, or social dimensions (Whitbourne, 1998). We'll consider four components of identity in this section: body image, feminist identity, ethnic identity, and self-esteem.

BODY IMAGE AND PHYSICAL ATTRACTIVENESS

In Chapter 3, we saw that physical attractiveness is more important for pre-school girls than for preschool boys. Compared to less attractive little girls, cute little girls are more likely to be patted and praised—and less likely to be hit and pushed. However, physical attractiveness is generally irrelevant for little boys (G. J. Smith, 1985).

This same emphasis on female attractiveness is exaggerated during ado-lescence. Young women constantly receive the message that good looks and physical beauty are the most important dimension for females (Galambos, 2004; Giles, 2003; Steinberg & Morris, 2001). Their skin must be clear, their teeth straight and gleaming, and their hair lustrous. They must also be slender. Attractiveness may be an especially important attribute in the United States and in other relatively wealthy countries (Gibbons, Brusi-Figueroa et al., 1997; Kirk & Okazawa-Rey, 2001). As we'll soon see in the section on ethnic identity, young women of color seldom see their own ethnic group represented in these advertisements.

Some North American young women are so concerned about being slender that they develop life-threatening eating disorders. (We will discuss these dis-orders and our culture's emphasis on thinness in more detail in Chapter 12.) This intense focus on body weight extends beyond those with eating disorders; it also has a substantial impact on the general population of adolescent females. For example, Polce-Lynch and her colleagues (1998) asked adolescents in the southeastern United States to name some things that made them feel bad about themselves. In this sample, 38% of the eighth-grade girls reported dissatisfac-tion with their bodies, in contrast to only 15% of the eighth-grade boys.

The media encourage this emphasis on beauty and slenderness, and young women are well aware of this message (Botta, 2003; Hofschire & Greenberg, 2002; Quart, 2003; C. A. Smith, 2004). Furthermore, controlled experiments have shown that women are less satisfied with their bodies if they have been looking at fashion magazines, rather than magazines showing normal-sized women (D. F. Roberts et al., 2004). Try Demonstration 4.2 on page 124 to appreciate the narrow view that teen magazines provide to female adolescents.

Unfortunately, young women's general self-concepts are often shaped by whether they believe they are attractive. Researchers have found that physical

Demonstration 4.2

REPRESENTATION
OF FEMALES IN
TEEN MAGAZINES

Locate several magazines intended for adolescent women. Currently, *Seventeen, YM, Teen People,* and *CosmoGirl!* are popular (Tyre, 2004). Glance through the magazine for photos of women in either advertisements or feature articles. What percentage of these women would be considered overweight? How many look nearly anorexic? Then inspect the magazines for ethnic representation. If you find any women of color, are they pale-skinned, with features typical of White women, or do they seem typical of their own ethnic group?

Notice the body posture of the women pictured. Would a young man look ridiculous in these positions? What percentage of the photos seems aimed at encouraging sexual relationships? How many of the women look competent? What other messages do these images provide for high-school females?

---

appearance is the strongest predictor of self-worth in females. For males, however, athletic competence is a stronger predictor of self-worth (Denner & Griffin, 2003; Kwa, 1994). Notice, then, that females feel valued for how their bodies *look*. In contrast, males feel valued for how their bodies *perform* in athletics and other activities that enhance their self-image.

In recent years, researchers have begun to discover that girls who participate in athletics can often escape from the dominant images presented to adolescent females. Not surprisingly, women athletes often have higher self-esteem than their nonathlete peers (Richman & Shaffer, 2000; Tracy & Erkut, 2002; J. Young & Bursik, 2000). Exercise also increases women's sense of control over their lives (Vasquez, 2002).

Young women's participation in sports has increased dramatically during recent decades. The media are now more likely to feature female athletes, and these images of strong women might make a difference. Adolescent women watching the victorious women athletes in sports such as basketball and soccer may realize that women's bodies can be competent and athletic rather than anorexic (Dowling, 2000; Strouse, 1999). Now try Demonstration 4.3 before you read further.

FEMINIST IDENTITY

In Chapter 1, we emphasized that **feminism** is a belief system in which women's experiences and ideas are valued. Feminists argue that women and men should be socially, economically, and legally equal (L. A. Jackson et al., 1996; Pollitt, 2004). In that chapter, we also identified several different approaches to feminism. In Chapter 2, we briefly noted that people have less favorable attitudes about feminists than about women in general. In the present chapter, we noted that adolescents have the capacity to think abstractly and to contemplate their personal identity. As a consequence, they can consider abstract questions such as "What do I believe about women's roles?" and "Am I a feminist?"

Demonstration 4.3

If you are a woman, rate each of the following items using a 5-point scale. (Rate an item 1 if you strongly disagree; rate the item 5 if you strongly agree.) If you are a man, think of a woman you know well who shares your ideas about women's issues, and try to answer the questionnaire from her perspective.

_____ 1. I want to work to make the world a fairer place for all people.

_____ 2. I have become increasingly aware that society is sexist.

_____ 3. I am very interested in women writers and other aspects of women's studies.

_____ 4. I think that most women feel happiest being a wife and mother.

_____ 5. I do not want to have the same status that a man has.

_____ 6. I am proud to be a strong and competent woman.

_____ 7. I am angry about the way that men and boys often treat me.

_____ 8. I am glad that women do not have to do construction work or other dangerous jobs.

_____ 9. I owe it to both women and men to work for greater gender equality.

_____ 10. I am happy being a traditional female.

Note: These items are similar to the 39-item Feminist Identity Development Scale, developed by Bargad & Hyde (1991). The reliability and validity of the items in this shortened version have not been established.

Most of the research about feminist values and identity has surveyed college students in late adolescence. We would welcome research on the development of a feminist identity from early adolescence through late adulthood, using a more diverse sample of young women.

In both the United States and Canada, people are likely to say that they support feminist ideas. However, they are reluctant to claim a **feminist social identity** by saying, "Yes, I am a feminist" (Anastasopoulos & Desmarais, 2000; Burn et al., 2000; Twenge & Zucker, 1999). Researchers have identified several factors that are associated with feminist beliefs. For example, people who support feminist beliefs are more advanced in their ego development than those who do not support these beliefs (Bursik, 2000). **Ego development** is a kind of psychological growth in which people develop a more complex view of themselves and of their relationships with other people.

People who have a feminist social identity are also more likely to be very knowledgeable about feminism, through friends, college classes, or feminist magazines and books. They are also more likely to have a positive evaluation of feminists (Henley et al., 1998; Liss et al., 2001; A. Reid & Purcell, 2004). In addition, females are more likely than males to consider themselves feminists

(Burn et al., 2000; Henderson-King & Zhermer, 2003; Toller et al., 2004). Finally, females who considered themselves to be extremely feminine—and males who considered themselves to be extremely masculine—are not likely to have a feminist social identity (Toller et al., 2004).

Some people claim that older women are much more likely than the current generation of adolescent females to call themselves feminists (Jowett, 2004). However, the research shows that generational differences are small (Peltola et al., 2004).

Now assess your answers to Demonstration 4.3 by looking at the end of the chapter (page 143). Also, answer one additional question: Do you consider yourself a feminist?

ETHNIC IDENTITY

We can define **ethnic identity** as people's sense that they belong to an ethnic group, as well as their attitudes and behaviors toward that group (Tsai et al., 2002; Yeh, 1998). Researchers have examined whether female and male adolescents differ in the strength of their ethnic identity. In general, they have found no consistent gender differences (e.g., Rotheram-Borus et al., 1996; Waters, 1996). However, young women of color may be more interested in maintaining their cultural traditions, in comparison to young men of color (K. K. Dion & Dion, 2004; Meece & Scantlebury, 2006).

Other researchers have focused on the nature of adolescents' ethnic identity rather than on gender comparisons. In general, young European American women are not concerned about their ethnic identity (Peplau et al., 1999; Poran, 2002; Waters, 1996). When being White is considered standard or normative, White individuals don't notice their privileged status.

Some young women of color may initially try to reject their ethnicity. Consider, for example, an African American woman's description of herself:

> For a long time it seemed as if I didn't remember my background, and I guess in some ways I didn't. I was never taught to be proud of my African heritage. Like we talked about in class, I went through a very long stage of identifying with my oppressors. Wanting to be like, live like, and be accepted by them. Even to the point of hating my own race and myself for being a part of it. Now I am ashamed that I ever was ashamed. I lost so much of myself in my denial of and refusal to accept my people. (Tatum, 1992, p. 10)

Sadly, the White-as-normative attitudes are strikingly evident in beauty contests. For instance, Vietnamese immigrant communities in the United States often organize beauty contests in which the winners are young Vietnamese women who look most like European Americans. In fact, many contestants even undergo plastic surgery so that their eyes, chin, and nose can look more "American" (Lieu, 2004). Furthermore, women who enter the "Miss India" pageant in India are expected to attend a 6-week training session that includes a near-starvation diet and skin bleaching so that they can look more "White" (Runkle, 2004).

However, some young women of color pursue information about their ethnic identity by reading about their ethnic group or exploring their family's history. These women often discover that their roots are deep, as a Mexican American woman explained:

> I also think of people as flowers. . . . The reason why I say this is because there are things in our lives constantly. But it goes farther back than my life here. It goes deeper into our past interior, and I think of that as my past history. And all those things impact me. I don't know all those things. But some I've been told about, and I can see the way my great-grandmother interacts with me, I hear the stories of my great-great-aunt, and it's all impacted me. (Ford, 1999, p. 85)

Researchers are just beginning to explore these complex issues about identity that arise at the intersection of ethnicity and gender.

SELF-ESTEEM

According to researchers, American culture emphasizes the importance of self-esteem (Crocker & Park, 2004a, 2004b). **Self-esteem** is a measure of how much you like and value yourself (Malanchuk & Eccles, 2006). Do adolescent males and females differ in self-esteem? As with ethnic identity, we cannot reach a clear-cut conclusion because the answer depends on several important factors.

During the 1990s, several popular books concluded that self-esteem drops sharply for females, relative to males, during high school (Pipher, 1994; Sadker & Sadker, 1994). Indeed, many researchers have reported a modest gender difference in adolescents' self-esteem (e.g., J. Frost & McKelvie, 2004; Quatman & Watson, 2001; Widaman et al., 1992). However, other researchers have reported that adolescent females and males have similar self-esteem, at least under some conditions (e.g., Kling & Hyde, 2001; Meece & Scantlebury, 2006; D. Wise & Stake, 2002).

With mixed results like these, how can we draw any conclusions? Fortunately, researchers who study gender comparisons can use a technique called meta-analysis. **Meta-analysis** provides a statistical method for integrating numerous studies on a single topic. Researchers first locate all appropriate studies on the topic. Then they perform a statistical analysis that combines the results from all these studies. The meta-analysis yields a single number that tells us whether a particular variable has an overall effect. For example, for self-esteem, a meta-analysis can statistically combine numerous previous studies into one enormous superstudy that can provide a general picture of whether gender has an overall effect on self-esteem.

Two important meta-analytic studies have been conducted on gender comparisons of self-esteem, each study based on more than 200 different gender comparisons (Kling et al., 1999; Major et al., 1999). Both studies concluded that the average male scores are slightly—but significantly—higher in self-esteem than the average female scores. However, when these two groups of researchers took a closer look, they found that the gender differences are minimal in childhood, early adolescence, and later adulthood; during late adolescence, gender differences are somewhat larger.

Furthermore, the gender differences in self-esteem are relatively large for European Americans, whereas Black females and Black males are generally more similar. These findings are consistent with other reports that Black females are higher in self-esteem than females from other ethnic groups (Denner & Griffin, 2003; Malanchuk & Eccles, 2006; Tracy & Erkut, 2002). Apparently, young African American women develop strategies for protecting their self-esteem when they are facing discrimination (Collins, 2002b).

In addition, Major and her colleagues (1999) found that gender differences are relatively large among lower-class and middle-class participants. In contrast, upper-class females and males from well-educated families are usually somewhat similar in their self-esteem.

In other words, gender differences in self-esteem are inconsistent, and they depend on several personal characteristics. We know that age is an important characteristic; a young woman in her late teens may feel especially constrained by our culture's gender roles (Major et al., 1999). Ethnicity is also important; Black women may use different cultural standards than other women when assessing their self-worth (Major et al., 1999). Social class is similarly important; well-educated families may conclude that gender bias is unfair, so female adolescents raised in these families may be encouraged to break through the gender roles (Major et al., 1999).

Section Summary

Self-Concept and Identity During Adolescence

1. Physical attractiveness is emphasized for adolescent women, and the current emphasis on thinness and beauty can lead to eating disorders and too much concern about personal appearance.

2. People who say they are feminists are likely to be familiar with feminism and to evaluate feminists positively; females are more likely than males to say they are feminists.

3. Young women of color may initially ignore their ethnic identity but strengthen it during adolescence; some adolescents may undergo plastic surgery or skin bleaching so that they can look more European American.

4. The average male may score slightly higher in self-esteem than the average female; this gender difference is relatively large in late adolescence, in European Americans, and in people with relatively little education.

EDUCATION AND CAREER PLANNING

In Chapter 3, we saw that young girls are often relatively invisible in the elementary-school classroom, whereas boys receive more attention. Now we'll examine young women's educational experiences and career planning. Chapter 5 explores gender comparisons in cognitive skills and achievement motivation, whereas Chapter 6 focuses on gender comparisons in social and personality characteristics. A background in these topics will prepare us to discuss women and employment in Chapter 7. In the current section, we explore young women's experiences in middle school and high school, early encounters with math and science, experiences in higher education, career choices, and the discrepancy between aspirations and reality.

Young Women's Experiences in Middle School and High School

A female seventh-grader described the complex challenge of blending school and social roles:

> For school we got an open mind, good grades, participation, we've got the attitude, a certain perspective. You have to suck up sometimes, you have to be quiet, you have to know certain people, you have to be yourself, you have to be attentive, on task, you have to study a lot. And for the crowd you have to wear the right clothes, you have to have the attitude, you have to be willing to bully people, you also have to suck up to, like, your friends or whatever, you have to be outgoing, daring, you have to know certain people . . . and sometimes you have to be mean. (J. Cohen et al., 1996, p. 60)

Some of the adolescent characteristics we've discussed in this chapter make it especially challenging for young women to achieve academic success. Their bodies are changing, they may be preoccupied with their physical appearance, and they may be tempted to starve themselves. They may also have low self-esteem. Many females in middle school (junior high) and high school feel invisible in the classroom (Levstik, 2001). When the academic environment is not friendly to young women, they will study less, choose less rigorous courses, and select less challenging careers (Arnold et al., 1996; L. M. Brown, 1998; Eccles, 2004).

Young women are most likely to maintain their academic aspirations if their middle schools or high schools make gender equality a priority, institute a mentoring system, have high expectations for young women, and encourage them to become leaders in their field (Cohen et al., 1996; Erkut et al., 2001; Fort, 2005b). In addition, these schools must emphasize both ethnic equality and social-class equality (V. C. Adair & Dahlberg, 2003; J. L. Hochschild, 2003; Ostrove & Cole, 2003). For example, a European American woman who had grown up in a low-income area vividly recalls a high-school vice principal who shouted to a busload of students, "Hogtrash. Every last one of you. You'll never amount to nothing" (N. Sullivan, 2003, p. 56).

Early Experiences in Math and Science

Zelda Ziegler remembers sitting in a high school classroom, preparing to take an engineering exam. She was the only female among those taking the test. The proctor stood in front of the room and announced that the exam would be reasonable. "Nobody would have trouble with it except for one person—and she knows who she is" (J. Kaplan & Aronson, 1994, p. 27). Fortunately, Ziegler was not discouraged by these words. She went on to earn a Ph.D. degree in chemistry and now acts as a mentor for young women interested in science.

Most high-school females do not face such overt sexism, but they typically experience subtle biases that discourage all but the most persistent young women. For example, math and science teachers may convey higher expectations to male students than to female students (Duffy et al., 2001; Piran & Ross, 2006). They may also give males more helpful feedback. Teachers may also emphasize examples that are more familiar to males than to females. In addition, teachers may fail to encourage talented females to pursue careers in math and science. Middle school is often the crucial time at which young women start to form negative attitudes toward these traditionally male courses (Eccles, 1997; Hanson & Johnson, 2000).

Several additional factors contribute to the gender differences in pursuing math and science:

1. Male peers may react negatively toward females who are interested in these areas (Brownlow et al., 2002; Stake, 2003).
2. Females often feel less competent and effective in these courses, even though they may actually perform very well (Erchick, 2001; L. L. Sax & Bryant, 2002; Tenenbaum & Leaper, 2003).
3. Parents tend to believe that boys are more skilled in science than girls are (Tenenbaum & Leaper, 2003).
4. Females are less likely to join extracurricular groups that focus on math and science, a factor that further increases the difference between males and females (L. L. Sax & Bryant, 2002).

Some school systems have developed innovative programs to encourage young females to pursue careers in math and the sciences (Stake, 2003). For example, Carolyn Turk (2004) describes her experiences in a program designed for high-school females who were interested in engineering. As she writes, "If I hadn't stumbled into that summer program, I wouldn't be an engineer" (p. 12). In these academic settings, young women can learn to take risks, make mistakes, develop a peer group, and enjoy being successful in a nontraditional area (Stake & Nickens, 2005).

In addition, parents can support their daughter's interest in nontraditional fields by seeking nonsexist career guidance. They can also encourage her college plans and value her academic interests (Betz, 2006; Song, 2001). Furthermore, teachers can identify young females who are gifted in science and math and then encourage parents to support their daughter's interest in these areas (Eccles et al., 2000; Reis, 1998).

HIGHER EDUCATION

In North America, women are currently more likely than men to pursue higher education. For example, 57% of all full-time university students in Canada are

Table 4.1	Male and Female Enrollment in U.S. Colleges and Universities in 2004, as a Function of Ethnic Group	
	Number of Students	
Ethnic Group	**Women**	**Men**
European American	6,434,800	4,988,000
Black	1,406,300	758,400
Latina/o	1,064,500	745,100
Asian	597,100	511,600
Native American	107,500	68,600

Source: Based on "The Nation: Students" (2006).

female (Statistics Canada, 2006). Women also constitute 56% of students enrolled in U.S. colleges and universities ("The Nation: Students," 2006). As Table 4.1 shows, this gender difference holds for all five major ethnic groups in the United States, although the gap is largest for Black women and men. Furthermore, you'll probably be surprised to learn that U.S. women now earn 51% of all the Ph.D. degrees awarded to U.S. citizens ("By the Numbers," 2006).

In contrast to the gender ratio for students, relatively few college professors are women. At present, only 39% of all full-time faculty members at U.S. colleges and universities are female ("The Nation: Faculty and Staff," 2006). If a young woman wants to pursue a science degree, female faculty members are even less visible. For instance, females constitute only 17% of the faculty in the 50 top-ranked chemistry departments in the United States (Kuck et al., 2004). Consequently, female students may receive a message that they have entered a male-dominated environment where they are not welcome. Is the college environment somewhat hostile to women? And what is college like for women of color?

THE ACADEMIC ENVIRONMENT.   In the early 1980s, some observers suggested that female students in higher education were experiencing a chilly classroom climate (e.g., R. M. Hall & Sandler, 1982). Where the concept of the **chilly classroom climate** persists, faculty members treat men and women differently in the classroom and women may feel ignored and devalued. As a result, some women may participate less in discussions and may be less likely to feel academically competent (Basow, 2004; Pascarella et al., 1997).

Several resources provide reports of the chilly classroom climate in higher education (Betz, 2006; Murray et al., 1999). For example, when a female nursing student asked a question about the topic a male professor had just discussed, the professor leaned over to one of the male students and said, "Whoa, that went right over her head, didn't it?" (Shellenbarger & Lucas, 1997, p. 156).

Research has not found consistent evidence for a chilly classroom climate (K. L. Brady & Eisler, 1995, 1999; M. Crawford & MacLeod, 1990). In general, gender discrimination is more likely in male-dominated disciplines such as math, science, and engineering (J. Steele et al., 2002). Furthermore, feminists and students of color are more likely than others to experience a chilly climate (Janz & Pyke, 2000).

WOMEN OF COLOR AND HIGHER EDUCATION.   As we saw in Table 14.1, Black women are much more likely than Black men to attend college. The reasons for this discrepancy are not clear, but theorists suggest that part of the problem is a cultural climate that values athletic ability and high salaries more than academic achievement in young males (Etson, 2003; Roach, 2001).

Students of color often receive the message that they do not fit well in a college setting (Gruber, 1999; P. T. Reid & Zalk, 2001). As one young Puerto Rican woman said, "People sort of see me differently because I'm Hispanic and I'm smart. I feel sometimes that they want to put me down. I have had several incidents where people will look at my skin color and think I'm dumb, and they immediately think 'She's not bright, she's not smart'" (Reis, 1998, pp. 157–158).

Students of color face multiple additional barriers. For instance, Asian families may be reluctant to let their daughter attend a college far from home (Zia, 2000). Financing a college education is often an issue for women of color, especially in immigrant families (De las Fuentes & Vasquez, 1999; hooks, 2000b).

In general, Native Americans are the ethnic group that we often know the least about. We also know little about their college attendance. However, an important program in the United States is called **tribal colleges**, which are 2- and 4-year institutions that provide a transition between native culture and the predominately European American "mainstream" culture. At present, there are 32 tribal colleges, almost all of them west of the Mississippi River. These colleges train Native American students—primarily women—in fields such as health care. After completing their education, most return to work in their own community ("New England Tribal College," 2004). In Canada, several dozen colleges and universities are actively recruiting Aboriginal students, and the government has also committed funds to Aboriginal higher education (Birchard, 2006).

Our discussion so far has focused on the difficulty of blending school with peer relationships, early experiences in math and science, and the challenges of higher education. Now let's turn to young women's career plans.

CAREER ASPIRATIONS

A variety of studies have asked adolescents about their career aspirations. In general, adolescent females and males have similar career goals. Here are some of the findings:

1. Adolescent males and females have equivalent aspirations with respect to advanced degrees, and they also aspire to similarly prestigious careers (e.g., Abele, 2000; Astin & Lindholm, 2001; C. M. Watson et al., 2002).

2. Adolescent females are more likely than adolescent males to choose careers that are nontraditional for their gender (Bobo et al., 1998; C. M. Watson et al., 2002). For example, Reis and her colleagues (1996) surveyed gifted adolescents. Of the females, 37% aspired to be doctors, whereas fewer than 1% of the males aspired to be nurses.

3. When considering their future careers, adolescent females are more likely than adolescent males to emphasize the importance of marriage and children (Debold et al., 1999; Mahaffy & Ward, 2002).

4. Parents are more likely to let daughters make their own decisions about careers. In one study of middle-school students, 88% of girls, compared with only 38% of boys, said that their parents had been allowing them to make their own occupational choices (Reis, 1998).

5. Adolescent females are more likely than adolescent males to report that they have been effective in gathering information about their future careers (Gianakos, 2001).

What personal characteristics are typical for women who aspire to high-prestige, nontraditional careers? Not surprisingly, they receive high grades in school (C. M. Watson et al., 2002). They also tend to be independent, self-confident, assertive, emotionally stable, and satisfied with their lives (Astin & Lindholm, 2001; Betz, 1994; Eccles, 1994). Notice that the young women who plan to pursue nontraditional careers typically have characteristics that should serve them well in these careers. In addition, their emotional stability and life satisfaction indicate that they are well adjusted. They also tend to express feminist attitudes and to transcend traditional gender roles (Flores & O'Brien, 2002; Song, 2001; Vincent et al., 1998).

Women who plan on prestigious nontraditional careers are likely to have parents who are well educated and from middle- or upper-class backgrounds (Kastberg & Miller, 1996). Their mothers are also likely to be employed outside the home and to have feminist beliefs (Belansky et al., 1992; J. Steele & Barling, 1996). Other influential background characteristics include a supportive and encouraging family, female role models, and work experience as an adolescent (Betz, 1994; Flores & O'Brien, 2002; Lips, 2004).

In this section, we have explored women's aspirations about future careers and the factors associated with nontraditional career choices. But how well do women's aspirations match their actual career pathways?

CAREER ASPIRATIONS VERSUS REALITY

Young women may enter middle school or high school with ambitious career goals. However, they may absorb the cultural messages about finding a boyfriend, so that they lose sight of these goals (Reis, 1998; C. M. Watson et al., 2002). For example, a seventh-grader commented about this topic:

> I don't know what has happened to some of my friends. Consider Lisa. She acts so different around boys. She gets all giggly and silly and seems to act like such a jerk. She's cooing and trying to be all sweet and everything. She's started to act like she

isn't smart at all. Her grades are horrible and she just isn't herself any more. (Reis, 1998, p. 130)

As you may recall from previous chapters, boys and men hold more traditional views about gender than do girls and women. As a result, a young woman in a romantic relationship may find that her boyfriend does not support her career ambitions, and she becomes a less dedicated student (Basow & Rubin, 1999).

Women may also be more likely than men to downscale their dreams as they move through college (Betz, 1994; Lips, 2004). For example, one study followed the lives of a group of Black women and a group of White women while they progressed through two universities in the South (Holland & Eisenhart, 1990). In two-thirds of both groups, the women's aspirations about careers diminished during their college years. Instead, they spent more time and energy on romantic relationships. As they increased their attention to romance, they grew more bored with schoolwork, producing further erosion of their career identities. Ultimately, their romantic relationships became far more important than their career-related education.

Most of the research in this area examines the career paths of relatively affluent women who can afford to go to college. Columnist Molly Ivins (1997) reminds us that the aspirations of these individuals are not relevant for many young women. Ivins described the situation of Shanika, who is 24 and unmarried and has three children. She has no high school degree, no job, and little prospect of obtaining either. When asked what she had dreamed before her children were born, she replied, "You know, I really didn't have a dream" (p. 12).

Section Summary

Education and Career Planning

1. Adolescent females must negotiate the conflicting demands of schoolwork and social relationships.

2. Teachers and school systems may treat young women in a biased fashion; they may also discriminate on the basis of ethnicity and social class.

3. Adolescent females may be discouraged from pursuing careers in science and math; however, some schools offer innovative programs to promote these nontraditional careers for women.

4. Women in higher education may sometimes encounter a chilly classroom climate, but current research has not documented widespread discrimination against college women.

5. Women of color sometimes report that they do not feel comfortable in academic environments, but some universities offer programs designed to be supportive.

6. Adolescent females are similar to adolescent males with respect to their aspirations for advanced degrees and prestigious careers, but females are more likely to choose nontraditional careers and to emphasize marriage and

children. Females also feel less parental pressure to choose a particular career, but they are more likely to gather career information effectively.

7. Factors associated with women's choice of a prestigious nontraditional career include high grades, self-confidence, emotional stability, and feminist beliefs. Other factors include parental education, mothers' employment and feminist beliefs, and supportive adults.

8. As women advance through middle school, high school, and college, they are likely to adopt less ambitious plans; in addition, romantic relationships may interfere with academic achievement.

INTERPERSONAL RELATIONSHIPS DURING ADOLESCENCE

So far in this chapter, we have explored three clusters of issues that are important to young women: (1) puberty and menstruation; (2) self-concept and identity; and (3) education and career planning. However, adolescent females are perhaps most concerned about their social interactions.

Consider Ruby, a 14-year-old African American, who has six younger siblings. Her narrative illustrates the centrality of interpersonal relationships for adolescent females. For example, she describes how the women in her family provide a circle of support when she wants to discuss her future plans: "[My mother] says if I want something, I can always accomplish it. I believe that, too. And my aunt and my grandmother. There's lots of people" (J. M. Taylor et al., 1995, p. 42). Ruby also emphasizes the support offered by her classmates, for example, when they elected her to a special team in her history class: "The kids are all—I guess they accepted me for that, so maybe they like me. . . . You know you're wanted" (p. 42).

In this final section of the chapter on adolescence, we will begin by exploring relationships with family members. Then we'll examine connections with peers, specifically in friendships and in love relationships.

FAMILY RELATIONSHIPS

If you believe the popular media, you might conclude that adolescents and their parents inhabit different cultures, interacting only long enough to snarl at each other. The data suggest otherwise (Zebrowitz & Montepare, 2000). Most adolescents, both females and males, actually get along well with their parents. They may disagree on relatively minor issues such as music or messy rooms. However, they typically agree on more substantive matters such as religion, politics, education, and social values (Graber & Brooks-Gunn, 1999; Smetana, 1996; Smetana et al., 2003). Furthermore, current theories emphasize the strong emotional bond between adolescents and their parents (W. A. Collins & Laursen, 2004).

The family is likely to be a strong basis of identification for adolescent females of color, especially if the family can serve as a source of resiliency when these young women experience ethnic or gender discrimination (Vasquez & De las Fuentes, 1999). The research also suggests that both in North America and in other cultures, adolescent females typically feel closer to their mothers than to their fathers (W. A. Collins & Laursen, 2004; Gibbons et al., 1991; Smetana et al., 2004).

In most areas, female and male adolescents report similar family experiences. However, you may remember that parents tend to discuss fear and sadness with their daughters but that they talk about anger with their sons (Chapter 3). Interestingly, adolescent females are much more likely than adolescent males to endorse statements such as "In our family, it's okay to be sad, happy, angry, loving, excited, scared, or whatever we feel" (Bronstein et al., 1996). These family discussions may encourage young women to emphasize their emotional experiences. We'll explore some of the consequences of this emphasis on emotions in Chapter 12, when we discuss depression.

As young women mature, they may begin to notice gender issues in their families. For example, young Latina and Portuguese American women report that their parents give young men many more privileges and much more freedom (Raffaelli, 2005; J. M. Taylor et al., 1995). They also report that their parents strictly forbid any sexual activity. The parents' concerns have important implications for young women's romantic relationships, a topic we'll discuss at the end of this chapter.

FRIENDSHIPS

In Chapter 6, we'll examine gender comparisons in friendship patterns during adulthood. We have less information about adolescent friendships. In general, females' friendships seem to be somewhat closer and more intimate than males' friendships. However, the gender differences are small, and some studies report no significant gender differences (L. M. Diamond & Dubé, 2002; Monsour, 2002; Zarbatany et al., 2000).

A more interesting question focuses on the importance of close friendships in the lives of adolescent females. Young women consider loyalty and trust to be essential in these friendships (B. B. Brown et al., 1997; L. M. Brown et al., 1999). For example, Lyn Mikel Brown (1998) studied a group of lower-class European American teenagers. These young women reported that their relationships with girlfriends provided a support system in an environment that often seemed hostile.

Another important part of young women's friendships is intimate conversations. A Latina teenager discusses her best friend: "I go to her because I wouldn't feel comfortable telling other people, you know, like, real deep personal things" (Way, 1998, p. 133).

Adolescent females face a major challenge as they try to develop a clear sense of themselves in relationships with others. Some emphasize interdependence with others; these young women may spend so much attention on their friends that they fail to take care of their own needs. Other young women are more independent; they are concerned about other people, but they do not compromise their own integrity for the sake of friends (Lyons, 1990).

The research on friendships illustrates a central choice that weaves through women's lives. At many turning points, from youth through old age, women face conflicts between doing something that is best for themselves or doing something for another person: a parent, a female friend, a male friend, or a spouse (Eccles, 2001).

In two later chapters of this book, we will examine topics related to women's focusing on themselves: cognitive ability and achievement (Chapter 5) and work (Chapter 7). Several other chapters emphasize women in relationships: social characteristics (Chapter 6), love relationships (Chapter 8), sexuality (Chapter 9), and pregnancy, childbirth, and motherhood (Chapter 10). As you'll see, women frequently have to balance their own needs and priorities against the wishes of other people who are important in their lives.

ROMANTIC RELATIONSHIPS

For most individuals, adolescence marks the beginning of romantic relationships. We'll explore these experiences in more detail in Chapter 8, but let's consider some of the issues that young women face in heterosexual and lesbian relationships during adolescence. Before you read further, try Demonstration 4.4 on page 138, which focuses on early heterosexual romances.

HETEROSEXUAL RELATIONSHIPS.   As you recall from Chapter 3, young girls and boys practice gender segregation; they tend to inhabit different worlds for many years. As a result, they reach early adolescence with only limited experience regarding the other gender (Compian & Hayward, 2003; Feiring, 1998).

How do young women figure out how they should interact with these unfamiliar young men in a romantic relationship? An important source of information is the media: movies, television, music, magazines, and computer games (J. D. Brown et al., 2006; Galician, 2004; J. R. Steele, 2002; Walsh-Childers et al., 2002). Not surprisingly, the media usually portray gender-stereotyped romances. The media also suggest that a boyfriend is an absolutely necessity for a high school female. Consider the title of a typical article in a magazine aimed at adolescent women: "Why Don't I Have a Boyfriend? (And How Do I Get One?)" (2001). This article suggests, for example, that if a young woman is too busy studying to meet a boyfriend, she should look around the library to find a likely candidate. These magazines also emphasize that young women must make themselves thin and beautiful to attract a desirable boyfriend. However, as we'll see shortly, these magazines focus exclusively on heterosexual relationships—lesbian relationships do not exist in those glossy pages.

If you believe the media reports that are directed toward adults, you would think that adolescent romance is rare, but adolescent sexuality is widespread. However, Hearn and her colleagues (2003) surveyed low-income African

Demonstration 4.4

For each of the following quotations, try to guess whether the person describing the love relationship is a male or a female. Then check the answers, which are listed at the end of the chapter.

_____ Person 1: "Um, we're both very easygoing. Um, we like a lot of affection. Um, not like public affection, but um, just knowing that we, we care for each other. Um, uh, it doesn't even have to be physical affection, just any type. We like cuddling with each other. Um, we enjoy going out and doing things with each other and each other's friends. . . . We enjoy high action things together. Um, pretty much, we have a very open relationship, and we can talk about anything."

_____ Person 2: "I think after a while, like, (person) following me around, and wanting to be with me all the time, and maybe the fact that I had a lot to say and had the power . . . I'd just, like, I don't know, I still think like that. I don't know why but (person) . . . was getting too serious by following me around all the time and, you know, wanting to spend every minute of the day. . . . You know I'm, like, 'I do have friends I need to talk to.' . . . I was just, like 'Aaah! Go away!'"

_____ Person 3: "It's like . . . you know . . . we love each other so much . . . it's great. We have so much fun. We get mad at each other sometimes, and, you know, we make up, and, you know, we hug. It's great. I mean (person) is wonderful! . . . We, like, we just have a lot of fun, and we have a lot of heartache, but it's perfect because of that, you know. If it was all fun all the time, what's wrong? And if it's bad all the time, something's wrong. It's right in the middle. It's right where it should be."

_____ Person 4: "I'm not really a relationship person. If I meet someone, I want to be able to, you know, to uh, you know . . . not have any restraints or anything. Basically, I run into someone who I think is cool and all that about twice a month. . . . The friends before are friends after. Most of them are probably physical. Um, I don't have any regrets."

Source: Based on Feiring (1998).

American and Latina females between the ages of 12 and 14. According to their results, 94% of these teenagers reported having had a crush on someone, but only 8% reported having had penile-vaginal intercourse.

Adolescent romantic relationships have only recently attracted the attention of serious researchers (Raffaelli, 2005; Steinberg & Morris, 2001). The researchers report tremendous individual differences in the gender typing of adolescents' romantic relationships, consistent with Theme 4 of this book (Hartup, 1999; Tolman, 2002). For example, if you check the answers to Demonstration 4.4, you're likely to find that some adolescents behave in a gender-stereotypical fashion but that some clearly transcend these stereotypes.

Research on early heterosexual romances suggests that these relationships typically last an average of about 4 months, but relationships last longer in late adolescence (B. B. Brown, 2004; Feiring, 1996). Both females and males are likely to describe their romantic partners in terms of positive personality traits, such as nice or funny. However, males are somewhat more likely to mention physical attractiveness, whereas females are somewhat more likely to emphasize personal characteristics, such as support and intimacy (Feiring, 1996, 1999b). In Chapter 8, we'll see that males' emphasis on attractiveness in a dating partner continues through adulthood.

In Chapter 9, we'll examine an important component of heterosexual romantic relationships during adolescence: decision making about sexual behavior. As we'll see, these decisions can have a major impact on a young woman's life, especially because they may lead to pregnancy and life-threatening sexually transmitted diseases.

Romantic relationships can also influence academic performance and career planning. Young women often spend many hours each week dreaming about romance, discussing romantic relationships with friends, and pursuing these relationships (Furman & Shaffer, 2003; Rostosky et al., 1999). Once a woman finds a boyfriend, she may arrange her life to be available to her boyfriend, to help him, and to participate in social activities he chooses (Holland & Eisenhart, 1990).

However, when a young woman has a boyfriend who respects her and values her ideas, these romantic relationships can encourage her to explore important questions about her identity and self-worth (Barber & Eccles, 2003; Furman & Shaffer, 2003; R. W. Larson et al., 1999). She can notice how her interactions with this boyfriend affect her own personality (Feiring, 1999a). She can also think about the qualities that she truly wants in an ideal long-term relationship (W. A. Collins & Sroufe, 1999). Clearly, this self-exploration will have an important impact on her personal values during adulthood, as well as her romantic relationships.

LESBIAN RELATIONSHIPS.　In Chapter 8, we will examine many aspects of lesbian relationships during adulthood. Adolescent women who are just beginning to discover their lesbian identity rarely see positive lesbian images in the movies or on television (O'Sullivan et al., 2001). Psychology researchers also pay more attention to adolescent gay males than to adolescent lesbians. As Theme 3 points out, females are less visible than males. In addition, psychology researchers typically focus on observable problems, and young lesbians are not at high risk for health problems such as pregnancy or AIDS (Welsh et al., 2000).

However, young lesbians are likely to hear negative messages about lesbians and gay males from their peers. In one study, 99% of lesbian and gay youth reported that they had heard anti-gay remarks in their schools ("Lesbian, gay, bisexual," 2001). Adolescent lesbians are also likely to be threatened or attacked (Prezbindowski & Prezbindowski, 2001). They may also receive negative messages from their parents, who sometimes believe that being gay or lesbian is a sin. However, some fortunate adolescents find a school or community support group for lesbian, gay, and bisexual young people (D'Augelli et al., 2002; L. M. Diamond et al., 1999). Furthermore, the American Academy of Pediatrics recently published a six-page article about how pediatricians can support and help gay, lesbian, and bisexual adolescents (Frankowski, 2004).

Young lesbians report that they were about 11 years old when they were first aware of their attraction to other females (D'Augelli et al., 2002). They frequently have a period of questioning their sexual orientation, often explaining to themselves that they are simply feeling an intense emotional connection with another female, rather than a sexual connection (Garnets, 2004a). Young lesbians are most likely to first "come out" to a friend (D'Augelli, 2003). If they come out to their parents at some point, they are more likely to disclose to their mother rather than to their father, according to surveys conducted in the United States and Canada (D'Augelli, 2002, 2003; Savin-Williams, 1998, 2001).

Consistent with Theme 4, young women have widely varying experiences when they come out to their parents. At first, parents may react with shock or denial (Savin-Williams, 2001). However, some young women reported a more positive reaction. As one teenager explained, "We've always been very close, very close, and talk about everything. No secrets from her! . . . This gave me hope in coming out to her. Shortly thereafter I told her I was dating Naomi. . . . But you know, she seemed to know it before I did!" (Savin-Williams, 2001, p. 67). Fortunately, most parents eventually become tolerant or even supportive of their daughters' lesbian relationships (Savin-Williams & Dubé, 1998).

As we'll see in Chapter 8, lesbians typically overcome most negative messages from their community and family, and they construct positive self-images (Owens, 1998). D'Augelli and his coauthors (2002) surveyed 552 lesbian and bisexual high-school females in the United States and Canada. They found that 94% of these young women reported that they were glad to be lesbian or bisexual.

In Chapter 3 and in this chapter, we have considered how children and adolescents develop gender typing. We pointed out in Chapter 3 that children develop elaborate ideas about gender throughout their childhood, especially because their family, their peers, their schools, and the media often provide clear gender messages. In this chapter, we have examined how puberty and menstruation help define young women's views of themselves. We have also noted that gender may influence an adolescent's body image, feminist identity, ethnic identity, and self-esteem. Gender also has important implications for an adolescent's career planning and interpersonal relationships.

In the following chapters, we will change our focus to examine adult women. We'll first explore gender comparisons in cognitive and achievement areas (Chapter 5) and in personality and social areas (Chapter 6). Then we'll consider women in work settings (Chapter 7) as well as in social relationships (Chapters 8, 9, and 10). In Chapters 11, 12, and 13, we will focus on issues women face with respect to health, psychological disorders, and violence. We will return to a developmental framework in Chapter 14, when we consider women's journeys during middle age and old age. In our final chapter, we'll examine some trends in gender issues that we are facing in the twenty-first century.

Section Summary

Interpersonal Relationships During Adolescence

1. Despite some disagreements, adolescent women generally get along well with their families; they typically feel closer to their mothers than to their fathers.

2. Compared to adolescent men, adolescent women may have friendships that are somewhat more intimate.

3. Adolescents' heterosexual relationships show wide individual differences in the extent to which they are gender stereotyped. Young women may spend a great deal of time in their romantic relationships; these relationships can encourage them to explore important questions about identity.

4. Adolescent lesbians often hear negative messages from classmates and parents; experiences differ widely when lesbians come out to their parents. Most adolescent lesbian and bisexual young women are positive about their sexual orientation.

CHAPTER REVIEW QUESTIONS

1. In the section on menstruation, we examined two topics that are occasionally mentioned in the popular media: menstrual pain and premenstrual syndrome (PMS). What did you learn in this section that was different from the impressions the media convey?

2. Throughout this book, we have discussed the social constructionist perspective, in which people construct or invent their own versions of reality based on prior experiences and beliefs. How does this perspective help explain the following issues: (a) premenstrual syndrome, (b) young women's emphasis on slenderness, and (c) heterosexual romantic relationships?

3. We emphasize in this textbook that research findings about gender comparisons often vary, depending on operational definitions (e.g., how you measure the relevant variables). How is this statement relevant when we consider the research on feminist identity and ethnic identity?

4. In this chapter, we have argued that some people—but not everyone—may treat young women in a biased fashion while guiding and educating them. Summarize the information

on these issues. If you were conducting a large-scale study on gender biases during high school and college, what other issues, not mentioned here, would you consider examining?

5. In portions of this chapter, we examined ethnic comparisons. Describe information about relevant comparisons, including age of menarche, self-esteem, and experiences with higher education.

6. Compare adolescent males' and females' career aspirations. What factors influence these aspirations for young women? Although we did not consider similar research on young men, speculate about whether these same factors influence the aspirations of adolescent males.

7. Relate the material in the section on self-concept to the material on career aspirations and to the material on social interactions. Focus on the struggle between commitment to one's own pursuits and commitment to social relationships.

8. We mentioned parents in connection with nontraditional careers, family relationships, and romantic relationships. Discuss this

information and speculate how parents can also be important in a young woman's attitudes toward menstruation, feminist identity, and ethnic identity.

9. Imagine that you are teaching high school and that a group of teachers has obtained a large grant for a program on improving the lives of female adolescents. Review the topics in this chapter, and suggest 8 to 10 important topics that this program should address.

10. The next two chapters focus on gender comparisons in academic performance and interest about achievement (Chapter 5), as well as in social and personality characteristics (Chapter 6). To prepare for these two chapters, make a list comparing young women and men on these dimensions. Be sure to include the experiences in academic settings prior to high school, early experiences in math and science, career aspirations, and friendships.

KEY TERMS

*adolescence (112)

*puberty (112)

*menarche (112)

*secondary sex characteristics (113)

*ovaries (114)

*ova (114)

*uterus (114)

*feedback loop (115)

*ovulation (116)

*dysmenorrhea (116)

*prostaglandins (116)

*premenstrual syndrome (PMS) (117)

*confederate (121)

*identity (123)

*feminism (124)

*feminist social identity (125)

*ego development (125)

*ethnic identity (126)

*self-esteem (127)

*meta-analysis (127)

*chilly classroom climate (131)

*tribal colleges (132)

 Note: The terms asterisked in the Key Terms section serve as good search terms for InfoTrac@ College Edition. Go to http://infotrac.thomsonlearning.com and try these added search terms.

RECOMMENDED READINGS

Adair, V. C., & Dahlberg, S. L. (Eds.). (2003). *Reclaiming class: Women, poverty, and the promise of higher education in America.* Philadelphia: Temple University Press. This book explores how social class impacts the college experiences of women; several chapters examine how "welfare reform" has decreased many women's access to higher education in the United States.

Brown, J. D., Steele, J. R., & Walsh-Childers, K. (Eds.). (2002). *Sexual teens, sexual media: Investigating media's influence on adolescent sexuality.* Mahwah, NJ: Erlbaum. Some of the media forms that this book examines include prime-time television, daytime talk shows, movies, and teen magazines.

Chrisler, J. C., Golden, C., & Rozee, P. D. (Eds.). (2004). *Lectures on the psychology of women* (3rd ed.). Boston: McGraw-Hill. Several chapters in this excellent book are relevant to the topic of

adolescence. Some especially relevant chapters discuss gender in the classroom, women's body image, women and sport, menstruation, and lesbian relationships.

Lerner, R. M., & Steinbert, L. (Eds.). (2004). *Handbook of adolescent psychology* (2nd ed.). Hoboken, NJ: Wiley. Especially relevant chapters in this handbook include ones on puberty, sex, gender roles, adolescents and the media, parent-adolescent relationships, and adolescents' relationships with their peers.

O'Reilly, P., Penn, E. M., & deMarrais, K. (Eds.). (2001). *Educating young adolescent girls.* Mahwah, NJ: Erlbaum. The scope of this book is broader than the standard meaning of education because it also includes chapters on young women with disabilities, adolescent lesbians, and romantic relationships.

ANSWERS TO THE DEMONSTRATIONS

Demonstration 4.3: You can informally assess your feminist identity by adding together the ratings that you supplied for Items 1, 2, 3, 6, 7, and 9 and by subtracting the ratings that you supplied for Items 4, 5, 8, and 10. Higher scores indicate a stronger feminist identity.

Demonstration 4.4: Person 1 is a male; Person 2 is a female; Person 3 is a female; Person 4 is a male.

ANSWERS TO THE TRUE-FALSE STATEMENTS

1. False (p. 116); 2. False (p. 117); 3. False (p. 126); 4. False (pp. 127–128); 5. False (pp. 129–130); 6. True (p. 131); 7. True (p. 132); 8. True (p. 135); 9. False (p. 136); 10. True (p. 140).

© Ron Levine/Getty Images

5 | Gender Comparisons in Cognitive Abilities and Attitudes About Success

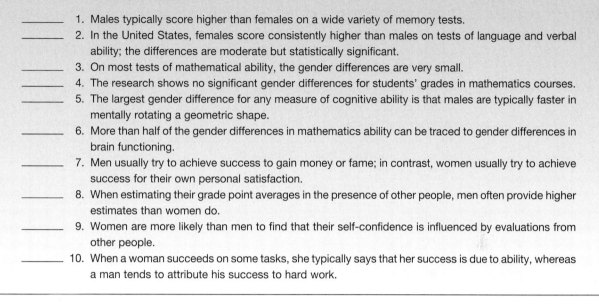

True or False?

_____ 1. Males typically score higher than females on a wide variety of memory tests.

_____ 2. In the United States, females score consistently higher than males on tests of language and verbal ability; the differences are moderate but statistically significant.

_____ 3. On most tests of mathematical ability, the gender differences are very small.

_____ 4. The research shows no significant gender differences for students' grades in mathematics courses.

_____ 5. The largest gender difference for any measure of cognitive ability is that males are typically faster in mentally rotating a geometric shape.

_____ 6. More than half of the gender differences in mathematics ability can be traced to gender differences in brain functioning.

_____ 7. Men usually try to achieve success to gain money or fame; in contrast, women usually try to achieve success for their own personal satisfaction.

_____ 8. When estimating their grade point averages in the presence of other people, men often provide higher estimates than women do.

_____ 9. Women are more likely than men to find that their self-confidence is influenced by evaluations from other people.

_____ 10. When a woman succeeds on some tasks, she typically says that her success is due to ability, whereas a man tends to attribute his success to hard work.

Shortly before I began to write this chapter, the front page of the *Boston Globe* featured an article about economist Dr. Lawrence Summers, the president of Harvard University (Bombardieri, 2005). Summers had been invited to address a conference sponsored by the National Bureau of Economic Research, and he chose to discuss why there are so few high-ranking women in science and engineering at the most prestigious universities.

According to Summers, one of the reasons why male faculty members are more successful at Harvard than female faculty members in science and engineering is that women do not have the same innate ability as men in those disciplines. Summers then proposed that some gender differences in abilities—which researchers had previously attributed to socialization—might really be explained by genetic factors (Summers, 2005). The Harvard faculty later voted "no confidence" in Dr. Summers, and he resigned in February 2006 (R. Wilson, 2006). Unfortunately, Dr. Summers had not read the research on gender comparisons in mathematics ability.

When people who are not experts discuss gender comparisons in thinking, they almost always emphasize gender differences, ignoring the evidence for gender similarities. In addition, they often suggest biological factors to explain these gender differences. People who study the psychology of women need to know the research in this area because it demonstrates that men and women are remarkably similar in most of these cognitive skills (Theme 1). Furthermore, the popular media also highlight biological explanations for the small number of gender differences, consistent with our culture's current emphasis on biology. You need to know, however, that social and cultural explanations play a more important role than biology does.

In the present chapter, we will explore two broad questions regarding gender comparisons:

1. Do women and men differ in their cognitive abilities?
2. Do women and men differ in their attitudes related to motivation and success?

By addressing these two questions, we will gain some background information needed to answer another important question. In Chapter 7, we'll see that men and women tend to pursue different careers. For example, men are much more likely than women to become engineers. Can we trace this gender difference in career choice to major cognitive differences (such as ability in math) or to major differences in motivation (such as attitudes about success)? We will focus here on the school-related comparisons that assess intellectual abilities and achievement motivation. In contrast, in Chapter 6, we will emphasize interpersonal gender comparisons, specifically, social and personality characteristics. Can we trace gender differences in career preferences to gender differences in some important personality qualities, such as communication patterns, helpfulness, and aggressiveness?

BACKGROUND ON GENDER COMPARISONS

Before we address any of these specific gender comparisons, we need to consider some research issues that are relevant here and in Chapter 6. We'll first examine several cautions about the way psychologists conduct their research and interpret it. Then we'll briefly describe the meta-analysis approach to summarizing a large number of studies that focus on the same topic.

CAUTIONS ABOUT RESEARCH ON GENDER COMPARISONS

As we saw in Chapter 1, a variety of biases can have a powerful effect when psychologists conduct research about either women or gender comparisons. In addition, we need to be cautious about interpreting the results. Let's consider five specific cautions that are relevant to the current chapter:

1. People's expectations can influence results.
2. Biased samples can affect results.
3. The scores of males and females typically produce overlapping distributions.
4. Researchers seldom find gender differences in all situations.
5. The cognitive gender differences are not large enough to be relevant for your career choice.

Let's look at each caution in more detail.

1. People's expectations can influence results. As we noted in Chapter 1, biases can interfere at every stage of the research process. For example, researchers who expect to find gender differences will often tend to find them.

The participants also have expectations, including expectations about cognitive gender differences (Caplan & Caplan, 1999; Nosek et al., 2002). We considered this issue in Chapter 2, in connection with stereotype threat.

2. Biased samples can affect results. Almost all the research on cognitive abilities focuses on college students (D. F. Halpern, 2000). We know almost nothing about adults who don't attend college. In addition, most of the research on gender comparisons examines European American samples in the United States and Canada (Eccles et al., 2003; McGuinness, 1998). Our conclusions about gender comparisons might be different if the research participants were more diverse.

3. The scores of males and females typically produce overlapping distributions. To discuss the concept of overlap, we need to consider frequency distributions. A **frequency distribution** tells us how many people in a sample receive each score.

Imagine that we give a vocabulary test to a group of women and men and that we use their scores to construct a frequency distribution for each gender, as Figure 5.1 shows. Notice the tiny section in which the frequency distribution for the males overlaps with the frequency distribution for the females. In Figure 5.1, males and females received the same scores only in one small region, roughly between 54 and 66. When the two distributions show such a small overlap, this pattern tells us that the two distributions are very different. As you can see in this figure, the average woman received a score of 80, whereas the average man received a score of 40.

In real life, however, distributions of female and male characteristics rarely show the separation illustrated in Figure 5.1. They are much more likely to show a large overlap (Eccles et al., 2003; Gallagher & Kaufman, 2004b; A. J. Stewart & McDermott, 2004), as Figure 5.2 illustrates. Notice that males and females receive the same scores in the large region that extends roughly between 35 and 85. As we have often emphasized in our discussion of Theme 1, men and women are reasonably similar, which means that their scores will overlap considerably. Notice in Figure 5.2 that the average woman received a score of 63 and that the average man received a score of 57.

This 6-point difference between the average scores looks trivial when we compare it to the difference within each distribution, a range of about 50 points. As Theme 4 emphasizes, women differ widely from one another in cognitive abilities; men also show wide variation (A. J. Stewart & McDermott, 2004).

4. Researchers seldom find gender differences in all situations. You are certainly familiar with this issue from our earlier discussion of Theme 1. Throughout this chapter as well, you will notice that we cannot make general statements about gender differences. Instead, the gender differences often disappear when we test certain kinds of people or when we look at particular

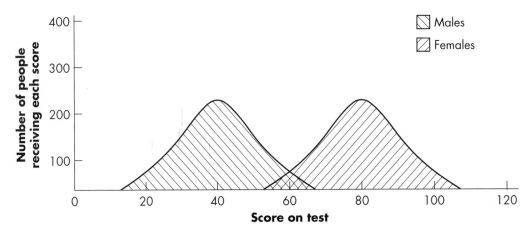

FIGURE 5.1 | SCORES ACHIEVED BY MALES AND FEMALES ON A HYPOTHETICAL TEST. THE SMALL OVERLAP INDICATES A LARGE GENDER DIFFERENCE.

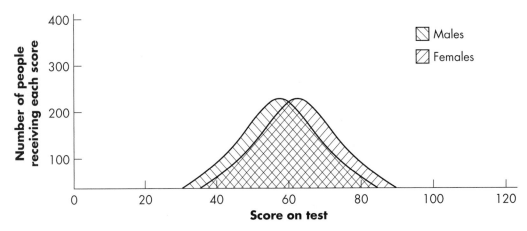

FIGURE 5.2 | SCORES ACHIEVED BY MALES AND FEMALES ON A HYPOTHETICAL TEST. THE LARGE OVERLAP INDICATES A SMALL GENDER DIFFERENCE.

situations (D. F. Halpern, 2006; Hyde & Mezulis, 2001; B. Lott, 1996). This observation suggests that gender differences can be modified; they are not inevitable (D. F. Halpern, 2004a). In short, many men and women have remarkably similar psychological characteristics in many situations.

5. *The cognitive gender differences are not large enough to be relevant for your career choice.*   For instance, women's scores may be slightly lower than men's scores on some tasks that require spatial skills. For example, 7% of males and 3% of females typically place in the top 5% of the population (Hyde, 1981). In other words, about 30% of the people with superior spatial abilities are female.

Some people argue that women seldom pursue careers in engineering because they lack spatial skills. At present, only 12% of U.S. engineers are women (Bureau of Labor Statistics, 2004c). This 12% is much lower than the 30% we would expect if high spatial ability were the only requirement for becoming an engineer. We need to search for additional explanations if we want to account for the small number of women in such fields as engineering.

THE META-ANALYSIS APPROACH TO SUMMARIZING MULTIPLE STUDIES

When psychologists want to obtain an overview of a specific topic, they typically review the research by examining all the studies on that topic. For many years, psychologists who wanted to draw general conclusions about gender comparisons used the box-score approach to reviewing research. When using the **box-score approach** (also called the **counting approach**), researchers read through all the appropriate studies on a given topic and draw conclusions based on a tally of their outcomes. Specifically, how many studies show no gender differences, how many show higher scores for women, and how many show higher scores for men? Unfortunately, however, the box-score approach often produces ambiguous tallies. Suppose that researchers locate 16 relevant studies; 8 of these studies find no gender differences, 2 show higher scores for women, and 6 show higher scores for men. One researcher might conclude that no gender differences exist, whereas another might conclude that men score somewhat higher. The box-score approach does not provide a systematic method for combining individual studies.

Meta-analysis, the more useful alternative, provides a statistical method for combining numerous studies on a single topic. Researchers first try to locate all appropriate studies on the topic. Then they perform a statistical analysis that combines the results from all these studies. This analysis calculates the size of the overall difference between two groups of people, such as females and males. For example, for verbal ability, a meta-analysis can combine numerous previous studies into one enormous superstudy that can provide a general picture of whether gender has an overall effect on verbal ability.

A meta-analysis yields a number known as effect size, or d. For instance, if the meta-analysis of numerous studies shows that males and females received exactly the same overall score, the d would be zero. Now consider the d for the gender difference in height; here, the d is 2.0. This is a huge difference! In fact, the overlap between the male and female distributions for height is only 11% (Kimball, 1995).

Compared to a d of 2.0, the d values for psychological gender comparisons are relatively small. In an important study, Janet Hyde (2005a) examined 128 different meta-analysis measures that focused on gender comparisons in cognitive skills. She found that 30% of these gender comparisons were in the "close-to-zero" range (d less than 0.11), 48% had a small effect size ($d = 0.11$ to 0.35), 15% had a moderate effect size ($d = 0.36$ to 0.65), and only 8% had a large effect size (d greater than 0.65). In other words, the clear majority of these gender comparisons showed either no difference or a small gender difference. With all these important methodological issues in mind, let's now consider the actual research on cognitive gender comparisons.

Section Summary

Background on Gender Comparisons

1. In considering research on gender comparisons, we need to emphasize that expectations and biased samples can influence results.

2. Frequency distributions for the scores of males and females typically show a large overlap, so that most females and males receive similar scores.

3. Gender differences that are present in some situations are typically absent in others; also, the cognitive gender differences are not large enough to be relevant when people make career choices.

4. In contrast to the earlier box-score approach, the meta-analysis technique provides a systematic statistical method for integrating studies on a single topic and for drawing conclusions about that topic. This technique demonstrates that few gender comparisons show a large difference.

COGNITIVE ABILITIES

We'll begin our examination of the research by focusing on cognitive abilities. Later in the chapter, we will focus on topics related to achievement motivation. In this current section, we'll first examine some areas that show gender similarities, and then we'll focus on four kinds of cognitive abilities for which we have some evidence of gender differences: (1) memory, (2) verbal ability, (3) mathematics ability, and (4) spatial ability.

COGNITIVE ABILITIES THAT SHOW NO CONSISTENT GENDER DIFFERENCES

Before we examine the four areas that show occasional gender differences, let's first consider some general categories where gender similarities are typical.

GENERAL INTELLIGENCE.   One major area in which females and males are similar is general intelligence, as measured by total scores on an IQ test (e.g., Geary, 1998; D. F. Halpern, 2001; Herlitz & Yonker, 2002; Stumpf, 1995). Many intelligence tests have been constructed by eliminating items on which gender differences are found. As a result, the final versions of the intelligence tests usually show gender similarities. Other research also shows gender similarities in general knowledge about history, geography, and other basic information (Meinz & Salthouse, 1998).

Furthermore, let's dispel a popular belief. The media often claim that women are better than men at "multitasking," or performing two tasks at the same time. However, researchers in cognitive psychology have not found systematic gender differences in this area (D. E. Meyer, personal communication, 2005).

COMPLEX COGNITIVE TASKS.   Several other challenging intellectual tasks show no overall gender differences. For example, males and females are equally competent when they form concepts and when they solve a variety of complex problems (Kimura, 1992; Meinz & Salthouse, 1998). Males and females are also similar in their performance on a variety of creativity tasks (Baer, 1999; Ruscio et al., 1998).

We have seen that women and men are typically similar in their general intelligence and complex cognitive abilities. Keep these important similarities in mind as we explore the four areas in which modest gender differences have sometimes been identified.

MEMORY ABILITY

Do women and men differ in their ability to remember information? As you will see throughout this chapter, the best answer is typically, "It depends." Specifically, women are better on some memory tasks, men are better on other tasks, and the two genders are similar on still other tasks. Furthermore, I have not been able to locate any meta-analysis of gender comparisons in memory skills. Therefore, I'll describe some recent studies on different kinds of tasks.

In one kind of memory task, people see a list of words. After a delay, they are asked to remember the words. In general, women are somewhat more accurate on this kind of memory task (Herlitz et al., 1997, 1999; Herlitz & Yonker, 2002; Larsson et al., 2003; Meinz & Salthouse, 1998). However, the nature of the words on the list may make a difference (Herrmann et al., 1992).

For instance, Colley and her colleagues (2002) gave women and men a list of items to remember. The list was labeled either "Grocery store" or "Hardware store." The items on the list were equally likely for both kinds of stores (for example, *nuts, salt,* and *disinfectant*). This study included many different gender comparisons. However, we will consider the results for students who received neutral instructions before seeing the list of words. As you can see from Figure 5.3, women recalled many more items than men from the "grocery list," but women and men recalled a similar number of items from the "hardware list."

In another kind of memory task, people are asked to remember events, rather than words. Again, the pattern of gender differences depends on the nature of the material. For example, David Rubin and his colleagues (1999) found that men were more accurate than women in remembering which teams competed in previous World Series and which candidate lost each presidential election, consistent with the stereotype that men are more interested in sports and politics. However, these researchers found no gender differences in remembering who won the Academy Awards.

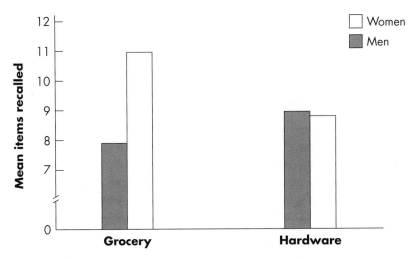

FIGURE 5.3 | PERFORMANCE ON A MEMORY TASK, AS A FUNCTION OF PARTICIPANTS' GENDER AND THE KIND OF MEMORY TASK.

Sources: Based on Colley et al. (2002).

Furthermore, women are more accurate than men in remembering events from their own lives (Colley et al., 2002; Fivush & Nelson, 2004). This gender difference is consistent with the stereotype that women are more interested in social and emotional issues. Also, as you might recall from Chapter 3, mothers are more likely to discuss emotional topics with their daughters, rather than their sons. As a result, girls have more opportunities to practice remembering these personal events (Fivush & Nelson, 2004).

Let's now shift to memory tasks for nonverbal material. Women tend to be more accurate than men in recognizing faces (Herlitz & Yonker, 2002; Lewin & Herlitz, 2002). Women also seem to be more accurate in recognizing odors (Larsson et al., 2003). However, men and women are similar in remembering abstract shapes (Herlitz & Yonker, 2002).

We cannot draw any clear-cut conclusions about gender differences in memory until a meta-analysis has been conducted. However, the pattern of gender differences suggests that both males and females have an advantage in the areas for which they have greater familiarity or expertise. The general research in cognitive psychology shows that people with expertise in a specific area remember that material much more accurately than nonexperts (Matlin, 2005).

VERBAL ABILITY

Females score somewhat higher than males on a small number of verbal tasks, although the overall gender similarities are more striking. Let's look at three areas of research: general studies, standardized language tests, and research on reading disabilities.

GENERAL VERBAL ABILITY.   Some research suggests that girls have larger vocabularies than boys have before the age of 2, but these gender differences disappear by 3 years of age (N. Eisenberg et al., 1996; Huttenlocher et al., 1991; Jacklin & Maccoby, 1983). The similarities are more striking than the differences when we consider young school-age children (Cahan & Ganor, 1995; Maccoby & Jacklin, 1974). Therefore, if you plan to teach elementary school, the girls and boys in your class should be comparable in their language skills.

When we consider adolescents and adults, the research shows gender similarities in such areas as spelling, vocabulary, word associations, and reading comprehension (Collaer & Hines, 1995; D. F. Halpern, 1997; Hedges & Nowell, 1995; Ritter, 2004). In some specific areas, the gender differences demonstrate statistical significance but not practical significance (see page 24). For example, females seem to be somewhat better at **verbal fluency**, or naming objects that meet certain criteria, such as beginning with the letter S (D. F. Halpern, 2000, 2001; D. F. Halpern & Tan, 2001).

In recent years, females have scored higher on tests of writing ability (Geary, 1998; D. F. Halpern, 2000, 2004a; Pajares et al., 1999). However, it isn't clear whether this gender difference has practical implications for women's success in the classroom and on the job.

We emphasized earlier that meta-analysis is the ideal statistical tool for combining the results of a number of studies on a specific topic. Janet Hyde and Marcia Linn (1988) conducted a meta-analysis on overall gender comparisons in verbal ability. The average effect size (d) was only 0.11, just slightly favoring females. This value is so close to 0 that Hyde and Linn concluded that overall gender differences do not exist. Other researchers have reached the same conclusions, based on standardized test scores for U.S. students (Feingold, 1988; Hedges & Nowell, 1995; Willingham & Cole, 1997). Ironically, researchers have studied the two general areas in which females occasionally have the advantage—verbal abilities and memory—less extensively than spatial or mathematical skills (D. F. Halpern, 2000). An up-to-date meta-analysis would help us understand whether any gender differences in verbal ability are noteworthy.

Let's consider some tests that are especially relevant for college students. For instance, you may have taken the SAT when you applied for college admission. The verbal portion of this test covers skills such as reading comprehension and vocabulary. Gender differences on this part of the SAT are minimal. For example, in 2003, the average SAT verbal score was 503 for women and 512 for men ("The Nation: Students," 2004). Gender differences are also minimal for the Advanced Placement examinations in English language, English literature, and all foreign languages (Stumpf & Stanley, 1998).

We've looked at gender comparisons in general verbal ability, from preschool up to college. Let's now explore the related topic of reading disabilities.

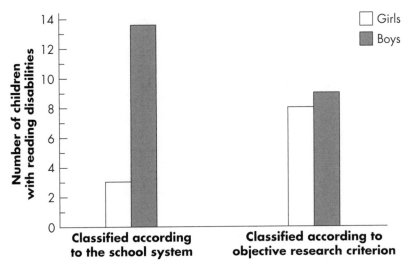

FIGURE 5.4 | NUMBER OF BOYS AND GIRLS WITH READING DISABILITIES, ACCORDING TO THE SCHOOLS' CRITERION AND THE OBJECTIVE RESEARCH CRITERION.

READING DISABILITIES. Some research suggests that males are more likely than females to be labeled as having language problems. For instance, school systems report reading disabilities about five times as often for boys as for girls (D. F. Halpern, 2000).

An important study by Sally Shaywitz and her colleagues (1990) used more objective methods to categorize students. According to these researchers, the term **reading disability** refers to poor reading skills that are not accounted for by the level of general intelligence. Therefore, they defined reading disability in objective, statistical terms.[1] The target population for this study included children in 12 cities throughout the state of Connecticut.

When the school systems evaluated the two gender groups, they classified roughly four times as many boys as having reading disabilities. You can see this enormous gender difference at the left side of Figure 5.4. This 4:1 ratio was consistent with earlier reports (D. F. Halpern, 2000). Then Shaywitz and her colleagues recalculated the data, using the objective statistical criterion for reading disabilities. With this criterion, roughly the same number of boys and girls met the criterion of having reading disabilities.

Why do the schools identify reading problems in so many more boys than girls? Shaywitz and her colleagues (1990) proposed that teachers target more active, less attentive boys as having reading disabilities. These boys may be

---

[1]Specifically, the researchers used a child's IQ to predict what his or her score should be on a standardized test of reading achievement. Any child whose actual score on the reading test was more than 1.5 standard deviations below the predicted score was categorized as having a reading disability. A score that was 1.5 standard deviations below the prediction meant that the child had a reading score in the bottom 7% of all those children at his or her IQ level.

referred to a reading clinic on the basis of their behavior, rather than their poor reading skills. An equally disturbing problem is that many girls probably have genuine reading disabilities, but they sit quietly in their seats and hide their disabilities (J. T. E. Richardson, 1997a). These well-behaved, neglected girls will miss out on the additional tutoring in reading that could help them thrive in school. As Chapter 3 emphasized, girls are often invisible in our schools, and they lose out on educational opportunities.

Throughout this section on verbal skills, we have seen a general pattern of minimal gender differences, based on a variety of measures. In addition, gender differences in reading disabilities can be traced—at least partly—to a bias in teachers' referrals to reading clinics.

MATHEMATICS ABILITY

Mathematics is the cognitive ability that receives the most attention from both researchers and the popular press. Media reports would lead you to expect large gender differences favoring males. Instead, as you'll see, most of the research shows gender similarities in math ability, and females actually receive higher grades in math courses. Males perform substantially better than females only on the mathematics section of the SAT.

GENERAL MATHEMATICS ABILITY. Most comparisons of males' and females' ability on mathematics achievement tests show gender similarities, although males may perform better on some problem-solving tasks (Feingold, 1988; Geary, 1998; Hedges & Nowell, 1995). Consider, for example, a meta-analysis of 100 studies, based on standardized-test scores of more than 3 million people. (This analysis did not include math SAT scores, which we'll consider shortly.) By averaging across all samples and all tests, Hyde and her colleagues (1990) found a d of only 0.15. (See Figure 5.5.) As you can see, the two distributions are almost identical.

The National Center for Education Statistics (2004) reported the scores for eighth-grade students on a standardized mathematics test. The report did not discuss whether any gender differences were statistically significant. However, part of this report included average scores from 34 different countries throughout the world. Interestingly, the boys' average was higher than the girls' average in 16 countries, the girls' average was higher than boys' average in 16 countries, and girls and boys had the same averages in 2 countries.

GRADES IN MATHEMATICS COURSES. I often ask students in my classes to raise their hands if they have heard that males receive higher average scores on the math section of the SAT. The hands fly up. Then I ask how many have heard that females receive higher average grades in mathematics courses. The hands all drop. In fact, representative studies show that females earn higher grades in fifth-, sixth-, eighth-, and tenth-grade mathematics as well as in college math courses (S. Beyer, 1999a; Crombie et al., 2005; D. F. Halpern, 2004a, 2006; Kimball, 1989, 1995; Willingham & Cole, 1997). Females also earn higher

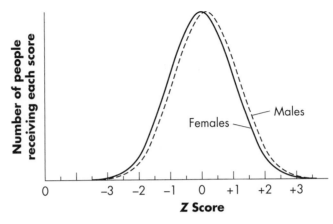

FIGURE 5.5 | PERFORMANCE OF FEMALES AND MALES ON ALL MATHEMATICS TESTS EXCEPT THE SAT, SHOWING AN EFFECT SIZE (d) OF 0.15.

Sources: From Hyde, J. S., et al. (1990). Gender differences in mathematics performance: A meta-analysis. *Psychological Bulletin, 107,* 139–155. © 1990 by the American Psychological Association. Reprinted with permission.

grades in related areas, such as high-school science courses and college-level statistics (C. I. Brooks, 1987; Brownlow et al., 2000; D. F. Halpern, 2004a; M. Stewart, 1998).

Meredith Kimball (1989, 1995) proposed that females perform better when dealing with familiar situations, such as exams on material covered in a mathematics course. In contrast, males perform better when dealing with unfamiliar situations, especially the kinds of math problems included on the SAT. In any event, Kimball points out that females' high grades in math courses deserve wider publicity. This publicity would encourage females, their parents, and their teachers to be more confident about girls' and women's competence in mathematics.

THE SAT.   Of all the research in cognitive gender differences, the topic that has received the most media attention is performance on the math portion of the SAT. For instance, the data for 2003 show that women received an average score of 503, in contrast to 537 for men ("The Nation: Students," 2004).

However, is the math SAT test a valid index of ability in mathematics? A test has high **validity** if it measures what it is supposed to measure. For example, the SAT is supposed to predict students' grades in college courses. The SAT has high *overall* validity because it does predict college grades. However, the math portion of the SAT has a specific validity problem because it predicts that women will receive lower grades in college math courses than they actually do receive (De Lisi & McGillicuddy-de Lisi, 2002; Leonard & Jiang, 1999; Spelke, 2005; Willingham & Cole, 1997). For example, Wainer and Steinberg (1992) matched males and females in terms of the grades that they earned in college mathematics courses. Then the researchers looked back at the math SAT scores that these students had earned. They found that the women had received math SAT scores that were an average of 33 points lower than those of the men with whom they were matched. For example, suppose that Susan Jones and Robert Smith both received a B in their college calculus course. Looking back at their math SAT scores, we might find that Susan had a score of 600, compared to 633 for Robert. Susan's math SAT score would have substantially underestimated her grade in calculus. Based on validity studies such as these, some colleges and universities have stopped using the SAT or have modified the math SAT requirements (Hoover, 2004; Linn & Kessel, 1995).

SPATIAL ABILITY

Most people are familiar with the first two cognitive abilities discussed in this chapter: verbal ability and mathematics ability. Spatial abilities are less well known. **Spatial abilities** include understanding, perceiving, and manipulating shapes and figures. Spatial ability is important in many everyday activities, such as playing electronic games, reading road maps, and arranging furniture in an apartment.

Most researchers agree that spatial ability is not unitary (Caplan & Caplan, 1999; Chipman, 2004). Instead, it has several different components: Spatial visualization, spatial perception, and mental rotation. Most researchers also agree that mental rotation tests are the only spatial tasks that reveal large gender differences. Let's consider each of these components separately.

SPATIAL VISUALIZATION. Tasks that use **spatial visualization** require complex processing of spatially presented information. For example, an embedded-figure test requires you to locate a particular pattern or object that is hidden in a larger design. Demonstration 5.1a illustrates three examples of an embedded-figure test. As a child, you may have tried similar games, perhaps searching for faces in a picture of a woodland scene.

Many individual studies and meta-analyses have shown that males and females perform fairly similarly on tasks requiring spatial visualization (e.g., Hedges & Nowell, 1995; Sanz de Acedo Lizarraga & García Ganuza, 2003; Scali & Brownlow, 2001; Scali et al., 2000). For example, one meta-analysis of 116 studies produced a d of 0.19, a small gender difference suggesting that males are slightly better on this task (Voyer et al., 1995). Glance again at Figure 5.5 for a graph of a similar effect size ($d = 0.15$). As you can see, the overlap for the two distributions is substantial.

Let's consider one component of spatial visualization, the ability to learn map information. Some studies find that males perform better, but other similar studies report no gender differences (Beatty & Bruellman, 1987; Bosco et al., 2004; C. Davies, 2002; Galea & Kimura, 1993; Henrie et al., 1997; Lawton & Kallai, 2002). Related research indicates that males are better than females in finding their way back to the starting point from a distant location. However, other similar studies reveal no gender differences (Lawton, 1996; Lawton et al.,

Demonstration 5.1

EXAMPLES OF
TESTS OF SPATIAL
ABILITY

Try these three kinds of tests of spatial ability.

a. *Embedded-Figure Test*. In each of the three units, study the figure on the left. Then cover it up and try to find where it is hidden in the figure on the right. You may need to shift the left-hand figure to locate it in the right-hand figure.

b. *Water-Level Test*. Imagine that this woman is drinking from a glass that is half-filled with water. Draw a line across the glass to indicate where the water line belongs.

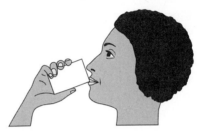

c. *Mental Rotation Test*. If you mentally rotate the figure on the left-hand side, which of the five figures on the right-hand side would you obtain?

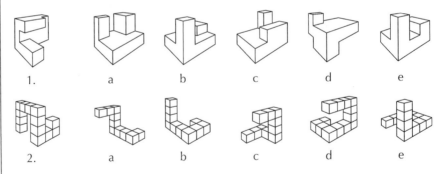

The answers to these three tests appear at the end of the chapter.

1996; Lawton & Morrin, 1999; Saucier et al., 2002; Schmitz, 1999). As you can see, the picture is mixed; gender differences are not consistent.

SPATIAL PERCEPTION. In **spatial perception** tests, participants are asked to identify a horizontal or vertical location without being distracted by irrelevant information. One example of this skill, a water-level test, appears in Demonstration 5.1b. The rod-and-frame test also assesses spatial perception; in this test, participants sit in a darkened room and look at a single rod, which is surrounded by a rectangular frame. The participants are instructed to adjust the rod so that it is in a true vertical position, without being distracted by the cues from the obviously tilted frame. Meta-analyses of gender comparisons for spatial perception show that males receive somewhat higher scores; effect sizes are in the range of 0.40 (Nordvik & Amponsah, 1998; Voyer, Nolan, & Voyer, 2000; Voyer, Voyer, & Bryden, 1995). However, one study found no gender differences on the water-level test (Herlitz et al., 1999). Still another study found that gender differences were erased following a brief training session (Vasta et al., 1996).

MENTAL ROTATION. A test of **mental rotation** measures the ability to rotate a two- or three-dimensional figure rapidly and accurately. The two problems of Demonstration 5.1c illustrate this skill. The mental rotation task produces the largest gender differences of all skills, when measured in terms of performance speed. The effect sizes are generally in the range of 0.50 to 0.90 (D. F. Halpern, 2001, 2004a; Nordvik & Amponsah, 1998; Ritter, 2004). Even though the gender differences for mental rotation tasks are relatively large, we still need to keep the data in perspective. An effect size as large as 0.90 is certainly larger than any other cognitive effect size. However, 0.90 is trivial compared to the effect size of 2.00 for height, discussed earlier (Kimball, 1995). Also, some studies in Canada, the United States, and Spain report no consistent gender differences (Brownlow & Miderski, 2002; Brownlow et al., 2003; D. F. Halpern & Tan, 2001; Loring-Meier & Halpern, 1999; Robert & Chevrier, 2003; Sanz de Acedo Lizarraga & García Ganuza, 2003).

Other research shows that gender differences on mental rotation tasks depend on how the task is described to participants. For example, Sharps and his colleagues (1994) found that men performed much better than women when the instructions emphasized the usefulness of these spatial abilities in stereotypically masculine professions, such as piloting military aircraft. When the instructions emphasized how these abilities could help in stereotypically feminine occupations, such as interior decoration, the gender differences disappeared.

Furthermore, Favreau (1993) pointed out that statistically significant gender differences often arise from studies in which most males and females actually receive similar scores. Look at Figure 5.6, which Favreau derived from earlier research by Kail and his colleagues (1979). As you can see, most males and females received scores between 2 and 8. The statistically significant gender difference can be traced almost entirely to 20% of the females who had very slow mental rotation speeds (Favreau & Everett, 1996).

What can we conclude about spatial abilities? Even the most well-established gender difference—mental rotation—turns out to be elusive. The gender differences seem to decrease when the instructions emphasize that a spatial skill is related to a traditionally feminine area of interest. Furthermore, difficulty on this task seems to be limited to a small proportion of females. In

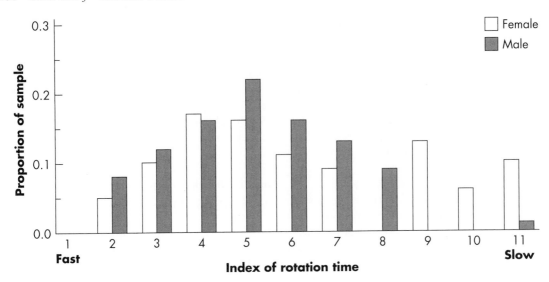

FIGURE 5.6   AMOUNT OF TIME REQUIRED TO MENTALLY ROTATE A GEOMETRIC FIGURE, SHOWING A LARGE OVERLAP BETWEEN MALES' SCORES AND FEMALES' SCORES. (NOTE: FASTER SCORES REPRESENT BETTER PERFORMANCE.)

Sources: Based on Favreau (1993) and Kail et al. (1979).

short, this erratic gender difference should not have major implications for women's lives—and it certainly cannot explain why only 12% of U.S. engineers are female.

EXPLAINING THE GENDER COMPARISONS

We began this chapter by considering a large number of cognitive skills on which males and females are similar. Then we saw that the gender differences for most cognitive skills are minimal. However, the gender differences on some mathematical and spatial tasks are somewhat larger, so we need to consider some potential reasons for the difference.

Let's first consider the biological explanations and then turn to the social explanations. However, as Diane Halpern (2004a) emphasizes, the biological factors and learning experience can influence each other. For instance, if you take several math courses, in which you solve numerous complex math problems, then this learning experience will influence the structure of the neurons in your brain. Once the structures in your brain are well developed, you will be more skilled in solving math problems. This increased skill can lead you to choose additional learning experiences in mathematics. As you read the following information, keep in mind that the biological and social factors cannot be divided into two completely separate lists (D. F. Halpern & Ikier, 2002).

BIOLOGICAL EXPLANATIONS.   It's ironic that the media and some researchers are extremely eager to embrace a biological explanation (Brescoll & LaFrance,

2004), even though gender differences are not well established.[2] Dr. Lawrence Summers clearly supported a biological approach (see page 145). In a clear presentation of biological perspectives, Diane Halpern (2000) divided the biological explanations into three major categories: genetics, sex hormones, and brain organization. Let's consider each of these.

1. A genetic explanation suggests that spatial ability might be a recessive trait carried on the X chromosome. However, research has not supported this idea that genetic factors directly produce cognitive gender differences (D. F. Halpern, 2000; J. T. E. Richardson, 1997b).

2. Hormones are critically important before birth and during puberty. Could the level of hormones in males and females also account for gender differences in cognitive skills? Here, the results are often complex or contradictory (Hampson & Moffat, 2004; J. T. E. Richardson, 1997b). For example, men seem to perform better on spatial tasks if they have low levels of male hormones, whereas women seem to perform better if they have high levels of these hormones (Kimura, 1987).

3. The last category of biological explanations focuses on brain organization. Many researchers who favor biological explanations tend to emphasize gender differences in brain lateralization. **Lateralization** means that the two halves (or hemispheres) of the brain function somewhat differently. In humans, the left hemisphere typically specializes in language or verbal tasks, whereas the right hemisphere typically specializes in spatial tasks. (For easy recall, remember that *left* and *language* both begin with the letter *l*.) For most people, either hemisphere can process both language and spatial material. However, the left hemisphere tends to be faster and more accurate on language tasks, and the right hemisphere tends to be faster and more accurate on spatial tasks.

A typical lateralization theory might argue that males use only the right hemisphere to perform spatial tasks, whereas females may use both hemispheres to perform all cognitive tasks (Gur et al., 1999; D. F. Halpern, 2000; M. Hines, 2004). According to this argument, when females work on a spatial task, a smaller portion of the right hemisphere is available to process spatial information. As a result, they perform the spatial problem more slowly.

However, the research does not provide convincing evidence that males actually *do* have more complete lateralization. For example, one study was widely cited as "proof" that men's brains show more lateralization

---

[2]Biological factors—such as genetics and brain structure—are clearly important in accounting for individual differences in various cognitive abilities. For example, these biological factors help explain why some people (both male and female) earn high scores on a math test, whereas other people (again both male and female) earn low scores. As emphasized in this discussion, however, biological factors cannot adequately account for gender differences.

(B. A. Shaywitz et al., 1995). The popular media failed to emphasize that only 11 of the 19 female participants showed the balanced-hemisphere pattern proposed by lateralization theory (Favreau, 1997).

Still other studies report gender similarities in lateralization or else only weak gender differences (D. F. Halpern & Collaer, 2005; Medland et al., 2002). However, you'll never read about them in your local newspaper. For instance, Frost and her colleagues (1999) studied language processing in a large sample of males and females. The brain-imaging data revealed gender similarities: *Both* groups—women and men—showed strong lateralization, with most activity in the left hemisphere (Gernsbacher & Kaschak, 2003). In addition, even if we could demonstrate major gender differences in brain lateralization, no one has yet shown that these brain differences actually *cause* the gender differences on cognitive tests (D. F. Halpern, 2000; Hyde, 1996b; Hyde & Mezulis, 2001).

Conceivably, at some time in the future, researchers might identify a biological component that helps explain gender differences. However, we need to remember that the differences requiring explanation are neither widespread nor extraordinarily large. Indeed, biological explanations may be more powerful than they need to be to explain such small and inconsistent gender differences (J. B. Caplan & Caplan, 2004). Relying on biological explanations is like trying to kill a fly with a baseball bat when a subtler instrument, such as a fly swatter, would be more appropriate.

Furthermore, Diane Halpern and her coauthors (2004) make an important point. As we'll see on page 163, mathematically talented boys usually spend more time on math activities than mathematically talented girls. This extra math experience can actually change the structure of the brain. We therefore need to be cautious about assuming that males and females are born with differently structured brains.

SOCIAL EXPLANATIONS.   Many theorists have provided social explanations for cognitive gender differences. These explanations can be divided into two categories: (1) different experiences for males and females and (2) different attitudes among males and females.

Experience with a subject clearly influences a person's competence. If you've had frequent experience with maps and other spatial tasks, you'll perform a mental rotation task relatively quickly and accurately (M. Crawford & Chaffin, 1997; D. F. Halpern & Ikier, 2002; Sanz de Acedo Lizarraga & García Ganuza, 2003). Let's examine these gender differences in experience.

1. When elementary textbooks show how people use mathematics, they often include more pictures of boys than girls. The girls may also be shown primarily in helping roles (Kimball, 1995). Similarly, computer magazines include more pictures of males than females. When women *are* shown, the text of the ad is likely to include a stereotypical comment, such as the attractive colors produced by the printer (Burlingame-Lee & Canetto, 2005). These ads imply

that females focus on superficial "feminine" aspects of computers, rather than their usefulness in math and science. As Chapters 2 and 3 emphasized, images of competent females can boost the performance of girls and women. If they have more positive images, role models, and experiences, they may realize that females can excel in mathematics and related areas (Marx & Roman, 2002; R. L. Pierce & Kite, 1999).

2. Parents and teachers may provide different experiences for males and females (Wigfield et al., 2002). For example, parents spend more time explaining science concepts to their sons than to their daughters (Crowley et al., 2001).

3. Males and females now take a similar number of math courses during high school (Chipman, 2004; De Lisi & McGillicuddy-De Lisi, 2002). However, they differ in the amount of experience they have with mathematics and spatial activities outside school. Boy who are highly talented in math spend more time on math-related activities, compared to equally talented girls (D. F. Halpern, 2000; Newcombe et al., 2002; Voyer et al., 2000). Boys are also more likely to belong to a chess club, be members of a math team, learn about numbers in sports, and have more experience with computers (J. Cooper & Weaver, 2003; Hyde, 1996a; J. E. Jacobs et al., 2004). However, Gilbert and her colleagues (2004) describe an intervention project, which successfully increased young women's experience with computers and technology.

We have reviewed three ways in which males and females may differ in mathematics *experience*. Let's now turn to another social explanation, which focuses on gender differences in *attitudes* about mathematics.

1. Parents' and teachers' attitudes may influence their children's self-confidence indirectly. For instance, if parents hold strong stereotypes about females' poor performance in math, they may convey these stereotypes to their daughters (J. E. Jacobs et al., 2004; Räty, 2003; Räty et al., 2002). Teachers may have especially low expectations for Black and Latina girls (S. Jones, 2003).

2. By the age of 11—or even earlier—boys often perceive themselves as more competent in math than girls do, even though boys may actually receive lower grades (Byrnes, 2004; Crombie et al., 2005; J. E. Jacobs et al., 2002; Skaalvik & Skaalvik, 2004). In addition, boys typically have more positive attitudes toward mathematics than girls do (E. M. Evans et al., 2002). However, we must be careful not to oversimplify the situation. Consistent with the theme of individual differences, women vary widely in their reactions toward math, and some women have very positive attitudes (J. B. Caplan & Caplan, 2004; Oswald & Harvey, 2003).

3. By about the age of 10, many students believe that math, computers, and science are primarily associated with males (J. Cooper & Weaver, 2003; Räty

et al., 2004; J. L. Smith et al., 2005; T. J. Smith et al., 2001). As noted in Chapter 3, people tend to prefer activities that are consistent with their gender role. Accordingly, many females may avoid math because it seems "too masculine."

4. Stereotype threat may decrease females' performance on mathematics and spatial tests. In Chapter 2, we introduced the concept of **stereotype threat**; if you belong to a group that is hampered by a negative stereotype—and you are reminded about your group membership—your performance may suffer (Davies & Spencer, 2004; K. L. Dion, 2003; C. M. Steele et al., 2002). Suppose that a young woman is about to take the mathematics test of the SAT. Stereotype threat can operate on important math tests like the SAT because, as Susan Chipman (2004) wrote, "It is clear that many people *do not want to believe* that girls and women can be good at mathematics" (p. 18).

As this young woman sits down, she thinks to herself, "This is a test where women just can't do well." She is likely to have many more negative thoughts than a young man with similar math ability (Cadinu et al., 2005). As a result, she might make more errors on this important test. (Be sure to review the important study by Shih and her colleagues, 1999, about stereotype threat, discussed on pages 68–69.)

Researchers have conducted numerous studies about stereotype threat (e.g., Good et al., 2003; D. F. Halpern & Tan, 2001; Schmader, 2002; J. L. Smith, 2004; Smith et al., 2005; Smith & White, 2002; J. Steele et al., 2002). Most of them report that females earn lower scores when stereotype threat is present than when it is absent. In a representative study, Good and her colleagues (2003) examined the math performance of seventh-grade girls who had been assigned a college-student mentor. In one condition, the mentors provided information about how intelligence is flexible, so that people can learn how to improve their skills. The girls in this condition earned significantly higher math scores than the girls in a control condition, whose mentors talked about an irrelevant topic. Now look back at Harvard President Summers's comments on page 145. How might these widely publicized remarks contribute to stereotype threat for females?

We have examined a large number of biological and social factors that can contribute to the gender differences in spatial and mathematics tasks. We do not currently have a cohesive explanation for the way in which the pieces of the puzzle fit together in accounting for the gender differences. However, as Janet Hyde and Amy Mezulis (2001) concluded, "If the extensive examination of gender differences over the past several decades has taught us anything, it may be that gender differences are (1) often small in magnitude and (2) low in frequency compared with the vast similarities between the sexes" (p. 555). Furthermore, not one of these cognitive gender differences is so substantial that it has major implications for the career performance of women and men, a topic we will explore in Chapter 7.

Section Summary

Cognitive Abilities

1. No consistent gender differences are found in areas such as general intelligence, concept formation, problem solving, or creativity.

2. On memory tasks, males and females are most skilled in the areas with which they are familiar.

3. At present, gender differences in verbal skills and reading disabilities are minimal.

4. Gender differences in mathematics ability are negligible on most tests. Females generally receive higher grades than males in their math courses. Males receive higher scores on the SAT mathematics test, a test that underpredicts women's college math grades.

5. Gender differences are minimal on spatial visualization tasks, moderate on spatial perception tasks, and more substantial on mental rotation tasks. Still, most males and females receive similar scores on mental rotation tests. Also, gender differences on spatial tasks disappear when people receive training and when the task is described as a feminine one.

6. Biological explanations for gender differences in cognitive skills include genetics, hormones, and brain organization (e.g., brain lateralization); current research does not strongly support any of these explanations.

7. Social explanations for gender differences in cognitive skills include several that emphasize gender differences in experience (illustrations in books and magazines, treatment by adults, and extracurricular activities). Several other social explanations focus on math attitudes (parents' and teachers' attitudes, perceptions of math competence, beliefs about math being masculine, and stereotype threat).

ACHIEVEMENT MOTIVATION AND ATTITUDES ABOUT SUCCESS

In the preceding discussion of gender comparisons in cognitive abilities, we concluded that men and women are generally similar in their thinking skills. The cognitive differences are never large enough to explain the tremendous imbalances in the gender ratios found in many professions. Some observers argue that these imbalances can be traced, instead, to women's lack of motivation; perhaps women simply don't want to achieve. In this section, we'll explore **achievement motivation**, which is the desire to accomplish something on your own and to do it well (Hyde & Kling, 2001).

As Arnold Kahn and Janice Yoder (1989) noted, many theorists have tried to explain women's absence from certain prestigious fields in terms of personal "deficiencies" that inhibit their achievement. However, females earn higher grades in school than males do. They are also less likely than males to drop out of school and more likely to enroll in college (Eccles et al., 2003). As we'll see in this section, the research reveals gender similarities in almost every area related to achievement. Personal deficiencies cannot explain the gender differences in career patterns; in Chapter 7, we will explore several more valid explanations.

BIASES IN THE RESEARCH ON ACHIEVEMENT MOTIVATION

Before examining the research on achievement motivation, we should note two important biases in this field. First, the tasks that measure attitudes about success are usually stereotypically masculine (Todoroff, 1994). Success may be represented by achievement in a prestigious occupation, academic excellence, or other accomplishments associated with traditionally masculine values. Achievements that are associated with traditionally feminine values receive little or no attention. An adolescent woman may manage to entertain a group of six toddlers so that they are all playing cooperatively. However, psychologists don't typically include this kind of accomplishment among the topics of achievement motivation. As Theme 3 emphasizes, topics that are traditionally associated with women are underrepresented in the psychological literature.

A second bias applies to most of psychology. Nearly all research on achievement motivation is conducted with college students. Researchers ignore nonacademic settings, older populations, people of color, and populations outside North America (Dabul & Russo, 1998; Mednick & Thomas, 1993). Think how achievement motivation might be defined in a Latin American culture that places more emphasis on the well-being of the community (Hyde & Kling, 2001). Perhaps achievement motivation might be measured in terms of a person's ability to work well with others or a person's knowledge about the community's history. As you read through this section, keep these limitations in mind.

Let's begin our exploration of motivation by discussing gender similarities in people's desire for achievement and in their concerns about the negative consequences of success. We'll see that women and men sometimes differ in self-confidence, although gender similarities are often reported. We'll also see that women and men usually provide similar explanations for their achievements.

ACHIEVEMENT MOTIVATION

To measure achievement motivation, researchers often ask the study participants to look at drawings of people in various situations and then to create stories based on these drawings. A person receives a high achievement motivation score if these stories emphasize working hard and excelling. The research, conducted with both Black and White participants, shows that males and females are similar in achievement motivation (Eccles et al., 2003; Hyde & Kling, 2001; Krishman & Sweeney, 1998; Mednick & Thomas, 1993).

COMPLETING A STORY	## Demonstration 5.2

Write a paragraph in response to one of the following beginning sentences.

If you are a female, complete this sentence with a paragraph: "After first-term finals, Anne finds herself at the top of her medical school class."

If you are a male, complete this sentence with a paragraph: "After first-term finals, John finds himself at the top of his medical school class."

Males and females are also similar in their **intrinsic motivation**, which is your tendency to work on a task for your own satisfaction, rather than for rewards such as money or praise (Grolnick et al., 2002). Furthermore, males and females are equally likely to emphasize motivation when they describe important events in their lives (Travis et al., 1991).

Try Demonstration 5.2 before reading further.

FEAR OF SUCCESS

So far, our discussion of achievement motivation has emphasized how people are motivated to achieve success. Research about achievement motivation has also explored whether some people are afraid of this kind of successful achievement. At the end of the 1960s, Matina Horner proposed that women are more likely than men to be afraid of success (e.g., Horner, 1968, 1978).

More specifically, Horner proposed that a woman who is high in **fear of success** is afraid that success in competitive achievement situations will produce unpleasant consequences, including unpopularity and a loss of femininity. Men are not afraid of success, Horner said, because achievement is part of the masculine gender role.

When Horner used a technique such as the one Demonstration 5.2 illustrates, she found that women tended to write stories in which a successful woman was socially rejected. Men tended to write stories in which a successful man's hard work brought rich rewards. The popular press was delighted: At last, here was a reason to justify why women were less successful than men!

In the years following Horner's original study, however, the research has shown fairly consistent gender similarities in the fear of success (e.g., Hyde & Kling, 2001; Krishman & Sweeney, 1998; Mednick & Thomas, 1993; Naidoo, 1999). If theorists are searching for a powerful explanation for women's absence from prestigious occupations, they will need to look beyond fear of success (Hyde & Kling, 2001).

CONFIDENCE IN YOUR OWN ACHIEVEMENT AND ABILITY

Self-confidence is another concept that is intertwined with achievement motivation. As we'll see, gender differences do sometimes emerge in two areas: (1) Men often report more self-confidence than women do, and (2) men's self-confidence may be less influenced by the evaluations provided by other people.

Demonstration 5.3

REACTIONS TO
COMMENTS FROM
OTHER PEOPLE

Imagine that you have given a presentation on a project to an important group of people. Afterward, someone approaches you and says that you did a very good job: You used wonderful examples, and your ideas were interesting. Someone else rejects everything you had to say and disagrees with all your proposals. Then a third person comments, not on the content of your presentation but on your excellent speaking style.

How much would the feedback from these other people influence your self-confidence? Would your confidence rise or fall, depending on the nature of the comments, or would your self-evaluations tend to remain fairly constant?

Source: Based on T. Roberts (1991, p. 297).

LEVEL OF SELF-CONFIDENCE.   Several studies suggest that men are sometimes more self-confident about their ability than women are (Eccles et al., 2003; Furnham, 2000; Furnham et al., 1999; Pulford & Colman, 1997).[3] In a representative study, Pallier (2003) administered a test of general knowledge to college students. Compared to the females, the males gave much higher estimates of their scores on this test, even though Pallier found no gender differences in their actual accuracy.

Researchers have found that gender differences in self-confidence are larger when people make public estimates rather than private estimates (J. Clark & Zehr, 1993; Daubman et al., 1992; Lundeberg et al., 2000). Women are especially likely to give low estimates for their grade point average when another student has already announced that he or she has low grades (Heatherington et al., 1993, 1998). One possible explanation is that women are more likely than men to be modest when they are with other people (Daubman et al., 1992; Wosinska et al., 1996).

Gender differences in self-confidence are also larger on a task that is considered traditionally masculine, rather than neutral or traditionally feminine (S. Beyer, 1998; S. Beyer & Bowden, 1997; Eccles et al., 2003). For instance, Brownlow and her colleagues (1998) compared the strategies of contestants on the TV game show "Jeopardy." On stereotypically masculine topics, men bet a higher percentage of their earnings than the women did. On neutral and stereotypically feminine topics, men and women used similar betting strategies.

Now try Demonstration 5.3 above before reading further.

SELF-CONFIDENCE AND EVALUATION PROVIDED BY OTHERS.   Researchers have reported some gender differences in self-confidence. Now let's consider a second issue, focusing on the *stability* of a person's self-confidence. Specifically, Tomi-Ann

---

[3]People sometimes assume that women are underconfident. An alternative viewpoint is that men are overconfident and that women have the appropriate level of self-confidence (Hyde & Mezulis, 2001; Tavris, 1992).

Roberts and Susan Nolen-Hoeksema (1989, 1994) demonstrated that comments from other people influence women's self-confidence. In contrast, men's self-confidence is more stable. Compared to these findings, how did you respond to Demonstration 5.3?

In an important study on responses to others' comments, Roberts and Nolen-Hoeksema (1989) asked students to work on a series of challenging cognitive tasks. After several minutes, the participants rated their self-confidence in terms of the likelihood that they could do well on the task. A few minutes later, half of the participants—chosen at random—received positive comments from the researcher (e.g., "You are doing very well" or "You are above average at this point in the task"). The other half of the participants received negative comments ("You are not doing very well" or "You are below average at this point in the task"). Several minutes later, they all rated their self-confidence a second time.

Figure 5.7 shows the change in self-confidence between the first and the second rating period. Notice that the men's self-confidence ratings were not significantly changed by the nature of the comments other people made. In

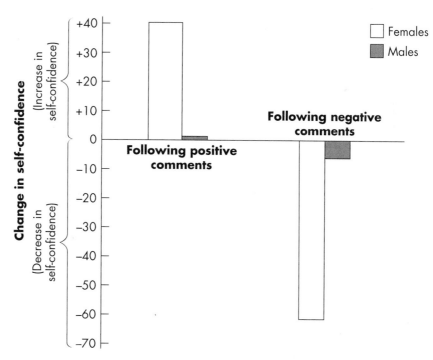

FIGURE 5.7   CHANGE IN SELF-CONFIDENCE, FOLLOWING EITHER POSITIVE OR NEGATIVE COMMENTS. (NOTE: NEGATIVE NUMBERS INDICATE A DECREASE IN SELF-CONFIDENCE; POSITIVE NUMBERS INDICATE AN INCREASE.)

Sources: Based on T. Roberts and Nolen-Hoeksema (1989).

Demonstration 5.4

EXPLAINING
SUCCESSFUL
PERFORMANCE

Think about the last time you received a good grade on a test. A number of different factors could have been responsible for your success. Four possible factors are listed below. You have 100 points to divide among these four factors. Assign points to reflect the extent to which each factor contributed to your success; the points must add up to 100.

_____ I have high ability for the subject that was covered on that test.

_____ I put a lot of effort into studying for that test.

_____ The test was easy.

_____ It was just luck.

---

contrast, the women's self-confidence rose dramatically after receiving positive comments, and it fell even more dramatically after receiving negative comments.

This research has been replicated in the workplace, after bank employees had been evaluated by their supervisor (M. Johnson & Helgeson, 2002). Once again, women were more responsive to the feedback from other people. But why should men and women react differently to people's comments? One reason is that women are more likely than men to believe that other people's evaluations are accurate assessments of their performance (Johnson & Helgeson, 2002; Roberts & Nolen-Hoeksema, 1994). Furthermore, women are more likely to use the information from these evaluations in assessing their own performance, even when the evaluations are not accurate (Van Blyderveen & Wood, 2001).

When I first read about these gender differences in response to others' comments, I confess that I was dismayed. Men apparently trust their own judgments, whereas women seem to adjust their self-confidence in response to whatever comments they happen to hear. But then I recalled the male-as-normative issue, discussed on page 66 in Chapter 2 (Tavris, 1992). Maybe we shouldn't conclude that men are stable and that women are fickle. Instead, men may be overly rigid, not questioning their initial judgment. In contrast, women may be appropriately flexible, willing to listen and to respond to new information. Ideally, people *should* respond to evaluations from well-informed experts.

ATTRIBUTIONS FOR YOUR OWN SUCCESS

Be sure to try Demonstration 5.4 before reading further. This demonstration asks you to make attributions about your own performance on an achievement task. **Attributions** are explanations about the causes of your behavior. When you have been successful on an achievement task, you generally attribute that success to some combination of four factors: (1) ability, (2) effort, (3) task easiness, and (4) luck. Keep your own answers to Demonstration 5.4 in mind as we examine the research on gender comparisons in attribution patterns.

Incidentally, this topic of attributions may seem familiar, because we examined a similar topic in connection with gender stereotypes in Chapter 2. In that chapter, we saw that the *gender of the stimulus* often influences attributions. Specifically, when people make judgments about men, they tend to attribute the success of men to their high ability; however, when they make judgments about women, they tend to attribute the success of women to other factors, such as an easy task or luck. In this chapter, however, we are examining the *gender of the subject.* In particular, we will examine whether women and men use different attributions when judging their own success.

Several early studies suggested that males are more likely than females to give credit to their ability (e.g., Deaux, 1979). However, two meta-analyses concluded that gender differences in attributional patterns are minimal (D. Sohn, 1982; Whitley et al., 1986). Other research and reviews of the literature also conclude that women and men are similar in the reasons they provide for their success or failure (Mednick & Thomas, 1993; Russo et al., 1991; Travis et al., 1991; Wigfield et al., 2002).

In short, attributions for success usually show the same pattern of gender similarities that we observed in our earlier discussion of cognitive abilities, achievement motivation, and fear of success. (Remember, however, that gender differences are somewhat common in areas related to self-confidence.) Although gender similarities in attributions are most common, gender differences appear in some groups and some situations:

1. In general, males and females have similar attribution patterns from early adolescence through early adulthood. However, for adults over the age of 25, men are more likely than women to say, "I did well because I have high ability" (Mezulis et al., 2004).
2. In public settings, men are more likely than women are to attribute success to their high ability. When men and women provide attributions in private, their responses may be similar (J. H. Berg et al., 1981).
3. Men are more likely than women are to cite ability as an explanation for their success on stereotypically masculine tasks, such as grades in natural science, mathematics, and business courses (C. R. Campbell & Henry, 1999; A. K. F. Li & Adamson, 1995). In contrast, women are more likely than men are to use ability explanations on stereotypically feminine tasks, such as comforting a friend or earning high grades in an English course (S. Beyer, 1998/1999; R. A. Clark, 1993).

At the beginning of this section on achievement motivation, we saw that theorists have often favored a "women are deficient" rationale to explain why women are less likely than men to hold prestigious positions in society. However, the discussion of attributions reveals the same pattern we have seen throughout most of this chapter. Consistent with Theme 1, women and men are typically similar. When gender differences do emerge, they can usually be traced to characteristics of the social setting or the task. With attribution patterns, the gender differences are so small and readily modifiable that a blame-the-person explanation does not seem useful.

We have emphasized in this chapter that women resemble men in both cognitive ability and motivational factors. In Chapter 6, we will continue our search for explanations about the lack of women in prestigious occupations. Specifically, we will consider gender comparisons in social and personality characteristics. Then, in Chapter 7, we will turn our attention to women's work experiences to try to identify external factors that account for gender differences in employment patterns.

Section Summary

Achievement Motivation and Attitudes About Success

1. The research on topics related to achievement motivation usually focuses on stereotypically masculine tasks and White college students living in North America.

2. Women and men are similar in their achievement motivation and intrinsic motivation.

3. Women and men are also similar in their fear of success.

4. Men are sometimes more self-confident than women on achievement tasks, especially those involving public estimates of self-confidence and traditionally masculine tasks.

5. Comments from other people are more likely to influence women's self-confidence than men's.

6. Women and men tend to use similar attributions when explaining their successes. However, gender differences may emerge (a) for adults older than 25, (b) when making statements in public, and (c) when performing gender-stereotyped tasks.

CHAPTER REVIEW QUESTIONS

1. Suppose that your local newspaper carries the headline: "Test Shows Males More Creative." The article reports that males had an average score of 78 on a creativity test compared to an average score of 75 for females. Based on the cautions discussed at the beginning of this chapter, why would you be hesitant to conclude that the gender differences in creativity are substantial?

2. Recall the cognitive abilities for which researchers have reported no consistent gender differences. Think of several men and several women whom you know well. Do the conclusions about those abilities match your observations about these individuals?

3. Imagine that a third-grade teacher tells you that the girls in her class have much better reading abilities than the boys. What would you answer, based on the information in this chapter?

4. The sections on mathematics and spatial abilities revealed inconsistent gender differences. Which areas showed the smallest gender differences, and which showed the largest? Which potential biological and social explanations might account for these differences?

5. Imagine that your local newspaper features an article about gender differences in math ability. You decide to write a letter to the editor; describe four points that you would emphasize in your letter.

6. Suppose that a woman you know has read an article about fear of success in a popular magazine marketed to young business-women. She asks you whether the article is correct: Do women have a significantly higher fear of success than men do? Answer her with the information from this chapter.

7. The research on topics related to achievement motivation illustrates how gender differences rarely apply to all people in all situations. Describe some variables that determine whether gender differences will occur in self-confidence and in attributions for one's own success. Although the research on fear of success shows gender similarities, which of these variables could also apply to fear of success?

8. We discussed two factors that influence whether women and men differ with respect to self-confidence in achievement settings. Keeping these factors in mind, think of a concrete situation in which gender differences are relatively large. Then think of an example of a situation in which gender differences should be minimal.

9. In Chapter 6, we'll see that—in comparison to men—women are somewhat more attuned to the emotions of other people. How is this sensitivity to emotions related to an observation in the current chapter that women are somewhat more attuned to social factors and other people's emotions when they make judgments about self-confidence and attributions for success? Also, how is sensitivity to others related to the discussion of self-confidence on pages 167 to 170?

10. To solidify your knowledge in preparation for the chapter on women and work (Chapter 7), think of a prestigious profession that employs relatively few women. Review each of the cognitive abilities and motivational factors discussed in this chapter. Do any of these factors sufficiently explain the relative absence of women in that profession?

KEY TERMS

*frequency distribution (147)

*box-score approach (149)

counting approach (149)

*meta-analysis (149)

*verbal fluency (153)

*reading disability (154)

*validity (156)

*spatial abilities (157)

*spatial visualization (157)

*spatial perception (158)

*mental rotation (159)

*lateralization (161)

*stereotype threat (164)

*achievement motivation (165)

*intrinsic motivation (167)

*fear of success (167)

*attributions (170)

 Note: The terms asterisked in the Key Terms section serve as good search terms for InfoTrac College Edition. Go to http://infotrac.thomsonlearning.com and try these added search terms.

RECOMMENDED READINGS

Gallagher, A. M., & Kaufman, J. C. (Eds.). (2004). *Gender differences in mathematics: An integrative psychological approach.* New York: Cambridge University Press. I strongly recommend this book, which includes 15 chapters that address the research on gender and math. It's not clear why the editors chose the term "gender differences," rather than "gender comparisons." However, if Dr. Lawrence Summers had read this book, he might still be the president of Harvard.

Halpern, D. F. (2000). *Sex differences in cognitive abilities* (3rd ed.). Mahwah, NJ: Erlbaum. Diane Halpern writes about gender comparisons in a clear and interesting fashion; she emphasizes that gender differences arise from a combination of biological and social factors.

Wigfield, A., & Eccles, J. S. (Eds.). (2002). *Development of achievement motivation*. San Diego: Academic Press. Surprisingly few books in the current decade focus on topics related to achievement. Therefore, this book is especially useful for a general orientation about achievement as well as information about gender comparisons.

Worell, J. (Ed.). (2001). *The encyclopedia of women and gender*. San Diego: Academic Press. I strongly recommend this two-volume encyclopedia for college libraries, especially because the entries are written by prominent researchers and theorists in the field of psychology of women. Particularly relevant for the current chapter are the chapters on achievement and gender difference research.

ANSWERS TO THE DEMONSTRATIONS

Demonstration 5.1: a.1: Rotate the pattern so that it looks like two mountain peaks, and place the leftmost segment along the top-left portion of the little white triangle. a.2: This pattern fits along the right side of the two black triangles on the left. a.3: Rotate this figure about 100 degrees to the right, so that it forms a slightly slanted *z*, with the top line coinciding with the top line of the top white triangle. b. The line should be horizontal, not tilted. c. 1c, 2d.

ANSWERS TO THE TRUE-FALSE STATEMENTS

1. False (pp. 151–152); 2. False (pp. 152–155); 3. True (p. 155); 4. False (pp. 155–156); 5. True (p. 159); 6. False (pp. 160–162); 7. False (p. 167); 8. True (p. 168); 9. True (pp. 168–170); 10. False (pp. 170–171).

© Getty Images

6 | Gender Comparisons in Social and Personality Characteristics

True or False?

_____   1. Gender differences in social behavior tend to be especially small when people's other roles (e.g., work roles) are emphasized.

_____   2. In college students' social conversations, men tend to be more talkative than women.

_____   3. Women tend to look at their conversational partners more than men do, especially when talking with someone of the same gender.

_____   4. In general, women are more helpful to other people than men are.

_____   5. Women are consistently more interested in infants than men are, according to several different measures of interest.

_____   6. The research shows that women make moral decisions on the basis of caring relationships with others, whereas men make moral decisions on the basis of laws and regulations.

_____   7. According to self-reports, men are just as satisfied with their friendships as women are.

_____   8. One consistent gender difference is that men are more aggressive than women.

_____   9. The current research shows that male leaders are more likely than female leaders to encourage employees to develop their potential strengths.

_____ 10. Men are more likely to be persuaded by a woman who uses tentative language than by a woman who uses assertive language.

As I was browsing through some issues of *People* magazine, the title of one article caught my eye: "Uncommon Valor." Think of the word *valor*. Don't you envision a heroic man rescuing a weeping woman? However, the stories were refreshingly gender balanced. Yes, 24-year-old Ryan Lane had rescued five people from a flood in Kansas. Also, two teenagers named Jonathan Griswold and Clay Cheza had tackled a classmate who had aimed a handgun at the students in his English class. However, the feature story described how Roxanna Vega, 16 years old, rescued her young cousins after their mother had deliberately driven over a cliff. When the car crashed, Roxanna had broken her back, ankle, and arm, yet she struggled up the 160-foot cliff to get help from passing motorists (Jerome & Meadows, 2003).

In Chapter 5, we saw that gender similarities are common when we consider cognitive abilities and achievement. In this chapter about social and personality characteristics, we'll once again observe occasional small to moderate gender differences but many gender similarities (Eagly, 2001; M. C. Hamilton, 2001; J. D. Yoder & Kahn, 2003). For example, we'll see that males are typically more likely than females to be heroic rescuers, although the overall differences in helping behavior are not large (S. W. Becker & Eagly, 2004).

In this chapter, we will explore gender comparisons in three areas: (1) communication patterns, (2) characteristics related to helping and caring, and (3) aggression and power. Before you read further, turn to pages 146–148 and re-read the five cautions about research on gender comparisons in cognitive skills. These cautions are also relevant when we consider gender comparisons in social and personality characteristics.

We'll see that the social constructionist perspective is especially useful in examining social behavior, as we emphasize several times throughout this textbook. According to the **social constructionist approach,** we construct or invent our own versions of reality, based on prior experiences, social interactions, and beliefs. The social constructionist approach often focuses on language as a mechanism for categorizing our experiences—for example, our experiences about gender (Eckert & McConnell-Ginet, 2003; K. J. Gergen & Gergen, 2004).

A colleague provided an excellent example of the way we construct personality characteristics (K. Bursik, personal communication, 1997). Quickly answer the following question: Who are more emotional, men or women? Most people immediately respond, "Women, of course" (J. R. Kelly & Hutson-Comeaux, 2000). But what kinds of emotions did you consider? Only sadness and crying? Why don't we include anger, one of the primary human emotions? When a man pounds his fist into a wall in anger, we don't comment, "Oh, he's so emotional." Our culture constructs the word *emotional* to emphasize the emotions typically associated with women.

Notice, too, that we interpret a behavior differently, depending upon who is displaying the behavior. Suppose that you are walking to a classroom, and you see someone sitting alone and crying. If the person is a male, you are likely to think that he is upset about a genuinely important problem (L. Warner & Shields, 2007). Now imagine that the person is a female. Would you judge her problem to be equally important?

As we'll see in the final section of this chapter, social constructionism also shapes the way we view aggression; we define the word *aggression* primarily in terms of the kinds of aggression associated with men. The social constructionist approach forces us to consider alternative interpretations of viewing our language and our social interactions (K. J. Gergen & Gergen, 2004).

Every day, we construct what it means to be male and female in our society. When social constructionists examine gender, they focus on a central question: How does our culture create gender and maintain it in our interpersonal relationships and communication patterns (M. M. Gergen, 2001; Shields, 2002)?

You and I do not construct gender independently. Instead, our culture provides us with schemas and other information. All this information operates like a set of lenses through which we can interpret the events in our lives (Bem, 1993; Shields, 2002). In Chapters 2 and 3, we examined how the media provide cultural lenses for both adults and children. Females are typically represented as gentle, nurturant, and submissive, whereas men are represented as independent, self-confident, and aggressive. Our culture has established different social roles for women and men, so we should find that people usually want to uphold these ideals (Eagly, 2001; Popp et al., 2003; Shields, 2005).

As you read this chapter, keep in mind some of the gender comparison issues we raised in Chapter 5. For example, we saw that the social setting influences people's self-confidence and their attribution patterns. However, the social setting has a relatively modest impact on cognitive and achievement tasks because people typically perform these tasks in relative isolation. The social setting is more important when we consider social and personality characteristics. Humans talk, smile, help, and act aggressively in the presence of other people. The social setting provides a rich source of information that people examine to make sense out of the world (J. D. Yoder & Kahn, 2003). If the social setting has such an important influence on whether people act in a gender-stereotyped fashion, then a characteristic such as "nurturant" is not an inevitable, essential component of all females. Furthermore, a characteristic such as "aggressive" is not an inevitable, essential component of all males.

Several factors related to the social setting have an important influence on the size of the gender differences in social and personality characteristics (Aries, 1996; M. C. Hamilton, 2001; J. B. James, 1997; Wester et al., 2002; J. D. Yoder & Kahn, 2003). Here are some examples:

1. *Gender differences are usually largest when other people are present.* For instance, women are especially likely to react positively to infants when other people are nearby.
2. *Gender differences are generally largest when gender is prominent and other shared roles are minimized.* For example, at a singles bar, gender is emphasized strongly, and gender differences are likely to be large. In contrast, at a professional conference of accountants—where men and women occupy the same job—the work role will be emphasized, and gender differences will be small.
3. *Gender differences are usually largest when the behavior requires specific gender-related skills.* For example, men might be especially likely to volunteer to change a tire or perform a similar skill traditionally associated with men in our culture.

Notice, then, that gender differences are especially prominent when a social setting encourages us to think about gender and to wear an especially strong set of gender lenses. In other social settings, however, women and men usually behave with remarkable similarity. Our exploration of social characteristics in this chapter will focus on three clusters: (1) communication patterns, (2) characteristics related to helping and caring, and (3) characteristics related to aggression and power.

COMMUNICATION PATTERNS

The term *communication* typically suggests verbal communication, or communication with words. Many people have strong gender stereotypes about this topic; for example, they often think that women are more talkative than men are. The research results may surprise you.

Communication can also be nonverbal. **Nonverbal communication** refers to all human communication that does not use words, such as eye and hand movements, tone of voice, facial expression, and even how far you stand from another person. Nonverbal communication can effectively convey messages of power and emotion. However, when we hear the word *communication,* we typically think of verbal communication, rather than nonverbal communication. Still, research has uncovered some substantial gender differences in nonverbal communication that are worth exploring.

Both verbal and nonverbal communication are essential in our daily interactions. Unless you are reading this sentence before breakfast, you have already today spoken to many people, smiled at others, and perhaps avoided eye contact with still others. Let's now examine gender comparisons in verbal and nonverbal communication.

VERBAL COMMUNICATION

John Gray's best-selling book, *Men Are From Mars, Women Are From Venus,* claims that men and women "almost seem to be from different planets, speaking different languages" (Gray, 1992, p. 5). However, Gray's book is based on speculation and informal observations rather than actual research. In reality, within each gender, we find great variation in verbal communication patterns, and social factors influence whether we observe gender differences (Aries, 1998; Athenstaedt et al., 2004; R. C. Barnett & Rivers, 2004; R. Edwards & Hamilton, 2004; Shields, 2002; Thomson et al., 2001). Let's consider the research.

TALKATIVENESS. According to the long-standing stereotype, women chatter for hours (Holmes, 1998). In reality, however, several studies show no gender differences in the length of college students' conversations with their friends or their written descriptions of vivid memories (Athenstaedt et al., 2004; Niedźwieńska, 2003). Men and women are also equally talkative when they are being interviewed on talk shows (Brownlow et al., 2003). In other research, males are *more* talkative than women, based on data gathered in elementary classrooms, college classrooms, and college students' conversations (Aries, 1998; M. Crawford, 1995; Eckert & McConnell-Ginet, 2003; Romaine, 1999; Thomson et al., 2001). In short, the research shows mixed results, but it does not support the "talkative female" stereotype.

INTERRUPTIONS. Suppose that you are telling a story about meeting a famous person. A listener interrupts after your first two sentences to say, "Oh, that sounds like the time I . . .". When researchers look at this kind of intrusive interruption, they find that men tend to interrupt more than women (K. J. Anderson & Leaper, 1998; Athenstaedt et al., 2004).

Also, the research on interruptions sometimes compares high-status men in conversation with low-status women. This research typically finds that men interrupt more than women do. However, power, not gender, could explain the interruptions (R. C. Barnett & Rivers, 2004; Romaine, 1999). Other studies suggest that men interrupt significantly more often than women do in conversations with strangers and in competitive task settings. Still, gender differences may be minimal in other settings (Aries, 1996, 1998; Athenstaedt et al., 2004; C. West & Zimmerman, 1998b).

LANGUAGE STYLE.   Some theorists suggest that women's language style is very different from men's (e.g., Lakoff, 1990; Tannen, 1994). In reality, the gender differences are more subtle (Mulac et al., 2001; Thomson et al., 2001; Weatherall, 2002). Men are likely to curse more often and to use a larger vocabulary of obscene words (Jay, 2000; Pennebaker et al., 2003; Winters & Duck, 2001). However, other research shows only minimal gender differences in politeness during conversations or in writing style (D. Cameron et al., 1993; S. Mills, 2003; D. L. Rubin & Greene, 1994; Timmerman, 2002).

How about hesitant phrases such as "I'm not sure" or "It seems to be"? A review of the literature suggests that women are more likely than men to use this speech pattern (Mulac et al., 2001). However, Carli (1990) demonstrated the importance of the social setting. She found that people rarely used these hesitant phrases when they were talking with another person of the same gender. In contrast, when a woman was talking with a man, the woman was much more likely than the man to use this speech pattern.

THE CONTENT OF LANGUAGE.   We have discussed how women and men talk, but what do they talk about? R. A. Clark (1998) asked female and male students at the University of Illinois to report on all topics mentioned in their most recent conversation with a student of the same gender. As Figure 6.1 shows,

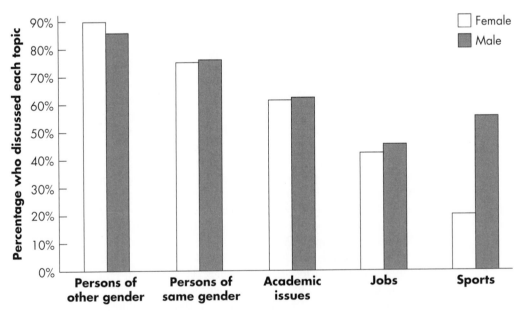

FIGURE 6.1   PERCENTAGE OF WOMEN AND MEN WHO DISCUSSED EACH OF FIVE TOPICS IN A RECENT CONVERSATION WITH A FRIEND OF THE SAME GENDER.

Source: Based on R. A. Clark (1998).

the gender similarities are striking. In fact, the only statistically significant gender difference is in talking about sports. Research has also demonstrated gender similarities when men and women are interviewed on talk shows (Brownlow et al., 2003).

Let's consider one other important point about conversations. In our list of three generalizations about gender comparisons, we noted that gender differences are small when other roles are emphasized. S. A. Wheelan and Verdi (1992) observed professionals in business, government, and service-oriented occupations who were attending a four-day group relations conference—a setting in which work-related roles would be prominent. The researchers found that men and women were similar in the number of statements that challenged the leadership and also in the number of statements that supported other people's remarks.

The groups in Wheelan and Verdi's study met for many hours; most other studies have recorded relatively brief conversations. In Chapter 2, we saw that stereotypes are especially likely to operate when people do not have enough information about a person's qualifications. When people initially meet each other, these stereotypes may inhibit a competent woman's comments. As time passes, however, other group members begin to appreciate the woman's

Demonstration 6.1

**GENDER
DIFFERENCES IN
BODY POSTURE**

Which of these figures is a girl, and which is a boy? What cues are you using when you make your decision?

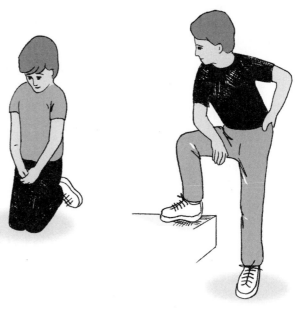

remarks, and their expectations become less gender based. As a consequence, gender differences may grow smaller as conversations become longer. By looking at a wide range of conversations, Aries (1998) confirmed that gender is a relatively unimportant factor in conversational content when groups have met for a long time.

NONVERBAL COMMUNICATION

Try turning off the sound on a television game show and observing the non-verbal behavior. You could read a transcript of the conversation between Mr. Game Show Host and Ms. Contestant, and yet that transcript would fail to capture much of the subtle communication between these two people. The nonverbal aspects of conversation are extremely important in conveying social messages. As we'll note later in this section, gender differences are often sub-stantial in certain kinds of nonverbal behavior, such as personal space, body position, and smiling.

Let's examine several components of nonverbal communication, beginning with the nonverbal messages that people send by means of their personal space, body posture, gaze, and facial expression. A fifth topic, decoding ability, examines gender comparisons in *interpreting* these nonverbal messages. As we'll see throughout this section, gender differences in nonverbal communication are typically larger than other kinds of gender dif-ferences (J. A. Hall, 1998). We'll also consider individual differences in non-verbal communication as well as explanations and implications of these gender comparisons.

Be sure to try Demonstration 6.1 before you read any further.

PERSONAL SPACE.   The term **personal space** refers to the invisible boundary around each person that other people should not invade during ordinary social interactions. You are probably most aware of personal space when a stranger comes too close and makes you feel uncomfortable. In general, women have smaller personal-space zones than men (Briton & Hall, 1995; LaFrance & Henley, 1997; Payne, 2001). As a result, when two women are talking to each other, they typically sit closer together than two men do. In the world of work, high-status individuals occupy larger physical work spaces than low-status individuals (Bate & Bowker, 1997). In general, the executives (mostly men) occupy spacious offices, whereas the low-ranking employees (mostly women) work in relatively crowded conditions.

BODY POSTURE.   Gender differences in body posture develop early in life. The drawings in Demonstration 6.1 were traced from yearbook pictures of two fifth-graders, and then other cues about gender—such as clothing—were equated. The figure on the left can be easily identified as a girl, whereas the one on the right is clearly a boy. A glance through magazines will convince you of further gender differences in body posture. Notice that females keep their legs together, with their arms and hands close to their bodies. In contrast, males sit and stand with their legs apart, and their hands and arms move away from their bodies. Men look relaxed; even when resting, women keep their postures more tensely contained (Bate & Bowker, 1997; J. A. Hall, 1984). When talking to another person, women are more likely than men to maintain an erect body posture (J. A. Hall et al., 2001).

Notice how this observation meshes with the gender differences we have discussed. Men often use more conversational space in their verbal interactions because they may talk for longer and they may interrupt more often. Similarly, men use more personal space (distance from other people), and their own postures require greater physical space. As Demonstration 6.1 illustrates, even young children have mastered "gender-appropriate" body language.

GAZE. When we consider gaze, gender as a subject variable is important. Research shows that females gaze more at their conversational partners than males do (Briton & Hall, 1995; LaFrance & Henley, 1997). This gender difference emerges during childhood; young girls spend more time looking at their conversational partners.

Gender as a stimulus variable seems to be even more powerful than gender as a subject variable. Specifically, people gaze at females more than they gaze at males (J. A. Hall, 1984, 1987). As a result, two women speaking to each other are likely to have frequent eye contact. In contrast, two men in conversation are likely to avoid looking at each other for long periods of time. Prolonged eye contact is relatively uncommon between two men.

FACIAL EXPRESSION. Gender differences in facial expression are substantial. The most noticeable difference is that women smile more than men do (L. R. Brody & Hall, 2000; J. A. Hall et al., 2000; J. A. Hall et al., 2001). In a recent meta-analysis of 418 gender comparisons of smiling frequency, the d was 0.41 (LaFrance et al., 2003).

The magazines you examine in Demonstration 6.2 are likely to reveal smiling women and somber men. An inspection of yearbooks will probably

Demonstration 6.2

GENDER
DIFFERENCES
IN SMILING

For this demonstration, you will first need to assemble some magazines that contain photos of people. Inspect the photos to identify smiling faces. (Let's define a smile as an expression in which the corners of the mouth are at least slightly upturned.) Record the number of women who smile, and divide it by the total number of women to calculate the percentage of women who smile. Repeat the process to calculate the percentage of men who smile. How do those two percentages compare? Does the gender comparison seem to depend on the kind of magazine you are examining (e.g., fashion magazine versus news magazine)?

Next, locate a high-school or college yearbook. Examine the portraits, and calculate the percentages of women and of men who are smiling. How do these two percentages compare?

confirm this gender difference (J. Mills, 1984; Ragan, 1982). Ragan examined nearly 1,300 portrait photographs and found that women were nearly twice as likely as men to smile broadly. In contrast, men were about eight times as likely as women to show no smile.

Gender differences are especially large when strangers interact (LaFrance et al., 2003). Furthermore, the gender differences are relatively large when people pose, for instance for a yearbook photo, or when they know that someone is videotaping them. In contrast, women and men have more similar facial expressions in candid photos (J. A. Hall et al., 2001; LaFrance et al., 2003). The gender differences in smiling have important social implications. For example, we know that positive responses, such as smiling, can affect the person who receives these pleasant messages. Specifically, the recipients begin to act in a more competent fashion (P. A. Katz et al., 1993; Word et al., 1974). When a typical man and woman interact, the woman's smiles and other positive reactions may encourage a man to feel competent and self-confident (Athenstaedt et al., 2004). However, the typical man does not smile much to encourage a woman.

The gender difference in smiling also has a dark interpretation. You may have noticed that some women smile bravely when someone makes fun of them, tells an embarrassing joke in their presence, or sexually harasses them. In fact, social tension is a strong predictor of smiling in women. In other words, women often smile because they feel uncomfortable or embarrassed in the current social setting, not because they are enjoying the social interaction (J. A. Hall & Halberstadt, 1986; LaFrance et al., 2003).

In Chapter 3, we discussed how adults can be biased when they interpret infants' facial expressions. Specifically, when a baby has an unhappy expression, adults who believe that the baby is a boy may tend to label that expression "anger" (Plant et al., 2000). In contrast, adults who believe that the baby is a girl may tend to label that expression "fear" (Condry & Condry, 1976). We find a similar effect when people judge adults' facial expressions. Algoe and her colleagues (2000) asked college students to make judgments about the facial expressions of adult males and females in photographs. These photos were carefully chosen so that the males and the females showed similarly intense emotions.

As part of this study, Algoe and her colleagues (2000) asked people to judge a photo of either an angry man or an angry woman. In both cases, the person was described as an employee involved in a workplace incident. Figure 6.2 shows that the male was judged to be somewhat angrier than the female. Even more interesting, however, is that the angry female was judged to be showing a moderate amount of fear, much more than the angry male. Apparently, when people look at an angry woman, they perceive that she is actually somewhat afraid.

Other research demonstrates that people also perceive more sadness than anger in a female's ambiguous facial expression. In contrast, they perceive more anger than sadness in a male's ambiguous facial expression (Plant et al., 2004).

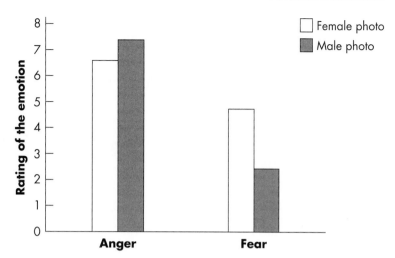

FIGURE 6.2 | RATINGS OF ANGER AND FEAR WHEN JUDGING THE PHOTO OF AN ANGRY FEMALE OR MALE EMPLOYEE. (NOTE: MINIMUM RATING = 0; MAXIMUM RATING = 8.)

Source: Based on Algoe et al. (2000).

DECODING ABILITY.   So far, we have seen evidence of gender differences in several kinds of nonverbal behavior: personal space, body posture, gaze, and facial expression. Decoding ability is different because it requires receiving messages rather than sending them. **Decoding ability** refers to competence in looking at another person's nonverbal behavior and figuring out what emotion that person is feeling. A person who is a skilled decoder can notice a friend's facial expression, posture, and tone of voice and deduce whether that person is in a good mood or a bad mood.

According to reviews of the research, females are more likely than males to decode nonverbal expressions accurately (L. R. Brody & Hall, 2000; McClure, 2000; Shields, 2002). For example, one meta-analysis of the research yielded a moderate effect size ($d = 0.41$); women were better decoders in 106 of 133 gender comparisons (J. A. Hall, 1984; J. A. Hall et al., 2000).

During infancy, baby girls are more skilled than baby boys in visually discriminating between adults' facial expressions, although the explanation for this gender difference is not clear (McClure, 2000). During childhood and adolescence, females are better decoders than males (Bosacki & Moore, 2004; McClure, 2000). The gender difference for adults also holds true cross-culturally, as evidenced by studies conducted in countries as varied as Greece, New Guinea, Japan, and Poland (Biehl et al., 1997; J. A. Hall, 1984). Incidentally, the research in Canada and the United States typically examines European Americans. It would be interesting to see whether the gender differences are consistent in all ethnic groups.

So far, we have focused on gender differences in decoding emotion from facial expressions. Bonebright and her colleagues (1996) examined people's

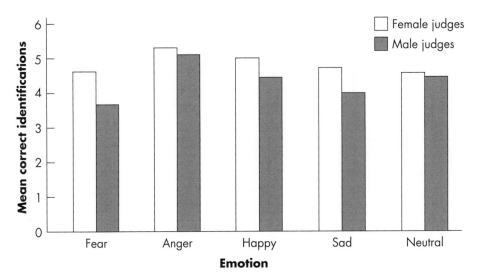

FIGURE 6.3 | MALE AND FEMALE ACCURACY IN DECODING EMOTIONS FROM VOCAL CUES. (NOTE: MAXIMUM SCORE = 6.)

Source: From Bonebright, T. L., Thompson, J. L., & Leger, D. W. (1996). Gender stereotypes in the expression and perception of vocal effect. *Sex Roles, 34,* 429–445 (Figure 1). Reprinted with permission.

ability to decode emotion from vocal cues. They instructed trained actors to record paragraph-long stories, each time using their voice to portray a specified emotion—fear, anger, happiness, or sadness—or neutrality. Then, undergraduate students listened to each recorded paragraph and tried to determine which emotion the speaker was trying to portray. As you can see from Figure 6.3, women were more accurate than men in decoding voices that expressed fear, happiness, and sadness; these gender differences were small but consistent. No gender differences were found for anger—the one emotion where we might have expected men to be more accurate—or for neutral expressions.

POTENTIAL EXPLANATIONS FOR GENDER DIFFERENCES IN COMMUNICATION

We need to keep in mind the large individual differences within each gender (R. Edwards & Hamilton, 2004), consistent with Theme 4 of this book. For example, women differ from one another in the size of their personal-space zones, their body posture, gazing, facial expression, and decoding ability. These within-gender variations are so large that you can probably think of several women whose communication style is more "masculine" than the average male. For instance, you may know some women who rarely smile and other women who have no idea what emotions you are feeling unless you make a public announcement.

Even though individual differences are substantial, we need to explain the gender differences in some kinds of verbal and nonverbal communication. Specifically, men often talk more, interrupt more, have larger personal-space zones, use more relaxed postures, gaze less, and smile less; they also tend to be less skilled at decoding other people's facial expressions. Given these reasonably large gender differences, we should expect that theorists would have developed coherent theoretical explanations. Unfortunately, they have not. Let's consider two general approaches, which primarily address the gender differences in decoding ability and in smiling.

POWER AND SOCIAL STATUS EXPLANATIONS.   Researchers such as Marianne LaFrance and her coauthors have argued that the single most effective explanation for gender differences in communication is that men have more power and social status in our culture (A. J. Stewart & McDermott, 2004). Powerful people are allowed to talk at length; less powerful people must listen. Powerless people should use phrases such as "I'm not sure" and "I suppose" when talking with powerful people. Powerful people also have large personal-space zones that less powerful people should not penetrate. Powerful people can sprawl in a chair in a relaxed body position. Powerful people don't need to smile, whereas low-power people must often smile, even if they do not feel happy (Athenstaedt et al., 2004; Hecht & LaFrance, 1998, LaFrance et al., 2003; Pennebaker et al., 2003).

Marianne LaFrance and Nancy Henley (1997) were especially interested in explaining the gender differences in decoding ability. They argued that low-power individuals must be especially attentive to powerful individuals so that they can respond appropriately. Imagine a male boss and his low-ranking male assistant. The assistant must be vigilant for signs of unhappiness on his boss's face because those signs suggest that the boss shouldn't be interrupted or brought any bad news. In contrast, the boss doesn't need to be equally sensitive. According to the power-based explanation, the boss has little to gain from decoding his assistant's facial expression.

LaFrance and Henley (1997) argued that our current culture usually assigns dominant status to men and subordinate status to women. As a consequence, even when a man and a woman are equivalent in other characteristics, such as age and occupation, the man will generally have more power. With that status, the man will use the verbal and nonverbal communication patterns that are characteristic of bosses, leaving the woman in the position of a relatively submissive assistant.

However, LaFrance and her colleagues (2003) pointed out that gender differences can be minimal when people have similar power and status, as point 2 on page 178 emphasizes. Specifically, their meta-analysis demonstrated that men and women have more similar patterns of smiling when they are sharing the same role.

SOCIAL LEARNING EXPLANATIONS.   Judith Hall and her colleagues believe that social status and power cannot account for the gender differences in nonverbal decoding ability (J. A. Hall & Halberstadt, 1997; J. A. Hall et al., 2000; J. A. Hall et al., 2001). For example, Hall and her colleagues (2001) found that high-status university employees smiled just as much as low-status university employees.

Instead, researchers such as Hall and her colleagues argue that our culture provides roles, expectations, and socialization experiences that teach males and females how to communicate (Athenstaedt et al., 2004; J. A. Hall et al., 2000; Pennebaker et al., 2003; Weatherall, 2002). In other words, these researchers emphasize a social learning approach, which we discussed in Chapter 3. As children grow up, for instance, they are reinforced for behavior that is consistent with their gender. They are also punished for behavior that is more typical of the other gender. Thus, a young girl may be scolded and told, "Let's see a smile on that face!" when she has been frowning. If she values others' approval, she will probably smile more often. The girl also notices that females often smile and gaze intently at their conversational partners. In contrast, a boy will be criticized if he uses "feminine" hand gestures, and he can certainly notice stereotypically masculine body movements by watching the men in his family, his community, and the media. Young girls also learn that they are supposed to pay attention to people's emotions, so they are likely to develop sensitivity to facial expressions. In addition, young girls learn that they are supposed to look out for people's emotional well-being, and a smile makes people feel welcome and accepted.

CONCLUSIONS.   As with so many debates in psychology, both perspectives are probably at least partially correct. My own sense is that the power hypothesis and the social learning approach combine fairly well to explain the gender differences in the communications that people send to others. However, the social learning approach seems more relevant than the power hypothesis in explaining people's ability to receive and decode emotions in other people. Consistent with J. A. Hall and Halberstadt's (1997) argument, I've known some executives and other high-power individuals who are skilled at reading other people's emotions from relatively subtle cues. Social sensitivity makes some people popular, and so they rise to positions of power.

Even if we aren't certain about the explanations, some gender differences remain. What should we do about them? Women do not have to smile when they are unhappy, and they do not need to occupy the smallest possible space on a couch. With respect to verbal communication, women should feel comfortable claiming their fair share of the conversation. Men can interrupt less, and they can stop invading women's personal space. They can also smile more, and they can sit so that they occupy less space.

In discussing how communication patterns can be changed, we must remember that women should not necessarily strive to be more masculine in their behavior. This reaction would assume that male behavior must be normative. I recall a recent article in a magazine—intended for women executives—that urged woman to master high-powered, masculine verbal and nonverbal behavior. However, as we'll see later in the chapter, this strategy may backfire. Furthermore, we should not assume that women are the ones who need to change their behavior. Instead, we should note that men may have learned inappropriate communication strategies. They have much to gain from adopting some of the strategies typically associated with women.

Section Summary

**Communication
Patterns**

1. The social constructionist perspective helps us understand how language shapes our ideas about gender; it also explains why our culture has different standards for the ideal social behavior of women and men.

2. Gender differences are largest when other people are present, when gender roles are emphasized, and when a task requires gender-related skills.

3. Men often talk more than women; in some circumstances, they also interrupt more.

4. With respect to language style, women may be less likely than men to use profanity; also, women use hesitant phrases (e.g., ''I suppose'') more in speech with men than in speech with other women.

5. Gender differences in conversational topics are usually minimal.

6. Women generally have smaller personal-space zones than men do, and their posture is less relaxed.

7. Compared to males, females often gaze more at their conversational partners, especially when speaking with someone of the same gender.

8. Women usually smile more than men do, but their smiles may indicate social tension rather than pleasure. However, people may misread women's angry facial expressions as being partly fearful.

9. Women are generally more accurate than men at decoding nonverbal messages that other people send.

10. Some gender differences in communication can be traced to gender differences in power; however, social learning explanations (e.g., roles, expectations, and socialization) are equally important.

11. To change communication patterns, we must not emphasize how women should become more ''masculine''; instead, men would profit from adopting some of the strategies that are usually associated with women.

CHARACTERISTICS RELATED TO HELPING AND CARING

Take a moment to form a mental image of a person helping someone else. Try to picture the scene as vividly as possible. Now inspect your mental image. Is this helpful person a male or a female?

In North America, we have two different stereotypes about gender differences in helpfulness. Males are considered more helpful in activities requiring heroism; they are supposed to take risks, even to help strangers. In contrast, females are considered more helpful and generous in offering assistance and emotional support to family members and close friends (Barbee et al., 1993).

Demonstration 6.3

A Personal Dilemma

Suppose you have been looking forward for some time to watching a special television program: an old movie you have always wanted to see, a sports championship game, or a special program such as "Masterpiece Theater." Just as you are all settled in and the show is about to begin, your best friend calls and asks you to help with something you had promised several days ago you would do—for example, painting a room or hanging wallpaper. You had assumed that your friend would need you sometime during the week, but had not expected it to be right now. You want nothing else but to stay in your comfortable chair and watch this show, but you know your friend will be disappointed if you do not come over to help (R. S. Mills et al., 1989). For purposes of this demonstration, assume that you cannot record the program for future viewing. What would you choose to do in this dilemma?

For many years, psychologists ignored helpfulness in long-term close relationships, where so many of our everyday interactions occur (Eagly & Wood, 1991). In later chapters, we'll explore how women provide this less visible kind of helpfulness when we discuss child care (Chapter 7), love relationships (Chapter 8), and care of elderly relatives (Chapter 14).

Furthermore, women's paid employment often emphasizes this low-visibility kind of helpfulness. Women are more likely than men to choose occupations in the "helping professions," such as nursing and social work. In summary, helpfulness actually includes both the high-visibility activities that are stereotypically masculine and also the less visible activities that are stereotypically feminine. Let's consider several topics related to helping and caring: altruism, nurturance, empathy, moral judgments involving other people, and friendship. Try Demonstration 6.3 before you read further.

ALTRUISM

Altruism means providing unselfish help to others who are in need, without anticipating any reward. Research with children and with adults shows gender similarities (N. Eisenberg et al., 1996). For example, one meta-analysis of 182 gender comparisons yielded an overall effect size (d) of only 0.13 (Eagly & Crowley, 1986). Gender similarities are common, although men are more helpful on tasks that are physically dangerous or require expertise in a traditionally "masculine" area (Fiala et al., 1999; M. C. Hamilton, 2001).

Let's consider a representative study that showed gender similarities. Researchers distributed questionnaires to adult visitors at a Canadian science museum (R. S. L. Mills et al., 1989). Each person read three stories, such as the one in Demonstration 6.3, and was instructed to choose between two specified options. According to the results of this study, both women and men selected the altruistic choice 75% of the time. In other words, the researchers found no gender differences in responses to this hypothetical scenario not involving danger.

A recent article by Selwyn Becker and Alice Eagly (2004) examined helpfulness in more dangerous situations. Specifically, they studied **heroism,** which they defined as risking one's life for the welfare of other people. For example, they considered the list of Carnegie Hero Medal recipients. This award is given to individuals in the United States and Canada who risk their own life to save the lives of other people (e.g., from drowning or electrocution). Becker and Eagly discovered that 9% of these individuals were female. The second category of heroes focused on individuals who earned the title "Righteous Among the Nations," non-Jews who risked their lives during the Nazi holocaust to save Jews. For this category, 61% were female. Finally, they considered individuals whose helpfulness was less dangerous, although still very risky. Again, the majority of these individuals were female. For instance, 57% of "living kidney donors" were women. In other words, women are somewhat more likely than men to undergo pain and potential medical problems, so that they can help another person.

Alice Eagly and her colleagues believe that the pattern of gender differences in helpfulness can be explained by social roles (S. W. Becker & Eagly, 2004; Eagly, 2001; Eagly et al., 2000). A **social role** refers to a culture's shared expectations about the behavior of a group that occupies a particular social category, for example, the social category "men." Men typically have greater size and strength than women, which means that they are more likely to perform activities requiring these physical characteristics, such as saving someone from drowning. Their heroism is also more public.

In contrast, the social-role explanation points out that women's social role is partly based on their giving birth to children. They are therefore more likely to take care of children, most often in a home setting. Their kind of heroism is less likely to require physical strength and more likely to occur in private. For example, most people who rescued Jews during the Nazi holocaust were very careful to conceal their heroism. In summary, then, both men and women can be heroic, but the nature of their heroism is somewhat different.

NURTURANCE

Nurturance is a kind of helping in which someone gives care to another person, usually someone who is younger or less competent. The stereotype suggests that women are more nurturant than men. In fact, women rate themselves higher on this characteristic than men do (Feingold, 1994; P. J. Watson et al., 1994).

Here's a related question: Do females find babies more interesting and engaging than males do? As we've seen before, the answer to this question depends on the operational definitions that researchers use. For example, women and men are equally responsive to babies when the operational definition requires a physiological measure (e.g., heart rate) or a behavioral measure (e.g., playing with the baby). However, when the operational definition is based on self-report, women rate themselves as being more attracted to babies (Berman, 1980; M. C. Hamilton, 2001).

Judith Blakemore (1998) examined whether preschool girls and boys differ in their interest in babies. She asked parents to observe their children interacting with an unfamiliar baby on three separate occasions—for example, when a family with a baby came to visit in the home. As an additional precaution, each parent was also instructed to find another person who could simultaneously observe the preschoolers' behavior; Blakemore found that the parents' ratings were highly correlated with the other observers' ratings. The analysis of the ratings showed that preschool girls scored higher than boys in their amount of nurturance toward the baby, degree of interest in the baby, and kissing and holding the baby.

However, Blakemore noted that some parents had rated themselves as being tolerant of "girl-like behavior" in their sons. Interestingly, these parents tended to have sons who were highly interested in babies and very nurturant toward these babies. Notice, then, that preschool girls are often higher than boys on behavioral measures of both nurturance and interactions with a baby, although some preschool boys can overcome the stereotypes.

EMPATHY

You show **empathy** when you understand the emotion that another person is feeling and when you experience that same emotion. When empathic people watch someone lose a contest, they can experience the same feelings of anger, frustration, embarrassment, and disappointment that the loser feels. According to the stereotype, women are more empathic than men. However, researchers typically find substantial gender differences only when the results are based on self-reports (Cowan & Khatchadourian, 2003; N. Eisenberg & Lennon, 1983; N. Eisenberg et al., 1996; P. W. Garner & Estep, 2001). The research findings will remind you of our discussion about responsiveness to babies:

1. *Females and males are equally empathic when the operational definition requires physiological measures.* Specifically, measures such as heart rate, pulse, skin conductance, and blood pressure typically show no gender differences in empathy.
2. *Females and males are equally empathic when the operational definition requires nonverbal measures.* For example, some studies have measured empathy in terms of the observer's facial, vocal, and gestural measures. A typical study examines whether children's facial expressions change in response to hearing an infant cry. Using this nonverbal measure, boys and girls usually do not differ in their empathy.
3. *Females are more empathic than males when the operational definition is based on self-report.* To assess empathy, a typical questionnaire includes items such as "I tend to get emotionally involved with a friend's problems." Studies with adolescents and adults usually find that females report more empathy than do males. Furthermore, males who rate themselves relatively high in "feminine characteristics" also report that they are high in empathy (Karniol et al., 1998).

In related research, K. J. K. Klein and Hodges (2001) examined empathic accuracy. A person is high in empathic accuracy if she or he can correctly guess which emotions another person is experiencing. In the control condition, women earned higher scores in empathic accuracy. However, women and men were equally accurate if (a) they received feedback on their accuracy or (b) if they were paid when their empathic accuracy was high.

In summary, the research demonstrates that gender differences in self-reported empathy are far from universal. As we have emphasized, we cannot answer the question of whether males or females are more empathic unless we know how empathy is measured and whom we are studying. Once again, we see an illustration of Theme 1: Gender differences certainly are not found in every condition.

Moral Judgments About Social Relationships

Do males and females tend to make different kinds of decisions when they make moral judgments that have implications for other people's lives? We'll explore this controversial topic in some detail because it has important consequences for helping and caring. First, let's consider some theoretical background, emphasizing the important contributions of Carol Gilligan. Then we'll review other research, which generally supports the similarities perspective. Finally, we'll summarize the issues.

THEORETICAL BACKGROUND.   Several prominent feminist theorists have argued that gender differences in moral judgments are large. They also emphasize that the characteristics traditionally associated with women have been undervalued (e.g., Gilligan, 1982; Jordan, 1997). These theorists favor the **differences perspective,** which tends to exaggerate gender differences; they view males and females as being different and as having mutually exclusive characteristics. Their relational model is also consistent with cultural feminism. As we discussed in Chapter 1, **cultural feminism** emphasizes the positive qualities that are presumably stronger in women than in men—qualities such as nurturing and caring for others.

The **similarities perspective,** in contrast, tends to minimize gender differences, arguing that males and females are generally similar. As you know from Theme 1, this book typically favors a similarities perspective. The similarities perspective is most consistent with the framework of **liberal feminism;** by de-emphasizing gender roles and increasing equal rights laws, the gender similarities will increase still further. Those who favor the similarities perspective admire some aspects of Gilligan's model, which we'll discuss next. However, supporters of the similarities perspective argue that women and men are fairly similar in their concerns about helping and caring; the two genders do not live on separate planets.

Carol Gilligan eloquently expressed the differences perspective in her 1982 book, *In a Different Voice*. Gilligan's book was partly a feminist response to the research by Lawrence Kohlberg (1981, 1984). Kohlberg had argued that men are more likely than women to achieve sophisticated levels of moral development. Gilligan (1982) criticized the masculine bias in the moral dilemmas that Kohlberg had tested. For our purposes, however, the most interesting aspect of her book is that she provided a feminist approach to moral development (Clinchy & Norem, 1998). According to Gilligan, women are *not* morally inferior to men, but they do "speak in a different voice." Gilligan emphasized that women's voices have been ignored by mainstream psychology. We must remember this important point, even if research does not consistently support her actual theories (R. C. Barnett & Rivers, 2004).

Gilligan (1982) contrasted two approaches to moral decision making. The **justice approach** emphasizes that an individual is part of a hierarchy in which some people have more power and influence than others. Gilligan proposed that men tend to emphasize justice and the legal system when making moral decisions. In contrast, the **care approach** emphasizes that individuals are interrelated with one another in a web of connections. Gilligan proposed that women tend to favor the care perspective, in which life is based on connections with others.

Numerous feminists, including many from disciplines outside psychology, embraced Gilligan's emphasis on gender differences (described by Kimball, 1995). It's likely that Gilligan's theory was especially appealing to nonpsychologists because it matched people's stereotypes that men are hierarchical and women are interconnected (Brabeck & Shore, 2002; Schmid Mast, 2004). However, many psychologists argued that men and women are more likely to show similar styles of moral reasoning. The dissenters also pointed out that if we were to glorify women's special nurturance and caring, men would be less likely to recognize and develop their own competence in that area (H. Lerner, 1989; Tavris, 1992).

SUBSEQUENT RESEARCH. A variety of studies have been conducted to examine gender comparisons in moral reasoning. An occasional study reports that women are somewhat more likely than men to adopt a care perspective (e.g., Crandall et al., 1999; Finlay & Love, 1998). However, most of the results support the similarities perspective: Men and women typically respond similarly (e.g., Brabeck & Brabeck, 2006; Brabeck & Shore, 2002; W. L. Gardner & Gabriel, 2004). In addition, the individual differences are substantial. For example, boys who are high in traditionally feminine characteristics are likely to emphasize the care approach, echoing the results we saw in the discussion of nurturance on pages 191–192 (Karniol et al., 2003). Furthermore, a meta-analysis by Jaffee and Hyde (2000) found gender similarities in 73% of the 160 studies they examined. The *d* was 0.28, indicating a small gender difference.

Let's consider a study by Skoe and her coauthors (2002). In one part of this study, college students rated the importance of moral dilemmas that focused on the care approach, as well as moral dilemmas that focused on the justice approach. Women thought that the "care dilemmas" were slightly more important than the "justice dilemmas." However, men thought that the "care dilemmas" were *much* more important than the "justice dilemmas." These results contradict Gilligan's proposal that women are more likely than men to focus on caring and interpersonal relationships.

Some critics of Gilligan's theory argue that her approach is based on European American values (e.g., Brabeck & Brabeck, 2006; Brabeck & Satiani, 2001; Lykes & Qin, 2001). For example, Brabeck (1996) interviewed teenage boys in Guatemala. When asked about the characteristics they most valued, they emphasized helping other people and improving the community. Critics also argue that we cannot carefully examine gender comparisons in moral judgments unless we understand the social setting and context in which people make these judgments (Brabeck & Shore, 2002; J. D. Yoder & Kahn, 2003).

SUMMARY OF MORAL JUDGMENTS. Carol Gilligan contributed an important framework by emphasizing our responsibility to other people and our interconnections with them. She emphasized that the standard theory had downplayed the ethic of care, a value traditionally associated with women. However, the current research does not support the idea of major gender differences in moral judgment. I'm more persuaded by the research that demonstrates how men and women respond similarly to a wide variety of moral dilemmas. Men and women seem to live in the same moral world. This generalization is especially true when men and women provide judgments about similar moral dilemmas and when we consider the values of people who are not European American. We share the same basic values that include both justice and care (Brabeck & Shore, 2002; Kunkel & Burleson, 1998).

FRIENDSHIP

For many decades, psychologists ignored the topic of friendship; aggression was a much more popular topic! However, in recent years, many books and articles have discussed issues relevant to gender differences in friendship (e.g., Fehr, 2004; Foels & Tomcho, 2005; Monsour, 2002; Winstead & Griffin, 2001). Let's consider two components of gender comparisons in friendship: (1) Are there gender differences in the nature of women's and men's friendships? (2) Do women and men help their friends in different ways?

THE NATURE OF WOMEN'S AND MEN'S FRIENDSHIPS. Try to create a mental image of two women who are good friends with each other, and think about the nature of their friendship. Now do the same for two men who are good friends. Are female-female friendships basically different from male-male friendships? You can probably anticipate the conclusion we will reach in this section: Although gender differences are observed in some components of friendship, gender similarities are more striking.

We find gender similarities when we assess what friends do when they get together. Specifically, both female friends and male friends are most likely to just talk. They are generally less likely to work on a specific task or project together. And they rarely meet for the purpose of working on some problem that has arisen in their friendship (Duck & Wright, 1993; Fehr, 2004; P. H. Wright, 1998). Another gender similarity is that females and males report the same degree of satisfaction with their same-gender friendships (Brabeck & Brabeck, 2006; Crick & Rose, 2000; Foels & Tomcho, 2005). However, females also value physical contact with the friend, whereas—no surprise—males mentioned this less often (Brabeck & Brabeck, 2006).

According to research in both Canada and the United States, women and men typically believe that self-disclosure increases the intimacy of a friendship (Fehr, 2004; Monsour, 1992). When you engage in **self-disclosure**, you reveal information about yourself to another person. Both women and men also emphasize emotional expressiveness, communication skills, unconditional support, and trust (Monsour, 1992; P. H. Wright, 1998).

Other research suggests that women typically value self-disclosure somewhat more than men. Dindia and Allen (1992) conducted a meta-analysis of 205 studies, which reported on 23,702 people. The *d* was 0.18, a small effect size, with women disclosing somewhat more than men. Recent studies generally report that women are slightly more self-disclosing (Dindia, 2002; Fehr, 2004).

Why should women tend to be more self-disclosing? One reason is that women value talking about feelings more than men do; as we've already discussed, females receive greater training in emotions. In addition, North Americans have gender-related norms about self-disclosure. Men may *want* to self-disclose. However, they choose not to share their private feelings with other men, especially if they are guided by our culture's anti-gay messages (Fehr, 2004; Winstead & Griffin, 2001; P. H. Wright, 1998).

Recent research by Beverley Fehr (2004) compares women's and men's perspectives on qualities that are important for a close, intimate friendship. Try Demonstration 6.4 now to see whether you can predict which characteristics women rate higher than men do.

Demonstration 6.4

CHARACTERISTICS OF INTIMATE FRIENDSHIPS

Beverley Fehr (2004) conducted a study at the University of Winnipeg in which she asked female and male students to indicate how important certain characteristics would be for an intimate friendship. For five of the items below, females gave higher ratings to the characteristics than males did; for the remaining five, females and males supplied similar ratings of importance. Select the five characteristics that you think revealed gender differences. The answers appear at the end of this chapter, on page 208.

1. If I need to talk, my friend will listen.
2. If I have a problem, my friend will listen.
3. If someone was insulting me or saying negative things behind my back, my friend would stick up for me.
4. No matter who I am or what I do, my friend will accept me.
5. Even if it feels as though no one cares, I know my friend does.
6. If I need to cry, my friend will be there for me.
7. If something is important to me, my friend will respect it.
8. If I do something wrong, my friend will forgive me.
9. If I need cheering up, my friend will try to make me laugh.
10. If something is bothering me, my friend will understand how I feel.

Source: Based on Fehr (2004).

How Women and Men Help Their Friends. Several articles and books focus on how people help their friends in real-life settings. These studies often find that women are more helpful (Belansky & Boggiano, 1994; D. George et al., 1998; S. E. Taylor, 2002). For example, George and his colleagues (1998) asked 1,004 community residents to describe a recent situation in which they helped a friend of the same gender. Compared to men, women reported spending more time helping their friend. Also, Belansky and Boggiano (1994) reported gender differences in the kind of help people would offer. For example, a scenario in their study described a friend from high school who was considering dropping out of school. Women were likely to say that they would encourage the friend to talk about the situation. Men were likely to split their votes between two strategies: the "let's talk about it" strategy and a problem-solving strategy such as encouraging the friend to make a list of pros and cons about dropping out.

Several recent studies have explored whether women and men differ in the kind of emotional support they offer their friends. As you might expect, the research shows that the gender differences are subtle rather than widespread. For example, Erina MacGeorge and her colleagues (2004) analyzed several studies and found that both women and men are much more likely to offer sympathy or advice to a worried friend, rather than changing the subject or telling the friend not to worry. However, women's comments to their friends show somewhat more emotional sensitivity, compared to men's comments (MacGeorge et al., 2003). Furthermore, men are somewhat more likely than women to blame male friends for a problem they have (MacGeorge, 2003). Taking everything into account, MacGeorge and her coauthors (2004) comment on the idea of two different cultures—a Mars culture and a Venus culture—that cannot communicate with each other. As these researchers conclude, "The different cultures thesis is a myth that should be discarded" (p. 143).

Section Summary

Characteristics Related to Helping and Caring

1. Overall gender differences in helpfulness are not strong; men are more likely to help on dangerous tasks and on tasks requiring expertise in masculine areas. When helping friends, gender differences may be minimal or women may help more.

2. The research on heroism is consistent with Eagly's social role theory, which says that the gender differences in helping patterns can be traced to women's and men's current work roles and family responsibilities.

3. In general, women and men do not differ in nurturance or in responsiveness to babies; preschool girls may show more interest in infants than most preschool boys do; however, boys who have been reared in nontraditional households are very nurturant toward babies.

4. In general, women and men do not differ in empathy; gender similarities are common for physiological and nonverbal measures, but women are typically

more empathic on self-report measures. Women and men have equal empathic accuracy when people receive feedback and when they receive payment for accurate responses.

5. Carol Gilligan (1982), a proponent of the differences perspective, has suggested that men favor a justice approach, whereas women emphasize a care approach.

6. Most research supports a similarities perspective, especially when people make moral judgments about the same kind of situation and when considering the values of cultures other than European American groups.

7. Men and women have similar friendship patterns in terms of the activities that friends engage in when they get together and in terms of satisfaction with their friendships; women are typically somewhat more self-disclosing than men are.

8. Men and women tend to give similar kinds of emotional support to their friends.

CHARACTERISTICS RELATED TO AGGRESSION AND POWER

We have seen that the research on helping and caring does not allow a simple, straightforward conclusion about gender differences. The situation is similar for attributes associated with aggression and power.

In the previous section, we focused on characteristics that are stereotypically associated with females. In this section, we will focus on characteristics that are stereotypically associated with males. An important central topic in this cluster is **aggression,** which we'll define as any behavior directed toward another person with the intention of doing harm (J. W. White, 2001).

Let's begin by considering some issues raised by social constructionists about the nature of aggression, and next we'll examine the research on aggression. Then we'll shift our focus from aggression to power, as we look at the topics of leadership and persuasion.

GENDER AND AGGRESSION: THE SOCIAL CONSTRUCTIONIST PERSPECTIVE

As we saw in the introduction to this chapter, social constructionists argue that we humans actively construct our views of the world. This point also holds true for theorists and researchers trying to make sense out of human behavior. As a result, researchers who are studying aggression are guided by the way scholars have constructed the categories. The customary language has limited the way that researchers tend to view aggression (Marecek, 2001a; Underwood, 2003; J. W. White, 2001). Consequently, the cultural lenses that researchers wear will often restrict their vision.

In particular, researchers have often constructed aggression so that it is considered a male characteristic. To appreciate this point, reread the definition of aggression in the second paragraph of this section. What kinds of aggression do you visualize—hitting, shooting, and other kinds of physical violence? However, aggression can be verbal as well as physical. If you are a typical college student, you are much more likely to experience verbal aggression, instead of physical aggression (Howard & Hollander, 1997). An unkind remark may not require a trip to the hospital, but it can have a profound effect on your self-esteem. Still, our cultural lenses usually prevent us from seeing the kinds of aggression that might be more common in females.

Social constructionists point out that each culture devises its own set of lenses (K. J. Gergen & Gergen, 2004; Matsumoto & Juang, 2004). As a result, cultures may differ in their construction of social behaviors, such as aggression. Consider the egalitarian culture on the island of Vanatinai, a remote island near New Guinea in the South Pacific (Lepowsky, 1998). In this remarkable culture, both girls and boys are socialized to be self-confident but not aggressive. During Lepowski's 10 years of research, she discovered only five acts of physical violence, and women were the aggressors in four of these incidents. In a culture that discourages aggression, gender differences may disappear.

Closer to home, M. G. Harris (1994) reported on female members of Mexican American gangs in the Los Angeles area. The young women she interviewed stated that they had joined the gang for group support but also because of a need for revenge. One young woman emphasized, "Most of us in our gangs always carry weapons. Guns, knives, bats, crowbars, any kind. . . . Whatever we can get hold of that we know can hurt, then we'll have it" (p. 297). In a subculture that admires physical aggression, gender differences may disappear as both females and males adopt violent tactics (Jack, 1999a; Miller-Johnson et al., 2005).

Throughout this exploration of aggression, keep in mind the cultural lenses that we wear. Also, remember that how we frame our questions has an important influence on the answers we obtain.

PHYSICAL AGGRESSION VERSUS RELATIONAL AGGRESSION

As we have discussed, our cultural lenses typically encourage us to see aggression from a male perspective, which emphasizes physical aggression. As you might expect, **physical aggression** is aggression that could physically harm another person. In general, males are more likely than females to demonstrate physical aggression.

Let's examine the research on gender comparisons in crime rates, an important index of physical aggression. The data on crime show that men are more likely than women to be the offenders in almost every category of criminal behavior (C. A. Anderson & Bushman, 2002). For example, in the United States, men account for 73% of the arrests for violent crime, including murder, robbery, and assault (U.S. Census Bureau, 2006). In Canada, men account for 84% of those who are charged with a violent crime (Statistics

Canada, 2006). We'll return to this topic in Chapter 13 when we consider domestic violence.

In both Canada and the United States, the media are eager to point out how the number of women in prison has been rapidly rising. However, the media have been reporting an increase for more than 25 years (S. R. Hawkins et al., 2003). In fact, this increase is a well-established trend.

What can we conclude from these data on criminal behavior? Women are clearly capable of committing atrociously violent murders (C. L. Meyer & Oberman, 2001). Women have also committed other horrifying acts of aggression. For instance, when U.S. newspapers reported that American soldiers had been terrorizing Iraqi prisoners, one of the most chilling photos showed petite and perky Lynndie England. She had a wide grin on her face, as she dragged a naked Iraqi man around on a leash (Cocco, 2004). Yes, women may be somewhat more likely to commit crimes now than in earlier eras. Still, the bottom line is that gender differences in physical aggression remain relatively large.

Now let us consider a different kind of aggression, one that threatens interpersonal relationships (e.g., Crick, Casas, & Nelson, 2002; Crick, Grotpeter, & Bigbee, 2002; A. J. Rose et al., 2004; Underwood, 2003). **Relational aggression** is aggression that could harm another person through intentionally manipulating interpersonal relationships, such as friendships (Crick et al., 2004). For example, someone may spread a lie about a person or intentionally exclude a person from a group. This type of aggression is especially likely in children between the ages of 10 and 12. Relational aggression is often more common in females than in males (Archer, 2004; Archer & Coyne, 2005; Geiger et al., 2004). Furthermore, girls are more likely than boys to report that relational aggression is very upsetting (Crick & Nelson, 2002).

In a representative study, Jamie Ostrov and his colleagues (2004) studied 3- to 5-year-old children who attended a preschool program. These researchers observed groups of three same-gender children, who had been instructed to use a crayon to color in a picture—such as a cartoon of Winnie the Pooh—on a white sheet of paper. Each observation period began by placing three crayons in the center of the table. One crayon was an appropriate color, such as an orange crayon for coloring Winnie the Pooh. However, the other two crayons were white—clearly useless for coloring on white paper. As you might expect, the children in this condition wanted to have the orange crayon, rather than a white one, and they tried different tactics to take this crayon away from the child who was currently using it.

Trained observers recorded measures of physical aggression, such as hitting or pushing another child. They also recorded measures of relational aggression, such as spreading rumors about a child or ignoring a child.

As you can see from Figure 6.4, the boys were more likely than the girls to use physical aggression. However, the girls were more likely than the boys to use relational aggression. For example, in one group of three girls, Girl 3 is holding the only useful crayon. Girl 1 said to Girl 2, "I gotta tell you something" (p. 367). She then got out of her seat to whisper something in Girl 2's

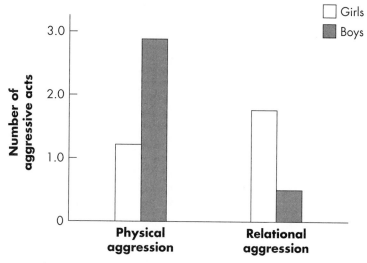

FIGURE 6.4 | THE NUMBER OF ACTS OF PHYSICAL AND RELATIONAL AGGRESSION DELIVERED BY BOYS AND GIRLS.

Source: Based on Ostrov et al. (2004).

ear. Studies like these help us to reinterpret the myth of the nonaggressive female. However, in emphasizing females' use of relational violence, we must not lose sight of the harmful consequences of males' physical violence. No one would argue that a woman gossiping is equivalent to a man breaking someone's arm.

GENDER AND AGGRESSION: OTHER IMPORTANT FACTORS

So far, we have seen that males may be relatively high in physical aggression but that females are relatively high in relational aggression. What other factors play a role in gender comparisons?

For many years, psychologists seemed convinced that males are consistently more aggressive than females. However, a breakthrough in our understanding of gender and aggression came from a classic review of previous studies, conducted by Ann Frodi and her colleagues (1977). According to the studies they examined, males were often found to be more aggressive. However, only 39% of these studies showed males being more aggressive than females for all the research conditions. The analysis by Frodi and her colleagues has now been joined by additional research and meta-analyses (e.g., Archer, 2004; Bettencourt & Miller, 1996; L. R. Brody, 1999; G. P. Knight et al., 1996). These reports inform us that gender differences depend on factors such as operational definitions and the social context. Let's consider these two factors:

1. Gender differences are relatively large when measuring spontaneous aggression. Men are more likely than women to show spontaneous, unprovoked aggression—the kind of aggression that cannot be traced to a

specific cause. In contrast, suppose that a person has been insulted, which provides a specific excuse for an aggressive response. In this case, both men and women are likely to respond aggressively. With provoked aggression, no gender differences are observed (C. A. Anderson & Bushman, 2002; Archer, 2004; L. R. Brody, 1999).

2. Gender differences are relatively large when the individuals know each other. For example, in a study by Lightdale and Prentice (1994), a pair of participants played a video game in which each person dropped bombs on the competitor's target. When the two participants did not know each other beforehand, no gender differences were observed. However, when the participants had briefly met before the game began, men played the game significantly more aggressively than women did. Here's one possible explanation for the gender difference in this condition: Compared to the men, women may have felt more empathy for someone they had met, so the women might have been more reluctant to treat their opponents in an aggressive fashion (Carlo et al., 1999).

When you think about gender and aggression, keep in mind the general principle that the psychological characteristics of males and females always show a substantial overlap (Archer, 2004). For example, some studies have compared boys and girls on measures of observed physical aggression (e.g., Archer, 2004; Favreau, 1993; Frey & Hoppe-Graff, 1994). Gender differences should be relatively large in these studies because they measure physical violence. Still, most of the boys and girls were similarly nonaggressive, and the gender differences could be traced to a small number of aggressive boys.

Also keep in mind that researchers and theorists emphasize the kinds of aggression that are stereotypically masculine. They seldom explore those domains in which women may be more aggressive. As a result, people tend to believe that females are rarely aggressive. The myth of the nonaggressive female has several disadvantages for North American society:

1. If women see themselves as weak and nonaggressive, some of them may believe that they cannot defend themselves against men's aggression (J. W. White & Kowalski, 1994).
2. Because competitiveness is associated with aggression, some women may be denied access to professions that value competition.
3. Aggressiveness may be seen as normal for males, so some men may choose not to inhibit their aggressive tendencies.

In short, both women and men suffer when we hold stereotyped views of the gender differences in aggression.

LEADERSHIP

So far, we have considered only the negative characteristics associated with power, such as physical and relational aggression. In contrast, leadership can be an important positive role associated with power. Let's consider two

Demonstration 6.5

LEADERSHIP STYLES

Imagine that you have completed college, and you are applying for a job. Try to imagine what characteristics your new boss will have. Place a check mark in front of every item you would *most* like to see in an ideal boss.

_____ 1. My boss will be optimistic and enthusiastic about the organization's goals.

_____ 2. My boss will give rewards when employees do satisfactory work.

_____ 3. My boss will have personal characteristics that encourage me to respect him or her.

_____ 4. My boss will focus on mentoring employees and will try to figure out what each person needs.

_____ 5. My boss will wait until a problem becomes serious before trying to fix the problem.

_____ 6. My boss will communicate with employees about the values of the organization's mission.

_____ 7. My boss will pay special attention to employees' mistakes.

Now read the section on leadership to determine which leadership style you prefer.

Source: Based on Eagly et al. (2003) and Powell & Graves (2003).

questions about gender and leadership: Do women and men differ in their style of leadership, and do they differ in their leadership effectiveness? But first, try Demonstration 6.5.

LEADERSHIP STYLE.   Current researchers who study leadership often refer to two effective kinds of leadership styles (Eagly et al., 2003; Powell & Graves, 2003). Leaders who have a **transformational style of leadership** will inspire employees, gain their trust, and encourage them to develop their potential skills. The name "transformational" makes sense because these leaders encourage employees to *transform* themselves. In Demonstration 6.5, items 1, 3, 4, and 6 represent a transformational boss. In contrast, leaders who have a **transactional style of leadership** will clarify the tasks that employees must accomplish, rewarding them when they meet the appropriate objectives and correcting them when they do not meet these objectives. The name "transactional" makes sense because the leader focuses on straightforward exchanges: "If you do X, I will give you Y." In Demonstration 6.5, items 2, 5, and 7 represent a transactional style. Alice Eagly and her colleagues (2003) conducted a meta-analysis of 45 studies that focused on gender comparisons in leadership style. As you might predict, the results were complex. However, women leaders tended to receive slightly higher scores on the transformational dimension, with *d* values that averaged 0.10. Women were also slightly higher on the "reward" aspect of transactional leadership (item 2), but slightly lower on the other aspects of transactional leadership (items 5 and 6).

An article in a mental health newsletter summarized the meta-analysis and argued that the world "might be in better shape if women were more often in charge" ("Do women make better leaders?," 2004, p. 7). However, I was impressed that the research tended to indicate gender similarities. Furthermore, gender similarities in leadership style are even stronger when we compare men and women who occupy similar roles in an organization (Eagly & Johannesen-Schmidt, 2001).

LEADERSHIP EFFECTIVENESS.   Which gender is actually more effective in the leadership role? Eagly and her coauthors (2003) performed a meta-analysis of the research conducted with an assessment technique called the Multifactor Leadership Questionnaire (MLQ). Females scored somewhat higher than males on the MLQ ($d = .22$).

But how do people rate female leaders, compared to male leaders? A variety of surveys suggests that more people say they would prefer to work for a male, rather than a female (Eagly, 2003; Eagly & Carli, 2003; Eagly & Karau, 2002; Powell & Graves, 2003). Other research shows that female leaders receive especially negative ratings when they use a power-oriented leadership style or when they claim to be an expert about a stereotypically masculine topic (Chin, 2004; Lips, 2001; J. Yoder et al., 1998). Traditionally masculine males are especially likely to give negative ratings to female leaders (Rivero et al., 2004).

All this research on leadership ability has important implications for women and work, the topic of our next chapter. Specifically, the research tells us that women are—if anything—somewhat more effective as leaders. However, the research also tells us that people react differently to male and female leaders, consistent with Theme 2.

Unfortunately, however, few of the studies on leadership examine ethnic factors. We don't know, for example, whether Black men and women differ in their leadership style. We also don't know whether ethnicity has an influence on people's ratings of male and female leaders. For instance, would people be especially likely to downgrade an Asian American woman or Latina woman if she held a leadership position in a traditionally masculine field?

PERSUASION

Suppose that you want to persuade a clerk in a grocery store to locate an item for you, and he refuses to be helpful. What persuasion strategy would you be likely to use? Carothers and Allen (1999) found that male and female students who were high in masculinity were more likely than other students to say that they would threaten to complain to the manager. In contrast, the other students preferred a more gentle approach.

How do people respond to the persuasive efforts of men and women? In general, the research shows that men are more persuasive than women (Carli, 2001; Carli & Eagly, 2002). This gender difference can be partly traced to stereotypes about women. As we saw in Chapter 2 (pp. 55–56), people think women are friendly and nice, but not especially competent. When women try to influence other people—and they therefore violate this stereotype—they may encounter problems (Carli & Bukatko, 2000).

Our discussion of leadership pointed out that female leaders are downgraded if they appear too powerful and masculine. Similarly, women may be less persuasive if they appear too masculine. For example, men are not persuaded by women who use assertive language. Instead, they are persuaded when women use the kind of tentative language we discussed earlier, such as "I'm not sure" (Buttner & McEnally, 1996; Carli, 1990, 2001). Interestingly, though, *women* are often more persuaded by a woman who uses assertive language than by a woman who uses tentative language (Carli, 1990). A female politician who plans to give a persuasive speech to voters therefore faces a double bind: If she is too assertive, she'll lose the males, but if she is too tentative, she'll lose the females!

Other research shows this same pattern of gender differences in response to a competent, assertive woman (Carli & Eagly, 2002). For example, Dodd and her colleagues (2001) asked students to read a vignette focusing on a conversation among three friends: one woman and two men. In the story, one of the men makes a sexist comment, and the woman either ignores it or confronts it. The results of the study showed that the male students liked the woman more if she ignored the comment rather than confronted it. In contrast, the female students liked the woman more if she confronted the comment rather than ignored it.

Women also face a problem if they use nonverbal behavior that appears too masculine. An interesting analysis by Linda Carli and her colleagues (1995) compared women who used a competent nonverbal style and men who used the same style. A competent nonverbal style includes a relatively rapid rate of speech, upright posture, calm hand gestures, and moderately high eye contact when speaking. A male audience was significantly more influenced by a man who used this competent style than by a woman who used this same style. According to other research, women are more successful if they act modest. In contrast, men are more successful if they are boastful and self-promoting (Carli & Eagly, 2002; Rudman, 1998). Again, behavior associated with high status is not acceptable when used by a person with low status (Carli, 1999; Carli & Bukatko, 2000; Rudman, 1998).

As you can see, subtle sexism persists in social interactions. A competent woman finds herself in a double bind. If she speaks confidently and uses competent nonverbal behavior, she may not persuade the men with whom she interacts. But if she speaks tentatively and uses less competent nonverbal behavior, she will not live up to her own personal standards—and she might not persuade other women. Keep this issue in mind when you read about women's work experiences in Chapter 7.

Throughout this chapter, we have compared women and men on a variety of social and personality characteristics. For example, we noted occasional gender differences in communication patterns, helpfulness, aggression, and leadership. However, gender similarities are typically more common. Furthermore, every characteristic we discussed demonstrates a substantial overlap in the distribution of female and male scores.

In summary, we can reject the claim that men and women are from different planets and have little in common. The title of John Gray's (1992) book, *Men Are From Mars, Women Are From Venus,* was certainly enticing enough to produce a best-seller. However, its message does not match the gender similarities found in psychology research. Furthermore, in Chapter 7, we'll continue to search for factors that could explain why women are seldom employed in certain high-prestige occupations and why women are treated differently from men in the workplace. In the chapter you've just read, we have seen that major gender differences in social and personality characteristics cannot explain these discrepancies.

Section Summary

Characteristics Related to Aggression and Power

1. The social constructionist perspective points out that North American scholars have emphasized the stereotypically masculine components of aggression. They have usually ignored the kinds of aggression that might be more common in females; they have also paid little attention to gender similarities in other cultures and subcultures.

2. Researchers currently differentiate between two kinds of aggression. Males are typically higher in physical aggression, whereas females are typically higher in relational aggression.

3. Gender differences in aggression are inconsistent. These gender differences are relatively large when spontaneous aggression is measured and when individuals know each other.

4. When leaders adopt a transformational style, they inspire employees, gain their trust, and encourage them to develop their skills. When leaders adopt a transactional style, they clarify employees' tasks, reward them when they meet objectives, and correct them when they do not meet objectives. Compared to men, women are slightly more likely than men to adopt a transformational style and to reward employees who meet objectives. In contrast, men are somewhat more likely to clarify employees' tasks and to correct employees for not meeting objectives.

5. Females score somewhat higher than males on an assessment of leadership effectiveness, although research suggests that more people say they would prefer to work for a male than for a female. Female leaders are especially likely to be downgraded when they act in a traditionally masculine fashion and when they are rated by traditionally masculine males.

6. Men and women generally use similar persuasion strategies, but women face a double bind when they want to be persuasive. If they appear stereotypically masculine, they won't persuade men; if they appear less assertive and more stereotypically feminine, they won't persuade women.

CHAPTER REVIEW QUESTIONS

1. In the discussion of communication styles, we pointed out that men seem to take up more space than women, whether we use the word *space* to refer to physical space or, more figuratively, conversational space. Discuss this point, making as many gender comparisons as possible.

2. Imagine that two college students—a male and a female—are sitting next to each other on a bench somewhere on your college campus. They have never met before, but they begin a conversation. Compare the two genders with respect to verbal communication (talkativeness, interruptions, language style, language content) and nonverbal communication (personal space, posture, gaze, facial expression, decoding ability).

3. Turn back to Chapter 3, and review the social learning and cognitive developmental approaches to gender development (pp. 85–87). Point out how these two approaches could explain each of the gender differences in verbal and nonverbal communication. How could the power explanation and the social status explanation in this chapter (p. 187) account for most gender differences in communication?

4. The social constructionist perspective emphasizes that our cultural lenses shape the way we ask questions. In particular, these lenses influence the choices that psychologists make when they select topics for research. Summarize the topics of helpfulness, aggression, leadership, and persuasion, pointing out how the nature of the results could be influenced by the kinds of issues studied in each area (e.g., aggression in stereotypically masculine areas versus stereotypically feminine areas).

5. According to stereotypes, women care about interpersonal relationships, whereas men care about dominating other people. As with many stereotypes, this contrast contains a grain of truth. Discuss the grain of truth with respect to helping, friendship, aggression, leadership,

and persuasion. Then point out the number of similarities shared by males and females.

6. What kinds of factors influence gender differences in aggression? Combining as many factors as possible, describe a situation in which gender differences are likely to be exaggerated and a situation in which they are likely to be minimal.

7. Some researchers argue that gender differences are likely to emerge in areas in which men and women have had different amounts of practice or training. Using the chapter outline on page 175, point out how differential practice can account for many of the gender differences.

8. Page 178 lists three circumstances under which we tend to find large gender differences in social and personality characteristics. Describe what these factors would predict about gender comparisons in the following situations: (a) A male professor and a female professor who have similar status are discussing a professional article they have both read; what are their likely patterns of gaze? (b) A group of male and female students are asked to talk about the nurturing support that they have given to a younger sibling. (c) A lecture hall is filled with people, and the VCR is not working; the speaker asks for volunteers to figure out the problem. Who will help?

9. In most of this chapter, we focused on the topic of gender of the subject. However, we also discussed the gender of the stimulus. How do people react to male and female leaders and to females who are trying to influence other people? Why is the phrase "double bind" relevant to this question?

10. To solidify your knowledge in preparation for studying women and work (Chapter 7), think of a profession in which relatively few women are employed. Review each of the social and personality characteristics that this chapter discusses. Note whether any of these factors provides a sufficient explanation for the relative absence of women in that profession.

KEY TERMS

*social constructionist approach (177)

*nonverbal communication (178)

*personal space (182)

*decoding ability (185)

*altruism (190)

heroism (191)

*social role (191)

*nurturance (191)

*empathy (192)

*differences perspective (193)

cultural feminism (193)

*similarities perspective (193)

*liberal feminism (193)

*justice approach (194)

care approach (194)

*self-disclosure (196)

*aggression (198)

*physical aggression (199)

*relational aggression (200)

transformational style of leadership (203)

transactional style of leadership (203)

 Note: The terms asterisked in the Key Terms section serve as good search terms for InfoTrac College Edition. Go to http://infotrac.thomsonlearning.com and try these added search terms.

RECOMMENDED READINGS

Barnett, R., & Rivers, C. (2004). *Same difference: How gender myths are hurting our relationships, our children, and our jobs.* New York: Basic Books. This is the book to buy for friends who believe that men and women come from different planets. In contrast to the standard pop psychology, Barnett and Rivers' book critically evaluates the gender-difference myths in areas such as emotions, power, and helping behavior.

Eckert, P., & McConnell-Ginet, S. (2003). *Language and gender.* New York: Cambridge University Press. Here is an excellent book that approaches language and gender from the perspective of linguistics, rather than psychology; it also conveys the subtlety of gender comparisons in language use.

Shields, S. A. (2002). *Speaking from the heart: Gender and the social meaning of emotion.* New York: Cambridge University Press. Stephanie Shields argues that emotion is at the core of our ideas about gender; her book is a concise, interesting, and well-informed exploration of this topic. Every college library should have a copy of this book.

Underwood, M. K. (2003). *Social aggression among girls.* New York: Guilford. In the current decade, many books have been published about aggression in girls and women. Most are intended for either a general audience or for researchers. This book is my current favorite because it is both readable and scholarly.

ANSWERS TO THE DEMONSTRATIONS

Demonstration 6.4. The statements that females were more likely than males to endorse are numbers 1, 2, 5, 6, and 10. No gender differences were found for numbers 3, 4, 7, 8, and 9.

ANSWERS TO THE TRUE-FALSE STATEMENTS

1. True (p. 178); 2. True (p. 179); 3. True (p. 183); 4. False (pp. 190–191); 5. False (p. 191); 6. False (pp. 194–195); 7. True (p. 195); 8. False (pp. 199–202); 9. False (p. 203); 10. True (p. 205).

7 | WOMEN AND WORK

True or False?

_____   1. Most U.S. women who have been on welfare—and then find jobs—are living below the poverty level.

_____   2. Researchers have found that the U.S. affirmative action policy has led to numerous cases of reverse discrimination against males.

_____   3. Although women earn lower incomes than men, the discrepancy can be explained by gender differences in education, specific occupation, and number of years of full-time employment.

_____   4. Men who are employed in traditionally female occupations—such as nursing—are often quickly promoted to management positions.

_____   5. If a woman in Latin America makes clothes in a U.S.-run sweatshop (a factory that violates labor laws), she typically earns about $1.00 an hour.

_____   6. Women and men in the same profession, such as medicine, are typically fairly similar in their cognitive and personality characteristics.

_____   7. Women in blue-collar jobs are usually dissatisfied with their work, especially because their salaries are so much lower than the salaries of other employed women.

_____   8. Research in both the United States and Canada shows that women spend about twice as long as men on household chores.

_____   9. Children in day-care centers have normal cognitive development compared to children cared for at home by their mothers; however, they have substantially more social and emotional problems.

_____   10. Because of their numerous responsibilities, employed women are more likely than nonemployed women to experience problems with their physical and psychological health.

Several relevant issues caught my attention as I prepared to write this chapter about women and work. My daughter, who works in the San Francisco Bay Area, sent me information about gender bias in a nearby sheriff's department. Only 13 of the 243 law enforcement deputies are females, and their male colleagues brag publicly about driving the women out of their department. Meanwhile, the female deputies report that the men often sexually harass them, and the harassers are often promoted (Women's Justice Center, 2005).

Soon afterward, a student in my psychology of women course forwarded an e-mail about "Equal Pay Day." According to data from 2004, U.S. women earn $.76 for every $1.00 that U.S. men earn (National Committee on Pay Equity, 2005). In other words, suppose that a man works for a full year and earns a salary of $30,000. A comparable woman would earn a salary of $22,800 during the same time period. To earn a total of $30,000, this woman would need to work for one full year . . . and then she would need to work until April 19 of the following year—roughly $3\frac{1}{2}$ months longer than the man!

Then I was glancing through my class notes related to women and work to locate additional material for this chapter. I discovered a note from a student who described her mother's experience with gender discrimination. Her mother—whom we will call Ms. W.—had worked with the same small business for 14 years. She knew every aspect of the business, from supervising the factory to managing the office. Several years ago, Ms. W. learned that her boss had decided to hire another man to help with some of her work. This man had the same educational credentials and much less job experience, yet he would earn twice the salary that Ms. W. was earning. Furthermore, Ms. W. would be responsible for training this new employee. At this point, Ms. W. decided to return to school, and she is currently completing her R.N. degree.

As we will see throughout this chapter, the gender differences in work-related skills and characteristics are often small, consistent with Theme 1 of this book. However, consistent with Theme 2, women and men are often treated differently. Women frequently face barriers with respect to hiring, salary, treatment, and advancement in the workplace.

We'll begin this chapter by exploring some general information about women and work, and next we'll consider several kinds of discrimination in the workplace. We'll then look at a variety of traditional and nontraditional occupations. In the final section of the chapter, we'll discuss how women coordinate their employment with family responsibilities.

BACKGROUND FACTORS RELATED TO WOMEN'S EMPLOYMENT

To remove any confusion, we first need to introduce some terms related to work. The general term **working women** refers to two categories:

1. **Employed women,** or women who work for pay. Employed women may receive a salary or be self-employed.
2. **Nonemployed women,** or women who are unpaid for their work. They may work for their families, in their homes, or for volunteer organizations, but they receive no money for these services.

As this chapter demonstrates, employment has become an increasingly important part of women's lives in North America. For example, in 1970, 43% of women over the age of 16 were employed, and that percentage has now increased to 60% (Bureau of Labor Statistics, 2004c). In Canada, about 58% of women over the age of 15 are employed (Statistics Canada, 2006). However, employment rates differ widely for other countries. Some representative employment rates for women are 38% for Mexico, 48% for Japan, 49% for France, 54% for Brazil, and 73% for Ghana (United Nations, 2006).

Here is another change: In some fields once reserved for men, the number of women has increased dramatically. Well into the twentieth century, women were barred from many medical schools. For years, Yale University Medical School clung to men-only admissions by arguing that the facilities did not include women's bathrooms (M. R. Walsh, 1990). As recently as 1983, only 29% of U.S. medical school graduates were women. Currently, 46% of medical school graduates are women (American Medical Association, 2005). The numbers of women in law schools and veterinary schools have also increased dramatically. We'll be well into the twenty-first century before an equal number of practicing doctors, lawyers, and veterinarians are female. However, the large percentage of women currently in the professional pipeline is encouraging.

In this chapter, we will examine areas in which women have made progress in recent decades, as well as areas in which women still face disadvantages. Let's begin this first section by considering some basic information about women's employment. Then we'll briefly explore two issues that are critical for women who are seeking employment: welfare and discrimination in hiring.

GENERAL INFORMATION ABOUT EMPLOYED WOMEN

What situations or characteristics predict whether a woman works outside the home? One of the best predictors of women's employment is her educational background. As you can see from Figure 7.1, U.S. women with at least a master's degree are much more likely than women with less than four years of high school to be employed outside the home (Bureau of Labor Statistics, 2004c). Education and employment are also highly correlated in Canada (Statistics Canada, 2006).

Several decades ago, one of the best predictors of a woman's employment was whether she had young children. However, the current U.S. data show that married women with children under the age of 3 do not differ from other married women in their rate of employment (Bureau of Labor Statistics, 2004c).

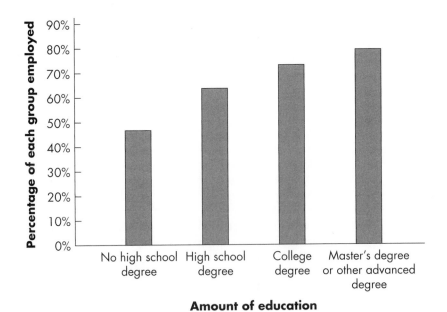

FIGURE 7.1   PERCENTAGE OF WOMEN IN THE U.S. LABOR FORCE, AS A FUNCTION OF EDUCATION.

Source: Based on Bureau of Labor Statistics (2004c).

The current data also show that ethnicity is not strongly related to participation in the labor force. For example, U.S. data show employment for 59% of European American women, 58% of Latina women, 62% of Black women, and 59% of Asian women (Bureau of Labor Statistics, 2004c). One group of women who face different barriers to employment are immigrant women. Many of these women are not fluent in the language of their new country. Their educational degrees, professional licenses, and work experience in another country may not be given full credit when they apply for a North American job (Berger, 2004; Naidoo, 2000).

Many immigrant women have little formal education. For instance, in the last two decades, 12% of the Asian women who immigrated to the United States had less than a ninth-grade education; the comparable figure for U.S.-born European American women is 5%. Immigrant women are likely to find low-paying work on the assembly line or in domestic settings (Hesse-Biber & Carter, 2000; Naidoo, 2000; Phizacklea, 2001). For example, about 500,000 women are domestic workers in New York City, where they may earn as little as $200 a month by working 18-hour days, with no days off (Das Gupta, 2003).

Immigrants from some countries are relatively well educated. For instance, of the Asian women in Canada, 47% have had at least some university education, in contrast to only 30% of women who list their ethnicity as "Canadians" (Finnie et al., 2005). In general, however, immigrants' salaries are significantly lower than nonimmigrants with comparable training (Berger, 2004; Hesse-Biber & Carter, 2000).

In summary, education and immigrant status are related to women's employment situation. However, two factors that are *not* related to employment are parental status and ethnicity.

WOMEN AND WELFARE

In the United States, an important long-term debate has focused on mothers who are not currently employed. If they do not find employment after an "appropriate" period of time, should the welfare payments for their children be suspended? This debate is especially crucial because welfare policy has important effects on women's lifetime prospects for employment.

The previous policy, called the Aid to Families with Dependent Children (AFDC) program, was created to provide welfare payments for children whose parents could not supply economic support. Although that program was far from perfect, it did benefit numerous low-income families. In 1996, President Clinton signed legislation that abolished AFDC and created a new program, called Temporary Assistance for Needy Families (TANF). This legislation includes many changes that jeopardize economically poor women. For example, individuals can only receive welfare for a lifetime maximum of 5 years. This plan assumes that welfare recipients are basically lazy, undisciplined women who will achieve dignity by taking a minimum-wage job (P. Kahn et al., 2004; Madsen, 2003).

The long-term goal of the U.S. welfare policy should be that a mother can earn enough money for the family to be self-sufficient (Kahne, 2004). Unfortunately, this is not the current goal. Furthermore, women in the TANF program are specifically discouraged from pursuing education beyond the level of high school (Belle, 2004; Ratner, 2004).

In addition, each of the 50 states is now allowed to decide which individuals are desperate enough to need financial assistance. Some states have imposed harsh barriers (P. Kahn & Polakow, 2004). TANF has had tragic consequences for many women, especially because most former recipients—who are currently employed—still live below the U.S. federal poverty line (P. Kahn & Polakow, 2004). For example, suppose that a college student who is a mother wants to escape from an abusive marriage. If she leaves the marriage and applies for welfare to support her children, she will be forced to leave college and earn a minimum wage in a low-level job (Evelyn, 2000).

However, a few states have emphasized that welfare should include the option of higher education. For example, the state of Maine created the "Parents as Scholars" program. This program allows TANF recipients to attend college, with the long-term goal of empowering them and helping them move out of poverty. Here is a comment from a 39-year-old woman, now a college senior with a 3.7 grade point average:

> My self-esteem has greatly improved. For most of my life I believed I was not intelligent enough to go to college. When I began school I was very nervous and stressed about whether I could succeed; I have! I now feel confident in my ability to think, process, and produce answers both academically and personally. (Deprez et al., 2004, p. 225)

You already know from Figure 7.1 that a woman's education is one of the best predictors of her employment. Compared to college graduates, women without college degrees are significantly more likely to live in poverty (Deprez et al., 2004; Mathur et al., 2004). The current TANF policy will not solve the employment problem. Research shows that this policy also has important consequences for the children of these women. If mothers are poorly educated, then their children are likely to have more cognitive and behavioral problems (Deprez et al., 2004; A. P. Jackson et al., 2000). The current welfare program is obviously shortsighted for both women and their children.

DISCRIMINATION IN HIRING PATTERNS

Consider the following study. Rhea Steinpreis and her colleagues (1999) wrote to psychology professors, asking them to evaluate the qualifications of a potential job candidate. All the professors received the same, identical resume; however, half the resumes used the name "Karen Miller" and half used the name "Brian Miller." Of those who thought that the candidate was female, 45% said that they would hire her. Of those who thought that the candidate was male, 75% said that they would hire him. Incidentally, female professors were just as likely as male professors to demonstrate this biased hiring pattern. This evidence of discrimination is especially worrisome because psychology professors are well aware of the research on gender stereotypes (Powell & Graves, 2003).

The term **access discrimination** refers to discrimination used in hiring—for example, rejecting well-qualified women applicants or offering them less attractive positions. Once women have been hired, they may face another kind of discrimination, called treatment discrimination, which we'll discuss later in this chapter. In later chapters, we will encounter additional examples of access discrimination during hiring when we consider women with disabilities (Chapter 11) and women who are overweight (Chapter 12).

WHEN DOES ACCESS DISCRIMINATION OPERATE? As you might guess, the research on access discrimination is complex. Several factors determine whether women face access discrimination when they apply for work.

1. Employers who have strong gender-role stereotypes are more likely to demonstrate access discrimination. In general, decision makers who endorse traditional gender roles tend to avoid hiring women (Masser & Abrams, 2004; Powell & Graves, 2003). In addition, people who consider themselves strongly religious are likely to have negative attitudes toward employed women (Harville & Rienzi, 2000).

2. Access discrimination is particularly likely to operate when women apply for a prestigious position. For example, the Canadian government designed a program of awarding research grants to attract outstanding professors to Canadian universities. Unfortunately, only 17% of the approximately 1,000 awards have gone to women, although 26% of all full-time Canadian faculty members are female (Birchard, 2004). Furthermore, one study analyzed more than 30,000 employees of financial services organizations (Lyness & Judiesch, 1999). According to the results, men were likely to be hired at senior-level positions. In contrast, women were more likely to be hired at lower positions and promoted—years later—to the higher positions.

3. Access discrimination often operates for both women and men when they apply for "gender-inappropriate" jobs. In general, employers select men for jobs when most of the current employees are male, and they select women when most of the employees are female (Lorber, 1994; Powell & Graves, 2003).

For example, Peter Glick (1991) mailed employment questionnaires to personnel officers and career placement consultants. He asked them to read the job applications and make judgments about the applicants' suitability for 35 specific jobs. Glick then calculated the respondents' preferences for male versus female applicants. The respondents showed a clear preference for male applicants when 80% to 100% of the employees in an occupation were male. They showed weaker preferences for male applicants in an occupation with equal numbers of males and females. When the clear majority (80–100%) of employees were female, the respondents preferred female applicants.

These data suggest that employers would tend to select a male for an executive position in a corporation, but they would prefer a female as a worker in a day care center. These two examples of discrimination are not really equivalent, however, because the positions that favor men actually pay more and are more prestigious.

4. Access discrimination is particularly likely to operate when the applicant's qualifications are ambiguous. For instance, employers will hire a man rather than a woman when both candidates are not especially qualified for a job. In contrast, employers are less likely to discriminate against a woman if they have abundant information that she is well qualified and if her experience is directly relevant to the proposed job (Powell & Graves, 2003).

In summary, a woman is less likely to be considered for a job when the evaluators hold strong stereotypes, when the position is prestigious, and when the job is considered appropriate for males. She is also less likely to be considered when information about her qualifications is insufficient or unclear.

HOW DOES ACCESS DISCRIMINATION OPERATE? We examined gender stereotypes in some detail in Chapter 2. Unfortunately, people's stereotypes about women may operate in several ways to produce access discrimination (C. C. Bauer & Baltes, 2002; Cramer et al., 2002; Heilman, 2001; Padavic & Reskin, 2002; Powell & Graves, 2003).

1. Employers may have negative stereotypes about women's abilities. An employer who believes that women are typically unmotivated and incompetent will probably react negatively to a specific woman candidate.
2. Employers may assume that the candidate must have certain stereotypically masculine characteristics to succeed on the job. Female candidates may be perceived as having stereotypically feminine characteristics, even if they are actually assertive and independent. An employer may misperceive a woman as being deficient in these ideal characteristics. As you know from Chapter 2, people's stereotypes can bias their memory and their judgment.
3. Employers may pay attention to inappropriate characteristics when female candidates are being interviewed. The interviewer may judge a woman in terms of her physical appearance, secretarial skills, and personality, and they might ignore characteristics relevant to the executive position she is seeking. In this situation, called **gender-role spillover,** beliefs about gender roles and characteristics spread to the work setting (Cleveland et al., 2000). Employers are likely to emphasize the kinds of stereotypically female traits we discussed in Chapter 2.

In each case, notice that stereotypes encourage employers to conclude that a man ought to receive a particular position. In fact, they may hire a moderately qualified man, instead of a somewhat more qualified woman (Powell & Graves, 2003).

WHAT IS AFFIRMATIVE ACTION? Affirmative action is designed to reduce access discrimination and other workplace biases. According to the current federal law in the United States, every company that has more than 50 employees must establish an affirmative action plan. **Affirmative action** means that an employer must make special efforts to consider qualified members of under-represented groups during hiring and promotion decisions (Cleveland et al., 2000; Crosby et al., 2003). Affirmative action also means that the employer has actively worked to remove any barriers that prevent genuine equality of opportunity. Most often, the underrepresented groups are women and people of color.

The average U.S. citizen is not well informed about affirmative action (Crosby & Clayton, 2001; Crosby et al., 2003; Konrad & Linnehan, 1999). You are likely to hear talk-show hosts or politicians claiming that the government is forcing companies to hire unqualified women instead of qualified men. They may also claim that the government sets quotas, for instance, about the specific number of Black individuals that a company must hire. Neither of these claims is correct. Instead, affirmative action specifies that companies must encourage applications from the underrepresented groups and that these companies must make a good-faith effort to meet the affirmative action goals they have set.

The goal of affirmative action is to make sure that fully qualified women and people of color are given a fair consideration in the workplace, to compensate for past or present discrimination (Cleveland et al., 2000; Vasquez, 1999). For example, a company's administrators may discover that the company employs a smaller number of women than the data indicate to be available for a specific job title. The administrators must then analyze their procedures to see whether or not the hiring procedures are somehow biased (Sincharoen & Crosby, 2001).

Research demonstrates that those U.S. companies with affirmative action programs—and Canadian companies with a similar program called Employment Equity—do indeed have greater workplace equality for women and people of color (Crosby et al., 2003; Konrad & Linnehan, 1999). Also, women perceive that they are more fairly treated when they work for a corporation that has hired a relatively large number of women (Beaton & Tougas, 1997).

Some people think that affirmative action will produce **reverse discrimination**, in which a woman would be hired instead of a more highly qualified man. However, according to a study of 3,000 U.S. affirmative action court cases, only 3 cases represented reverse discrimination. Unfortunately, though, conservative politicians and commentators distort the truth by claiming that affirmative action is clearly unfair to men (Crosby et al., 2003; Hesse-Biber & Carter, 2000; Salinas, 2003).

Section Summary

Background Factors Related to Women's Employment

1. Women's employment status is influenced by factors such as education and immigrant status; parental status and ethnicity are not strongly related to being employed.

2. The current TANF policy on welfare has long-term consequences for women's lives; for example, women may be forced to leave a career-oriented college program to earn money in a low-level job.

3. Women are especially likely to experience access discrimination when (a) the employer has strong stereotypes, (b) the position is prestigious, (c) they apply for a stereotypically masculine position, and (d) their qualifications are ambiguous.

4. Gender stereotypes encourage access discrimination because employers (a) have negative stereotypes about women, (b) believe women lack "appropriate" stereotypically masculine characteristics, and (c) may pay attention to characteristics that are irrelevant for the positions women are seeking.

5. Affirmative action policy specifies that companies must make appropriate efforts to consider qualified members of underrepresented groups in work-related decisions.

DISCRIMINATION IN THE WORKPLACE

So far, we've discussed one kind of discrimination against women: the *access discrimination* women face when applying for a job. A second problem, **treatment discrimination**, refers to the discrimination women encounter after they have obtained a job. Let's examine salary discrimination, promotion discrimination, other workplace biases, and the discrimination that lesbians experience in the workplace. We'll also consider what people can do to combat workplace discrimination.

SALARY DISCRIMINATION

The most obvious kind of treatment discrimination is that women earn less money than men do. As of 2004, as we noted earlier, U.S. women who worked full time earned only 76% of the median[1] annual salary of men (National Committee on Pay Equity, 2005). Let's make this discrepancy more vivid: The average female college graduate will earn $1.2 million less during her lifetime than the average male college graduate, if both of them work full time (E. F. Murphy, 2005).

---

[1]The median is the exact midpoint of a distribution; in this case, it is a dollar amount above which half the men were receiving higher salaries and below which half were receiving lower salaries.

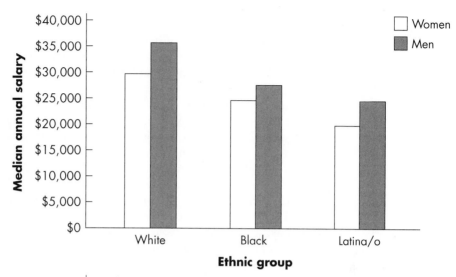

FIGURE 7.2 | U.S. MEDIAN ANNUAL SALARIES FOR FULL-TIME EMPLOYMENT, AS A FUNCTION OF GENDER AND ETHNIC GROUP.

Source: Based on Bureau of Labor Statistics (2004c).

As Figure 7.2 shows, the gender gap in salaries holds true for European Americans, Blacks, and Latinas/os (Bureau of Labor Statistics, 2004c; Padavic & Reskin, 2002). Other data show a similar gender gap for Asian Americans (Mishel et al., 2004); however, comparable data for Native American workers do not seem to be available.

Canadian workers also experience a gender gap. In 2003, for instance, Canadian women who worked full time earned only 71% of the average[2] annual salary of men (Statistics Canada, 2006). Unfortunately, one of the fastest growing employment fields in Canada is in part-time and temporary work, where women's salaries are unpredictable and job security is minimal (De Wolff, 2000). Salary discrimination cannot be explained by gender differences in education (Powell & Graves, 2003; Statistics Canada, 2006). Women earn substantially lower salaries at every educational level. For instance, one analysis showed that men with associate degrees actually earn about $200 more each year than women with bachelor's degrees (Bureau of Labor Statistics, 2004a). In other words, these women attend college for approximately 2 more years than these men do, and the women then earn lower salaries.

One important reason for the discrepancy in salaries is that men enter jobs that pay more money. Lawyers, who are usually male, earn more than twice as much as social workers, who are usually female. However, males earn more

---

[2]In contrast to the median, the average is calculated by adding together every person's salary and dividing by the number of people. Because the U.S. data and the Canadian data used different measures to represent the typical salary, they cannot be directly compared.

than females, even in the same job (Lips, 2003; E. F. Murphy, 2005). For instance, male lawyers have a median annual income of $84,000 versus $73,000 for female lawyers. Male social workers have a median annual income of $38,000 versus $36,000 for women (Bureau of Labor Statistics, 2004a).

Other variables that can explain part of the wage discrepancy include gender differences in the number of years of work experience and family responsibilities. However, studies conducted in the United States and Canada demonstrate that women are simply paid less than men, even when other factors are taken into account (Drolet, 2001; Fogg, 2003; Padavic & Reskin, 2002; D. Robinson, 2001; U.S. General Accounting Office, 2003).

Researchers have reported similar wage gaps in countries other than the United States and Canada. For instance, in Great Britain, Switzerland, and Germany, women earn between about 65% and 75% of men's pay. The gap is even larger in Japan, where women earn about 50% of men's pay. However, in countries such as Norway, Denmark, and Australia, women earn close to 90% of men's pay (Padavic & Reskin, 2002; Powell & Graves, 2003). The salary gap is smaller in countries in which the government has instituted a policy of pay equity.

Let's look at two more specific aspects of the salary gap: (1) a concept called comparable worth and (2) women's reactions to receiving lower pay.

COMPARABLE WORTH.   Most people are willing to agree that a man and a woman with equivalent performance at the same job should receive the same salaries. That is, women and men should receive equal pay for equal work.

Comparable worth is more complicated. The concept of **comparable worth** argues that women and men should receive equal pay for different jobs when those different jobs are comparable—that is, the jobs require equal training and equal ability (Lips, 2003; J. Peterson, 2003; D. Robinson, 2001).

People who favor comparable worth legislation point out that we can attribute much of the gender gap in wages to **occupational segregation**; as we noted, men and women tend to choose different occupations. Specifically, "women's jobs" (such as nurses and secretaries) pay less than "men's jobs" (such as auto mechanics and electricians). Consistent with Theme 3 of this book, the work that women do is devalued in terms of the actual dollar value placed on their accomplishments in the workplace. In other words, these female-stereotypical jobs pay less, simply because it is women—and not men—who do this work (Lips, 2003; E. F. Murphy, 2005; J. Peterson, 2003).

In general, the strategy behind comparable worth is to pay the same salaries for "men's jobs" and "women's jobs" that have been matched on characteristics such as education, previous experience, skills, level of danger, and supervisory responsibilities (Lips, 2003; Roos & Gatta, 1999). By this reasoning, a woman with a bachelor's degree who works with children in a daycare center should earn a larger salary than a mechanic with a high-school degree who works with air conditioners. So far, however, comparable worth legislation has had only limited success.

Demonstration 7.1

GENDER COMPARISONS IN SALARY REQUESTS

Ask a number of friends to participate in a brief study. Ideally, you should recruit at least five males and five females. (Make sure that the two groups are roughly similar in average age and work experience.) Ask them the following question:

"I want you to imagine that you are an undergraduate who has been employed as a research assistant to Dr. Johnson, who is a professor of psychology. You will be working with him all summer, entering data that are being collected for a summer research project. What hourly salary do you believe would be appropriate for this summer job?"

When you have gathered all the data, calculate the average wage the males suggested and the average wage the females suggested.

The text lists the salary requests that students provided in a study several years ago. Do you find a similar wage gap in the requests you gathered?

Source: Based on Bylsma and Major (1992).

REACTIONS TO LOWER SALARIES. How do women feel about their lower salaries? One answer to this question comes from research in which women and men decide how much they ought to receive for doing a particular job. According to research in both the United States and Canada, women choose lower salaries, suggesting that they are satisfied with less money (Bylsma & Major, 1992; Desmarais & Curtis, 1997a, 1997b; Heckert et al., 2002; Hogue & Yoder, 2003; McGann & Steil, 2006).

Now try Demonstration 7.1, which illustrates a classic study by Bylsma and Major (1992). These researchers found that male and female undergraduates who received no additional information gave very different salary requests. Specifically, men asked for an average of $6.30, whereas women asked for an average of $5.30. In a study that was similar but more recent, Hogue and Yoder (2003) found that men asked for an average of $10.27, whereas women asked for $7.48. With respect to salary, men seem to have a greater sense of **entitlement**; based on their membership in the male social group, they believe that they have a right to high rewards (McGann & Steil, 2006; Steil et al., 2001).

How do women react to the gender gap in wages? Both women and men know that women actually earn lower wages (McGann & Steil, 2006). However, women are typically more concerned about women's lower wages than men are (Browne, 1997; Desmarais & Curtis, 2001). For instance, Reiser (2001) asked 1,000 men and women a variety of questions that focused on anger. She found that 62% of the women and only 38% of the men agreed with the statement, "It makes me angry when men have greater job opportunities and rewards than women" (p. 35). Still, isn't it surprising that 38% of the women and 62% of the men were *not* concerned about this inequity?

Why should women be relatively happy about their low salaries? One reason may be that women often fail to acknowledge that they have the right skills for the job (Hogue & Yoder, 2003). Another important reason is that women may want to believe that the world is a just and fair place in which people receive what they deserve (Sincharoen & Crosby, 2001; A. J. Stewart & McDermott, 2004). In contrast, if a woman acknowledges that she is underpaid, then she must explain this inequity. She may be reluctant to conclude that her boss and the organization that employs her are villains. Unfortunately, if she continues to deny her personal disadvantage, she is not likely to work for pay equity and other social justice issues.

DISCRIMINATION IN PROMOTIONS

Wal-Mart employs more women than any other company in the United States. In 2001, Wal-Mart employees filed a lawsuit against their company, and they presented more than 100 declarations. Many of these declarations emphasized Wal-Mart's discrimination against women with respect to promotions. For instance, a woman who was seeking a promotion was told, "You aren't part of the boy's club, and you should raise a family and stay in the kitchen" (Hawkes, 2003, p. 53). Wal-Mart executives also claimed that men are more aggressive about working for advancement within the company; if they were to promote women, this would mean lowering the company's standards.

The female employees at Wal-Mart had clearly bumped into the glass ceiling. The **glass ceiling** is a presumably invisible barrier that seems to prevent women and people of color from reaching the top levels in many professional organizations (Atwater et al., 2004; Betz, 2006; Powell & Graves, 2003). The data persuasively confirm that women encounter glass ceilings in a variety of professions. Compared to men, women are less likely to be promoted to management positions in fields such as college teaching and business (Agars, 2004; Fischer & van Vianen, 2005; "Tenure Denied," 2005). Basically, when managers think about the term *manager,* they typically picture another male (Burk, 2005; Schein, 2001; Sczesny, 2003).

Labor theorists have constructed a different metaphor to describe a related situation. The metaphor of the **sticky floor** describes the situation of women who are employed in low-level, dead-end jobs with no chance of promotion (Gutek, 2001). Many women are office workers, cashiers, and waitresses. They are likely to remain in these jobs throughout their work life, never being considered for positions with greater responsibility (Padavic & Reskin, 2002). In fact, these women have no opportunity to even see a glass ceiling, and they certainly will not bump into it.

A third metaphor describes another component of gender bias. The **glass escalator** phenomenon applies to men who enter fields often associated with women, such as nursing, teaching, library science, and social work; in these occupations, men are often quickly promoted to management positions (Furr, 2002; Padavic & Reskin, 2002; J. D. Yoder, 2002). The glass escalator whisks them up to a more prestigious position. For example, a male teacher in elementary special education was asked about his career choice. He replied, "I am extremely marketable in special education. That's not why I got into the field. But I am extremely marketable because I am a man" (C. L. Williams, 1998, p. 288).

In short, women generally face discrimination with respect to promotion (Eagly & Karau, 2002; Whitley & Kite, 2006). The three stereotypes that we mentioned on page 216 in connection with hiring patterns also operate when women want to advance in their occupations (Sczesny, 2003). After reviewing the research on treatment discrimination, Mark Agars (2004) concluded, "It is clear that substantial discrepancies in gender distributions at high levels of organizations are attributable, at least in part, to gender stereotypes" (p. 109).

OTHER KINDS OF TREATMENT DISCRIMINATION

In addition to discrimination in salary and promotions, women experience treatment discrimination in other areas (Benokraitis, 1998; Cleveland et al., 2000; Lyness & Thompson, 1997). For example, several studies show that women in the workplace are more likely than men to receive a negative evaluation (e.g., Gerber, 2001; Heilman, 2001). Chapter 2 pointed out that women sometimes (although not always) are downgraded for their performance. The research on evaluation in the workplace confirms a point we made throughout Chapter 6: Women are especially likely to be downgraded if they are seen as assertive, independent, and unfeminine (Atwater et al., 2001; Eagly & Karau, 2002; Richeson & Ambady, 2001).

Other analyses show that women are especially likely to receive negative workplace ratings (relative to men) when the rater is somewhat preoccupied with other tasks or when the rater makes a delayed rating, some time after observing the individual (R. F. Martell, 1991, 1996). In the real world, executives frequently rate their employees under distracted or delayed conditions—with unfortunate consequences for women!

For women teaching at colleges and universities, students provide other forms of treatment discrimination. For instance, students rate young male professors as more conscientious and interested in their material compared to young female professors (Arbuckle & Williams, 2003). Sometimes the treatment discrimination depends on the gender of the students. For example, male students are generally more likely than female students to give their female college professors poor ratings on their teaching performance (Basow, 2004). In addition, students often assume that their male professors have had more education than their female professors (J. Miller & Chamberlin, 2000). When students address their female professors who have Ph.D. degrees, they are likely to call them "Miss _____" or "Ms. _____," instead of "Dr. _____" (Benokraitis, 1998; Wilbers et al., 2003).

Another form of treatment discrimination is **sexual harassment,** or "deliberate or repeated comments, gestures, or physical contacts of a sexual nature that are unwanted by the recipient" (American Psychological Association, 1990, p. 393). (We'll discuss sexual harassment in detail in Chapter 13.) Women frequently experience this kind of treatment discrimination on the job. Some harassers specifically tell women that sexual favors are a prerequisite for job advancement. Other harassers' messages are more subtle. However, they still convey the message that women are sexual objects, rather than competent employees.

Another potential kind of treatment discrimination is less dramatic, although it has important implications. Specifically, coworkers may make negative gender-related comments that indicate women are second-class citizens. For example, a Black female firefighter recalled her first encounter with her White male supervisor:

> The first day I came on, the first day I was in the field, the guy told me he didn't like me. And then he said: "I'm gonna tell you why I don't like you. Number one, I don't like you cuz you're Black. And number two, cuz you're a woman." And that was all he said. He walked away. (J. D. Yoder & Aniakudo, 1997, p. 329)

You won't be surprised to learn, then, that women are often more likely than men to report negative interactions in the workplace (Betz, 2006; Blau & Tatum, 2000; Fassinger, 2002). In addition, women may be excluded from informal social interactions both at work and after hours. People may conduct business at these events, and they may exchange important information. Women of color are especially likely to be left out of the social interactions and mentoring (Fasssinger, 2002; Lyness & Thompson, 2000). Furthermore, the friendships that are strengthened outside work may provide access to prestigious assignments and career advancement. In addition to facing other forms of discrimination, women certainly do not have equal opportunities in informal social interactions.

DISCRIMINATION AGAINST LESBIANS IN THE WORKPLACE

In Chapter 2, we noted that **heterosexism** is a bias against lesbians, gay males, and bisexuals—any group that is not heterosexual. Lesbians frequently face heterosexism in the workplace. A lesbian mortgage broker remarked about the effects of heterosexism on her career:

> I was on the fast track in my company—I was on special committees, getting bonuses, the whole works. Somehow my employer found out that I had a female domestic partner and—pow!—it took no time before I was fired. Despite my not being out and being considered an attractive woman, the mere fact of my being a lesbian was enough to get me fired. There was no law to protect me from this. (Blank & Slipp, 1994, p. 141)

As you might guess, many employers refuse to hire individuals who are known to be gay. For example, public schools often discriminate against hiring lesbians, gays, and bisexuals as teachers. The unjustified argument is that these individuals may try to persuade young people to adopt a nonheterosexual orientation. Furthermore, in some parts of the United States, employers can fire employees for any reason they choose, including being a lesbian or a gay male (Horvath & Ryan, 2003; Peplau & Fingerhut, 2004).

The research suggests that people who are open and accepting of their gay identity are higher in self-esteem (Walters & Simoni, 1993). Sadly, many jobs seem to require that gay individuals remain in the closet. Many lesbians and gay men say they spend so much energy trying to hide their sexual orientation that their work is less productive (Blank & Slipp, 1994; Hambright & Decker, 2002).

Should lesbians, gay men, and bisexuals disclose their sexual orientation to potential employers? Openness makes sense for people who plan to be "out" in their work setting, especially for people who would not choose to work in a heterosexist environment (Wenniger & Conroy, 2001). However, some lesbians prefer to receive the job offer first and then come out gradually to coworkers. As you know from this chapter, bias is less likely when people are already familiar with an employee's work.

Some recent research provides interesting perspectives on lesbians and their work experiences. For instance, several studies show that lesbian workers earn higher salaries than heterosexual female workers. One explanation is that lesbians are almost twice as likely as married women to have at least a bachelor's degree, and education is correlated with a person's income. Another explanation is that lesbians are more likely than other women to pursue nontraditional careers, which also pay better than traditionally feminine careers (Peplau & Fingerhut, 2004).

In a related study, undergraduates rated the qualifications of a potential job applicant, on a scale from 0 to 100. Except for gender and sexual orientation, the job applicant's characteristics were identical. The students gave a rating of 85 to the heterosexual man, 81 to the gay man, 80 to the lesbian woman, and 76 to the heterosexual woman (Horvath & Ryan, 2003). These results are not especially hopeful for anybody other than heterosexual men, except for the fact that there was only a 9-point range among all four ratings.

WHAT TO DO ABOUT TREATMENT DISCRIMINATION

The title of this section is daunting: How can we possibly try to correct all the forces that encourage gender discrimination in the workplace? A few guidelines may be helpful with respect to the actions of both individuals and institutions.

Individuals can have an impact on their own work experiences as well as on the experiences of other women:

1. Women should be aware of the conditions in which stereotypes are least likely to operate, for example, when the job applicant's qualifications are clear cut rather than ambiguous. Find work you enjoy, and develop skills and experiences that are especially relevant to your occupation (O'Connell, 2001). You should also know your legal rights (Dworkin, 2002).

2. Join relevant organizations, use the Internet, and make connections with other supportive people (Padavic & Reskin, 2002; Wenniger & Conroy, 2001). Feminist organizations may be especially helpful. In a study by Klonis and her colleagues (1997), female psychology professors reported

that they experienced feminism as "a life raft in the choppy, frigid waters of gender discrimination" (p. 343).

3. Locate someone who has achieved success in your profession; ask whether she can serve as a mentor (O'Connell, 2001; Quick, 2000). Employees who have mentors are likely to be especially successful and satisfied with their occupation (Padavic & Reskin, 2002).

In reality, however, individuals cannot overcome the entire problem of gender discrimination. Institutions must change. It is often in their best interests to become more diversified. For example, a company's sales may increase if their workplace diversity resembles the diversity in the real world outside that company (Cleveland et al., 2000; Powell & Graves, 2003). In addition, gender discrimination is legally prohibited. Organizations that are truly committed to change can take the following precautions:

1. Understand affirmative action policies and take them seriously; make sure that women are well represented in the pool of candidates for hiring and promotion. Develop guidelines within the organization (Bronstein & Farnsworth, 1998; Eberhardt & Fiske, 1998).

2. Appoint a task force to examine gender issues within the organization. The chief executive must make it clear that the group's recommendations will be valued and carried out (Cleveland et al., 2000). Managers should receive incentives if they are successful in meeting diversity goals. Diversity training workshops are useful if their objective is genuine change (Powell & Graves, 2003).

3. Train managers so that they can evaluate candidates fairly, reducing gender stereotypes (Gerber, 2001). Managers who rate employees should ask themselves questions such as "How would I evaluate this performance if the person were a man rather than a woman?" (Valian, 1998, p. 309).

Realistically, creating gender-fair work experiences requires a massive transformation of our culture, beginning with nonsexist child rearing, acceptance of feminist concerns, and appreciation for the contributions of women and other underrepresented groups. Comparable worth must also become the standard policy (J. D. Yoder, 2000). A truly gender-fair work world would also provide a national child-care plan, and it would ensure that men would perform an equal share of child-care and housework responsibilities—a topic we'll examine at the end of this chapter.

Section Summary

Discrimination in the Workplace

1. Women earn lower salaries than men; the wage gap remains, even when such factors as occupation and work experience are taken into account.

2. "Comparable worth" means that women and men should receive the same pay for occupations that require similar training and skill.

3. Men typically feel entitled to a higher salary than women do; also, women may fail to express concern about being underpaid.

4. Women experience discrimination in terms of promotion; three related kinds of gender discrimination are called the glass ceiling, the sticky floor, and the glass escalator.

5. Women may also experience other kinds of treatment discrimination, such as lower evaluations from supervisors and (in the case of professors) from students; women may also face sexual harassment and exclusion from social interactions.

6. Lesbians are especially likely to experience workplace discrimination; they may be fired because of their sexual orientation, and they may feel it necessary to hide their sexual orientation.

7. The actions of individuals and institutions can address treatment discrimination, but a genuine solution must depend on more widespread societal change.

WOMEN'S EXPERIENCES IN SELECTED OCCUPATIONS

We have seen that women face access discrimination when they apply for work. They also encounter a variety of treatment discriminations once they are employed. In this section, we will examine women's work experiences in several specific occupations.

On the news in North America, we hear about women who are physicians, heads of corporations, and steelworkers. Women who are nurses, cashiers, and cafeteria workers do not make headlines. Even though the majority of employed women hold jobs in clerical and service occupations, the work of millions of these women is relatively invisible.

Let's begin by discussing some traditionally female occupations. Then we'll examine two areas in which fewer women are employed: the traditionally male professions and traditionally male blue-collar work. After discussing why women are so scarce in nontraditional occupations, we'll consider homemakers, who are among the least visible female workers.

Employment in Traditionally Female Occupations

Table 7.1 lists some representative traditional occupations and shows the percentage of workers who are women. Roughly half of all female professional or technical workers are in traditional areas such as nursing and pre-college teaching.

This observation does not imply that something is wrong with traditionally female occupations. In fact, our society's children would probably be better off if occupations such as child care and teaching elementary school were more

TABLE 7.1 | PERCENTAGE OF WORKERS IN SELECTED TRADITIONALLY FEMALE OCCUPATIONS WHO ARE WOMEN

Occupation	Percentage of Workers Who Are Women
Secretary	99%
Dental hygienist	98
Bank teller	87
Elementary schoolteacher	83
Librarian	83

Source: Bureau of Labor Statistics (2004c).

highly valued. However, women in traditionally female jobs frequently confront real-world problems, such as low income, under-utilization of abilities, and lack of independence in decision making.

Similar employment patterns operate in Canada. For example, 70% of all employed women work in teaching, health-care occupations such as nursing, clerical positions, or occupations such as sales or service. In contrast, only 31% of employed men work in one of these areas (Statistics Canada, 2004).

Keep in mind, though, that the work considered traditional for women may be quite different in developing countries. About 80% of women in Western Europe work in service occupations, but in sub-Saharan Africa, 65% of the women in the labor force work in agriculture (United Nations, 2000). We even see different work patterns within the same continent. For example, consider two West African countries. In Sierra Leone, the men are responsible for the rice fields; in Senegal, women manage the rice fields (Burn, 1996).

Perhaps the only characteristic that all these traditionally female occupations have in common is relatively low pay. As we discussed in connection with welfare, many of these workers earn wages that are below the poverty level. Writer Barbara Ehrenreich (2001) tried to see how she could survive working as a waitress and a hotel maid, for $6 to $7 an hour. She found that the only way to make ends meet was to work seven days a week . . . and hope that she didn't have to buy a new pair of shoes or repair her car. Ehrenreich emphasized that most women must also raise children on these low salaries.

You probably know many women who work as secretaries, librarians, and other occupations listed in Table 7.1. Let's consider two traditionally female jobs with which you may be less familiar: domestic work and work in the garment industry. Consistent with Theme 3, this kind of women's work is generally invisible; women do the work, but few people notice (Zandy, 2001). Furthermore, women are especially likely to be exploited in these jobs.

DOMESTIC WORK.   Many women emigrate from the Caribbean, Latin America, and other developing companies. They come to the United States to live and work in private homes, doing domestic work until they can earn a green card, which will allow them to find better jobs. They may be expected to work every day, with no time off, for a fraction of the minimum-wage salary. Many of the women report that their employers insult them, do not let them leave the house, and treat them much like modern-day slaves (B. Anderson, 2003; Boris, 2003; Zarembka, 2003). For example, one woman reported:

> I work hard. I don't mind working hard. But I want to be treated with some human affection, like a human being. . . . I don't get any respect. . . . Since I came here this woman has never shown me one iota of . . . human affection as a human being. (Colen, 1997, p. 205)

GARMENT WORK. Several years ago, I showed my psychology of women class a video about sweatshops. (A **sweatshop** is a factory that violates labor laws regarding wages and working conditions.) I then asked how many students were familiar with the sweatshop problem. One young Chinese American woman, whom I will call "Ling," kept her hand raised. Then she said, "I worked in a sweatshop in New York City." Ling described the inhumane working conditions in this clothing sweatshop, and I later asked her to write down some of the details. Ling wrote that, at the age of 17, she was urged to quit high school so that she could work longer hours. She then worked every day at this sweatshop, from about 8:00 in the morning until as late as 1:00 the next morning—with just a 15-minute break for lunch. Ling's two younger siblings, ages 14 and 16, worked in the same sweatshop after school, until 10:00 at night. Several months later, Ling's mother began working on a garment, without asking for the supervisor's permission. The supervisor then punched her mother in the chest, and the family called the police to report this assault. The manager fired the entire family.

Ling was one of the fortunate ones. She took this opportunity to complete high school and then enroll at SUNY Geneseo. As Ling wrote:

> Unfortunately, many young people still work there in order to live in the United States, and they are still suffering long working hours, low wages, and terrible working conditions. They are losing their sense of being interesting human beings day by day, and becoming boring and dehumanized machine-like humans. . . . After all these experiences, my American dream is that all workers deserve to have humane working conditions, living wages so that they can survive, and reasonable working hours, and that we will make better changes until these basic needs are met for all workers of all occupations.

Fortunately, Ling's story has a positive outcome. She graduated from my college with a strong academic record, and she is now employed as a union organizer. However, sweatshops operate in many North American cities, from Los Angeles to Toronto (Bains, 1998; Bao, 2003; I. Ness, 2003). These sweatshops typically employ recent immigrants from Asia and Latin America.

Furthermore, about half of all the clothing you can purchase in the United States was made in another country, typically under extremely poor working

© Getty Images

Burmese women stitch sports clothing in a garment factory for a Taiwanese company in Hlaing Tharyar, Myanmar. They make an average wage of 50 cents a day, which is a fairly normal salary.

conditions. In Latin America, these sweatshops are called *maquiladoras* (pronounced mah-kee-lah-*door*-ahs) or *maquilas*, and they are typically run by U.S. corporations. In Latin America, a young woman may earn only 16 cents an hour, which cannot cover the cost of her food and housing (Bilbao, 2003). The work hours are also inhumane. In a typical sweatshop in China, the women work from 7:00 A.M. to 10:00 P.M. (Ngai, 2005). As one woman commented, "In the eyes of the managers, workers are merely stuff that can be thrown away at will" (Ngai, 2005, p. 183).

These women have no possibility of pursuing an education, saving money, or training for a better job. In addition to the long hours, low pay, and unsafe working conditions, the women who work in these sweatshops often experience sexual harassment and physical abuse. If they try to organize a union, they may be fired; many have even received death threats (Bender & Greenwald, 2003a; Bilbao, 2003).

The sweatshop issue cannot be addressed without looking at our economic system to discover who is making the greatest profits from our clothing industry. You can obtain more information from the websites of organizations that promote sweatshop reform, such as the Chinese Staff and Workers' Association, the National Mobilization Against Sweatshops, the National Labor Committee, and the Ain't I a Woman?! Campaign. To bring the sweatshop issue closer to home, try Demonstration 7.2.

WHERE WERE YOUR CLOTHES MADE?	## Demonstration 7.2
	Go to your closet or your dresser, and search each item of clothing for a label indicating where it was made. Record each location. What percentage was made in the United States or Canada, and what percentage was made in other countries? Later, when you have the opportunity, look in your college bookstore or other location that sells caps and sweatshirts featuring your college's logo. Where were these items made?

EMPLOYMENT IN TRADITIONALLY MALE PROFESSIONS

Ironically, we have more information about the relatively small number of women employed in "the male professions" than we have about the much larger number of women employed in traditionally female jobs. Unfortunately, this emphasis on nontraditional professions creates an impression that employed women are more likely to be executives than clerical workers. A more accurate picture of reality appears in Table 7.2, which lists the percentage of workers who are women in several prestigious occupations. Use Table 7.1 to compare the two groups.

Incidentally, you'll note that I used the phrase *prestigious occupations* to refer to the male-dominated professions. Glick and his colleagues (1995) asked college students to rate the prestige of various occupations. Those rated most prestigious were all professions that employ more men than women.

Let's consider some of the characteristics of women in traditionally male professions. Then we'll examine the climate in which these women work.

CHARACTERISTICS OF WOMEN IN TRADITIONALLY MALE PROFESSIONS. In general, the women who work in stereotypically masculine occupations are similar to the men in that area. For example, Lubinski and his colleagues (2001) sent questionnaires to males and females enrolled in the most prestigious U.S. graduate programs in math and science. The males and females reported highly similar academic experiences and attitudes toward their future careers. To some extent, this similarity may occur because only those women with personal

TABLE 7.2 | PERCENTAGE OF WORKERS IN SELECTED TRADITIONALLY MALE PROFESSIONS WHO ARE WOMEN

Occupation	Percentage of Workers Who Are Women
Mechanical engineer	10%
Dentist	19
Architect	20
Computer programmer	26
Lawyer	29

Source: Bureau of Labor Statistics (2004c).

characteristics appropriate for that occupation would choose it for a career and persist in it (Cross & Vick, 2001). For example, women who pursue non-traditional careers tend to be high achieving and self-confident in their specific area of expertise (L. L. Sax & Bryant, 2003).

As we would expect, women and men in the same profession tend to be similar in cognitive skills. For example, Cross (2001) found that men and women in science and engineering had earned similar scores on standardized tests as well as similar grades in graduate school. Other research shows that men and women have corresponding professional expectations, motivation, fascination with the discipline, and work involvement (R. C. Barnett & Rivers, 2004; Burke, 1999; T. D. Fletcher & Major, 2004; Preston, 2004). However, one area in which gender differences often appear is general self-confidence (Cross, 2001). This finding is not surprising. As we observed in Chapter 5, men may be more self-confident than women in some achievement settings.

THE WORKPLACE CLIMATE FOR WOMEN IN TRADITIONALLY MALE PROFESSIONS. In Chapter 4, we saw that some young female students may face a chilly climate in their academic classrooms. The chilly climate continues for many women in their graduate training and in their professions (Bergman & Hallberg, 2002; Betz, 2006; Fort, 2005b; Janz & Pyke, 2000; Preston, 2004; Steeh, 2002; R. Wilson, 2003). For instance, when women apply for jobs, they may find that they are evaluated in terms of their physical appearance, rather than their job-related competence (Dowdall, 2003). After women are hired, they may feel that their male colleagues have negative attitudes toward women and ignore women's contributions (Bergman, 2003; Bergman & Hallberg, 2002; Preston, 2004).

Earlier in this chapter, we noted several forms of treatment discrimination. Unfortunately, treatment discrimination has an important effect on the professional environment. For instance, Dr. Frances Conley (1998), a prominent neurosurgeon, described how the male neurosurgeons would attempt to kiss her neck while she was scrubbing up, call her "honey" in front of patients, and brag about their sexual conquests. One neurosurgeon would sometimes invite her to go to bed with him, thrust his pelvis forward, look down at his genitals, and directly ask his genitals whether they would like that experience.

We saw in Chapter 6 that women are downgraded if they are too self-confident and assertive; this principle also applies in the world of work (Kite et al., 2001; Rudman & Glick, 1999). Furthermore, Heilman and her colleagues (2004) asked students to rate employees who were described in vignettes. They found that the students liked the male and female employees equally when the quality of their work was somewhat ambiguous. In contrast, when both employees were clearly successful, the students liked the male employee much more than the female employee. In other words, a woman who is confident, assertive, and competent may encounter negative reactions from her coworkers.

Another problem for women in these traditionally male professions is that men may treat them in a patronizing fashion (Preston, 2004). For instance, one female astronomer remarked, "You will go through three or four days of professional meetings and never once hear the word 'her' used. Every scientist is 'he' " (Fort, 2005b, p. 187). At times, male colleagues may be astonishingly sexist. For example, a male chemistry professor announced out loud to another man, "Why do you bother with women? They're almost as bad as foreigners" (Gleiser, 1998, p. 210). Obviously, this professor showed not only sexism but also U.S.-centered nationalism. In short, women in traditionally male professions receive many messages that they are not really equal to their male colleagues.

EMPLOYMENT IN TRADITIONALLY MALE BLUE-COLLAR JOBS

Several years ago, Barbara Quintela's job as a secretary had paid $10 an hour. When her husband left her—and their five children—she managed to persuade a school administrator to let her enroll in a high-school training program for electricians. After a grueling interview with eight hostile administrators, she was accepted into an apprenticeship program that would eventually pay $22 an hour. As she says, "I like getting dirty, running wires, digging ditches, getting into crawl spaces. I would never want to go back to being a secretary. I can't afford to be a secretary" (J. C. Lambert, 2000, p. 6). Most women in blue-collar jobs report that the pay is attractive, especially compared to the salaries for traditionally feminine jobs.

Most of the information on working women describes women in such traditionally male professions as medicine and law. In contrast, the information on women in blue-collar jobs is scanty. Women are slowly entering blue-collar fields, and the percentages are still small. Table 7.3 lists some representative employment rates for women in these jobs.

Women in blue-collar jobs report that they are often held to stricter standards than their male coworkers. For example, a Black woman firefighter was forced by her White male supervisor to recertify after her vehicle skidded into a pole during an ice storm. In contrast, a male colleague received no penalty when his vehicle accidentally killed an elderly pedestrian who was crossing a street (J. D. Yoder & Aniakudo, 1997). Women firefighters frequently comment that

TABLE 7.3 | PERCENTAGE OF WORKERS IN SELECTED TRADITIONALLY MALE BLUE-COLLAR OCCUPATIONS WHO ARE WOMEN

Occupation	Percentage of Workers Who Are Women
Automobile mechanic	1%
Pest control employee	1
Carpenter	2
Firefighter	3
Bulldozer operator	5

Source: Bureau of Labor Statistics (2004c).

they would probably have to keep proving—for the rest of their lives—that they are competent workers (J. D. Yoder & Berendsen, 2001). Men often claim that women are physically unable to handle the work (P. Y. Martin & Collinson, 1998). Another study of women firefighters discovered that only 3 out of 44 women said that they had never experienced sexist reactions on the job (J. D. Yoder & McDonald, 1998). Furthermore, sexual harassment is common (S. Eisenberg, 1998).

Fortunately, some women report that they develop good working relationships with their male colleagues (Padavic & Reskin, 2002; J. D. Yoder, 2002). For instance, a White female firefighter described the bond she shared with her Black male coworkers:

> It's neat. Because I think a lot of them . . . we kind of have a bond, too. And they understand more what I go through than a White guy would. So, yeah. They're pretty together guys. They've come through the fire too, I think, in a lot of ways. (J. D. Yoder & Berendsen, 2001, p. 33)

Other women mention additional advantages to blue-collar work, such as a sense of pride in their own strength and satisfaction in doing a job well (Cull, 1997; S. Eisenberg, 1998). Some also enjoy serving as a role model and encouraging young women to pursue work in nontraditional areas (Coffin, 1997).

WHY ARE WOMEN SCARCE IN CERTAIN OCCUPATIONS?

Why do relatively few women work in the traditionally male professions or in the traditionally male blue-collar jobs? Researchers have identified two major classes of explanations. According to **person-centered explanations** (also called the **individual approach**), female socialization encourages women to develop personality traits that are inappropriate for these occupations (Hesse-Biber & Carter, 2000; Riger & Galligan, 1980). One example of a person-centered explanation would be to claim that women are somehow less motivated than men. However, as we saw in Chapter 5, women and men are similar in areas related to motivation and achievement.

Most current research and theory in the psychology of women supports a second explanation for the scarcity of women. According to **situation-centered explanations** (or the **structural approach**), the characteristics of the organizational situation explain why women are rarely employed in these traditionally masculine occupations; personal skills or traits cannot be blamed (Hesse-Biber & Carter, 2000; Riger & Galligan, 1980). For example, access discrimination may block women's opportunities. If women do manage to be hired, they face several kinds of treatment discrimination, such as the glass ceiling that blocks promotion (Powell & Graves, 2003). Also, people in prestigious positions may be unwilling to help new female employees.

Notice that the person-centered explanations and the situation-centered explanations suggest different strategies for improving women's employment conditions. For example, if a woman aspires to a management position in a corporation, the person-centered explanations propose that women should

Demonstration 7.3

EVALUATING A
JOB DESCRIPTION

Based on the following description, would you be tempted to apply for this job?

Requirements: Intelligence, energy, patience, social skills, good health. *Tasks:* At least 20 different occupations. *Hours:* About 100 hours per week. *Salary:* None. *Holidays:* None (must remain on standby 24 hours a day, 7 days a week). *Opportunities for Advancement:* None (experience in this occupation will not impress future employers). *Fringe Benefits:* Food, clothing, and shelter generally provided, but any additional bonuses will depend on the financial standing and good nature of the employer. No pension plan. *Job Security:* None (layoffs are likely; further food and shelter may not be supplied).

Source: Based on Bergmann (2003) and Chesler (1976).

take courses in handling finances, conducting meetings, and assertiveness training.

In contrast, the situation-centered explanations propose strategies designed to change the situation, not the person. For instance, companies should train managers to use objective rating scales (Gerber, 2001). They should also enforce affirmative action policies, and they should promote women to high-ranking positions (Etzkowitz et al., 2000).

Although these suggestions sound excellent, they will not occur spontaneously. Executives need to realize that corporations will benefit if they hire competent women and treat them fairly (Etzkowitz et al., 2000; Powell & Graves, 2003; Strober, 2003). When executives publicly state that a female employee is competent, other employees will also value her contributions (Yoder, 2002). Before you read further, be sure that you try Demonstration 7.3.

HOMEMAKERS

You probably recognized that the unappealing job description in Demonstration 7.4 lists the duties of a wife and mother. A **homemaker** is someone who works full time as an unpaid laborer in maintaining a home and providing service for other family members (Lindsey, 1996). About 20% of adult women in the United States are full-time homemakers (Hesse-Biber & Carter, 2000). In the next section of this chapter, we'll see that even women with full-time paying jobs continue to do far more than their share of housework and child care. Here, we will focus on the diversity of responsibilities that homemakers perform.

Research on homemakers is scarce. As Theme 3 argues, topics associated almost exclusively with women tend to be invisible. Also, by definition, homemaking is unpaid, and our culture values work that earns money (Bergmann, 2003; Hesse-Biber & Carter, 2000).

We do know that the variety of tasks included in homemaking is so extensive that any list will necessarily be incomplete. Here is just a fraction of the responsibilities: providing emotional support to other family members, shopping for food; preparing meals; washing dishes; making household purchases; cleaning the house; washing, ironing, and mending clothes; tending to the garden; taking care of the car; preparing children for school; transporting children; preparing children for bed; disciplining children; hiring child-care help; planning for holidays; managing household finances; and volunteering in the community (Bergmann, 2003; Lindsey, 1996).

We do not need to dwell on the unpleasant nature of many tasks performed by homemakers. Any job is frustrating if it must be repeated just as soon as it is finished or if it typically has no clear-cut standards of completion. (Is the kitchen floor ever really clean enough?)

In short, our discussion of working women in this chapter must acknowledge the tremendous amount of time and effort women devote to housework. Unfortunately, the tasks are extensive, repetitive, often frustrating, and low in prestige.

Section Summary

Women's Experiences in Selected Occupations

1. Most employed women occupy traditionally female jobs, such as clerical and service work.

2. Women are especially likely to be exploited in two low-income, traditionally female jobs: domestic work and work in the garment industry (including sweatshops).

3. Women who are employed in traditionally male professions are generally similar to the men in these professions in terms of academic experiences, personal characteristics, and cognitive skills; however, the women are often lower in self-confidence.

4. Many women in traditionally male professions face treatment discrimination, sexist attitudes, and patronizing treatment.

5. Women in blue-collar jobs may face biased treatment from the men on the job, but they value the salary and the sense of pride they gain from their work.

6. Person-centered explanations argue that women are underrepresented in traditionally male occupations because they lack the relevant personality characteristics.

7. Situation-centered explanations provide a more appropriate explanation for the findings; they emphasize that the structure of organizations prevents women's success.

8. The work of homemakers is relatively invisible, complex, and time consuming.

Demonstration 7.4

DIVISION OF
RESPONSIBILITY
FOR HOUSEHOLD
TASKS

Think about a married heterosexual couple with whom you are familiar; it might be your parents, the parents of a close friend, or your own current relationship with someone of the other gender. For each task in the following list, place a check mark to indicate which member of the pair is primarily responsible. Is this pattern similar to the division of housework we are discussing in this chapter?

Task	Wife	Husband
Shopping for food	_____	_____
Cooking	_____	_____
Washing the dishes	_____	_____
Laundry	_____	_____
Vacuuming	_____	_____
Washing the car	_____	_____
Gardening	_____	_____
Taking out the trash	_____	_____
Paying the bills	_____	_____
Household repairs	_____	_____

COORDINATING EMPLOYMENT WITH PERSONAL LIFE

Most college women plan to combine a career with family life (Hoffnung, 1993, 2004; Novack & Novack, 1996). However, according to R. C. Barnett and Rivers (2004), the popular media claim that an employed woman with a family must be a total wreck. Every day, she must juggle multiple commitments, to her work, her spouse, her children, and her housework. Furthermore, the media claim that gender differences are enormous. Therefore, women should not trust their husbands to show any competence in taking care of their children. The media also imply that numerous women are quitting their jobs to escape the time crunch and enjoy life at home.

However, these articles in popular magazines are typically based on small samples of White, upper-class women (Prince, 2004). As we have noted throughout this textbook, reality often differs from the myth presented by the media. In this section, we'll see that employed women may find it challenging to combine their many roles, but they are not dropping out of their careers by the thousands, as some magazine articles imply. Let's see how employment influences three components of a woman's personal life: (1) her marriage, (2) her children, and (3) her own well-being.

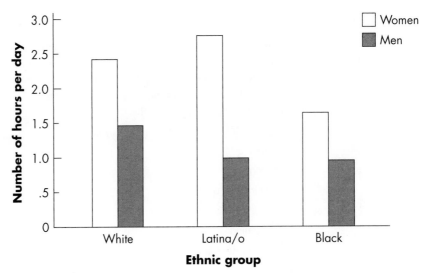

FIGURE 7.3 | U.S. AMOUNT OF TIME SPENT ON HOUSEWORK, AS A FUNCTION OF GENDER AND ETHNIC GROUP.

Source: Based on Bureau of Labor Statistics (2004b).

MARRIAGE

In 53% of all married couples in the United States, both the wife and the husband are employed (Bureau of Labor Statistics, 2004c). The comparable figure for Canada is 67% (Statistics Canada, 2006). Try Demonstration 7.4 on page 237 before you read further, and then we'll consider two questions:

1. How do families divide their household responsibilities?
2. Does employment influence marital satisfaction?

PERFORMING HOUSEHOLD TASKS.   Throughout this chapter, we've often noted that women are treated unfairly in the world of work. When we consider how married couples divide household tasks, we find additional evidence of unfairness. For example, the Bureau of Labor Statistics (2004b) studied a U.S. sample of approximately 21,000 women and men. Figure 7.3 shows that women in White, Latina/o, and Black families spend more time than men on housework. These researchers then subtracted the number of hours and minutes each person spent on the job. Compared to women, men had an average of 36 more minutes each day to devote to leisure and sports.

What happens when both the wife and the husband are employed? Several studies in the United States suggest that men do somewhat more housework if they are married to employed women. However, men still perform between only 30% and 40% of the household tasks in two-job families (Coltrane & Adams, 2001a; Crosby & Sabattini, 2006; Perry-Jenkins et al., 2004). An analysis of the 2001 Census data for Canada shows that men performed a median of about 7 hours of housework each week, in contrast to a median of about 13 hours for women (Statistics Canada, 2005c). The same pattern has also been observed in Great Britain, China, and Japan (Brush, 1998).

Women are much more likely than men to do the cooking, cleaning, laundry, dishwashing, and shopping. The only indoor chore that men are more likely to do is household repair (Galinsky & Bond, 1996; Landry, 2000). Another issue is that men seldom take responsibility for noticing when a household task needs to be done; instead, the typical husband waits for his wife to remind him (Coltrane & Adams, 2001a). Also, many men do not acknowledge how little housework they do; only 52% of men in one study agreed with the statement "Men typically don't do their share of work around the house" (Reiser, 2001, p. 35). Earlier in the chapter, we noted a wage gap between the salaries of employed men and women. Because women spend so much time on housework, there is also a leisure gap for employed men and women (Coltrane & Adams, 2001a).

What factors influence the division of household tasks? As Figure 7.3 shows, U.S. women in all three major ethnic groups do more housework than men do. However, the discrepancy is often largest for Latina/o couples (Bureau of Labor Statistics, 2004b; Stohs, 2000). Another factor is the couple's belief system. Research in the United States and in 13 European countries shows that men tend to share the housework more equally if they are nontraditional and politically liberal (Apparala et al., 2003; Sabattini & Leaper, 2004).

How do the men explain their lack of responsibility for household tasks? Although many men may be more sensitive, one man explained, "People shouldn't do what they don't want to do. . . . And I don't want to do it" (Rhode, 1997, p. 150). Earlier in this chapter, we noted that men often feel entitled to higher salaries than women receive. Apparently, many men also feel entitled to leave the housework to their wives (Crosby & Sabattini, 2006; Steil, 2000). Furthermore, even college students tend to believe that men are entitled to perform less than half of the housework (Swearingen-Hilker & Yoder, 2002). Surprisingly, many women do not express anger toward their greater work in the home (Dryden, 1999; Perry-Jenkins et al., 2004), just as they fail to acknowledge that they are underpaid (see pages 221–222).

SATISFACTION WITH MARRIAGE. In general, a woman's employment status does not influence her marital satisfaction or the stability of her marriage (Viers & Prouty, 2001; L. White & Rogers, 2000). For example, Stacy J. Rogers (1996) analyzed data from a national sample of 1,323 women, all married continuously to the same men and all with at least one child living at home. She found no statistically significant difference between employed and nonemployed women, with respect to the reported quality of their marriage. Furthermore, there is no correlation between an increase in a woman's salary and a couple's likelihood of divorce (Rogers & DeBoer, 2001). Some studies even show that marriages are more stable if the woman is employed (R. C. Barnett & Hyde, 2001).

However, marital satisfaction is related to other work-related factors. For example—no surprise!—employed women are usually happier with their

Demonstration 7.5

COLLEGE
STUDENTS' PLANS
ABOUT CAREERS
AND PARENTHOOD

Conduct an informal survey of your friends, ideally at least five females and five males. (Select people who would feel comfortable discussing this topic with you.) Ask them each individually the following questions:

1. After you have finished your education, do you plan to seek employment? How many hours would you expect to work each week?
2. After you have finished your education, do you see yourself becoming a parent? (If the answer is no, you do not need to ask additional questions.)
3. Suppose that you and your partner have a 1-year-old child. How many hours a week would you expect to work outside the home? How many hours a week would you expect your partner to work outside the home?
4. How many hours a week do you expect to spend taking care of the baby? How many hours a week would you expect your partner to spend in child care?

Note the percentage of respondents who plan to be employed when they are the parents of a 1-year-old child. If you surveyed both women and men, did you notice any differences in their patterns of responses?

---

marriage if their husbands perform a relatively large percentage of the housework (Coltrane & Adams, 2001b; Padavic & Reskin, 2002; Steil, 2000). In contrast, women whose husbands are doing relatively little housework are at risk for depression (C. E. Bird, 1999), as we'll see in Chapter 12.

In summary, women who work outside the home may be busier than nonemployed women. However, the two groups of women seem to be equally satisfied with their marriages.

CHILDREN

In the United States and Canada, most surveys of young women show that they expect to combine a career with motherhood (Davey, 1998; Hoffnung, 1999, 2000, 2004). However, in an occasional study, young women may report that they plan to give up their career once they have children (Riggs, 2001). Try Demonstration 7.5, to explore this question with your own friends.

The reality is that most North American mothers do work outside the home. In the United States, 72% of mothers with children under the age of 18 are currently employed (Bureau of Labor Statistics, 2004c). The data are comparable for Canada, where 70% of mothers with children under the age of 16 are currently employed (Statistics Canada, 2004). These observations suggest two important questions concerning the children of employed women:

1. How are the child-care tasks divided in two-parent families?
2. Does a mother's employment influence children's psychological adjustment?

TAKING CARE OF CHILDREN.   In the previous section, we saw that women perform more housework than men do. Who's taking care of the children? The research suggests that U.S. and Canadian fathers have substantially increased their child-care responsibilities since similar studies were conducted 30 years ago (R. C. Barnett, 2004; Milkie et al., 2002; Pleck & Masciadrelli, 2004).

Still, researchers conclude that mothers perform most of the child care. For example, a large-scale study of U.S. residents included data on adults who had children younger than 18 years of age. In this study, the men spent about 50 minutes a day in child care, in contrast to 1 hour and 45 minutes for the women (Bureau of Labor Statistics, 2004b). Other studies provide similar data; mothers perform between 60% and 90% of child-care tasks (Laflamme et al., 2002; Pleck & Masciadrelli, 2004; Statistics Canada, 2005c). If we combine the hours spent on housework and the hours spent on child care, we see that mothers devote many more hours working in the home, in comparison to fathers (Bureau of Labor Statistics, 2004b; M. Fine & Carney, 2001).

When fathers perform a high proportion of the child care, children show greater cognitive and social skills than when fathers seldom provide child care. The children are also higher in self-esteem, and they have fewer behavioral problems (Coltrane & Adams, 2001b; Deutsch et al., 2001; L. W. Hoffman & Youngblade, 1999). Apparently, children benefit from having two caring adults actively involved in their lives. Furthermore, fathers who spend more time in child care are healthier and more caring of other people than are uninvolved fathers. These fathers also have better relationships with their children (hooks, 2000a; Pleck & Masciadrelli, 2004). In other words, both fathers and children may benefit from the time they spend together.

Francine Deutsch and her colleagues have studied married couples who share their child-care activities reasonably equally (Deutsch, 1999, 2001; Deutsch & Saxon, 1998a, 1998b). These parents describe the difficulty of breaking out of the traditional patterns of child care. However, many fathers report the unexpected benefits of sharing child care. For example, a fire inspector who is married to a secretary commented:

> [I've gained] time with my wife. I mean it's not much time, but whatever time there is in the evening. If one of us had to do everything, then we wouldn't have the time together. I enjoy spending time with my wife too (as well as the kids). It's crazy sometimes, crazy most days, but I love my life. I love the way it is and I can't see living any other way. (Deutsch, 1999, p. 134)

Many women have no partner who can—even theoretically—share in the care of the children. Mothers who are single, separated, divorced, or widowed typically work outside the home for economic reasons. For these women, the logistical problems of arranging for child care and transporting children become even more complicated. In addition, unmarried mothers usually have sole responsibility for nurturing their children, helping them with homework, and disciplining them.

MATERNAL EMPLOYMENT AND CHILDREN. College students tend to believe that a mother's employment has a negative impact on her children (Bridges & Etaugh, 1995, 1996). Mothers who do not work outside the home also believe that children are harmed by their mother's employment (Johnston & Swanson, 2002, 2004). The research contradicts this belief. We need to emphasize that the topic of maternal employment and children's adjustment is complex. The nature of our conclusions depends on a wide variety of variables, such as the quality of the child-care program, the age of the child, the economic background of the family, and the mother's sensitivity to her child's needs (Brooks-Gunn et al., 2002; Marshall, 2004; NICHD Early Child Care Research Network, 2001, 2002, 2004).

In general, the cognitive development of children who have been in a day-care setting is similar to that of children cared for by their mother at home. For low-income families, high-quality day care may provide cognitive advantages (Loeb et al., 2004; Marshall, 2004; NICHD Early Child Care Research Network, 2001). Furthermore, children in high-quality day care are generally more cooperative, and they have fewer behavior problems (Marshall, 2004; NICHD Early Child Care Research Network, 2001, 2002; Weinraub et al., 2001).

In addition, most infants who spend time in a day-care center have the same kind of emotional closeness to their mothers as do children whose mothers do not work outside the home. The only exception is children who have poor-quality day care and whose mothers are not sensitive to their needs (L. W. Hoffman, 2000; NICHD Early Child Care Research Network, 1999, 2001; Weinraub et al., 2001).

Employed mothers tend to encourage their children to be independent (Johnston & Swanson, 2002). Furthermore, children whose mothers work outside the home have an important advantage: Their mothers provide models of competent women who can achieve in the workplace (Coontz, 1997; L. W. Hoffman & Youngblade, 1999). In general, the research shows that children of employed mothers are not as gender stereotyped as children who are cared for in the home by their mothers (Etaugh, 1993; L.W. Hoffman, 2000).

In summary, the overall picture suggests that children's development is not substantially affected by nonmaternal care (Erel et al., 2000; L. W. Hoffman, 2000). However, U.S. families face a problem. Children clearly benefit from good day care, but high-quality child care at a reasonable price is not widely available (Brooks-Gunn et al., 2002; Coontz, 1997). We claim that children are a top priority. However, the government does not subsidize child care—a particular problem for low-income families. For example, in the United States, migrant workers harvest 85% of our hand-picked fruit and vegetables (Kossek et al., 2005). Suppose that you were a migrant worker, and affordable child care was not available. Would you bring your children to work with you, where they would be exposed to rain, excessive heat, and pesticides?

In many European countries, parents can enroll their children in a variety of programs at no cost or at a minimal charge (Poelmans, 2005). However, the United States is one of a few industrialized countries that does not have comprehensive child-care policies (Bub & McCartney, 2004; Marshall, 2004). Children are clearly not a top priority in this country.

PERSONAL ADJUSTMENT

We have examined both the marriages and the children of employed women. But how are the women themselves doing? Do they experience role strain? How is their physical and mental health?

ROLE STRAIN. A female physician who directs an inner-city medical clinic for adolescents commented about her life: "I don't know any professional woman in her 40s who feels her life is balanced. At that age, we are all overcommitted. Perhaps we figure it out in our 50s" (Asch-Goodkin, 1994, p. 63).

This woman is describing **role strain**, which occurs when people have difficulty fulfilling all their different role obligations. For example, in research with both Canadian nurses and Canadian physicians, women reported excessive workloads and high levels of role strain (Bergman et al., 2003; K. Thorpe et al., 1998). According to U.S. research, women in every ethnic group experience some kind of role strain.

Employed women often experience role strain in the form of conflict between a job and family responsibilities (Crosby & Sabattini, 2006; Greenhaus & Parasuraman, 2002; Powell & Graves, 2003). However, employed women often say they would miss their work identity if they stopped working outside the home. As one mother remarked, "I've considered at times not working. After giving birth I didn't, and I realized I needed that outside stimulation . . . for my own self-concept" (Brockwood et al., 2001, p. 58).

PHYSICAL HEALTH. We might imagine that role strain could lead to poor physical health for employed women. However, the data suggest that employed women are, if anything, healthier than nonemployed women (Cleveland et al., 2000; Crosby & Sabattini, 2006). Only one group of employed women has substantial health problems: women who have low-paying or unrewarding jobs, several children, and an unsupportive husband (R. C. Barnett & Rivers, 1996; Cleveland et al., 2000; Noor, 1999).

MENTAL HEALTH. If you believe the picture painted by the media, you can easily imagine a bleary-eyed woman who arrives home from a grueling day at work just in time to feed the dog, change the baby's diapers, and set the dinner table. This woman, it would seem, has every right to be depressed and unhappy. However, as we'll see in this section, employed women are typically as happy as nonemployed women. If their work role is an important part of their self-concept, employed women are often happier and better adjusted (Betz, 2006; L. W. Hoffman, 2000; Martire et al., 2000). Many women enjoy the challenge of a difficult task and the enormous pleasure of successfully achieving a long-term occupational goal.

Furthermore, many women find that their multiple roles provide a buffer effect (R. C. Barnett & Hyde, 2001; Betz, 2006; S. J. Rogers & DeBoer, 2001). Specifically, employment acts as a buffer against the stress of family problems, and family life acts as a buffer against problems at work. When these roles are generally positive, the benefits of multiple roles seem to outweigh the disadvantages (J. D. Yoder, 2000).

Research also demonstrates that woman's self-esteem is enhanced by employment. In general, employed women report a greater sense of competence, accomplishment, and life satisfaction, compared to nonemployed women.

Employed women are also less likely to be depressed or anxious (Betz, 2006; Cleveland et al., 2000; S. J. Rogers & DeBoer, 2001).

Little cross-cultural information is available on employed women's multiple roles. One exception is a study conducted in South Korea by Park and Liao (2000). This research compared married female professors with female homemakers who were married to professors. Park and Liao's results showed that the female professors experienced greater role strain, but also greater feelings of gratification—similar to the general trend of North American research.

In one large-scale study, R. C. Barnett (1997) studied 300 married couples, all of whom worked outside the home. She found that women who had challenging and rewarding jobs coped well with problems at home, such as frustrating child-care issues. Another study demonstrated that French Canadian women were significantly higher in self-esteem if their occupations gave them the opportunity to work independently and to feel accomplished. These characteristics of their jobs were more important than salary in determining self-esteem (Streit & Tanguay, 1994). However, women who have low-status or unrewarding jobs typically report lower general life satisfaction and greater levels of distress (Noor, 1996).

We cannot ignore the fact that employed women experience a leisure gap; their housework and child-care responsibilities are much greater than those of employed men (D. L. Nelson & Burke, 2002). Women cannot solve this problem by simply learning how to manage their time more effectively. Instead, couples need to navigate through work-family conflicts so that they can share the workload more equally (Crosby & Sabattini, 2006; MacDermid et al., 2001; Nevill & Calvert, 1996).

Most important, our society needs to acknowledge the reality of employed women and dual-earner families (R. C. Barnett, 2001). Companies need to design genuinely family-friendly policies for their employees (Padavic & Reskin, 2002; Rosin & Korabik, 2002). As R. C. Barnett and Rivers (1996) emphasized:

> The facts are clear: Women are working and will do so in even greater numbers in the near future. They are not going home. Paid employment has a positive impact on the physical and emotional health of women, and trying to get them to work part-time or relinquish their commitment to work will harm—not improve—their health. (p. 38)

Section Summary

Coordinating Employment With Personal Life

1. Among North American families, men do only about 30% to 40% of the household tasks, although many women do not express anger about their greater workload.

2. In general, a woman's satisfaction with her marriage is not influenced by whether she works outside the home.

3. In North America, women perform the clear majority of child-care tasks; however, both children and their fathers benefit from fathers' involvement with child care.

4. In general, children in day care do not experience disadvantages with respect to cognitive abilities, social development, or attachment, and they may develop more flexible beliefs about gender.

5. The quality of day care has an important influence on children's psychological development; unfortunately, many families cannot afford high-quality day care.

6. Employed women may experience role strain from conflicting responsibilities, but many report that their work enhances their feeling of competence.

7. Employed women are as healthy and as well adjusted psychologically as nonemployed women; women with satisfying jobs seem to be even healthier and better adjusted.

CHAPTER REVIEW QUESTIONS

1. In many ways, women's work experiences have changed dramatically during the past few decades. Turn to the chapter outline on page 209 and describe which factors have changed and which ones have stayed reasonably constant.

2. Where did you learn your previous information about women and welfare: from other classes, from the media, or from people you know? Which aspects of this chapter's discussion match your previous information, and which aspects are new?

3. Based on this chapter's examination of access discrimination, describe a situation in which a woman would be especially likely to face access discrimination when she applies for a job. What four factors would make a woman least likely to face access discrimination? How would affirmative action operate in hiring situations?

4. What kinds of treatment discrimination do women usually face in the workplace? Discuss the research on this topic, and supplement it with some of the issues mentioned in the section on women's experiences in selected occupations.

5. Some people claim that the wage gap can be entirely explained by the fact that women are more likely than men to stop working once they have children and that women have less education. How would you answer this claim, and how would you explain the concept of comparable worth?

6. Compare the experiences of employed women and employed men with respect to the glass ceiling, the sticky floor, and the glass escalator. Also compare the personal characteristics of men and women in the same occupation.

7. Outline the two general kinds of explanations that have been offered for women's underrepresentation in certain jobs (pp. 234–235). Review the section summaries in Chapters 5 and 6, and note which explanation is most supported by the evidence from cognitive and social gender comparisons.

8. Suppose that you know several women who earn lower salaries than comparable men in the same company, yet they don't seem very upset by the discrepancy. How would you explain why they are not outraged? What similar process operates when a woman

considers the gap in the amount of house-work and child care that she and her husband perform?

9. Imagine that you are a 25-year-old woman and that you have decided to return to your former job after the birth of your first baby. A neighbor tells you that your child will probably develop psychological problems if you work outside the home. Cite evidence to defend your decision.

10. Imagine that you are part of a new task force in your state or province. This task force has been instructed to make recommendations to improve the situation of women in the work-place. Based on the information in this chap-ter, make a list of 8 to 10 recommendations.

KEY TERMS

*working women (211)

*employed women (211)

*nonemployed women (211)

*access discrimination (215)

gender-role spillover (216)

*affirmative action (217)

*reverse discrimination (217)

treatment discrimination (218)

*comparable worth (220)

*occupational segregation (220)

*entitlement (221)

*glass ceiling (222)

*sticky floor (222)

*glass escalator (222)

*sexual harassment (223)

*heterosexism (224)

*sweatshop (229)

*maquiladoras (maquilas) (230)

person-centered explanations (234)

*individual approach (234)

situation-centered explanations (234)

*structural approach (234)

*homemaker (235)

*role strain (243)

 Note: The terms asterisked in the Key Terms section serve as good search terms for InfoTrac College Edition. Go to http://infotrac.thomsonlearning.com and try these added search terms.

RECOMMENDED READINGS

Bender, D. E., & Greenwald, R. A. (Eds.). (2003). *Sweatshop USA: The American sweatshop in historical and global perspective*. New York: Routledge. At present, this book provides the most comprehensive overview of the sweatshop problem. It emphasizes historical and current-day perspectives on sweatshops in the United States, but it also discusses "offshore" sweatshops in other countries.

Ehrenreich, B. (2001). *Nickel and dimed: On (not) getting by in America*. New York: Metropolitan Books. This book is ideal for anyone who thinks that a person can survive on the minimum wages paid for service jobs. Ehrenreich is a superb writer, and she compassionately describes both her own work experiences and those of her coworkers.

Murphy, E. F. (2005). *Getting even: Why women don't get paid like men—and what to do about it*. New York: Simon & Schuster. Evelyn Murphy served as the Lieutenant Governor of Massachu-setts from 1987 to 1991, and she has also held executive positions in corporations. This well-written book provides information about the gender gap—and steps that individuals can take to bridge the gap.

Polakow, V., Butler, S. S., Deprez, L. S., & Kahn, P. (Eds.). (2003). *Shut out: Low income mothers and higher education in post-welfare America*. Albany, NY: State University of New York Press. I recommend this book to anyone who wonders whether the current U.S. welfare policy is work-ing. I especially appreciated the diversity of women who contributed chapters to this book.

Powell, G. N., & Graves, L. M. (2003). *Women and men in management* (3rd ed.). Thousand Oaks, CA: Sage. This well-written textbook provides a clear overview of the topic. Some especially relevant chapters focus on career development, gender discrimination, and leadership.

ANSWERS TO THE TRUE-FALSE STATEMENTS

1. True (p. 214); 2. False (p. 217);
3. False (pp. 219–220); 4. True (p. 222);
5. False (p. 230); 6. True (pp. 231–232);
7. False (pp. 233–234); 8. True (pp. 238–239);
9. False (pp. 241–242); 10. False (pp. 243–244).

8 | LOVE RELATIONSHIPS

© Margaret W. Matlin, Ph.D.

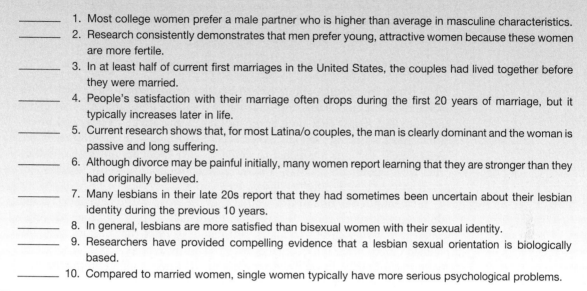

True or False?

_____ 1. Most college women prefer a male partner who is higher than average in masculine characteristics.

_____ 2. Research consistently demonstrates that men prefer young, attractive women because these women are more fertile.

_____ 3. In at least half of current first marriages in the United States, the couples had lived together before they were married.

_____ 4. People's satisfaction with their marriage often drops during the first 20 years of marriage, but it typically increases later in life.

_____ 5. Current research shows that, for most Latina/o couples, the man is clearly dominant and the woman is passive and long suffering.

_____ 6. Although divorce may be painful initially, many women report learning that they are stronger than they had originally believed.

_____ 7. Many lesbians in their late 20s report that they had sometimes been uncertain about their lesbian identity during the previous 10 years.

_____ 8. In general, lesbians are more satisfied than bisexual women with their sexual identity.

_____ 9. Researchers have provided compelling evidence that a lesbian sexual orientation is biologically based.

_____ 10. Compared to married women, single women typically have more serious psychological problems.

Just before I began to write this chapter on love relationships, my husband and I ordered tickets to see the Chicago Lyric Opera's production of the classic Verdi opera, "Rigoletto." Here's the plot: A lovely young woman named Gilda has been seduced by the Duke of Mantua. The evil Duke has seduced numerous other young women, so it is ironic when he sings, "La donna é mobile," an aria about the fickleness of women. Gilda's father, Rigoletto, is enraged, and he hires an assassin to kill the Duke. However, the night is dark, and Rigoletto discovers that the assassin has killed Gilda instead. Almost every grand opera focuses on some aspect of romantic relationships.

This week on television, the soap opera "Soñar No Cuesta Nada" features Señora Roberta, trying to hide her lover—the doctor—when her husband arrives unexpectedly. And our local movie theater is playing "Mr. and Mrs. Smith," a comedy about two assassins who are married to each other. Meanwhile, every magazine at the supermarket checkout counter is speculating that the two actors in that movie—Brad Pitt and Angelina Jolie—are more than "just good friends."

No matter how many times we hear about "boy meets girl," we go back for more. You can probably think of a few grand operas, soap operas, or movies about power or danger or money. However, these are clearly outnumbered by themes about love (Fletcher, 2002; Hedley, 2002a, 2002b). The previous chapter focused on women and work, a central issue in the lives of contemporary women. In Chapters 8, 9, and 10, we'll examine women's close personal relationships as we consider love, sexuality, and motherhood. Our four major topics in the current chapter about love relationships are (1) dating and living together, (2) marriage and divorce, (3) lesbians and bisexual women, and (4) single women. As you'll see, these four categories are much more fluid than they may initially seem.

DATING AND LIVING TOGETHER

We'll begin by talking about heterosexual relationships—the category we encounter most frequently in the media. We should note, though, that many heterosexuals report that they never thought much about their sexual orientation. After all, being "straight" is considered normative in our culture. When heterosexual students are asked to describe their thoughts on the issue, they often write comments such as "I never gave consideration to my sexual identity; it just came naturally" (Eliason, 1995, p. 826).

Incidentally, the title of this section uses the word *dating*. However, many adolescents currently report that they are more likely to hang out together or go somewhere with a group of males and females rather than have a formally planned date (Baca Zinn & Eitzen, 2002; O'Sullivan et al., 2001; Wekerle & Avgoustis, 2003). Still, we'll refer to "dating" because popular culture has not yet invented a substitute term.

Let's consider the characteristics that heterosexual women and men want in an ideal romantic partner; we'll then discuss two explanations for gender differences in this area. Next, we'll compare women and men with respect to several characteristics of the love relationship. Our final two topics will be couples who live together and couples who break up.

THE IDEAL ROMANTIC PARTNER

Before you read this section on ideal partners, try Demonstration 8.1. You may be convinced that you can tell whether a man or a woman wrote these personal ads, but be sure to check the answers. Let's first consider North American studies on this topic and then explore research from other cultures.

NORTH AMERICAN RESEARCH.   What do women and men want in their romantic partner? The answer depends on whether they are discussing a sexual partner or a marriage partner. Regan and Berscheid (1997) asked undergraduates at a Midwestern university to rank a variety of personal characteristics in terms of their desirability for (a) a partner for sexual activity and (b) a partner for a long-term relationship such as marriage. Table 8.1 shows the five most important characteristics for each type of relationship for females judging males and for males judging females.

As you can see, both women and men emphasized physical attractiveness when judging an ideal sexual partner. However, a statistical analysis showed that men were more likely than women to rank physical attractiveness as the most important characteristic.

Notice, however, that the preferred characteristics shift when people judge an ideal marriage partner. Here, the gender differences are small, because both

Demonstration 8.1

This demonstration contains excerpts from advertisements in the personals column of *City Newspaper* (Rochester, New York). Each excerpt describes the kind of person the writer of the ad is looking for. I have left out any mention of the gender of the ideal partner; otherwise, this portion of the ad is complete. In front of each description, put an F if you think the writer of the ad is female or an M if you think the writer is male.

_____ 1. I am seeking a friend first and then maybe more. Warmth, intelligence, and sense of humor all pluses.

_____ 2. I'm looking for someone who is successful, but not a workaholic, with great sense of humor, healthy, honest, faithful, able to make commitment.

_____ 3. I am seeking a new best friend to laugh with. Interests include: movies, cards, antiques, the outdoors.

_____ 4. I'm looking for a 30-something nonsmoker. Trail-climbs and off-road bike by day, and share romantic cultured evenings. Friends first.

_____ 5. Looking for fun-loving single White Jewish [person] who enjoys dancing and dining.

_____ 6. I'm seeking a single White Protestant [person], 45–55 years old, who wants to share music, cooking, football Sundays, weekend trips, and holiday fun. Love of walking and biking a plus. Smoking will get you nowhere.

_____ 7. I'm seeking a single White [person] under 34 to share a life of kindness, togetherness, friendship, and love.

_____ 8. [Ad writer] seeks single [person], 26–35, race unimportant. Must like dancing, dining, movies, and cuddling, for exciting Fall romance. Will not be disappointed.

_____ 9. Looking for career-oriented self-confident individual who desires to share a variety of outdoor activities, including bicycling, skiing, backpacking, gardening.

_____ 10. Seeking Black [person] 20's–40's who's honest, intelligent, positive, loving, caring, and tender for a relationship.

Check the accuracy of your answers at the end of this chapter (page 288).

---

women and men value honesty, good personality, and intelligence. However, men do mention physical attractiveness as the third most important characteristic for a marriage partner.

Other research confirms that physical appearance is extremely important when people first meet a potential romantic partner. Also, attractiveness and slimness are especially important when men are judging women (Fletcher, 2002; J. H. Harvey & Weber, 2002; Regan et al., 2000; Travis & Meginnis-Payne, 2001). We will return to this topic later in this book, when we discuss reactions to women with disabilities (Chapter 11) and women who are overweight (Chapter 12).

TABLE 8.1   CHARACTERISTICS THAT MALES AND FEMALES CONSIDER MOST IMPORTANT FOR A SEXUAL PARTNER AND A MARRIAGE PARTNER, LISTED IN ORDER OF IMPORTANCE

	Females Judging Males	Males Judging Females
Sexual partner	Physically attractive	Physically attractive
	Healthy	Healthy
	Attentive to my needs	Overall personality
	Sense of humor	Attentive to my needs
	Overall personality	Self-confident
Marriage partner	Honest or trustworthy	Overall personality
	Sensitive	Honest or trustworthy
	Overall personality	Physically attractive
	Intelligent	Intelligent
	Attentive to my needs	Healthy

Source: Regan, P. C., & Berscheid, E. (1997). Gender differences in characteristics desired in a potential sexual and marriage partner. *Journal of Psychology & Human Sexuality, 9,* 32 (Table 1). Haworth Press, Inc., 10 Alice Street, Binghamton, NY 13904.

How accurate were you in guessing the gender of the people who wrote the personal ads in Demonstration 8.1? You may have hesitated because several of these ads could have been written by either a male or a female. In general, systematic studies of personal ads in both the United States and Canada confirm that men are more likely than women to emphasize physical attractiveness in describing an ideal partner. In contrast, women are more likely than men to emphasize financial status. However, both men and women tend to specify that an ideal partner should be warm, romantic, kind, and sensitive and also have a good sense of humor (Green & Kenrick, 1994; Lance, 1998; E. J. Miller et al., 2000). Furthermore, Theme 4 operates in the choice of a romantic partner; there is more variation *within* each gender than *between* the genders.

You may wonder whether women are looking for strong, dominant men or for nice guys. Urbaniak and Kilmann (2003) found that female undergraduates were much more likely to prefer a man who said he was "kind and attentive and doesn't go for all that macho stuff," rather than a man who said he knew how to get what he wants and "doesn't go in for all that touchy-feely stuff" (p. 416). Other research about hypothetical romantic partners reported similar results (Desrochers, 1995; Jensen-Campbell et al., 1995). Furthermore, Burn and Ward (2005) found that college women were more satisfied with their romantic relationships if their male partner was low in traditionally masculine characteristics. Any reader of this textbook who happens to be a kind, considerate male—in search of a female partner—will be pleased to know that nice guys finish first, not last!

CROSS-CULTURAL RESEARCH.   Most of the participants in research on ideal partners have been White men and women living in the United States and Canada. When we move beyond groups with European origins, we often find different patterns for romantic relationships (Hamon & Ingoldsby, 2003). For example, many marriages in India are arranged by the couple's parents. However, as the two people become better acquainted, either the man or the woman may have the right to veto the prospective spouse (Medora, 2003; Pasupathi, 2002). What happens when young men and women immigrate to North America? In many cases, a woman—or her family—places a matrimonial advertisement in newspapers. Here is a representative ad from the website of *India Abroad* (2005):

> 33/5′6″, beautiful, highly accomplished Surgeon, Certified USA/Canada, Punjabi Arora. Currently Asst Professor/Staff Surgeon USA. Proposals invited from tall, never married, similarly qualified and highly successful MD Specialists or Engineers/ Attorneys (doctorate level from top schools and in top management positions).

Different cultures value somewhat different characteristics in a marriage partner. In general, however, women are more likely than men to say that a partner should be well educated and have good financial prospects. In contrast, men are more likely than women to say that a partner should be physically attractive (Higgins et al., 2002; Sprecher et al., 1994; Winstead et al., 1997).

In a representative cross-cultural study, Hatfield and Sprecher (1995) asked college students in the United States, Russia, and Japan to rate a number of characteristics that might be important in selecting a marriage partner. Gender similarities were found for many characteristics. However, Figure 8.1 shows that women in all three cultures are more likely than men to emphasize financial prospects in a spouse. Figure 8.2 shows that men in all three cultures are more likely than women to emphasize physical attractiveness.

EXPLANATIONS FOR GENDER DIFFERENCES IN PREFERENCE PATTERNS

One of the most controversial topics in the research on love relationships is whether evolutionary explanations can account for gender differences in romantic preferences. The **evolutionary-psychology approach** argues that various species gradually change over the course of many generations so that they can adapt better to their environment. A basic principle of this approach is that both men and women have an evolutionary advantage if they succeed in passing on their genes to the next generation.

Evolutionary psychologists argue that the evolutionary approach can explain why men and women have somewhat different views about ideal mates (Buss, 1995, 2000; A. Campbell, 2002; Fletcher, 2002; Geary, 1998). Specifically, men should be driven to prefer young, attractive, healthy-looking women because those women are most likely to be fertile. Therefore, these women will pass on the men's genes to the next generation. Contrary to the evolutionary perspective, however, the research actually shows that ratings of women's attractiveness are not correlated with health or fertility (Kalick et al., 1998; Tassinary & Hansen, 1998).

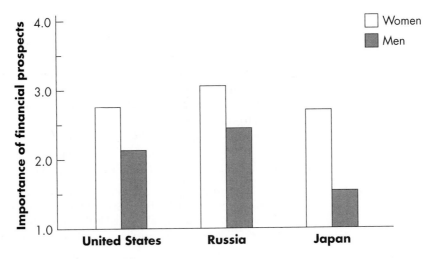

FIGURE 8.1 | IMPORTANCE OF FINANCIAL PROSPECTS IN A SPOUSE, FOR WOMEN AND MEN IN THREE CULTURES.

Source: Hatfield and Sprecher (1995).

Evolutionary psychologists also propose that women try to select a partner who will be committed to a long-term relationship. After all, women must make sure that the children are provided with financial resources. According to this argument, women look for reliable men who also have good incomes. Evolutionary psychologists emphasize that culture has little influence on gender differences in mate selection (Buss, 1998).

Many feminist psychologists object to the evolutionary approach. They argue, for example, that the theory is highly speculative about evolutionary forces that operated many thousands of years ago (Eagly & Wood, 1999). Feminists also point out that the evolutionary approach has failed to identify any genetic mechanism for these proposed gender differences (Hyde, 2002). In addition, evolutionary psychology cannot account for same-gender relationships (Surra et al., 2004). Also, the research shows that men are just as interested as women in long-term relationships (L. C. Miller et al., 2002; Popenoe & Whitehead, 2002). For example, in one study at a California university, 99% of female students and also 99% of male students said that they planned to be in a long-term relationship with just one sexual partner (Pedersen et al., 2002).

An explanation that sounds much more credible to me—and to most other feminists—emphasizes that social factors can effectively explain gender differences in preference patterns. According to the **social-roles approach,** men and women often occupy different social roles, they are socialized differently, and they experience different social opportunities and social disadvantages (Eagly & Wood, 1999; S. S. Hendrick, 2006; Johannesen-Schmidt & Eagly, 2002). For example, women have more limited financial resources in our culture, as we saw in Chapter 7. As a result, women are forced to focus on a partner's ability to earn money.

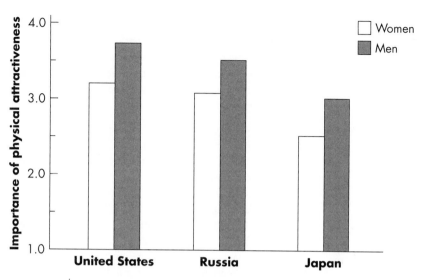

FIGURE 8.2 | IMPORTANCE OF PHYSICAL ATTRACTIVENESS IN A SPOUSE, FOR WOMEN AND MEN IN THREE CULTURES.

Source: Hatfield and Sprecher (1995).

In support of the social roles approach, research demonstrates that women are especially likely to prefer high-income men if they live in countries where women have limited educational and financial opportunities (Eagly & Wood, 1999; Kasser & Sharma, 1999). In contrast, in more egalitarian countries, women can earn their own incomes, so they don't need to seek wealthy husbands. Contrary to the predictions of evolutionary psychology, culture does affect mate preferences (Travis & Meginnis-Payne, 2001).

An important argument comes from social-roles theorists: Gender differences in mate preferences are not inevitable. For example, if women's social status in our own culture improves, women may place less emphasis on financial resources and more emphasis on factors such as physical attractiveness (Hatfield & Sprecher, 1995). A final point favoring the social-roles approach is that the differences in mate preferences between cultures are typically larger than the differences in mate preferences between genders (K. K. Dion & Dion, 2001b).

CHARACTERISTICS OF HETEROSEXUAL LOVE RELATIONSHIPS

We have looked at women's and men's ideal romantic partners. However, do women and men differ in their thoughts about an established love relationship? Furthermore, what factors predict satisfaction with a love relationship?

GENDER COMPARISONS. To some extent, women and men emphasize different aspects of love in their current romantic relationships. For example, women are significantly more likely than men to say that they have a relationship based on friendship (K. L. Dion & Dion, 1993; Nicotera, 1997; Sprecher & Sedikides,

Demonstration 8.2

If you are currently in a love relationship, rate the following statements based on that relationship. Alternatively, rate a previous love relationship that you experienced or a love relationship of a couple whom you know fairly well. For each statement, use a scale in which 1 = strongly disagree and 5 = strongly agree. Then add up the total number of points. In general, high scores reflect a love relationship that is strongly based on friendship.

_____ 1. My love for my partner is based on a deep, long-lasting friendship.
_____ 2. I express my love for my partner through the activities and interests we enjoy together.
_____ 3. My love for my partner involves solid, deep affection.
_____ 4. An important factor in my love for my partner is that we often laugh together.
_____ 5. My partner is one of the most likable people I know.
_____ 6. The companionship I share with my partner is an important part of our love.
_____ 7. I feel I can really trust my partner.
_____ 8. I can count on my partner in times of need.
_____ 9. I feel relaxed and comfortable with my partner.

Source: Based on Grote and Frieze (1994).

1993). When describing their romantic relationship, women are more likely than men to report commitment, liking, and satisfaction—all positive emotions. However, women also report more sadness, depression, hurt, and loneliness. In other words, compared to men, women seem to experience a wider range of both positive and negative emotions (Impett & Peplau, 2005; Sprecher & Sedikides, 1993).

However, in many other respects, the gender similarities are more striking. For example, both women and men typically say that the essential features of their love relationships are trust, caring, honesty, and respect (C. Hendrick & Hendrick, 1996; Rousar & Aron, 1990). Both women and men also report similar strategies for maintaining a romantic relationship, such as acting cheerful toward the partner and expressing love for this person. Still, the research suggests that women actually perform more of this "relationship-maintenance work" (Impett & Peplau, 2005; Steil, 2001a).

FACTORS RELATED TO SATISFACTION WITH THE RELATIONSHIP.   Before you read further, try Demonstration 8.2, which is based on a study by Grote and Frieze (1994). This questionnaire assesses the friendship dimension of a love relationship. We just noted some gender differences in emphasizing friendship. Other research suggests that both men and women are more satisfied with their love relationships if they are based on friendship (Grote & Frieze, 1994; J. H. Harvey & Weber, 2002). People who had friendship-based relationships also reported a greater degree of reciprocal understanding. In addition, relationships based on friendship lasted longer.

In Chapter 6, we saw that women are sometimes more likely than men to disclose personal information about themselves. In their romantic relationships, however, women and men have similar self-disclosure patterns (Hatfield & Rapson, 1993). In addition, both men and women are more satisfied with their love relationship if both partners are skilled at expressing their emotions (Lamke et al., 1994; Sternberg, 1998). The strong, silent male or the mysteriously uncommunicative female may look appealing in the movies. However, in real life, people prefer a person with sensitivity and other interpersonal skills.

LIVING TOGETHER

The term **cohabitation** refers to unmarried people who live together and who have a continuing emotional and sexual relationship (Rice, 2001b; Smock & Gupta, 2002). Other legal terms include *unmarried-couple household*, *common-law relationship*, and—the term used most often in Canada—*common-law union*. All these terms sound more like a business arrangement than a romantic relationship! According to recent data, about 5 million heterosexual couples in the United States report that they are living together; this number is probably an underestimate (U.S. Census Bureau, 2005). In Canada, 13% of women between the ages of 25 and 44 are currently living with a man to whom they are not married (Statistics Canada, 2000).

In the United States, the number of couples who were living together at the end of the 1990s was about ten times as many as the number at the beginning of the 1990s (Popenoe, 2004). The current U.S. data show that Blacks and Latinas/os are more likely than Whites to favor cohabitation. In Canada, French Canadians are more likely than Canadians from other ethnic backgrounds to choose cohabitation (Le Bourdais & Juby, 2002; Smock & Gupta, 2002; Statistics Canada, 2002). However, cohabitation is even more common in France and in Scandinavian countries than in North America (Kiernan, 2002).

In more than half of current first marriages in the United States, couples had lived together before marriage (Smock & Gupta, 2002). According to research in the United States and Canada, couples who live together before marriage are more likely to get divorced than those who have not lived together (Smock & Gupta, 2002; Surra et al., 2004). Does this mean that a couple should avoid living together because it is likely to cause divorce? An equally likely explanation is that people who live together before marriage are relatively nontraditional. Nontraditional people may also feel fewer constraints about seeking a divorce (Smock & Gupta, 2002; Surra et al., 2004).

BREAKING UP

A man and a woman have been dating for about a year. Then they break up. Who suffers more? Try Demonstration 8.3 before you read further.

Choo and her coauthors (1996) studied a sample of students at the University of Hawaii. Unlike a typical sample from the continental United States, most of the participants were Asian Americans. The students were asked to think back on a romantic relationship that had broken up and to assess their

Demonstration 8.3

Think about a person you once dated and felt passionate about, but then the two of you broke up. Read each of the items below, and place an X in front of each strategy you frequently used to cope with the breakup. (If you have not personally experienced a breakup, think of a close friend who has recently broken up with a romantic partner, and answer the questionnaire from that person's perspective.)

_____ 1. I tried to figure out what I might have done wrong.

_____ 2. I took alcohol or drugs.

_____ 3. I talked to my friends, trying to figure out if there was anything we could do to save the relationship.

_____ 4. I thought about how badly my partner had treated me.

_____ 5. I kept busy with my schoolwork or my job.

_____ 6. I told myself: "I'm lucky to have gotten out of that relationship."

_____ 7. I engaged in sports and other physical activities more than usual.

Source: Based on Choo et al. (1996).

emotional reactions immediately after the breakup. Men and women reported similar negative emotions (anxiety, sadness, and anger) as well as similar guilt. As Choo and her colleagues (1996) point out, "Men and women are more similar than different. In most things, it is not gender, but our shared humanity that seems to be important" (p. 144).

You may be surprised to learn that women felt more joy and relief following the breakup. How can we explain the results? The research by Choo and her coauthors suggests that women are usually more sensitive to potential problems in a relationship. In other words, women may have anticipated the breakup and worried about some danger signs. For instance, as Chapter 6 noted, women are relatively skilled in decoding facial expressions. In contrast, a man may not recognize signs of sadness or anger in a woman's facial expression. As a result, a woman may be less shocked and more relieved when the breakup does occur.

Both women and men are likely to experience ambivalence after the end of a romantic relationship (J. H. Harvey & Weber, 2002). For instance, a young woman described her emotions when she saw her former high-school boyfriend, a year after breaking up:

> I saw Jim for two days before I left for my sophomore year of college. There was something bittersweet about the whole thing. I hadn't seen him in so long and it felt so comfortable to be back with him even if it was for a short time. . . . I was proud that I didn't need him any more. I felt more grown up. Even though I didn't need him, I still wanted him back with me too. I was flooded with memories of the past, some good, some not so good. (N. M. Brown & Amatea, 2000, p. 86)

How do women and men cope with a breakup? Choo and her colleagues (1996) asked their respondents to recall how they had responded to the end of their love relationship. Demonstration 8.3 shows some of the items. The researchers found that women and men were equally likely to blame themselves for the breakup (Questions 1 and 3 of Demonstration 8.3). They were also equally likely to take alcohol and drugs following the breakup (Question 2). Men were more likely than women to try to distract themselves from thinking about the breakup (Questions 5 and 7). However, women were somewhat more likely than men to blame their partner for the breakup (Questions 4 and 6).

Why were women more likely than men to blame their partner for the breakup? Choo and her colleagues suggested one possibility: Women typically work harder than men do to maintain a relationship. When a breakup occurs, women may realistically blame their partner for not investing more effort in the relationship.

Section Summary

Dating and Living Together

1. Both women and men value physical attractiveness as an important characteristic for an ideal sexual partner, but men emphasize it more; both women and men value characteristics such as honesty and intelligence in an ideal marriage partner, but men still emphasize attractiveness more than women do.

2. To explain why men emphasize physical attractiveness in a romantic partner—and why women emphasize good financial prospects—evolutionary psychologists theorize that each gender emphasizes characteristics that are likely to ensure passing their genes on to their offspring.

3. According to the social-roles explanation for men's emphasis on physical attractiveness, men and women typically occupy different social roles. They are socialized differently, and they also have different opportunities and costs; furthermore, the differences are not inevitable.

4. Women are somewhat more likely than men to say that their love relationship is based on friendship; they also report a wider range of emotions in their relationships. Most other gender differences in evaluations of love relationships are minimal.

5. Relationships are more satisfying if they are based on friendship and if both partners can express their emotions.

6. The number of cohabiting couples has increased dramatically in recent decades; in more than half of first marriages in the United States, couples had lived together before marrying.

7. When couples break up, women and men experience similar negative emotions. However, women are more likely than men to experience joy and relief; they are also more likely to blame their partner for the breakup.

MARRIAGE AND DIVORCE

Our theme of individual differences in women's lives is especially important when we discuss women's experiences with marriage. Consider how two women describe their marriages. An interviewer asked one woman to describe her marriage, two years after the wedding:

> I really don't understand it. We used to enjoy spending time together, whether we went out to a party, had dinner with some friends, or just spent the night at home watching TV. It didn't matter what we did; just the fact that we were together made me happy. These days, Edgar doesn't seem to want to spend time with me anymore. I try to think of things that we could do together that would be fun and I make all sorts of suggestions to him, but he never wants to do anything, except stay at home and watch TV. . . . It's like his romantic side is gone. (J. Jones et al., 2001, p. 328)

Contrast that description with the observations of feminist author Letty Cottin Pogrebin (1997) about her own marriage. Recalling her parents' troubled marriage, she had originally vowed to remain single. However, she now describes being happily married for 34 years. As Pogrebin emphasizes, for many women, marriage can be a source of strength and joy:

> All I know is what I've had—34 years with a devoted partner who is my lover and closest friend. I know how it feels to live with someone whose touch excites, whose counsel calms, whose well-being matters as much as my own. I know that simple contentment is a kind of euphoria, that the familiar can be as intoxicating as the exotic, and that comfort and equality are, over the long haul, greater aphrodisiacs than romanticized power plays. I know how soul-satisfying it is to love someone well and deeply and to be loved for all the right reasons. I know how much more layered life is when everything is shared—sorrow and success, new enthusiasms, old stories, children, grandchildren, friends, memory. . . . We're what's called a good fit. (p. 37)

In Canada, the average ages for a first marriage are 28 years for women and 30 years for men (Statistics Canada, 2006). Furthermore, 90% of Canadian women between the ages of 40 and 69 have been married at least once (Statistics Canada, 2002).

In the United States, the average ages for a first marriage are somewhat younger—25 years for women and 27 years for men (Surra et al., 2004). As of 2003, 63% of U.S. women were married, a decrease from earlier eras (Coontz, 2005; Simon & Altstein, 2003; U.S. Census Bureau, 2005). Figure 8.3 shows the percentages of married women in three major ethnic groups of U.S. residents (U.S. Census Bureau, 2005). The percentages of divorced women are also listed in this figure. Unfortunately, however, the most current data do not include information about Asian Americans or Native Americans.

Let's begin our examination of marriage and divorce by first discussing marital satisfaction. Then we'll look at the distribution of power in marriage and marriage patterns among women of color. Our final topic in this section is the realities of divorce.

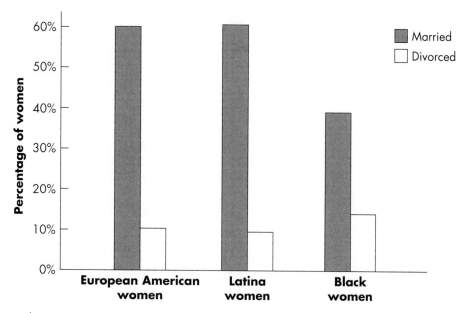

FIGURE 8.3 | PERCENTAGES OF WOMEN (AGE 15 OR OLDER) WHO LABEL THEIR STATUS AS MARRIED AND DIVORCED, IN THREE MAJOR ETHNIC GROUPS OF U.S. RESIDENTS.

Source: Based on data from U.S. Census Bureau (2005, Table 51).

MARITAL SATISFACTION

How happy are women with their marriages? Let's see how marital satisfaction changes over time, how men and women compare in terms of marital satisfaction, and how certain characteristics are associated with happy marriages.

SATISFACTION DURING VARIOUS PERIODS OF MARRIAGE. Think of the words *newlywed* and *bride*. These words may suggest associations such as bliss, radiance, obliviousness to the rest of the world, and complete happiness. Surveys show that individual differences are great, but young married couples are perhaps the happiest people in any age group (Karney & Bradbury, 2004; Karney et al., 2001).

About one or two years after the wedding, many married people report being less romantic and more dissatisfied. They may discover that they had different expectations for marriage (J. Jones et al., 2001; Noller & Feeney, 2002). Women are also likely to resent that they perform more housework than their husbands (S. E. Smith & Huston, 2004), an inequity we emphasized in Chapter 7. As we also saw in that chapter, women do even more of the work after children are born; during this period, women may become less satisfied with the marriage (K. K. Dion & Dion, 2001b).

People who have been married 20 to 24 years tend to be the group that is least satisfied with their marriage. However, marital satisfaction generally improves during the next decade, once the children have left home (J. Jones et al., 2001; Koski & Shaver, 1997). Couples who have been married at least 35 years also report relatively little conflict in their relationship (Bachand & Caron, 2001; Levenson et al., 1994). The reasons for this increased satisfaction are not clear, but they may include factors such as reduced conflict over parenting issues after the children leave home, as well as an increase in economic resources.

GENDER COMPARISONS IN MARITAL SATISFACTION.   A survey of college students asked them to estimate what percentage of their future identity would be devoted to being a marriage partner. Both women and men supplied an average figure of 30% (Kerpelman & Schvaneveldt, 1999).

Once people are married, women report more extreme levels of emotion than men do. Specifically, women report more positive emotions (W. Wood et al., 1989). However, women are also more likely than men to report major depression, as we'll see in Chapter 12.

Regarding satisfaction with marriage, women are somewhat more likely than men to report that their marriage did not live up to their visions of an ideal relationship (Vangelisti & Daily, 1999). Also, women are more sensitive than men to problems in their marital relationships (K. K. Dion & Dion, 2001b; W. Wood et al., 1989). This sensitivity is consistent with our earlier observation that women are better than men at anticipating potential problems in a dating relationship. In general, however, current researchers tend to emphasize gender similarities in marital satisfaction (Kurdek, 2005).

CHARACTERISTICS OF HAPPY, STABLE MARRIAGES.   In a happy, long-lasting marriage, both the wife and the husband feel that their emotional needs are fulfilled, and each partner enriches the life of the other. Both people understand and respect each other, as noted in Pogrebin's (1997) comment at the beginning of this section. Each person also understands and values the other person's cultural background (Gaines & Brennan, 2001; Leeds-Hurwitz, 2002).

Researchers have found that a variety of psychological characteristics are correlated with happy, stable marriages (Bradbury et al., 2001; Cobb et al., 2001; Cutrona et al., 2005; Donaghue & Fallon, 2003; Fincham, 2004; Perry-Jenkins et al., 2004; Prager & Roberts, 2004; Steil, 2001a; Wickrama et al., 2004):

1. Good communication skills and understanding.
2. A greater number of positive comments and expressions of affection, rather than negative comments and reactions.
3. Strong conflict-resolution skills.
4. Trust in the other person.
5. Mutual support.
6. The belief that each spouse is genuinely concerned about the other person's well-being.
7. Flexibility.

8. Equal sharing of household tasks.
9. Equal sharing in decision making.

Happily married couples even interpret their spouse's actions differently than unhappy couples do. For example, suppose that Jack gives a gift to his wife, Mary. If Mary is happily married, she is likely to think to herself, "How wonderful! Jack wanted to do something nice for me." However, if Mary is unhappily married, she might think, "He's probably giving me these flowers because he's feeling guilty about something." Unpleasant interactions can also be explained in either a positive or a negative light. These explanatory patterns could make a happy marriage even happier, but they could encourage more conflict in an unhappy marriage (Fincham, 2004; Karney & Bradbury, 2004; Karney et al., 2001).

DISTRIBUTION OF POWER IN MARRIAGES

In Chapter 7, we discussed how women are increasingly likely to work outside the home. However, most husbands still have more power in a marriage than wives do. Let's see how men's and women's salaries can influence the balance of power in a marriage. Then, we'll discuss how power is distributed in North American marriages.

SALARY AND POWER. To some extent, money is power. Men who earn higher salaries than their wives usually have much more power within a marriage (N. M. Brown & Amatea, 2000; Deutsch et al., 2003).

Wives who are employed have more power in decision making than non-employed wives have. In earlier eras, women were often embarrassed if they earned more than their husbands. Currently, however, women with higher incomes tend to be proud of their earning power (Deutsch et al., 2003). Still, many of these women do not have an equal voice in financial matters, if they have a traditional marriage. Although they may bring the family more income than their husbands do, their husbands still make most of the financial decisions (Steil, 1997, 2001b).

PATTERNS OF POWER DISTRIBUTION. We have emphasized individual differences throughout this book, and the variation in marital roles is also substantial (N. M. Brown & Amatea, 2000). In a **traditional marriage,** the husband is more dominant than the wife, and both partners maintain traditional gender roles. The wife can make decisions about housework and child care, but the husband has the ultimate authority in family decisions. He also controls the money. Traditional marriages are especially common among people from a traditional religious background (Impett & Peplau, 2005; Peplau, 1983; S. E. Smith & Huston, 2004). However, in recent decades, the typical marriage is somewhat less traditional (Amato et al., 2003). Because husbands are still likely to have more power than wives, most U.S. and Canadian marriages could probably be categorized somewhere along a continuum between a traditional marriage and an egalitarian marriage.

In an **egalitarian marriage,** both partners share power equally, without traditional gender roles. The wife and the husband have equal responsibility for housework, child care, finances, and decision making. Egalitarian marriages also emphasize companionship and sharing. These marriages are based on a true friendship in which both partners really understand and respect one another (Impett & Peplau, 2005; Peplau, 1983).

In an egalitarian marriage, the man and the woman share many of the same interests, and they know how to resolve conflicts fairly (Peplau, 1983). For example, a husband who had been married 16 years remarked:

> I started out pretty traditional. But over the years it made sense to change. We both work, and so we had to help each other with the kids. . . . And we worked together at church, and we both went whole hog into the peace program. So that got shared. I don't know; you can't design these things. You play fair, and you do what needs doing, and pretty soon you find the old ways don't work and the new ways do. (P. Schwartz, 1994, p. 31)

Marriage and Women of Color

We do not have a large number of systematic studies about marriage patterns for people from ethnic groups that are not European American. However, some resources provide partial information. Throughout this section, keep in mind the diversity within each group (Baca Zinn & Eitzen, 2002; Chan, 2003; Diggs & Socha, 2004). For instance, Latin American families in North America differ from one another because of the wide range of family income, education, country of origin, location of current residence, and level of acculturation.

Latinas.   In general, Latinas/os emphasize that they have an important obligation to their family (de las Fuentes et al., 2003; Parke, 2004; Torres, 2003). One of the key concepts often discussed in connection with Latinas/os is *machismo* (pronounced mah-*cheez*-mo). Social scientists have traditionally defined *machismo* as the belief that men must show their manhood by being strong, sexual, and even violent—clearly dominant over women in relationships (de las Fuentes et al., 2003; Ybarra, 1995). The machismo perspective also emphasizes that men should not do housework (Hurtado, 2003).

The parallel concept for women is *marianismo* (pronounced mah-ree-ah-*neez*-mo) Social scientists have traditionally defined *marianismo* as the belief that women must be passive and long suffering, giving up their own needs to help their husbands and children (de las Fuentes et al., 2003; Hurtado, 2003). *Marianismo* is based on the Catholic representation of the Virgin Mary, who serves as a role model for Latina women. *Machismo* and *marianismo* complement each other in a traditional Latina/o marriage:

> Love and honor your man—cook his meals, clean his house, be available and ready when he wants to have sex, have and care for his children, and look the other way at

marital infidelities. . . . In return, he will agree to protect you and your children, work, pay the bills. (M. Fine et al., 2000, p. 96)

How well do *machismo* and *marianismo* capture the relationship between Latinos and Latinas in the current era? Latinas/os do report less egalitarian attitudes than Whites or Blacks. Recent immigrants to North America are likely to emphasize traditional values (Steil, 2001b; Torres, 2003). However, the stereotype of the dominant husband and the submissive wife does not apply to most Latin American families (Baca Zinn & Wells, 2000; Matsumoto & Juang, 2004; Roschelle, 1998). Fewer than half of Latinos and Latinas believe that marriages should adopt this pattern of inequity. Furthermore, both Latina women and Latino men believe that they can effectively influence their partners by being honest and by talking with each other (Beckman et al., 1999).

The *marianismo* model also fails to describe women's roles for the millions of economically poor Latinas who must take a job to survive. Women who pick crops or work in factories cannot remain passive or totally focused on their husbands and children. In short, many Latinas and Latinos have created marital patterns that are different from the models that *marianismo* and *machismo* values suggest.

BLACK WOMEN. In the 1960s, U.S. government officials created the term **Black matriarchy** to refer to women's domination in Black families. Women in Black families were supposed to be so dominant that they presumably emasculated Black men and encouraged other family problems (Baca Zinn & Eitzen, 2002; Gadsden, 1999; R. L. Taylor, 2000).

Much of the early research focused on the most economically poor Black families. The researchers then generalized from that selected sample to all Black families. Basically, Black women were being unfairly criticized for having the motivation to work outside the home and still be strong figures in their own homes (P. H. Collins, 1990; Gadsden, 1999; L. B. Johnson, 1997).

The research does not support the idea of a Black matriarchy (Dodson, 1997; L. B. Johnson, 1997). For example, Oggins and her colleagues (1993) showed that both Black families and White families saw husbands as having slightly more power than wives. Some researchers have examined decision-making power in African American families (J. L. McAdoo, 1993; Parke, 2004). Most of these families are close to the egalitarian model. The husband and the wife contribute equally to decisions about what car to buy, what house to buy, child rearing, and other similar issues. In summary, the Black matriarchy is not a useful concept in explaining Black families.

ASIAN AMERICAN WOMEN. Asian American parents expect their children to marry someone from their own ethnic group (Chan, 2003), and the children typically do so. For example, a study of marriages within the Korean American community in Los Angeles found that 92% involved someone who was Korean by birth or descent (Min, 1993). About 60% married a Korean partner who had been living in the United States. However, about 30% brought their marriage partners from Korea. Marriages between Korean Americans and recent emigrants from Korea are likely to have many adjustment problems. For example, Korean American women who bring in husbands from Korea are likely to find that their spouses have extremely traditional ideas about gender roles.

Conflict between traditional customs in the home country and contemporary gender roles in North America undermines many marriages of recent immigrants (Chan, 2003; K. K. Dion & Dion, 2001a; Naidoo, 1999). Consider a Korean couple who immigrated to the United States and now work together in a family business. The husband comments:

> After she started working her voice got louder than in the past. Now, she says whatever she wants to say to me. She shows a lot of self-assertion. She didn't do that in Korea. Right after I came to the U.S., I heard that Korean wives change a lot in America. Now, I clearly understand what it means. (Lim, 1997, p. 38)

In contrast, consider his wife's comments:

> In Korea, wives tend to obey their husbands because husbands have financial power and provide for their families. However, in the U.S., wives also work to make money as their husbands do, so women are apt to speak out at least one time on what they previously restrained from saying. (Lim, 1997, p. 38)

We've noted the relative power of the wife and the husband in Latina/o, Black, and Korean couples. When couples immigrate to the United States from India, the traditional wife is supposed to quietly obey her husband and in-laws. She should also be self-sacrificing and uncomplaining (Gupta, 1999; Tran & Des Jardins, 2000). These couples divide decision-making power along gender stereotypical lines (Parke, 2004). Specifically, wives are primarily responsible for decisions concerning food and home decoration. In contrast, husbands are primarily responsible for decisions requiring large sums of money, such as buying a car and deciding where to live (Dhruvarajan, 1992).

In summary, Latina/o, Black, and Asian American families are guided by cultural traditions that vary widely, consistent with Theme 4 of this book. However, in this discussion, we can also see that women from all three cultures are creating their own marriage styles that differ greatly from these traditions.

DIVORCE

So far, most of our discussion has focused on relatively upbeat topics such as dating, living together, and marriage. As you know, however, divorce has become more common in North America during recent decades. According to current predictions, between 40% and 65% of first marriages recently taking place in the United States and Canada will end in divorce (Kitzmann & Gaylord, 2001; Popenoe & Whitehead, 2002; Statistics Canada, 2002). In the United States, as Figure 8.3 on page 261 shows, the different ethnic groups have somewhat different divorce rates. The highest rate is for Blacks, the lowest for Asian Americans (Kitzmann & Gaylord, 2001; U.S. Census Bureau, 2005).

Even though attitudes toward divorce are not as negative as they were several decades ago, the divorce experience is still traumatic for most people. Let's consider three aspects of divorce: (1) the decision to divorce, (2) psychological effects, and (3) financial effects.

THE DECISION TO DIVORCE.   Who is more likely to seek divorce, men or women? Folk wisdom might suggest that the men are most eager to leave a marriage. However, you'll recall that women are more likely to foresee problems in a dating relationship. In fact, the data show that wives initiate divorce more often than husbands do (Rice, 2001a). For instance, one survey focused on men and women who had experienced a divorce when they were between 40 and 69 years old. The results showed that 66% of women said that they had asked for the divorce, in contrast to 41% of men. Furthermore, 14% of women said that the request for a divorce had surprised them, in contrast to 26% of men. The three major reasons that women listed for a divorce were physical or emotional abuse, infidelity, and drug or alcohol abuse (Enright, 2004). In Chapter 13, we will discuss detailed information about the abuse of women.

Women sometimes report that they contemplated a divorce for years. Consider the following example:

> Jane Burroughs knew 10 years into her marriage that it wasn't working. She and her husband argued constantly. He made all the decisions; she felt she had no say. But instead of divorcing, she stayed for 21 more years, when her children were grown. . . . Burroughs, now 58, concedes it was the most difficult experience of her life and one that triggered conflicting emotions. (Enright, 2004, p. 62)

PSYCHOLOGICAL EFFECTS OF DIVORCE.   Divorce is especially painful because it creates so many different kinds of transitions and separations in addition to the separation from a former spouse (Baca Zinn & Eitzen, 2002; Ganong & Coleman, 1999). When a woman is divorced, she may be separated from friends and relatives previously shared by the couple. She may also be separated from the home she has known and from her children. In addition, people are likely to judge a divorced woman negatively (Etaugh & Hoehn, 1995).

Divorce is one of the most stressful changes a person can experience (Enright, 2004; Kitzmann & Gaylord, 2001). Depression and anger are often common responses, especially for women (Kaganoff & Spano, 1995; J. M. Lewis et al., 2004). Adjustment to divorce is complex and occurs over an extended time (M. A. Fine, 2000). In addition, mothers typically need to help children cope with the reality of divorce (J. M. Lewis et al., 2004).

However, divorce can lead to some positive feelings. Women who felt constrained by an unhappy marriage may also feel relief (Baca Zinn & Eitzen, 2002). As one woman said, "For me, the divorce was not difficult. I had been living in loneliness for years by the time my marriage ended, so that being alone felt uplifting, free" (Hood, 1995, p. 132). Many women also report that their divorce lets them know they are stronger than they had thought. In fact, some say that misfortune actually had a long-range positive effect (Bursik, 1991a, 1991b; Enright, 2004; McKenry & McKelvey, 2003).

FINANCIAL EFFECTS OF DIVORCE.   Despite the occasional positive effects of divorce, one consequence is painful: A woman's financial situation is almost always worse following a divorce, especially if she has children (Rice, 2001a). In Canada, two-thirds of divorced single mothers and their children live in poverty (Gorlick, 1995). In the United States, less than half of divorced fathers actually pay the mandated child support (Baca Zinn & Eitzen, 2002; Stacey, 2000). Black mothers are even more likely than White mothers to face financial problems (McKenry & McKelvey, 2003).

In summary, divorce can provide an opportunity for women to appreciate their strength and independence. Unfortunately, however, many divorced women find that economic inequities create real-life emergencies for themselves and their children.

Section Summary

Marriage and Divorce

1. Marital satisfaction is high during the newlywed period; it may drop shortly thereafter. Satisfaction is lowest during the first 20 to 24 years of marriage, and then it may increase after the children have left the home.

2. Women are more likely than men to report positive emotions about their marriage, but they are also more sensitive than men to marital problems.

3. Happy marriages are more common among people who have strong communication skills and conflict-resolution skills, who trust and support each other, and who share equally.

4. Power within a marriage tends to be related to spouses' salaries. Marriages can be categorized along a continuum between traditional and egalitarian.

5. Although some Latinas and Latinos emphasize *machismo* and *marianismo* in their marriages, a large percentage of them advocate more egalitarian marital patterns. Research with Black families does not support the concept of the Black matriarchy. Asian American families are likely to experience conflicts between traditional Asian values and contemporary North American gender roles.

6. Women are more likely than men to initiate divorce, most often because of physical or emotional abuse, infidelity, and drug or alcohol abuse.

7. Divorce is almost always stressful, especially because it creates depression and anger. Some women experience positive effects, such as relief and a sense of strength. However, most divorced women experience financial problems that can have serious implications for their well-being.

LESBIANS AND BISEXUAL WOMEN

Rita and Sandy, a lesbian couple together for 16 years, describe their relationship here. Reflecting on their first 10 years, Rita describes how she had thought that their relationship could not get any better:

> And now, between ten and sixteen years, I'm thinking, this is just excellent! Our relationship is just getting deeper and deeper and more loving and more loving, and of course, like any relationship, we've had our roller coaster. We've had our ups and downs and we'll continue to have our problems and work them out. It's hard to describe the deepness of the love. It keeps growing and growing and growing. So I can't imagine what it's going to be like in another sixteen years.

Then Sandy adds:

> And we're grateful for each other and we're both very verbal about thanking each other and being grateful to each other, respecting each other. I think that's really important. (Haley-Banez & Garrett, 2002, pp. 116–117)

A **lesbian** is a woman who is psychologically, emotionally, and sexually attracted to other women. Most lesbians prefer the term *lesbian* to the term *homosexual*. They argue that *lesbian* acknowledges the emotional components of the relationship, whereas *homosexual* focuses on sexuality. The term *lesbian*—like the term *gay*—is more proud, political, healthy, and positive (Kite, 1994). Some psychologists use the term **sexual minority** to refer to anyone (female or male) who has a same-gender attraction (L. M. Diamond, 2002); sexual minority includes lesbians, gay males, bisexual females, and bisexual males. As we'll see in this section, our discussion of sexual orientation emphasizes love, intimacy, and affection as well as sexual feelings.

In Chapter 1, we introduced the term **heterosexism**, or bias against lesbians, gay males, and bisexuals—groups that are not heterosexual. In North American culture, an important consequence of heterosexism is that we judge heterosexual relationships differently from lesbian, gay, and bisexual relationships (S. D. Smith, 2004). Try Demonstration 8.4 to appreciate how heterosexist thinking pervades our culture.

An important point is that researchers in psychology no longer consider lesbians to be invisible. In fact, while preparing this chapter, I conducted a search on a resource called PsycINFO. Impressively, 928 professional articles had been published with the term *lesbian* in the title, between January 2000 and June 2005.

In Chapter 2, we examined heterosexism and bias based on sexual orientation; in Chapter 4, we discussed the coming-out experience of adolescent lesbians, and in Chapter 7, we emphasized anti-lesbian prejudice in the workplace. In upcoming chapters, we will discuss sexuality issues among lesbians (Chapter 9), the research on lesbian mothers (Chapter 10), and the experiences of lesbians whose life partners have died (Chapter 14).

In this section of Chapter 8, we'll first discuss the psychological adjustment of lesbian women. Next we'll explore several characteristics of lesbian relationships, the experiences of lesbian women of color, and the fluid nature of

Demonstration 8.4

HETEROSEXIST THINKING

Answer each of the following questions, and then explain why each one encourages us to reassess the heterosexist framework.

1. Suppose that you are walking to class at your college and you see a man and a woman kissing. Do you think, "Why are they flaunting their heterosexuality?"
2. Close your eyes and picture two women kissing each other. Does that kiss seem sexual or affectionate? Now close your eyes and imagine a woman and a man kissing each other. Does your evaluation of that kiss change?
3. Suppose that you have an appointment with a female professor. When you arrive in her office, you notice that she is wearing a wedding ring and has a photo of herself and a man smiling at each other. Do you say to yourself, "Why is she shoving her heterosexuality in my face?"
4. If you are heterosexual, has anyone asked you, "Don't you think that heterosexuality is just a phase you'll outgrow once you are older?"
5. In all the public debates you've heard about sexual orientation, have you ever heard anyone ask any of the following questions:
   a. The divorce rate among heterosexuals is now about 50%. Why don't heterosexuals have more stable love relationships?
   b. Why are heterosexual men so likely to sexually harass or rape women?
   c. What really causes heterosexuality?

Sources: Based partly on L. Garnets (2004a) and Herek (1996).

sexual orientation. We'll then address the legal status of lesbian relationships, as well as information about bisexual women. Our final topic will be potential explanations for sexual orientation.

THE PSYCHOLOGICAL ADJUSTMENT OF LESBIANS

In 1973, the American Psychiatric Association decided that homosexuality should no longer be listed as a disorder in its professional guidebook, the *Diagnostic and Statistical Manual* (J. F. Morris & Hart, 2003; Schuklenk et al., 2002).

A large number of studies have shown that the average lesbian is as well adjusted as the average heterosexual woman (J. F. Morris & Hart, 2003; Peplau & Garnets, 2000). In a representative study, Rothblum and Factor (2001) compared the mental health of 184 pairs of lesbian women and their heterosexual sisters. The results showed that the two groups were equivalently well adjusted, except that the lesbian women were higher in self-esteem.

According to other research, lesbians and heterosexual women are similar on almost all psychological dimensions, except that lesbians score higher on positive characteristics such as "being self-sufficient," "being self-confident," and "making decisions easily" (Garnets, 2004a; Peplau & Garnets, 2000). Furthermore, lesbian couples and heterosexual couples are equally effective in resolving relationship conflicts (Kurdek, 2004).

As our discussion of heterosexism and sexual prejudice emphasized in Chapter 2, many sexual minority individuals are victims of hate crimes. Not surprisingly, lesbians, gays, and bisexuals who have experienced hate crimes are likely to report depression, anxiety, and substance abuse (Bontempo & D'Augelli, 2002; Herek et al., 1999; I. L. Meyer, 2003). In other words, hatred has real-life consequences for the well-being of thousands of women and men. Surprisingly, however, lesbian women are not at greater risk for suicide than heterosexual women (I. L. Meyer, 2003; Remafedi et al., 1998). In light of the sexual prejudice problem, we should be surprised that lesbians and gay men do not have high rates of psychological dysfunction (J. F. Morris & Hart, 2003).

Students in my classes sometimes ask whether people who accept their lesbian or gay identity are better adjusted. The research shows that people who accept their lesbian identity have higher self-esteem than those who have not accepted their lesbian identity (Garnets, 2004a; J. F. Morris et al., 2001).

Many lesbians create their own communities, and warm, supportive networks develop from the "families" they choose. These communities are especially helpful when lesbians are rejected by their birth families (Esterberg, 1996; Haley-Banez & Garrett, 2002). However, lesbians are more satisfied with their lives and less depressed if their family and friends support their lesbian identity (Beals & Peplau, 2005).

CHARACTERISTICS OF LESBIAN RELATIONSHIPS

For most North Americans—lesbian, gay male, bisexual, or heterosexual—being in a love relationship is an important determinant of their overall happiness (Peplau et al., 1997). Surveys suggest that between 40% and 65% of lesbians are currently in a steady romantic relationship (Peplau & Beals, 2004). In other words, many lesbians consider being part of a couple to be an important aspect of their life.

Let's now look more closely at several aspects of lesbian relationships. Specifically, how do most lesbian relationships begin? How is equality emphasized in these relationships? How happy are lesbian couples? How do they respond when the relationship breaks up?

THE BEGINNING OF A RELATIONSHIP. Lesbian women want many of the same qualities in a romantic partner that heterosexual women emphasize. These include characteristics such as dependability and good personality (Peplau & Beals, 2004). The research suggests that most lesbian couples begin their relationship as friends and then fall in love (Peplau & Beals, 2004; S. Rose, 2000; Savin-Williams, 2001). For many young women, a romantic relationship is a major milestone in coming out and identifying as a lesbian (M. S. Schneider, 2001).

An important hallmark of a strong friendship is emotional intimacy. As we'll see, lesbian couples are likely to emphasize emotional closeness. In contrast, physical attractiveness is relatively unimportant as a basis for a lesbian love relationship. In fact, when lesbians place personal ads in newspapers, they rarely emphasize physical characteristics (Peplau & Spalding, 2000; C. A. Smith & Stillman, 2002).

EQUALITY IN LESBIAN RELATIONSHIPS.   The balance of power is extremely important in lesbian relationships, and couples are happier if both members of the pair contribute equally to the decision making (Garnets, 2004a). We saw earlier that salary is an important determinant of power for heterosexual couples. However, salary isn't closely related to power among lesbian couples (Peplau & Beals, 2004). In general, lesbians try to avoid letting their salaries influence the balance within a relationship.

In Chapter 7, we saw that women do most of the housework in heterosexual marriages, even when both the husband and the wife work full time. As you might expect, lesbian couples are especially likely to emphasize that housework should be divided fairly (Oerton, 1998; Peplau & Spalding, 2000).

SATISFACTION.   The research on lesbian couples shows that their satisfaction with their relationship is much the same as for heterosexual couples and gay male couples (Kurdek, 1998; C. J. Patterson, 1995; Peplau & Beals, 2004). Try Demonstration 8.5 before you read further.

Demonstration 8.5 contains some of the questions from a survey, designed by Lawrence Kurdek (1995a), that measures relationship commitment. In this survey, Kurdek's sample of lesbian couples had commitment scores that were similar to the scores of married couples. The results also showed that the lesbian couples were more committed to the relationship than were heterosexual couples who were dating but not living together.

Psychological intimacy is likely to be strong in lesbian couples (Mackey et al., 2000). One woman described this sense of caring and intimacy:

> What has been good is the ongoing caring and respect and the sense that there is somebody there who really cares, who has your best interest, who loves you, who knows you better than anybody, and still likes you . . . and just that knowing, that familiarity, the depth of that knowing, the depth of that connection [make it] so incredibly meaningful. There is something spiritual after awhile. It has a life of its own. This is what is really so comfortable. (Mackey et al., 2000, p. 220)

BREAKING UP.   We do not have extensive information about how lesbian partners break up their love relationships. However, the general pattern seems to be similar to the heterosexual breakup pattern (Kurdek, 1995a; Peplau & Beals, 2001). The common reasons for breaking up include conflict, loneliness, feeling emotionally distant from the partner, and differences in interests, background, and attitudes about sex (Kurdek, 1995b; Peplau et al., 1996).

When relationships break up, lesbian women report the same mix of negative and positive emotions that heterosexual women experience (Kurdek, 1991). However, the breakup of a lesbian relationship typically differs from the breakup of a heterosexual marriage. In the current U.S. culture, certain factors are more likely to keep heterosexual couples from splitting apart, such as the cost of divorce, joint investments in property, and concerns about children

Demonstration 8.5

ASSESSING COMMITMENT TO A RELATIONSHIP

Answer the following questions about a current or a previous love relationship. Or, if you prefer, think of a couple you know well, and answer the questionnaire from the perspective of one member of that couple. Use a rating scale where 1 = strongly disagree and 5 = strongly agree. These questions are based on a survey by Kurdek (1995a). This is a shorter version. Turn to page 288 to see which relationship dimensions these items assess.

Rating   **Question**

_____ 1. One advantage to my relationship is having someone to count on.

_____ 2. I have to sacrifice a lot to be in my relationship.

_____ 3. My current relationship comes close to matching what I would consider my ideal relationship.

_____ 4. As an alternative to my current relationship, I would like to date someone else.

_____ 5. I've put a lot of energy and effort into my relationship.

_____ 6. It would be difficult to leave my partner because of the emotional pain involved.

_____ 7. Overall, I derive a lot of rewards and advantages from being in my relationship.

_____ 8. Overall, a lot of personal costs are involved in being in my relationship.

_____ 9. My current relationship provides me with an ideal amount of equality.

_____ 10. Overall, alternatives to being in my relationship are appealing.

_____ 11. I have invested a part of myself in my relationship.

_____ 12. It would be difficult to leave my partner because I would still feel attached to him or her.

Source: Based on Kurdek, L. A. (1995a). Assessing multiple determinants of relationship commitment in cohabitating gay, cohabitating lesbian, dating heterosexual, and married heterosexual couples. *Family Relations, 44*, 261–266. (Table 1). Copyright © 1995 by the National Council on Family Relations, 3989 Central Ave. NE, Suite 550, Minneapolis, MN 55421. Reprinted with permission.

(Beals et al., 2002; Peplau & Beals, 2004). In addition, lesbian couples are less likely to have support for their relationship from other family members—a factor that often keeps heterosexual couples together.

Consider another point that several lesbian friends have mentioned to me. Lesbians are likely to derive substantial emotional support from their partner, especially because they experience relatively little emotional support from heterosexuals. When their relationship breaks up, there are not many people with whom they can share their sorrow. In addition, their heterosexual friends often consider this loss to be less devastating than the breakup of a heterosexual relationship.

LESBIAN WOMEN OF COLOR

Lesbians of color often comment that they face a triple barrier in U.S. society: their ethnicity, their gender, and their sexual orientation (R. L. Hall & Greene,

2002; J. F. Morris, 2000; J. F. Morris et al., 2001). Lesbians who have immigrated to the United States and Canada face even greater barriers. For example, they may have been persecuted in the country from which they came (Espín, 1999). Now, these women struggle with cultural differences, and the new culture may have different ideas about lesbians from those in their country of origin.

Many lesbians of color face an extra barrier because their culture has even more traditional views of women than does mainstream European American culture. For example, Black churches often show sexual prejudice toward lesbian and gay individuals (Cole & Guy-Sheftall, 2003; B. Greene, 2000a). In addition, a Latina lesbian cannot fulfill the roles that are expected of the Latina woman—such as being obedient to her husband and rearing her children in a traditional fashion (Torres, 2003). The lesbian woman doesn't propagate the race, and she doesn't serve men in either a domestic or a sexual capacity. As a result, she becomes marginalized both within and outside her own culture (Gaspar de Alba, 1993).

Another issue is that some cultures may be more traditional than European American culture with respect to discussing sexuality. For example, Asian cultures typically believe that sexuality shouldn't be discussed (C. S. Chan, 1997; Takagi, 2001). Asian parents may also feel that a lesbian daughter has rejected their cultural values (Hom, 2003).

In addition, many heterosexual people of color believe that only European Americans face the "problem" of having gays and lesbians (Fingerhut et al., 2005; J. F. Morris, 2000). Furthermore, ethnic sexual minorities are typically more worried than White sexual minorities that their parents will reject them because of their sexual orientation (Dubé et al., 2001). As a result of these two factors, gays and lesbians of color are even less visible than in European American communities.

How do lesbian women of color feel about their own relationships? Peplau and her colleagues (1997) sent questionnaires to Black lesbians throughout the United States. Three-quarters of the women responded that they were "in love" and felt very close to their romantic partner. They also reported that they were quite satisfied with the relationship; the mean score was 5.3 on a scale where the maximum was 7.0.

Today, an increasing number of lesbian women of color can find organizations and community groups that provide support (J. F. Morris, 2000). However, these groups are more likely in urban regions of North America. For example, Mariana Romo-Carmona (1995) explained that Latina lesbians in the New York City area can watch a TV program featuring Latina lesbians, read brochures on health care written in Spanish by Latina lesbians, and march in the Puerto Rican Day parade with a contingent of lesbian and gay Latinas/os. Racism and heterosexism may still be present, but these groups can provide a shared sense of community.

Some regions of North America have Asian American lesbian and gay social organizations, support groups for parents of Asian American lesbian and gay children, and conferences that focus on relevant issues. However, critics emphasize that much work still needs to be done to include lesbian and gay perspectives within the framework of contemporary Asian American issues (Duong, 2004; Fingerhut et al., 2005; Takagi, 2001).

Women of color who are lesbians often create positive environments for themselves, even though they might appear to be living on the margins of North American society. They refuse to let themselves be confined by labels, they develop powerful friendships, and their activism strengthens their lives, as well as the lives of lesbian communities (R. L. Hall & Fine, 2005).

THE FLUIDITY OF FEMALE SEXUAL ORIENTATION

During the 1990s, researchers who were interested in the topic of lesbian and gay sexual orientation favored a straightforward model. Specifically, a young person would feel discontent about her or his heterosexual relationships. Then she or he would enter a period of sexual questioning, which would end with the adoption of a lesbian, gay, or bisexual identity. Current researchers realize that this model is too simplistic because it does not acknowledge the diverse pathways by which sexual orientation develops, especially for women (Baumeister, 2000; L. M. Diamond, 2002, 2003b, 2005; Peplau, 2001; Vohs & Baumeister, 2004). One problem with the older research is that most of the sexual minority individuals who had shared their stories were openly gay males who were exclusively attracted to other men. Consistent with Theme 3 of this textbook, earlier research focused on sexual minority men rather than on sexual minority women.

Current studies demonstrate that sexual orientation can be a fluid, changing process rather than a rigid category. Consider, for example, the research of Lisa M. Diamond (2000, 2002, 2003b, 2005). She began by interviewing 80 women between the ages of 18 and 25 who had identified themselves as "non-heterosexual women," a term that could include lesbian and bisexual women. Diamond located these women in college courses on sexuality, in college campus groups, and in community events sponsored by lesbian, gay, and bisexual organizations.

Diamond continued to interview these women over a period of 8 years. Of the women who had identified themselves as lesbians in the first interview, some described a "classic" development of their lesbian identity. These **stable lesbians** had focused on girls and women during childhood, and this interest had continued during adolescence. However, a larger number of women in Diamond's study could be classified as **fluid lesbians** because they had questioned or changed their lesbian sexual identity at some point. Consider the following description, provided by one woman who could be classified as a fluid lesbian:

> After I graduated from college . . . I found myself, not necessarily only attracted to both sexes, but also slightly more open-minded to the notion that maybe . . . maybe I can find something in just a person, that I don't necessarily have to be attracted to one sex versus the other. (L. M. Diamond, 2005, p. 126)

Interestingly, many of the women in Diamond's research also emphasized that they disliked having to fit themselves into someone else's labels or categories.

In this chapter, we have emphasized the variation in women's romantic relationships, consistent with Theme 4. As we've just seen, the current research also suggests that a woman's sexual orientation can vary throughout her lifetime. In the last part of this section on lesbian and bisexual women, we will see the implications of this fluidity for theories of sexual orientation.

LEGAL STATUS OF LESBIAN RELATIONSHIPS

Linda Garnets is a professor at UCLA, and she conducts research about lesbian relationships. She describes her personal perspective:

> I am in a 22-year relationship that I know is a life partnership, but it has no legal status because same-gender marriages are illegal. My partner and I cannot be jointly covered by insurance, inheritance laws, or hospital visitation rules. . . . A good friend of ours was dying, and the hospital would only let her partner of 12 years see her if she pretended to be her sister. She was not considered "immediate family" by the hospital rules. (Garnets, 2004a, p. 172)

Currently, lesbian couples living in the United States generally cannot marry or form legally recognized partnerships. The exceptions can be found only in a few states (Schindehette et al., 2004).

Why would a lesbian couple want to be married? One obvious reason is personal: Two women want to recognize their commitment to each other. Another reason is political: They want to overcome the heterosexist bias that makes lesbians invisible (Garnets, 2004a). A third reason is practical: In the United States, two people who are married can receive more than 1,000 federal and state benefits and protections, in comparison to two people who are an unmarried couple (Garnets, 2004b). The American Psychological Association examined the research in 2004 and concluded that same-gender partners deserved the same marriage rights that male-female partners can obtain (American Psychological Association, 2004; Farberman, 2004).

As of 2006, same-gender marriages are permitted in Canada, the Netherlands, Belgium, Spain, and South Africa. A more limited "partnership" is legally recognized in countries such as Denmark, Sweden, Hungary, and Portugal (Hamon & Ingoldsby, 2003; Merin, 2002; J. Thorpe, 2005). Meanwhile, in the United States, attitudes toward lesbian and gay marriage have been growing more positive. For instance, a Gallup poll showed that 31% of respondents supported same-sex marriages in December 2003, and the percentage increased to 42% by May 2004 (Younge, 2004). Now try Demonstration 8.6 to provide more information about attitudes toward same-gender marriages.

ATTITUDES TOWARD LESBIAN MARRIAGES	## Demonstration 8.6 First, answer the following questions yourself: Susan Brown and Jessica Smith met shortly after they graduated from college in 1990. They fell in love, and in 1991, they decided to live together. They consider themselves to be life partners and would like to get married. Do you believe that they should have the right to be married? Why or why not? Now, decide whether you would feel comfortable asking some of your friends these questions. If so, present this vignette to several people. Do you see any overall pattern in their responses?

BISEXUAL WOMEN

Heather Macalister, a psychology professor, describes her personal perspectives on sexual attraction:

> Growing up I assumed I was straight, as most of us do, and when I was about seventeen I discovered that some of the people I was attracted to were women. I was pretty excited about this. I thought it was neat to be open-minded, a free-thinker, to place other criteria for attraction above gender or sex. I frankly never considered referring to myself as "bisexual." It wasn't until later when the cumbersome "I'm open-minded, a free-thinker. I place other criteria for attraction above gender or sex!" left people confused that I began using the label "bisexual" for their cognitive convenience. But I still feel like it's missing something. I'm not hung up on gender or sex or sexual orientation, and I'm just attracted to whomever I'm attracted to. (Macalister, 2003, pp. 29–30)

A **bisexual woman** is a woman who is psychologically, emotionally, and sexually attracted to both women and men; a bisexual woman therefore refuses to exclude a possible romantic partner on the basis of that person's gender (Berenson, 2002; Macalister, 2003). Consistent with the discussion on pages 275–276, a woman is more likely to have been attracted to both women and men than to have been attracted only to women throughout her life (L. M. Diamond, 2002, 2005; Rust, 2000). We'll see that bisexuality presents a dilemma for a culture that likes to construct clear-cut categories (Macalister, 2003).

IDENTITY ISSUES AMONG BISEXUAL WOMEN. Most bisexual women report that they felt attracted to men at an earlier age than they felt attracted to women (R. C. Fox, 1996; Weinberg et al., 1994). Weinberg and his colleagues believe that bisexuals actively work to make sense of their sexual interests—that is, to construct their bisexuality. Given the heterosexist bias in our culture, these individuals would certainly find it easier to make sense out of their heterosexual desires before they acknowledge any same-gender interests.

Bisexual women often comment that the nature of the attraction may differ, too, as one woman explains: "I feel a greater physical attraction to men, but a greater spiritual/emotional attraction to women" (Rust, 2000, p. 212). In short, bisexuality creates a fluid identity rather than a clear-cut life pathway (Rust, 2000; M. J. K. Williams, 1999).

Although little research has been conducted on the adjustment of bisexual women, they do not seem to have unusual difficulties (R. C. Fox, 1997; Ketz & Israel, 2002). Also, bisexual women and lesbian women are equally satisfied with their current sexual identity (Rust, 1996). Bisexuals who come from a background of mixed ethnicity often find that their mixed heritage is consistent with their bisexuality. After all, their experience with ethnicity has taught them from an early age that our culture constructs clear-cut ethnic categories. As a result, they are not surprised to encounter our culture's clear-cut categories of sexual orientation (Duong, 2004; Rust, 2000).

ATTITUDES TOWARD BISEXUAL WOMEN.   Bisexual women often report rejection by both the heterosexual and the lesbian communities. Because of sexual prejudice, heterosexuals may condemn bisexuals' same-gender relationships. In fact, heterosexuals rate bisexual women more negatively than they rate lesbian women (Herek, 2002b; Whitley & Kite, 2006). Many heterosexuals also believe that bisexuals are frequently unfaithful to their partners (Ketz & Israel, 2002; Peplau & Spalding, 2000). In contrast, lesbians often argue that bisexual women are "buying into" heterosexism, and so they deny that they are lesbians (Herdt, 2001; Ketz & Israel, 2002; Peplau & Spalding, 2000). As a result, both heterosexuals and lesbians often act as if the bisexual group were invisible (Robin & Hamner, 2000).

In Chapter 2, we emphasized that people like to have precise categories for males and females, fitting everyone neatly into one category or the other. Prejudice against lesbians can be partly traced to the fact that lesbians violate the accepted rules about categories: A person is not supposed to have a romantic relationship with someone who belongs to the same category. Bisexuals provide an additional frustration for people who like precise categories. After all, bisexuals cannot even be placed into the neat category of lesbians, a group that clearly violates the rule about categories. The concept of bisexuality is frustrating to people who have a low tolerance for ambiguity.

THEORETICAL EXPLANATIONS ABOUT SEXUAL ORIENTATION

When we try to explain how lesbians develop their psychological, emotional, and sexual preference for women, we should also consider another question: How do *heterosexual* women develop their psychological, emotional, and sexual preference for men? Unfortunately, theorists rarely mention this question.[1] Because of our culture's heterosexist bias, it is considered both natural and normal for women to be attracted exclusively to men. This assumption

---

[1]One exception is an excellent article by Hyde and Jaffee (2000), which suggests that adolescent women are encouraged toward heterosexuality by means of traditional gender roles and numerous anti-gay messages.

implies that lesbianism is unnatural and abnormal, and abnormalities require an explanation (Baber, 2000; Nencel, 2005).

In reality, however, heterosexuality is more puzzling. After all, research in social psychology shows that we prefer people who resemble ourselves, not people who are different. On this basis, we should actually prefer those of our own gender.

Articles in the popular press proclaim that biological factors can explain the mystery of being lesbian or gay. In reality, we do not have strong evidence for a biological explanation for the sexual orientation of lesbians or bisexual women. Meanwhile, psychologists who favor sociocultural explanations are developing theories about the ways in which social forces and our thought processes may shape our sexual orientations. Let's begin by considering the biological explanations, and then we'll summarize the sociocultural explanations.

BIOLOGICAL EXPLANATIONS.   Researchers who favor biological explanations are much more likely to study gay men than lesbian women. For example, a recent article in the *Wall Street Journal* was titled "Brain Responses Vary by Sexual Orientation, New Research Shows" (2005). However, lesbians were invisible in this study because it discussed only gay men. Other research examines nonhuman species of individuals exposed to abnormal levels of prenatal hormones. These research areas are too far removed to offer compelling explanations for women's sexual orientation.

Other research examines normal humans to determine whether genetic factors, hormonal factors, or brain structures determine sexual orientation (e.g., Hershberger, 2001; LeVay, 1996; Savic et al., 2005). Some of the research suggests, for example, that a particular region on the X chromosome may contain genes for homosexuality. However, this research focuses almost exclusively on gay males, not lesbians or bisexuals (Peplau, 2001; Savic et al., 2005). Many of these studies also have serious methodological flaws that other researchers have pointed out (e.g., J. M. Bailey et al., 2000; J. Horgan, 2004; Hyde & DeLamater, 2006; L. Rogers, 2001).

Let's consider one of the few studies on genetic factors that looked at lesbians. Bailey and his colleagues focused on lesbians who happened to have an identical twin sister (J. M. Bailey et al., 2000). Of these lesbians, 24% had lesbian twin sisters. This is a fairly high percentage. However, if genetic factors guarantee sexual orientation—and each twin pair has identical genes—why isn't that figure closer to 100% (L. Rogers, 2001)? Other conceptually similar research shows weak support for the biological approach to women's sexual orientation (J. M. Bailey et al., 1993; Hyde, 2005b; Pattatucci & Hamer, 1995).

In short, biological factors may be responsible for a small part of women's sexual orientation; however, few studies examine lesbians or bisexual women. We should note, incidentally, that research suggests somewhat stronger support for the role of biological factors in male sexual orientation (Baumeister, 2000; Fletcher, 2002; Hershberger, 2001; Vohs & Baumeister, 2004). Clearly, however, the popular press has overemphasized the importance of biological factors in explaining sexual orientation in women (J. Horgan, 2004).

SOCIOCULTURAL EXPLANATIONS. The recent research and theory suggest that women's sexual orientation is more influenced by sociocultural and situational factors than by biological factors (Baumeister, 2000; L. M. Diamond, 2003b; Vohs & Baumeister, 2004). Let's consider two related theories that explain how these sociocultural factors might operate: (1) the social constructionist approach and (2) the intimate careers approach. As you read about these two approaches, you'll note that they are compatible with each other; we do not need to choose one and reject the other. Furthermore, notice how these sociocultural explanations emphasize the individual differences among women in their erotic orientations (Vohs & Baumeister, 2004).

The **social constructionist approach** argues that our culture creates sexual categories, which we use to organize our thoughts about our sexuality (Baber, 2000; Bohan, 1996; C. Kitzinger & Wilkinson, 1997). Social constructionists reject an essentialist approach to sexual orientation. In other words, sexual orientation is not a fundamental aspect of an individual that must be acquired either before birth or in early childhood.

The social constructionists propose that, based on their life experiences and cultural messages, most North American women initially construct heterosexual identities for themselves (Baber, 2000; Carpenter, 1998). However, some women review their sexual and romantic experiences and decide that they are either lesbian or bisexual (Bociurkiw, 2005; L. M. Diamond, 2003b).

The social constructionist approach argues that sexuality is both fluid and flexible, consistent with our earlier discussions. For example, women can make a transition from being heterosexual to being lesbian by re-evaluating their lives or by reconsidering their political values (C. Kitzinger & Wilkinson, 1997).

To examine the social constructionist approach, Celia Kitzinger and Sue Wilkinson (1997) interviewed 80 women who had previously identified themselves as heterosexuals for at least 10 years and who, at the time of the study, strongly identified themselves as lesbians. These women reported how they re-evaluated their lives in making the transition. For example, one woman said:

> I was looking at myself in the mirror, and I thought, "That woman is a lesbian," and then I allowed myself to notice that it was me I was talking about. And when that happened, I felt whole for the first time, and also absolutely terrified. (p. 197)

However, we need to emphasize an important point: Some lesbians believe that their sexual orientation is truly beyond their conscious control (Golden, 1996). These women had considered themselves different from other females at an early age, usually when they were between 6 and 12 years old.

In short, the social constructionist approach acknowledges that the categories *heterosexual, bisexual,* and *lesbian* are fluid and flexible. This approach also explains how some women consciously choose their sexual category.

A second sociocultural explanation, called the *intimate careers approach,* emphasizes the diversity of women's sexual orientations as well as the variation within many women's life course. This approach has been proposed by Letitia Anne Peplau, a prominent researcher in the area of lesbian and gay relationships (Peplau, 2001; Peplau & Garnets, 2000). Peplau suggests that we can use people's occupational career development as a metaphor for the way our romantic interests and sexual orientations develop. For instance, think about two of your friends who have taken different pathways in developing their career interests. Perhaps one friend has been interested in psychology for as long as she can remember. Another friend may have pursued majors in biology and sociology, before deciding on a psychology major.

By adopting the metaphor of occupational careers, the **intimate careers approach** suggests that we humans take a variety of pathways as we develop our intimate relationships. For instance, you may know one woman who is exclusively heterosexual, another is exclusively lesbian, and another is bisexual. The intimate careers approach also emphasizes that different people may currently hold the same sexual orientation for a variety of reasons (L. M. Diamond, 2003c). For example, you may know one woman who has been attracted to women for as long as she can remember. Another woman may have considered herself to be heterosexual throughout her early adulthood; then she developed an intense friendship with another woman, which grew into a lesbian relationship. Although the details of this approach need to be developed, it is certainly consistent with our theme about individual differences.

In reality, then, we don't yet have a satisfying comprehensive theory that considers the wide variety of women's sexual and romantic identities. To construct a theory, we need carefully conducted research that focuses on women who are heterosexual, as well as women who are lesbians and bisexuals. The most comprehensive theory of sexual orientation may actually include a biological predisposition that encourages some women to develop a lesbian or bisexual orientation (L. M. Diamond, 2003c). However, social experiences may determine which women will choose lesbian or bisexual identities and which women will choose heterosexual identities. This comprehensive theory would also specify that sexual identities are typically fluid. Sexual orientation is not a clear-cut category but a continuing process of self-discovery.

Section Summary

Lesbians and Bisexual Women

1. Lesbians are women who are psychologically, emotionally, and sexually attracted to other women; however, our heterosexist culture judges heterosexual relationships differently from other romantic relationships.

2. Research demonstrates that lesbians and heterosexual women are equally well adjusted; lesbians who accept their lesbian identity are typically higher in self-esteem.

3. The research shows that most lesbian relationships begin with friendship and that lesbian couples tend to emphasize emotional closeness. Lesbian

couples are happier when decision making is evenly divided; lesbian couples and heterosexual couples are equally satisfied with their relationships.

4. Lesbian couples and heterosexual couples have fairly similar emotional reactions to breaking up; however, legal factors are more relevant in preventing heterosexual breakups.

5. Lesbian women of color are more reluctant than European American lesbians to disclose their sexual orientation if their ethnic community has conservative values; however, many lesbian women of color have organized support groups.

6. The majority of lesbians report having had a fluid pattern of sexual identity, with some heterosexual interest, rather than a consistent lesbian identity.

7. Same-gender marriages are illegal in most of the United States; however, many lesbian couples want to marry to make their mutual commitment more visible, to overcome heterosexism, and to achieve legal equality.

8. Bisexual women illustrate that romantic attractions are often flexible; unfortunately, these women may face rejection by both the lesbian and the heterosexual communities.

9. Biological research examines whether genetic factors, hormonal factors, and brain structures determine sexual orientation. However, the research seldom focuses on lesbians or bisexuals; we do not currently have persuasive evidence that biological factors are responsible for a major part of women's sexual orientation.

10. Researchers have proposed two mutually compatible sociocultural explanations: (a) the social constructionist approach emphasizes that sexual orientation is flexible, and women can reconstruct their identity to make transitions between heterosexual and lesbian orientations; and (b) the intimate careers approach also emphasizes the flexible nature of women's sexual orientation, in terms of both individual differences among women and in terms of changing experiences within each woman's life course.

SINGLE WOMEN

According to the current data, 21% of women—18 years of age and older—have never married (U.S. Census Bureau, 2005). The comparable figure for Canada is 27% (Status of Women Canada, 2000). Although the category "single women" includes those who have never married, it also overlaps with many groups we have already considered. For example, this category includes women who are in dating or cohabiting relationships. Women who are separated or divorced are also included. So are lesbians and bisexual women who are not currently married. Finally, some of these single women are widows, a group whom we will consider in Chapter 14.

Demonstration 8.7

Imagine that a friend has invited you to a family picnic with her extended family. She is giving you a brief description of each relative who will be there. For one relative, Melinda Taylor, she says, "I really don't know much about her, but she is in her late 30s and she isn't married."

Try to form a mental image of Melinda Taylor, given this brief description.

Compare her with the average woman in her late 30s, using the following list of characteristics. In each case, decide whether Melinda Taylor has more of the characteristic (write *M*), the same amount of the characteristic (write *S*), or less of the characteristic (write *L*).

_____ friendly

_____ bossy

_____ intelligent

_____ lonely

_____ disorganized

_____ attractive

_____ warm

_____ good sense of humor

_____ good conversationalist

_____ unhappy

_____ feminist

_____ politically liberal

Do you see any pattern to your responses?

In this section on single women, we will focus on women who have never married because they are not considered elsewhere in the book. However, the other groups of women mentioned in the previous paragraph share some of the same advantages and disadvantages these never-married women experience. Before you read further, try Demonstration 8.7.

CHARACTERISTICS OF SINGLE WOMEN

Psychologists and sociologists seldom study single women, even though they constitute a substantial percentage of adult women (M. S. Clark & Graham, 2005; B. M. DePaulo, 2006; B. M. DePaulo & Morris, 2005). The data show that single women are slightly more likely than married women to work outside the home (Bureau of Labor Statistics, 2004c). Many single women are highly educated, career-oriented individuals. These women often report that being single allows them flexible work hours and geographic mobility (DeFrain & Olson, 1999).

Many single women have chosen not to marry because they never found an ideal partner. For example, *Time* magazine conducted a survey of 205 never-married women. One question asked, "If you couldn't find the perfect mate, would you marry someone else?" (T. M. Edwards, 2000, p. 48). Only 34% of these women replied that they would choose to marry a less-than-perfect spouse. Other women remain single because they believe that happy marriages are difficult to achieve (Huston & Melz, 2004).

Research suggests that single, never-married women receive the same scores as married women on tests measuring psychological distress (N. F. Marks, 1996). Furthermore, single women score higher than married women on measures of independence. However, single women score lower than married women on tests of self-acceptance (N. F. Marks, 1996). Other research shows that single women and married women are similar in their life span, and both tend to live longer than divorced women (Fincham & Beach, 1999; Friedman et al., 1995). In summary, single women are generally well adjusted, and they are often satisfied with their single status.

ATTITUDES TOWARD SINGLE WOMEN

What kinds of answers did you provide in Demonstration 8.7? Also, think about the comments aimed at never-married women when you were growing up. The word **singlism** refers to bias against people who are not married (B. M. DePaulo & Morris, 2005). For example, single women report that they received less respect and poorer service at restaurants, compared to married women (Byrne & Carr, 2005). Research by Bella DePaulo and Wendy Morris (2005) shows that college students tend to describe single people as lonely, shy, unhappy, insecure, and inflexible. However, these college students also describe single people as being sociable and friendly, so the students acknowledge some positive characteristics.

Remaining single is currently more respectable than it was in earlier eras (Baca Zinn & Eitzen, 2002). One reason is that women are more likely to be single, partly due to an increase in the number of well-educated, economically self-sufficient women (Whitehead, 2003). In 1970, only 10% of 25- to 29-year-old women were unmarried, compared to 40% by 2003 (DeFrain & Olson, 1999; U.S. Census Bureau, 2005). Many current television programs also represent single women in a positive fashion.

ADVANTAGES AND DISADVANTAGES OF BEING SINGLE

Among the advantages to being single, women most often mention freedom and independence (DeFrain & Olson, 1999; B. M. DePaulo & Morris, 2005; K. G. Lewis & Moon, 1997). Single people are free to do what they want, according to their own preferences. In fact, single women are more likely than married women to spend their time in leisure activities, travel, and social get-togethers (Lee & Bhargava, 2004). Single women also have more freedom to choose the people with whom they want to spend time (B. M. DePaulo & Morris, 2005).

Single women also mention that privacy is an advantage for them. They can be by themselves when they want, without the risk of offending someone. By learning to be alone with themselves, many women also say that they have developed a greater level of self-knowledge (Brehm, Miller et al., 2002).

When women are asked about the disadvantages of being single, they frequently mention loneliness (T. M. Edwards, 2000; Rouse, 2002; Whitehead, 2003). One woman reported, "I am not a widow, but I'm the same as a widow. I'm a woman living alone, going home to an empty house" (K. R. Allen, 1994, p. 104).

Single people sometimes mention that they feel at a disadvantage in communities where couples predominate—a situation that some humorously call the "Noah's Ark Syndrome." Our culture seems to believe that it's abnormal for a woman to be alone in a social situation (Watrous & Honey-church, 1999).

However, most single women create their own social networks of friends and relatives (Rouse, 2002). Many have a housemate with whom they can share joys, sorrows, and frustrations. One woman described an advantage to her social world, in terms of "having friends that care for you as a person and not as part of a couple" (K. G. Lewis & Moon, 1997, p. 123). In summary, single women frequently develop flexible support systems for caring and social connection.

SINGLE WOMEN OF COLOR

We noted that little research has been conducted on the general topic of single women. Sadly, single women of color are virtually invisible in the psychology research. This observation is especially ironic because 37% of Black women and 24% of Latina women have never married, in contrast to only 18% of European American women (U.S. Census Bureau, 2005).

In some ethnic communities, unmarried women serve a valuable function. For example, in Chicana (Mexican American) culture, an unmarried daughter is expected to take care of her elderly parents or to help out with nieces and nephews (Flores-Ortiz, 1998).

Asian American single women are also frequently expected to fulfill the unmarried-daughter role (Ferguson, 2000; Newtson & Keith, 1997). Many Asian American women also report that they choose to remain single because they want to pursue an advanced education or because they have not found an appropriate marriage partner (Ferguson, 2000).

Somewhat more research has been conducted with Black women who are single. The research shows, for example, that many Black women prefer to remain single, rather than to marry a man who currently has limited employ-ment possibilities (Baca Zinn & Eitzen, 2002; Jayakody & Cabrera, 2002).

Supportive friendships often provide invaluable social interactions for single Black women. One study focused on the support networks of Black unmarried and married women in Richmond, Virginia (D. R. Brown & Gary, 1985). These women were asked about the number of friends and relatives with whom they maintained close contact. The unmarried respondents emphasized that other family members were extremely important in their lives. Roughly two-thirds of the women mentioned kin as their closest relationship, and about one-quarter of the women mentioned female friends. Single Black women also find friends who support their accomplishments in the workplace. For example, Black professional women described many ways in which their friends had provided encouragement (Denton, 1990).

Researchers in past years have failed to provide a balanced description of attitudes, social conditions, and behaviors of single women. In the next few decades, we may achieve a more complete understanding of the diversity of single women from all ethnic backgrounds. Furthermore, as Bella DePaulo and Morris (2005) emphasize, "Enlightened citizens come to realize that you don't need to be a man to be a leader, you don't need to be straight to be normal, you don't need to be White to be smart, and you don't need to be coupled to be happy" (p. 78).

Section Summary

Single Women

1. Although researchers typically do not study single women, they are fairly similar to married women on various measures of adjustment and health.

2. "Singlism" refers to bias against people who are not married. Single women report some discrimination; college students also indicate some negative attitudes about single people.

3. Single women tend to value their privacy and their freedom to pursue their own leisure activities, but they mention that loneliness is a disadvantage; most single women create alternative social networks.

4. Unmarried Latina and Asian women are often expected to take care of family members. Black single women emphasize the importance of family members and friends in providing close relationships and support, both socially and on the job.

CHAPTER REVIEW QUESTIONS

1. From time to time throughout this book, we have discussed the topic of attractiveness. How important is attractiveness in heterosexual relationships and in lesbian relationships?

2. At several points in this chapter, we discussed cross-cultural studies as well as research focusing on North American women of color. Summarize this research with respect to the following topics: (a) the ideal romantic partner, (b) marriage, (c) lesbian women, and (d) single women of color.

3. What is evolutionary psychology, and how does it explain women's and men's choices for an ideal romantic partner? Why is it inadequate in explaining romantic relationships in the current century? How can the social-roles theory account for that research? Finally, why would evolutionary psychology have difficulty accounting for lesbian relationships?

4. The issue of power was discussed several times in this chapter. Summarize the relationship between money and power in marriage, the division of power in traditional and egalitarian marriages, and the importance of balanced power in lesbian relationships. Also discuss how power operates for married women of color.

5. Discuss how this chapter contains many examples of the theme that women differ widely from one another. Be sure to include topics such as patterns of living together, reactions to divorce, sexual orientation, and the social relationships of single women.

6. Discuss gender comparisons that were described throughout this chapter, including the ideal sexual partner, the ideal marriage partner, reactions to breaking up, satisfaction with marriage, and the decision to seek a divorce.

7. We noted that people who like clear-cut categories are often frustrated by lesbians and bisexual women. Discuss the fluid nature of sexual orientation, mentioning the research of Lisa Diamond, the experiences of bisexual women, and the two sociocultural theories about sexual orientation.

8. Lesbians, bisexuals, and single women all have lifestyles that differ from the norm. What are people's attitudes toward women in these three groups?

9. Imagine that you are having a conversation with a friend from your high school, whom you know well. This friend says that she thinks that lesbians are more likely than heterosexual women to have psychological problems and relationship difficulties. She also opposes same-gender marriages. How could you address her concerns by using information from this chapter?

10. Suppose that you continue to talk with the high-school friend mentioned in Question 9, and the conversation turns to people who have never married. She tells you that she is worried about a woman you both know who doesn't seem to be interested in dating or finding a husband. How would you respond to your friend's concerns?

KEY TERMS

*evolutionary-psychology approach (253)

*social-roles approach (254)

*cohabitation (257)

*traditional marriage (263)

*egalitarian marriage (264)

*machismo (264)

*marianismo (264)

Black matriarchy (265)

*lesbian (269)

*sexual minority (269)

*heterosexism (269)

stable lesbians (275)

fluid lesbians (275)

*bisexual woman (277)

social constructionist approach (280)

intimate careers approach (281)

singlism (284)

 Note: The terms asterisked in the Key Terms section serve as good search terms for InfoTrac College Edition. Go to http://infotrac.thomsonlearning.com and try these added search terms.

RECOMMENDED READINGS

Conger, R. D., Lorenz, F. O., & Wickrama, K. A. S. (Eds.). (2004). *Continuity and change in family relations: Theory, methods, and empirical findings*. Mahwah, NJ: Erlbaum. This book focuses specifically on how relationships change over time; the chapters on change and continuity in marriage are especially relevant to the current chapter.

DePaulo, B. M. (2006). *Singled out: How singles are stereotyped, stigmatized, and ignored, and still live happily ever after*. New York: St. Martin's Press. Every time I revise this textbook, I hope to find new books that deserve a recommendation! Bella DePaulo is a social psychologist, and her book combines scholarly research with interesting narratives. I'm planning to give the book to several single friends who have experienced "singlism."

Leeds-Hurwitz, W. (2002). *Wedding as text: Communicating cultural identities through ritual*. Mahwah, NJ: Erlbaum. I was fascinated by this author's descriptions of how couples in her study included cultural symbols in their wedding ceremonies, using interesting conceptions that you definitely won't find in the traditional bridal magazines.

Rose, S., & Hall, R. (2005). Innovations in lesbian research [Special section]. *Psychology of Women Quarterly*, 29 (2), 119–187. This issue of *Psychology of Women Quarterly* features seven articles about topics such as stable versus fluid lesbian identity, well-being among lesbians, and the lives of elderly Black lesbians.

Vangelisti, A. L. (Ed.). (2004). *Handbook of family communication*. Mahwah, NJ: Erlbaum. I strongly recommend this excellent resource, which discusses such topics as mate selection and communication in marriage, in lesbian and gay families, and in divorced families.

ANSWERS TO THE DEMONSTRATIONS

Demonstration 8.1: 1. F; 2. F; 3. M; 4. M; 5. F; 6. F; 7. M; 8. F; 9. M; 10. M.

Demonstration 8.5: Kurdek's (1995a) questionnaire, the Multiple Determinants of Relationship Commitment Inventory, assesses six different components of love relationships. On the shortened version in this demonstration, each of six categories is represented with two questions: Rewards (Questions 1 and 7), Costs (Questions 2 and 8), Match to Ideal Comparison (Questions 3 and 9), Alternatives (Questions 4 and 10), Investments (Questions 5 and 11), and Barriers to Leaving the Relationship (Questions 6 and 12). High relationship commitment was operationally defined in terms of high scores on Rewards, Match to Ideal Comparison, Investments, and Barriers to Leaving and low scores on Costs and Alternatives.

ANSWERS TO THE TRUE-FALSE STATEMENTS

1. False (p. 252); 2. False (p. 253); 3. True (p. 257); 4. True (pp. 261–262); 5. False (pp. 264–265); 6. True (pp. 267–268); 7. True (pp. 275–276); 8. False (p. 278); 9. False (pp. 279–280); 10. False (p. 284).

© Simon Marcus/Corbis

9 | SEXUALITY

True or False?

_____ 1. A small sexual organ called the clitoris plays a major role in a woman's orgasms.

_____ 2. The gender differences in sexual desire are larger than most other gender differences.

_____ 3. In the current decade, people consistently judge a sexually active unmarried male more positively than a sexually active unmarried female.

_____ 4. Most U.S. parents say that they want high-school sex education courses to discuss birth control.

_____ 5. Almost all women have very positive memories about their first experience of sexual intercourse.

_____ 6. A woman who discusses her sexual likes and dislikes with her partner is likely to be more satisfied with her sexual relationships than a woman who does not disclose this information.

_____ 7. When a woman has difficulty reaching orgasm, one common reason is that she is worried about losing control over her emotions.

_____ 8. During sexual activity, women often tend to worry about their physical attractiveness.

_____ 9. An adolescent female in the United States is more than twice as likely to become pregnant as an adolescent female in Canada.

_____ 10. When women with an unwanted pregnancy have an abortion, they typically do not experience serious psychological consequences.

On the day I began editing this chapter about sexuality, I happened to walk past the magazine racks of a drugstore. The "women's section" oozed with sexual messages. A headline from *Self* proclaimed "The Best Sex Ever: Make It Happen." *Glamour* was even more alluring, with its claim, "The Sex Stuff Women Keep Secret: We've Got 3,000 X-Rated Confessions." However, *Cosmopolitan* won the contest. One headline shouted, "Naughty Sex: 8 Hot New Positions We've Never Published Before." Others on the same cover boasted "How to Keep Your Guy *Totally* Turned on by You," "The Sexiest Things to Do After Sex," and "Four Facts Men Wish Their Girlfriends Knew."

Our North American culture is so intrigued with sexuality that we might expect people to be well informed about the topic—but studies suggest otherwise. Mariamne Whatley and Elissa Henken (2000) asked people in Georgia to share some of the "information" they had heard about a variety of sexual topics. Some people believed, for instance, that a woman can become pregnant from kissing, from dancing too close to a man, or when having sexual intercourse during her menstrual period (rather than midcycle). Other people reported that when gynecologists have conducted pelvic exams, they have discovered snakes, spiders, or roaches living in women's vaginas. Still others told how they had heard that a tampon, inserted into the vagina, can travel into a woman's stomach. Apparently, people can be seriously misinformed about pregnancy and women's sexual anatomy!

Our chapter begins with some background information about sexuality. (However, I will assume you know that the vagina is not connected to the stomach.) In the second section, we'll discuss sexual attitudes and behavior. We'll briefly describe sexual disorders in the third section, and in the final section, we'll examine the topics of birth control and abortion. (In Chapter 11, we will discuss the related issue of sexually transmitted diseases.)

BACKGROUND ON WOMEN'S SEXUALITY

In most of this chapter, we focus on people's attitudes toward sexuality and on women's sexual behavior; sexuality is much more than just a biological phenomenon (Easton et al., 2002; Marecek et al., 2004). To provide an appropriate context for these topics, however, we need to address some background questions. What theoretical approaches to sexuality are currently most prominent? What parts of a woman's body are especially important in her sexual activities? What sexual responses do women typically experience? Furthermore, are there gender differences in sexual desire?

THEORETICAL PERSPECTIVES

Feminist psychologists have pointed out that discussions about sexuality often represent a limited view of the topic (L. M. Diamond, 2004; Marecek et al., 2004; Tiefer, 2004). For instance, consistent with Theme 3, researchers pay relatively little attention to female sexuality. Instead, researchers frequently consider men's sexual experiences to be the normative standard. This androcentric emphasis is reflected in descriptions of sexuality in several textbooks designed for middle-school and high-school students. For example, these books approach the sex organs from the male perspective. In one textbook, for example, the word *penis* is defined as "the male sexual organ," whereas *vagina* is defined as "receives penis during sexual intercourse" (cited in C. E. Beyer et al., 1996). Also, notice the heterosexist bias. Consistent with much of the sexuality research, the woman's partner is assumed to be a man.

Another bias in the discussion of sexuality is that sexual experiences are often viewed from a purely biological framework, so that hormones, brain structures, and genitals occupy center stage (Tolman & Diamond, 2001a; J. W. White et al., 2000). Furthermore, such discussions often assume that these biological processes apply universally to all women (Peplau, 2003; Tiefer, 2004).

This overemphasis on biology is consistent with the essentialist perspective. As we discussed in Chapter 1, **essentialism** argues that gender is a basic, stable characteristic that resides within an individual. According to the essentialist perspective, all women share the same psychological characteristics (Marecek et al., 2004). Essentialism ignores the widespread individual differences in women's sexual responses, consistent with Theme 4 of this textbook (Baber, 2000). When researchers adopt this essentialist perspective, they often neglect the social and cultural framework, which is especially important because sexuality is so prominent in our popular culture.

In contrast to the essentialist perspective, social constructionism emphasizes that social forces have a major impact on our sexuality. As we discussed in Chapters 1 and 6, **social constructionism** argues that individuals and cultures construct or invent their own versions of reality based on prior experiences, social interactions, and beliefs. For example, in North American culture, males are supposed to have sexual desires, but females' sexual desires are rarely mentioned (Tolman, 2002). However, in another culture, women may be considered highly sexual (Easton et al., 2002; Fontes, 2001; Tiefer, 2004).

According to social constructionists, our cultures even construct the basic sexual vocabulary (Marecek et al., 2004). For instance, consider the phrase "to have sex." Most North American women use this term to refer only to sexual intercourse with a man, even if that experience was not sexually pleasurable (Rothblum, 2000). These women probably would not say that two people "had sex" if their sexual activity was limited to oral sex. Let's briefly discuss women's sexual anatomy and sexual responses, as well as the important topic of sexual desire. Then, in the remaining sections, we will consider women's sexual attitudes and behaviors in greater detail.

FEMALE SEXUAL ANATOMY

Figure 9.1 shows the external sexual organs of an adult female. The specific shapes, sizes, and colors of these organs differ greatly from one woman to the next (Foley et al., 2002). Ordinarily, the labia fold inward, so that they cover the vaginal opening. In this diagram, however, the labia fold outward to show the urethral and vaginal openings.

Mons pubis is a Latin phrase referring to the fatty tissue in front of the pubic bone. At puberty, the mons pubis becomes covered with pubic hair. The labia majora are the "large lips," or folds of skin, located just inside a woman's thighs. Located between these two labia majora are the labia minora, or "small lips."

Notice that the upper part of the labia region forms the clitoral hood, which covers the clitoris. As we will see later in this section, the **clitoris** (pronounced *klih*-tuh-riss) is a small sensitive organ that plays a central role in

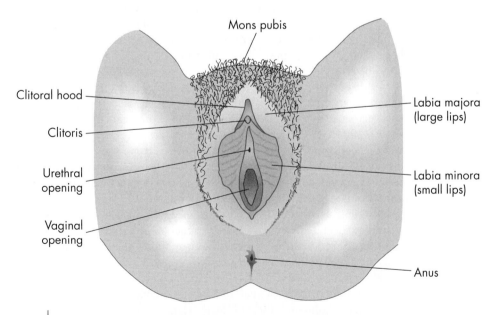

FIGURE 9.1 | FEMALE EXTERNAL SEXUAL ORGANS.

women's orgasms. The clitoris has a high density of nerve endings, and its only purpose is to provide sexual excitement (Foley et al., 2002).

Urine passes through the urethral opening. Notice that the vaginal opening is located between the urethral opening and the anus. The **vagina** is a flexible canal through which menstrual fluid passes. During heterosexual intercourse, the penis enters the vagina. The vagina also provides a passageway during the normal birth of an infant. At this point, you may want to return to Figure 4.1, on page 115, to review several important internal organs that are relevant for women's sexuality.

SEXUAL RESPONSES

Women report a variety of reactions during sexual activity, and they emphasize that emotions and thoughts are extremely important. Certain visual stimuli, sounds, and smells can either increase or decrease arousal (L. L. Alexander et al., 2004). Let's consider the general phases that many women experience during sexual activity, and then we'll discuss some gender comparisons.

GENERAL PHASES.   William H. Masters and Virginia Johnson (1966) wrote a book, called *Human Sexual Response*, which summarized their research on individuals who readily experienced orgasms during sexual activity. As you can imagine, these findings should not be overgeneralized; sexuality shows much more variety than the neatly ordered sequence of events that Masters and Johnson described (L. L. Alexander et al., 2004; Basson, 2006; Foley et al., 2002). Masters and Johnson described four phases, each focusing on changes in the genitals. As you read about these phases, keep in mind a caution raised by C. Wade and Cirese (1991): "The stages are not like the cycles of an automatic washing machine; we are not programmed to move mechanically from one stage to another" (p. 140).

Masters and Johnson called the first phase the excitement phase. During the **excitement phase**, women become sexually aroused by touching and erotic thoughts. During the excitement phase, blood rushes to the genital region, causing **vasocongestion** (pronounced vaz-owe-kun-*jess*-chun), or swelling resulting from the accumulation of blood. Vasocongestion causes the clitoris and the labia to enlarge as they fill with blood; it also produces droplets of moisture in the vagina.

During the **plateau phase**, the clitoris shortens and draws back under the clitoral hood. The clitoral region is now extremely sensitive. The clitoral hood is moved, either by thrusting of the penis or by other touching. The movement of the clitoral hood stimulates the clitoris.

During the **orgasmic phase**, the uterus and the outer part of the vagina contract strongly, at intervals roughly a second apart. (Figure 4.1, on page 115, shows the female internal organs, with the uterus located above the vagina.) A woman generally experiences between 3 and 10 of these rapid contractions during an orgasm (Foley et al., 2002).

During the **resolution phase**, the sexual organs return to their earlier unstimulated size. The resolution phase may last 30 minutes or more.

However, females may have additional orgasms without going directly into the resolution phase.

You'll notice that the clitoris is extremely important when women experience an orgasm (L. L. Alexander et al., 2004; Crooks & Baur, 2005). As Masters and Johnson (1966) observed, orgasms result from stimulation of the clitoris, either from direct touching in the clitoral area or from indirect pressure—for example, from a partner's thrusting penis. Physiologically, the orgasm is the same, no matter what kind of stimulation is used (Hyde & DeLamater, 2006).

Current feminist researchers and theorists emphasize that women's views of sexuality do not focus simply on genitals and orgasms during sexual activity (Conrad & Milburn, 2001; J. W. White et al., 2000). As Naomi McCormick (1994) wrote:

> Cuddling, self-disclosing, even gazing into a partner's eyes are highly valued by women. A feminist vision of sexuality considers whole people, not just their genitals. Intellectual stimulation, the exchange of self-disclosures, and whole body sensuality may feel just as "sexy" as orgasms. (p. 186)

GENDER COMPARISONS IN SEXUAL RESPONSES.   The studies by Masters and Johnson and by more recent researchers allow us to conclude that women and men are reasonably similar in the nature of their sexual responses. For example, women and men experience similar phases in their sexual responses. Both men and women experience vasocongestion, and their orgasms are physiologically similar.

In addition, women and men have similar psychological reactions to orgasm. Read Demonstration 9.1 and try to guess whether a man or a woman wrote each passage. Vance and Wagner (1977) asked people to guess which descriptions of orgasms were written by women and which were written by men. Most respondents were unable to guess at better than a chance level. Another gender similarity is that women can reach orgasm as quickly as men when the clitoral region is directly stimulated (Tavris & Wade, 1984). We need to emphasize, however, that women typically do not consider "faster" to be "better"!

In general, then, men and women are reasonably similar in these internal, physiological components of sexuality. However, we'll see that gender differences are larger in some other aspects of sexuality, such as sexual desire and its consequences.

SEXUAL DESIRE

If your high-school discussions about "sex education" were typical, you learned some basic information about the anatomy of sex organs, and the rest of the messages focused on "just say no," including the dangers of pregnancy and sexually transmitted diseases. You were unlikely to hear the phrase "sexual desire," especially in connection with females (Tolman, 2002). One definition of **sexual desire** is "a need or drive to seek out sexual objects or to engage in sexual activities" (L. M. Diamond, 2004, p. 116). A variety of sex hormones

Demonstration 9.1

PSYCHOLOGICAL REACTIONS TO ORGASM

Try to guess whether a female or a male wrote each of the following descriptions of an orgasm. Place an F (female) or an M (male) in front of each passage. The answers appear at the end of the chapter, on page 321.

_____ 1. A sudden feeling of lightheadedness followed by an intense feeling of relief and elation. A rush. Intense muscular spasms of the whole body. Sense of euphoria followed by deep peace and relaxation.

_____ 2. To me, an orgasmic experience is the most satisfying pleasure that I have experienced in relation to any other types of satisfaction or pleasure that I've had, which were nonsexually oriented.

_____ 3. It is like turning a water faucet on. You notice the oncoming flow but it can be turned on or off when desired. You feel the valves open and close and the fluid flow. An orgasm makes your head and body tingle.

_____ 4. A buildup of tension which starts to pulsate very fast, and there is a sudden release from the tension and a desire to sleep.

_____ 5. It is a pleasant, tension-relieving muscular contraction. It relieves physical tension and mental anticipation.

_____ 6. A release of a very high level of tension, but ordinarily tension is unpleasant, whereas the tension before orgasm is far from unpleasant.

_____ 7. An orgasm is a great release of tension with spasmodic reaction at the peak. This is exactly how it feels to me.

_____ 8. A building of tension, sometimes, and frustration until the climax. A tightening inside, palpitating rhythm, explosion, and warmth and peace.

Source: Based on Vance and Wagner (1977, pp. 207–210).

are associated with sexual desire, but social and cultural factors are similarly important. In most North American communities, for instance, teenage females are not supposed to feel sexual desire (Tolman & Diamond, 2001a).

Feminist researchers are beginning to conclude that the gender differences in sexual desire are larger than most other psychological gender differences (e.g., Diamond, 2004; Hyde & DeLamater, 2006; Hyde & Oliver, 2000). Compared to women, men (a) think about sex more frequently; (b) want sexual activities more frequently; (c) initiate sexual activities more frequently; (d) are more interested in sexual activities without a romantic commitment; and (e) prefer a greater number of sexual partners (Impett & Peplau, 2003; T. A. Lambert et al., 2003; Mosher & Danoff-Burg, 2005; Peplau, 2003; Vohs & Baumeister, 2004).

How can we explain these gender differences in sexuality? One factor is obvious. A nude woman rarely sees her clitoris, and she may not even know where to find it. A nude man can see his penis by simply looking down. He may therefore think about masturbating, so he may be more familiar with sexual sensations (Hyde & DeLamater, 2006). Obviously, too, women are more concerned about pregnancy than men are. As we'll soon see, the double standard may also inhibit women's sexual activities. However, gender differences in hormones are probably not relevant (Hyde & DeLamater, 2006).

Furthermore, some portion of these gender differences might be traceable to using male-normative standards—for instance, focusing on sexual intercourse rather than other measures of sexual desire (Peplau, 2003). In the next decade, researchers may draw more clear-cut conclusions about gender comparisons in sexual desire. Furthermore, they may pay more attention to gender comparisons in the subjective *quality* of sexual desire, rather than simply the *strength* of sexual desire (Tolman & Diamond, 2001a).

As our theme of individual differences suggests, some women may be higher than most men with respect to sexual desire. However, the gender differences in sexual desire will help us understand several topics throughout this chapter, such as masturbation, sexual scripts, and a sexual disorder called low sexual desire.

Section Summary

Background on Women's Sexuality

1. Feminist psychologists argue that discussions of sexuality have paid relatively little attention to women's perspectives and that the discussions overemphasize biological factors (consistent with essentialism) rather than social and cultural factors (consistent with social constructionism).

2. The clitoris is a sexual organ that plays a major role in women's orgasms.

3. Emotions, thoughts, and sensory stimuli are central to women's sexual responses. Individual differences are large, and sexual responses do not follow a rigid sequence; Masters and Johnson (1966) described four phases of sexual response: excitement, plateau, orgasm, and resolution.

4. Female orgasms are similar whether they are produced by direct stimulation of the clitoris or by indirect stimulation; current theorists emphasize aspects of sexuality other than genitals and orgasms.

5. Women and men are similar in their psychological reactions to orgasm, but men are often higher in some components of sexual desire.

SEXUAL ATTITUDES AND BEHAVIOR

The previous section emphasized the biological side of sexuality—the swelling genitals and the contracting uterus. Let's now turn to the humans who possess these sex organs as we address several questions, such as these: What are people's attitudes about sexuality? How are these attitudes reflected in sex education aimed at young people? What sexual experiences do people report? Before you read further, however, try Demonstration 9.2 on page 297.

Demonstration 9.2

JUDGMENTS
ABOUT SEXUAL
BEHAVIOR

Suppose you discover some information about the sexual behavior of a 25-year-old unmarried person whom you know slightly. Questions 1 through 4 provide information about four possible people. Rate the person in terms of this person's *moral values*. Try to rate each person separately, without considering the other three persons.

1	2	3	4	5

Poor moral values   Good moral values

_____ 1. A man who has had no sexual partners
_____ 2. A man who has had 19 sexual partners
_____ 3. A woman who has had no sexual partners
_____ 4. A woman who has had 19 sexual partners

Source: Based on M. J. Marks and Fraley (2005).

ATTITUDES ABOUT FEMALE AND MALE SEXUALITY

In the current era, most North Americans believe that nonmarital intercourse is acceptable, for example, in a committed relationship. In one cross-cultural study, only 12% of Canadian participants and 29% of U.S. participants said that sex before marriage is always wrong (Widmer et al., 1998). However, attitudes varied widely across the 24 countries in this study. Less than 5% of respondents in Austria, Germany, and Sweden said that premarital sex was always wrong, in contrast to 35% in Ireland and 60% in the Philippines.

In North America, men typically have more permissive attitudes toward sex than women do (Brehm et al., 2002; N. M. Brown & Amatea, 2000; Hyde & Oliver, 2000). For example, a meta-analysis conducted by Oliver and Hyde (1993) demonstrated that men are significantly more permissive about premarital sex; the *d* for this gender difference was a substantial 0.81. That is, gender as a *subject variable* is important.

How about gender as a *stimulus variable*? Do people judge a man's sexual behavior differently from a woman's sexual behavior? Before the 1960s, most North Americans held a **sexual double standard:** They believed that premarital sex was inappropriate for women, but it was excusable or even appropriate for men. In general, the prime-time television dramas still demonstrate the double standard (Aubrey, 2004). However, in real life, the double standard is less common (Crooks & Baur, 2005; Marks & Fraley, 2005; Milhausen & Herold, 1999). For example, both genders believe that premarital intercourse is equally appropriate for both men and women if a couple is engaged to be married (Hatfield & Rapson, 1996).

Michael Marks and R. Chris Fraley (2005) provide some current information about the sexual double standard. Demonstration 9.2 is a greatly simplified version of their study; also, each of the participants in their study rated only one person. These researchers tested both undergraduate students and people who responded to their questionnaire on the Internet. The participants in both samples gave a lower rating to a person who had 19 sexual partners, compared to a person who had zero sexual partners. Surprisingly, the participants supplied about the same ratings for the male target as for the female target. In other words, they did *not* find evidence of a sexual double standard. It is not clear whether researchers would discover a sexual double standard if participants completed the survey in a face-to-face setting, rather than on the Internet.

However, in many cultures outside North America, the double standard frequently has life-threatening consequences for women. For example, in some Asian, Middle Eastern, and Latin American cultures, a man is expected to uphold the family honor by killing a daughter, a sister, or even a mother who is suspected of engaging in "inappropriate" sexual activities (Crooks & Baur, 2005; P. T. Reid & Bing, 2000; Whelehan, 2001). They typically ignore the same sexual activity in a male family member.

SEXUAL SCRIPTS

A script for a play describes what people say and do. A **sexual script** describes the social norms for sexual behavior, which we learn by growing up in a culture (Bowleg et al., 2004; DeLamater & Hyde, 2004; Mahay et al., 2002). In the twenty-first century, our North American culture provides a sexual script for heterosexual couples: Men initiate sexual relationships. In contrast, women are expected either to resist or to comply passively with their partner's advances (Baber, 2000; Impett & Peplau, 2002, 2003; Morokoff, 2000). According to the traditional script, for example, the woman is supposed to wait for her date to kiss her; she does not initiate kissing. Only one person is in charge in this script-based kind of relationship. Even in a long-term relationship or marriage, the male's erotic schedule may regulate sex.

Two kinds of relationships do not follow the traditional sexual script. For instance, women in egalitarian relationships feel free about expressing their erotic interests, and they also feel free to decide not to have sex (Peplau, 2003).

Furthermore, as we will see in Chapter 13, men sometimes violate the standard sexual script. They may continue to make sexual advances, ignoring their partner's indication that these advances are not welcome. The male may use coercion, for example, by saying that he will break off a relationship if his girlfriend doesn't have sex with him (Brehm et al., 2002). The most coercive sexual interaction is **rape**, which is forced sexual intercourse, without consent. As we discuss in Chapter 13, a woman can be raped—not just by a stranger—but also by an acquaintance, a boyfriend, or even a husband.

In some cases, it's not clear whether a man and a woman are following a sexual script. Consider, for example, a 35-year-old woman who described how her partner felt that she "should be very accessible and happy to have sex with him when he chooses to" (Bowleg et al., 2004, p. 75). Does this quotation represent the standard script, or does it sound like coercion?

SEX EDUCATION

Take a moment to think about your early ideas, experiences, and attitudes about sexuality. Was sex a topic that produced half-suppressed giggles in the school cafeteria? Did you worry about whether you were too experienced or not experienced enough? Sexuality is an important topic for adolescents and many preadolescents. In this section, we will examine how children and adolescents learn about sexuality—at home, at school, and from the media.

PARENTS AND SEX EDUCATION. Young women are much more likely to hear about sexuality from their mothers than from their fathers (Baumeister & Twenge, 2002; Raffaelli & Green, 2003). Furthermore, parents are not likely to talk about pleasurable aspects of sexuality (Conrad & Milburn, 2001; Tolman & Diamond, 2001a, 2001b). As a consequence, certain topics are never discussed. For example, fewer than 1% of students in a college human sexuality course had heard a parent mention the word *clitoris* (Allgeier & Allgeier, 2000). Other women recall hearing mixed messages from their parents, such as "Sex is dirty," and "Save it for someone you love" (O'Sullivan et al., 2001; K. Wright, 1997).

Some studies have examined parent-child communications among women of color. Latina and Asian American adolescents often report that sex is a forbidden topic with their parents, who may have conservative ideas about dating (Chan, 2004; Hurtado, 2003; Raffaelli & Green, 2003). Black mothers seem to feel more comfortable than Latina or European American mothers in speaking to their daughters about sexuality. For example, one Black mother reported, "I can't remember a specific age when I first talked. . . . I'm real open with my daughter as far as sex and things like that" (O'Sullivan et al., 2001, p. 279).

SCHOOLS AND SEX EDUCATION. What do our school systems say about sexuality? Many sex education programs focus on the reproductive system, in other words, an "organ recital." Students don't hear about the connections between sexuality and emotions. They rarely hear about gay and lesbian perspectives, and many programs avoid discussion of contraceptives. As a result, sex education in school often has little impact on students' sexual behavior (Easton et al., 2002; Feldt, 2002; T. Rose, 2003).

In recent years, many school programs emphasize an oversimplified "just say no" approach. These abstinence-only programs typically include misinformation (Bartell, 2005; Wagle, 2004). They also fail to reduce teenagers' sexual activity or their rate of sexually transmitted diseases (Daniluk & Towill, 2001; S. L. Nichols & Good, 2004: Schaalma et al., 2004; Tolman, 2002). Still, the U.S. government spends about $300 million each year on these ineffective programs (Hahn, 2004).

However, some communities in the United States have developed a more comprehensive approach to sexual education. In addition to providing relevant information, these programs address values, attitudes, and emotions.

They also provide strategies for making informed choices about sexuality (B. L. Barber & Eccles, 2003; Florsheim, 2003). A comprehensive educational program helps students to develop skills and behaviors, such as how to discuss contraceptives with a partner and how to actually use them. Teenagers who participate in these comprehensive programs—as opposed to the abstinence-only programs—typically postpone sexual relationships until they are older, and they also have a lower pregnancy rate (S. L. Nichols & Good, 2004; Tolman, 2002).

We often hear reports about parents protesting sex education in the schools. Surprisingly, however, most parents acknowledge that high-school sex education classes should take a comprehensive approach (Hahn, 2004). For example, one large-scale U.S. survey reported that 94% of parents wanted the classes to include information about how to deal with pressure to have sex, 90% wanted information on birth control, and 79% wanted information on abortion (Hoff & Greene, 2000; S. L. Nichols & Good, 2004).

THE MEDIA.   According to a survey, many teenagers report that they have learned information about sexual issues from the media: 40% pointed to television and movies, and 35% mentioned magazines (Hoff & Greene, 2000). The Internet is also an important source of information—and misinformation—about sexuality, though it has not been studied extensively (G. Cowan, 2002; Escobar-Chaves et al., 2005; Lambiase, 2003).

Most media research focuses on the magazines. For example, the magazines that young women read tend to provide narrowly defined sexual scripts about how they can make themselves alluring to young men (J. L. Kim & Ward, 2004). Meanwhile, the magazines that young men read tend to teach them that women are sex objects, and men can improve their sex lives by taking specific steps (C. N. Baker, 2005; L. D. Taylor, 2005).

According to M. J. Sutton and his colleagues (2002), the average adolescent witnesses about 2,000 sexual acts in the media each year. Unfortunately, adolescents probably won't learn accurate information from the media. One study noted that the risks of pregnancy or sexually transmitted diseases are mentioned in less than 0.01%—that's 1 in 10,000—of the sexual portrayals in television or the movies ("Pediatrician Testifies," 2001). The clear majority of popular programs also do not show any consequences—either positive or negative—for sexual activity (Cope-Farrar & Kunkel, 2002).

Furthermore, young women often report feeling that they cannot attain the perfect look portrayed in the media images of female sexuality. In one discussion group, Latina women were especially likely to say that they could not measure up to the European American images (Dello Stritto & Guzmán, 2001). Furthermore, these media images often suggest that young women are a combination of innocence and seductiveness (Kilbourne, 2003; J. L. Kim & Ward, 2004). For instance, one ad shows a young woman dressed in an old-fashioned white dress, but the dress is unbuttoned and pulled down over one shoulder. How can a real-life teenager make sense of this mixed message to be both sexually innocent and sexually active?

SEXUAL BEHAVIOR IN HETEROSEXUAL ADOLESCENTS

Adolescent females are more likely to have early heterosexual experiences if they reached puberty before most of their peers (Bergevin et al., 2003; Weichold et al., 2003). Other important predictors of females' early experiences include low self-esteem, poor academic performance, poor parent-child relationships, poor parent-child communication, extended exposure to sexually explicit media, poverty, and early use of alcohol and drugs (Crockett et al., 2002; Escobar-Chaves et al., 2005; Farber, 2003; Furman & Shaffer, 2003; Halpern, 2003; Sieverding et al., 2005; Spencer et al., 2002).

Ethnicity is also related to adolescent sexual experience. In the United States, for example, Black female adolescents are likely to have their first sexual intercourse one or two years before European American or Latina female adolescents (Joyner & Laumann, 2002; O'Sullivan & Meyer-Bahlburg, 2003; P. T. Reid & Bing, 2000). Asian American female adolescents are typically the least likely to have early sexual experiences (Chan, 2004). In Canada, adolescents born in other countries and immigrating to Canada are much less likely than Canada-born adolescents to have early sexual experiences (Maticka-Tyndale et al., 2001).

As you might imagine, peer pressure encourages some teenagers to become sexually active (Kaiser Family Foundation, 2003; O'Sullivan & Meyer-Bahlburg, 2003). These teenagers risk unwanted pregnancies and sexually transmitted diseases—topics we'll examine later in this chapter and in Chapter 11. In other words, biological, psychological, and cultural variables all have an impact on young women's sexual experiences (Crockett et al., 2002).

For many adolescents, decisions about sexuality are critically important in defining their values (Tolman, 2002). For instance, one young woman was neither judgmental nor prudish, but she had decided not to be sexually active as a teenager. As she explained:

> I have certain talents and certain gifts, and I owe it to myself to take care of those gifts. I'm not going to just throw it around, throw my body around. And I see that sexuality is part of that. The sexual revolution—I guess we grew up in that—I think a lot of it has cheapened something that isn't cheap. (Kamen, 2000, pp. 87–88)

Romance novels portray idealized images of young women being blissfully transformed by their first sexual experience. However, many women do not have positive memories of their first intercourse (Conrad & Milburn, 2001; Tiefer & Kring, 1998). The experience may also be physically painful (Tolman, 2002). Furthermore, about 10% of high-school females say that they were forced to have sexual intercourse (Centers for Disease Control and Prevention, 2004a; S. L. Nichols & Good, 2004).

Some young women, in contrast, recall a highly positive experience:

> We were totally in love. We wanted this to be the best experience of our lives. We were at his apartment and we had done everything right. We had talked about it, planned for it, saw this as the highest expression of our joint future. He was very caring, very slow with me. I felt empowered, beautiful. It was a great night. (P. Schwartz & Rutter, 1998, p. 97)

In summary, young women often learn about sexuality in a less-than-ideal way. As we saw earlier in this section, parents, schools, and the media seldom help young people make informed decisions about sexuality. In addition, many young women's early sexual experiences may not be as romantic or joyous as they had hoped.

SEXUAL BEHAVIOR IN HETEROSEXUAL ADULTS

Any survey about sexual behavior inevitably runs into roadblocks. How can researchers manage to obtain a random sample of respondents who represent all geographic regions, ethnic groups, and income levels—on a sensitive topic such as sexuality (Dunne, 2002)? Sociologist Edward Laumann and his colleagues (1994) conducted one of the most respected U.S. surveys of sexual behavior. They interviewed 3,432 adults about a wide range of topics. The results showed, for example, that 17% of men claimed to have had more than 20 sexual partners during their lifetime, in contrast to 3% of women.

A meta-analysis of 12 earlier studies confirmed a general trend for men to report a somewhat greater number of sexual partners, with a d of 0.25 (Oliver & Hyde, 1993). In all these surveys, men probably overreport their number of sexual partners, whereas women probably underreport (P. Schwartz & Rutter, 1998).

Surveys also show that masturbation is much more common for men than for women (Hyde & Oliver, 2000; Vohs & Baumeister, 2004). Oliver and Hyde (1993) reported a d of 0.96, a much larger gender difference than others we've discussed in this book. For instance, in the survey by Laumann and his colleagues (1994), 27% of men and 8% of women reported that they masturbated at least once a week. As researchers note, it's strange that this risk-free sexual activity is missing from many women's sexual scripts (Baber, 2000; Shulman & Horne, 2003). Some of the gender differences in masturbation can be traced to the more obvious prominence of the male genitals (Oliver & Hyde, 1993) and to gender differences in sexual desire, discussed on pages 294–295. The gender differences with respect to masturbation may well have some important theoretical significance as well as practical implications for male and female sexuality.

COMMUNICATION ABOUT SEXUALITY

We mentioned earlier in this section that parents often feel uncomfortable talking about sex with their children. Actually, most couples also feel uncomfortable talking with *each other* about sexual activity. Most people try to communicate their sexual desire by nonverbal communication, such as kissing or touching. Women are somewhat more likely than men to use verbal messages, such as asking if their male partner has a condom (Hickman & Muehlenhard, 1999).

One problem, however, is that it's difficult to convey some messages about sexuality. Suppose that you are a female, and you want to convey to a male, "I'm not certain whether I'm interested in sexual activity." Most women report that they have trouble communicating this message verbally (Brehm et al., 2002; O'Sullivan & Gaines, 1998). Now try imagining how you would convey

Demonstration 9.3

The items listed in this demonstration were shown to women students at a large state university in the Northeast. The women were asked to rate each item, using a scale where 1 = disagree strongly and 5 = agree strongly. Your task is to inspect each item and estimate the average rating that the women supplied for that item (e.g., 2.8). When you have finished, check page 321 to see how the women actually responded. (Note: This demonstration is based on Morokoff et al., 1997, but it contains only 6 of the 18 items; the validity of this short version has not been established.)

_____ 1. I let my partner know if I want my partner to touch my genitals.

_____ 2. I wait for my partner to touch my breasts instead of letting my partner know that's what I want.

_____ 3. I give in and kiss if my partner pressures me, even if I already said no.

_____ 4. I refuse to have sex if I don't want to, even if my partner insists.

_____ 5. I have sex without a condom or latex barrier if my partner doesn't like them, even if I want to use one.

_____ 6. I insist on using a condom or latex barrier if I want to, even if my partner doesn't.

Source: From Morokoff, P. J., et al. (1997). Sexual Assertiveness Scale (SAS) for women: Development and validation. *Journal of Personality and Social Psychology, 73*, 804 (appendix). © 1997 by the American Psychological Association. Reprinted with permission.

this ambivalent message *nonverbally* to a romantic partner, and you can anticipate some communication difficulties. Women may try to communicate this uncertainty, but men may not understand the message (Tolman, 2002).

One important development in the area of sexual communication focuses on women's sexual assertiveness (P. B. Anderson & Struckman-Johnson, 1998). Previous research had suggested that women may hesitate to say no to men's sexual advances because they don't want to hurt their partner's feelings. Patricia Morokoff and her colleagues (1997) developed a Sexual Assertiveness Scale for women. Try Demonstration 9.3, which includes some of the questions from the Sexual Assertiveness Scale. Then check the answers at the end of the chapter. Were you fairly accurate in predicting the women's answers? Did this exercise provide any new insights into your own communication patterns with respect to sexual activity?

Another important topic focuses on sexual self-disclosure. For instance, E. Sandra Byers and Stephanie Demmons (1999) surveyed Canadian college students who had been dating for at least 3 months. These researchers found that respondents were reluctant to talk with their partner about the sexual activities that they liked or disliked. However, those who provided more self-disclosure were likely to be more satisfied with the sexual aspects of their relationship. This correlation is consistent with some information from Chapter 8: Married couples are more satisfied with their relationship if they have good communication skills.

LESBIANS AND SEXUALITY

Most of this chapter focuses on heterosexual relationships. Is sexuality different in lesbian relationships? As you can anticipate, it is more challenging to find a representative sample of lesbian women who are willing to be interviewed. The research suggests that lesbian couples value nongenital physical contact, such as hugging and cuddling (Klinger, 1996; McCormick, 1994). However, our North American culture tends to define sexual activity in terms of genital stimulation and orgasm. Researchers with that operational definition of sexual activity might conclude that lesbian couples are less sexually active than heterosexual couples or gay male couples (L. M. Diamond, 2003a; Peplau & Beals, 2001). This conclusion would be especially true for couples who have been together for many years (Haley-Banez & Garrett, 2002; Vohs & Baumeister, 2004).

When lesbians do engage in genital sexual activity, they are more likely than heterosexual women to experience an orgasm. Some possible explanations for this difference are that lesbian couples may communicate more effectively and be more sensitive to each other's preferences. They may also engage in more kissing and caressing than heterosexual couples do (Hatfield & Rapson, 1996; Herbert, 1996).

Laura S. Brown (2000) wrote that lesbians are like the early mapmakers who must construct their own maps about the unknown territories of lesbian sexuality. After all, the well-established maps—or scripts—represent heterosexual territory. Also, some adolescent lesbians mention that they had to keep their sexual desires hidden. Later, when they entered a romantic relationship, they found it difficult to express these desires. An additional challenge is that our culture does not tolerate evidence of sexual affection between two women in public places. I recall a lesbian friend commenting that she feels sad and resentful that she and her partner cannot hold hands or hug each other in public, and kissing would be unthinkable.

OLDER WOMEN AND SEXUALITY

Women's reproductive systems change somewhat as women grow older. As we'll discuss in Chapter 14, estrogen production drops rapidly at menopause. As a result, the vagina loses some of its elasticity and may also produce less moisture (Foley et al., 2002). However, these problems can be at least partly corrected by using supplemental lubricants. Also, women who have been sexually active throughout their lives may not experience vaginal changes (Hyde & DeLamater, 2006). Furthermore, it's worth questioning a popular belief that a decrease in hormone levels causes a decrease in sexual interest; no solid research supports that proposal (Kingsberg, 2002; Rostosky & Travis, 2000).

Researchers often report that the *frequency* of genital sexual activity declines as heterosexual and lesbian women grow older (Burgess, 2004; Dennerstein et al., 2003). However, a woman's age doesn't have a strong influence on her *enjoyment* of sex (Burgess, 2004; Laumann et al., 2002). The best predictors of a woman's sexual satisfaction are her feeling of well-being and her emotional closeness with her partner, rather than more "biological" measures such as vaginal moisture (Bancroft et al., 2003).

In a study by Mansfield and her colleagues (1998), many older women emphasized the importance of "sweet warmth and constant tenderness" and "physical closeness and intimacy." As one woman wrote, "Touching, hugging, holding, become as or more important than the actual sex act" (p. 297). Notice, then, that these studies emphasize a broad definition of sexuality, rather than a focus on the genitals.

In general, older women maintain the physiological capability to experience an orgasm as well as an enthusiastic interest in sexual relationships. However, they may no longer have a partner. In addition, some heterosexual older women may have male sexual partners who are no longer able to maintain an erection. These men may stop all caressing and sexual activities once intercourse is not possible (Ellison, 2001; Kingsberg, 2002; Leiblum & Segraves, 2000).

Another problem is that North Americans seem to think that older women should be asexual. Our culture has constructed images of grandmothers baking cookies in the kitchen, not cavorting around in the bedroom. In some cultures that are generally negative about sexuality, such as the people of Uttar Pradesh in Northern India, older women are expected not to be sexually active. In contrast, in sex-positive cultures, such as the San of Africa or Chinese Taoists, sexuality is considered healthy for the elderly (Whelehan, 2001).

Sexuality seems to be condemned more in older women than in older men (C. Banks & Arnold, 2001). People often view a sexually eager older woman with suspicion or disgust. A manufacturer of lingerie has tried to revise this view with ads of older women in lacy underwear and quotes such as "Time is a purification system that has made me wiser, freer, better, some say sexier. Are those the actions of an enemy?" Of course, this advertising strategy may not be motivated by altruism or feminist convictions. Still, the ads may help to change views about women's sexuality in later life.

Section Summary

Sexual Attitudes and Behavior

1. Most North Americans believe that sex before marriage is acceptable in some circumstances. The double standard about sexuality is no longer widespread in North America. However, in some Asian, Middle Eastern, and Latin American cultures, a woman may be killed for suspected sexual activity, whereas a man is allowed sexual freedom.

2. Sexual scripts specify what women and men in a certain culture are supposed to do in sexual interactions; for example, men are supposed to take the initiative in sexual activity.

3. Young people typically report that their parents do not discuss pleasurable aspects of sexuality as part of sex education. Many schools adopt "abstinence-only" sex education programs; they usually fail to explore the topics most relevant to adolescents. More comprehensive school programs discuss emotions and decision-making strategies. The media frequently portray sexuality, but they seldom show the consequences of sexual activity.

4. Most women report that their first experience with intercourse was not positive; about 10% of women report that their first experience was forced intercourse.

5. The research shows that men report more sexual partners than women do and that men are much more likely to report masturbating.

6. Couples seem to experience difficulty communicating about sexual issues; an important component of communication is sexual assertiveness; couples who discuss their preferences about sexual activities are more likely to be satisfied with the sexual aspects of their relationships.

7. Lesbian couples typically value nongenital physical contact; compared to heterosexual women, they are more likely to experience an orgasm, perhaps because of better communication.

8. Many older women experience subtle changes in their sexual responding, but not necessarily decreased enjoyment; however, lack of a partner is often an important obstacle to older women's sexual activities.

SEXUAL DISORDERS

A **sexual disorder** is a disturbance in sexual arousal or in sexual responding that causes mental distress (L. L. Alexander et al., 2004; Hyde & DeLamater, 2006). As you might guess, it's difficult to estimate how many women experience these sexual problems. However, one survey sampled 1,749 sexually active women in the United States. According to the women's reports, 43% of the women had sexual experiences that were less than ideal (Laumann et al., 2002). Sexual dissatisfaction was especially high among women who had little education and women who experienced general depression or economic problems. Furthermore, sexual problems may arise because people are simply too tired at the end of the day (Deveny, 2003; Shifren & Ferrari, 2004).

In this section on sexual disorders, we first examine two of the more common sexual problems in women: low sexual desire and female orgasmic disorder. Then we will see how traditional gender roles are partly responsible for sexual problems. Finally, we'll discuss therapy for sexual problems, including some thought-provoking questions raised by feminist theorists and researchers (e.g., Kaschak & Tiefer, 2001; Tiefer, 2004).

Low Sexual Desire

As the name suggests, a woman with **low sexual desire** (also called **hypoactive sexual desire disorder**) has little interest in sexual activity, and she is distressed by this lack of desire (Basson, 2006; Hyde & DeLamater, 2006; LoPiccolo, 2002). Earlier in this chapter, we noted that women maybe somewhat lower in sexual desire than men. One woman who reported low sexual desire had been happily married for 31 years, and she reported that her husband was a gentle and considerate lover. However, she remained entirely passive during love-making. In fact, she kept her mind busy creating menus and making shopping lists (H. S. Kaplan, 1995).

A disorder of low sexual desire may be caused by a variety of psychological factors, including a more general problem such as depression or anxiety (Wincze & Carey, 2001). A woman who is not satisfied with her romantic partner or their relationship may also experience little sexual desire (Hyde & DeLamater, 2006; O'Sullivan et al., 2006; Schnarch, 2000).

Low sexual desire is one of the most common sexual problem that lesbians face. In many cases, a lesbian couple may have a harmonious social relationship. However, they no longer have sexual interactions because the more sexually interested member of a lesbian couple is reluctant to pressure her less enthusiastic partner (M. Nichols, 2000).

Female Orgasmic Disorder

A woman with **female orgasmic disorder** experiences sexual excitement, but she does not reach orgasm. Exactly what constitutes an orgasm problem? Some women want to have an orgasm every time they engage in sexual activity. Others are satisfied if they feel emotionally close to their partner during sexual activity. The diagnosis of female orgasmic disorder should not be applied if a woman is currently satisfied with her situation. For example, suppose that a woman reaches orgasm through clitoral stimulation, but not during intercourse. If she feels satisfied with her sexual experiences, most feminist sex therapists would say that she should not be diagnosed with female orgasmic disorder (Hyde & DeLamater, 2006).

One common cause of female orgasmic disorder is that women who are accustomed to inhibiting their sexual impulses have difficulty overcoming their inhibitions, even in a relationship where sex is approved. Other women have orgasm problems because they are anxious about losing control over their feelings (LoPiccolo, 2002). They may be embarrassed about experiencing such intense pleasure. Still others are easily distracted during sexual activity. They may suddenly focus on a distant noise rather than on the sexual sensations (Wincze & Carey, 2001). And many women may not have orgasms because their partners do not provide appropriate sexual stimulation. Unfortunately, female orgasmic disorder is a relatively common sexual problem (Baber, 2000; Heiman, 2000).

How Gender Roles Contribute to Sexual Disorders

Sexual problems are extremely complex. Some are caused by a painful medical problem or a side effect of medication (Wincze & Carey, 2001). The problems may also be caused by a psychological trauma experienced many years earlier (Offman & Matheson, 2004). Other psychological factors include low self-esteem and problems in a couple's interactions (Crooks & Baur, 2005).

Gender roles, stereotypes, and biases may also contribute to sexual problems. As feminists have pointed out, a heterosexual marriage is typically an unequal playing field, with the man having more power (Tiefer, 1996; Tolman & Diamond, 2001b). Here are some reasons that gender roles can create or intensify sexual problems (Baber, 2000; Crooks & Baur, 2005; Foley et al., 2002; LoPiccolo, 2002; Morokoff, 1998):

1. Many people believe that men should be sexual and aggressive, whereas women should be asexual and passive; people therefore believe that women don't need to enjoy sexual activity.
2. Our culture emphasizes the length, strength, and endurance of a man's penis (Zilbergeld, 1999). When a man focuses on these issues, he probably won't think about how to make the interactions pleasurable for his partner.
3. Because of the emphasis on male sexuality, researchers know how physical illness and drugs affect men's sexual responses. However, they know much less about their effects on female sexuality. Consistent with Theme 3 of this book, women are relatively invisible.
4. Women are hesitant to appear selfish by requesting the kind of sexual activity they enjoy, such as tender caresses or clitoral stimulation. Stereotypes suggest that women should give rather than request.
5. Physical attractiveness is emphasized more for females than for males, and so women may focus on their physical appearance, rather than on their own sexual pleasure.

Let's consider this last point in more detail. We discussed the importance of female attractiveness in the sections on adolescence and dating. Furthermore, we'll encounter this issue again in Chapter 12 in connection with eating disorders and in Chapter 14, on older women.

The reality is that many men may prefer to think about women's bodies as they are airbrushed into perfection in a magazine like *Playboy,* rather than the bodies that belong to the women they know. Gary R. Brooks (1997) referred to this problem as the "Centerfold Syndrome." Women who feel less than perfectly attractive—that is, almost all women—may worry about their physical appearance. Women may therefore experience **self-objectification,** by adopting an observer's view of their body—as if their body were an object (T. Roberts & Waters, 2004). In a cleverly designed study, Tomi-Ann Roberts and Jennifer Gettman (2004) encouraged one group of young women to think about words related to their body's competence, such as *health, energetic,* and *strong.* Young women in a second group were encouraged to think about "objectifying" words such as *attractive, shapely,* and *slender.* Compared to the women in the "physical competence" condition, those in the "objectifying" condition were more ashamed, disgusted, and anxious about themselves. The women in the "objectifying" condition were also less positive about the physical aspects of sexuality.

In summary, our culture emphasizes men's sexuality, focusing on male genitals and the treatment of male sexual problems. In contrast, women's sexual enjoyment receives little attention. In addition, self-objectification encourages women's sexual problems.

THERAPY FOR SEXUAL DISORDERS

In 1970, Masters and Johnson introduced a kind of sex therapy called sensate focus. **Sensate focus** encourages couples to focus on their sensual experiences and to avoid trying to quickly reach a goal such as orgasm. Partners touch and stroke so that they can discover sensitive areas on their own body and on their partner's body, and they are encouraged to focus on these pleasant sensations (LoPiccolo, 2002; Wincze & Carey, 2001). Later in the therapy, clitoral masturbation is encouraged for female orgasmic problems.

Sensate focus is widely used in sex therapy, even though few studies have been conducted to document its effectiveness (Christensen & Heavey, 1999). It may sometimes be helpful, but it doesn't offer a complete answer (Wincze & Carey, 2001). For example, this approach may not pay enough attention to the tender, loving, and caring aspects of lovemaking (Tiefer, 2004).

Sex therapists have developed many other techniques (e.g., LoPiccolo, 2002). For example, **cognitive-behavioral therapy** combines behavioral exercises, such as those that Masters and Johnson (1970) suggested, with therapy techniques that emphasize people's thoughts about sexuality. In a popular technique called **cognitive restructuring,** the therapist tries (1) to change people's inappropriately negative thoughts about some aspect of sexuality and also (2) to reduce thoughts that interfere with sexual activity and pleasure (Basson, 2006; Wincze & Carey, 2001).

However, all of these traditional approaches to sex therapy may be too limited. Leonore Tiefer (1996, 2001, 2004), one of the leading feminist sex therapists, points out that sexual problems must be addressed from a broad social perspective rather than by focusing on biological aspects:

> The amount of time devoted to getting the penis hard and the vagina wet vastly outweighs the attention devoted to assessment or education about sexual motives, scripts, pleasure, power, emotionality, sensuality, communication, or connectedness. (Tiefer, 2001, p. 90)

So far, unfortunately, sex therapists have not devised a comprehensive program that addresses gender inequalities in a relationship while also correcting specific problems in sexual responding. An ideal comprehensive program would award equal value to women's and men's pleasurable experiences. Tenderness, emotional closeness, and communication are also essential (Basson, 2006; O'Sullivan et al., 2006).

Section Summary

Sexual Disorders

1. A woman who has a disorder called "low sexual desire" has little interest in sexual activity and is unhappy about the situation. Depression, other psychological problems, and relational issues may contribute to this disorder.

2. A woman who has female orgasmic disorder feels sexual excitement but does not experience orgasm. Psychological factors (e.g., anxiety about losing control) and inadequate sexual stimulation are often responsible.

3. Gender roles contribute to sexual disorders in several ways: (a) Women aren't supposed to be interested in sex; (b) male gender roles create problems; (c) sexuality research emphasizes male sexuality; (d) women are hesitant to request their preferred sexual stimulation; and (e) physical attractiveness is emphasized for females more than for males, so that females may experience self-objectification.

4. Masters and Johnson's (1970) sensate focus therapy may sometimes be helpful and so may cognitive-behavioral therapy techniques such as cognitive restructuring.

5. A feminist perspective on sex therapy emphasizes that the traditional approaches are too narrow; instead, therapy should adopt a broader perspective that includes gender equality, tenderness, and communication.

BIRTH CONTROL AND ABORTION

Birth control and abortion are highly controversial topics in the current century. The most publicized data about birth control and abortion in the United States typically focus on teenagers. Unfortunately, U.S. adolescents are more likely to give birth than adolescents in any other industrialized country in the world (Singh & Darroch, 2000; United Nations, 2005b). In Table 9.1 on page 311, you can see estimated birthrates for Canada, the United States, and many countries in Western Europe. (We'll discuss the abortion rates in Table 9.1 later in this chapter.)

Figure 9.2 shows estimates of the outcomes for the more than 800,000 teen pregnancies in the United States each year (Alan Guttmacher Institute, 2004).[1] A young woman who does not experience a miscarriage or a stillbirth must make an extremely important decision: Should she carry the pregnancy to term, or should she seek an abortion? Should she choose marriage, or should she become a single mother? Should she give up her baby for adoption?

In this section, we will first discuss women's decisions about contraception, and then we'll look at some information about abortion and other alternatives.

---

[1]Unfortunately, no comparable analysis is available for the options faced by pregnant teenagers in Canada. However, as Table 9.1 shows, a teenager in Canada is less than half as likely as a U.S. teenager to become pregnant. Also, the abortion rate is somewhat lower in Canada.

TABLE 9.1	ANNUAL RATE OF ADOLESCENT BIRTHS (PER 1,000 WOMEN, AGES 15–19) FOR CANADA, THE UNITED STATES, AND 10 COUNTRIES IN WESTERN EUROPE.

Country	Birth Rate	Abortion Rate
Belgium	14	5
Canada	20	21
Denmark	8	14
France	9	10
Germany	10	4
Italy	7	5
Netherlands	8	4
Norway	11	19
Spain	9	5
Sweden	7	17
United Kingdom	29	18
United States	49	29

Note: Several countries in Western Europe are missing because data on abortion were not available.
Source for birth data: United Nations (2005b).
Source for abortion data: Reproduced with the permission of The Alan Guttmacher Institute from Singh, S., & Darroch, J. E. (2000). Adolescent pregnancy and childbearing: Levels and trends in developed countries. *Family Planning Perspectives, 32,* 14–23 (data selected from Table 2, p. 16).

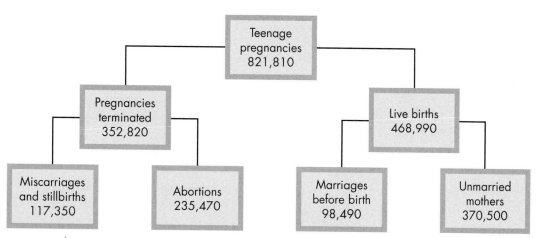

FIGURE 9.2	ESTIMATED OUTCOMES FOR PREGNANT U.S. TEENAGERS (AGES 15–19) IN 2000.

Source: Calculations based on data from Alan Guttmacher Institute (2004) and Farber (2003).

Because this is a psychology textbook, we will primarily focus on women's experiences. Still, we need to keep in mind that issues such as teen pregnancy have widespread political and economic consequences, for instance in the billions of dollars that the United States spends each year in costs related to teen pregnancy. For example, in New York State, every dollar spent on family planning saves at least three dollars later, just on the cost of prenatal and newborn care (Family Planning Advocates of New York State, 2005).

BIRTH CONTROL METHODS

If a sexually active woman uses no form of birth control whatsoever, she has an 85% chance of becoming pregnant within 1 year (Hatcher et al., 2004). Table 9.2 describes the major forms of birth control, together with some information about their effectiveness. You'll note that abstinence is the only method of birth control that is 100% effective in preventing pregnancy. In earlier decades, people who recommended abstinence might have been considered prudish. However, in the current era, sexual intercourse presents not only a substantial risk of pregnancy for women but also a significant risk of contracting a deadly disease. As we will discuss in Chapter 11, very few birth

TABLE 9.2 | MAJOR BIRTH CONTROL METHODS.

Method	Effectiveness When Used Consistently	Possible Side Effects and Disadvantages
Abstinence	100% effective	No physical disadvantages (assuming no sperm contact whatsoever).
Tubal ligation (severing of female's fallopian tubes)	99% effective	Minor surgical risk; typically not reversible; possible negative emotional reactions.
Vasectomy (surgery to prevent passage of male's sperm)	99% effective	Minor surgical risk; typically not reversible; possible negative emotional reactions.
Oral contraceptives (synthetic hormones taken by woman)	97–99% effective	Slight risk of blood-clotting disorders, particularly for women over 35 and smokers; other medical side effects possible; must be taken regularly.
Condom (sheath placed on penis)	85–95% effective	Must be applied before intercourse; may decrease pleasure for male.
Diaphragm and spermicidal cream	70–95% effective	Must be applied before intercourse; may irritate genital area.
Spermicidal creams (but no condom or diaphragm)	75–80% effective	Must be applied before intercourse; may irritate genital area.

Note: For more information, consult L. L. Alexander et al. (2004), Crooks and Baur (2005), Hatcher et al. (2004), and Hyde and DeLamater (2006).

control methods can reduce the risk of AIDS. Even condoms cannot completely prevent the transmission of this disease. Yes, they make sex safer, but not completely safe.

Incidentally, Table 9.2 does not list two behavioral birth control methods: (1) withdrawal (removal of the penis before ejaculation) and (2) the rhythm method, also known as natural family planning (intercourse only when a woman is least fertile). These methods are not listed because their effectiveness is unacceptably low: less than 80% (Alan Guttmacher Institute, 2005; Foley et al., 2002; Hatcher et al., 2004).

Let's focus on the psychological aspects of birth control. We need to consider the personal characteristics related to using birth control, the obstacles that prevent its use, and family planning in developing countries.

WHO USES BIRTH CONTROL?

Many heterosexual women who are sexually active use either an unreliable birth control method (such as foam, withdrawal, or rhythm) or no contraception at all. Because they do not always use effective birth control methods, many women have unplanned pregnancies. We saw, for example, that approximately 800,000 U.S. teenagers become pregnant each year. If we consider women of all ages in the United States, about half of all pregnancies were unintended at the time of conception (Alan Guttmacher Institute, 2005).

Here are some relevant factors related to women's birth control use:

1. Social class. Women from the middle and upper socioeconomic classes are more likely to use birth control (Allgeier & Allgeier, 2000; Farber, 2003).
2. Ethnicity. In the United States, birth control use is higher for European American women and Asian women than for Latina women and Black women (Kaiser Family Foundation, 2003). We do not have comparable data about other ethnic groups.
3. Level of education. Women who have had at least some college education are somewhat more likely than other women to use birth control (E. Becker et al., 1998). However, according to one study, only 52% of women who had at least a master's degree reported that they consistently used contraception (Laumann et al., 1994). In other words, about half of these well-educated women could face an unplanned pregnancy.
4. Personality characteristics. Research on adolescents shows that young women are more likely to use contraceptives if they are high in self-esteem and if they dislike taking risks (E. Becker et al., 1998; N. J. Bell et al., 1999).

OBSTACLES TO USING BIRTH CONTROL

Why are half of all U.S. pregnancies unplanned? The problem is that many obstacles stand in the way of using effective birth control. A woman who avoids pregnancy must have adequate knowledge about contraception. She must also have access to it, and she must be willing to use it on a consistent basis. In Canadian and U.S. surveys of sexually active young adults, only about 25% to 40% reported using a contraceptive when they last had intercourse (Fields, 2002; Statistics Canada, 2000).

In more detail, here are some of the obstacles to using birth control:

1. Parents and educators often avoid discussing birth control with young people because they "don't want to give them any ideas." As a result, many young people are misinformed or have gaps in their knowledge (Feldt, 2002; Kaiser Family Foundation, 2003; Tolman, 2002).
2. Some young women cannot obtain contraceptive services or products, so they use less reliable forms of birth control (Feldt, 2002; Hyde & DeLamater, 2006). Other women in the United States have no health insurance, or their health insurance does not cover birth control (Alan Guttmacher Institute, 2001).
3. Many young women have sexual intercourse without much planning. In a survey of Canadian female college students going to Florida over spring break, 13% reported that they had sex with someone they had just met (Maticka-Tyndale et al., 1998). In a sample of U.S. college students, 26% reported having had intercourse with someone they had met earlier the same night. Casual sex does not encourage conversations and careful planning about contraception strategies (M. Allen et al., 2002; Hyde & DeLamater, 2006; S. L. Nichols & Good, 2004).
4. People may not think rationally about the consequences of sexual activity. For example, sexually inexperienced women often believe that they themselves are not likely to become pregnant during intercourse (Brehm et al., 2002; Hyde & DeLamater, 2006). A survey of adolescents in the United States revealed another example of irrational thinking. For instance, 67% of adolescent females in this sample reported that they use condoms "all the time," yet only 50% of them said that they had used condoms during the last time they had sexual intercourse (Kaiser Family Foundation, 2003). A Canadian survey reported a similar discrepancy (H. R. L. Richardson et al., 1997).
5. Traditional women believe that, if they were to obtain contraception, they would be admitting to themselves that they planned to have intercourse and are therefore not "nice girls" (Luker, 1996; Tolman, 2002). In fact, college students downgrade a woman who is described as providing a condom before sexual intercourse (D. M. Castañeda & Collins, 1998; Hynie et al., 1997).
6. People often believe that birth control devices will interrupt the love-making mood, because they are not considered erotic or romantic (Perloff, 2001). Condoms and other contraceptives are seldom mentioned in movies, television, romantic novels, and magazines, as Demonstration 9.4 shows. We can see a woman and a man undressing, groping, groaning, and copulating. The one taboo topic seems to be contraception! Interestingly, women who read romance novels are especially likely to have negative attitudes toward contraception (Diekman et al., 2000).

Demonstration 9.4

CONTRACEPTION
AS A TABOO
TOPIC

For the next two weeks, keep a record of the number of times you see or hear about couples in sexual relationships in the media. Monitor television programs, movies, stories in magazines, books, and the Internet, as well as any other source that seems relevant. In each case, note whether contraceptives are mentioned, shown, or even hinted at.

---

7. Many young women are forced to have sexual intercourse, often with a much older man (Centers for Disease Control and Prevention, 2004a). When a 14-year-old female has a partner who is a 21-year-old male, she is unlikely to persuade him to wear a condom.

Earlier in the chapter, we noted that schools must develop more comprehensive sex education programs. Communities need to be sure that adolescents receive appropriate information before they become sexually active. We also need to change people's attitudes toward contraception. People might use contraceptives more often if the women in soap operas were shown discussing birth control methods with their gynecologists and if the macho men of the movie screen carefully adjusted their condoms before the steamy love scenes.

CONTRACEPTION AND FAMILY PLANNING IN DEVELOPING COUNTRIES

In the United States, 74% of couples who are of childbearing age use some kind of contraceptive. The percentage is almost identical for Canada: 73%. How about developing countries throughout the world? The data vary widely. Fewer than 5% of couples use contraceptives in Ethiopia, Angola, and many other African countries. However, in Cuba, 70% of couples use contraceptives—almost the same as in North America (Neft & Levine, 1997; Stout & Dello Buono, 1996). Even in some countries that are predominantly Catholic, the rates of contraceptive use are high (Neft & Levine, 1997). These countries include France (81%), Brazil (78%), and Italy (78%).

One of the best predictors of contraceptive use in developing countries is the female literacy rate (Winter, 1996). For example, if we consider the entire country of India, 31% of high-school-age girls are in school, and the average adult woman has 3.7 children. Kerala is one of the states in India. In Kerala, 93% of high-school-age girls are in school, and the average adult woman has only 2.0 children (B. Lott, 2000). That number is nearly identical to the average number for U.S. women, which is 1.9 (Townsend, 2003).

When women are well educated, they are likely to take control of their lives and make plans for the future. By limiting their family size, they can increase their economic and personal freedom—and not contribute to the world's overpopulation (P. D. Harvey, 2000). They can also provide better care for the children they already have.

The use of contraceptives throughout the world has been rising steadily, with between 50% and 60% of couples practicing contraception (David &

Russo, 2003; Townsend, 2003). Still, an estimated 120 million married couples throughout the world do not have access to family planning (García-Moreno & Türmen, 1995). When we add the millions of unmarried couples who also have no available family planning, the numbers are staggering. In fact, in the next 5 minutes, about 950 women throughout the world will have conceived a pregnancy that is not wanted (David & Russo, 2003). Each woman will probably need to make choices about continuing with a pregnancy, giving the child up for adoption, or having an abortion. Let's now explore the controversial topic of abortion and the alternatives.

ABORTION

Before 1973 in the United States, many abortions were performed illegally, often by untrained individuals in unsanitary conditions. Each year, an estimated 200,000 to 1,200,000 illegal abortions were performed and about 10,000 women died from these illegal abortions (Gorney, 1998). Before 1973, countless women also attempted to end an unwanted pregnancy themselves. They swallowed poisons such as turpentine, and they tried to stab coat hangers and other sharp objects through the cervix and into the uterus (Baird-Windle & Bader, 2001; Gorney, 1998).

In 1973, the U.S. Supreme Court's *Roe v. Wade* decision stated that women have the legal right to choose abortion. However, throughout North America, health-care professionals who perform abortions have been harassed or even murdered by so-called pro-life groups. Abortion clinics have also been bombed (Baird-Windle & Bader, 2001; Feldt, 2002; Quindlen, 2001b). In 1998, anti-abortionists murdered gynecologist Barnett Slepian in Amherst, New York, about an hour's drive from my home.

It's worth noting that cigarette smoking nearly doubles a woman's chances of having a miscarriage and losing her baby (Ness et al., 1999). However, pro-life groups have not yet harassed the tobacco companies.

Let's emphasize an important point: *No one recommends abortion as a routine form of birth control.* We need to provide more comprehensive education about sexuality so that women do not need to consider the abortion alternative (Adler et al., 2003). As you can see from Table 9.1 on page 311, the adolescent abortion rate is higher in the United States and Canada than in all other countries on this list. Worldwide, about 50 million abortions are performed each year for women of all ages. About 40% of these abortions are illegal (Caldwell & Caldwell, 2003; C. P. Murphy, 2003; United Nations, 2000). Worldwide, about 120 women die every 5 minutes from an unsafe abortion (David & Russo, 2003). Most of these abortions could have been avoided by using effective birth control methods.

About one-quarter of all pregnancies in the United States and Canada are terminated by means of a legal abortion (Singh et al., 2003; Statistics Canada, 2000). Compared to women who continue an unwanted pregnancy, pregnant women who seek abortions are more likely to be single women from middle-class or upper-class backgrounds (S. S. Brown & Eisenberg, 1995; L. Phillips, 1998).

Abortion may be a controversial issue, but one aspect of abortion is not controversial: its safety. A woman in the United States is about 30 times more likely to die as a result of childbirth than as a result of a legal abortion (Adler et al., 2003). As a general rule, women who have abortions performed shortly after conception have fewer medical complications, and they recover more quickly than women who had later abortions (Allgeier & Allgeier, 2000). In contrast to this objective information about methods, numbers, and safety, we must now consider the more difficult topics, focusing on the psychological aspects of abortion.

PSYCHOLOGICAL REACTIONS TO AN ABORTION.   Most women report that their primary reaction following an abortion is relief (David & Lee, 2001; Russo, 2004). Some women experience sadness, a sense of loss, or other negative feelings. Consistent with Theme 4 of this textbook, individual differences in emotional reactions are large (Major et al., 1998; Russo, 2004). However, studies show that the typical woman who has an abortion suffers no long-term effects, such as problems with depression, anxiety, or self-esteem (N. E. Adler et al., 2003; E. Lee, 2003; C. P. Murphy, 2003; Russo, 2004).

What factors are related to psychological adjustment following an abortion? In general, women who cope most easily are those who have the abortion early in their pregnancy (Allgeier & Allgeier, 2000). Another important psychological factor related to adjustment is **self-efficacy**, or a woman's feeling that she is competent and effective (Major et al., 1998). Not surprisingly, adjustment is also better if the woman's friends and relatives can support her decision (N. E. Adler & Smith, 1998; David & Lee, 2001). A medical staff that is helpful and supportive during the abortion also contributes to good adjustment (De Puy & Dovitch, 1997, p. 56).

CHILDREN BORN TO WOMEN WHO WERE DENIED ABORTIONS.   In many cases, a woman wants to obtain an abortion, but circumstances (such as lack of money) prevent the abortion. As a result, many women will give birth to children who are not wanted. Let's focus on these unwanted children: How do they develop psychologically under these circumstances?

Abortion has been legal in the United States since 1973, so researchers cannot accurately examine that question in this country. However, several studies in other countries provide some answers. Consider a long-term study conducted with 220 children whose mothers were denied abortions in the former Czechoslovakia (David et al., 1988; David et al., 2003). Each of these children was carefully matched—on the basis of eight different variables such as social class—with a child from a wanted pregnancy. As a result, the two groups were comparable.

The study showed that, by 9 years of age, the children from unwanted pregnancies had fewer friends and responded poorly to stress, compared to children from wanted pregnancies. By age 23, the children from unwanted pregnancies were more likely to report that their mothers were not interested in them. These children were also likely to receive psychological treatment. In addition, they had more marital difficulties, drug problems, conflicts at work, and trouble with the legal system (David et al., 1988). Ongoing research about these two groups continues to show psychological problems when these unwanted children are adults, whereas the wanted children have relatively few problems (David & Lee, 2001; David et al., 2003).

Other similar studies show that many mothers of unwanted children continue to report negative emotions and a lack of concern about those children many years later (J. S. Barber et al., 1999; Sigal et al., 2003). These implications for children's lives should be considered when governments try to make informed decisions about abortion policies.

ALTERNATIVES TO ABORTION. Unplanned pregnancies can be resolved by methods other than abortion. For example, people who oppose abortion often suggest the alternative of giving the baby up for adoption, and this might be an appropriate choice for some women. However, adoption may create its own kind of trauma and pain when the birth mother continues to feel guilty (David & Lee, 2001; Feldt, 2002; MariAnna, 2002). One woman who gave up her daughter for adoption commented two years later:

> I'm sad that I don't see her—the first steps, the first tooth. I'm missing everything, missing her discovering life. I love her, I love her to death. If tomorrow they were to call and say there's a problem, we need a heart, we need something, I'm there. I wouldn't even think twice about it. If that means I have to give my life for her, I'll do it. (Englander, 1997, p. 114)

Another alternative is to deliver the baby and choose the motherhood option. In many cases, an unwanted pregnancy can become a wanted baby by the time of delivery. However, hundreds of thousands of babies are born each year to mothers who do not want them. This situation can be destructive for both the mother and the child. In the United States, most adolescents who choose to give birth are currently choosing to become single mothers (Farber, 2003; Florsheim et al., 2003). Unfortunately, most unmarried teenage mothers encounter difficulties in completing school, finding employment, fighting poverty, obtaining health care, and facing the biases that unmarried mothers often confront in our culture (Hellenga et al., 2002; MariAnna, 2002; S. L. Nichols & Good, 2004).

We have seen that none of these alternatives—abortion, adoption, or motherhood—is free of problems. Instead, family planning seems to create less psychological pain than the other alternatives.

Section Summary

Birth Control and Abortion

1. More than 800,000 U.S. adolescent females become pregnant each year; pregnancy rates are much lower in Canada and Western Europe.

2. No birth control device offers problem-free protection from pregnancy and sexually transmitted diseases.

3. Many heterosexual, sexually active women do not use reliable birth control methods. Female contraceptive use is related to social class, ethnicity, education, self-esteem, and risk taking.

4. Couples avoid using birth control because of inadequate information, unavailable contraceptive services, inadequate planning, irrational thinking, reluctance to admit they are sexually active, and the feeling that birth control devices are not romantic. A man who is sexually assaulting a woman is unlikely to wear a condom.

5. Some developing countries have instituted family planning programs, whereas others do not support these programs. Literacy is highly correlated with women's contraceptive use.

6. Before *Roe v. Wade*, thousands of U.S. women died each year from illegal abortions; legal abortions are much safer than childbirth.

7. Following an abortion, most women experience a feeling of relief; adjustment is best when the abortion occurs early in pregnancy, when the woman feels competent, and when friends, family, and the medical staff are supportive.

8. Children born to women who have been denied an abortion are significantly more likely to experience psychological and social difficulties than children from a wanted pregnancy.

9. In general, giving up a child for adoption is not an emotionally satisfactory alternative; women who choose the motherhood option also face many difficulties. Pregnancy prevention is therefore the preferable solution.

CHAPTER REVIEW QUESTIONS

1. At several points throughout this chapter, we have seen that sexuality has traditionally been male centered. Address this issue, focusing on topics such as (a) theoretical perspectives on sexuality, (b) sexual scripts, and (c) sexual problems. Also, compare how the essentialist perspective and the social constructionist perspective approach sexuality.

2. In the first section of this chapter, we noted that men and women differ more in the intensity of sexual desires than in most other areas. What are some of the potential consequences of this difference, with respect to sexual behavior and sexual disorders?

3. In many sections of this chapter, we discussed adolescent women. Describe the experiences a young woman might face as she discusses sexuality with her parents, listens to a sex education session in her high school, has her first sexual experience, makes decisions about contraception, and tries to make a decision about an unwanted pregnancy.

4. How are gender roles relevant in (a) the initiation of sexual relationships, (b) sexual activity, (c) sexual problems, (d) therapy for sexual problems, and (e) decisions about contraception and abortion?

5. What information in this chapter would be helpful for a sexually active woman to know regarding communication about sexuality, self-objectification, and methods of birth control?

6. Describe attitudes about sexuality in the current era. Does the sexual double standard still hold true in North America in the twenty-first century?

7. What information do we have about sexuality among lesbians, including sexual activity and sexual problems? Why would a male-centered approach to sexuality make it difficult to decide what "counts" as sexual activity in a lesbian relationship? Why is this same problem relevant when we consider older women and sexual activities?

8. Describe the two sexual problems discussed in this chapter. Why might older women be especially likely to experience these problems? Also, summarize the kinds of therapeutic approaches currently used to treat sexual problems.

9. Imagine that you have received a large grant to reduce the number of unwanted pregnancies, at the high school you attended. What kinds of programs would you plan, to achieve both immediate and long-term effects?

10. What information do we have about the safety of abortion, the psychological consequences to the woman, and consequences for children whose mothers had been denied an abortion?

KEY TERMS

*essentialism (291)

*social constructionism (291)

*clitoris (292)

*vagina (293)

excitement phase (293)

vasocongestion (293)

plateau phase (293)

orgasmic phase (293)

resolution phase (293)

*sexual desire (294)

*sexual double standard (297)

*sexual script (298)

*rape (298)

*sexual disorder (306)

*low sexual desire (307)

*hypoactive sexual desire disorder (307)

female orgasmic disorder (307)

*self-objectification (308)

*sensate focus (309)

*cognitive-behavioral therapy (309)

*cognitive restructuring (309)

*self-efficacy (317)

 Note: The terms asterisked in the Key Terms section serve as good search terms for InfoTrac College Edition. Go to http://infotrac.thomsonlearning.com and try these added search terms.

RECOMMENDED READINGS

Brown, J. D., Steele, J. R., & Walsh-Childers, K. (Eds.). (2002). *Sexual teens, sexual media: Investigating media's influence on adolescent sexuality.* Mahwah, NJ: Erlbaum. Here is an excellent collection of 13 chapters about the kind of "information" that adolescents learn from the media, including television, magazines, movies, and the Internet.

Florsheim, P. (Ed.). (2003). *Adolescent romantic relations and sexual behavior: Theory, research,* *and practical implications.* Mahwah, NJ: Erlbaum. This book considers the romantic and the sexual aspects of adolescents' lives, focusing on both male-female and same-gender couples.

Hyde, J. S., & DeLamater, J. D. (2006). *Understanding human sexuality* (9th ed.). Boston: McGraw-Hill. Janet Hyde and her husband, John DeLamater, have written a clear, comprehensive, and interesting textbook about sexuality, from a feminist perspective.

Tiefer, L. (2004). *Sex is not a natural act and other essays*. Boulder, CO: Westview Press. I strongly recommend this book, which provides a feminist perspective on sexuality—rather than a biological/medical approach. The book includes some theoretical essays, but also some intended for the general public.

Tolman, D. L. (2002). *Dilemmas of desire: Teenage girls talk about sexuality*. Cambridge, MA: Harvard University Press. I recommend this book because it provides an opportunity to learn about young women's thoughts regarding their sexuality, rather than the dangers of disease and pregnancy.

ANSWERS TO THE DEMONSTRATIONS

Demonstration 9.1: 1. F; 2. M; 3. F; 4. F; 5. M; 6. M; 7. M; 8. F.

Demonstration 9.3: 1. 2.7; 2. 2.7; 3. 4.2; 4. 4.1; 5. 4.6; 6. 4.4.
(Note that a woman who is high in sexual assertiveness would provide high ratings for Items 1, 4, and 6; she would provide low ratings for Items 2, 3, and 5. Also note that respondents answered numbers 5 and 6 inconsistently—both having sex without a condom and insisting on a condom.)

ANSWERS TO THE TRUE-FALSE STATEMENTS

1. True (pp. 292–293); 2. True (p. 295); 3. False (pp. 297–298); 4. True (p. 300); 5. False (p. 301); 6. True (p. 303); 7. True (p. 307); 8. True (pp. 308–309); 9. True (pp. 310–311); 10. True (p. 317).

10 | PREGNANCY, CHILDBIRTH, AND MOTHERHOOD

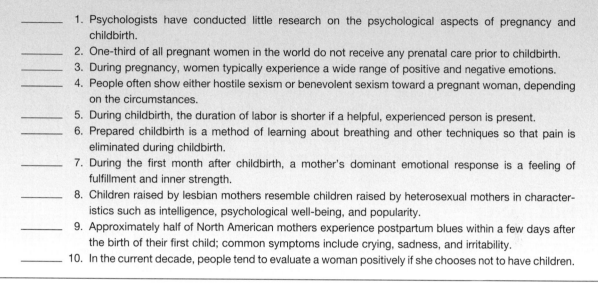

True or False?

——————— 1. Psychologists have conducted little research on the psychological aspects of pregnancy and childbirth.

——————— 2. One-third of all pregnant women in the world do not receive any prenatal care prior to childbirth.

——————— 3. During pregnancy, women typically experience a wide range of positive and negative emotions.

——————— 4. People often show either hostile sexism or benevolent sexism toward a pregnant woman, depending on the circumstances.

——————— 5. During childbirth, the duration of labor is shorter if a helpful, experienced person is present.

——————— 6. Prepared childbirth is a method of learning about breathing and other techniques so that pain is eliminated during childbirth.

——————— 7. During the first month after childbirth, a mother's dominant emotional response is a feeling of fulfillment and inner strength.

——————— 8. Children raised by lesbian mothers resemble children raised by heterosexual mothers in characteristics such as intelligence, psychological well-being, and popularity.

——————— 9. Approximately half of North American mothers experience postpartum blues within a few days after the birth of their first child; common symptoms include crying, sadness, and irritability.

——————— 10. In the current decade, people tend to evaluate a woman positively if she chooses not to have children.

Dr. Ingrid Johnston-Robledo is a psychologist who is young, European American, and married. She was also visibly pregnant at the time she wrote a chapter on motherhood (Johnston-Robledo, 2000). She commented on the contradictory messages she received from others, depending on the social context in which they saw her:

> I am greeted by strangers who smile at me with approval. They are seemingly pleased with my choice and ability to fulfill the role of mother. Sometimes these perfect strangers (usually women who have been through this themselves) actually stop me to touch my belly, attempt to figure out the sex of the fetus based on my shape, or ask me plenty of pregnancy-related questions. . . . However, when I am accompanied by my Puerto Rican husband and bicultural toddler, people react to me differently. Their glances are neutral or they appear curious, to put it politely. They may be thinking . . . "they're probably not married" or "look, there she is, pregnant again." The other day a man walked by us and said to his companion as he pointed at us, "See, there it is . . . that's the problem, that's what I'm talking about right there." Were we walking examples of a social ill? (p. 129)

As we'll see throughout this chapter, women are likely to receive mixed messages about childbirth and motherhood.

The world currently has more than 6 billion inhabitants, each of whom was produced by a woman's pregnancy. Shouldn't the sheer frequency of this personally important event make it a popular topic for psychological research? However, the topic of pregnancy is almost invisible in psychology (Greene, 2004; Johnston-Robledo & Barnack, 2004; Rice & Else-Quest, 2005; Stanton et al., 2002). Each year, psychologists write a limited number of journal articles on issues such as teen pregnancy, unwanted pregnancy, and drug abuse or violence during pregnancy. In contrast, psychologists tend to ignore the experiences of women who are happy to be pregnant and are looking forward to being mothers (Matlin, 2003).

The media provide another context in which the motherhood sequence is invisible. In Chapter 8, we saw that the theme of love dominates music, television, and entertainment. Sexuality—the focus of Chapter 9—is equally prominent. However, pregnancy and childbirth are relatively invisible topics, consistent with Theme 3, and the subtleties of mother-infant relationships are rarely explored in depth.

Let's examine these phases of reproduction in more detail. As you'll see, each phase has important psychological components.

PREGNANCY

What are the major biological components of pregnancy? How do women react to pregnancy, both emotionally and physically? Also, how do other people react to pregnant women? Finally, how do women combine pregnancy with their employment?

THE BIOLOGY OF PREGNANCY

Typically, the egg and the sperm unite while the egg is traveling down a fallopian tube. Interestingly, even an act that seems as value free as the joining of the egg and the sperm may be represented in a gender-biased fashion. You probably learned from your high-school biology textbook that the male sperm penetrates the female egg. However, this description is inaccurate because the egg is much more active during fertilization. In fact, part of the egg reaches out and draws the sperm inward. The egg then penetrates the head of the sperm, distributing the sperm's genetic material throughout the egg (Crooks & Baur, 2005; E. Martin, 2001; Rabuzzi, 1994).

The fertilized egg continues along the fallopian tube, floats around in the uterus for several days, and then may implant itself in the thick tissue that lines the uterus. If a fertilized egg does not implant itself, then this tissue is sloughed off as menstrual flow. This is the same menstrual flow that occurs when an egg has not been fertilized. However, if implantation does occur, this tissue provides an ideal environment in which a fertilized egg can develop into a baby.

Shortly after the fertilized egg has implanted itself, the placenta begins to develop. The **placenta**, which is connected to the growing embryo, is an organ that allows oxygen and nutrients to pass from the mother to the embryo. The placenta also helps transport the embryo's waste products back to the mother's system. This amazing organ even manufactures hormones. By the end of her pregnancy, a woman's estrogen and progesterone levels are much higher than they were before her pregnancy (L. L. Alexander et al., 2004).

Typically, a woman first suspects she is pregnant when she has been sexually active and then misses a menstrual period. A pregnancy test is necessary to confirm that she is pregnant because a woman can be pregnant and have a menstrual period or she can miss a menstrual period for reasons other than pregnancy (L. L. Alexander et al., 2004; Hyde & DeLamater, 2006).

Prenatal care is essential for identifying and treating any complications related to pregnancy as well as for providing relevant information. However, only 65% of pregnant women in developed regions of the world receive prenatal care. In developing countries, that percentage is even lower. In Afghanistan, for instance, only 8% of women have at least one prenatal visit during their pregnancy (United Nations, 2000).

PHYSICAL REACTIONS DURING PREGNANCY

Pregnancy affects virtually every organ system in a woman's body, although most of the consequences are relatively minor. The most obvious changes are weight gain and a protruding abdomen. During pregnancy, many women also report breast tenderness, frequent urination, and fatigue (L. L. Alexander et al., 2004; Hyde & DeLamater, 2006).

Nausea is another especially common symptom during the first trimester. It is often called morning sickness, even though it may occur at any time of the day (Feeney et al., 2001; Murkoff et al., 2002). Surveys suggest that 70% to 90% of all pregnant women will experience nausea at some point in their pregnancy (Q. Zhou et al., 1999).

Our general theme about the wide range of individual differences holds true with pregnancy as with other phases in women's lives (Stanton et al., 2002). For instance, the majority of women are less interested in sexual activity during pregnancy, but some actually report more interest in sex (Haugen et al., 2004; Hyde & DeLamater, 2000; Murkoff et al., 2002; P. Schwartz, 2000). Furthermore, "pregnant couples" often enjoy other forms of sexual expression.

EMOTIONAL REACTIONS DURING PREGNANCY

> All I seem to think about is the baby. . . . I'm so excited. I'd love to have the baby right now. Somehow this week I feel on top of the world. I love watching my whole tummy move. (Lederman, 1996, p. 35)

> I think I, in a sense, have a prepartum depression—already! . . . Over Easter, when I was home from teaching, it just really hit me how I would be home like that all the time. . . . I was very depressed one day just kind of anticipating it and realizing how much of a change it was going to be, because I had been really active with my teaching, and it had been a pretty major part of my life now for four years. (Lederman, 1996, p. 39)

These quotations from two pregnant women illustrate how individual women respond differently to the same life event, consistent with Theme 4. In pregnancy, the situation is extremely unpredictable because each woman may experience a wide variety of emotions during the 9 months of her pregnancy. For example, those two quotations, although different in emotional tone, could have come from the same woman.

POSITIVE EMOTIONS. For many women, the news that they are pregnant brings a rush of positive emotions, excitement, and anticipation. Many women report feeling wonder and awe at the thought of having a new, growing person inside their own bodies. In a study of married couples, many husbands also shared this sense of wonder in creating a new life (Feeney et al., 2001).

Most married women also sense that other people approve of their pregnancy, as we noted at the beginning of the chapter. After all, women are supposed to have children, so friends and family members typically offer social support (Morling et al., 2003).

For many women, pregnancy represents a transition into adulthood. They may describe a sense of purpose and accomplishment about being pregnant (Leifer, 1980). Another positive emotion is the growing sense of attachment that pregnant women feel toward the developing baby (Bergum, 1997; Condon & Corkindale, 1997). One woman reported:

> When I had my first scan, the man explained everything, like this is his leg, this is his foot, little hands, little head. I couldn't see his other leg and asked "Where's his other leg then?" Then they pushed him round and showed me his other leg. It was quite nice. That's when you realize you are having a baby, when you actually see it on the scan. (Woollett & Marshall, 1997, p. 189)

In addition, many pregnant women find pleasure in anticipating the tasks of motherhood and child rearing, which they believe will provide a tremendous source of satisfaction. As we'll see in the section on motherhood, their expectations may be different from reality.

NEGATIVE EMOTIONS. Pregnant women typically express some negative feelings, fears, and anxieties, such as concern about the pain of childbirth (Feeney et al., 2001; Melender, 2002; L. J. Miller, 2001). Some women report that their emotions are fragile and continually changing. However, the clear majority of women remain within the normal emotional range of emotions during pregnancy. Most women adapt well, and the stress levels do not harm the developing fetus (DiPietro, 2004; Johnston-Robledo & Barnack, 2004; Stanton et al., 2002).

Another potential problem is that a woman's self-image may deteriorate as she watches her body grow bigger (Philipp & Carr, 2001). Women often say that they feel fat and ugly during pregnancy, especially because North American culture values slimness.

Interestingly, however, these women's romantic partners may feel otherwise. For example, C. P. Cowan and Cowan (1992) questioned married couples who were expecting a baby. They noted that most husbands respond positively. For instance, one man named Eduardo was looking at his wife, and he remarked, "The great painters tried to show the beauty of a pregnant woman, but when I look at Sonia, I feel they didn't do it justice" (p. 59). Fortunately, many women are able to overcome our culture's concern about weight. They are excited to see their abdomen swell, to feel the baby move, and to anticipate a healthy pregnancy.

Women may worry about their health and bodily functions (Johnston-Robledo & Barnack, 2004). These anxieties are heightened by the increasing evidence that smoking, alcohol, a variety of drugs, and environmental contaminants can harm the developing fetus (T. Field, 1998; R. B. Ness et al., 1999; Newland & Rasmussen, 2003; Streissguth et al., 1999). Incidentally, studies in both the United States and Canada show that many pregnant women try to stop smoking cigarettes during their pregnancy, but it's difficult to break this addiction (N. Edwards & Sims-Jones, 1998). About 11% of all women continue to smoke throughout their pregnancy. The smoking rate is highest for Native American and White women and lowest for Latina and Asian women (Arias et al., 2003; Hoyert et al., 2000).

An important part of women's negative reactions to pregnancy is caused by other people beginning to respond differently to them, as we will see in the next section. They are categorized as "pregnant women"—that is, women who have no identity aside from the responsibility of a growing baby (Philipp & Carr, 2001). Women may also begin to see themselves in these terms.

Naturally, however, a woman's overall response to pregnancy depends on factors such as her physical reactions to pregnancy, whether the pregnancy was planned, her relationship with the baby's father, and her economic status (Barker et al., 2000; Hyde & DeLamater, 2000; Tolman, 2002; Webster et al., 2000). We can understand predominantly negative emotions from an unmarried, pregnant 16-year-old whose boyfriend and family have rejected her and who must work as a waitress to earn an income. Her problems will be intensified if she is one of the thousands of pregnant women in the United States who cannot afford prenatal care (S. E. Taylor, 2002; P. H. Wise, 2002). We can also understand predominantly positive emotions from a happily married 26-year-old who has hoped for this pregnancy for 2 years and whose family income allows her to buy the stylish maternity clothes that she can wear to her interesting, fulfilling job (Feeney et al., 2001).

During pregnancy, some women will experience a **miscarriage,** or an unintended termination of pregnancy, before the fetus is developed enough to survive after birth. For instance, in Figure 9.2 (p. 311), we saw that—each year—an estimated 15% of pregnant teenagers in the United States experience a miscarriage. We cannot provide an accurate estimate of miscarriage rates for teenagers or for pregnant women of any age because a large percentage of miscarriages occur during early pregnancy, outside a medical setting. As you can imagine, some women will experience extreme grief about this loss (McCreight, 2005). Others feel a sense of relief or else mixed emotions.

In summary, a woman's emotional reaction to pregnancy can range from excitement and anticipation to worry, a loss of identity, and grief (Statham et al., 1997). Consistent with Theme 4 of this book, the individual differences can be enormous. For most women, pregnancy is a complex blend of both pleasant and unpleasant reactions.

ATTITUDES TOWARD PREGNANT WOMEN

Most women experience three major gynecological events: menarche, pregnancy, and menopause. Menarche and menopause are highly private events, which women discuss only with intimate acquaintances. In contrast, pregnancy is public, especially in the last trimester. The quotation at the beginning of the chapter noted that strangers may feel free to pat the stomach of a pregnant woman and offer unsolicited comments to her. Can you imagine these same people taking such liberties with a woman who was *not* pregnant?

Some recent research by Michelle Hebl and her colleagues (2006) shows that people's attitudes toward pregnant women depend on the context. These researchers arranged for young women to go to a retail store, in two different contexts. In half of the situations, the woman was instructed to ask if she could apply for a job. In the other half, the woman was instructed to ask for help in choosing a gift for her sister. The second variable in this study was whether or not the woman looked pregnant. Half the time in each situation, the woman wore a "pregnancy prosthesis," which had been professionally constructed to resemble the stomach of a woman who was 6- to 7-months pregnant. The other half of the time, the woman did not wear a prosthesis. Meanwhile, observers unobtrusively watched and coded the way that the store employee interacted with the woman.

In Chapter 2, we discussed two kinds of sexism that people are likely to display toward women. **Hostile sexism,** the more blatant kind of sexism, is based on the idea that women should be subservient to men and should "know their place." When the woman in this study asked to apply for a job, the store employees showed significantly more hostile sexism to the pregnant-looking woman than to the non-pregnant-looking woman. After all, this woman is pregnant, and she shouldn't be out looking for a job! Other studies have confirmed this bias against hiring a pregnant woman for a job (Bragger et al., 2002).

Benevolent sexism, the more subtle kind of sexism, argues for women's special niceness and purity. When the woman in the study by Hebl and her colleagues asked for help in buying a gift, the employees showed significantly more benevolent sexism to the pregnant-looking woman than to the non-pregnant-looking woman. After all, this woman is pregnant, so she needs extra help; the store employees were overly helpful and even patronizing. Other research confirms that people are especially likely to help a pregnant woman, for example, if she has dropped her keys (Walton et al., 1988).

In another study, Horgan (1983) measured people's attitudes toward pregnant women by checking where maternity clothes were located in department stores. The expensive, high-status stores placed maternity clothes near the lingerie and loungewear. This arrangement suggests an image of femininity, delicacy, luxury, and privacy. In contrast, the less expensive, low-status stores placed maternity clothes near the uniforms and the clothing for overweight women. This placement implies that pregnant women are fat, with a job to do. Try Demonstration 10.1, a modification of Horgan's study.

Demonstration 10.1

ATTITUDES
TOWARD
PREGNANT
WOMEN,
AS ILLUSTRATED
IN DEPARTMENT
STORES

Select several nearby stores that sell maternity clothes. Try to obtain a sample of stores that vary in social status, and visit each store. (You may want to come prepared with a "shopping for a pregnant friend" cover story.) Record where the maternity clothes are placed. Are they near the lingerie, the clothes for overweight women, the uniforms, or someplace else?

Also notice the nature of the clothes themselves. In the 1970s, the clothes were infantile, with ruffles and bows. Clothes are now more like clothing for nonpregnant women. Do the different kinds of stores feature different styles?

Finally, check on the price of the clothing. How much would a pregnant woman's wardrobe be likely to cost, assuming that she will need maternity clothes during the last 6 months of her pregnancy?

EMPLOYMENT DURING PREGNANCY

Several decades ago, European American women in the United States and Canada typically stopped working outside the home once they became pregnant. However, Black women have had different expectations. Being a good mother never meant that a woman should stay at home full time (P. H. Collins, 1991). In developing countries, pregnant women are often expected to work in the fields or to perform other physically exhausting tasks, sometimes until labor begins (S. Kitzinger, 1995).

In North America in the current decade, many women plan to have both a career and children, especially if the women are college graduates (Hoffnung, 2003, 2004). The research shows that pregnant women often continue at their jobs until shortly before their due date (Hung et al., 2002; Mozurkewich et al., 2000).

According to the research, a woman's pregnancy will typically not be affected if her job involves normal physical exertion (Hung et al., 2002; Klebanoff et al., 1990). However, she is slightly more likely to have a premature delivery if her job is physically demanding, if she works on the night shift, and if her job involves prolonged standing without the opportunity to sit down (Mozurkewich et al., 2000).

Section Summary

Pregnancy

1. Pregnancy and childbirth receive little attention in psychological research and in the media.

2. At the beginning of pregnancy, the fertilized egg implants itself in the tissue that lines the uterus, and the placenta develops shortly afterward.

3. Although individual differences are great, several common physical reactions to pregnancy include weight gain, fatigue, and nausea.

4. Women vary greatly in their emotional reactions to pregnancy. Positive emotions include feelings of excitement and wonder, a sense of purpose, growing attachment, and the anticipated pleasure of motherhood.

5. Negative emotions include fragile emotions, concerns about physical appearance, health worries, and concern about other people's reactions. An unknown percentage of pregnant women also experience a miscarriage.

6. When people interact with a woman who looks pregnant, they tend to show hostile sexism if she is doing something considered nontraditional, such as applying for a job. They show benevolent sexism if she is doing something traditionally feminine, such as shopping for a gift.

7. Most women can work outside the home without affecting their pregnancy; however, a physically demanding job and nonstandard work hours are associated with a slightly higher risk of premature delivery.

CHILDBIRTH

Women in the United States currently have an average of 2.1 children, and Canadian women have an average of 1.6 children (United Nations, 2005b). In other words, childbirth is extremely common in North America. However, psychologists virtually ignore this important event. Interesting topics, such as women's emotions during childbirth, are almost invisible. In fact, most of our information comes from nursing journals. Let's consider the biology of childbirth and emotional reactions to childbirth. Then we'll consider some current practices that are likely to improve women's childbirth experiences.

The Biology of Childbirth

Labor for childbirth begins when the uterus starts to contract strongly. The labor period is divided into three stages. During the first stage, the uterus contracts about every 5 minutes. Also, the dilation of the cervix increases to about 10 centimeters (4 inches), a process that may last anywhere from a few hours to at least a day (L. L. Alexander et al., 2004; Feeney et al., 2001).

The second stage of labor lasts from a few minutes to several hours. The contractions move the baby farther down the vagina. When a woman is encouraged to push during this second stage, she usually says that this is the most positive part of labor (Crooks & Baur, 2005). Women report feelings of strong pressure and stretching during this stage. The contractions often become extremely painful and stressful (Soet et al., 2003). During the second stage, the mother's progesterone levels begin to drop. This stage ends when the baby is born. The photograph on page 331 illustrates the end of the second stage of labor.

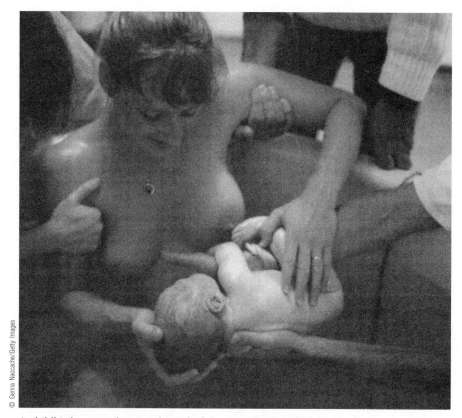

A childbirth scene, showing the end of the second stage of labor.

The third stage of labor, which usually lasts less than 20 minutes, is clearly an anticlimax. The placenta separates from the uterine wall, and then it is expelled along with some other tissue that had surrounded the fetus. The levels of estrogen and progesterone drop during this third stage, so that both of them are drastically lower than they were several hours earlier.

Social factors can profoundly affect the health of both the mother and her newborn ("Challenging Cases," 2004; Hoyert et al., 2000). In a study conducted in Ireland, for example, pregnant women participated in a program that included customized childbirth classes and a nurse assigned to each woman for the entire childbirth experience. Labor was 2.7 hours shorter for this group than for a similar group of women who had the standard treatment (Frigoletto et al., 1995). Another study in a hospital in the African nation of Botswana reported that women required significantly less pain medication if they had been accompanied by a female relative during labor and delivery (Madi et al., 1999).

For women in many cultures—as diverse as Scandinavian countries and Mayan communities in Latin America—childbirth is considered a normal process rather than a medical achievement. In these cultures, women expect to have attendants with them during childbirth (DeLoache & Gottlieb, 2000; Klaus et al., 2002; Whelehan, 2001). Many North American hospitals now offer a doula (*doo*-lah) option. A **doula** is a woman experienced in childbirth who provides continuous support to a family throughout labor and delivery ("Challenging Cases," 2004).

Currently, 29% of all deliveries in the United States and 17% in Canada are performed by cesarean section (Canadian Institute for Health Information, 2004; Hoyert et al., 2000; Diony Young, 2003). In a **cesarean section** (pronounced sih-*zare*-ee-un; abbreviated as **C-section**), the physician makes an incision through the woman's abdomen and into the uterus to deliver the baby.

Some cesarean sections are necessary if a vaginal delivery would be risky—for example, because the baby's head is larger than the mother's pelvis (L. L. Alexander et al., 2004). However, a C-section carries health risks for both a mother and her baby (R. Walker et al., 2002). A C-section can also be a traumatic experience (Johnston-Robledo & Barnack, 2004). Critics argue that the rate of C-sections is high because they are more convenient for the medical staff and other similar reasons (M. C. Klein, 2004; Diony Young, 2003).

A woman normally gives birth after 40 weeks' gestation. A **preterm birth** is defined as less than 37 weeks' gestation, and a preterm birth places a child at risk for medical complications. The research in the United States shows that women with little education and overly thin women are at risk for a preterm birth. Also, Black women are almost twice as likely as White, Latina, and Asian mothers to have a preterm birth. After adjusting for factors such as the age of the mother and her level of education, Black women are still more likely than other women to have a preterm birth. Researchers have not yet figured out why ethnicity should be an important factor, but it may involve differences in health prior to pregnancy (R. L. Goldenberg & Culhane, 2005; Haas et al., 2005).

EMOTIONAL REACTIONS TO CHILDBIRTH

Women's emotional reactions to the birth of their child can vary as widely as their reactions to pregnancy (Johnston-Robledo & Barnack, 2004; Wuitchik et al., 1990). For some women, childbirth can be a peak experience of feeling in tune with the birth. For instance, one woman described her intense joy when her firstborn arrived:

> I have never had such a high as after he was born! I guess it's the first child; you're so up for the whole thing. I think I could have flown if I had tried. . . . I have never felt that way about anything else at all: not getting married, not my other kids, nothing. (Hoffnung, 1992, p. 17)

Another woman describes how she coped with pain by focusing on the child who would be born:

> I don't think one should focus on the pain, that women should have to experience pain. But in the pain there is an experience of being inward and involved in feeling the pain—not enjoying it but taking hold, enduring, or whatever you do to handle it—and knowing that it is going to produce a child. (Bergum, 1997, p. 41)

Fathers who participate in the birth of their child may also experience intense joy, as in this description, which a new father offered:

> I couldn't have imagined the incredibly powerful feelings that engulfed me when I saw Kevin slip out of Tanya. I was right there, and this was my son! All the next day whenever he began to cry or nurse, I was in tears. I'm still transfixed watching him. It's the most amazing experience I ever had. (C. P. Cowan & Cowan, 1992, p. 71)

ALTERNATIVE MODELS OF CHILDBIRTH

Many healthcare advocates suggest that the childbirth experience can be made more comfortable and emotionally satisfying for women. The most widely used approaches, called **prepared childbirth,** feature the following elements (L. L. Alexander et al., 2004; Allgeier & Allgeier, 2000; Hyde & DeLamater, 2006):

1. Education about pregnancy and childbirth, to reduce fear and dispel myths.
2. Relaxation techniques and exercises designed to strengthen muscles.
3. Controlled breathing techniques, which distract attention away from the pain of the contractions.
4. Social support throughout childbirth from the baby's father, the mother's partner, or a person trained as a caregiver.

People who emphasize prepared childbirth point out that this method does not eliminate pain. Childbirth is still a stressful experience. However, women who have had a helpful companion present during childbirth are significantly more satisfied with the childbirth experience (Dannenbring et al., 1997). Prepared childbirth seems to provide a number of substantial benefits (Chalmers, 2002; Diony Young, 1982). The mothers report more positive attitudes, less anxiety, and reduced pain. They also require less medication.

The technology of childbirth has made impressive advances during the past 50 years. Death rates are lower for both mothers and infants. An unfortunate side effect of this high-tech approach, however, is that births in hospitals may focus on expensive equipment, fetal monitoring, and sanitizing every part of the mother (Chalmers, 2002; Howell-White, 1999; Wolf, 2001).

In contrast to the high-tech approach, the **family-centered approach** in the United States and Canada emphasizes that safe, high-quality health care can be delivered while focusing on the woman's sense of individuality and her autonomy, as well as her family's psychosocial needs (C. R. Phillips, 2000; "Spotlight on Canada," 2000; Diony Young, 1982, 1993). The family-centered approach acknowledges that some high-risk pregnancies may require special technology. However, the vast majority of births are normal. Instead of focusing exclusively on the medical aspects of childbirth, the family-centered approach insists that professionals should realize that childbirth is an important psychological event in which a family is born and new relationships are formed. Mothers, not technology, should be at the center of the childbirth experience (Chalmers, 2002; Dahlberg et al., 1999; Pincus, 2000).

Demonstration 10.2

Locate women who had babies very recently, about 10 years ago, about 20 years ago, and in some year long before you were born. If possible, include your own mother or close relatives in your interview. Ask each of these women to describe her childbirth experience in as much detail as possible. After each woman has finished, you may wish to ask some of the following questions, if they were not already answered:

1. Were you given any medication? If so, do you remember what kind?
2. How long did you stay in the hospital?
3. Did the baby stay with you in the room, or was she or he returned to the nursery after feedings?
4. Was a relative or friend allowed in the room while you were giving birth?
5. When you were in labor, were you encouraged to lie down?
6. Did you have "prepared childbirth"?
7. Do you recall any negative treatment from any of the hospital staff?
8. Were you treated like a competent adult?
9. Do you recall any positive treatment from any of the hospital staff?
10. If you could have changed any one thing about your childbirth experience, what would that have been?

Some of the changes that promote the family-centered approach include the following (M. C. Klein, 2004; Kozak & Weeks, 2002; Pincus, 2000; Soet et al., 2003; Van Olphen-Fehr, 1998; Diony Young, 1982, 1993):

1. The physician should not artificially induce labor simply because it may be more convenient.
2. Women should have special birthing rooms to make the birth experience more pleasant.
3. A supportive family member, friend, or doula should be present.
4. Women should move around during labor, and they can choose to sit upright during childbirth.
5. Hospital birth practices that have no health benefits should be modified. These include routine enemas and shaving the genital area.
6. Anesthetics should not be used unless necessary or desired.
7. Health-care providers must be empathic individuals who can encourage women's sense of empowerment during childbirth.

The family-centered approach to childbirth emphasizes that the mother's wishes should be taken seriously. This approach helps redistribute power, so that women in childbirth have more control over their own bodies. Women can make decisions about how they want to give birth, rather than being passive and infantilized.

Try Demonstration 10.2 to learn about the childbirth experiences of several women you know. Also, can you detect any changes in childbirth procedures for women with the most recent birth experiences?

Section Summary

Childbirth

1. The three stages in labor are dilation of the cervix, childbirth, and expulsion of the placenta. Social factors can influence the duration of labor and the amount of pain medication required.

2. Two potential problems during childbirth are cesarean sections and preterm births.

3. Reactions to childbirth vary widely. Some women report an intensely positive experience; others focus on coping with the pain.

4. Prepared childbirth emphasizes education, relaxation, exercise, controlled breathing, and social support; this approach generally produces a more satisfying childbirth experience.

5. The family-centered approach to childbirth focuses on supporting women in labor; it discourages the unnecessary use of high-technology procedures.

MOTHERHOOD

The word *motherhood* suggests some stereotypes that are well established, although contradictory; we'll consider these stereotypes in the first part of this section. Next we'll see how those stereotypes contrast with reality. We'll also examine the motherhood experience of two groups of women outside the mainstream of European American heterosexual mothers: women of color and lesbian women. We'll then focus on two issues of concern to many women who have just given birth: postpartum depression and breast feeding. The final topics in this chapter focus on the decision about returning to the workplace, the option of deciding not to have children, and the problem of infertility.

STEREOTYPES ABOUT MOTHERHOOD

For most people, the word *motherhood* inspires a rich variety of pleasant emotions such as warmth, strength, protectiveness, nurturance, devotion, and self-sacrifice (Ganong & Coleman, 1995; Johnston & Swanson, 2003b; Swanson & Johnston, 2003). According to the stereotype, a pregnant woman is expected to be joyously upbeat, eagerly anticipating the blessed event. Motherhood is portrayed as happy and satisfying, a notion that is perpetuated by media images of the "Perfect Mother" (Johnston-Robledo, 2000; Maushart, 1999; J. Warner, 2005). Furthermore, the motherhood stereotype emphasizes that a woman's ultimate fulfillment is achieved by becoming a mother (P. J. Caplan, 1998, 2000, 2001; Johnston & Swanson, 2003b).

The motherhood stereotype also specifies that a mother will feel perfectly competent as soon as she sees her newborn, and her "natural" mothering skills will take over (Johnston & Swanson, 2003b; Johnston-Robledo, 2000). She is also completely devoted to her family, and she shows no concern for her own personal needs (S. J. Douglas & Michaels, 2004; Ex & Janssens, 2000; Johnston & Swanson, 2003b). As you might imagine, many mothers feel guilty when they cannot live up to this impossible standard of perfect mothering (P. J. Caplan, 2001; S. J. Douglas & Michaels, 2004; J. Warner, 2005).

North American culture is actually ambivalent about motherhood, although the negative aspects are generally less prominent. The media exaggerate the faults of some mothers, while simultaneously ignoring their positive attributes. Also, when children develop a psychological problem, therapists usually blame the mother, not the father (P. J. Caplan, 2000, 2001). You'll recall from Chapter 2 that women in classical mythology and religion are sometimes saints and sometimes villains. Stereotypes about mothers provide similar images of these two extremes (P. J. Caplan, 2001).

THE REALITY OF MOTHERHOOD

Many lofty phrases pay tribute to motherhood, but the role is actually accorded low prestige (P. J. Caplan, 2000; Hoffnung, 1995). Our society really values money, power, and achievement—rather than motherhood (J. Warner, 2005). In reality, mothers do not receive the appreciation they deserve.

None of the stereotypes captures the rich variety of emotions that mothers actually experience. Columnist Anna Quindlen (2001a) describes this perspective:

> My children have been the making of me as a human being, which does not mean that they have not sometimes been an overwhelming and mind-boggling responsibility. . . I love my children more than life itself. But just because you love people doesn't mean that taking care of them day in and day out isn't often hard, and sometimes even horrible. (p. 64)

Before you read further, try Demonstration 10.3, which we'll discuss later in this chapter. Let's now explore the reality of motherhood in more detail. We'll first consider a long list of negative factors and then examine the more abstract, but intensely positive factors.

NEGATIVE FACTORS.   A newborn infant certainly creates pressures and stress for the mother. Here are some of the negative factors that women often mention:

1. Child care is physically exhausting, and sleep deprivation is also common (Cusk, 2002; Huston & Holmes, 2004; J. F. Thompson et al., 2002). Because infant care takes so much time, new mothers often feel that they can accomplish very little other than taking care of the infant.
2. Roughly 35% of all infants in the United States are born to women who are not married (Hoyert et al., 2000). The father may not live in the same house, and the mother may not have adequate income to raise children.

Demonstration 10.3

INFANT MORTALITY RATE

Look at the list of 15 countries below, and think about which ones are likely to have a low infant mortality rate (i.e., a low rate of an infant dying within the first year of life). All 15 countries have at least a reasonably good health-care system, and their infant mortality rates range between 3 and 7 infant deaths per 1,000 infants. Rate these countries, placing a 3 in front of the countries that you think would have the lowest rates, so they are the *safest* for infants. Place a 7 in front of the countries that you think would have the highest rates, so they are the *least safe* for infants. Continue rating the 15 countries, using a scale that ranges from 3 to 7. The answers appear at the end of the chapter.

_____ Australia	_____ Japan	_____ Belgium
_____ Greece	_____ France	_____ Czech Republic
_____ Cuba	_____ Sweden	_____ Ireland
_____ Israel	_____ Germany	_____ Poland
_____ Denmark	_____ United States	_____ Canada

Note: These data represent infant mortality rates for 2003, the most recent international data available.

Source: United Nations (2005a).

3. Fathers who do live in the same home usually help much less with child rearing than mothers had expected. As we noted in Chapter 7, mothers take the major responsibility for child care, including less pleasant tasks such as changing diapers (Gjerdingen & Center, 2005; Milkie et al., 2002; Rice & Else-Quest, 2006).

4. For several weeks after childbirth, women report that they feel leaky and dirty, coping with after-birth discharges. They are also likely to feel pain in the vaginal area and in the uterus (J. F. Thompson et al., 2002).

5. New mothers seldom have training for the tasks of motherhood; they often report feeling incompetent. As a result, they may wonder why no one warned them about the difficulty of child care or how their life would change after the baby was born (Fuligni & Brooks-Gunn, 2002; Gager et al., 2002; J. Warner, 2005).

6. Pregnant women often create a vision of the glowing baby they expect to cuddle in their arms. In reality, babies cry much more than parents expect, and they do not smile until they are about 2 months old (Feeney et al., 2001).

7. Because mothering is done at home, mothers of newborns may have little contact with other adults (Johnston & Swanson, 2006). Friends and extended family may not be available to provide support. A single mother may regret that she has no social interactions. This kind of isolation further encourages the invisibility of women, already an important issue throughout this book.

8. Because the woman's attention has shifted to the newborn, her romantic partner may feel neglected. Many mothers comment that their husbands make them feel guilty about not being adequate. However, parents and nonparents are equally positive about the quality of their marriage (Huston & Holmes, 2004).

9. Women feel disappointed in themselves because they do not match the standards of the ideal mother, the completely unselfish and perfect woman. She is our culture's stereotype of motherhood—but no one really lives up to that stereotype (P. J. Caplan, 2000; Quindlen, 2005a).

Among all these negative factors is another one—so horrifying that I cannot simply add it to the end of the preceding list. However, the reality is that a large number of infants die at an early age. The most common measure is called the **infant mortality rate,** which is the annual number of deaths prior to the first birthday, per 1,000 live births. For instance, in Angola, Liberia, Mali, Sierra Leone, and other sub-Saharan African countries, more than 100 out of every 1,000 infants die before their first birthday (United Nations, 2005a). Some so-called developed countries also have a much higher child death rate than most people expect. Check your responses to Demonstration 10.3 against the answers on page 353. Did you guess that the United States has the worst record among the 15 countries on this list?

POSITIVE FACTORS.   Motherhood also has its positive side, although these qualities may not predominate early in motherhood. Some women discover that an important positive consequence of motherhood is a sense of their own strength. As one woman told me, "I discovered that I felt very empowered and confident, like, 'Don't mess with me! I've given birth!'" (T. Napper, personal communication, 1998). Sadly, we often focus so much on childbirth's negative consequences for women that we fail to explore the life-enhancing consequences. As one woman wrote:

> I had a child at 46. Before that, although I loved being with other people's children, anytime something went wrong and the child irritated me, I would think to myself, How could I ever stand the full-time responsibility of being a mother? Somehow, becoming a mother changed that. There is an intangible, indescribable bond intrinsic to the relationship, which in the long run transcends the petty everyday irritating occurrences. (Boston Women's Health Book Collective, 2005, p. 311)

Parents often point out that children can be fun and interesting, especially when they can look at the world from a new viewpoint, through the eyes of a child. In addition, one mother explained how her children developed an important part of her personality: "My kids have opened up emotions in me that I never knew were possible; they have slowed down my life happily" (Villani, 1997, p. 135). Many women point out that having children helped them to identify and develop their ability to nurture (Bergum, 1997).

We also need to acknowledge that many fathers are very competent in caring for their children (R. C. Barnett & Rivers, 2004; Deutsch, 1999). Many fathers also express their admiration and affection for their partner. In these families, marital satisfaction increases after children are born (Shapiro et al., 2000). Many mothers and fathers say that they enjoy the sense of unity and feeling like a family (Feeney et al., 2001).

Summarizing the comments of many mothers, Hoffnung (1995) wrote:

> The role of mother brings with it benefits as well as limitations. Children affect parents in ways that lead to personal growth, enable reworking of childhood conflicts, build flexibility and empathy, and provide intimate, loving human connections. . . . They expand their caretakers' worlds by their activity levels, their imaginations, and their inherently appealing natures. Although motherhood is not enough to fill an entire life, for most mothers, it is one of the most meaningful experiences in their lives. (p. 174)

If you were to ask a mother of an infant to list the positive and negative qualities of motherhood, the negative list would probably contain more items and more specific details. Most mothers find that the positive side of motherhood is more abstract, more difficult to describe, and yet more intense (Feeney et al., 2001). The drudgery of dirty diapers is much easier to talk about than the near ecstasy of realizing that this complete human being was once part of your own body, and now this baby breathes and gurgles and hiccups independently.

Also, shortly after birth, babies develop ways of communicating with other humans. The delights of a baby's first tentative smile are undeniable. An older baby can interact even more engagingly with adults by making appropriate eye contact and conversational noises. Most mothers also enjoy watching their babies develop new skills. They also value the intimate, caring relationships they develop with their children (Feeney et al., 2001). Motherhood has numerous joyous aspects. Unfortunately, our society has not yet devised creative ways to diminish the negative aspects so that we can appreciate the joys more completely.

MOTHERHOOD AND WOMEN OF COLOR

The U.S. Census Bureau (2005) provides information for each major ethnic group about the average number of children that a woman would be expected to have in her lifetime. (Keep in mind that many women in each group do not have any children.) These ethnic-group differences are smaller than many people expect: 2.1 for White and Black women, 2.3 for Asian women, 2.5 for Native Americans, and 2.8 for Latina women.

The data on family size may be fairly similar, but the motherhood experiences of women of color often differ from the European American experience. Unfortunately, these mothers are still surprisingly invisible in the social science research, even in the more comprehensive resources about women of color (Hellenga et al., 2002).

Several theorists have pointed out the stabilizing influence of extended families in Black culture (Kirk & Okazawa-Rey, 2001; H. P. McAdoo, 2002; Parke, 2004). These networks of grandmothers, aunts, siblings, and close family friends are especially important among economically poor mothers (P. H. Collins, 1991).

The extended family is also important for Latina/o families (Cisneros, 2001; Harwood et al., 2002; Matsumoto & Juang, 2004). For instance, many immigrants from Latin America move in with relatives who are already established in North America. As a result, young Latina/o children are likely to be cared for by members of their extended family (Leyendecker & Lamb, 1999; Parke, 2004). In Chapter 8, we saw that *marianismo* is the belief among Latinas/os that women must be passive and long suffering, giving up their own needs to help their husbands and children (de las Fuentes et al., 2003; Hurtado, 2003). Ginorio and her colleagues (1995) emphasized that real-life Latina mothers are not passive; instead, they hold substantial power within the family. Furthermore, Latina mothers are currently reshaping their roles and becoming more independent, especially as they enter the workforce in increasing numbers.

Some ethnic groups emphasize values in motherhood that would not be central for European American mothers. For example, many North American Indians emphasize the continuity of generations, with grandmothers being central when their daughters give birth (A. Adams, 1995). Consider Theresa, an Aboriginal woman living on the west coast of Canada. Theresa describes how her mother responded to the birth of Theresa's daughter:

> My mother came the day after she was born. She said, "I'm so proud of you. And I'm so happy that now you have a friend for yourself the way I have a friend for myself in you." And that really is how it is. My daughter's been a friend to me for a long time. (D. Morrison, 1987, p. 32)

Asian American perspectives on motherhood depend on the family's country of origin and the number of generations that the family has lived in North America (Parke, 2004). However, cultural beliefs may conflict with the U.S. medical model when women from Asia emigrate to the United States. For instance, Hmong women who have come to the United States from Southeast Asia are horrified at the prospect of being examined by a male obstetrician when they are pregnant. Other procedures, such as providing a urine sample, may seem terrifying to a Hmong woman, even if they are routine to European Americans (Symonds, 1996).

As P. H. Collins (1994) points out, our knowledge about motherhood will not be helped by claiming that the experiences of women of color are more valid than the experiences of White middle-class women. Instead, Collins emphasized that examining motherhood "from multiple perspectives should uncover rich textures of differences. Shifting the center to accommodate this diversity promises to recontextualize motherhood and point us toward feminist theorizing that embraces differences as an essential part of commonality" (p. 73).

LESBIAN MOTHERS

Lesbians become mothers by a variety of pathways. The largest number are women who had a child in a heterosexual relationship and later identified themselves as lesbians. Other lesbians decide to conceive by donor insemination, and still others adopt their children. Some lesbians are single parents; others live with their female partner (C. J. Patterson, 2003). As you might imagine, it's difficult to estimate how many lesbians are raising children. According to one estimate, about 40% of U.S. lesbian couples are raising children (Human Rights Campaign, 2003). Although comparable Canadian data are not available, an estimated 200,000 lesbian mothers live in Canada (Walks, 2005).

Several studies have compared the parenting styles of lesbian mothers and heterosexual mothers. The two groups are similar in characteristics such as their parenting quality, enthusiasm about child rearing, warmth toward children, and self-esteem (Golombok et al., 2003; S. M. Johnson & O'Connor, 2002; C. J. Patterson, 2003). However, compared to heterosexual mothers, lesbian mothers in one study were more likely to engage in imaginative play with their children and less likely to spank them (Golombok et al., 2003).

Other research—including a meta-analysis by M. Allen and Burrell (2002)—has compared the adjustment of children raised in lesbian households and children raised in heterosexual households. According to studies in both the United States and Canada, the children in the two groups are similar in characteristics such as intelligence, development, self-esteem, psychological well-being, popularity with peers, and positive feelings about their family (Foster, 2005; Golombok et al., 2003; S. M. Johnson & O'Connor, 2002; C. J. Patterson, 2003; Savin-Williams & Esterberg, 2000; Stacey & Biblarz, 2001; M. Sullivan, 2004; Tasker & Golombok, 1995).

My students often ask whether children raised by lesbians have trouble being accepted by the wider community, especially because of the problem of sexual prejudice. Although some children feel uncomfortable talking about their mothers' sexual orientation, most are positive about their mothers' nontraditional relationships (S. M. Johnson & O'Connor, 2001; C. J. Patterson & Chan, 1999; Tasker & Golombok, 1997). Many children also report that they are more accepting of all kinds of diversity, compared to the children of heterosexual parents (D. Johnson & Piore, 2004; C. J. Patterson, 2003; Peplau & Beals, 2004).

Numerous studies demonstrate that children raised by lesbian mothers are similar in psychological adjustment to children raised by heterosexual mothers.

As we have seen, the research confirms that children raised by lesbians are well adjusted and that they do not differ substantially from children raised by heterosexuals. In light of these findings, professional organizations have emphasized that the courts should not discriminate against lesbian mothers in custody cases and that lesbians should be allowed to adopt children (e.g., American Academy of Pediatrics, 2002a, 2002b; American Psychological Association, 2004).

However, in many parts of the United States, same-gender parents cannot legally adopt a child (C. J. Patterson, 2003; Peplau & Beals, 2004). Lesbian parents also face discrimination in numerous ways that heterosexual parents would never anticipate. For example, a hospital security guard refused to let two lesbian parents visit their child in the pediatric ward of a California hospital. As the guard said, the regulations allowed "only parents" on the ward (M. Sullivan, 2004, p. 177).

BREAST FEEDING

Currently, about 70% of North American mothers breast-feed their newborn infants, and 25% to 35% nurse their babies for at least 6 months (Callen & Pinelli, 2004). Mothers who breast-feed are likely to be better educated than mothers who bottle-feed (Heck et al., 2003; J. A. Scott et al., 2004; Slusser & Lange, 2002). Mothers who are in their 30s or older are also more likely than younger mothers to breast-feed (J. A. Scott et al., 2004; Slusser & Lange,

2002). According to surveys, European American and Asian American mothers are most likely to breast-feed, Latina mothers are less likely, and Black mothers are least likely to breast-feed their infants (Kruse et al., 2005; R. Li & Grummer-Strawn, 2002; Slusser & Lange, 2002).

As you might expect, women are more likely to nurse successfully if their friends and the hospital staff members are supportive and encouraging (Dennis, 2002; Kruse et al., 2005). Early encouragement in breast feeding is also more likely in hospitals that favor vaginal births, rather than cesarean sections (Rowe-Murray & Fisher, 2002).

Some health-care workers have devised programs to encourage mothers to breast-feed. For instance, researchers in Brazil found that mothers who had seen a video about breast feeding were more likely than mothers in a control group to breast-feed until their infants were at least 6 months old (Susin et al., 1999). In other research, low-income mothers were more likely to breast-feed if they had received guidance from women who had successfully breast-fed their own infants (e.g., Ineichen et al., 1997; Schafer et al., 1998). For example, one Black woman described her feelings for her third child, whom she had breast-fed with the help of a counselor:

> Yes, I love all my children and I'm close to them, but there's something special with me and him. It's like he's part of me, and he's still a part of me. I have what he needs. I give it to him, nobody makes it for me. I give it to him. I'm the reason that he's healthy. (Locklin & Naber, 1993, p. 33)

Mothers who breast-feed typically report that nursing is a pleasant experience of warmth, sharing, and openness (Houseman, 2003; Lawrence, 1998). In contrast, mothers who bottle-feed their babies are more likely to emphasize that bottle feeding is convenient and trouble free.

The research demonstrates that human milk is better for human infants than is a formula based on cow's milk. After all, evolution has encouraged the development of a liquid that is ideally designed for efficient digestion. Breast milk also protects against allergies, diarrhea, infections, and other diseases (American Academy of Pediatrics, 2001; Slusser & Lange, 2002). In addition, breast feeding offers some health benefits for mothers, such as reducing the incidence of breast cancer and ovarian cancer (Lawrence, 1998; Slusser & Lange, 2002).

Because of the health benefits, health professionals should try to encourage breast feeding. This precaution is especially valid in developing countries where sanitary conditions make bottle feeding hazardous. However, the health professionals should not make mothers feel inadequate or guilty if they choose to bottle-feed their babies (L. M. Blum, 1999; Else-Quest et al., 2003; Lawrence & Lawrence, 1998).

POSTPARTUM DISTURBANCES

As we noted earlier, mothers are supposed to be delighted with their young infants, anticipating a blissful motherhood. However, a significant number of women develop psychological disturbances during the **postpartum period,** which extends from 0 to 6 weeks after birth. Take a moment to glance back over the list of nine negative factors on pages 336–338. Imagine that you are a new mother who is exhausted from childbirth; you are also experiencing most of these factors. In addition, suppose that your infant is not yet old enough to smile delightfully. Under these stressful circumstances, you can easily imagine how emotional problems could arise (Mauthner, 2002).

Two different kinds of postpartum problems occur relatively often. The most common kind of problem is called **postpartum blues** or **maternity blues**, a short-lasting change in mood that usually occurs during the first 10 days after childbirth. Roughly half of new mothers in North America experience postpartum blues, and it occurs in many different cultures (G. E. Robinson & Stewart, 2001). Common symptoms include crying, sadness, insomnia, irritability, anxiety, and feeling overwhelmed (O'Hara & Stuart, 1999). Postpartum blues are probably a result of the emotional letdown following the excitement of childbirth, combined with the sleeplessness and other life changes that a new baby brings. Most women report that the symptoms are gone within a few days. However, it is important for women to be well informed about this problem (Mauthner, 2002; G. E. Robinson & Stewart, 2001).

Postpartum depression (also called **postnatal depression**) is a more intense and serious disorder, typically involving feelings of extreme sadness, fatigue, sleep disturbances, despair, lack of interest in enjoyable activities, loss of interest in the baby, and feelings of guilt (Kendall-Tackett, 2005; Mauthner, 2002). Postpartum depression usually begins to develop within 6 months after childbirth, and it may last for many months (G. E. Robinson & Stewart, 2001). Depressed mothers tend to interact less effectively with their infants, placing them at risk for health and psychological problems (Bartlett et al., 2004; Hay et al., 2003; P. S. Kaplan et al., 2002; Kendall-Tackett, 2005).

Postpartum depression affects about 10% to 15% of women who have given birth (P. S. Kaplan et al., 2002; Kendall-Tackett, 2005; L. J. Miller, 2002). It is also reported in many different cultures (e.g., des Rivieres-Pigeon et al., 2004; E. Lee, 2003; Wang et al., 2005; Webster et al., 2003). One U.S. mother described her experience with postpartum depression:

> To not have any hope. . . . It's like you're suffocating or you're in a little prison. . . . And to wake up and to dread the day, I think, was the most hardest for me. To get up and go, "Oh, my God, I've got to go through another day." I mean, I never thought about killing myself. I never had those thoughts. I just thought I wanted to dig a big hole and have no one ever find me. (Mauthner, 2002, p. 189)

Postpartum depression is similar to other kinds of depression that are not associated with children. In fact, it may be the same as other forms of depression (G. E. Robinson & Stewart, 2001; Stanton et al., 2002). We will explore depression in more detail in Chapter 12. Fortunately, most cases of depression can be successfully treated.

Social factors are also important, according to research in the United States, Canada, and Europe. For instance, women who experience major life stress during pregnancy are more likely to develop postpartum depression. As a result, low-income women are at risk (L. J. Miller, 2002; G. E. Robinson & Stewart, 2001).

Women who lack social support from a partner, relatives, or friends are also likely to develop postpartum depression (Feeney et al., 2001; G. E. Robinson & Stewart, 2001; Thorp et al., 2004). In contrast, researchers found a low rate of postpartum depression among Hmong women who had emigrated from Southeast Asia to a community in Wisconsin (S. Stewart & Jambunathan, 1996). The researchers also noted that these women received high levels of support from their spouses and family members in this community.

Furthermore, Lavender and Walkinshaw (1998) conducted a well-controlled study with new mothers who were predominantly European American. Half of the women (the control group) received no special treatment. The other half talked for about 1 to 2 hours with a midwife who offered support and informal counseling. Three weeks later, the women in the control group were six times as likely to score in the "very depressed" region of the depression scale, compared with those who had received counseling. If other research finds similar results, then a program of supportive counseling would be useful for mothers at risk for depression.

The origins of both postpartum blues and postpartum depression are controversial. We noted that the levels of progesterone and estrogen drop sharply during the last stages of childbirth. The levels of other hormones also change during the weeks following childbirth. Women's popular magazines are likely to emphasize these hormonal factors as a cause of psychological disorders (R. Martínez et al., 2000). However, the relationship between hormonal levels and postpartum disorders is inconsistent and not very strong (Mauthner, 2002; G. E. Robinson & Stewart, 2001). In contrast, as we just discussed, social factors do play an important role in postpartum disturbances.

Also, keep in mind that many women do not experience either the blues or depression following the birth of their baby. Earlier in this chapter, we noted that some women experience little discomfort and few psychological problems during pregnancy. In Chapter 4, we pointed out that many women do not have major premenstrual or menstrual symptoms, and we'll see in Chapter 14 that most women pass through menopause without any trauma. In short, women differ widely from one another. The various phases in a woman's reproductive life do not inevitably bring emotional or physical problems.

RETURNING TO EMPLOYMENT AFTER CHILDBIRTH

Should women return to working outside the home after the birth of a child? The popular media and public opinion basically suggest a "can't win" dilemma. If you have a young child, you should stay home and be a full-time mother. However—especially if you are well educated—you should work outside the home, rather than wasting all that education by not living up to your potential (Johnston & Swanson, 2003a, 2004; Rice & Else-Quest, 2006). There's a further complication: Suppose that a woman does decide to return to working outside the home after she has given birth. People often judge employed mothers to be less competent than employed women who have no children (Cuddy & Fiske, 2004; Ridgeway & Correll, 2004).

We have seen abundant evidence for Theme 4 throughout this chapter: During pregnancy, childbirth, and motherhood, women differ widely from one another. Marjorie H. Klein and her colleagues (1998) discovered individual differences in women's reactions to combining motherhood and employment. These researchers surveyed 570 women in two Midwestern cities; each woman had recently given birth. Overall, they found that the length of the women's maternity leave—before returning to work—was not correlated with mental health measures such as depression, anxiety, anger, and self-esteem.

However, Klein and her colleagues then conducted a separate analysis for women who considered their employment an important part of their identity. For these women, a longer maternity leave was associated with a higher score on the depression measure. For some women, staying home with a baby on an extended maternity leave may actually be harmful if the women really value their work role.

In another part of the same study, Klein and her colleagues (1998) compared the mental health of three groups of women: homemakers, women employed part time, and women employed full time. One year after childbirth, these three groups of women did not differ on measures of depression, anxiety, anger, or self-esteem.

We saw in Chapter 7 that children do not experience increased problems if someone other than their mother takes care of them. Similarly, mothers who choose to return to the workplace are no more likely than other mothers to experience mental health problems. In fact, women who are engaged in more than one role (e.g., mother and employee) often have better physical and psychological health than women who have only one role (R. C. Barnett & Hyde, 2001). In short, mothers should assess their own personal situations and preferences in order to make decisions about this crucial question.

DECIDING WHETHER TO HAVE CHILDREN

As recently as the 1970s, most married women did not need to make a conscious decision about whether to have a child. Almost all married women anticipated becoming mothers, with little awareness that they actually had a choice. However, attitudes have changed. In the United States, for example, about 25% of women will never have children (Warren & Tyagi, 2003). Some of these women may choose not to have children because they are unmarried. Other women may not have children because they, or their partners, are infertile.

Let's consider how other people view these "childfree" women. We'll also explore some advantages and disadvantages of deciding not to have children.

ATTITUDES TOWARD WOMEN CHOOSING NOT TO HAVE CHILDREN.   Many people believe that all women should have children, a viewpoint called **compulsory motherhood**

Demonstration 10.4

For this demonstration, you will need some volunteers—ideally, at least five persons for each of the two scenarios described. Read the following paragraph aloud to half of the volunteers, either individually or in a group.

> Kathy and Tom are an attractive couple in their mid-forties. They will be celebrating their twentieth wedding anniversary next year. They met in college and were married the summer after they received their undergraduate degrees. Tom is now a very successful attorney. Kathy, who earned her Ph.D. degree in social psychology, is a full-time professor at the university. Kathy and Tom have no children. They are completely satisfied with their present family size because they planned to have no children even before they were married. Because both have nearby relatives, they often have family get-togethers. Kathy and Tom also enjoy many activities and hobbies. Some of their favorites are biking, gardening, and taking small excursions to explore nearby towns and cities.

After reading this paragraph, pass out copies of the rating sheet below and ask volunteers to rate their impression of Kathy.

Follow the same procedure for the other half of the volunteers. However, for the sentence "Kathy and Tom have no children" and the following sentence, substitute this passage: "Kathy and Tom have two children. They are completely satisfied with their present family size because they planned to have two children even before they were married."

Compare the average responses of the two groups. Do they rate Kathy as more fulfilled if she is described as having two children? Does she have a happier and more rewarding life?

1	2	3	4	5
Less fulfilled				More fulfilled

1	2	3	4	5
Very unhappy				Very happy

1	2	3	4	5
Unrewarding life				Rewarding life

Source: From Mueller, K. A., & Yoder, J. D. (1997). Gendered norms for family size, employment, and occupation: Are there personal costs for violating them? *Sex Roles, 36,* 211. Reprinted by permission of Kluwer.

(Boston Women's Health Book Collective, 2005; Coltrane, 1998). A few decades ago, a young woman who did not plan to have children would have been viewed very negatively. Attitudes toward childfree women are still somewhat negative (P. J. Caplan, 2001; Mueller & Yoder, 1999). For example, Demonstration 10.4 is a modified version of two scenarios tested by Karla Mueller and Janice Yoder

| TABLE 10.1 | RATINGS OF A CHILDFREE WOMAN AND A WOMAN WITH TWO CHILDREN, ON THREE DIFFERENT CHARACTERISTICS | |

	Rating of Woman in Scenario	
Characteristic	Childfree Woman	Woman With Two Children
Fulfillment	4.0	4.4
Happiness	3.5	4.3
Rewarding life	3.5	4.2

Note: 5 is the highest level of the attribute.

Source: From Mueller, K. A., & Yoder, J. D. (1997). Gendered norms for family size, employment, and occupation: Are there personal costs for violating them? *Sex Roles, 36,* 216. Reprinted by permission of Kluwer.

(1997). These researchers found statistically significant differences in the way college students in Wisconsin rated the women in the two scenarios. Table 10.1 shows the results on the three dimensions included in this demonstration. I suspect that the ratings for the childfree woman would be somewhat more negative in a general population that includes nonstudents.

Married couples also report that they receive advice about the ideal family size from many different people, including their parents, friends, and acquaintances (Boston Women's Health Book Collective, 2005; Casey, 1998; Mueller & Yoder, 1999). Childfree couples are informed that they are self-centered and too career oriented. Couples with one child are told—incorrectly—that an only child will face emotional problems. Couples with four or more children are told that they are basically crazy, because they won't be able to pay enough attention to each child (Blayo & Blayo, 2003; Kantrowitz, 2004).

Notice, then, that our culture seems to admire only a narrow range of options. A couple may have two or three children, but many people will criticize them for fewer than two or more than three. Interestingly, however, Mueller and Yoder (1999) also studied married couples and found that family size was not correlated with the couples' actual satisfaction. In other words, those with no children were just as happy as those with one, two, three, or more children.

ADVANTAGES AND DISADVANTAGES OF BEING CHILDFREE. Married couples provide many reasons for not wanting to have a child (Boston Women's Health Book Collective, 2005; Casey, 1998; Ceballo et al., 2004; Megan, 2000; Townsend, 2003; Warren & Tyagi, 2003):

1. Parenthood is an irrevocable decision; you can't take children back to the store for a refund.
2. Some women and men are afraid that they will not be good parents.
3. Some couples realize that they genuinely do not enjoy children.

4. Some couples are reluctant to give up a satisfying and flexible lifestyle for a more child-centered orientation.
5. Children can interfere with educational and vocational plans.
6. Raising children can be extremely expensive, especially if they will attend college.
7. People can spend time with other people's children, even if they don't have children of their own.
8. Some couples do not want to bring children into a world threatened by overpopulation, nuclear war, terrorism, and other serious global problems.

Still, people who are enthusiastic about parenthood provide many reasons for having children (Boston Women's Health Book Collective, 2005; Ceballo et al., 2004; C. P. Cowan & Cowan, 1992; McMahon, 1995):

1. Parenthood offers a lifelong relationship of love and nurturance with other human beings; children can enrich people's lives.
2. Parents have a unique chance to be responsible for someone's education and training; in raising a child, they can clarify their own values and instill them in their child.
3. Parents can watch their children grow into socially responsible adults who can help the world become a better place.
4. Parenthood is challenging; it offers people the opportunity to be creative and learn about their own potential.
5. Through parenting, people can fulfill their relationship with their spouse, and they can become a "family."
6. Children can be a source of fun, pleasure, and pride.

INFERTILITY

You probably know a woman who has wanted to have children, but pregnancy does not seem to be a possibility. For example, one woman wrote:

> How had having a baby, getting pregnant, become such an obsession with me? All I could think was that there must be a mechanism that clicks in once you try to get pregnant that, instead of allowing you to accept that you cannot, compels you to keep trying, no matter what the odds or cost. . . . I never would have suspected, until I tapped into it, just how powerful the desire could be. (Alden, 2000, p. 107)

By the current definition, **infertility** is the failure to conceive after 1 year of sexual intercourse without using contraception (Carroll, 2005; Pasch, 2001). An estimated 10% to 15% of couples in the United States are infertile (Beckman, 2006; A. L. Nelson & Marshall, 2004).

Some women manage to reconcile their initial sadness. Consider the conclusion reached by the woman in the previous quote: "It came to me that it really was a choice between two good things—having a child and not having a child. Our life without a child seemed good to me. I caught a glimpse that it was what was right for us, for the best" (Alden, 2000, p. 111). Other women, who had looked forward to children as a central part of their married lives, experience stress and a real sense of loss. However, comparisons of fertile and infertile women show that the two groups do not differ in their marital satisfaction or self-esteem (Beckman, 2006; Stanton et al., 2002).

Still, the research does suggest that women who are infertile show higher levels of distress and anxiety than fertile women (L. L. Alexander et al., 2004; Stanton et al., 2002). We need to emphasize an important point: According to researchers, the infertility causes the distress and anxiety. Distress and anxiety do not cause infertility. Also, individual differences in psychological reactions to infertility are substantial, consistent with Theme 4 of this book (Stanton et al., 2002).

One source of psychological strain for people facing infertility is that they may live with the constant hope, "Maybe next month. . . ." They may see themselves as "not yet pregnant" rather than as permanently childless. As a result, they may feel unsettled, caught between hopefulness and mourning the child they will not have.

Women of color face an additional source of strain when they experience infertility. For example, Ceballo (1999) interviewed married African American women who had tried to become pregnant for many years. These women often struggled with racist health-care providers who seemed astonished that a Black woman should be infertile. As these women explained, European Americans seem to believe that infertility is "a White thing" because they believe that Black women should be highly sexualized, promiscuous, and fertile. One woman pointed out how she began to internalize these racist messages; she almost believed that she was "the only Black woman walking the face of the earth that cannot have a baby." Unfortunately, psychologists know little about the impact of infertility on the lives of women of color (Pasch, 2001; Stanton et al., 2002).

Many couples who are concerned about infertility decide to consult health-care professionals for an "infertility workup," which includes a medical examination of both partners. About half of couples who seek medical treatment will eventually become parents (A. L. Nelson & Marshall, 2004). They will use one of a wide variety of reproductive technologies, which are often stressful and extremely expensive; health insurance plans rarely cover the cost (Beckman & Harvey, 2005; Boston Women's Health Book Collective, 2005).

However, many women will not become pregnant, even after medical treatment, or they may experience miscarriages. Eventually, some will choose to adopt (Ceballo et al., 2004). Others will decide to pursue other interests. A woman who might have focused on the regret of infertility in earlier eras can now shift her emphasis away from what is not in her life, so that she can fully appreciate the many positive options available in her future (Alden, 2000).

Section Summary

Motherhood

1. The stereotypes about motherhood reveal our ambivalence about mothers: Mothers are supposed to feel happy and contented, but they are also blamed for children's problems.

2. Motherhood has a strong negative side because mothers may feel exhausted, overworked, physically uncomfortable, incompetent, unrewarded, isolated, and disappointed by their failure to become the "ideal mother." In addition, especially in developing countries, a substantial number of children die before they are 1 year of age.

3. Motherhood also has a strong positive side; the benefits include a sense of women's own strength, pleasurable interactions with the baby, and increased nurturing skills, as well as abstract, intense joys.

4. Compared to White women, women of color may have different motherhood experiences. Black mothers often have the benefit of the extended family; Latinas must combat the values implied by *marianismo;* North American Indians may emphasize the continuity of motherhood; Asian women who have emigrated to the United States may encounter conflicts between their cultural beliefs and U.S. medical practice.

5. Research on lesbian mothers reveals that they do not differ from heterosexual mothers in their parenting skills or the adjustment of their children.

6. Breast feeding provides benefits for a mother's interactions with her infant, as well as for the health of both the infant and the mother.

7. About half of new mothers experience the short-term depression called postpartum blues; between 10% and 15% experience the more severe postpartum depression.

8. The psychological well-being of mothers of infants is similar for homemakers, women employed part time, and women employed full time; those with multiple roles may even experience benefits to their physical and psychological health.

9. At present, attitudes toward childfree women are somewhat negative; attitudes toward women with large families are also somewhat negative.

10. Childfree couples say that the disadvantages of parenthood include the irrevocability of the decision to have a child, the interference with lifestyle and work, and the expenses.

11. Couples who want to have children cite advantages such as the pleasurable aspects of children, the opportunity to educate children, and the challenge of parenthood.

12. Women who are infertile are similar to women with children in terms of their marital satisfaction and self-esteem, but they may be more anxious; many women manage to refocus their lives when infertility seems likely.

CHAPTER REVIEW QUESTIONS

1. Pregnancy and childbirth both involve biological processes. However, social factors are also very influential. Describe how social factors can operate during pregnancy and childbirth.

2. This chapter emphasizes ambivalent feelings and thoughts more than any other chapter in the book. Address the issue of ambivalence with respect to six topics: (a) emotional reactions to pregnancy, (b) emotional reactions to childbirth, (c) the reality of motherhood, (d) the decision to have children, (e) returning to the workplace after childbirth, and (f) reactions to infertility.

3. Describe how people react to pregnant women. How might these reactions contribute to women's emotional responses to pregnancy? Be sure to discuss both hostile and benevolent sexism.

4. Contrast the high-tech approach to childbirth with the family-centered approach. Which of these characteristics would be likely to make women feel more in control of their experience during childbirth?

5. Throughout this chapter, we have seen that stereotypes often do not match reality. Address this issue with respect to some of the problems of motherhood.

6. In the chapter on women and work (Chapter 7), we discussed Francine Deutsch's (1999) research on families in which the mother and father take almost equal responsibility for child care. Obviously, men cannot experience pregnancy or childbirth. However, based on the information in this chapter, describe how an ideal father would offer the best possible support during pregnancy and childbirth.

What would this father do, once the baby is born, so that the mother's postpartum period is as positive as possible?

7. What are the stereotypes about women of color who are mothers, and how is reality different from these stereotypes? What are the stereotypes and the reality for lesbian mothers?

8. Childbirth educators have made impressive changes in the way childbirth is now approached. However, motherhood is still extremely stressful. Imagine that our society valued motherhood enough to fund programs aimed at decreasing the difficulties that women experience during the early weeks after a baby is born. First, review those sources of stress. Then describe an ideal program that would include education, assistance, and social support.

9. Psychologists have conducted less research on pregnancy, childbirth, and motherhood than on any other topic in this book. Review this chapter, and suggest possible research projects that could clarify how women experience these three important events in their lives.

10. As we pointed out in this chapter, women often face a no-win situation with respect to decisions about childbearing and employment. Consider the options for three categories of women: married, lesbian, and single. What kinds of prejudices would be aimed at each category of women (e.g., a lesbian who decides to have children and to be employed full time)? Can any of these women win the complete approval of society?

KEY TERMS

*placenta (324)

*miscarriage (327)

hostile sexism (328)

benevolent sexism (328)

doula (332)

*cesarean section
  (C-section) (332)

*preterm birth (332)

*prepared childbirth
  (333)

*family-centered approach (333)

*infant mortality rate (338)

*marianismo (340)

*postpartum period (343)

*postpartum blues (344)

*maternity blues (344)

*postpartum depression (344)

*postnatal depression (344)

*compulsory motherhood (346)

*infertility (349)

 Note: The terms asterisked in the Key Terms section serve as good search terms for InfoTrac College Edition. Go to http://infotrac.thomsonlearning.com and try these added search terms.

RECOMMENDED READINGS

Biernat, M., Crosby, F. J., & Williams, J. C. (Eds.). (2004). The maternal wall: Research and policy perspectives on discrimination against mothers [Special issue]. *Journal of Social Issues, 60* (4). The *Journal of Social Issues* publishes special issues about a variety of social-justice concerns, and many of them focus on the psychology of women and gender. This particular special issue examines a wide variety of biases against employed women who are mothers.

Birth: Issues in Perinatal Care. This quarterly journal provides an interdisciplinary perspective on topics that psychologists have generally ignored. The articles examine women's experiences during pregnancy, childbirth, and the postpartum period; they also discuss innovative childbirth programs.

Feeney, J. A., Hohaus, L., Noller, P., & Alexander, R. P. (2001). *Becoming parents: Exploring the bonds between mothers, fathers, and their infants.* New York: Cambridge University Press. Here's a book that focuses on many aspects of the transition to parenthood in a study of Australian married couples. The book is scholarly, but it also offers some wonderful quotations from the parents.

Mauthner, N. S. (2002). *The darkest days of my life: Stories of postpartum depression.* Cambridge, MA: Harvard University Press. Natasha Mauthner interviewed British and U.S. mothers who were experiencing postpartum depression. She selected some especially poignant quotations from these mothers, and her book emphasizes the social and cultural issues that encourage postpartum depression.

ANSWERS TO THE DEMONSTRATIONS

Demonstration 10.3: Note: The name of each country is followed by its infant mortality rate (the number of infant deaths during 1 year per 1,000 live births). Australia, 6; Greece, 4; Cuba, 6; Israel, 5; Denmark, 3; Japan, 3; France, 4; Sweden, 3; Germany, 4; United States, 7; Belgium, 4; Czech Republic, 4; Ireland, 6; Poland, 6; Canada, 5.

ANSWERS TO THE TRUE-FALSE STATEMENTS

1. True (p. 323); 2. True (p. 325); 3. True (pp. 325–327); 4. True (p. 328); 5. True (p. 331); 6. False (p. 333); 7. False (pp. 336–338); 8. True (p. 341); 9. True (p. 344); 10. False (pp. 347–348).

11 | WOMEN AND PHYSICAL HEALTH

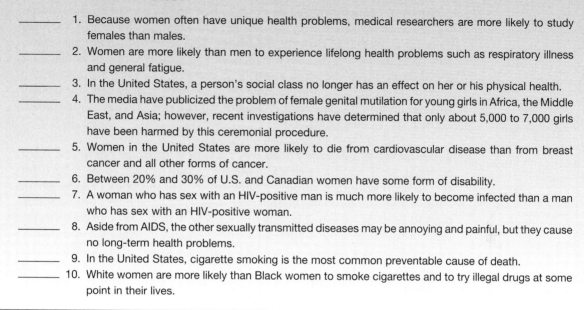

True or False?

_____ 1. Because women often have unique health problems, medical researchers are more likely to study females than males.

_____ 2. Women are more likely than men to experience lifelong health problems such as respiratory illness and general fatigue.

_____ 3. In the United States, a person's social class no longer has an effect on her or his physical health.

_____ 4. The media have publicized the problem of female genital mutilation for young girls in Africa, the Middle East, and Asia; however, recent investigations have determined that only about 5,000 to 7,000 girls have been harmed by this ceremonial procedure.

_____ 5. Women in the United States are more likely to die from cardiovascular disease than from breast cancer and all other forms of cancer.

_____ 6. Between 20% and 30% of U.S. and Canadian women have some form of disability.

_____ 7. A woman who has sex with an HIV-positive man is much more likely to become infected than a man who has sex with an HIV-positive woman.

_____ 8. Aside from AIDS, the other sexually transmitted diseases may be annoying and painful, but they cause no long-term health problems.

_____ 9. In the United States, cigarette smoking is the most common preventable cause of death.

_____ 10. White women are more likely than Black women to smoke cigarettes and to try illegal drugs at some point in their lives.

A woman named Samantha describes her relationship with her husband, Michael: "We love each other passionately and often. While the disability does, in reality, affect how we do things and what we are able to do together, it does not define our relationship. Assumptions are always the problem. People can assume that because I am disabled, that my sexuality and my ability to enjoy and participate in sex have been taken away from me. It is fun to be part of an education process aimed at challenging this perception." Samantha has quadriplegia, which means that all four limbs are paralyzed (Boston Women's Health Book Collective, 2005, p. 216).

This chapter explores both the stereotypes and the realities of women with disabilities. We will also consider information about women's health status, sexually transmitted infections, and substance abuse. These topics are part of **health psychology**, an interdisciplinary area in psychology that focuses on the causes of illness, the treatment of illness, illness prevention, and health improvement (Brannon & Feist, 2004; Gurung, 2006; Sarafino, 2006). Why should women's health problems require special attention in a psychology course? In this chapter, we will emphasize three major reasons that health issues are related to the psychology of women and gender.

1. Gender makes a difference in the kinds of illness that people experience. One theme of this book is that psychological gender differences are typically small. However, several biological gender differences have important consequences for women's health. Some consequences are obvious. For example, women may need to worry about cancer of the ovaries or the uterus, but not prostate cancer.

Some consequences are more subtle. For example, the female body has more fat and less fluid than the male body. This gender difference has important consequences for alcohol metabolism. Specifically, women's bodies have less fluid in which the alcohol can be distributed. So, even if a man and a woman weigh the same and consume the same amount of alcohol, the woman will end up with a higher level of alcohol in her blood (L. L. Alexander et al., 2004; L. H. Collins, 2002a).

2. Gender makes a difference in the way a disease is diagnosed and treated.   For example, we'll see that men are more likely than women to be treated for certain heart problems, consistent with Theme 2 of this book (Travis, 2005). Also, health-care providers consider the normative or standard disease symptoms to be those occurring in males (Benrud & Reddy, 1998). In contrast, the same disease may cause a different set of symptoms in females. For example, AIDS can affect a woman's reproductive system. Ironically, women's disease symptoms are often considered deviations from the norm, consistent with our discussion of the normative male, on page 40 (Porzelius, 2000).

Gender also makes a difference in the way certain diseases are viewed. For example, researchers in previous decades rarely studied osteoporosis, a bone disease found predominantly in women. As Theme 3 emphasizes, topics important to women are often invisible.

However, one cluster of women's health problems has received abundant attention: women's reproductive systems (N. G. Johnson, 2001). A physician in the late 1800s captured this perspective: "Woman is a pair of ovaries with a human being attached, where man is a human being furnished with a pair of testes" (cited by Fausto-Sterling, 1985, p. 90).

3. Illness is an important part of many women's experience.   A textbook on the psychology of women must explore both gender comparisons and the life experiences of women. Sadly, health problems are a major concern for many women, and they become an increasingly central force as women grow older. According to estimates, more than 80% of women who are 55 or older experience at least one chronic health problem (Meyerowitz & Weidner, 1998; Revenson, 2001).

In this chapter, we will explore several important components of women's physical health. In the first section, we examine how gender is related to both health care and health status. In the second section, we will emphasize the theme of variability among women, as we examine the lives of women with disabilities. In the last two sections, we will consider sexually transmitted infections and substance abuse. The topics in this chapter may initially seem unrelated. However, they all focus on two central issues: How does gender influence people's physical health, and how are women's lives influenced by their health?

THE HEALTH CARE AND HEALTH STATUS OF WOMEN

Theme 2 of this book states that women are treated differently from men. The biases against women in the health-care system provide still further evidence for that theme, both in North America and in developing countries. In this section, we will also examine gender comparisons in life expectancy and in general health as well as several diseases that have an important impact on women's lives.

Biases Against Women

The medical profession has consistently been biased against women. Both women physicians and women patients have often been mistreated. A fascinating book by Mary Roth Walsh (1977) features a title based on a 1946 newspaper advertisement: "Doctors Wanted: No Women Need Apply." The book documents the long history of attempts to keep women out of medical schools and medical practice. Even today, women are still underrepresented as chairpersons of academic departments in medical schools and in management positions in health-care organizations (Ketenjian, 1999a; Robinson-Walker, 1999).

On the bright side, 46% of current medical school graduates are women, in contrast to only 9% in 1969 (American Medical Association, 2005; N. Eisenberg et al., 1989). Now that women constitute such a large percentage of medical students, discrimination will probably decrease (Manderson, 2003b).

Nevertheless, the medical profession and the health-care system show several biases against women patients. As you read about these biases, keep in mind three cautions: (1) Not every doctor is biased against women, (2) some female doctors *are not* feminists, and (3) some male doctors *are* feminists. What are the biases that operate in health care so that women patients often become second-class citizens?

1. Women have often been neglected in medicine and in medical research. For example, one study analyzed all illustrations of men and women in medical textbooks, omitting those about gynecology and reproduction. Men were almost four times as likely as women to be pictured in these illustrations (Mendelsohn et al., 1994). Consistent with Theme 3, the male body has been considered normative, and it serves as the standard. With this perspective, medical experts have often assumed that women are basically identical to men, except that they are smaller . . . and of course they have different reproductive processes (L. L. Alexander et al., 2004).

Furthermore, health-care providers' decisions about women's health may be based on research that does not represent women. For instance, five large-scale studies showed that a low dose of aspirin reduces the risk of a heart attack. However, three of those studies included no women, and the other two studies did not test enough women to permit conclusions. In fact, when a large-scale study was finally conducted with women, the researchers reported that a low dose of aspirin did *not* reduce the rate of heart attacks in women (Ridker et al., 2005).

Fortunately, this neglect of women has outraged many health-care consumers and some legislators. Medical educators are now encouraging medical schools to emphasize women's health as part of the regular curriculum (Fonn, 2003; N. Rogers & Henrich, 2003). Since the early 1990s, the U.S. National Institutes of Health and many other organizations require that funded research must include both women and members of ethnic minorities (L. L. Alexander et al., 2004; N. G. Johnson, 2001). Also, activist organizations such as The Society for Women's Health Research (2006) encourage women to become better informed about recent research and health-care strategies.

These measures won't immediately correct the centuries of neglect that health-care professionals have shown toward women. However, women's health problems are now more visible. Health care is one area where feminist concerns have had a clear impact on women's lives.

2. Gender stereotypes are common in medicine.   In Chapter 2, we introduced many of the popular beliefs about men and women. The medical profession remains attached to many of these stereotypes. For example, the advertisements in medical journals seldom show women in a work setting (J. W. Hawkins & Aber, 1993). In addition, many physicians do not consider women's complaints to be as serious as men's complaints. Physicians may believe that women are more emotional than men or that women will not be able to understand information about their medical problems (Chrisler, 2001). Gender stereotypes keep women from receiving appropriate medical treatment.

3. Medical care provided to women is often irresponsible or inadequate. Women sometimes receive too much health care, but sometimes they receive too little (Livingston, 1999). Specifically, some surgical procedures are performed too often. We saw in Chapter 10 that cesarean sections are performed too often during childbirth, and we'll see later in this section that hysterectomies are also more common than they need to be. As we noted earlier, the medical profession emphasizes women's reproductive systems.

In contrast, when we consider diseases that affect both women and men, the women often receive too little health care. For example, women are less likely than men to receive diagnostic testing or surgical treatment for the same severity of coronary heart disease (Gan et al., 2000; Travis, 2005). The combination of "too much care" and "too little care" means that women often receive inappropriate treatment.

4. Physician-patient communication patterns often make women feel relatively powerless.   In Chapter 6, we saw that men often interrupt women in ordinary conversations. When the man is a physician and the woman is a patient in a medical setting, women may feel especially powerless (Manderson, 2003b; Porzelius, 2000). Many health-care plans limit a patient's visit to 15 minutes. This policy discourages women from asking questions and understanding medical procedures. In addition, physicians may miss information that would be useful for diagnosis and treatment (Boston Women's Health Book Collective, 2005; Klonoff & Landrine, 1997).

Fortunately, some research indicates no gender biases in physicians' conversational style (Roter & Hall, 1997). For example, one woman described her communication pattern with her doctor:

> Friends now marvel at my close relationship with my current doctor and my ability to talk back, question, and disagree with him and his colleagues. He respects me and trusts me to tell him what is going on, and I, in turn, trust him to listen, make suggestions, and consult with me before any action is taken. (Boston Women's Health Book Collective, 2005, p. 715)

GENDER COMPARISONS IN LIFE EXPECTANCY

Let's now shift our focus to a more general question: What is the life expectancy for women and for men? Figure 11.1 shows the gender gap for three groups of people in North America. Furthermore, researchers find a gender gap in **mortality** (or death rate) in all ethnic groups in the United States. The gender gap also occurs in virtually every country in the world, despite the substantial health problems that women experience in developing countries (Costello & Stone, 2001; U.S. Census Bureau, 2005). Notice that the gender gap in Figure 11.1 is small but consistent.

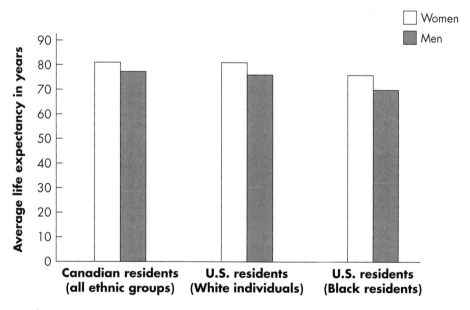

FIGURE 11.1 | AVERAGE LIFE EXPECTANCY FOR INDIVIDUALS BORN IN 1990, IN THREE NORTH AMERICAN POPULATIONS.

Sources: Statistics Canada (2005b); U.S. Census Bureau (2005).

But *why* do women live longer? The answer includes biological, social, and environmental factors (Stanton & Courtenay, 2004; D. R. Williams, 2003). For example, females' second X chromosome may protect them from some health problems (Landrine & Klonoff, 2001). Gender differences in activities and lifestyles are also likely. For example, men are more likely to die from suicide, homicide, and motor vehicle accidents. Men also consume more fatty and salty food than women do. In addition, more men than women are exposed to dangerous conditions at work, as is the case for coal miners and factory workers (Stanton & Courtenay, 2004; D. R. Williams, 2003). As we'll see later in the chapter, North American men are currently more likely to die of AIDS.

In both the United States and Canada, another factor that clearly contributes to women's longevity is that women visit their health-care providers more often than men do (Stanton & Courtenay, 2004; Statistics Canada, 2000; D. R. Williams, 2003). We saw in earlier chapters that women are somewhat more attuned to emotions and to problems in a relationship. Compared to men, women also may be more sensitive to internal signals that might foreshadow health problems (Addis & Mahalik, 2003; R. Martin & Suls, 2003; Stanton & Courtenay, 2004). In contrast, the male gender role encourages men to be physically "tough," rarely complaining about minor symptoms. Women may consult physicians during the early stages of a disease, before it becomes fatal.

GENDER COMPARISONS IN OVERALL HEALTH

We have seen that women have an advantage with respect to mortality, or death rate. However, women in both the United States and Canada have a disadvantage with respect to **morbidity**, which is defined as generalized poor health or illness. The research shows that women are more likely than men to have problems such as obesity, anemia, and respiratory illness. Women are also more likely to experience lifelong illnesses, headaches, and general fatigue (Chrisler, 2001; Field & Brackin, 2002; Statistics Canada, 2006).

Some of this gender difference is easy to explain: women live longer than men, so they are more likely to have non-fatal illnesses associated with old age (Crimmins et al., 2002). Some of the difference can probably be traced to the fact that morbidity is usually assessed by self-report (Brannon & Feist, 2004; Chrisler, 2001; Skevington, 2004). A woman may be more likely than a man to report that she is bothered by her arthritis.

Other explanations for the gender differences in morbidity are not so obvious. For example, women are the primary victims of rape, and women who have been raped are very likely to experience health problems during the years following the attack (N. G. Johnson, 2004). In addition, an estimated 22 million U.S. women are physically abused at some point during their lifetime by a boyfriend, spouse, or domestic partner (M. C. Roberts et al., 2004). Elderly women are also more likely than elderly men to be victims of elder abuse (Whitbourne, 2001). Economic factors also contribute to the gender differences in morbidity, as we'll see in the following discussion. In a variety of ways, then, women are more likely than men to experience illness and poor health.

How Social Class Influences U.S. Women's Health

Social class can be measured in terms of a person's occupation, income, or education. No matter how social class is measured, it is correlated with both morbidity and mortality (Adler & Conner Snibbe, 2003; Gallo & Matthews, 2003; Pappas et al., 1993). One important factor in these correlations is the quality of health care. No country's health-care system is perfect. For example, Canadian researchers point out that that their own system should emphasize disease prevention, rather than focusing primarily on treatment (Arnett et al., 2004; Romanow & Marchildon, 2003). However, Canada and other industrialized countries provide universal health care to its citizens, whereas the United States does not.

Unfortunately, more than 46 million U.S. citizens—especially women—do not have any health insurance (U.S. Census Bureau, 2007). Furthermore, men are more likely than women to have private insurance provided by their employers; private insurance furnishes the best health-care benefits (Brannon & Feist, 2004). In contrast, women are more likely to have Medicaid insurance—which offers second-class benefits—or no insurance at all (Chrisler, 2001; Landrine & Klonoff, 2001). Women of color are especially likely to receive second-class health care (Brannon & Feist, 2004; Landrine & Klonoff, 2001). For instance, about 40% of Latinas have no health-care insurance (Pérez-Stable & Nápoles-Springer, 2001). Realistically, health insurance sometimes makes a difference between life and death.

Many factors other than the quality of a person's health insurance help to explain the influence of social class on morbidity and mortality. For example, low-income housing is often constructed in locations with high levels of toxic materials. Also, low-income families often live in noisy, crowded environments; these factors are associated with poor health (Adler & Conner Snibbe, 2003; Csoboth, 2003). As you can imagine, poverty is also associated with negative thoughts and emotions. These psychological factors lead to heart disease, as well as other health problems (Adler & Conner Snibbe, 2003; Gallo & Matthews, 2003). In summary, any attempt to improve the health-care system in the United States—for both women and men—must emphasize the direct and indirect effects of social class.

Health Issues for Women in Developing Countries

In developing countries, women face more severe biases than in North America. In fact, many women in other countries do not need to be concerned about a health professional treating them in a biased manner because they will never even meet a physician, a nurse, or any person trained in health care. When resources are scarce, females are especially likely to suffer (Marton, 2004). Data gathered in Asia, Africa, and the Middle East demonstrate that parents are significantly more likely to seek medical care for a son than for a daughter. For example, boys in India are more than twice as likely as girls to receive medical treatment (Landrine & Klonoff, 2001). In many developing countries, only the wealthiest females have access to medical care.

Women in developing countries usually have inadequate nutrition and health care. Females currently constitute 70% of the world's population who typically have too little to eat ("Join the Global Effort," 2005; Marton, 2004). Therefore, they face a relatively high chance of dying as a result of pregnancy or childbirth. For example, during childbirth, an African woman living in either Niger or Sierra Leone is about 130 times more likely to die than a woman living in the United States—and about 360 times more likely to die than a woman living in Canada (World Health Organization, 2005b).

One of the most widely discussed issues related to women's health in some developing countries is female genital mutilation. **Female genital mutilation** (also called **female genital cutting**) involves cutting or removing the female genitals. This procedure removes part or all of the clitoris. In some cultures, the labia minora are also removed, and the labia majora are then stitched together. (See Chapter 9, Figure 9.1, for a review of female external sexual organs.) This more drastic procedure leaves only a tiny opening to allow both urine and menstrual blood to pass out of the body (S. M. James & Robertson, 2002; Kalev, 2004; Whelehan, 2001).

Female genital mutilation is a challenging issue to resolve. On the one hand, some people say that North Americans should not cast judgments about a cultural practice in another country. On the other hand, female genital mutilation clearly creates health problems for girls and women. The operation is extremely painful. It can also cause severe blood loss and infections (often leading to death), damage to other organs, and difficulty during childbirth (S. M. James & Robertson, 2002; Schiffman & Castle, 2005; Thrupkaew, 1999).

Some people use the phrase *female circumcision* to refer to female genital mutilation. However, this term is misleading because it suggests a relatively minor operation similar to male circumcision—cutting off the foreskin from the tip of the penis, without damaging the penis (S. M. James & Robertson, 2002). The male equivalent of the more drastic version of female genital mutilation would require removal of the entire penis and part of the skin surrounding the testicles (Toubia, 1995; Whelehan, 2001).

In about 30 countries throughout the world, approximately 100 million girls and women have experienced genital mutilation (Kalev, 2004; Walley, 2002; Whelehan, 2001). Most of these women live in Africa, the Middle East, and Asia. However, many have emigrated to Canada, the United States, and Europe (Nour, 2005).

The operation is usually performed when the young girl is between the ages of 4 and puberty. The girl is typically held down by female relatives. Meanwhile, an older woman performs the operation, often using an unsterilized razor blade, piece of glass, or sharp rock (Kalev, 2004). According to people in cultures that practice female genital mutilation, this procedure makes the genitals cleaner (Nour, 2005). People also believe that the operation reduces sexual activity outside marriage. Indeed, women do experience less sexual pleasure if the clitoris has been removed (Walley, 2002).

The World Health Organization and other prominent health groups have condemned the practice of female genital mutilation. Some countries have reduced the percentage of females who experience the procedure, using culturally sensitive educational techniques (El-Bushra, 2000; Gunning, 2002; Walley, 2002).

CARDIOVASCULAR DISEASE, BREAST CANCER, AND OTHER SPECIFIC HEALTH PROBLEMS

So far, we have seen that gender makes a difference for both mortality and morbidity. Women live longer, but they experience more illness during their lifetime. Let's now examine several specific diseases and health problems that are important in women's lives. The first problem, cardiovascular disease, affects women's lives because it is the most common cause of death for women. The other three problems—breast cancer, cancer of the reproductive system, and osteoporosis—occur either exclusively or more frequently in women. Therefore, we need to examine these specific diseases in our discussion of women's health.

CARDIOVASCULAR DISEASE.   The term **cardiovascular disease** includes disorders of the heart (such as heart attacks) and the blood vessels (such as strokes, which occur for blood vessels in the brain). Cardiovascular disease is the major cause of death for U.S. women. In fact, it is more deadly than all forms of cancer combined (Travis & Compton, 2001). Each year, cardiovascular disease kills about 500,000 women in the United States and about 27,000 women in Canada[1] (L. L. Alexander et al., 2004; Hansen, 2002; Statistics Canada, 2000).

Many people think that heart disease is a man's illness, but that myth is not correct. Men are likely to experience heart disease earlier than women do, but women run about the same risk by the time they reach 75 years of age (Brannon & Feist, 2004). In addition, Black women are more likely than White women to die of heart disease (Brannon & Feist, 2004).

An important problem is that men typically report chest pain when they are having a heart attack. Women may report chest pain, but they also report symptoms such as breathlessness (Skevington, 2004). Health professionals may fail to recognize heart attacks in women if they are searching for the "classic" male symptoms.

Furthermore, as we discussed at the beginning of this chapter, men are more likely than women to receive diagnostic testing or surgical treatment for heart disease. For example, men are twice as likely as women to receive bypass surgery, even when both genders have the same medical profile (Travis, 2005).

Researchers are also much more likely to study cardiac problems in men than in women (Boston Women's Health Book Collective, 2005; Travis & Compton, 2001). As a result, we don't know much about how to prevent women from facing heart problems. For example, since the 1980s, physicians

---

[1]For comparison, it is helpful to know that the U.S. population is roughly nine times that of Canada. Notice that heart disease kills a higher proportion of women in the United States than in Canada.

have recommended low doses of aspirin to protect men from heart attacks. However, comparable research on women was not published until about 20 years later. This research showed that low-dose aspirin had no effect on heart attacks in women, but it did significantly reduce women's risks of strokes (Ridker et al., 2005).

What can people do to help prevent heart disease? Some precautions include a diet that is low in salt, cholesterol, and saturated fats, maintenance of a reasonable body weight, and regular exercise (Brannon & Feist, 2004; Oldenburg & Burton, 2004). As we'll discuss later in the chapter, women who smoke also run a high risk of heart disease.

BREAST CANCER.   At the beginning of this chapter, we noted that gender makes a difference in the way certain diseases are viewed. We've just seen that many people don't associate heart disease with women. The one disease in women that receives widespread publicity is breast cancer.

Breast cancer is definitely an important problem that requires extensive medical research, and we all know women who have struggled with this disease. Still, health psychologists are uncertain why both medical researchers and the general public focus more on breast cancer than on other illnesses that are actually more dangerous for women. One important factor is our culture's emphasis on breasts as an essential part of being a woman. As a result, a woman who has had a breast removed (or partly removed) is viewed as being less female (Chrisler, 2001; Saywell, 2000).

Approximately 180,000 women in the United States are diagnosed with breast cancer each year, and about 40,000 U.S. women will die from the disease (Backus, 2002; Compas & Luecken, 2002). Also, about 19,000 Canadian women will be diagnosed with breast cancer annually, and about 4,300 Canadian women will die from the disease (Canadian Cancer Society, 2005a). Perhaps the most personally relevant statistic is this: If you are a woman in the United States or Canada—and you live to the age of 80—you have a 12% chance of developing breast cancer at some point in your lifetime (Canadian Cancer Society, 2005a; Compas & Luecken, 2002; Wymelenberg, 2000). Before you read further, however, try Demonstration 11.1 on page 365.

Regular, systematic breast self-examination is an important strategy for detecting cancer. Early detection of breast cancer is important because the chances of a cure are very high if the disease is diagnosed at an early stage. If you are a woman over the age of 20, you should examine your breasts at least once a month (L. L. Alexander et al., 2004; Keitel & Kopala, 2000). Women who are menstruating should examine their breasts about a week after their menstrual period is over because breasts are likely to have normal lumps during menstruation. Figure 11.2 on page 366 provides instructions.

Breasts can also be examined using technological methods. For example, a **mammogram** is an X-ray of the breast—a picture of breast tissue—taken while the breast tissue is flattened between two plastic plates (L. L. Alexander et al., 2004). Women over the age of 50 should have a screening mammogram every year or two to detect lumps that are too small to detect by self-examination.

Demonstration 11.1

Think about and answer the following questions concerning breast cancer and its relevance in your life.

1. When was the last time you heard or saw a discussion of breast cancer? Was the discussion a general one, or did it provide specific information about how to conduct a breast self-examination or where to go for a mammogram?
2. Have you seen any notices about breast self-examination or mammograms (for example, in public buildings or at the student health service)?
3. If a woman in your home community wanted to have a mammogram, do you know where she would go? (If you don't, you can find a nearby location by calling the American Cancer Society at 800-227-2345 or by visiting its website at www.cancer.org to find a nearby location.)
4. Think about several women over the age of 50 who are important to you. Have you ever discussed breast cancer or mammograms with them? If not, try to figure out how you might raise these issues with them soon, or identify another person who could make certain that these women have had a recent mammogram.

However, it's not yet clear whether women under the age of 50 would benefit from mammograms (Aiken et al., 2001).

Unfortunately, many women over the age of 50 do not have regular mammograms. Women of color have especially low rates for mammogram screening (Borrayo, 2004; Gotay et al., 2001). For example, only about 50% of Asian American women in one study reported having had a mammogram, in contrast to 70% of European American women (Helstrom et al., 1998). Asian American women may be less likely to have mammograms for several reasons. Many do not speak English or do not have health insurance that would cover the cost of the procedure. But perhaps the major reason is that many Asian American women are taught from an early age not to discuss topics related to sexuality, so breast cancer is an especially forbidden topic of conversation (Ketenjian, 1999b).

Latina women may also be reluctant to perform breast self-examination or seek breast cancer screening by a health-care provider—especially if they endorse traditional health beliefs. For instance, many women of Mexican descent believe that it would be indecent for a health-care provider to see their unclothed breasts (Borrayo, 2004; Borrayo & Jenkins, 2001, 2003; Borrayo et al., 2001).

The most common procedure for treating breast cancer is currently a **lumpectomy**, surgery that removes the cancerous lump and the immediate surrounding breast tissue. Radiation therapy or chemotherapy might also be used (L. L. Alexander et al., 2004). Fortunately, with earlier detection and more sophisticated procedures, women are significantly less likely to die from breast cancer now than in earlier decades (Backus, 2002).

Naturally, the diagnosis and treatment of breast cancer cause some fear, anxiety, grief, depression, and anger. The treatment cycle is physically painful

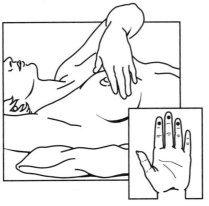
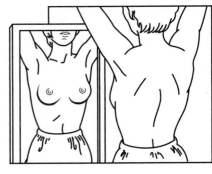

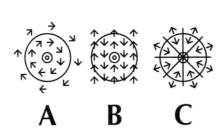

1. Lie down and put a pillow under your right shoulder. Place your right arm behind your head.

2. Use the finger pads of the three middle fingers on your left hand to feel for lumps or thickening. Your finger pads are the top third of each finger.

3. Press hard enough to know how your breast feels. If you're not sure how hard to press, ask your health care provider. Or try to copy the way your health care provider uses the finger pads during a breast exam. Learn what your breast feels like most of the time. A firm ridge in the lower curve of each breast is normal.

4. Move around the breast in a set way. You can choose either the circle (A), the up and down line (B), or the wedge (C). Do it the same way every time. It will help you to make sure that you've gone over the entire breast area, and to remember how your breast feels each month.

5. Now examine your left breast using right hand finger pads.

You might want to check your breasts while standing in front of a mirror right after you do your BSE each month. You might also want to do an extra BSE while you're in the shower. Your soapy hands will glide over the wet skin making it easy to check how your breasts feel.

FIGURE 11.2 | PERFORMING A BREAST SELF-EXAM (BSE).

Source: American Cancer Society (2003).

and difficult, and it is a socially lonely experience (Andersen & Farrar, 2001; Compas & Luecken, 2002; Spira & Reed, 2003). Women may feel exhausted for several months during and after treatment (Kaelin, 2005).

As you might expect, women who have been treated for breast cancer differ widely in their reactions (Rosenbaum & Roos, 2000; Spira & Reed, 2003; Yurek et al., 2000). In addition, these women are likely to report major fluctuations in their emotions from day to day. Some women continue to worry. For instance, a 70-year-old African American woman had chemotherapy, and she was cancer-free four years later. However, she still had persistent concerns about cancer: "It's just there, and I can't get it out of my brain, and it's just something that I've just learned to live with. It's just like sometime you wished you could just put your brain under a faucet and just wash the kinks out because it's just sticking there" (Rosenbaum & Roos, 2000, p. 160).

Fortunately, most women who have had surgery tend to cope well, especially if they have supportive friends and family members (Andersen & Farrar, 2001; Bennett, 2004; Compas & Luecken, 2002). For instance, in one study of Black women only 2 months after surgery, 62% reported that they were in very good spirits (Weaver, 1998).

Women often emphasize that the breast cancer experience forced them to clarify their values and to decide where to concentrate their future energies (Backus, 2002). As one woman commented on her personal transformation: "When you are diagnosed with breast cancer, you become an elder, no matter what your age. Through the events that occur, the decisions you make, the reevaluating and refocusing, you acquire wisdom and strength" (McCarthy & Loren, 1997, p. 195).

REPRODUCTIVE SYSTEM CANCER AND HYSTERECTOMIES.   Several kinds of cancer often affect women's reproductive systems. For example, **cervical cancer** affects the lower portion of the uterus. (Figure 4.1, on page 115 shows the cervix.)

In North America, women seldom die from cervical cancer. A major reason is a highly accurate screening test called the Pap smear, administered during routine gynecology examinations. In the **Pap smear test,** the gynecologist takes a sample of cells from the cervix to see whether they are normal, precancerous, or cancerous (L. L. Alexander et al., 2004). When cervical cancer is detected early, it is highly curable (Burns, 2001; Robertson et al., 2003; Schiffman & Castle, 2005). Gynecologists recommend that all women who are sexually active or who have reached the age of 18 should have an annual Pap smear. However, many young women do not know why Pap smears are important (Blake et al., 2004). This deadly disease is not limited to older women!

In Canada, about 75% of women over the age of 18 have had a Pap smear within the last three years (Statistics Canada, 2000). Most European American women in the United States have routine Pap smears, but millions without health insurance do not have this test on a regular basis (Landrine & Klonoff, 2001). For example, a 45-year-old woman remarked:

> My Mother's Day present this year was and is the best I've had in a while. My daughter got me a free Pap test. . . . She knew it had been years since I had one.

My family's history is riddled with cancer. We don't have health insurance because it's not affordable. (Feldt, 2002, p. 92)

As we noted earlier in this chapter, U.S. women experience much more severe health problems if they do not have insurance.

Compared to European American women, Latinas and other women of color are more likely to die from cancer of the cervix—especially because they are less likely to have had this screening test (Borrayo et al., 2004; Rimer et al., 2001). Throughout the world, cancer of the cervix is one of the major causes of death, especially because women in developing countries do not have access to Pap smears (World Health Organization, 2005a).

We noted at the beginning of the chapter that gender influences the way a disease is treated and that women's reproductive systems receive more attention than other health concerns. The best example of this principle is the high rate of hysterectomies in the United States. A **hysterectomy** is the surgical removal of a woman's uterus (Elson, 2004). Some hysterectomies are advisable—for example, when advanced cancer cannot be treated by more limited surgery. However, many surgeons remove a woman's uterus when other less drastic treatments would be effective. As a result, about one-third of all U.S. women can expect to have a hysterectomy at some point in their lifetime. This rate is much higher than in other developed countries (Elson, 2004). Women need appropriate information about the alternatives before making decisions about whether they should have a hysterectomy.

Some hysterectomies are medically necessary. Also, some women who have had hysterectomies experience only minimal psychological or physical symptoms. Consistent with our theme of individual differences, however, some women report that the hysterectomy removed an important part of their identity as a woman (Elson, 2004; Todkill, 2004). Clearly, the medical community needs to examine its policies on this widespread operation.

Another disorder of the reproductive system has not received the attention it deserves. In the United States, cancer of the ovaries has the highest rate of death of all gynecological cancers (L. L. Alexander et al., 2004; Burns, 2001). Unfortunately, no screening test for this disorder has yet been developed that is both reliable and valid. Furthermore, the symptoms include cramping, abdominal cramping, and vomiting—so people are likely to attribute the symptoms to a less serious health problem. As a result, most ovarian cancers are not discovered until they are in an advanced stage and the cancer has spread to other parts of the body (Boston Women's Health Book Collective, 2005; Robb-Nicholson, 2004). Most women's health issues now receive greater attention than in earlier decades. However, ovarian cancer is one major disease that requires much more research.

Osteoporosis. In the disorder called **osteoporosis** (pronounced oss-tee-owe-poe-*roe*-siss), the bones become less dense and more fragile. Women are roughly four times more likely than men to develop this disorder, depending on how it is assessed (L. L. Alexander et al., 2004; Fausto-Sterling, 2005). Osteoporosis is common among older women, especially postmenopausal women. Osteoporosis makes fractures much more likely, even from just tripping and falling in the bathroom. Hip fractures resulting from osteoporosis create major problems, especially because they often cause long-term disability (Raisz, 2005).

Women can reduce the risk of osteoporosis by doing regular weight-bearing exercises, such as walking or jogging. Even young women need to take adequate calcium and vitamin D to build strong bones, and they need to continue this precaution throughout their lives (Boston Women's Health Book Collective, 2005). In addition, the National Osteoporosis Foundation and other professional organizations recommend a bone-density test when women reach the age of 65 (Raisz, 2005).

Section Summary

The Health Care and Health Status of Women

1. Women's health is a crucial issue for several reasons: (a) Women experience different illnesses than men, (b) gender influences the way a disease is treated, and (c) illness is an important factor in women's lives.

2. Biases against women include the neglect of women in medicine, the prevalence of gender stereotypes in medicine, inadequate or irresponsible medical care, and problems in the physician-patient relationship.

3. U.S. women in all ethnic groups live longer than men do; this gender difference also occurs in Canada. However, women report more health problems than men do.

4. In the United States, social class is related to a person's health status; women of color are especially likely to receive inadequate health care.

5. Women in developing countries often experience inadequate nutrition and health care. Female genital mutilation threatens the health of about 100 million girls and women.

6. Cardiovascular disease is the most common cause of death in women; precautions such as proper diet and exercise are important.

7. In the United States and Canada, about 12% of women who live to the age of 80 will develop breast cancer in their lifetime. However, the chances for survival are high if the cancer is detected early; most women cope remarkably well with breast cancer.

8. Pap smears are very effective in detecting early uterine cancer; hysterectomies may be advisable in some cases, but many are performed without sufficient medical justification. Ovarian cancer is an especially deadly disease.

9. Osteoporosis often leads to serious bone fractures in postmenopausal women.

WOMEN WITH DISABILITIES

We have seen that women and men have somewhat different health-care experiences, and they also have somewhat different patterns of illness. Now let's consider how gender can be relevant when we consider individuals with disabilities.

BACKGROUND INFORMATION ON DISABILITY STUDIES

One important theme of this book is that women vary widely from one another. We have already examined some factors that create variability: ethnicity, country of residence, social class, and sexual orientation. Disability is an additional dimension of variability. **Disability** refers to a physical or mental impairment that limits a person's ability to perform a major life activity in the manner considered normal (Asch , 2004; Cook, 2003; Korol & Craig, 2001). In general, the term *person with a disability* is preferable to *disabled person* (Humes et al., 1995). *Person with a disability* emphasizes someone's individuality first and the disability second.

Another theme in this book is that women are relatively invisible. Until recently, women with disabilities were nearly invisible within the discipline of women's studies. Fortunately, however, several current books are now available in the field of disability studies (M. E. Banks & Kaschak, 2003; Braithwaite & Thompson, 2000; G. A. King et al., 2003b; C. Lewis et al., 2002; Olkin & Pledger, 2003; B. G. Smith & Hutchison, 2004; Snyder et al., 2002). **Disability studies** is an interdisciplinary field that examines disabilities from the perspective of social sciences, natural science, the arts, and media studies (Brueggemann, 2002; B. G. Smith, 2004). Disability studies is also growing internationally, in countries as diverse as Uganda, El Salvador, and Nepal (C. Lewis et al., 2002).

By some estimates, 21% of women in the United States have disabilities (Asch et al., 2001). As you might expect, elderly women are especially likely to have a disability. For instance, consider Canadian women, age 65 and older, who live at home. An estimated 26% of these women live with a disability (Statistics Canada, 2000). Consistent with our earlier discussion of morbidity, the average Canadian man will live with a disability for 8 years, whereas the average Canadian woman will live with a disability for 11 years (Statistics Canada, 2005a).

The variation within the disability category is tremendous. In fact, the term *women with disabilities* is simply a social construct that links together unrelated conditions (Mason et al., 2004; Olkin, 2004). In reality, life experiences may be very different for a woman who is blind, a woman who is missing an arm, and a woman who is recovering from a stroke (Asch, 2004; B. G. Smith, 2004). Still, many people judge individuals with a disability primarily in terms of that disability. As Y. King (1997) remarked, the popular culture assumes that being disabled is what these individuals *do* and *are*: "She's the one in the wheelchair."

When we consider the topic of disabilities, we need to remind ourselves about a unity between women with disabilities and women without disabilities. Many people do not currently live with a disability. However, everyone could become disabled in a matter of seconds through an accident, a stroke, or a disease (Garland-Thomson, 2004). As Lisa Bowleg (1999) pointed out, people who are not disabled should adopt the label "temporarily abled."

Theorists often note that women typically live on the margins of a world in which men occupy the central territory. In many ways, women with disabilities live on the margins of those margins. As a result, they may feel that the culture considers them invisible (A. M. Bauer, 2001; Goldstein, 2001; Kisber, 2001). Women of color who have disabilities experience a triple threat, in which they constantly face sexism, racism, and **ableism**, which is discrimination on the basis of disability (Nabors & Pettee, 2003).

But how are disabilities related to gender? Why would the life of a woman with a disability be different from the life of a man with a disability? The following discussions of education, work, and social relationships demonstrate that disabilities can exaggerate the differential treatment of women and men.

EDUCATION AND WORK PATTERNS OF WOMEN WITH DISABILITIES

Women with disabilities face barriers in pursuing an education beyond high school. According to one U.S. survey, for example, only 15% of women with a disability hold at least a bachelor's degree, in contrast to 33% of women without a disability (Schur, 2004). A variety of barriers on college campuses make it difficult to pursue an education beyond high school. For example, women with disabilities often cannot find accessible buildings, wheelchair-friendly sidewalks, sign-language interpreters, and other support services.

Currently, 44% of U.S. women with a disability are employed; the comparable figure for men is 49%. In other words, the employment rates for these two groups are similar (Schur, 2004). However, in both the United States and Canada, people with disabilities are much less likely to be employed than people without disabilities (MacKinnon et al., 2003; Schur, 2004).

Gender and disability combine in unique ways to discriminate in the workplace against women with disabilities (Mason et al., 2004; Schur, 2004). For example, Mary Runté (1998) described how her disability does not allow her to use her hands. Her supervisor did not invite her to attend an important meeting because he assumed that any female would need to serve as a note-taker—a function she could not perform. As she wrote, "The glass ceiling for a disabled woman turns her office into a crawl space" (p. 102).

As you might imagine, women with disabilities often encounter economic difficulties. For example, women with disabilities have average incomes that are only 60% of the average income of men with disabilities (Schur, 2004). Women with disabilities are also unlikely to receive adequate retirement benefits. Disabilities can increase the size of the male-female wage gap.

In Chapter 7, we discussed the dilemma lesbians face in the workplace: Should they come out of the closet and risk discrimination? Should they try to pass, even though this option requires them to hide an important part of their identity? Women with invisible disabilities face a similar dilemma (Garland-Thomson, 2004; G. A. King et al., 2003a; Kleege, 2002). For instance, a woman with multiple sclerosis may not look disabled, but she may tire easily or experience numbness or memory problems. Should she tell her boss and risk patronizing comments or job discrimination? Or should she try to hide her disability, risking exhaustion or criticism for being lazy? In Chapter 7, we examined many biases that employed women face; these problems are intensified for women with disabilities.

PERSONAL RELATIONSHIPS OF WOMEN WITH DISABILITIES

Throughout this book, we have emphasized how women are judged by their physical attractiveness. Many North Americans have fairly rigid ideas about attractiveness. As a result, they consider many women with disabilities to be unattractive (D. Crawford & Ostrove, 2003; Mason et al., 2004). Consequently, women with disabilities are likely to be excluded from the social world as well as from some aspects of the employment world (Asch et al., 2001; A. Sohn, 2005). Heterosexual women with disabilities are less likely to date and to marry. In fact, 28% of women with disabilities live alone, in contrast to 8% of women without disabilities (Olkin, 2004; Schur, 2004).

Even less is known about the love relationships of lesbian women with disabilities. However, the research suggests that many of them also have limited romantic opportunities (Asch & Fine, 1992; Chinn, 2004).

Ynestra King (1997) described an interesting example of this bias against women with disabilities, with respect to romantic relationships. When she is sitting down, her disability is invisible; when she stands up, it's obvious she has difficulty walking. She commented on the reactions in social settings:

> It is especially noticeable when another individual is flirting and flattering, and has an abrupt change in affect when I stand up. I always make sure that I walk around in front of someone before I accept a date, just to save face for both of us. Once the other person perceives the disability, the switch on the sexual circuit breaker often pops off—the connection is broken. "Chemistry" is over. I have a lifetime of such experiences, and so does every other disabled woman I know. (p. 107)

Many North Americans assume that people with physical disabilities are not interested in sex or not capable of engaging in sexual activity (D. Crawford & Ostrove, 2003; Dotson et al., 2003; Olkin, 2004). Women with disabilities often complain that they do not receive adequate counseling about sexuality (Asch et al., 2001).

Furthermore, women's own sexual desires are likely to be ignored (A. Sohn, 2005). A woman who has a spinal disorder described a conversation she had with a gynecologist before her adolescence. She asked whether she would be able to have satisfying sexual relations with a man. He replied, "Don't worry, honey, your vagina will be tight enough to satisfy any man" (Asch et al., 2001, p. 350). Apparently, he did not even consider this woman's own sexual satisfaction!

Nonromantic friendships are also difficult. For instance, women who have friends with disabilities will often avoid certain topics of discussion. These censored areas may include sexuality, dating, and childbearing. Some women with disabilities point out that their friends seem to avoid trying to understand what it's like to live with a disability (Wendell, 1997).

Throughout this book, we have examined how biases can have harmful effects for individuals in a less favored social group. In addition to women, we have seen how people may be mistreated on the basis of ethnic group and sexual orientation. As disability activists increase their publicity, we will become more informed about this additional kind of discrimination (Kreston, 2003). According to Rosemarie Garland-Thomson (2004), "Disability, like gender and race, is everywhere, once we know how to look for it" (p. 100).

Section Summary

Women With Disabilities

1. Until recently, women with disabilities were often ignored; however, disability studies is a relatively active discipline.

2. Women with disabilities are diverse, yet they experience similar discrimination in a society that exhibits both sexism and ableism. Disabilities tend to exaggerate the differential treatment of women and men.

3. Women with disabilities may face barriers in education, discrimination in the workplace, and economic problems.

4. Women with invisible disabilities face a dilemma about whether to reveal their disabilities in the workplace.

5. Women with disabilities are often excluded from the social world of love relationships, sexual desires, and friendships.

AIDS AND OTHER SEXUALLY TRANSMITTED DISEASES

Sexually transmitted infections have major implications for women's health. For instance, thousands of North American women acquire AIDS each year from their sexual partners. In this section, we will emphasize AIDS. However, we will also briefly look at the consequences for women of five other sexually transmitted diseases: (1) human papillomavirus, which is also called HPV or genital warts, (2) chlamydia, (3) genital herpes, (4) gonorrhea, and (5) syphilis.

BACKGROUND INFORMATION ON AIDS

Acquired immunodeficiency syndrome (AIDS) is a viral disease spread by infected blood, semen, or vaginal secretions; this disease destroys the body's normal immune system (Blalock & Campos, 2003). AIDS is caused by the

human immunodeficiency virus (HIV), which has the potential to destroy part of the immune system. In particular, HIV invades white blood cells and reproduces itself. HIV then destroys those white blood cells—the very cells that coordinate the immune system's ability to fight infectious diseases (L. L. Alexander et al., 2004; Kalichman, 2003).

Women are much more vulnerable to sexually transmitted diseases than men are. By current estimates, a woman who has unprotected sexual intercourse with an HIV-infected man is between two and eight times more likely to contract HIV, compared to a man who has unprotected sexual intercourse with an HIV-infected woman (R. W. Blum & Nelson-Mmari, 2004; Gurung, 2006; E. M. Murphy, 2003). One reason for this gender difference is that the concentration of HIV is much greater in semen than in vaginal fluids.

Women's rates are increasing for HIV/AIDS and other sexually transmitted infections. In the United States and Canada, between 15% and 20% of HIV-positive individuals are female (AVERT, 2005; Ciambrone, 2003). In other parts of the world, even greater percentages are female. For instance, in the African countries south of the Sahara desert, an average of 55% of HIV-positive individuals are female. In Botswana, for example, 36% of the entire population is HIV positive. Literally hundreds of thousands of women and girls die of AIDS each year in Botswana (Coates & Szekeres, 2004; Townsend, 2003).

By the end of 2005, an estimated 440,000 U.S. males and 86,000 U.S. females had died of AIDS. Furthermore, by the end of 2005, an estimated 342,000 males and 127,000 females were living with HIV/AIDS (Centers for Disease Control and Prevention, 2005). The outlook is even grimmer when we consider the situation worldwide. Currently, an estimated 2,900,000 people have died from AIDS (Global Health Facts, 2006). In fact, throughout the world, AIDS is the second leading cause of death in adolescents and young adults. Only traffic and other accidents are more deadly (R. W. Blum & Nelson-Mmari, 2004).

Figure 11.3 shows the increasing number of AIDS deaths among U.S. women since 1991. Ethnicity is also related to the likelihood of an AIDS diagnosis. In the United States, the incidence of AIDS is relatively high among Black women; in fact, Black females account for 69% of the females who are HIV positive (Grassia, 2005). The incidence is somewhat lower among Latinas and equally low among Asian American, Native American, and European American women (Centers for Disease Control, 2005; McNair & Prather, 2004; Nichols & Good, 2004). In Canada, Black women and Aboriginal (Canadian Indian) women have a higher incidence of AIDS than White or Asian women (Loppie & Gahagan, 2001; Ship & Norton, 2001).

Let's now consider how the AIDS is transmitted, as well as the medical and psychological consequences of AIDS. Then we'll explore how the disease can be prevented.

The Transmission of AIDS

Anyone who engages in risky sexual behavior with an infected person can get AIDS. According to surveys, people believe that they can judge which sexual

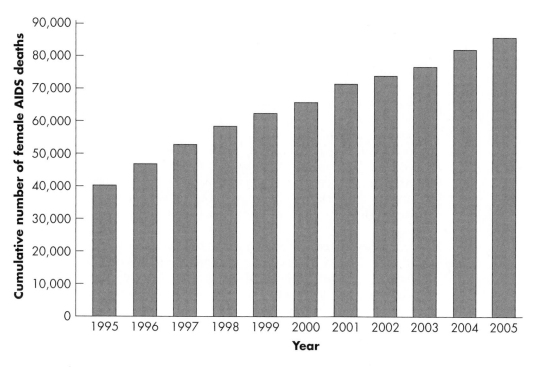

FIGURE 11.3 | CUMULATIVE AIDS DEATHS AMONG FEMALES OF ALL AGES AND ALL ETHNIC GROUPS IN THE UNITED STATES, 1995–2005.

Source: Centers for Disease Control (2002, 2005).

partners look like they might have HIV infection (L. D. Cameron & Ross-Morris, 2004). Unfortunately, however, it is impossible to tell whether a person is infected just by looking at her or him (Blalock & Campos, 2003).

Most women are infected with HIV because they used injected drugs or because they had vaginal or anal intercourse with a man who is infected (Ickovics et al., 2001; Kalichman, 2003). An important observation is that heterosexual transmission of AIDS is much more likely in women than in men. This trend is especially likely for Latina women. In fact, only 1% of Latino men in one sample acquired AIDS through heterosexual transmission, in contrast to 42% of Latina women (D. Castañeda, 2000a).

Gay and bisexual men who have had anal intercourse with men without condom protection are at high risk for becoming infected. However, women who have sex only with women and who do not use injected drugs are at relatively low risk for becoming infected (Kalichman, 2003; Peterkin & Risdon, 2003).

MEDICAL ASPECTS OF HIV AND AIDS

Many HIV-positive individuals have no symptoms at first, and so they do not realize that they are infected. In fact, some people may not experience any signs of infection for as long as 10 years. They then develop symptoms, such as swollen lymph glands, fatigue, rashes, unexplained fevers, unintentional weight loss, and diarrhea (L. L. Alexander et al., 2004; Kalichman, 2003). Both men and women may have these symptoms if they are HIV positive.

In addition, women who are HIV positive are likely to develop vaginal infections and cervical cancer (Herbert & Bachanas, 2002). Because the medical community tends to operate from a male-as-normative model, these gynecological symptoms were not included in the original list of diagnostic signs of AIDS. As a result, many women are misdiagnosed, and they may not receive early treatment (Ciambrone, 2003; Truthout, 2005). Furthermore, health-care providers are likely to test people for HIV if they belong to groups that are at high risk for AIDS. In contrast, they seldom offer to test a European-American female who is a college graduate (I. Ingber, personal communication, 2005).

People who are HIV positive are highly contagious during the initial stages of the infection, even if they have no symptoms (Blalock & Campos, 2003). As a result, HIV-positive individuals can spread the disease to other people without realizing that they are doing so.

It may take 10 years or longer for an HIV infection to develop into AIDS (Kalichman, 2003). A diagnosis of AIDS is made when a person's immune level drops below a specified level. At this point, people are seriously ill because of the symptoms mentioned earlier and because other infections have taken advantage of a severely weakened immune system (Blalock & Campos, 2003). Another problem is that HIV can damage the central nervous system, producing psychological problems such as memory loss, cognitive problems, and depression (Blalock & Campos, 2003; F. J. González, 2001; Herbert & Bachanas, 2002).

Drug therapies have been developed that prolong life for HIV-positive people. As a result, many people living with AIDS now cope with a long-term illness (Coates & Szekeres, 2004). However, low-income individuals often have no access to those expensive medications. Women are also less likely than men to use these medications, at least partly for financial reasons (Blalock & Campos, 2003; Ciambrone, 2003). These new drugs are seldom available to people in developing countries with the highest rates of HIV infection (Cowley, 2004; D'Adesky, 2004).

PSYCHOLOGICAL ASPECTS OF HIV AND AIDS

As you might imagine, HIV-positive individuals are likely to experience depression, anxiety, anger, and fear (Blalock & Campos, 2003; F. J. González, 2001). One woman described her reactions when she received her diagnosis: "Total shock, you just go numb. . . . Nothing meant anything to me. Of course, immediately you've got a death sentence; that's just what you stand there thinking" (Ciambrone, 2003, p. 24).

Some women experience a new perspective on life that is more hopeful. For instance, one woman who became an HIV/AIDS activist commented:

My goal now is to try to help other people that have this virus and let them know that you can plan for the future—life does go on, not to give up. I've always learned that if you're a fighter you'll be okay. You have to fight and you have to want to live. . . . When I finally started accepting the fact and telling people, I felt like a big burden was lifted off of my shoulder. It's like, boy, I can say it and not really be ashamed. (Ciambrone, 2003, p. 72)

People living with AIDS often report that they are stunned by insensitive reactions from other people (Ciambrone, 2003; Gahagan & Loppie, 2001). For example, family members may show no sympathy (Derlega et al., 2003). A 32-year-old Canadian woman was asked whether her family had been helpful. She replied, "Are you kidding, if I ask my family for help, they say stuff like you did this to yourself and now you want us to clean up after you? I don't talk to them anymore" (Gahagan & Loppie, 2001, p. 119).

However, some women are surprised by the messages of support. For example, Runions (1996) described how she had belonged to a fundamentalist Christian church. When she went public with her personal story about AIDS, many church members wrote to her. "The letters were warm and accepting and forgiving. Bridges that I thought had been damaged beyond repair appeared to have been strengthened by the shock of my illness" (p. 67).

Be sure you have tried Demonstration 11.2 before reading further. This demonstration assesses your personal feelings about using condoms.

Demonstration 11.2

ATTITUDES TOWARD CONDOM USE

Imagine a heterosexual woman between the ages of 18 and 35. She is sexually active, and she is not in a long-term relationship. Answer the following questions from the perspective of this woman:

1. How do you feel about condom use in general?
2. When was the last time that you had sexual intercourse?
3. Did you request that your sexual partner use a condom on that occasion?
4. How do you think that this sexual partner feels about using a condom?
5. Do you feel comfortable talking with your sexual partners about using condoms?
6. Do you typically carry a condom with you when you go out on a social occasion?
7. Where do you buy condoms?
8. Is it embarrassing for you to purchase condoms?
9. Suppose that you have been drinking and that you are about to have sexual intercourse. Would you remember to use a condom?
10. Suppose that your sexual partner says that he does not want to use a condom. What would you do?

Source: Based on Perloff (2001).

PREVENTING AIDS

At present, we have no cure for AIDS, so the only available alternative is to prevent it. Unfortunately, people in the United States are becoming less concerned about this health problem (E. Douglas, 2001). Furthermore, AIDS prevention is difficult, at both the individual and the global level (Jenkins, 2000; TK Logan et al., 2002; Oldenburg & Burton, 2004).

One problem with AIDS prevention is that many people think, "It can't happen to me!" (Dudley et al., 2002; Perloff, 2001). When people have consumed alcohol, they especially underestimate their own personal risk (L. D. Cameron & Ross-Morris, 2004). Many people also believe that they can avoid AIDS by asking a potential sexual partner about his or her HIV status. However, research with HIV-positive individuals revealed that as many as 40% of them had not disclosed their HIV status to their sexual partners (Ciambrone, 2003; Stein et al., 1998). Furthermore, some people say that they would lie about their HIV status to have sex (Noar et al., 2004).

You can probably anticipate another problem. Many people are HIV positive and don't know it. So a woman may be having sex with a man who doesn't realize he is HIV positive or who may not realize that he had sex with an HIV-positive individual two months before. Basically, if a woman decides to have sex, her sexual partner is not only that individual but also all of that individual's former partners . . . and their partners!

As we saw in Chapter 9, the abstinence-only, "Just say no" approach to safer sex does not reduce teen pregnancy; it also does not reduce HIV transmission (Coates & Szekeres, 2004). Any AIDS-prevention program must include comprehensive sex education that emphasizes condom use. It must also emphasize strategies for reducing risky sexual interactions, as well as active participation in role-play exercises (I. Ingber, personal communication, 2005; B. T. Johnson et al., 2003; Marín, 2003).

Condoms can help to limit the spread of the AIDS epidemic. However, surveys show that less than 40% of women reported that they always used condoms during sexual intercourse (Kaiser Family Foundation, 2003; Noar et al., 2004). In Demonstration 11.2, we noted some of the reasons that prevent people from consistently using condoms. In our culture, people are reluctant to discuss condom use with their potential sexual partners (Kaiser Family Foundation, 2003; Perloff, 2001).

An important problem with condom use is that men control whether they will use a condom. Throughout the world, men and women in most sexual relationships do not divide power equally. As a result, many women may not feel that they can safely insist that their partner wear a condom (R. W. Blum & Nelson-Mmari, 2004; Ciambrone, 2003; Marín, 2003). In the United States, Latino men are especially likely to control decisions about condom use during intercourse. A program designed only for Latina women may therefore be unsuccessful (D. Castañeda, 2000a). Any AIDS prevention program must be sensitive to the culture of the individuals that the program serves (L. A. Beatty et al., 2004; Jipguep et al., 2004).

Even regular condom use does *not* guarantee protection against AIDS because condoms can break or slip (L. L. Alexander et al., 2004). There is no perfectly safe sex, only safer sex. However, a condom is certainly better than no protection at all.

So far, the United States has lagged behind other industrialized countries in encouraging condom use and other AIDS-prevention programs. However, the international research shows that some developing countries successfully reduced HIV rates by emphasizing widespread education about HIV/AIDS and condom use (Commonwealth Secretariat, 2002; D'Adesky, 2004). Education about HIV/AIDS is especially difficult in developing countries because of low literacy rates (Nyanzi et al., 2004).

Other Sexually Transmitted Diseases

AIDS has attracted far more attention during the current era than all the other sexually transmitted diseases (STDs) combined (R. W. Blum & Nelson-Mmari, 2004). However, these other diseases are especially important for women because women are more likely than men to be infected from a single sexual encounter. Studies in Canada, for example, show that young women are three to seven times more likely than young men to have chlamydia, gonorrhea, or syphilis (Statistics Canada, 2000). Sexually transmitted infections also produce fewer detectable symptoms in women than in men (Jadack, 2001).

In addition, women suffer the most severe long-term consequences of sexually transmitted diseases. For example, many women who do not seek early treatment for these infections will become infertile, or they may pass the infection on to a newborn (L. L. Alexander et al., 2004; R. W. Blum & Nelson-Mmari, 2004). An additional problem is that diseases such as gonorrhea and syphilis can produce lesions in the skin, making it easier for the HIV virus to enter the body.

Table 11.1 lists five diseases that have particularly important consequences for women's lives. They are **HPV** (**human papillomavirus,** or **genital warts**), **chlamydia** (pronounced klah-*mih*-dee-uh), **genital herpes** (*her*-peas), **gonorrhea** (gon-uh-*ree*-uh), and **syphilis** (*siff*-ih-liss).

HPV deserves additional attention because it is the most common of the sexually transmitted diseases in the United States, especially among people between the ages of 15 and 24 (Moscicki, 2005). One study focused on women in college who reported never having sexual intercourse. Of those who then had intercourse, 30% acquired HPV within one year (Moscicki, 2005; Winer et al., 2003). Unfortunately, however, many people are unfamiliar with this disease. For instance, 87% of adolescents in a Canadian study had never heard of HPV (Dell et al., 2000). In other words, many young women may be infected with HPV; even though they do not recognize the name of this disease, they may eventually develop deadly cervical cancer, as discussed on page 367 of this chapter (Hillard & Kahn, 2005). According to recent research, however, a large sample of college women did not contract HPV if their sexual partners consistently used condoms (Winer et al., 2006). Furthermore, the Pap smear

TABLE 11.1 | SEXUALLY TRANSMITTED DISEASES (STDs) OTHER THAN AIDS

Disease	Description (for Women)	Consequences (for Women)
HPV (Genital Warts)	Caused by the human papilloma virus; small, often painless swellings in the genital area; very common in young women; can be treated and sometimes curable.	Can lead to cervical cancer, which may lead to death. Can be passed on to newborn during delivery.
Chlamydia	Common in young women; often no symptoms, but may cause painful urination and vaginal discharge; curable.	Can lead to infertility. Can be passed on to newborn during delivery.
Genital Herpes	Painful genital blisters, several attacks per year; can be treated, but is not currently curable.	Can lead to cervical cancer, which may lead to death. Can be passed on to newborn during delivery.
Gonorrhea	May produce vaginal discharge and pelvic pain but may not have visible symptoms; curable.	Can lead to infertility. Can be passed on to newborn during delivery.
Syphilis	Painless sores; may produce rash on the body, but may not have visible symptoms; curable.	Can be passed on to fetus prenatally and to newborn during delivery.

Sources: Based on L. L. Alexander et al. (2004), Foley et al. (2002), Hyde & DeLamater (2006), "New CDC Data" (2005), Rupp et al. (2005).

test (see page 367) is now getting more publicity, so women are more likely to receive treatment at an early stage of infection.

Women who are considering a sexual relationship need to worry not only about pregnancy, but also about the very real threat of sexually transmitted infections. Some of them may simply be uncomfortable or painful. However, others may cause recurrent health problems for a woman and potential danger to her infant. Most tragically, a sexual relationship with a person who has a sexually transmitted disease might literally be deadly.

Section Summary

AIDS and Other Sexually Transmitted Diseases

1. Acquired immunodeficiency syndrome (AIDS) is caused by the human immunodeficiency virus (HIV). AIDS has killed hundreds of thousands of North Americans; the number of cases among women has risen dramatically in recent years. AIDS is especially widespread among women in sub-Saharan Africa.

2. Most women are infected with HIV because they injected drugs or because they had vaginal or anal intercourse with an infected man.

3. People who are HIV positive may be very contagious; however, they may initially have no symptoms, so they often spread the disease. If they can afford to obtain expensive medicines, they can live much longer.

4. People living with AIDS are likely to be depressed, anxious, angry, and fearful.

5. Currently, AIDS cannot be cured. Sexually active people should know that condoms do not offer complete protection; in addition, because of power inequities, women often cannot safely insist that their partner wear a condom. AIDS prevention programs must be sensitive to the culture of the intended audience.

6. Other sexually transmitted diseases can be passed on to a newborn; they include the following:
   a. HPV (human papillomavirus or genital warts) is a common infection among young people, which can lead to cervical cancer
   b. chlamydia, which can cause infertility
   c. genital herpes, which is not curable and can lead to cervical cancer
   d. gonorrhea, which can cause infertility
   e. syphilis, which may be difficult to detect in women

WOMEN AND SUBSTANCE ABUSE

Substance abuse is an important topic in the psychology of women for the three reasons mentioned at the beginning of the chapter. First, the pattern of substance abuse is somewhat different for women and men, as we'll soon see. Second, substance abuse is treated differently in men and women (L. A. Beatty et al., 2006; Lex, 2000). For example, physicians seem to be less effective in identifying problems with alcohol and illegal drugs when the patient is a woman. In addition, the screening tests that identify substance-abuse problems are based on male norms. The tests neglect common female risk factors, such as being a victim of sexual abuse or family violence (TK Logan et al., 2002; Rheingold et al., 2004; S. H. Stewart & Israeli, 2002). The final reason that substance abuse is important is that these substances commonly cause illness and death in women.

SMOKING

Cigarette smoking is the largest preventable cause of death in the United States and other developed countries (Steptoe & Wardle, 2004). About 178,000 American women die each year from diseases related to smoking (Centers for Disease Control, 2004b). Lung cancer is the best advertised consequence of cigarette smoking, especially because only 15% of people survive more than five years after being diagnosed with lung cancer (Springen, 2004). Each year, about 44,000 U.S. women die of lung cancer (Centers for Disease Control, 2004b). For reasons that are not clear, smoking increases the chance of lung cancer more for women than it does for men (Cowley & Kalb, 2005; Henschke & Miettinen, 2004).

Women who smoke are also more likely than nonsmokers to die of emphysema and other lung diseases, several different kinds of cancer, heart disease, and strokes. Smoking also has gynecological consequences. Women who smoke increase the risk of cervical cancer, infertility, miscarriages, premature birth, and early menopause. Furthermore, babies born to smokers weigh less than babies born to nonsmokers (L. M. Cohen et al., 2003; Dodgen, 2005; Steptoe & Wardle, 2004).

Older women who smoke also increase their chances of developing osteoporosis and hip fractures (Dodgen, 2005; Steptoe & Wardle, 2004). According to a Canadian study, the average female smoker has a life expectancy of 75, in contrast to 85 for a female nonsmoker (Bélanger et al., 2002). You can see why some people say that the tobacco industry is a business that kills its best customers!

Many nonsmoking women also suffer because of their husband's or partner's smoking habits. For example, nonsmoking women married to men who smoke are significantly more likely to develop lung cancer and heart disease than women married to nonsmokers (Brannon & Feist, 2004; L. M. Cohen et al., 2003; Dodgen, 2005).

Cigarette smoking is clearly addictive. For instance, long-term smokers seldom quit smoking, even with carefully designed smoking-cessation programs (T. B. Baker et al., 2004; Dodgen, 2005; Hettema et al., 2005).

In the United States, 22% of women and 26% of men smoke cigarettes (American Cancer Society, 2005). Canadian rates are somewhat lower, with 17% for women and 22% for men (Canadian Cancer Society, 2005b). Ethnicity has a major effect on smoking rates. For example, the current rates for U.S. women are 41% for Native Americans, 22% for White women, 19% for Black women, 11% for Latina women, and only 6% for Asian American women (Centers for Disease Control, 2004b).

Why would young women want to start smoking, given the serious problems it causes? Peer influence is a major factor for adolescent females (L. L. Alexander et al., 2004; T. B. Baker et al., 2004). Furthermore, teenage females often report that they smoke to control their weight and keep slim (L. M. Cohen et al., 2003; C. S. Pomerleau et al., 2001; Saules et al., 2004). Interestingly, only 4 to 9% of Black females who are seniors in high school are cigarette smokers (Gotay et al., 2001; Husten, 1998). One reason for this low smoking rate could be that Black female teenagers are less likely than White female teenagers to be obsessed with their weight and physical appearance (C. S. Pomerleau et al., 2001).

In Chapter 2, we saw that advertisements help perpetuate gender stereotypes, and in Chapter 12 we'll see how ads also contribute to eating disorders in women. The U.S. tobacco industry currently spends more than $15 billion a year on tobacco marketing and advertising, especially targeting teenagers (Cowley & Kalb, 2005; Nichols & Good, 2004). Tragically, the cigarette ads contribute to the deaths of hundreds of thousands of women by appealing to their interests in staying slim and looking glamorous. As Kilbourne (1999) said, "Of all the lies that advertising tells us, the ones told in cigarette ads are the most lethal" (p. 180). Demonstration 11.3 asks you to analyze current cigarette ads.

Demonstration 11.3

Between now and the end of this academic term, try to analyze any cigarette advertisements you encounter in the media. (If you discover that your favorite magazine doesn't carry cigarette ads, write a thank-you letter to its editor!) If you do locate cigarette ads, does even one ad show a woman who is not slender? Are the women in these ads young or old? Keeping in mind the ethnic groups that are *least* likely to smoke, are any ethnic groups represented more frequently than they are represented in the population? What are the women doing in these ads? What message do these ads present about how cigarettes can improve your social life or your enjoyment of life? Cigarette ads sometimes portray violent messages, sexual innuendoes, and the promise of freedom. Does your sample of these advertisements support this observation?

ALCOHOL ABUSE

A 30-year-old woman, reflecting on her life, wrote the following passage:

> I used to think I couldn't be an alcoholic. I had a good job and I drank only wine. I certainly don't look like an alcoholic, whatever that look is. It took a long time for me to admit that I really was dependent on that wine. I needed it every day just to dull the world. (L. L. Alexander et al., 2004, p. 496)

Alcohol abuse refers to a pattern of alcohol use that repeatedly leads to significant impairment (Sher et al., 2005). Impairment includes missing work or school, arrests for alcohol-related crimes, or family problems (Erblich & Earleywine, 2003). Try Demonstration 11.4 before you read further.

PROBLEMS CAUSED BY ALCOHOL. Alcohol has many direct effects on women's health. They include liver disease, ulcers, brain damage, high blood pressure, heart attacks, strokes, cognitive problems, and various cancers (L. L. Alexander, 2004; Brannon & Feist, 2004; M. D. Wood et al., 2001). Children born to alcoholic mothers are likely to have **fetal alcohol syndrome**, which is characterized by facial abnormalities, retarded physical growth, psychological abnormalities, and mental retardation (Sher et al., 2005; M. D. Wood et al., 2001).

Alcohol also affects women's health indirectly. For example, alcohol is a contributing factor in about 16,000 U.S. automobile fatalities each year. Furthermore, when men drink heavily, they are more likely to rape or physically abuse women (Abbey, 2002; L. H. Collins, 2002a; Steptoe & Wardle, 2004). Alcohol abuse also increases the number of deaths from workplace injuries, drowning, fires, violent crimes, and suicide (Jersild, 2002; M. D. Wood et al., 2001).

GENDER AND ALCOHOL. According to U.S. estimates for 18- to 45-year-olds, about 4% of women and 9% of men are alcohol abusers (Sher et al., 2005). However, the gender ratio may change in the future. Surveys of U.S. high school students show that females drink slightly *more* frequently than males

Demonstration 11.4

Answer each of the following questions as accurately as possible.

1. Think about your behavior during the last two weeks. How many times have you had four or more drinks in a row if you are female or five or more drinks in a row if you are male? (The operational definition of a "drink" is 12 ounces of beer or a wine cooler, 4 ounces of wine, or 1.25 ounces of liquor.)

2. Since the beginning of this school year, how many times have you personally experienced each of the following problems as a consequence of drinking alcohol?
   a. Had a hangover
   b. Missed a class
   c. Fell behind in schoolwork
   d. Did something you later regretted
   e. Forgot what you did
   f. Argued with friends
   g. Had unplanned sexual activity
   h. Failed to use protection when you had sex
   i. Damaged property
   j. Got into trouble with campus or local police
   k. Got injured or hurt
   l. Required medical treatment for an alcohol overdose

Source: Based on Wechsler et al. (1994).

(Centers for Disease Control, 2004a). Alcohol companies are working hard to increase alcohol consumption among females because their magazine ads focus more on underage females than underage males (Jernigan et al., 2004).

Studies on college campuses reveal that more males than females abuse alcohol, although the gender difference is not enormous. For example, Wechsler and his colleagues (1994) collected survey data from 17,592 students at 140 representative colleges throughout the United States. One of the most striking findings was the large percentage of students who had engaged in **binge drinking** (defined as five or more drinks in a row for males and four or more drinks in a row for females) during the preceding two weeks. (The researchers specified fewer drinks for women because their body weight is generally lower.) The results showed that 50% of the males and 39% of the females could be categorized as binge drinkers.

Surveys on college campuses also show the behavioral consequences of drinking. Specifically, those who frequently binge are likely to report doing something they later regretted. They also report that they engaged in unplanned sexual activity and unprotected sexual intercourse (L. A. Beatty et al., 2006; Canterbury, 2002; Wechsler et al., 1994).

In discussing gender and alcohol, we need to expand on a topic mentioned at the beginning of this chapter. Research shows that, when a male and a female with the same body weight consume the same amount of alcohol, the woman will have a significantly higher blood alcohol level (L. L. Alexander et al., 2004; L. H. Collins, 2002a). This means that a 150-pound woman who drinks 2 ounces of whiskey will have a higher blood alcohol level than a 150-pound male friend who drinks 2 ounces of the same whiskey. In other words, women need to be more careful than men about limiting their alcohol consumption.

Gender differences are also relevant when people seek treatment for alcohol problems. Families are more likely to deny that female family members have a problem with alcohol. Physicians are also less likely to identify problem drinking in female patients than in male patients (Blume, 1998). In addition, society disapproves more strongly if a woman gets drunk at a party. Women may therefore be more reluctant to admit they have a drinking problem (L. A. Beatty et al., 2006; L. H. Collins, 2002a; Springen & Kantrowitz, 2004). Consistent with Theme 2, people react differently to male alcohol abusers than to female alcohol abusers.

OTHER SUBSTANCE-ABUSE PROBLEMS

Smoking and alcohol abuse are the two most common forms of substance abuse, but women also abuse other substances such as prescription medicines. Adult women are more likely than adult men to abuse sedatives and tranquilizers (L. L. Alexander et al., 2004; Canterbury, 2002; Merline et al., 2004). These drugs are socially acceptable—after all, a doctor prescribes them. On page 358, for example, we noted that health professionals often give women too much medical attention. In this case, they may be over-prescribing mind-altering medication to women who don't really need these drugs.

When we consider illicit drugs, however, the picture changes, because adult men are more likely to use these drugs. For example, a U.S. nationwide survey of adults showed that 42% of men and 30% of women reported using an illegal drug at some time in their life (Kilbey & Burgermeister, 2001). These drugs included marijuana, cocaine, heroin, and LSD. Other surveys reported similar gender differences for adults who abuse drugs (Lex, 2000; Merline et al., 2004). One reason for these gender differences is that females are judged more harshly than males for using these drugs. Also, males are more likely to know someone who sells illegal drugs (J. Warner et al., 1999). However, the gender gap in illegal-drug use has been shrinking in recent years (L. A. Beatty et al., 2006).

In a survey of high school students, males and females were equally likely to have tried illegal drugs (Centers for Disease Control, 2004a). Another trend that would surprise many people is that European American female students were more likely than Black female students to have tried illegal drugs at some point in their lives (Centers for Disease Control, 2004a). In contrast to the typical stereotype, a young woman who is experimenting with drugs is likely to be a European American female.

Women may also metabolize illegal drugs differently than men do, but little research has been conducted on this topic. In addition, few substance-abuse programs are designed to help women (L. L. Alexander et al., 2004; L. A. Beatty et al., 2006). Once again, women at risk for health problems are invisible, and their health needs are often ignored.

In this chapter, we have examined many health issues that are central to women's lives. We began by considering general health-care issues, showing that women are often second-class citizens in the United States. Women in developing countries face the risks of poor health care, complications during pregnancy, and female genital mutilation. In contrast, cardiovascular disease and cancer are primary concerns for women in North America. We also saw that women with disabilities experience exaggerated discrimination. In addition, women in the current era are increasingly likely to contract AIDS and other sexually transmitted infections. Finally, many women have problems with smoking, alcohol, and illegal substances. Feminist concerns have helped to make women's health problems more visible. However, information about these health problems is still incomplete.

Section Summary

Women and Substance Abuse

1. In the current decade, women are almost as likely as men to smoke cigarettes, a problem that has literally deadly consequences for women's health.

2. Adult women are less likely than adult men to be alcohol abusers, but female abusers face the risks of numerous health problems for themselves and fetal alcohol syndrome for their children. Furthermore, people are more likely to ignore alcohol problems in females than in males.

3. Women are more likely than men to abuse prescription drugs, whereas men are more likely than women to abuse illegal drugs.

CHAPTER REVIEW QUESTIONS

1. This chapter starts by discussing four general trends in the medical treatment of women. Consult pages 357–359 and provide additional information about each of these trends.
2. At the beginning of this chapter, we also examined gender comparisons in mortality, morbidity, and use of the health-care system. Summarize this information, and describe how these factors may be related.
3. One of the themes of this book is that men and women are treated differently. Apply this theme to the following topics: (a) biases against women in health care, (b) women with disabilities, (c) diagnosis of specific diseases, and (d) substance-abuse problems.

4. What are some of the specific health problems that women are likely to face, and how can women reduce the chances of developing these life-threatening problems? What are other serious problems for women who smoke or abuse alcohol?
5. What is a disability, and how do women with disabilities differ from one another? In what ways does the life of a woman with a disability differ from the life of a woman who is not disabled?
6. Imagine that you are counseling high-school females about AIDS and other sexually transmitted diseases. Describe each of them and explain why sexually active women should be concerned about this health problem.

7. Some people argue that the sexually transmitted diseases are biologically "sexist"; that is, they hurt women more than they hurt men. Provide some examples to support this statement. How does this statement also apply to smoking and alcohol abuse?

8. How is social class relevant when we consider health care, mortality, and the life expectancy for people with AIDS? How is ethnicity relevant when we consider women's life expectancy, women in developing countries, the incidence of AIDS, and substance abuse?

9. Explain why gender comparisons are complicated when we consider the topic of substance abuse. Before you had read the section on substance abuse, what did you believe about gender comparisons in this area?

10. One theme of this book is that women are relatively invisible. Relate this theme to topics such as the general research on women's health and the specific research on women with disabilities and on women with substance-abuse problems. In what areas are women unusually visible?

KEY TERMS

*health psychology (355)

*mortality (359)

*morbidity (360)

*female genital mutilation (362)

female genital cutting (362)

*cardiovascular disease (363)

*mammogram (364)

*lumpectomy (365)

*cervical cancer (367)

*Pap smear test (367)

*hysterectomy (368)

*osteoporosis (368)

*disability (370)

disability studies (370)

*ableism (371)

*acquired immunodeficiency syndrome (AIDS) (373)

*human immunodeficiency virus (HIV) (374)

*human papillomavirus (HPV) or genital warts (379–380)

*chlamydia (379–380)

*genital herpes (379–380)

*gonorrhea (379–380)

*syphilis (379–380)

*alcohol abuse (383)

*fetal alcohol syndrome (383)

*binge drinking (384)

 Note: The terms asterisked in the Key Terms section serve as good search terms for InfoTrac College Edition. Go to http://infotrac.thomsonlearning.com and try these added search terms.

RECOMMENDED READINGS

Alexander, L. L., LaRosa, J. H., Bader, H., & Garfield, S. (2004). *New dimensions in women's health* (3rd ed.). Sudbury, MA: Jones and Bartlett. Here's an excellent introductory textbook about women's health that is comprehensive, clearly written, and interesting.

Ciambrone, D. (2003). *Women's experiences with HIV/AIDS: Mending fractured selves*. Binghamton, NY: Haworth. Of all the volumes about women and HIV/AIDS, Ciambrone's book provided the most informative and compassionate perspective, with numerous well-chosen quotations from women's experiences with this disease.

Manderson, L. (Ed.). (2003). *Teaching gender, teaching women's health: Case studies in medical and health science education*. Binghamton, NY: Haworth. Manderson's book is an excellent introduction to the issue of emphasizing gender in medical education, especially because it includes several chapters with an international perspective.

Smith, B. G., & Hutchison, B. (Eds.). (2004). *Gendering disability*. New Brunswick, NJ: Rutgers University Press. I strongly recommend this book as an introduction to disability studies. It includes theoretical, historical, and psychological perspectives on the topic of women with disabilities.

ANSWERS TO THE TRUE-FALSE STATEMENTS

1. False (p. 357); 2. True (p. 360); 3. False (p. 361); 4. False (pp. 362–363); 5. True (p. 363); 6. True (p. 370); 7. True (p. 374); 8. False (p. 380); 9. True (p. 381); 10. True (p. 382).

© Getty Images

12 | WOMEN AND PSYCHOLOGICAL DISORDERS

True or False?

_____ 1. Women in the United States and Canada are two to three times more likely than men to experience major depression; however, researchers typically report gender similarities in other countries.

_____ 2. In the United States and Canada, men are more likely than women to attempt suicide and also to die from suicide.

_____ 3. Women are more likely than men to seek therapy, and this factor explains about 60% of the apparent gender differences in depression.

_____ 4. After a distressing event occurs, women are more likely than men to think about their emotions and about the causes and consequences of that event.

_____ 5. People with anorexia nervosa are underweight, and they experience several physical problems; however, they are otherwise fairly well adjusted.

_____ 6. Because of their binge-eating episodes, people with bulimia nervosa are typically overweight.

_____ 7. By early elementary school, children show a bias against their overweight classmates.

_____ 8. Black women are typically more satisfied with their bodies than European American women are.

_____ 9. European Americans are more likely than people of color to use mental health services.

_____ 10. Feminist therapy emphasizes a fairly evenly distribution of power between the therapist and the client.

Katie, a shy 16-year-old, described her personal struggles with depression:

> The experience of depression is like falling into a deep dark hole that you cannot climb out of. You scream as you fall, but it seems like no one hears you. . . . Depression affects the way you interpret events. It influences the way you see yourself and the way you see other people. (Barlow & Durand, 2005, p. 205)

Jennifer, 17 years old, has an eating disorder. She described an early phase of this disorder:

> I was just under five feet, six inches and weighed 76 pounds. My hair was falling out and my skin was dry and flaky. People stared at me. Some said I looked like a victim of a concentration camp. I took these comments as compliments. I thought these people were jealous of my body, envied me for how much weight I had lost. Their comments reassured me—confirmed that I was doing a good job restricting my calories. I was successful. (Shandler, 1999, p. 24)

Like many people throughout the world, these two young women are experiencing **psychological disorders;** they have emotions, thoughts, and behaviors that are typically maladaptive, distressing to themselves, and different from the social norm (Barlow & Durand, 2005). As we'll see in this chapter, women are more likely than men to suffer from both depression and eating disorders. They are also more likely to seek therapy for these problems.

Men are more likely than women to experience other problems. We saw in Chapter 11 that men are currently more likely than women to abuse alcohol and other drugs. Men are also about three times more likely than women to have **antisocial personality disorder,** which is characterized by a variety of behaviors that clearly violate the rights of other people; these behaviors include excessive lying, impulsiveness, and aggressiveness (American Psychiatric

Association, 2000; Barlow & Durand, 2005; Nydegger, 2004). People with this disorder also believe that they are perfectly well adjusted and that the rest of the world has a problem.

If we compile overall tallies—and include all individuals with substance-abuse problems and antisocial personality disorder—then the incidence of psychological disorders in women and men is roughly similar (Nydegger, 2004; Wilhelm, 2006). Keep in mind, however, that the specific types of disorders may differ.

In this chapter, we will focus on two categories of disorders that are more common among women than men: depression and eating disorders. Then we will investigate both traditional and nontraditional approaches to treating psychological disorders.

DEPRESSION

Katie, the young woman introduced at the beginning of this chapter, is suffering from depression. A person with **major depressive disorder** has frequent episodes of hopelessness and low self-esteem; this person seldom finds pleasure in any activities (American Psychiatric Association, 2000; Whiffen & Demidenko, 2006). The World Health Organization lists depression as one of the five most prevalent health threats throughout the world (Sáez-Santiago & Bernal, 2003).

In North America, women are two to three times more likely than men to experience depression during their lifetime (Kornstein & Wojcik, 2002; Statistics Canada, 2006; Whiffen & Demidenko, 2006). Interestingly, no consistent gender differences in depression are found among young children (Crick & Zahn-Waxler, 2003; R. C. Kessler, 2006). However, around the time of puberty, females begin reporting more depressive symptoms than males. During students' first semester of college, for example, L. J. Sax and her coauthors (2002) found that 11% of women and 6% of men reported that they were frequently depressed. This gender difference continues throughout adulthood (Kornstein & Wojcik, 2002; Lapointe & Marcotte, 2000; Whiffen & Demidenko, 2006).

Gender differences in depression rates hold for all U.S. ethnic groups: White, Latina/o, Black, Asian American, and Native American (Nolen-Hoeksema, 2002; Sáez-Santiago & Bernal, 2003; Saluja et al., 2004). Research in Canada shows gender differences for people from British, European, and Asian ethnic backgrounds (K. L. Dion & Giordano, 1990; Kornstein & Wojcik, 2002).

Furthermore, cross-cultural studies report that women are more likely than men to experience depression in countries as varied as Sweden, Germany, Lebanon, Israel, Chile, South Korea, Taiwan, Uganda, and New Zealand (Frodi & Ahnlund, 1995; Kornstein & Wojcik, 2002; Nydegger, 2004; Whiffen & Demidenko, 2006; Wilhelm, 2006). Let's consider some of the characteristics of depression and then examine some explanations for the higher incidence of depression in women.

CHARACTERISTICS OF DEPRESSION

Depression is a disorder that includes the following emotional, cognitive, behavioral, and physical symptoms (J. R. DePaulo & Horvitz, 2002; Horowitz, 2004; Mann, 2005; Whiffen & Demidenko, 2006; Worell & Remer, 2003):

1. *Emotional symptoms*: feeling sad, gloomy, tearful, guilty, apathetic, irritable, and unable to experience pleasure.
2. *Cognitive symptoms*: thoughts of inadequacy, worthlessness, helplessness, self-blame, and pessimism about the future. These depressed thoughts interfere with normal functioning, so that the individual has trouble concentrating and making decisions.
3. *Behavioral symptoms*: decreased ability to do ordinary tasks, decreased productivity at work, neglected personal appearance, decreased interactions with other people, and sleep problems. Many depressed individuals attempt suicide. In the United States and Canada, women are typically—but not always—more likely than men to think about suicide and also to attempt suicide. However, men are more likely to die from suicide (Canetto, 2001b; Centers for Disease Control, 2004a; Nydegger, 2004). The gender difference in deaths from suicide rate is found in most developed countries, but not all of them (Kennedy et al., 2005; Range, 2006; Statistics Canada, 2006).
4. *Physical symptoms*: illnesses such as headaches, dizzy spells, fatigue, indigestion, and generalized pain. Weight gain or weight loss is also common.

We should emphasize that most people have occasional episodes of extreme sadness. For example, this sadness is considered normal when a close friend or family member dies. However, these symptoms normally do not continue many years after the loss. Women with major depression struggle with persistent depression, without relief (Whiffen & Demidenko, 2006). They are also likely to have other problems such as substance abuse, anxiety disorders, and eating disorders (Crick & Zahn-Waxler, 2003; J. R. DePaulo & Horvitz, 2002; Kornstein & Wojcik, 2002). These additional problems, in turn, make the depression even more intense.

There is no "typical" depressed woman. However, some characteristics tend to be associated with depression. For example, a woman is more likely to be depressed if she has several young children in the home or if her income is low (Whiffen, 2001). As you might imagine, women who are unhappily married are more likely than happily married women to be depressed (Kornstein & Wojcik, 2002).

Personality characteristics are also important. Women who are depressed are especially likely to have low self-esteem, traditional feminine gender typing, and little sense of control over their own lives (Hoffmann et al., 2004; Malanchuk & Eccles, 2006; Travis, 2006; Whiffen & Demidenko, 2006).

EXPLANATIONS FOR THE GENDER DIFFERENCE IN DEPRESSION

What are some of the explanations for the prevalence of depression among women? Let's begin with some biological explanations that were once thought to be important but no longer seem relevant. Then we will examine a much longer list of factors that do contribute to the gender differences in depression.

FACTORS NO LONGER CONSIDERED RELEVANT.   Several decades ago, many theorists believed that gender differences in biological factors could explain why women are more likely than men to be depressed. For example, perhaps the gender differences could be directly traced to biochemical factors, hormonal fluctuations, or some genetic factor associated with having two X chromosomes. However, careful reviews of the literature suggest that biological factors do not convincingly explain the greater prevalence of depression in women (Nolen-Hoeksema, 2002, 2003; Whiffen & Demidenko, 2006; Worell & Remer, 2003).[1]

Let's now consider some of the explanations that are currently thought to account for the gender differences in depression. As we frequently observe in psychology, human behavior is so complex that a single explanation is usually inadequate. All the following factors probably help to explain why the rate of depression is so much higher in women than in men.

GENDER DIFFERENCES IN SEEKING THERAPY.   Maybe you've thought about another potential explanation. In Chapter 11, we pointed out that women are more likely than men to seek medical help. Is it possible that women and men are equally depressed in the general population but that women are simply more likely to seek help from a therapist? Researchers have shown that women are somewhat more likely than men to seek therapy (Addis & Mahalik, 2003; Mosher, 2002; Winerman, 2005). However, researchers have also examined the incidence of depression in the general population. Women are still much more likely than men to be depressed (R. C. Kessler, 2006; Kornstein & Wojcik, 2002). In summary, we must search for additional factors to account for the large gender differences in depression.

DIAGNOSTIC BIASES IN THERAPISTS.   The research suggests that therapists tend to *overdiagnose* depression in women (Sprock & Yoder, 1997). That is, therapists are more likely to supply a diagnosis of major depression in women, compared to men with similar psychological symptoms. At the same time, therapists tend to *underdiagnose* depression in men (Sprock & Yoder, 1997; Whiffen, 2001). That is, therapists are guided by their stereotypes about men being "tough," so they are reluctant to conclude that men have depression. In addition, men may respond to depression by drinking excessively, so therapists may diagnose an alcohol problem, rather than depression (McSweeney, 2004; Wolk & Weissman, 1995). Therapists' bias is one reason why women are more likely to be diagnosed with depression. However, many other factors also contribute to the very real gender difference in depression.

---

[1]Researchers have established that biological factors can predispose individuals to develop depression (e.g., Mann, 2005). However, males and females are similarly affected by these biological factors. For example, women are no more likely than men to have a genetic background associated with depression.

GENERAL DISCRIMINATION AGAINST WOMEN.   Several general forms of discrimination seem to increase the incidence of depression in women (Belle & Doucet, 2003; Mendelson & Muñoz, 2006; Nydegger, 2004; M. T. Schmitt et al., 2002). In earlier chapters, we noted that women experience general discrimination and that their accomplishments are often devalued relative to those of men. As Klonoff and her colleagues (2000) discovered, female students who frequently experience sexist treatment are especially likely to report symptoms of depression.

Furthermore, in Chapter 7, we showed that women are less likely to be hired and promoted in the workplace. In many cases, women's work is also less rewarding and prestigious. Depression is especially likely when women face barriers in their careers and when their achievements do not seem to be valued. Discrimination against women—in everyday life and in the workplace—leads women to feel that they have relatively little control over their lives (Lennon, 2006; Nolen-Hoeksema, 2002; Travis, 2006).

VIOLENCE.   As we will emphasize in Chapter 13, many females are the targets of violence. Some girls are sexually abused during childhood. Some women face sexual harassment at school and at work. Their boyfriends or husbands may physically abuse them. Furthermore, a large number of women are raped, either by men they know or by men who are strangers. Interpersonal violence clearly contributes to depression (Koss et al., 2003; Mendelson & Muñoz, 2006; Travis, 2006).

A 30-year-old Latina teacher wrote the following account about how an acquaintance rape continues to affect her:

> I wake up three or four mornings a week in a state of terror. . . . My last dream reminded me of a bad experience I had in college when my date drove to an isolated part of town, held me down, and threatened to beat me up unless I had sex with him. I tried to get away, but couldn't. I gave up fighting. But my reactions don't make sense. That experience was 10 years ago, and I didn't react much at the time. . . . I didn't tell anyone until last week when I called the crisis line. I feel like I am going crazy. I just don't usually get this overpowered by things. (Worell & Remer, 2003, p. 204)

Not surprisingly, women are likely to feel depressed and anxious during the months after they have been raped (J. A. Hamilton & Russo, 2006). In fact, it is surprising that many women who are victims of violence manage to escape the symptoms of depression.

POVERTY.   Throughout this book, we have emphasized how social class influences psychological and physical well-being. In addition, people with economic problems are especially likely to have high levels of depression (Gallo & Matthews, 2003; Travis, 2006; Whiffen & Demidenko, 2006). Low-income women have far fewer options and choices than women with financial resources (Belle & Dodson, 2006; Belle & Doucet, 2003; Ehrenreich, 2001). We can understand why an unemployed woman who is trying to support three young children—with no assistance from a husband who has deserted the family—should experience depression. Once again, it is surprising that more low-income women do not experience depression (V. E. O'Leary & Bhaju, 2006).

HOUSEWORK.   Women who choose a traditional role as a full-time homemaker often find that their work is unstimulating and undervalued. This focus on caring for others may lead to depression (Kornstein & Wojcik, 2002; Lennon, 2006). On the other hand, women who work outside the home often have the equivalent of two jobs.

We saw in Chapter 7 that most women thrive when they are employed. However, some women who become overwhelmed with housework, in addition to a job, may develop depression (Lennon, 2006; Nolen-Hoeksema, 2001; Travis, 2006).

EMPHASIS ON PHYSICAL APPEARANCE.   Beginning in adolescence, some young women become excessively concerned about their physical appearance. As we'll see in the section on eating disorders, adolescent females often resent the weight they gain during puberty. They may find their changing body shape especially unappealing in an era when female fashion models are so painfully thin. This dissatisfaction may contribute to depression (Girgus & Nolen-Hoeksema, 2006; Travis, 2006; Whiffen & Demidenko, 2006). At this point, try Demonstration 12.1 before you read further.

Demonstration 12.1

RESPONSES TO
DEPRESSION

Suppose that you are in a depressed mood because of a recent personal event (e.g., an unexpectedly low grade on an exam, the breakup of a love relationship, or a quarrel with a close friend or relative). Check which of the following activities you are likely to engage in when you are depressed:

_____   1. Working on a hobby that takes concentration
_____   2. Writing in a diary about how you are feeling
_____   3. Getting away from everyone else to try to sort out your emotions
_____   4. Doing something with your friends
_____   5. Getting drunk
_____   6. Telling friends about how depressed you are
_____   7. Punching something
_____   8. Exercising or playing sports
_____   9. Writing a letter to someone describing your emotions
_____ 10. Engaging in reckless behavior (e.g., driving 10 miles over the speed limit)
_____ 11. Listening to music
_____ 12. Making a list of the reasons you are sad or depressed

When you have finished, count up how many of your responses fall into the first group: Items 2, 3, 6, 9, 11, and 12. Then count up the number that fall into the second group: Items 1, 4, 5, 7, 8, and 10. The text discusses the results.

Source: Based on Nolen-Hoeksema (1990).

WOMEN'S RELATIONSHIPS.   Women are more likely than men to feel responsible for making sure that their relationship is going well (Crick & Zahn-Waxler, 2003; Girgus & Nolen-Hoeksema, 2006; Nolen-Hoeksema, 2003). They may believe that they ought to be more unselfish in a relationship rather than expressing their own personal preferences (Jack, 2003; McGann & Steil, 2006; Whiffen & Demidenko, 2006). Latina girls and women may be especially self-sacrificing (Travis, 2006).

In addition, many women become overly involved in the problems of their friends and family members. We saw in Chapter 6 that women sometimes have closer relationships with their friends than men do. However, in some cases, women become so involved with others' problems that they actually neglect their own needs (Helgeson & Fritz, 1998; McMullen, 2003; Whiffen, 2001).

RESPONSES TO DEPRESSION.   So far, we have noted that a number of factors make depression more likely in women than in men. More women than men may seek therapy, and therapists may overdiagnose depression in women. In addition, many factors—general discrimination, poverty, violence, housework, concern about physical appearance, and interpersonal relationships—predispose women to depression.

Another major factor also encourages depression: Women often respond differently from men when they are experiencing a depressed mood. Demonstration 12.1 focused on responses to depression. You may recall from Chapter 3 that parents are much more likely to encourage girls—rather than boys—to contemplate why they are sad. This factor may contribute to the development of depression in women.

Susan Nolen-Hoeksema is the major researcher on responses to depression. She proposed that depressed women are more likely than depressed men to turn inward and focus on their symptoms. They contemplate the possible causes and consequences of their emotions, an approach called a **ruminative style** of response. For example, they worry about how tired they are, and they keep thinking about all the things that are wrong in their life (Nolen-Hoeksema & Jackson, 2001). Research confirms that women are significantly more likely than men to use ruminative strategies when they are depressed (Girgus & Nolen-Hoeksema, 2006; Mor & Winquist, 2002; Nolen-Hoeksema, 1990, 2003; Tamres et al., 2002). According to other research, people believe that women *should* acknowledge their sadness, *should* worry more than men, and *do* worry more than men (Broderick & Korteland, 2002; M. Conway et al., 2003; Marecek, 2006).

Furthermore, Nolen-Hoeksema proposed that rumination prolongs and intensifies a bad mood. Rumination tends to create a negative bias in people's thinking, so that pessimistic ideas come easily to mind. People are therefore more likely to blame themselves and to feel helpless about solving their problems. This pessimistic style increases the likelihood of more long-term, serious depression (Nolen-Hoeksema, 2002; Scher et al., 2004). We also saw in the previous section that women often worry about other people's problems. Women who tend to ruminate about all these problems often make their depressed mood even worse.

Now look at your responses to Demonstration 12.1. Naturally, no 12-item questionnaire can provide an accurate assessment of your style of responding to depression. However, if you checked more items in the first group, you may tend to have a ruminative style. In contrast, if you checked more items in the second group, you are probably more likely to distract yourself when you are depressed. (Incidentally, if you checked Item 1, 4, or 8, your distracting style may help lift you out of a depressed mood. However, if you checked Item 5 or 10, you should be concerned that your response style could endanger yourself and others.)

What should you do if you have a ruminative style? The next time you are depressed, think briefly about the problem and then do some activity that takes your mind away from your emotions. Wait until your depressed mood has lifted somewhat. Then you can begin to analyze the situation that made you depressed. When you are less depressed, you will be able to think more clearly about how to solve the problem and how to gain control over the situation. However, if your depression persists, you should seek help from a therapist.

CONCLUSIONS ABOUT GENDER AND DEPRESSION. Therapists may be able to help women readjust their ruminative style. But look at the other sources of gender difference, such as poverty, violence, and workload. These problems of our society cannot be typically addressed by therapists working one on one with their clients. People who are genuinely concerned about depression in women must pressure elected officials and join organizations that publicize these issues. If social inequities created the depression problem, then we must work to change these inequities.

Many mental health professionals in the current era strongly emphasize biological factors, which reside inside each person. When they treat depression, they simply prescribe an antidepressant such as Prozac, rather than address the problems in society. This shifting focus parallels the increasingly conservative politics in the United States. For example, we saw in Chapter 7 that the U.S. government's policy on welfare has changed. This policy suggests that women should be blamed for being poor; it's not the government's job to reduce poverty. In contrast, feminist psychologists emphasize a different strategy: To address psychological problems, we must acknowledge that these problems occur in a social context (Cosgrove & Caplan, 2004; Marecek, 2006; Nolen-Hoeksema et al., 1999). In fact, these societal problems are intertwined with the many other gender inequities discussed throughout this textbook.

Section Summary

Depression

1. Women are more likely than men to suffer from depression and eating disorders; men are more likely to have problems with substance abuse and antisocial personality disorder.

2. Depression is two to three times more common in women than in men; this gender difference has been reported in a variety of ethnic groups in North America and also in many other countries.

3. Depression includes feelings of sadness and apathy, thoughts of inadequacy and pessimism, decreased performance, a potential for suicide attempts, and physical complaints such as headaches and dizzy spells.

4. Depression is more likely if a woman has young children in the home, a low income, an unhappy marriage, and low self-esteem.

5. Gender differences in biological predisposition do not explain the gender differences in depression.

6. Some likely explanations for gender differences in depression include gender differences in seeking therapy, therapists' diagnostic biases, general discrimination, violence, poverty, housework, emphasis on physical appearance, personal relationships, and ruminative responses to depression. Attempts to reduce depression in women must emphasize societal problems.

EATING DISORDERS AND RELATED PROBLEMS

Frances M. Berg (2000) began her book on eating disorders with a thought-provoking comment:

> The number one wish of brilliant, ambitious young women is not to save the rain forests or succeed in a career, but to lose weight. . . . Why do modern women in the most affluent countries in the world live like starving people in a [developing country]? Why do they choose to be weak, apathetic and unable to fully contribute to their families, their careers, and their communities? Why, when instead they could be strong, capable, and caring women? (p. 15)

The truth is that most women in North America are preoccupied with their body weight. Many women may not have one of the life-threatening disorders we will discuss shortly. However, they often shift their lives away from social pleasures and professional concerns so that they can focus on their physical appearance and dieting.

Furthermore, symptoms of disordered eating occur on a continuum of severity (Calogero et al., 2005; Piran, 2001; Ricciardelli & McCabe, 2004). Anorexia nervosa, bulimia nervosa, and binge-eating disorder occupy the most extreme end of that continuum. However, many other females have varying degrees of body-image problems, so that we can place their disorders on the less extreme portion of that continuum.

In this section, we'll first consider anorexia nervosa, bulimia nervosa, and binge-eating disorder. Then we'll address the more general question of our culture's emphasis on being slim. Our final topic will be the related issues of being overweight and dieting. We need to emphasize in advance that being overweight is *not* a psychological disorder. However, the emphases on thinness and dieting—combined with the fear of being overweight—are major factors in creating eating disorders.

Anorexia Nervosa

At the beginning of this chapter, you read about a young woman who has anorexia nervosa. A person with **anorexia nervosa** has an extreme fear of becoming obese and also refuses to maintain an adequate body weight, defined as 85% of expected weight (American Psychiatric Association, 2000; Garfinkel, 2002). People with this disorder typically have a distorted body image (Garfinkel, 2002; Stice, 2002). For example, one young woman with anorexia nervosa weighed only 100 pounds, yet she said:

> I look in the mirror and see myself as grotesquely fat—a real blimp. My legs and arms are really fat and I can't stand what I see. I know that others say I am too thin, but I can see myself and I have to deal with this my way. (L. L. Alexander et al., 2001, p. 64)

Approximately 95% of those with anorexia nervosa are female, and between 0.5% and 4% of adolescent females experience anorexia nervosa. The typical age range for the onset of anorexia nervosa is 14–18 years, although concern about weight often begins many years earlier (Jacobi, Hayward et al., 2004; Jacobi, Paul et al., 2004). Anorexia occurs in both Western and non-Western cultures (Keel & Klump, 2003). In North America, this disorder is more common in White females than in Black women, but the data on other ethnic groups are inconsistent (Jacobi, Hayward, et al., 2004; O'Neill, 2003; Striegel-Moore et al., 2003).

Anorexia nervosa starts in a variety of ways. Some women with anorexia were initially slightly overweight. Then a comment from someone or even a query as innocent as "Are you gaining weight?" prompts them to begin a severe dieting program. Other women with anorexia trace the beginning of their disorder to a stressful life event, such as moving to a new school, or to a traumatic event, such as sexual abuse (American Psychiatric Association, 2000; Beumont, 2002). Many who develop this disorder tend to be rigid perfectionists who are eager to please other people (Guisinger, 2003; Polivy & Herman, 2002; Stice, 2002). Their self-esteem is also lower than in females who do not have eating disorders (Jacobi, Hayward et al., 2004; Jacobi, Paul et al., 2004).

One important medical consequence of anorexia nervosa is **amenorrhea** (pronounced ae-men-oh-*ree*-ah), or the cessation of menstrual periods. Other frequent medical consequences include heart, lung, kidney, and gastrointestinal disorders (American Psychiatric Association, 2000; Michel & Willard, 2003; D. E. Stewart & Robinson, 2001). Another common problem is osteoporosis, the bone disorder we discussed in Chapter 11. Osteoporosis afflicts women with anorexia because of their low estrogen levels and inadequate nutrition (Gordon, 2000).

Anorexia nervosa is an especially serious disorder because between 5% and 10% of people with anorexia die from it (American Psychiatric Association, 2000; Keel et al., 2003; P. F. Sullivan, 2002). Unfortunately, treatment for this disorder is difficult, especially because many people with anorexia also meet the criteria for major depression. When anorexia is treated during the early stages, about 75% of people can recover completely (Powers, 2002; P. F. Sullivan, 2002).

Anorexia nervosa illustrates the potentially life-threatening consequences of our culture's preoccupation with thinness. One father told me about his daughter, who was struggling with anorexia: "She'd rather be dead than fat."

BULIMIA NERVOSA

A person with **bulimia nervosa** is able to maintain a normal body weight (unlike a person with anorexia nervosa); however, she or he has frequent episodes of binge eating and typically uses inappropriate methods to prevent weight gain. Binge eating means consuming huge amounts of food, typically 2,000 to 4,000 calories at a time (M. Cooper, 2003; Garfinkel, 2002; Keel et al., 2001). The binge-eating episodes are usually secretive. People with bulimia nervosa then try to compensate for this huge food intake by vomiting or using laxatives (Stice, 2002). In between binges, they may diet or exercise excessively.

As with people with anorexia, those with bulimia tend to be depressed and low in self-esteem (M. Cooper, 2003; Jacobi, Paul et al., 2004; Keel et al., 2001). They are also obsessed about food, eating, and physical appearance. For example, a female college student with bulimia nervosa described her behavior:

> I've gone for donuts, then ice cream, and then I got two cheeseburgers, a large order of fries, and then decided that chocolate chip cookies sounded good. So I got some of those. And then I got hungry for a candy bar, but I couldn't decide which kind, so I got both . . . sometimes I'll just be a bottomless pit. . . . So then I go throw up immediately, as much as I can. (Kalodner, 2003, p. 76)

At least 90% of individuals with bulimia nervosa are female, and the disorder is especially common on college campuses. Between 1% and 5% of adolescent and young adult females develop bulimia (Jacobi, Hayward et al., 2004; National Institute of Mental Health, 2001; Piran, 2001). However, recognizing the presence of bulimia is difficult because people with bulimia typically maintain a normal body weight (Beumont, 2002). They do not stand out in a crowd.

The medical consequences of bulimia nervosa include gastrointestinal, heart, liver, metabolism, and menstrual-cycle problems (Andreasen & Black, 2001; M. Cooper, 2003; Kreipe & Birndorf, 2000). Bulimia nervosa is typically not as life threatening as anorexia nervosa. However, bulimia is difficult to treat effectively and it is associated with serious medical and psychological problems (R. A. Gordon, 2000; Keel et al., 2003; Tobin, 2000).

BINGE-EATING DISORDER

Psychologists and psychiatrists have recently proposed a third kind of eating disorder, although it has not yet been studied as thoroughly as anorexia nervosa and bulimia nervosa (M. Cooper, 2003; Schmidt, 2002). People with **binge-eating disorder** have frequent episodes of binge eating (at least two episodes each week for at least 6 weeks). During these binges, they consume huge amounts of food, and they feel that they cannot control these binges. Afterward, they typically feel depressed and disgusted with themselves. Unlike people with bulimia nervosa, they do not use inappropriate methods, such as vomiting or using laxatives, to compensate for the binges (Grilo, 2002; Michel & Willard, 2003; Stice, 2002). As a result, those with binge-eating disorder are typically overweight.

Between 1% and 4% of the general population suffers from binge-eating disorder. About 60% of these individuals are female. In other words, the majority are female, but the gender ratio is much less skewed toward females than the gender ratio for anorexia nervosa or bulimia nervosa (Grilo, 2002; Kalodner, 2003). The research also suggests that people with binge-eating disorder do not value thinness as much as people with the other two eating disorders (R. A. Gordon, 2000). People who have binge-eating disorders are likely to experience depression and low self-esteem, similar to those with anorexia nervosa and bulimia nervosa (Grilo, 2002; Jacobi, Hayward et al., 2004; Michel & Willard, 2003)

Let's briefly review the three kinds of eating disorders, and then we'll consider some cultural factors related to these disorders.

1. People with anorexia nervosa refuse to maintain appropriate body weight, so they are dangerously thin.
2. People with bulimia nervosa maintain normal body weight. However, they have frequent episodes of binge eating; they typically use inappropriate methods to prevent weight gain.
3. People with binge-eating disorder have frequent episodes of binge eating. However, they do not use inappropriate methods to prevent weight gain; they are typically overweight.

THE CULTURE OF THINNESS

Most North American females are concerned that they are overweight—even if they are not—a tendency called the **culture of thinness** (M. Cooper, 2003). As we saw in Chapter 4, adolescent females often develop an intense focus on body weight. Information about the culture of thinness helps us understand people with eating disorders, as well as those with less extreme concerns about thinness. We'll explore media images, discrimination against overweight people, and women's general dissatisfaction with their bodies. Finally, we'll focus on how women of color view their bodies.

MEDIA IMAGES. Kate Dillon (2000) recalled her earlier experience in fashion modeling. She was 5'11" and weighed only 125 pounds, yet she was instructed to lose 10 to 20 pounds. Women who seek treatment for eating disorders often report that the anorexic-looking models in fashion magazines were an important motivational force in encouraging their pursuit of thinness (Kalodner, 2003; Smolak & Striegel-Moore, 2001).

Research demonstrates that the media emphasize weight consciousness, slenderness, and dieting in young women—and young women are well aware of this message (Greenberg & Worrell, 2005; Quart, 2003; C. A. Smith, 2004). Other research on the media assesses how these images may influence women's views of their bodies. For instance, studies show that young women who frequently read fashion magazines or see images of slender women tend to be especially dissatisfied with their own bodies (M. Cooper, 2003; Greenwood & Pietromonaco, 2004; Henderson-King et al., 2001; Vaughan & Fouts, 2003).

DISCRIMINATION AGAINST OVERWEIGHT WOMEN.   Our society is biased against women who are overweight. For example, most people would hesitate before making a racist comment, but they might make a comment about an overweight woman (Brownell, 2005; Dittman, 2004; C. A. Johnson, 2005; Myers & Rothblum, 2004). Furthermore, consistent with Theme 2 of this book, people discriminate more strongly against overweight women than against overweight men (Greenberg et al., 2003; J. M. Price & Pecjak, 2003; Smolak, 2006).

Women who are overweight are also less likely to be hired than slender women. Overweight women also tend to earn lower salaries, and they experience other forms of job discrimination (Fikkan & Rothblum, 2005; Myers & Rothblum, 2004). People also think that overweight women are less likely than slender women to have a romantic partner (Greenberg et al., 2003). Even 5-year-olds report that they would prefer to be friends with a slender child rather than a heavier one. Beginning at an early age, then, children may be biased against their overweight peers (Latner & Schwartz, 2005; Rand & Resnick, 2000; Rand & Wright, 2000). Furthermore, overweight girls are teased more than overweight boys (Neumark-Sztainer & Eisenberg, 2005). Children's physical attractiveness can have widespread consequences for the way other people treat them (Langlois et al., 2000; Ramsey & Langlois, 2002).

However, this discrimination against overweight individuals may not operate as strongly when people judge women of color. For instance, in one study, White college students rated a heavier Black woman more positively than a slender Black woman (T. J. Wade & DiMaria, 2003).

FEMALES' DISSATISFACTION WITH THEIR BODIES.   In our culture, the ideal is the emaciated women who inhabit fashion magazines. As a result, many females feel unhappy about their bodies (Forbes et al., 2004; Kalodner, 2003; Markey, 2004). For instance, women are significantly more likely than men to be dissatisfied with their bodies (T. F. Davison & McCabe, 2005). In addition, normal-weight women often rate themselves as heavier than they really are (McCreary & Sadava, 2001). Furthermore, college women typically believe that they are heavier than other women (Sanderson et al., 2002). As a result, women often spend time worrying unnecessarily about their weight.

Research on children in preschool and elementary school now shows that many young girls are concerned about being fat and about dieting (Kalodner, 2003; Smolak, 2006). The Disney Corporation offers a "Little Mermaid" bathroom scale, encouraging young girls' preoccupation with dieting. As early as 5 years of age, girls who are overweight are more likely to have negative self-concepts compared to normal-weight girls (K. K. Davison & Birch, 2001).

Also, our current culture encourages young women to evaluate how their bodies appear in the eyes of their peers (Gapinski et al., 2003; Smolak, 2006). Women's current dissatisfaction with their bodies produces unhappiness. It also focuses their attention on relatively superficial characteristics and on themselves rather than on meaningful interactions with other people (F. M. Berg, 2000).

Some females are less concerned about their physical appearance. Compared to heterosexual women, lesbian women are generally more satisfied with their bodies (Moore & Keel, 2003; Rothblum, 2002). Also, lower-class European American women are less worried about thinness than are European American women from middle and upper income brackets (Bowen et al., 1999). Ethnicity is an additional variable that is sometimes related to body dissatisfaction. Let's see how women of color regard these body-image issues.

WOMEN OF COLOR, BODY IMAGE, AND THINNESS.   For many years, the research on body image focused on European American populations (Smolak & Levine, 2001). However, more current research provides some information about Latinas, Black women, and Asian American women.

In general, Black women are more satisfied with their body-image than are European American women (Bay-Cheng et al., 2002; B. D. Hawkins, 2005). Black women also believe that an average-weight woman is more attractive than a too-thin woman (Markey, 2004; Smolak & Striegel-Moore, 2001; E. A. Wise et al., 2001). However, the European American admiration for thinness might be spreading to Black individuals. We may soon see an increase in eating disorders among Black women (Markey, 2004; Polivy & Herman, 2002).

The research on Latina women reveals some contradictions. Some research suggests that European Americans are more preoccupied with thinness than Latinas are. However, other research reports that European American and Latina women have similar levels of body dissatisfaction (Bay-Cheng et al., 2002; Bowen et al., 1999). One reason for the inconclusive findings is the diversity within each ethnic group. For example, women from the Dominican Republic may not emphasize thinness. In contrast, women raised in upper-class Argentinean families may value thinness even more than European American women do (B. Thompson, 1994; J. K. Thompson et al., 1999). Factors such as social class, country of origin, and current place of residence undoubtedly influence how Latina women view their bodies.

The research on Asian Americans also reveals inconclusive findings. For example, one study showed that European American women have more negative body images than women whose parents had emigrated from Cambodia to the United States (Franzoi & Chang, 2002). However, other research shows that North American women—whose heritage is Chinese, Korean, Indian, and Pakistani—often report negative body images (Cachelin et al., 2000; Chand, 2002).

Surprisingly, the results cannot be explained by the amount of exposure to North American culture. For instance, a study of female undergraduate students in Western Canada found that length of time living in Canada was not correlated with their body-image satisfaction. Furthermore, European Canadian women actually had more *positive* body images than Asian and South Asian women did (Kennedy et al., 2004).

BEING OVERWEIGHT AND DIETING

A variety of different measures are used to assess whether an individual is overweight. Depending on the specific measure, between 33% and 61% of the adult population in the United States is overweight (Cogan & Ernsberger, 1999; Wadden et al., 2002). Being overweight is not classified as a mental disorder (Kalodner, 2003). However, we need to discuss the issue of being overweight because it is a central topic in many women's lives. In addition, the fear of becoming overweight is a major factor in anorexia nervosa and bulimia nervosa.

Research demonstrates that people who eat foods that are high in fat—and who also do not exercise sufficiently—are likely to face greater health risks than other people. In addition, overweight people are more likely than other people to be at risk for diabetes, cancer, and cardiovascular disease (Hu et al., 2004; J. M. Price & Pecjak, 2003; Wing & Polley, 2001). Earlier in this section, we pointed out that overweight people face another cluster of problems because of social and professional discrimination.

Unfortunately, losing extra weight is a major challenge. Some people take up smoking to suppress their appetites. However, we saw in Chapter 11 that smoking has enormous health risks. Also, people are at risk for heart problems if they repeatedly lose and regain weight (Ernsberger & Koletsky, 1999).

According to one estimate, approximately 40% of U.S. women (compared with 20% of men) were dieting to lose weight (F. M. Berg, 1999). North Americans can choose from thousands of different diet plans and products, and most of them are expensive. In addition, many of them are ineffective because people regain the lost weight (J. M. Price & Pecjak, 2003; Wadden et al., 2002). Think about this: If any of these programs were truly effective, then why are there so many other programs on the market? And if they really worked, then why are there so many fat people?

Unfortunately, most people who have lost weight tend to gain it back (J. M. Price & Pecjak, 2003; C. A. Smith, 2004). Dieting causes a change in metabolism. The dieter can survive on increasingly smaller portions of food. A "normal" food intake therefore causes weight gain. In addition, dieters may become so focused on food that they are tempted to binge (Polivy & McFarlane, 1998). For these reasons, many clinicians encourage their clients to accept themselves, avoid further weight gain, not focus on reaching a specific weight, and exercise moderately (Myers & Rothblum, 2004; C. A. Smith, 2004; Wing & Polley, 2001). Other clinicians suggest that overweight clients should not aim for an enormous weight loss. Instead, their goal should be a realistic weight loss—perhaps 10% of body weight—that can actually be achieved.

In this section on eating disorders, we have looked at four groups of people who are highly concerned about their weight:

1. People with anorexia try to lose weight, and they succeed, sometimes with fatal consequences.

2. People with bulimia fluctuate between gorging and dieting; their weight is usually normal, but their eating habits produce numerous other problems.
3. People with binge-eating disorder have frequent episodes of eating large amounts of food; they are typically overweight.
4. People who are overweight may try to lose weight, usually without success.

Think how the guilt and anxiety that all four groups associate with eating might be reduced if more women were encouraged to accept their bodies. We all need to focus less on weight issues. We also need to urge the media not to show so many anorexic female actors and models. Something is clearly wrong when normal-weight women begin dieting! Imagine, too, how much more positive we might feel if the women in the media had bodies that showed as much variety as the bodies we see in real life. Imagine how wonderful it would be to glance at the covers of magazines in the grocery store and not see guilt-inducing articles titled, "Finally—An Answer to Problem Thighs" or "How to Lose 15 Pounds in Just One Month!" Now that you are familiar with the issues related to eating disorders, try Demonstration 12.2.

Demonstration 12.2

ANALYZING YOUR OWN ATTITUDES TOWARD BODY SIZE

Answer each of the questions in this demonstration using the following scale:

1	2	3	4	5

Never   Frequently

_____ 1. I comment about my own weight to other people.

_____ 2. I compliment other people if they seem to have lost weight.

_____ 3. If someone has gained weight, I avoid commenting about this.

_____ 4. I make jokes about people who are overweight.

_____ 5. I encourage people to feel good about their bodies, even if they do not meet the cultural norms for being slender.

_____ 6. When looking at a fashion magazine, I am concerned that many of the models are too thin.

_____ 7. When someone makes a joke about fat people, I express my disapproval.

_____ 8. I eat relatively little food, so that I can keep thinner than average.

_____ 9. I compliment other people when they show self-control in their eating habits.

_____ 10. When looking at a magazine, I'm concerned that the photographs may be encouraging eating disorders.

Now calculate your score: Add together your ratings for Items 1, 2, 4, 8, and 9. From this sum, subtract your ratings for Items 3, 5, 6, 7, and 10. If your total score is low, congratulations! You have a positive attitude toward body-size diversity.

Source: Based on F. M. Berg (2000).

Section Summary

Eating Disorders and Related Problems

1. Many females have varying degrees of body-image problems. Anorexia nervosa, bulimia nervosa, and binge-eating disorder are at the extreme end of the continuum.

2. People with anorexia nervosa have an intense fear of becoming overweight, and they do not maintain an adequate body weight. They have numerous health problems, which may have fatal consequences.

3. People with bulimia nervosa binge frequently, but they maintain a normal weight because they vomit or use other methods to prevent weight gain. They typically have many health problems.

4. People with binge-eating disorder have frequent excessive binges, but they do not use inappropriate methods to maintain a normal weight.

5. The media present images of exaggerated thinness, and these images contribute to women's dissatisfaction with their bodies; both adults and children discriminate against overweight people.

6. Many women are dissatisfied with their bodies, although body dissatisfaction is less common among lesbians and Black women; the pattern of body images is not yet clear for Latina and Asian American women.

7. Being overweight is not a psychological disorder, but it has potential health and social consequences; dieting can be both difficult and potentially dangerous.

8. Recommended weight-loss strategies include moderate exercise and more realistic goals for losing weight.

TREATING PSYCHOLOGICAL DISORDERS IN WOMEN

So far, we have discussed two categories of psychological disorders that are more common in women than in men: depressive disorders and eating disorders. To keep this chapter a manageable length, I omitted a third category of psychological problems that are more common in women than in men. These are called **anxiety disorders,** conditions in which a person's anxiety is intense and persistent. For instance, women are about twice as likely as men to have a **specific phobia,** an extremely strong, persistent fear of something particular, such as snakes (American Psychiatric Association, 2000). In a second anxiety disorder, called **panic disorder,** recurrent panic attacks occur without warning. Women are two to three times as likely as men to experience panic disorder (American Psychiatric Association, 2000).

If a woman seeks help for psychological problems such as depression, eating disorders, or anxiety disorders, she will probably receive psychotherapy and/or treatment with a medication. **Psychotherapy** is a process in which a therapist aims to treat psychological problems and reduce distress, most often through verbal interactions (Gilbert & Kearney, 2006; Worell & Remer, 2003). Severely disturbed individuals who receive therapy are typically treated in hospitals or other psychiatric facilities. Others may receive psychotherapy for many years, but they can still function while living at home. Still others choose psychotherapy to help them during brief periods of stress in their lives.

Pharmacotherapy uses medication to treat psychological disorders. In recent years, researchers have developed new medications to help people cope with some psychological disorders. When used in conjunction with psychotherapy, these medications may be useful. However, they are sometimes prescribed inappropriately. We'll briefly discuss pharmacotherapy in this section, although we'll emphasize the psychotherapy approach to treating psychological disorders.

Let's first consider how sexism may influence psychotherapy, and then we will discuss psychotherapy with lesbians and bisexuals, as well as psychotherapy with low-income women and women of color. Our final two sections will examine traditional approaches to psychotherapy and feminist therapy.

Psychotherapy and Sexism

Throughout this book, Theme 2 has emphasized that people treat women and men differently. We might hope that therapists' professional training would make them highly sensitive to potential biases. However, the research suggests that women often experience gender bias during psychotherapy.

Gender and Misdiagnosis.   Earlier in this chapter, we noted the potential for sexism in diagnosing psychological disorders. Specifically, therapists may over-diagnose depression in women and under-diagnose depression in men (Sprock & Yoder, 1997). Another problem is that therapists often rely too heavily on *The Diagnostic and Statistical Manual of Mental Disorders* (American Psychiatric Association, 2000). Unfortunately, many of the guidelines in this manual have not been scientifically tested (P. J. Caplan & Cosgrove, 2004a; Houts, 2002; Spiegel, 2005; Wiley, 2004). In addition, therapists often ignore poverty, discrimination, and other cultural problems that contribute to depression in women (McSweeney, 2004). An additional problem is that health-care professionals may misdiagnose a woman's physical disorder as being "all in her head" (Di Caccavo & Reid, 1998; Klonoff & Landrine, 1997).

The Treatment of Women in Therapy.   Gender bias may lead to misdiagnosis and to inappropriate treatment in therapy. For example, therapists may view men as more competent than women in work settings (Gilbert & Scher, 1999). Therapists may also evaluate clients in terms of how well their behavior fits female and male gender stereotypes (P. J. Caplan & Cosgrove, 2004a). In addition, therapists may blame women for events beyond their control. In treating a woman who has been sexually abused, for instance, they may ask her what she did to encourage the attack. In summary, the same gender stereotypes and discriminatory behavior that operate throughout our culture may also influence therapists

SEXUAL RELATIONSHIPS BETWEEN THERAPISTS AND CLIENTS.   One of the principles of ethical conduct for psychologists and psychiatrists states that therapists must not disrupt their professional relationships with clients by engaging in any form of sexual intimacy with them (Bersoff, 2003; Fisher, 2003). Nonetheless, surveys show that about 4% of male therapists and 1% of female therapists have had sexual relationships with their clients (Pope, 2001). We need to emphasize that most psychotherapists are ethical people who firmly believe that sexual relationships with clients are forbidden (Bersoff, 2003; Pope, 2001). As you can imagine, however, a woman who has been sexually exploited by a therapist is likely to feel guilty, angry, and emotionally fragile. She will also have an increased risk for suicide (Gilbert & Rader, 2001; Pope, 2001).

Sexual relationships with clients are especially damaging because they demonstrate a violation of trust. They are also damaging because they represent situations in which a person with power takes advantage of someone who is relatively powerless and vulnerable (Fisher, 2003). We examine similar power inequities in Chapter 13, where we'll discuss sexual harassment, rape, and battering.

PSYCHOTHERAPY WITH LESBIAN AND BISEXUAL WOMEN

When lesbian and bisexual women visit a therapist, they should feel just as valued and respected as any other client. In fact, ethical principles specify that psychologists must attempt to eliminate **sexual prejudice,** a negative attitude toward individuals because of their sexual orientation. Therefore, therapists must be well informed about the research on sexual orientation and the importance of love relationships. They also should not try to change a person's sexual orientation. Therapists must also recognize that most lesbian and bisexual women experience prejudice. Furthermore, therapists must be aware that lesbian and bisexual women of color may experience different forms of sexual prejudice in their own ethnic communities (Greene, 2000b; T. L. Hughes et al., 2003). In addition, therapists must be knowledgeable about community resources and support groups that are available for lesbian and bisexual clients.

Therapists must also be aware of **heterosexism,** which is bias against lesbians, gay males, and bisexuals or any group that is not exclusively heterosexual. For example, heterosexual therapists must avoid the heterosexist assumption that a client's lesbian relationship is somehow less important than another client's heterosexual relationship (Gilbert & Rader, 2001; C. R. Martell et al., 2004; T. L. Rogers et al., 2003). Feminists believe that women should not be treated as second-class citizens in comparison to men. In addition, feminists believe that lesbians and bisexual women should not be treated as second-class citizens, in comparison to heterosexual women. Let's now consider how low-income women and women of color are also frequently treated as second-class citizens, in comparison to European American women with relatively high incomes.

PSYCHOTHERAPY AND SOCIAL CLASS

As we saw in Chapter 11, many women do not have health insurance. Furthermore, most insurance companies cover only a relatively small portion of the costs for mental health care (Aponte, 2004; Katon & Ludman, 2003; Travis & Compton, 2001). Women also earn less than men, so they cannot afford some of the options for psychotherapy that many men are likely to have (Gilbert & Rader, 2001; V. Jackson, 2005; Nydegger, 2004). The national health-care program in Canada is certainly more comprehensive than the U.S. system. However, the mental health coverage emphasizes pharmacotherapy, rather than psychotherapy (Romanow & Marchildon, 2003). As a result, many low-income women in the United States and Canada cannot afford psychological counseling. Even if they manage to obtain counseling, they need to overcome barriers such as time off from work, childcare arrangements, and transportation (V. Jackson, 2005; L. Smith, 2005).

Furthermore, psychotherapists often treat economically poor women in a classist fashion. For example, therapists may assume that a low-income woman simply needs basic resources—such as shelter and food—and she cannot benefit by discussing psychological problems such as loneliness and depression. A therapist may believe in the **myth of meritocracy,** that a person's social status indicates his or her abilities and achievements. In this case, a therapist might think that a client has financial problems because she has chosen not to work and not to pursue training for a better-paying job (L. Smith, 2005). Clearly, psychotherapists need to overcome classist beliefs, and they also need to receive professional training about social-class issues. Furthermore, these classist beliefs may be especially destructive for women of color.

PSYCHOTHERAPY WITH WOMEN OF COLOR

The United States and Canada are rapidly becoming two of the most ethnically diverse countries in the world. In the United States, for example, 97 million people (out of a total population of 300 million) say that they are Latina/o, Black, Asian, or Native American. In Canada, 5 million people (out of a total population of 32 million) consider their ethnic origins to be Asian, Aboriginal, Black, or Latin American. As a result, North American therapists need to be sensitive to ethnic-group differences in values and beliefs (Brooks et al., 2004; Sue, 2004).

One basic problem is that people of color are not as likely as European Americans to use mental health services. Some of the reasons for this under-usage include: (1) reluctance to recognize that help is necessary; (2) language and economic barriers; (3) suspicion about discussing personal problems with therapists, especially European American therapists; (4) the use of other culturally specific interventions, such as prayer (R. C. Kessler et al., 2005; K. E. Miller & Rasco, 2004a; L. Smith, 2005; Snowden & Yamada, 2005).

Most members of ethnic minority groups will not be able to choose therapists from their own background. Only about 6% of U.S. doctorate-level psychologists belong to ethnic minority groups (American Psychological Association, 2003). As a result, most people of color must consult therapists whose life experiences may be very different from their own. For instance, those therapists would not be personally familiar with the continuing racism that people of color face (Comas-Díaz, 2000; Sue & Sue, 2003).

You can probably anticipate another problem. Many people of color do not speak fluent English. Furthermore, most European American therapists are not fluent in a language other than English. Language can therefore be a major barrier for many people of color (Bemak & Chung, 2004; Sue & Sue, 2003). To make the situation more vivid—if your own first language isn't Spanish—imagine describing your psychological problems to a therapist who speaks only Spanish. You may be able to discuss the weather, but could you describe to a Latina therapist precisely how and why you feel depressed? Could you accurately capture the subtleties of your binge-eating disorder? All these factors help explain why people of color are less likely than European Americans to seek therapy and also why they are likely to drop out of therapy sooner (Snowden & Yamada, 2005).

Let's consider some of the important issues that arise in therapy for four different ethnic groups of women: Latinas, Blacks, Asian Americans, and Native Americans. Then we'll discuss some general therapeutic issues for women of color.

LATINAS. In earlier chapters, we noted that Latina/o culture sometimes emphasizes gender roles in terms of *marianismo* for women and *machismo* for men (Arredondo, 2004; Garcia-Preto, 2005; Sue & Sue, 2003). In a traditional family, a Latina woman is expected to remain a virgin until marriage. Once she is married, she must place her family's needs first. As a result, some Latina women may feel that they cannot accept a suggestion to spend more time addressing their own needs (G. C. N. Hall & Barongan, 2002).

Furthermore, some Latinas have come to North America as refugees from a country besieged by war and turmoil. For example, government repression in El Salvador during the 1980s resulted in more than 75,000 deaths, as well as numerous rapes, tortures, "disappearances," and other human rights abuses. A young woman who escaped from El Salvador may have seen her sister slaughtered, and she may have spent years in a refugee camp (Kusnir, 2005). Living through such traumatic circumstances often creates long-lasting stress-related disorders and other psychological problems. Well-meaning therapists, even if they are fluent in Spanish, may not be prepared to provide therapy for women who have lived through political upheaval.

BLACK WOMEN. Black women are likely to experience a kind of stress that is qualitatively different from the stress experienced by middle-class European American women. Specifically, Black women may report stressful factors such as extreme poverty, inadequate housing, and neighborhood crime (Black & Jackson, 2005; Sue & Sue, 2003; Wyche, 2001). Black women often experience discrimination. For example, 80% of adult Black women in one survey reported that other people had frequently made them feel inferior (D. R. Brown et al., 2003).

However, Black women may have an advantage over European American women because their heterosexual relationships are often more evenly balanced with respect to power (Black & Jackson, 2005; R. L. Hall & Greene, 2003; P. M. Hines & Boyd-Franklin, 2005). Still, they are at a disadvantage if they seek help from a European American therapist who accepts the myth of the Black matriarchy, which we discussed in Chapter 8 (Baca Zinn & Eitzen, 2002). Therapists should also resist the myth that all Black women are strong and resilient (P. T. Reid, 2000). That perspective would encourage therapists to believe that their Black female clients do not really require care for themselves. Furthermore, therapists should resist the myth that all Black women are economically poor, because an increasing percentage are upper-middle class (Sue & Sue, 2003).

ASIAN AMERICAN WOMEN.   We noted earlier that many Latina women are refugees from war and torture in their country of birth. Many Asian American women are also refugees. They escaped war and torture in Asian countries such as Cambodia, Laos, Sri Lanka, and East Timor (Bemak & Chung, 2004; Lee & Mock, 2005a; K. E. Miller & Rasco, 2004b). Many Asian Americans cannot find an interpreter who is fluent in both English and an Asian language (McKenzie-Pollock, 2005). For instance, during the 1970s and 1980s, Southeast Asian people who speak the Hmong language immigrated to Minnesota. More than 45,000 Hmong now live in the Minneapolis-St. Paul area. As you can imagine, there are not many interpreters who can speak English and Hmong, appreciating the subtleties of both languages (Go et al., 2004).

We need to re-emphasize that individual differences among Asian Americans are substantial. However, many Asian American families are strongly influenced by the traditional perspective that the male should be the powerful member of the household. These families often expect women to play a passive, subordinate role (Lee & Mock, 2005a; McKenzie-Pollock, 2005; Root, 2005).

Many researchers have tried to determine why Asian Americans are less likely than other ethnic groups to use mental health services. They have concluded that Asian Americans are just as likely as European Americans to have mental health problems (G. C. N. Hall & Barongan, 2002; Lee & Mock, 2005a, 2005b). However, an important cultural value in many Asian groups is to maintain the honor of the family and to avoid any possibility of bringing shame to one's relatives. Psychological problems may be judged especially harshly. As a result, a woman who enters psychotherapy is basically admitting that she has failed (G. C. N. Hall & Barongan, 2002; W. M. L. Lee, 1999; Shibusawa, 2005).

Several Asian American mental health centers are trying outreach programs, using culturally sensitive techniques. These centers have been reasonably successful in increasing the number of community residents who seek therapy (G. C. N. Hall & Barongan, 2002; McKenzie-Pollock, 2005).

NATIVE AMERICANS.   Among Native American and Canadian Aboriginal (Canadian Indian) women, two major mental health problems are the high rates of alcoholism and depression (G. C. N. Hall & Barongan, 2002; Sutton & Broken Nose, 2005; Tafoya & Del Vecchio, 2005; Waldram, 1997). Many theorists trace these problems to earlier governmental programs in both the United States and Canada (Sutton & Broken Nose, 2005; Tafoya, 2005; Tafoya & Del Vecchio, 2005). For example, many Native and Aboriginal children were taken from their families and placed in residential schools, where they were punished for speaking their own language (Tafoya, 2005). These programs encouraged children to assimilate into the European-focused mainstream and undermined the influence of the tribal elders.

Currently, unemployment and poverty are widespread in many Native communities (Winerman, 2004). The combination of all these factors is partly responsible for the high suicide rate. For example, the suicide rate among Canadian Aboriginal women is much higher than for other Canadian women (Statistics Canada, 2000; Waldram, 1997).

Tawa Witko is a Native American who decided to earn a Ph.D. degree in psychology. She then returned to live and work with the Lakota Sioux on their reservation in South Dakota. In addition to psychotherapy, she also provides counseling about substance abuse and domestic violence (Winerman, 2004). Fortunately, some European American therapists can work successfully in Native American and Canadian Aboriginal communities. They are more likely to succeed if they help to train community members to become mental health professionals (Wasserman, 1994).

GENERAL STRATEGIES FOR THERAPY WITH WOMEN OF COLOR.   Many therapists have suggested methods for European Americans who want to increase their skills in helping women of color. Graduate training programs have incorporated a number of these suggestions (American Psychological Association, 2003; Aponte, 2004; Cervantes & Sweatt, 2004; R. L. Hall & Greene, 2003; McGoldrick et al., 2005b; Sue & Sue, 2003; Wyche, 2001). As you'll see, many of these recommendations apply to *all* clients, not just women of color.

1. Search the client's history for strengths and skills that can facilitate the counseling process.
2. Show empathy, caring, respect, and appreciation for your client.
3. Learn about the history, experiences, religion, family dynamics, and cultural values of the client's ethnic group.
4. Understand that each ethnic category includes many cultures that can differ substantially from one another.
5. Be aware that some immigrants and other people of color might want to become more acculturated into the European American mainstream but that others want to connect more strongly with their own culture.
6. Communicate to the client that racism may have played a significant role in her life, and try to determine how the client has responded to this racism.

7. Hire bilingual staff members and paraprofessionals from the relevant ethnic communities; enlist other community professionals (e.g., school-teachers) to help identify relevant problems in the community.

TRADITIONAL THERAPIES AND WOMEN

Therapists approach their work from a variety of theoretical viewpoints. A therapist's viewpoint can influence his or her attitudes toward women, the techniques used in therapy, and the goals of therapy. We'll discuss two traditional psychotherapy orientations: the psychodynamic approach and the cognitive-behavioral approach. We'll also consider pharmacotherapy in this section.

PSYCHODYNAMIC APPROACH.   Psychodynamic therapy refers to a variety of approaches derived from Sigmund Freud's psychoanalytic theories, proposed in the early 1900s. During treatment, classic psychoanalysis requires the "patient" to free-associate, saying any thoughts that come to mind. The therapist's task is to interpret these thoughts (Andreasen & Black, 2001; D. Young, 2003). Like Freud's psychoanalysis, current **psychodynamic therapy** focuses on unconscious and unresolved conflicts stemming from childhood; however, it emphasizes social relationships more than Freud did (D. Young, 2003).

We need to discuss Freud's theories in connection with therapy because it has influenced our culture's perspectives on both women and psychotherapy (Bornstein, 2001). Interestingly, Freud himself admitted that his theories about women were the weakest part of his work (Slipp, 1993). However, this caution is seldom mentioned when supporters discuss Freudian theory.

Here are some components of Freud's approach that present problems for individuals who are concerned about women's mental health (P. J. Caplan & Cosgrove, 2004b; Chodorow, 1994; Enns, 2004a; Saguaro, 2000):

1. In Freudian theory, the masculine is the norm for humans, and the feminine is less important.
2. According to Freudian theory, women's lack of a penis leads them to experience more shame and envy than men; women realize that they are inferior to men. Freud also argued that women develop a less mature sense of justice because they do not fully resolve childhood conflicts.
3. Freud's approach argues that penis envy can be partially resolved by having a baby. If a woman decides not to have children, she would be judged to have a psychological disorder.
4. Mothers are the caretakers of young children. The Freudian approach blames mothers for the psychological problems that children experience, but it does not praise the positive aspects of mothers' interactions with their children.
5. Freud did not address issues such as social class or ethnicity, although we have seen that these have an important impact on women's experiences.

A major part of psychodynamic therapy sessions focuses on unconscious forces and childhood relationships—factors that presumably help therapists understand current psychological problems. This emphasis on the unconscious is not inherently biased against women. However, most feminist critics argue that the five points we just outlined would not encourage women to become more positive about themselves or more psychologically healthy.

Many modern psychodynamic theorists have redefined some of the classic Freudian concepts. You may want to read further about these more feminist approaches (Brabeck & Brabeck, 2006; Chodorow, 1999, 2000; Enns, 2004a; Jordan, 2000; Saguaro, 2000).

COGNITIVE-BEHAVIORAL APPROACH. According to **cognitive-behavioral therapy,** psychological problems arise from inappropriate thinking (cognitive factors) and inappropriate learning (behavioral factors). This approach encourages clients to try new behaviors (Powers, 2002). For example, a woman who is depressed and lonely might be encouraged to initiate within the next week at least five social interactions (Andreasen & Black, 2001). The cognitive-behavioral approach also asks clients to question any irrational thought patterns they may have. For instance, suppose that a woman is depressed because she feels she is not socially skilled. A therapist may help the woman to see alternative viewpoints, such as "Just because my friend ate lunch with someone else today, it doesn't mean that I'm a loser." Well-controlled research demonstrates that cognitive-behavioral therapy (CBT) can be as effective as medication in reducing depression (Craighead et al., 2002; Hollon & DeRubeis, 2004; Worell & Remer, 2003).

In addition, therapists frequently use a cognitive-behavioral approach to treat eating disorders (e.g., Kalodner, 2003; Wilfley & Rieger, 2003). Well-controlled research on bulimia nervosa shows that CBT is more effective than antidepressant medication, which is the standard pharmacotherapy for bulimia nervosa (Agras & Apple, 2002; C. T. Wilson & Fairburn, 2002). For example, a cognitive-behavioral therapist may help a client develop behavioral strategies to reduce her compulsive eating and her automatic thoughts about body image (M. Cooper, 2003; Kalodner, 2003). The therapist may also work with the client to reword negative statements (e.g., "My thighs are disgusting") into more neutral forms (e.g., "My thighs are the heaviest part of me").

Cognitive-behavioral therapy can also be useful for lesbian and gay male individual—for instance, in helping a lesbian develop strategies for dealing with heterosexist acquaintances (C. R. Martell et al., 2004). Furthermore, many cognitive-behavioral principles can be combined with feminist therapy (Worell & Remer, 2003). As we will discuss shortly, however, most cognitive-behavioral therapists work to change clients' own individual behaviors and inappropriate thoughts (Enns, 2004a). They typically do not discuss with the client the more general problem of society's widespread gender biases.

PHARMACOTHERAPY. As we noted earlier, pharmacotherapy treats psychological disorders by using medication. Our focus in this chapter is on psychotherapy, but other resources offer additional information about specific medications (e.g., Dunivin, 2006; Gitlin, 2002; Shatzberg et al., 2003).

Women are more likely than men to use sedatives, tranquilizers, and antidepressants (Nydegger, 2004; Travis & Compton, 2001). However, women may be more likely than men to experience the kinds of psychological disorders for which these medications are appropriate. Unfortunately, current research has not examined whether physicians may be overprescribing medication for their female clients.

In the current era, pharmacotherapy is an important component of treating most serious psychological disorders (Gitlin, 2002; Mann, 2005; Shatzberg et al., 2003). In many cases, medication can allow severely disturbed clients to be more receptive to therapy. However, the physician must carefully select the medication and discuss it with the client. Physicians and therapists must also monitor the dosage and side effects of any medications (Dunivin, 2006; Sramek & Frackiewicz, 2002; "Treating Depression," 2004). Furthermore, most therapists would argue that any client with a disorder serious enough to be treated with medication should receive psychotherapy as well (P. J. Caplan & Cosgrove, 2004b; Dunivin, 2006). Before reading further, be sure to try Demonstration 12.3.

Demonstration 12.3

PREFERENCES
ABOUT
THERAPISTS

Imagine that you have graduated from college and would like to consult a therapist for a personal problem you have developed. You feel that the problem is not a major one. However, you want to sort out your thoughts and emotions on this particular problem by talking with a psychotherapist. The following list describes characteristics and approaches that therapists may have. Place a check mark in front of each characteristic that you would look for in a therapist. When you are done, consult page 420 to see how to interpret your responses.

_____ 1. I want my therapist to believe that it's okay not to adopt a traditional gender role.

_____ 2. I would like my therapist to help me think about forces in our society that might be contributing to my problem.

_____ 3. I would like my therapist to believe that the client and the therapist should have reasonably similar power in a therapy situation.

_____ 4. My therapist should believe that women and men are similar in their capacity for assertiveness and their capacity for compassion.

_____ 5. I want my therapist to be well informed about the research on women and gender.

_____ 6. I think that my therapist should reveal relevant information about her or his own experiences, if the situation is appropriate.

_____ 7. I want my therapist to address relevant issues other than gender in our therapy sessions—issues such as age, social class, ethnicity, disability, and sexual orientation.

_____ 8. My therapist should encourage me to develop relationships in which the two individuals are fairly similar in their power.

_____ 9. I want my therapist to avoid interacting with me in a gender-stereotyped fashion.

Source: Based on Enns (2004a).

FEMINIST THERAPY

We have examined how therapists can use the psychodynamic approach, the cognitive-behavioral approach, and pharmacotherapy in treating psychological disorders. However, feminists emphasize that psychotherapy must be sensitive to gender issues.

Most therapists probably believe that therapy should be nonsexist. According to the principles of **nonsexist therapy,** women and men should be treated similarly rather than in a gender-stereotyped fashion (Worell & Johnson, 2001; Worell & Remer, 2003). The nonsexist therapy approach emphasizes that therapists must interact with female and male clients in an unbiased fashion. Furthermore, therapists should be familiar with the recent research on the psychology of women and the pervasiveness of sexism in our society (Enns, 2004a). However, feminist therapy goes beyond nonsexist therapy in order to address these social inequalities. Demonstration 12.3 highlighted some of the differences between nonsexist therapy and feminist therapy.

Feminist therapy has three important components: (1) Clients should be treated in a nonsexist fashion; (2) social inequalities should be considered when evaluating the factors that shape women's behavior, so the personal is political; and (3) the distribution of power between the client and the therapist should be as egalitarian as possible (Slater et al., 2003; Szymanski, 2003; Worell & Remer, 2003). Many recent books and other resources describe both the theory and the practice of feminist psychotherapy (e.g., Ballou & Brown, 2002; Enns, 2004a; R. L. Hall & Greene, 2003; Marecek, 2001b; Silverstein & Goodrich, 2003; Worell & Johnson, 2001; Worell & Remer, 2003). Let's consider how feminist therapy addresses two central issues: (1) social forces in our culture and (2) power in psychotherapy.

Several principles of feminist therapy point out how North American culture devalues women (Brabeck & Ting, 2000; Enns, 2004a; Goodrich, 2003; Marecek, 2001b; Nolen-Hoeksema, 2003; Rastogi & Wieling, 2005; Szymanski, 2003; Tien & Olson, 2003; Worell & Remer, 2003). Let's examine these important principles:

1. Feminist therapists believe that women are less powerful than men in our culture, and women therefore have an inferior status. Women have many strengths, and their major problems are *not* internal, personal deficiencies. Instead, the problems are primarily societal ones, such as sexism and racism.
2. Women and men should have equal power in their family and other social relationships.
3. Society should be changed to be less sexist; women should not be encouraged to adjust to a sexist society by being quieter and more obedient.
4. We must work to change those institutions that devalue women, including governmental organizations, the justice system, educational systems, and the structure of the family.
5. We also need to address inequalities with respect to ethnicity, age, sexual orientation, social class, and disabilities; gender is not the only important inequality.

Another crucial component of feminist therapy focuses on power issues within the therapeutic relationship. In traditional psychotherapy, therapists have much more power than clients. In contrast, feminist therapy emphasizes more egalitarian interactions (Enns, 2004a; Gilbert & Scher, 1999; Mahalik et al., 2000; Marecek, 2001b; Sommers-Flanagan & Sommers-Flanagan, 2003; Szymanski, 2003). Here are several ways to balance power between the therapist and the client:

1. Whenever possible, the therapist should try to enhance the client's power in the therapeutic relationship. After all, if women clients are placed in subordinate roles in therapy, the situation simply intensifies their inferior status.
2. Throughout therapy, clients are encouraged to become more self-confident and independent and to develop skills to help themselves.
3. The therapist believes that the client—rather than the therapist—is her own best expert on herself.
4. When appropriate, feminist therapists may share information about their own life experiences, reducing the power discrepancy. However, a therapist's primary tasks are listening and thinking, not talking.

Feminist therapy can be a powerful tool in encouraging clients to analyze their psychological problems and to develop their personal strengths. However, we have relatively little current research that examines the effectiveness of feminist therapy. We do know that female clients who consider themselves feminists are more satisfied when their therapist is a feminist (Marecek, 2001b). In other research, clients rated themselves higher on measures of self-esteem, personal control, and social activism, following therapy sessions with a feminist therapist (Worell & Johnson, 2001; Worell & Remer, 2003).

Ideally, all therapists should respect the value of women and should encourage egalitarian relationships. Szymanski and her colleagues (2002) found that only about one-quarter of male therapists considered themselves to be feminist therapists. Fortunately, several male therapists have outlined how feminist therapy can be useful when working with male clients (G. R. Brooks, 2003; Rabinowitz & Cochran, 2002). Therapists are supposed to improve the psychological well-being of human beings. Isn't it puzzling that many therapists are not more concerned about females having an equal right to be psychologically healthy? Why don't more therapists—and more psychologists—work actively to support feminist politicians, gender-fair legislation, and greater gender equality (Nolen-Hoeksema, 2003)?

Section Summary

**Treating
Psychological
Disorders
in Women**

1. Anxiety disorders constitute a third category of psychological disorders that are found more often in women than in men; these include specific phobias and panic disorder.

2. Gender stereotypes may encourage some therapists to misdiagnose some psychological disorders and to treat clients in a gender-biased fashion.

3. One clearly harmful violation of ethical conduct is a sexual relationship between a therapist and a client.

4. In treating lesbians and bisexual clients, therapists must be aware of problems caused by sexual prejudice and heterosexism.

5. Many low-income women cannot afford psychotherapy; furthermore, some therapists may treat clients in a classist fashion.

6. People of color are less likely than European Americans to use mental health services. Therapists must be aware of characteristics of diverse ethnic groups that may be relevant in therapy.

7. Therapists can increase their skills in helping women of color by a variety of methods, including searching the client's history for her personal strengths, learning more about her ethnic group, and being aware of diversity within her ethnic group.

8. The psychodynamic approach is based on Freudian theory, a framework that emphasizes childhood experiences and unconscious conflict. The Freudian approach considers men to be normative and women to be relatively immature. It blames mothers for their children's psychological problems.

9. Cognitive-behavioral therapy emphasizes restructuring inappropriate thoughts and changing behaviors; it is effective in treating depression, eating disorders, and other psychological problems.

10. Pharmacotherapy may help treat serious disorders, but it must be used with caution.

11. Nonsexist therapy treats women and men similarly, and it attempts to avoid gender-stereotyped behavior.

12. Feminist therapy proposes that (a) therapists must provide nonsexist therapy, (b) social inequalities have helped to shape women's behavior, and (c) power should be more equally divided between the therapist and the client.

CHAPTER REVIEW QUESTIONS

1. Describe the defining characteristics of major depression. What personal characteristics are most likely to be related to depression? Based on these characteristics, describe a woman who would be *unlikely* to experience depression.

2. What factors help to explain why women are more likely than men to develop depression? How could each factor be related to cultural and societal forces?

3. Describe typical characteristics of anorexia nervosa and bulimia nervosa, as well as their medical consequences. Explain why women with these two eating disorders would also be likely to experience depression. How does binge-eating disorder differ from these other two problems?

4. What is the "culture of thinness"? How might this emphasis help produce eating

disorders? What kind of women would be most likely to resist this cultural norm?

5. Discuss the information on ethnicity and body image. Then summarize the material on the unique concerns that women of color bring to a psychotherapy session. Why must therapists emphasize individual differences within every ethnic group?

6. Many women want to lose weight and not regain this lost weight. Describe why the issues of being overweight and dieting make these goals difficult.

7. Based on what you have read in this chapter, why does the classical approach of Sigmund Freud present major problems for those who favor a nonsexist or feminist approach to therapy?

8. Suppose that you are a feminist therapist working with a female client who is severely depressed. Imagine someone who would fit this description, and point out how you would use selected principles of feminist therapy to facilitate her recovery. How might social class be relevant in this situation?

9. Many therapists favor an eclectic approach to the treatment of psychological disorders, in which they combine elements of several approaches. If you were a therapist, how could you combine elements of cognitive-behavioral therapy and feminist therapy?

10. This chapter focused on psychological disorders. Some theorists point out that psychologists should place more emphasis on how individuals can achieve positive mental health, rather than just avoiding disorders. Based on the information in this chapter, describe the characteristics of an individual who is mentally healthy.

KEY TERMS

*psychological disorders (390)

*antisocial personality disorder (390)

*major depressive disorder (391)

ruminative style (396)

*anorexia nervosa (399)

*amenorrhea (399)

*bulimia nervosa (400)

*binge-eating disorder (400)

culture of thinness (401)

anxiety disorders (406)

specific phobia (406)

panic disorder (406)

*psychotherapy (406)

*pharmacotherapy (407)

*sexual prejudice (408)

*heterosexism (408)

myth of meritocracy (409)

*psychodynamic therapy (413)

cognitive-behavioral therapy (414)

nonsexist therapy (416)

*feminist therapy (416)

 Note: The terms asterisked in the Key Terms section serve as good search terms for InfoTrac College Edition. Go to http://infotrac.thomsonlearning.com and try these added search terms.

RECOMMENDED READINGS

Enns, C. Z. (2004). *Feminist theories and feminist psychotherapies* (2nd ed.). New York: Haworth. This new edition of Carolyn Enns's book includes descriptions of a variety of feminist theoretical approaches, as well as feminist therapy approaches. She also includes self-testing exercises to help readers clarify their own perspectives on these approaches.

Kalodner, C. R. (2003). *Too fat or too thin? A reference guide to eating disorders*. Westport, CT: Greenwood. I recommend this book for anyone who would like more information about eating disorders, as well as a solid background on sociocultural influences that encourage North Americans to emphasize slenderness.

McGoldrick, M., Giordano, J., & Garcia-Preto, N. (Eds.). (2005). *Ethnicity and family therapy* (3rd ed.). New York: Guilford. This resource includes chapters about more than 40 specific ethnic groups, such as Filipinos, Armenians, Brazilians, and Greeks. Each chapter addresses family characteristics and values, as well as issues related to therapy.

Nolen-Hoeksema, S. (2003). *Women who think too much: How to break free of overthinking and reclaim your life.* New York: Holt. Susan Nolen-Hoeksema has written an excellent resource for women experiencing depression; the book emphasizes ways of reducing rumination.

Worell, J., & Goodheart, C. D. (Eds.). (2006). *Handbook of girls' and women's psychological health: Gender and well-being across the life span.* New York: Oxford. I strongly recommend this handbook for every college or community library. It includes chapters that focus on psychological disorders, such as depression and other serious mental illnesses. Its 50 chapters cover numerous topics related to the lives of girls and women.

ANSWERS TO THE DEMONSTRATIONS

Interpreting Demonstration 12.3: Look at your answers to Demonstration 12.3, and count how many of the following items you endorsed: Items 1, 4, 5, and 9. If you checked most of these, you tend to appreciate a nonsexist therapy approach. Now count how many of the following items you endorsed: Items 2, 3, 6, 7, and 8. Add this second number to the previous total to get a grand total. If your score is close to 9, you tend to appreciate a feminist therapy approach, in addition to nonsexist therapy.

ANSWERS TO THE TRUE-FALSE STATEMENTS

1. False (p. 391); 2. False (p. 392); 3. False (p. 393); 4. True (p. 396); 5. False (pp. 399–400); 6. False (p. 400); 7. True (p. 402); 8. True (p. 403); 9. True (p. 409); 10. True (p. 416).

13 | VIOLENCE AGAINST WOMEN

True or False?

_____ 1. To label a remark "sexual harassment" from the legal standpoint, the person making the remark must specifically request some sort of sexual favor.

_____ 2. Women who have been sexually harassed typically say that the harassment was moderately unpleasant but it had no long-lasting emotional effects.

_____ 3. In most research, men are more accepting of sexual harassment than women are.

_____ 4. About 20% of North American women will be victims of a rape during their lifetime.

_____ 5. More than twice as many women as men report that they are afraid of walking alone at night.

_____ 6. The clear majority of rape victims were previously acquainted with the man who raped them.

_____ 7. According to research, virtually all mentally stable men say that they would never consider raping a woman.

_____ 8. Many women who have been abused report that the psychological abuse is more difficult than the physical abuse.

_____ 9. Unemployment increases the likelihood of partner abuse.

_____ 10. Most abusive relationships improve spontaneously, but therapy is recommended when the abuse is severe or long lasting.

Approximately 500,000 women in the United States are migrant farmworkers, and they earn low wages by picking fruits and vegetables in the field. Unfortunately, female farmworkers are about ten times more likely than other female workers to experience sexual harassment and sexual assault. For example, Olivia is a California farmworker who was repeatedly harassed and assaulted by her supervisor, Rene, also a Mexican American. He offered to drive her to the work site, and then he raped her. He also came to Olivia's home when her husband was at work, and raped her again, threatening to kill her if she told anyone. When she reported these incidents to the main office, the bosses protested that she had no proof. Sexual assault is so common for female farmworkers that one woman in Iowa told a lawyer, "We thought it was normal in the United States that in order to keep your job, you had to have sex" (Clarren, 2005, p. 42).

Olivia's story describes both sexual harassment and sexual assault, two of the topics of this chapter. Sexual harassment, sexual assault, and the abuse of women share important similarities. Obviously, all three involve some form of violence—either physical or emotional.

Furthermore, in all three situations, men typically possess more power than women. Sexual harassers are usually persons with power at work or in an academic setting (DeSouza & Fansler, 2003; Foote & Goodman-Delahunty, 2005). In rape and abusive situations, men typically have more physical power. Throughout their lives, people learn these messages about power and gender roles. In a sense, sexual harassment, rape, and the abuse of women all represent a tragic exaggeration of traditional gender roles.

An additional similarity focuses on entitlement, a concept we examined in Chapter 7, on women and work (p. 221). In our culture, many men have a sense of **entitlement;** based on their membership in the male social group, they believe they have a right to certain "privileges" and rewards when they interact with women (Baumeister et al., 2002; A. J. Stewart & McDermott, 2004). For instance, a high-ranking executive assumes he has the right to fondle his secretary. A male college student may feel little guilt about raping his girlfriend. A husband believes that he is entitled to punch his wife if she comes home late from work.

Furthermore, in all three kinds of victimization, women are left feeling even less powerful after the violence. They have been forced to accept unwanted sexual attention, or their bodies have been violated or beaten. Powerlessness is yet another variation on one of the themes of this book: Women are often treated differently from men.

Unfortunately, women seldom regain power by reporting the violence committed against them. Legal procedures are often embarrassing and humiliating; they invade a woman's right to privacy even further. All these acts of violence encourage women to become more silent and more invisible (Foote & Goodman-Delahunty, 2005; T. S. Nelson, 2002). The relative invisibility of women is a theme we have emphasized repeatedly throughout this book.

Another similarity across all three situations is that people often blame the victim (T. S. Nelson, 2002; J. W. White et al., 2001). A woman is sexually harassed because "those tight pants invite it." A woman is raped because she "asked for it" by her seductive behavior. A woman is beaten because "she probably did something to make her husband angry." In contrast, the aggressor is often perceived as behaving "like any normal male." Although attitudes are changing, the aggressor may receive little blame for the violence.

SEXUAL HARASSMENT

Sexual harassment refers to unwanted gender-related behavior, such as sexual coercion, offensive sexual attention, and hostile verbal and physical behaviors that focus on gender (Fitzgerald et al., 2001; Gutek et al., 2004). Most sexual harassment situations occur in either a work setting or a school setting. According to surveys, women are between two and seven times as likely as men to report that they have been sexually harassed (Foote & Goodman-Delahunty, 2005).

The American legal system now prohibits two kinds of sexual harassment. In the first kind, called **quid pro quo harassment,** a powerful individual in a university or an organization makes it clear that someone with less power must submit to sexual advances to obtain something, such as a good grade in a course, a job offer, or a promotion (Gutek et al., 2004; M. A. Paludi, 2004; Woodzicka & LaFrance, 2005).

The second kind of sexual harassment is called "hostile environment." **Hostile environment** applies to a situation in which the atmosphere at school or at work is so intimidating and unpleasant that a student or an employee cannot work effectively (Fitzgerald et al., 2001; Foote & Goodman-Delahunty, 2005;

Demonstration 13.1

Rate each of the six statements about sexual harassment, using the scale below. Then check the instructions at the end of the chapter, on page 458.

1	2	3	4	5
Strongly disagree				Strongly agree

_____ 1. Sexual harassment is clearly related to power.

_____ 2. Women often try to get ahead by encouraging a professor or a supervisor to be sexually interested in them.

_____ 3. Women don't have a sense of humor, and so they make a big deal out of sexual remarks and jokes in the classroom.

_____ 4. Most charges of sexual harassment are made by women who really have experienced harassment.

_____ 5. Women frequently use their sexuality to tease professors and supervisors.

_____ 6. When a female says "No" to a sexual advance from a male professor or supervisor, he should realize that she really does mean "No."

Source: Based on Mazer and Percival (1989) and Kennedy and Gorzalka (2002).

M. A. Paludi, 2004). Before you read further, try Demonstration 13.1, an exercise designed to assess your thoughts about sexual harassment.

Let's consider several examples of sexual harassment so that we can appreciate the variety of problems in this area.

1. Quid pro quo sexual coercion. A woman named Anna and her supervisor, Jason, were on a work-related trip. During this trip, Jason kept talking about sex and rubbing her shoulders and neck. She did not respond, and so he told her to loosen up. Anna later asked about opportunities in the company for promotion. Jason replied, "You'll need to loosen up and be a lot nicer to me before I can recommend you." Then he placed his arms around her waist and added, "Remember, I can make your life very easy or very difficult here" (Foote & Goodman-Delahunty, 2005, p. 54).

2. Hostile environment in an academic setting. At a university in Texas, a professor who taught courses in criminal justice was accused of kissing and hugging several female students. His comments were equally offensive. For example, he told one woman that "she would not know real happiness until she had sex with a married man like himself" (R. Wilson, 2004, p. A12). Notice that this example cannot be classified as quid pro quo harassment because the professor did not specify an academic reward for sexual activity.

3. Hostile environment in the workplace. In a study of Black female firefighters, more than 90% said that they had experienced unwanted sexual teasing, jokes, and remarks on the job (J. D. Yoder & Aniakudo, 1996). The women also reported that their male coworkers harassed them by pouring syrup into their firefighting boots and bursting in while they were using the toilet. It's likely that sexism and racism combined to create an especially hostile environment for these women.

Most of this section on sexual harassment examines how males sexually harass females whom they perceive to be heterosexual. Keep in mind, however, that lesbian women might be sexually harassed, for example, by males or by other women in positions of power. Males can also be sexually harassed by women or by other men. However, in the most common situation, a male is harassing a female (DeFour et al., 2003; Foote & Goodman-Delahunty, 2005; Hambright & Decker, 2002).

You may read reports about females being harassed by their male classmates, beginning in elementary school and continuing through college; women are also harassed by their peers in the workplace (Duffy et al., 2004; Strauss, 2003). In addition, women are harassed in public settings by whistles and sexually explicit comments. These forms of harassment are certainly worrisome. In this chapter, however, we will focus on two situations in which a female is being harassed by a male with higher status: (1) professors harassing students in college settings and (2) supervisors harassing employees in work settings. Both situations raise particular problems because they involve power inequities and reasonably long-term relationships between the woman and the harasser.

Why Is Sexual Harassment an Important Issue?

Sexual harassment is important for several reasons (Foote & Goodman-Delahunty, 2005; T. S. Nelson, 2002; Norton, 2002; M. A. Paludi, 2004; Piran & Ross, 2006):

1. Sexual harassment emphasizes that men typically have more power than women in our society.
2. Sexual demands are often coercive because women are offered economic or academic advantages if they comply and harmful consequences if they say no.
3. Sexual harassment dehumanizes women and treats them in a sexist fashion; women are seen primarily as sexual beings rather than as intelligent and skilled employees or students.
4. Women are often forced to be silent victims because they are afraid and they need to continue either in the workplace or at school.
5. If sexual harassment occurs in a public setting, without condemnation from supervisors, many onlookers will conclude that sexist behavior is acceptable.

How Often Does Sexual Harassment Occur?

It is extremely difficult to estimate how frequently sexual harassment occurs. The boundaries of sexual harassment are often unclear. Also, people are reluctant to use the label "sexual harassment," even when they have experienced clear-cut harassment (M. A. Paludi, 2004). Furthermore, many cases go unreported (Fitzgerald et al., 2001; Norton, 2002; Wenniger & Conroy, 2001).

Reports of sexual harassment on college campuses suggest that between 20% and 40% of undergraduate and graduate women students have been harassed (Dziech, 2003; Frank et al., 1998). The incidence of sexual harassment in the workplace varies widely throughout the United States and Canada, depending on the employment setting. Women employed in traditionally male occupations are especially likely to experience sexual harassment (DeSouza & Fansler, 2003; Foote & Goodman-Delahunty, 2005). For instance, women in the military frequently report sexual teasing, unwanted touching, and pressure for sexual favors. According to surveys, between 50% and 75% of women in the military said that they had experienced sexual harassment (T. S. Nelson, 2002; J. D. Yoder, 2001). Sexual harassment in the military is especially common during wartime (Gluckman et al., 2004).

Sexual harassment is not limited to North America. Reports come from countries such as England, Germany, the Netherlands, Pakistan, India, Taiwan, Argentina, and Turkey (Hodges, 2000; Kishwar, 1999; M. A. Paludi, 2004; J. Sigal et al., 2005). In all the cultures examined so far, one universal finding is that only a small percentage of women choose to report the sexual harassment (Fitzgerald et al., 2001).

Women's Reactions to Being Sexually Harassed

Sexual harassment is not simply a minor inconvenience to women; it can change their lives. If a woman refuses her boss's sexual advances, she may receive a negative job evaluation, a demotion, or a transfer to another job. She may be fired or pressured into quitting (Foote & Goodman-Delahunty, 2005; Kurth et al., 2000; T. S. Nelson, 2002). A woman who has been harassed in an academic setting may drop out of school or miss classes taught by the harasser (Duffy et al., 2004; Fogg, 2005).

How do women respond emotionally to sexual harassment? Most women experience anxiety, fear, self-doubt, embarrassment, helplessness, and depression. They may also feel ashamed, as if they were somehow responsible for the harassment (Fogg, 2005; Foote & Goodman-Delahunty, 2005; T. S. Nelson, 2002; Shupe et al., 2002; Woodzicka & LaFrance, 2005). In contrast, women are not as likely to feel responsible when they are victims of crimes such as robbery. Understandably, women who have been sexually harassed may become less self-confident about their academic or occupational abilities (Duffy et al., 2004; Osman, 2004). Common physical reactions include headaches, eating disorders, substance abuse, and sleep disturbances (Foote & Goodman-Delahunty, 2005; Lundberg-Love & Marmion, 2003; Piran & Ross, 2006).

The Public's Attitudes About Sexual Harassment

Susan Bordo (1998) recalled her experience with sexual harassment when she was a graduate student. One of her professors had laughingly said, "It's time for class, dear," patting her on the rear as they stood in the open doorway of a classroom filled with other students. When she described the episode to some of her close male friends, they acted casual about the harassment. As they replied, "Well, what did you expect? You don't exactly dress like a nun!" (p. B6).

Men are usually more accepting of sexual harassment than women are, in North American and throughout the world (De Judicibus & McCabe, 2001; Dziech, 2003; Russell & Trigg, 2004; Sigal et al., 2005). For example, Kennedy and Gorzalka (2002) asked students at a Canadian university to complete a 19-item questionnaire about sexual harassment that included items similar to those in Demonstration 13.1. They found that females were more likely than males to believe that sexual harassment is a serious problem.

What to Do About Sexual Harassment

How should we address the problem of sexual harassment? Let's consider how individual women and men can make a difference. Then we'll see how institutions can address sexual harassment.

Individual Action. What can an individual woman do when she has been sexually harassed? Here are some recommendations for students who are concerned about harassment in an academic setting (Fogg, 2005; M. A. Paludi, 2004):

1. Become familiar with your campus's policy on sexual harassment, and know which officials are responsible for complaints.
2. If a professor's behavior seems questionable, discuss the situation objectively with someone you trust.
3. If the problem persists, consider telling the harasser directly that his sexual harassment makes you feel uncomfortable. Another possible strategy is to send a formal letter to the harasser, describing your objections to the incident, and stating clearly that you want the actions to stop. Many harassment policies cannot be legally applied unless the harasser has been informed that the behavior is unwanted and inappropriate.
4. Keep records of all occurrences, and keep copies of all correspondence.
5. If the problem persists, report it to the appropriate officials on campus. An institution that takes no action is responsible if another act of harassment occurs after an incident is reported.
6. Join a feminist group on campus, or help to start one. A strong support group can encourage real empowerment, reduce the chances that other students will experience sexual harassment, and help to change campus policy on this important issue.

These six suggestions can also be adapted for the workplace; employed women can take similar steps to avoid and eliminate sexual harassment. If a harasser persists, threats of exposure to a superior may be necessary. Employees may need to file a formal complaint with a superior, a union official, or a personnel officer. Competent legal advice may also be necessary. Fortunately, a U.S. Supreme Court decision states that employers may be held financially liable when supervisors harass employees, even when the companies are not aware of the misconduct (Fitzgerald et al., 2001).

Some women who file a sexual harassment charge may find that their complaint is treated seriously and compassionately. Unfortunately, however, many women encounter an unsympathetic response from college administrators or company officials (Foote & Goodman-Delahunty, 2005; T. S. Nelson, 2002; Reese & Lindenberg, 1999). They might be told that the event was simply a misunderstanding or that the harasser is so competent and valuable that this "minor" incident should be forgotten. Many women report feeling completely isolated and alienated during this experience.

Students in women's studies courses often protest that nothing about sexual harassment seems fair. This viewpoint is absolutely correct. A woman shouldn't have to suffer the pain and embarrassment of sexual harassment, see the quality of her work decline, and then—in many cases—find that administrators, supervisors, and the legal system do not support her.

How Men Can Help.   Men who care about women and women's issues can be part of the solution. First, they themselves must avoid behaviors that women might perceive as sexual harassment. In addition, men should speak up when they see another man sexually harassing someone. Harassers may be more likely to stop if other males point out that they are offended by sexual harassment. Furthermore, men who work as supervisors or as counselors can support individuals who have been sexually harassed (T. S. Nelson, 2002).

If you are a male reading this book, think about what steps you might take if you hear that a woman is being sexually harassed by one of your male friends. It's difficult to tell a male friend that a woman may not enjoy his comments about her body. However, if you do not comment, your silence may be interpreted as approval. You can also offer compassion and support to a female friend who tells you that she has been sexually harassed.

Society's Response to the Harassment Problem.   Individual women and men need to take action against sexual harassment. However, to stop sexual harassment more effectively, *institutions* must be firmly committed to fighting the problem (Foote & Goodman-Delahunty, 2005; C. A. Paludi & Paludi, 2003). For example, women in the military typically report that their commanding officers do not treat sexual harassment as a serious problem that must be prevented (Firestone & Harris, 2003; T. S. Nelson, 2002). Clearly, most officers have not been firmly committed to stopping sexual harassment.

Universities and corporations need to develop clear policies about sexual harassment (Foote & Goodman-Delahunty, 2005; C. A. Paludi & Paludi, 2003; Wenniger & Conroy, 2001). They should also publicize these policies and training programs—with top administrators in attendance—on sexual harassment issues. Students and employees should receive information about procedures to follow if they believe they have been sexually harassed.

Public opinion also needs to be changed. People should realize that they must not blame women who are victims of sexual harassment. The public must also realize that sexual harassment limits women's rights and opportunities in academic and work settings. Men should know that women often do not appreciate uninvited sexual attention. In addition, behavior that a man regards as flirtation may feel more like sexual harassment to a woman (Norton, 2002). Some men who harass may not be aware that they are creating a problem. Others may believe that they have a sanction to harass because of good-natured responses from other men.

However, the real answer lies in the unequal distribution of power between men and women. If we really want to eliminate sexual harassment, we must move beyond the level of trying to convince individual harassers to alter their behavior. Instead, we need to change the uneven distribution of power that encourages sexual harassment.

Section Summary

Sexual Harassment

1. Sexual harassment, rape, and the abuse of women all focus on violence and power inequalities—situations in which men feel entitled to certain privileges. All of these behaviors make women feel less powerful and less visible, and women are also blamed for causing the violence.

2. Two categories of sexual harassment are (a) quid pro quo harassment and (b) harassment that creates a hostile environment.

3. Sexual harassment is an important issue because (a) it emphasizes gender inequalities, (b) it is coercive and dehumanizing, (c) it may force women to be silent victims, and (d) it may encourage onlookers to believe that sexist behavior is acceptable.

4. Sexual harassment occurs fairly often on college campuses and in the workplace; it is especially frequent for women in traditionally male occupations.

5. Women who have been sexually harassed often quit jobs or leave school; they may experience anxiety, fear, embarrassment, depression, shame, reduced self-confidence, and physical symptoms.

6. Men typically have more tolerant attitudes toward sexual harassment than women do.

7. When we consider how to reduce sexual harassment, we must move beyond the individual actions of women and men. Universities and corporations must develop well-publicized policies; the general public must be well informed about sexual harassment, as well as the general issue of the unequal distribution of power.

SEXUAL ASSAULT AND RAPE

Sexual assault is a broad term that includes sexual touching and other forms of unwanted sexual contact. Sexual assault is typically accompanied by psychological pressure or by physical threats (O. Barnett et al., 2005). For example, a man may say, "If you really loved me, you'd have sex with me," or he may threaten to break her arm if the woman does not comply.

Rape is a more specific kind of sexual assault. **Rape** can be defined as sexual penetration—without the individual's consent—obtained by force or by threat of physical harm, or when the victim is incapable of giving consent (Tobach & Reed, 2003; Wertheimer, 2003; Worell & Remer, 2003). Most of the discussion here will focus on rape. However, the inclusiveness of the term *sexual assault* helps us understand the many ways in which men have power over women's lives (J. W. White & Frabutt, 2006).

Although strangers commit some rapes, a rapist is more likely to be an acquaintance (Koss, 2003; J. W. White & Frabutt, 2006). In other words, women who are worried about rape need to be especially concerned about someone they already know rather than a stranger.

A rapist may even be a woman's husband. By some estimates, between 10% and 20% of wives have been raped by a husband or an ex-husband (Herrera et al., 2006; Koss, 2003). Unfortunately, only 17 countries in the world currently consider marital rape a crime (Women in Action, 2001).

The incidence of rape varies cross-culturally. Rape is typically more common in cultures where women are subordinate to men (Sanday, 2003; J. W. White & Post, 2003). In recent years, invading soldiers have systematically raped women in countries such as Bangladesh, Afghanistan, Cyprus, Guatemala, Peru, Somalia, Uganda, Rwanda, and Bosnia (Agathangelou, 2000; Barstow, 2001; Borchelt, 2005; Hans, 2004; Nikolic-Ristanovic, 2000). For example, about 2 million people in the Darfur region of Sudan have been forced to leave their homes and move to refugee camps. The women in these camps must walk great distances away from the camps to gather wood for cooking their food. Men from the attacking militias search for these women and systematically rape them (Doctors Without Borders, 2005; Obama & Brownback, 2006). Rape is therefore a weapon of war as well as a sexual attack on individual women (Agathangelou, 2000; Lalumiere et al., 2005).

How Often Does Rape Occur?

As you can imagine, estimating the incidence of rape is difficult. One problem is that surveys differ in their definitions of rape and sexual assault (Hamby & Koss, 2003). Another problem is that women are reluctant to indicate on a survey that they have been raped. Furthermore, only a fraction of rape victims report the crime to the police. In the United States, for instance, only about 5% to 20% of victims report the rape, depending on the group that is surveyed (Bachar & Koss, 2001; Herrera et al., 2006; J. W. White et al., 2001).

Demonstration 13.2

KNOWLEDGE ABOUT RAPE

For each of the following statements about rape, check the space that represents your response. The correct answers appear on page 458.

	True	False
1. Women who have had a sexual relationship with a man often try to protect their reputation by claiming they have been raped.	_____	_____
2. Women cannot always prevent being raped by resisting their attackers.	_____	_____
3. Men rape because they experience uncontrollable sexual urges.	_____	_____
4. Most women secretly want to be raped.	_____	_____
5. Most rapes are not reported to the police.	_____	_____
6. A woman who is sexually experienced will not really be damaged by rape.	_____	_____
7. Women provoke rape if they dress in a sexually seductive way.	_____	_____
8. Most reported sexual assaults actually were true cases of sexual assaults.	_____	_____
9. Sexual assaults usually occur in isolated areas, away from a woman's home.	_____	_____
10. You can tell whether someone is a rapist by his appearance or general behavior.	_____	_____

Source: Based partly on Worell and Remer (2003, p. 203).

In the United States, women report about 90,000 rapes to the police each year (U.S. Census Bureau, 2001)—certainly an underestimate of the true number of rapes. Current estimates in both the United States and Canada suggest that between 15% and 25% of women have been raped at some point during their lives (Felson, 2002; Herrera et al., 2006; Rozee, 2005; Tjaden & Thoennes, 2000; J. W. White & Frabutt, 2006). The data clearly demonstrate that rape is a real problem for women in North America.

Before you read further, try Demonstration 13.2 to assess your knowledge about rape. Then you can check the answers at the end of the chapter.

ACQUAINTANCE RAPE

Psychologists and other researchers are increasingly aware that a rapist is not likely to be a stranger attacking in a dark alley. Instead, a rapist may be your chemistry lab partner, your sister's boyfriend, a business acquaintance, or the boy next door. Surveys suggest that about 85% of rape victims knew the man who raped them (Koss, 2003). **Acquaintance rape** refers to rape by a person known to the victim who is not related by blood or marriage. For example, one woman was a senior in high school. A classmate had just asked her for a date, and she had turned him down.

> He got angry and told me that I was a tease and he slapped me across the face. So I pulled open the door to my car and tried to get away, but he grabbed my arm and forced me into the back seat. All I remember after that was crying and trying to push him off me. When he had finished he left me in the back seat of my car bleeding and barely conscious. (A. S. Kahn, 2004, p. 11)

Surveys suggest that about 15% of U.S. women will experience acquaintance rape. An additional 35% to 40% of women will experience some other form of sexual assault from an acquaintance (Rickert et al., 2004; J. W. White & Kowalski, 1998). However, women who have been raped by a boyfriend are less likely than other rape victims to describe the situation as a rape (Frieze, 2005; A. S. Kahn, 2004; A. S. Kahn et al., 2003; Z. D. Peterson & Muehlenhard, 2004). Specifically, researchers in Canada and the United States have studied groups of women who had been assaulted by an acquaintance and whose experience met the legal definition for rape. Among these women, only about 40% classified the assault as rape (A. S. Kahn & Andreoli Mathie, 2000; Shimp & Chartier, 1998). In other words, most of these women had indeed been raped, yet they did not apply that term to the assault. Furthermore, women raped by a boyfriend or another acquaintance are less likely than other rape victims to report the rape (Worell & Remer, 2003).

Some cases of acquaintance rape can probably be traced to a particular kind of miscommunication. Specifically, men are more likely than women to perceive other people as being seductive (Abbey et al., 2000, 2001; Henningsen, 2004). For example, Saundra may smile pleasantly when talking with Ted. To her, this nonverbal behavior is intended to convey platonic friendship. Nevertheless, Ted may interpret her behavior as a sexual invitation. Another kind of miscommunication is that some men believe that women want to have sex, even though they have said "No" (Osman, 2004).

Furthermore, sexually aggressive men are especially likely to misinterpret neutral behavior (V. Anderson et al., 2004; Bondurant & Donat, 1999; Felson, 2002). Unfortunately, however, this research has often been misconstrued. For example, the popular media often blame women for sending the wrong messages rather than acknowledging that men misinterpret the messages.

The findings on miscommunication have practical implications for both women and men. First, women should be aware that their friendliness may be misperceived by men. Second, men must learn that friendly verbal and non-verbal messages from a woman may simply mean "I like you" or "I enjoy talking with you." A smile and extended eye contact do not necessarily mean "I want to have a sexual relationship with you."

THE ROLE OF ALCOHOL AND DRUGS

By some estimates, at least half of rapes in the United States are associated with the use of alcohol by either the perpetrator or the victim (Abbey, 2002;

Davis et al., 2004; Marchell & Cummings, 2001). Alcohol clearly impairs people's ability to make appropriate decisions (Abbey et al., 2002). For instance, men who have been drinking tend to overestimate a woman's interest in sexual activity. Furthermore, women who have been drinking may be more likely to judge a sexually aggressive situation as being relatively safe (Testa & Livingston, 1999; J. W. White & Frabutt, 2006).

You may also have read about a drug called Rohypnol (pronounced row-*hip*-noll), sometimes called roofie or the date rape drug. Mixed with alcohol, Rohypnol increases the sensation of drunkenness (Dobbert, 2004; Wertheimer, 2003). In both the United States and Canada, the media have reported many cases in which Rohypnol or some similar drug has been slipped into a woman's drink. The effect is like an alcohol blackout; the woman typically has no recall of any events that occurred after she passed out, even a rape attack. Obviously, a drug-induced rape can have a devastating effect on a woman.

Women's Reactions to Rape

A woman's reaction to rape depends on the nature of the attack, whether she knows the assailant, the threat of danger, her stage in life, and other circumstances. However, almost all women who have been raped report that they were terrified, repulsed, confused, and overwhelmed while they were being raped (Lloyd & Emery, 2000). Many women are afraid that they will be seriously hurt (Raitt & Zeedyk, 2000; Ullman, 2000). In fact, about 25% of women are injured (Koss, 2003).

During the rape, some women report that they feel detached from their own body (Matsakis, 2003). One woman described her reaction to an acquaintance rape:

> The experience moved from heavy petting to forced intercourse. I realized that a fly on the wall watching would have seen two people making love. But inside I was horrified and remembered thinking to myself that this can't be happening to me. I felt like throwing-up, and I shriveled up inside of myself, so that the outside of my body and the parts he was touching were just a shell. (Funderburk, 2001, p. 263)

Short-Term Adjustment.   Women report a wide range of feelings during the first few weeks after a rape. Some women have an expressive style. They show their feelings of fear, anger, and anxiety by crying and being restless (A. S. Kahn & Andreoli Mathie, 2000; Lloyd & Emery, 2000; Matsakis, 2003). Others hide their feelings with a calm and subdued external appearance.

Once again, we must emphasize our theme of individual differences. For example, Michelle Fine (1997) described a 24-year-old mother who had just experienced a brutal gang rape. She showed little concern for herself and chose not to take legal action. As she told the staff members in the hospital emergency room: "Prosecute? No, I just want to get home. While I'm pickin' some guy out of some line, who knows who's messin' around with my momma and my baby" (p. 152).

Most rape victims feel helpless and devalued. Many women blame themselves for the rape (Funderburk, 2001; A. S. Kahn & Andreoli Mathie, 2000; Koss, 2003). For instance, one woman who had been raped by an acquaintance said, "I never thought of it as date rape until very recently. I just always thought of it as my fault that I let things get out of hand" (Lloyd & Emery, 2000, p. 119). Self-blame is a particularly troublesome reaction because, in nearly all cases, the woman did nothing to encourage the assault.

Immediately following a rape, a woman may experience physical pain, and she may also experience gynecological symptoms, such as vaginal discharge and generalized pain. Realistically, a woman who has been raped needs to worry about possible pregnancy, as well as AIDS and other sexually transmitted diseases (W. S. Rogers & Rogers, 2001). However, many women are too upset or too ashamed to seek medical attention. Women who do go to a hospital may be treated in a caring manner, but some report that the members of the hospital staff were unsympathetic (Boston Women's Health Book Collective, 2005; Wasco & Campbell, 2002).

A woman who has been raped must also decide whether to report the crime to the police. Women often decide not to make an official report because "it wouldn't do any good." They believe that the criminal justice system won't handle the case effectively, that officials won't believe them, and that they might be embarrassed by the verifying procedure. These fears may be realistic. The legal system often harasses and frightens women who have been raped, often minimizes their distress, and often blames victims rather than supporting them (Raitt & Zeedyk, 2000). In recent years, however, a growing number of women have reported that they were treated with compassion and respect.

LONG-TERM ADJUSTMENT. The effects of a rape do not disappear suddenly. The physical and mental aftereffects may last for years. Common physical health problems include pelvic pain, excessive menstrual bleeding, vaginal infections, complications during pregnancy, gastrointestinal problems, and headaches (Ullman & Brecklin, 2003; E. A. Walker et al., 2004; C. M. West, 2000). Depression, excessive weight loss, eating disorders, substance abuse, and sexual dysfunction are also common (Funderburk, 2001; Herrera et al., 2006; Ullman & Brecklin, 2003). Women who have been raped are also more likely to engage in high-risk sexual behavior (Rheingold et al., 2004; Ullman & Brecklin, 2003). They are also more likely to attempt suicide (Ullman, 2004).

Many rape victims also meet the criteria for a psychological disorder called **post-traumatic stress disorder (PTSD)**, a pattern of symptoms such as intense fear, heightened anxiety, and emotional numbing after a traumatic event (American Psychiatric Association, 2000; Cling, 2004; Ullman & Brecklin, 2003). A woman experiencing PTSD following a rape may report that she keeps re-experiencing the rape, either in nightmares or in thoughts intruding during daily activities. Her memories of the rape may seem vivid and emotionally intense (McNally, 2003b; Schnurr & Green, 2004). Once again, however, individual differences are striking. For instance, many women experience a decrease in psychological symptoms within 3 months of the assault, but some women will continue to have symptoms for several years (Frieze, 2005; Ozer & Weiss, 2004; Warshaw, 2001).

Many women seek professional psychotherapy to reduce persistent symptoms. Controlled studies indicate that several kinds of psychotherapy are effective. Many current approaches use components of the cognitive-behavioral approach (see p. 414 in Chapter 12). For example, the therapist may ask the client to gradually confront the painful memories. Then the therapist helps her manage the anxieties that arise as she creates a mental image of the traumatic event (Enns, 2004a). Group counseling can also be beneficial because women can share their concerns with others who have survived similar experiences (Funderburk, 2001).

Women who are raped can often manage to transform their terrifying experience in a way that makes them stronger, more determined, and more resilient (Slater et al., 2003). Many survivors choose to speak out against violence—for example, at a forum on a college campus. As Funderburk (2001) wrote:

> Besides being a therapeutic experience in its own right, speaking out helps transform self-blame to anger and can galvanize the campus to making a commitment to social change through education and awareness. (p. 278)

FEAR OF RAPE

In the previous sections, we focused on women who had been raped. However, we also need to consider that all women suffer because of the threat of rape (Beneke, 1997; Rozee, 2004). Young girls and elderly women can be raped. Furthermore, many women are raped in the "safety" of their own homes—the one location where they are supposed to feel most secure.

Surveys in both the United States and Canada confirm this perceived danger and fear of rape (Frieze, 2005; M. B. Harris & Miller, 2000). For instance, about 40% of women report that they feel unsafe when they are out alone at night, in contrast to only about 15% of men (Rozee, 2004; M. D. Schwartz & DeKeseredy, 1997; Statistics Canada, 2000). In fact, men are often astonished to learn about the large number of safety measures that women employ (Rozee, 2004). A related issue is that women take numerous precautions to avoid being raped by a stranger. They take significantly fewer precautions to avoid rape by an acquaintance, even though they correctly acknowledge that acquaintance rape is more common (Hickman & Muehlenhard, 1997).

Fear of rape controls women's behavior and restricts what they can do, no matter where they live. I teach at a college located in a small village in upstate New York farmland. Nevertheless, my female students do not feel safe if they are alone at night. Sadly, the fear of rape drastically reduces women's sense of freedom and power (Rozee, 2004).

Demonstration 13.3

Read the first scenario in this demonstration. Then decide who is responsible for the occurrence of the rape, John or Jane. If you believe that John is entirely responsible, assign a value of 100% to the John column and 0% to the Jane column. If they are both equally responsible, assign a value of 50% to each one. If Jane is entirely responsible, assign a value of 0% to the John column and 100% to the Jane column. Use any values between 0% and 100%, as long as the two values sum to 100. To make the situations comparable, assume that both John and Jane are college students in all five scenarios. After completing the first scenario, read and evaluate each subsequent one.

John   **Jane**

_____   _____   1. Jane is walking back to her dorm from the library at 9:00 p.m., taking a route that everyone considers safe. As she passes the science building, John leaps out, knocks her down, drags her to an unlit area, and rapes her.

_____   _____   2. Jane is at a party, where she meets a pleasant-looking student named John. After dancing for a while, he suggests they go outside to cool off. No one else is outside. John knocks her down, drags her to an unlit area, and rapes her.

_____   _____   3. Jane is at a party, and she is wearing a very short skirt. She meets a pleasant-looking student named John. After dancing for a while, he suggests they go outside to cool off. No one else is outside. John knocks her down, drags her to an unlit area, and rapes her.

_____   _____   4. Jane is on a first date with John, whom she knows slightly from her history class. After a movie, they go out for an elegant late-night meal. They decide to split the cost of both the movie and the meal. In the car on the way home, John stops in a secluded area. Jane tries to escape once she realizes what is happening, but John is much larger than she is, and he pins her down and rapes her.

_____   _____   5. Jane is on a first date with John, whom she knows slightly from her history class. After the movie, they go out for an elegant late-night meal. John pays for the cost of both the movie and the meal. In the car on the way home, John stops in a secluded area. Jane tries to escape once she realizes what is happening, but John is much larger than she is, and he pins her down and rapes her.

THE PUBLIC'S ATTITUDES ABOUT RAPE

Before you read further, try Demonstration 13.3 above, which examines your own perspectives on rape.

Women who are raped are often doubly victimized, first by the assailant and later by the attitudes of other people (R. Campbell & Raja, 2005; J. W.

White & Frabutt, 2006). The victim may find that her own family and friends, the court system, and society all tend to blame her and treat her negatively because of something that was not her fault. These responses are particularly damaging at a time when she needs help and compassion. In fact, this "second victimization" increases the likelihood that a woman will develop post-traumatic stress disorder (R. Campbell & Raja, 2005).

The legal system's treatment of rape is mostly beyond the scope of this book. However, we hear numerous reports of injustice and mistreatment. For example, a New York City judge recommended leniency for a man who had forcibly sodomized a woman who was retarded, because "there was no violence here" (Rhode, 1997, p. 122).

People differ in their attitudes about rape. For instance, people with traditional gender roles place a greater proportion of the blame on the rape victims (A. J. Lambert & Raichle, 2000; Simonson & Subich, 1999). Furthermore, men are more likely than women to blame the rape victims (Emmers-Sommer et al., 2005; W. H. George & Martínez, 2002; Workman & Freeburg, 1999). For example, Alan J. Lambert and Katherine Raichle (2000) asked students at a Midwestern university to read an acquaintance rape scenario in which students named Bill and Donna began talking at a party and then go to her apartment. They undress; Donna says she does not want to have sex, yet Bill continues, despite her continuous pleading. Participants were asked how much they thought each person could be blamed for what happened. As Figure 13.1 shows, males are somewhat more likely than females to blame Donna.

People's attitudes about rape also depend on the circumstances surrounding the assault. For instance, people are much more likely to blame the rape victim in a case of acquaintance rape than in a case of stranger rape (L. A. Morris, 1997; Wallace, 1999). Compare your answers to the first and second scenario in Demonstration 13.3 on page 436. In the first scenario, did you assign all (or almost all) of the blame to John? Did you shift the blame somewhat when Jane had known John for perhaps 30 minutes?

Next look at your response for scenario 3, in which Jane was wearing a short skirt. People are likely to hold a woman more responsible for a rape if she is wearing a short skirt rather than more conservative clothing (Workman & Freeburg, 1999).

Now see whether your assignment of blame differed for Scenarios 4 and 5. In general, people are more likely to hold a woman responsible for a rape if the man paid for the date (L. A. Morris, 1997; Parrot, 1999). Let's say that the evening cost $100. In Scenario 4, they therefore each paid $50. In Scenario 5, John paid $100. If John pays $50 extra, does he have the right to rape Jane?

Myths About Rape

Numerous myths about rape, rapists, and rape victims help shape attitudes toward rape that we have just examined. As you might imagine, these rape myths can intensify the anguish of a woman who has been raped.

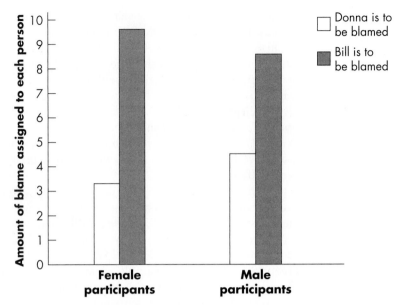

FIGURE 13.1 | RESPONSES TO AN ACQUAINTANCE RAPE SCENARIO, AS A FUNCTION OF THE PARTICIPANT'S GENDER. (NOTE: 0 = NOT AT ALL TO BE BLAMED; 10 = VERY MUCH TO BE BLAMED.)

Source: Based on A. J. Lambert and Raichle (2000).

Here are four of the more common myths:

Myth 1: Rapists are strangers—that is, people unknown to the victim. We noted earlier that about 85% of rapes are committed by acquaintances (Koss, 2003). However, the percentage may be even higher because women are less likely to report a rape that was committed by a person they know (Z. D. Peterson & Muehlenhard, 2004).

Myth 2: Only deviant men would consider raping a woman. Many people believe the myth that only men with serious psychological disorders would think about raping someone. This myth is not correct (Dobbert, 2004; Lalumiere et al., 2005; Rozee, 2004). For example, Osland and her colleagues (1996) gave a questionnaire about rape to undergraduate males at a small Midwestern college affiliated with a Protestant church. We might expect males at this kind of college to be especially repulsed by thoughts of sexual violence. However, 34% of them reported some likelihood to engage in rape or forced sex. In other words, the population of potential rapists includes many men who would ordinarily be judged "normal."

Myth 3: Women ask to be raped; they could avoid rape if they wanted to. Some people believe that women invite rape (Frieze, 2005; Matsakis, 2003; Worell

& Remer, 2003). According to one study, for example, 17% of undergraduates agreed with the statement that women provoke rape (B. E. Johnson et al., 1997). In addition, many advertisements glamorize rape. For example, one perfume ad that appeared in several teen magazines included a photo of a very young woman. The message that accompanied the photo said, "Apply generously to your neck so he can smell the scent as you shake your head 'no'" (Kilbourne, 1999, p. 213). Although the reasons are not clear, women of color are especially likely to be blamed for being raped (C. M. West, 2004; Wheeler & George, 2005).

Myth 4: Pornography has no effect on men's likelihood to rape. According to research, this myth is false. In fact, pornography that emphasizes violence can indeed be harmful (B. A. Scott, 2004; J. W. White & Frabutt, 2006).

Consider a study by Neil Malamuth (1998) that asked men whether they had ever been sexually aggressive toward a woman. Malamuth also assessed these men with respect to three risk factors, which he called hostile masculinity, promiscuity, and pornography consumption. The results showed that 72% of the men who were high in hostility, high in promiscuity, and *high* in pornography consumption reported at least one case of sexual aggression. In contrast, 44% of the men who were high in hostility, high in promiscuity, and *low* in pornography consumption reported any sexual aggression. We need to be cautious about confounding variables. However, this study showed that men who frequently viewed pornography had a much higher risk of sexual aggression in this sample.

Pornography is clearly a complex social, moral, and legal issue (B. A. Scott, 2004; J. W. White & Frabutt, 2006). Many men can view pornography without behaving violently toward women. However, pornography is not simply an innocent form of entertainment.

CHILD SEXUAL ABUSE

So far, we have focused on the sexual abuse of teenage and adult women. We also need to discuss child sexual abuse, which is one of the most devastating forms of sexual violence. For example, when Sashima was 9 years old, her mother's boyfriend moved into their house. At first, the boyfriend began by checking on Sashima during the night, and caressing her body. After several episodes, he began to touch her breasts and genitals, telling her constantly how much he loved her. He then attempted to have sexual intercourse with her. With the help of a concerned teacher, Sashima reported the events to child protective services. The boyfriend was later arrested (O. Barnett et al., 2005). The issue of child sexual abuse reminds us that adult women are not the only victims of violence; even young children are vulnerable.

Child sexual abuse is particularly cruel because, in most cases, children are abused by relatives, neighbors, and caretakers (Freyd et al., 2005). The abusers are the very individuals who should be protecting them, nurturing them, and acting in their best interests.

Definitions of child sexual abuse vary. Some definitions specify physical contact between the perpetrator and the child, and some do not. The incidence of child sexual abuse depends on the definition. Estimations are also difficult because only a fraction of the cases are reported (O. Barnett et al., 2005; Frieze, 2005; Ullman, 2003). Even so, estimates suggest that about 20% to 30% of all females in the United States and Canada had experienced child sexual abuse by the time they were 18 years old. Estimates are typically lower for males (O. Barnett et al., 2005; Herrera et al., 2006; Olio, 2004; Tudiver et al., 2002). According to current research, ethnicity does not have a consistent effect on the rate of child sexual abuse (Doll et al., 2004).

Incest is a particular kind of child sexual abuse; again, definitions vary. One accepted definition is that **incest** refers to sexual relations between biologically related individuals (Frieze, 2005). Unfortunately, relatives commit a large proportion of child sexual abuse incidents—including rape (Olafson, 2004; L. Phillips, 1998; J. W. White et al., 2001).

THE EFFECTS OF CHILD SEXUAL ABUSE.   Sexual abuse can profoundly affect a child, both immediately and over the long term. The immediate psychological consequences of child sexual abuse include fear, anger, depression, and guilt. Nightmares and other sleep disturbances are also common. As you might expect, many victims also stop trusting other people (Slater et al., 2003; Tudiver et al., 2002). The long-term consequences of child sexual abuse may include post-traumatic stress disorder (discussed on page 434), depression, anxiety disorders, eating disorders, substance abuse, and risky sexual behavior. Child abuse also affects the long-term physical health of adult women (O. Barnett et al., 2005; Duncan, 2004; Frieze, 2005; Herrera et al., 2006; McNally, 2003b; Ullman & Brecklin, 2003; Zurbriggen & Freyd, 2004).

THE RECOVERED-MEMORY/FALSE-MEMORY CONTROVERSY.   The topic of child sexual abuse has created a major debate among psychologists. When children have been sexually abused, some psychologists argue that children may forget their memory of that experience, but they may recover that memory when a later event triggers recall (the **recovered-memory perspective**). Other psychologists argue that many of these "recovered memories" are actually incorrect memories or stories that people constructed about events that never really happened (the **false-memory perspective**). This controversy has produced hundreds of articles, chapters, and books (e.g., Brainerd & Reyna, 2005; Enns, 2004b; M. Gardner, 2006; Loftus & Guyer, 2002a, 2002b; Lynn et al., 2003; Olio, 2004; Stoler et al., 2001; Zurbriggen & Freyd, 2004).

One major problem is that we cannot easily determine whether a memory of childhood abuse is accurate. Children are abused in private settings without witnesses. Also, we cannot conduct research about child sexual abuse in a fashion that is both realistic and ethical. We know from research on eyewitness testimony that people can be convinced to create a false memory for a trivial event that never happened. For example, researchers working with adults can plant a "memory" of a fictitious childhood event, such as spilling punch at a wedding. In follow-up interviews, these adults may claim that the event really did occur (Hyman et al., 1995; Loftus, 1997). However, the creation of these bland false memories is very different from the creation of memories about a trusted adult committing sexual abuse (L. S. Brown, 2004; Zurbriggen & Freyd, 2004).

Currently, psychologists in both the United States and Canada have begun to acknowledge the complexity of the issues. They argue that both recovered memory and false memory can occur (e.g., Enns, 2004b; Frieze, 2005; Matlin, 2005; Sivers et al., 2002).

Here are some general points:

1. In many cases, children can provide accurate testimonies about how they have been abused sexually (for instance, by a stranger), and they resist "remembering" false information that someone presented to them (Enns, 2004b; Goodman, 2005; Olafson, 2004).

2. In some cases, people who have truly experienced childhood sexual abuse may forget about the abuse for decades (Freyd et al., 2005; Goodman et al., 2003). Later, they may suddenly recover that memory. This recovered memory is especially likely when the abuser was a close relative or other trusted adult (L. S. Brown, 2004; Enns, 2004b; Schacter et al., 1999; Sivers et al., 2002; Zurbriggen & Freyd, 2004).

3. In some other cases, a therapist, a relative, or another person can implant misinformation about child sexual abuse, and an individual can mistakenly "remember" it. This false memory is especially likely when the misinformation is plausible and when it focuses on relatively trivial details (Pezdek, 2001; Stoler et al., 2001). Unfortunately, however, some individuals can "remember" an elaborate history of child abuse that did not actually happen (Brainerd & Reyna, 2005; McNally, 2003a).

The ongoing recovered-memory/false-memory debate should not distract us from our central concerns. Childhood sexual abuse is a critically important problem because close caregivers may cause trauma by using power inappropriately (Enns, 2004b; Olafson, 2004; Zurbriggen & Freyd, 2004).

The Prevention of Sexual Assault and Rape

We've examined several important characteristics of rape; what can people do to prevent it? Rape prevention is an issue both for individual women and for our entire society. Table 13.1, which lists some precautions that individual women can take, draws from much longer lists in several resources. More than 1,100 different rape-prevention strategies have been listed, and the advice is often confusing and conflicting (Corcoran & Mahlstedt, 1999; Fischhoff, 1992). Furthermore, no magic formula can prevent rape, although some strategies may reduce the dangers. Let's consider separately how women can help prevent rape by strangers and by acquaintances. Then we'll discuss how society can work to prevent rape.

	SAFETY PRECAUTIONS TO AVOID A RAPE CONFRONTATION
TABLE 13.1	WITH A STRANGER

Note: Read the section on individuals' prevention of rape by strangers (page 443) before you look at the following information.

General Precautions

1. Before an emergency arises, locate the nearest Rape Crisis Center or similar organization to obtain material on rape prevention.

2. Make certain that your consumption of alcohol or other drugs does not endanger your alertness. When women use drugs or alcohol before a rape attack, they typically experience more severe bodily injury.

3. Take a self-defense course, and learn the vulnerable body parts of a potential attacker.

4. If you are attacked, do not be afraid to be rude. Instead, yell loudly and throw any available object at the attacker.

Precautions at Home

1. Make certain to use secure locks on doors and windows.

2. Ask repairmen and deliverymen for identification before opening the door; do not let strangers inside your home to use your phone.

3. If you live in an apartment, don't enter the elevator with a strange man and don't enter a deserted basement or laundry room. Insist that the apartment manager keep hallways, entrances, and grounds well lit.

Precautions on the Street

1. When you are walking, walk purposefully; make it clear that you know your destination. Be alert to your surroundings.

2. Avoid being alone on the streets or on campus late at night; if you cannot avoid being alone, carry a whistle that will make a loud noise, or a "practical" weapon such as an umbrella, a pen, or keys.

3. If a car is following you, quickly turn around and then walk in the opposite direction to the nearest open store or neighbor.

Precautions in Cars and on Buses or Subways

1. Keep car doors locked, even when you are riding.

2. Keep your gas tank filled and the car in good working order. If you have car trouble, call 911 or other emergency number.

3. If you are being followed while driving, don't pull into your driveway. Instead, drive to the nearest police or fire station and honk your horn.

4. At bus or subway stations, stay in well-lit sections, near change booths or near a group of people.

Sources: Based on L. L. Alexander et al. (2001), Boston Women's Health Book Collective (2005), Crooks and Baur (2005), Parrot (1999), and Rozee (2005).

INDIVIDUALS' PREVENTION OF RAPE BY STRANGERS.   An important issue that is related to rape prevention can be called the blame-the-victim problem. Notice that many of the items in Table 13.1 will force women to limit their own freedom. Women should not hitchhike or walk in unlighted areas. Why should women— the potential victims—be the ones who have to restrict their behavior? This complaint cannot be answered satisfactorily (Koss, 2003; Rozee, 2004). The situation definitely *is* unjust. However, the reality is that rape is less likely if women take these precautions. This injustice also emphasizes that the real solutions would require changes in society, rather than modifying only one's personal behavior.

The research also shows that women significantly reduce their chances of being raped when they try to block, push, or incapacitate their assailants. Women who fight back are also likely to recover their psychological well-being more rapidly (Crooks & Baur, 2005; Gavey, 2005; Rozee, 2005).

Resources on rape avoidance also recommend training in self-defense, especially because self-defense affords women greater empowerment and personal competence (Crooks & Baur, 2005). In a rape situation, a woman must quickly assess the specific situation, as well as her own physical strength, before deciding whether to resist. However, even if a woman is raped, *it is never her fault.*

INDIVIDUALS' PREVENTION OF ACQUAINTANCE RAPE.   Women may feel comforted to think that they can protect themselves from rape by locking their doors and avoiding late-night walks in dangerous areas. But how will those precautions protect women from being raped by someone they know?

Unfortunately, women must use a different set of strategies to protect themselves from an acquaintance (Rozee, 2005). One precaution is to avoid a relationship with a man who talks negatively about women in general or with a domineering man who insults you and ignores what you say. These men are likely to ignore your refusals if you say you do not want to have sex (Adams-Curtis & Forbes, 2004; Crooks & Baur, 2005).

Some precautions on dating safety may sound obvious, but they can decrease the chances of acquaintance rape. When you are just getting to know someone, go to public places with a group of people. If possible, agree in advance that everyone will leave together at the end of the event. Limit your alcohol intake, and make sure that no one can slip a drug into your drink (Boston Women's Health Book Collective, 2005; Crooks & Baur, 2005). Also, take some time to think how you would respond if a situation becomes threatening. What would your options be? Throughout a relationship, communicate with your dating partner about any sexual activities that seem appropriate or inappropriate (Abbey, 2002).

In the previous section, we discussed effective ways of preventing rape by strangers. When the attacker is an acquaintance, he may respond to verbal assertiveness. For example, a woman can shout, "Stop it! This is rape, and I'm calling the police!" (Parrot, 1996, p. 226). Screaming or running away may also be effective.

In an ideal world, women could trust their dates, their classmates, and their friends. In the real world, the clear majority of men would never rape an acquaintance. However, some do, and women must be prepared for this possibility.

SOCIETY'S PREVENTION OF RAPE.   An individual may avoid rape by following certain precautions. However, solutions at the individual level mean that women will continue to live in fear of being raped (Rozee, 2004). To prevent rape, we need to take a broader approach, encouraging people to value women and men equally. We must acknowledge that a violent society—which often devalues women—will tend to encourage rape (O. Barnett et al., 2005; Christopher & Kisler, 2004). Our list starts with concrete suggestions and then considers some problems that require more fundamental changes (Abbey, 2002; Boston Women's Health Book Collective, 2005; Corcoran & Mahlstedt, 1999; DeKeseredy & Schwartz, 1998; Rozee, 2005):

1. Professionals who work with children must be alert for evidence of child sexual abuse. Schools also need to teach children about the sexual-abuse problem.
2. Hospitals and medical providers should be sensitive to the emotional and physical needs of girls and women who have been raped.
3. Laws must be reformed so that the legal process is less stressful and more supportive for the victims.
4. Education about rape needs to be improved, beginning in junior high or high school. Students need this information when they are young because they have already formed their attitudes toward rape by the time they reach college. Rape-prevention programs must emphasize that men *can* control their sexual impulses and that women are not to be blamed for rape (L. A. Anderson & Whiston, 2005; B. Fouts & Knapp, 2001).
5. Men's groups must become more involved in rape prevention (Binder, 2001). On some college campuses, fraternities will join together with campus women's groups to organize a rape awareness day or a "Take Back the Night" event (Abbey & McAuslan, 2004; Marine, 2004). Men and men's organizations need to remember this important quotation: "If you're not part of the solution, you're part of the problem."
6. Violence must be less glorified in the media. The violence in films, video games, television programs, and popular music is widely recognized, yet the situation has not improved in recent years (Dill et al., 2005; Escobar-Chaves et al., 2005; Kimmel, 2004; Rozee, 2004). We must emphasize that violent "entertainment" encourages aggression against women.
7. Ultimately, our society must direct more attention toward the needs of women. As we've emphasized throughout this book, women are relatively underpaid, powerless, and invisible. Their needs are often trivialized and ignored. Every woman should be able to feel that her body is safe from attack and that she has the same freedom of movement that men have. Our culture must not tolerate violence toward women.

Section Summary

Sexual Assault and Rape

1. Rape occurs in almost all cultures throughout the world; between 15% and 25% of women in the United States and Canada will be raped during their lifetime.

2. Frequently, women who have been raped by an acquaintance will not consider the assault to be a "real" rape. Some instances of acquaintance rape can be traced to misinterpretations of sexual interest.

3. Alcohol and other drugs increase the likelihood of sexual assault.

4. Women who have been raped report that, during the assault, they felt terrified, confused, and anxious. Afterward, victims often feel helpless and devalued. Long-term consequences for a rape victim may include post-traumatic stress disorder and physical health problems, although individual differences are prominent.

5. Because of the threat of rape, many women feel unsafe, and they restrict their activities.

6. A woman who has been raped may be blamed by her family, the legal system, and the general public; attitudes about rape depend on factors such as gender, gender-role beliefs, and whether a stranger or an acquaintance raped the woman.

7. Some myths about rape are not based on fact. In reality, rapists are often acquaintances; men who appear "normal" may consider rape; women do not ask to be raped; and pornography can increase the incidence of rape.

8. Child sexual abuse has both immediate and long-term effects on mental and physical health; some memories of child sexual abuse can be forgotten and then recovered later, but some adults may construct false memories of abuse that did not occur.

9. Safety precautions that prevent rape by a stranger typically limit women's freedom at home and in public places; it is important not to blame the victim of a rape attack.

10. Safety precautions for avoiding rape by an acquaintance include avoiding men who downgrade women; dating in groups at the beginning of a relationship; and being verbally assertive.

11. Ultimately, the number of rapes can be reduced only by greater societal attention to women's needs. The issues include reforming the medical, legal, and educational resources for rape victims. The media must reduce their emphasis on violence, and women's issues must receive more attention.

THE ABUSE OF WOMEN

Consider the following passage, in which a woman described how her husband had abused her:

> Little by little, he isolated me from my friends, he convinced me to quit working, he complained about how I kept the house, he kept track of the mileage on the car to make sure that I wasn't going anywhere. Eventually, when the beatings were regular and severe, I had no one to turn to, and I felt completely alone. (Boston Women's Health Book Collective, 2005)

The **abuse of women** refers to intentional acts that injure a woman; these acts include physical, psychological, and sexual abuse. (We discussed sexual abuse in the previous section.) The term *abuse of women* is broader than many similar terms. For example, the term *domestic violence* implies that two people are living together. Therefore, this term seems to exclude the kind of violence that often occurs in dating relationships, including high school and college students (DeKeseredy & Schwartz, 1998; J. Katz, Carino, & Hilton, 2002; J. W. White & Frabutt, 2006). The term *domestic violence* and the related term *battered women* also imply *physical* abuse (J. W. White et al., 2001). However, many women who have been abused report that the psychological abuse is the most destructive component of the abusive experience (Offman & Matheson, 2004; K. D. O'Leary & Maiuro, 2001).

Physical abuse can include hitting, kicking, burning, pushing, choking, throwing objects, and using a weapon. Emotional abuse can include humiliation, name calling, intimidation, extreme jealousy, refusal to speak, and isolating someone from friends and family members (D. A. Hines & Malley-Morrison, 2005; Straus, 2005). Another form of emotional abuse focuses on finances, for example, when a man withholds money or destroys his wife's credit cards (Castañeda & Burns-Glover, 2004; Martz & Saraurer, 2002).

Because of space limitations, in this section, we will focus on male violence against females. The research demonstrates that some females abuse their male partners. However, most research shows that men abuse their partners more frequently and more severely (DeKeseredy & Schwartz, 2002; Frieze, 2005; D. A. Hines & Malley-Morrison, 2005; McHugh, 2005; Statistics Canada, 2006). For example, men are about nine times as likely as women to assault a former spouse (Loseke & Kurz, 2005).

In addition, we will not examine abuse in lesbian relationships. However, other resources discuss this topic (e.g., D. A. Hines & Malley-Morrison, 2005; Ristock, 2002; J. W. White et al., 2001). Before you read further, try Demonstration 13.4.

HOW OFTEN DOES THE ABUSE OF WOMEN OCCUR?

Earlier in this chapter, we discussed the difficulty of estimating how many women experience sexual harassment and rape. Most women believe that they must not let others know that they have been abused; this silence prevents us from obtaining accurate data about violence in intimate relationships

Demonstration 13.4

As you can imagine, no simple questionnaire can assess whether a relationship shows signs of abuse. However, look at the following questions and see whether they may apply, either to a current relationship or to a previous relationship.

Does your partner:

1. Make fun of you or make demeaning comments when other people are present?
2. Tell you that everything is your fault?
3. Check up on you at work or other locations, to make certain that you are at the place where you said you'd be?
4. Make you feel unsafe in the current relationship?
5. Make you feel that he (or she) would explode if you did the wrong thing?
6. Act very suspicious about any potential romantic relationship with another person?
7. Try to keep you from developing nonromantic friendships with other people?
8. Try to make you do things you don't want to do?
9. Criticize you frequently?
10. Decide what you will wear, eat, or buy—when you have expressed a preference for something else?
11. Threaten to hurt you?
12. Intentionally hurt you physically?

Sources: Frieze (2005), Shaw and Lee (2001), and Warshaw (2001).

(Jiwani, 2000). According to estimates, however, about 20–35% of women in the United States and Canada will experience abuse during their lifetime (Christopher & Lloyd, 2000; Statistics Canada, 2006). To consider the statistics another way, male partners abuse 2 million to 3 million U.S. women each year (Koss et al., 2003; J. W. White & Frabutt, 2006).

Furthermore, between 30% and 55% of women who are treated in U.S. hospital emergency departments have injuries related to domestic violence (Warshaw, 2001). Even pregnancy does not protect women from abuse. Each year, between 15% and 20% of all pregnant women experience physical or sexual abuse (Berkowitz, 2005; Frieze, 2005; Logan et al., 2006).

As we mentioned earlier, abuse also occurs in dating relationships. According to Canadian and U.S. surveys, males abuse their girlfriends as early as elementary school and the abuse continues through high school and college (DeKeseredy & Schwartz, 1998, 2002; Frieze, 2005; J. Katz, Carino, & Hilton, 2002). For instance, a large-scale survey of Canadian university students revealed that 31% of the women had been pushed, grabbed, or shoved by someone they were dating. Psychological abuse was even more common: 65% of the women said they had been degraded in front of friends or family and 65% had experienced insults or swearing (DeKeseredy & Schwartz, 1998).

The problem of partner abuse is not limited to North America. The rate of abuse in European countries is similar to the North American rate (O. Barnett et al., 2005). Data gathered in Asia, Latin America, and Africa reveal even higher rates of abuse (e.g., O. Barnett et al., 2005; Krahé et al., 2005; Malley-Morrison, 2004; Stahly, 2004). Women are especially likely to experience abuse in the turmoil of a war or a natural disaster, such as the tsunami that hit southern Asia in 2004. As one woman said, "The silence regarding violence against women is louder than the tsunami waves" (Chew, 2005, p. 1).

In many countries, more than half of adult women reported that a partner had physically assaulted them. For example, an interviewer asked a man in South Korea if he had beaten his wife. He replied:

> I was married at 28, and I'm 52 now. How could I have been married all these years and not beaten my wife? . . . For me, it's better to release that anger and get it over with. Otherwise, I just get sick inside. (Kristof, 1996, p. 17A)

Notice, however, that this man never considered whether the abuse was also better for his wife.

THE DYNAMICS OF ABUSE

Most women are not abused continually. A cyclical pattern of abuse is more common, although certainly not universal (Downs & Fisher, 2005; Stahly, 2004; L. E. A. Walker, 2000, 2001). This **abuse cycle** typically has three phases: (1) the tension building phase, (2) the acute battering phase, and (3) the loving phase.

In the tension building phase, the physical abuse is relatively minor, but verbal outbursts and threats increase the tension. The woman often tries to calm her partner. She may try to keep his abuse from escalating by anticipating his whims. As one woman from rural Saskatchewan said, "You keep trying and you keep trying and you discover it doesn't matter what you do, it's not good enough. Like it's never enough" (Martz & Saraurer, 2002, p. 174).

When tension builds too high, the abuser responds with an acute battering incident, the hallmark of the second phase. The woman may be severely beaten. Even a trivial event can trigger a battering incident. For example, one wealthy professional man broke his wife's jaw when he discovered that one of the potted plants in their mansion had not been watered sufficiently (Stahly, 2004).

In the third phase, the abuser usually becomes charming and loving. He apologizes and promises that he will never be violent again. He may encourage his partner to forget the tension, uncertainty, and pain of the earlier two phases. Unfortunately, the cycle usually repeats itself, often with increasingly severe abuse and a shorter loving phase (Frieze, 2005; Harway, 2003; Slater et al., 2003).

WOMEN'S REACTIONS TO ABUSE

As you might expect, women typically react to abuse with fear, depression, and mistrust. Women who have been abused may be hyper-alert, searching for signs that their partner may be ready to strike again (Martz & Saraurer, 2002;

Statistics Canada, 2005). Understandably, women in long-term, violent relationships report that they are dissatisfied with these relationships (J. Katz, Kuffel, & Coblentz, 2002; S. L. Williams & Frieze, 2005). Women who have been abused typically feel anxious and low in self-esteem. About half of abused women develop depression, and some attempt suicide (Koss et al., 2003; Offman & Matheson, 2004; Stahly, 2004).

Abused women also experience many problems with their physical health. Women may suffer from bruises, cuts, burns, broken bones, and brain damage as a direct result of an assault. Abusers may even prevent women from seeking medical care. Many months afterward, women may still experience headaches, sleep disturbances, extreme fatigue, abdominal pain, pelvic pain, gynecological problems, and other chronic disorders (O. Barnett et al., 2005; Koss et al., 2001; Logan et al., 2006). Naturally, these physical problems may intensify their psychological problems. These physical problems may also prevent women from going to work, resulting in numerous additional problems (Mighty, 2004; Riger et al., 2004).

Characteristics Related to Abusive Relationships

Researchers have examined several factors related to the abuse of women. For example, some family characteristics may be associated with abuse. In addition, certain personal attributes are especially common among men who abuse their partners.

Family Variables Associated With Abuse.   Abuse of women is somewhat more common among low-income families, although the relationship between abuse and social class is complex (D. A. Hines & Malley-Morrison, 2005; Logan et al., 2006). However, no woman is immune. For example, a female professor at a prestigious college described her own experiences, when she was married to a well-educated man who was verbally and physically abusive for 12 years. When she finally left her husband, he committed suicide (Bates, 2005).

The relationship between ethnicity and family violence is both complex and inconsistent (Flores-Ortiz, 2004; Harway, 2003; Logan et al., 2006; C. M. West, 2002). Many analyses do not take social class into account, and we have just seen that social class is somewhat related to patterns of abuse. However, Statistics Canada (2006) noted that Aboriginal women are three times as likely as other Canadian women to report domestic violence.

In contrast, the number of reported cases of domestic abuse is relatively low in Asian American communities (O. Barnett et al., 2005; G. C. N. Hall, 2002). One reason may be that Asian American families are extremely reluctant to let anyone outside the immediate family know about domestic problems (McHugh & Bartoszek, 2000). Many Asian cultures believe that women should accept their suffering and endure their hardships, and this value system discourages women from reporting domestic violence (G. C. N. Hall, 2002; Tran & Des Jardins, 2000).

PERSONAL CHARACTERISTICS OF MALE ABUSERS.   One of the most commonly reported characteristics of male abusers is that they feel they are entitled to hurt their partners. From their egocentric perspective, their own needs come first (Birns, 1999). A good example of this male entitlement perspective is the Korean man who felt he was better off releasing his anger by beating his wife (p. 448).

Abusers are also likely to believe that the male should be the head of the family, along with other traditional concepts about gender roles (D. A. Hines & Malley-Morrison, 2005; J. W. White et al., 2001). Not surprisingly, abusers have more positive attitudes toward physical and verbal aggression, compared to men who are not abusers (D. A. Hines & Malley-Morrison, 2005; J. W. White & Frabutt, 2006). Furthermore, abusers are more likely than nonabusers to have witnessed family violence during childhood (D. A. Hines & Malley-Morrison, 2005; Martz & Sarauer, 2002; McHugh & Bartoszek, 2000).

Situational factors also increase the likelihood of partner abuse. For example, men who are unemployed have a relatively high rate of domestic violence (Frieze, 2005; Marin & Russo, 1999). Men whose friends endorse the abuse of women are also more likely to be aggressive (DeKeseredy & Schwartz, 1998).

Research also suggests that males who have a drinking problem are more likely to abuse women (D. A. Hines & Malley-Morrison, 2005; J. W. White & Frabutt, 2006). It's possible that alcohol plays an important role because it affects judgment and other cognitive processes. However, alcohol may not directly *cause* violence. For instance, some men simply use alcohol as an excuse for their violence (Gelles & Cavanaugh, 2005). A man might try to justify his violence by saying, "I don't know what got into me. It must have been the booze."

THE PUBLIC'S ATTITUDES ABOUT THE ABUSE OF WOMEN

In earlier chapters, we discussed the negative impact of the media on such issues as gender stereotypes and body images. However, North American research suggests that the media have had a generally positive impact on knowledge about domestic violence (Goldfarb, 2005; Rapoza, 2004). For example, 93% of U.S. residents in a nationwide survey said that they had learned from media coverage that domestic violence is a serious problem (E. Klein et al., 1997). We should be pleased when feminist educational efforts combine with the media and legal reform to change societal attitudes (Frieze, 2005; C. M. Sullivan, 2006; Yllö, 2005). In a Canadian public opinion survey, for instance, 77% of the respondents said that family violence should be an important priority for the federal government (Dookie, 2004).

In general, women are more likely than men to have negative attitudes toward the abuse of women. In contrast, men are more likely than women to say that a woman must have done something to deserve the punishment (Frieze, 2005; D. A. Hines & Malley-Morrison, 2005; Locke & Richman, 1999). A study by Nayak and her colleagues (2003) assessed attitudes toward men who physically abuse their wives. These researchers gathered data from college

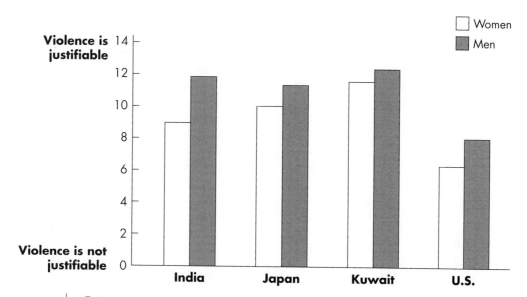

FIGURE 13.2 | COLLEGE STUDENTS' ATTITUDES ABOUT WHETHER A MAN'S PHYSICAL VIOLENCE TOWARD HIS WIFE IS JUSTIFIABLE, AS A FUNCTION OF GENDER AND COUNTRY OF RESIDENCE. (NOTE: HIGH SCORES = VIOLENCE IS JUSTIFIABLE; LOW SCORES = VIOLENCE IS NOT JUSTIFIABLE.)

Source: From M. B. Nayak et al. (2003).

classrooms in four countries: India, Japan, Kuwait (a Middle Eastern country where women could not vote at the time the study was conducted), and the United States. Figure 13.2 shows the students' tendency to believe that wives deserve to be physically abused. Consistent with the other research, the women in each country were less likely than the men to believe that wives deserved abuse. Furthermore, students in the United States were less likely than students in the other three countries to endorse abuse. However, are the cross-national differences as large as you would have expected?

MYTHS ABOUT THE ABUSE OF WOMEN

We have already discussed the evidence against several commonly accepted myths about the abuse of women. For example, each of the following myths is *not correct* because the research *contradicts* these myths:

1. Abuse is rare.
2. Men experience as much abuse as women.
3. Abuse is limited to the lower social classes.
4. Abuse is much more common among ethnic minority groups than among European Americans.

Let's examine some other myths. In each case, think about how the myth can lead people to blame women for being abused.

Myth 1: Abused women enjoy being beaten.   Sigmund Freud and other early theorists reasoned that women who remain in violent relationships enjoy the trauma of being abused. A portion of the general population still holds this belief. However, we have no evidence for this myth (Frieze, 2005; Stahly, 2004; L. E. A. Walker, 2000). Women do not enjoy being abused, just as women do not enjoy being raped.

Myth 2: Abused women deserve to be beaten and humiliated.   According to this myth, when a woman oversteps the boundaries of a proper girlfriend or wife, she ought to be beaten. In other words, people may blame the woman's behavior, not the man's response (O. Barnett et al., 2005). A student in my psychology of women course related an incident in which she had described a wife-abuse case to a group of friends. Specifically, a husband had seriously injured his wife because dinner was not ready as soon as he came home from work. A male friend in this student's group—whom my student had previously considered enlightened—responded, "Yes, but she really should have prepared dinner on time."

Myth 3: Abused women could easily leave, if they really wanted to.   This myth ignores both the interpersonal and the practical factors that prevent a woman from leaving a relationship. An abused woman may sincerely believe that her boyfriend or husband is basically a good man who can be reformed (Frieze, 2005).

Many abused women also face practical barriers. A woman may have no place to go, no money, and no way of escaping (O. Barnett et al., 2005; Frieze, 2005). Another practical concern is that the abuser may threaten to retaliate if she leaves. He often becomes even more violent after she has moved out of the home (O. Barnett et al., 2005; D. A. Hines & Malley-Morrison, 2005; Stahly, 2004).

How Abused Women Take Action

Some women remain in abusive relationships. They may seek support from family members or friends. For example, one woman described a helpful friend: "She had been through a similar relationship and it was nice that we could talk because she understood where I was coming from; she understood why I was still there even though I shouldn't be" (Martz & Saraurer, 2002, p. 178).

To some extent, a woman's strategies for handling abuse depend on her family background. For example, some families emphasize persevering in unpleasant situations and hiding domestic problems (O. Barnett et al., 2005; Ho, 1997). Community members and religious leaders may oppose the breakup of a marriage (McCallum & Lauzon, 2005). In these circumstances, women may be less likely to try to escape from an abusive relationship.

Let's discuss several options for women who have been abused: They can seek therapy, they can leave, or they can go to a shelter for abused women.

THERAPY.   An abusive relationship seldom improves spontaneously. In fact, as we noted earlier, violence frequently escalates in a relationship. Women often seek the services of therapists, who are usually aware that society's attitudes can encourage the abuse of women. Ideally, therapists who work with abused women will adopt a feminist-therapy approach (see pp. 416–417). Therapists should respect a woman's strengths and difficulties. They should also help women think about themselves with compassion rather than with criticism. Like other forms of women-centered therapy, this approach empowers women to pursue their own goals, rather than simply focusing on other people's needs (Ali & Toner, 2001; Frieze, 2005; Logan et al., 2006).

Consider the feminist-therapy approach that Rinfret-Raynor and Cantin (1997) used in working with French Canadian women who were abused. The therapists informed the women about their legal rights, helped them explore community resources, and conducted both individual and group therapy. A major message throughout therapy was that the abuser is responsible for the violence, not the victim. The therapists also worked to increase the women's self-esteem and sense of independence. Compared to women who had received standard nonsexist therapy, the women who had received feminist therapy experienced a greater decrease in physical violence.

In general, therapists believe that a man and a woman in a physically abusive relationship must not enter couples therapy together. If both meet at the same time with the therapist, the woman may say something during the session that the man will use as an excuse for battering when they return home (O. Barnett et al., 2005; Christensen & Jacobson, 2000; D. A. Hines & Malley-Morrison, 2005). However, some therapists report success if the couple seeks help before the violence escalates (D. A. Hines & Malley-Morrison, 2005).

DECIDING TO LEAVE A RELATIONSHIP.   Many women decide that abuse is too high a price to pay for the advantages of remaining in a relationship. Many women reach a crisis point after a particularly violent episode (Lloyd & Emery, 2000). For instance, one woman decided to leave after her husband broke her ribs (Martz & Saraurer, 2002).

Some women decide to leave after they have been attacked in front of their children. For example, one woman left after her husband threatened to kill her in front of her children. Others leave after their partner breaks a promise about stopping the abuse or after they realize that the relationship will not improve (O. Barnett et al., 2005; Jacobson & Gottman, 1998).

Unfortunately, people are so intrigued by the question, "Why do battered women stay?" that they forget to ask more important questions (Stahly, 2004). Some of these questions include "Why are violent men allowed to stay?" and "How can our society make it clear that emotional and physical abuse is not acceptable?"

SERVICES FOR ABUSED WOMEN.   Many communities in North America provide services for women who have been abused. Some communities also have shelters, where an abused woman and her children can go for safety, support, and information about social services available locally. Many shelters also offer counseling services and support groups for the residents (O. Barnett et al., 2005; C. M. Sullivan, 2006). Canada currently has about 500 shelters that focus on domestic violence (Statistics Canada, 2006). The United States—with about 9 times the population of Canada—currently has only about 2,000 shelters (D. A. Hines & Malley-Morrison, 2005). Shelters and other community organizations often sponsor presentations to schools and local groups to provide information about domestic violence—and to dispel the myths.

Unfortunately, these shelters operate on extremely limited budgets, and we need hundreds of additional shelters throughout North America. Thousands of women are turned away each year from shelters that are filled to capacity (L. E. A. Walker, 2001). Many of these women become homeless. Others return to their homes, where they risk being beaten once again. Ironically, as of January 20, 2007, the U.S. government has spent more than $360 billion on the Iraq War (National Priorities Project, 2007). As Logan and her coauthors (2006) emphasize, the abuse of women has affected many more people than any terrorist attack that the United States has experienced. However, our government is decreasing its funding for battered women's shelters, so they must struggle to locate funding from individuals and organizations in the community.

Society's Response to the Problem of Abuse

In recent years, the criminal justice system and the general public have become much more aware that abuse is a serious problem. Still, government policies have no consistent plan for providing shelters, services, and assistance for abused women. These policies also do not require counseling for the abusers. Government officials and agencies must publicize the fact that abuse of any kind is unacceptable. Colleges and high schools should require anti-violence campaigns that are very well publicized (Giordano, 2001; Kuffel & Katz, 2002). As Leonore Walker (2000) pointed out, "Domestic violence cannot be considered a private family matter. Its painful repercussions extend into the general community" (p. 218).

Community organizations are often silent about the issue of abused women. Imagine what could happen if church groups, parent-teacher associations, and service organizations (such as the Rotary Club and the Kiwanis) were to sponsor a program on domestic violence. These organizations often set the moral tone for a community, and they could send a strong message that abuse of women cannot be tolerated.

One positive development is that medical organizations are gradually paying more attention to the issue of the abuse of women (O. Barnett et al., 2005; Koss et al., 2001; Logan et al., 2006). For example, physicians are now being trained to screen all women by introducing the topic: "We're concerned about the health effects of domestic abuse, so we now ask a few questions of all our patients" (Eisenstat & Bancroft, 1999, p. 889). Health educators are also developing training materials. Physicians should be less likely to ignore the evidence of abuse now that a new norm of concern is being established.

Individual men can also make a difference (Goldrick-Jones, 2002; Poling et al., 2002). For example, James Poling describes how he and two male colleagues "moved from a lack of awareness of abusive behaviors, to a period of growing awareness because of the honest sharing of women about their experiences of violence, to belief in a set of principles that opened our eyes." As a result, they now incorporate anti-violence messages into the religious services that they conduct.

Concern about the abuse of women is emerging even more slowly in developing countries. For instance, most countries do not offer legal protection for women who have been abused (R. J. R. Levesque, 2001). Still, some of the efforts are encouraging. On a trip to Nicaragua, I found several resources on violence against women. One brochure, developed for church groups in Nicaragua, debunked common myths, such as that women deserve to be mistreated, that abuse is God's will, and that abuse occurs only in the lower class (M. West & Fernández, 1997). A brief handbook is also available to educate health-care workers about the problem of the abuse of women (Ellsberg et al., 1998).

Ultimately, however, any attempt to solve the problem of abuse must acknowledge that the power imbalance in intimate relationships reflects the power imbalance in our society (Goldfarb, 2005; Pickup, 2001). In addition, our culture trains some men to control their intimate partners through physical and emotional abuse. Some television programs, music videos, and other media reinforce the images of men's violence toward women. We can help to counteract these attitudes by encouraging the media to provide less violent entertainment (Kimmel, 2004). We must work toward a world in which violence is not directed at women as a group in order to keep them powerless.

Section Summary

The Abuse of Women

1. About one-quarter of women in the United States and Canada will experience abuse during their lifetime; abuse is also common in dating relationships; abuse is more likely in other countries, including some in Asia, Latin America, and Africa.

2. A common pattern is an abuse cycle, which begins with verbal outbursts and moderate physical abuse; then, tension builds toward an acute battering incident, followed by a period of calm and repentance.

3. Women who have been abused may feel afraid, anxious, and depressed, and they experience many physical health problems.

4. Abuse is somewhat correlated with social class, but its relationship with ethnicity is complex; male abusers typically have a sense of entitlement; unemployment is a risk factor for abuse.

5. Most North Americans consider abuse to be a serious issue; women are more likely than men to have negative attitudes about abuse, and country of residence is also related to attitudes.

6. Three myths about abused women that research does not support are that abused women enjoy being beaten, that they deserve to be beaten, and that they could easily leave the relationship.

7. Therapy for an abused woman focuses on reducing self-criticism and focusing on their own needs; women often decide to leave an abusive relationship after they reach a specific crisis point; shelters are helpful, but they are poorly funded and temporary.

8. Government policies have no uniform provisions about shelters or services for abused women; health-care providers now have better training about abuse issues.

9. As in other issues of violence, the problem of battered women cannot be resolved without seeking equality at the societal level and reducing violence in our culture.

CHAPTER REVIEW QUESTIONS

1. Throughout this chapter, we emphasized that people often blame the victims for events that are beyond their control. Describe how this process operates in sexual harassment, rape, and the abuse of women.

2. As the introduction to this chapter notes, a culture that values men more than women encourages some men to feel that they are entitled to certain privileges. Explain how this sense of entitlement is relevant in sexual harassment, rape, and the abuse of women.

3. In this chapter, we examined attitudes about sexual harassment, rape, and abuse. Identify any similarities that apply to all three topics. Also, comment on gender comparisons in these attitudes and the relationship between gender roles and these attitudes.

4. What are the two general categories of sexual harassment? Provide at least one example for each category, based on the recent media or on reports from friends. How do these examples illustrate why sexual harassment is an important issue?

5. Summarize the information about acquaintance rape and child sexual abuse. What does this information tell us about the balance of power and sexual violence in close personal relationships?

6. What are some of the common myths about sexual harassment, rape, and abuse? What do all these myths reveal about society's attitudes toward men and women?

7. What information do we have about sexual harassment, rape, and abuse, with respect to countries outside North America? Is this information substantially different from information about violence against women in North America?

8. Imagine that you have been appointed to a national committee to address the problems of sexual harassment, rape, and abuse. What recommendations would you make for government policy, the legal system, universities, business institutions, the media, and educational programs? Try to provide suggestions in addition to those mentioned in this chapter.

9. According to Theme 3, women are less visible than men in many important areas; topics important in women's lives are also considered relatively unimportant. How often had you heard about the topics of sexual harassment, rape, and abuse before the course for which you are reading this book? What are some factors that encourage these three topics to be relatively invisible?

10. Think about a high-school female whom you know well. Imagine that she is about to go off to college. What kind of information can you supply from this chapter that would be helpful for her to know, with respect to violence against women? Now think about a high-school male whom you know. If he were preparing to go to college, what information would you provide—both with respect to his avoiding violence against women and his role in supporting women who have experienced violence? (Better still, figure out how you can have an actual conversation about these topics with those individuals!)

KEY TERMS

*entitlement (423)

*sexual harassment (423)

*quid pro quo harassment (423)

*hostile environment (423)

*sexual assault (430)

*rape (430)

*acquaintance rape (431)

*post-traumatic stress disorder (PTSD) (434)

*incest (440)

recovered-memory perspective (440)

false-memory perspective (440)

*abuse of women (446)

*abuse cycle (448)

 Note: The terms asterisked in the Key Terms section serve as good search terms for InfoTrac College Edition. Go to http://infotrac.thomsonlearning.com and try these added search terms.

RECOMMENDED READINGS

Chrisler, J. C., Golden, C., & Rozee, P. D. (Eds.). (2004). *Lectures on the psychology of women* (3rd ed.). Boston: McGraw-Hill. This wonderful resource book includes 23 chapters on topics relevant to women's lives; the chapters on sexual harassment, fear of rape, pornography, and battered women are particularly relevant to the current chapter.

Foote, W. E., & Goodman-Delahunty, J. (2005). *Evaluating sexual harassment: Psychological, social, and legal considerations in forensic examinations.* Washington, DC: American Psychological Association. This book is intended as a resource for legal cases of sexual harassment. However, it also provides extensive information about survey results and psychological consequences of harassment.

Frieze, I. H. (2005). *Hurting the one you love: Violence in relationships.* Belmont, CA: Thomson Wadsworth. Irene Frieze is a highly respected psychologist who has published numerous research articles on sexual assault and the abuse of women. This clearly written book includes nine chapters on these topics; it also features three detailed case studies.

Logan, TK, Walker, R., Jordan, C. E., & Leukefeld, C. G. (2006). *Women and victimization: Contributing factors, interventions, and implications.* Washington, DC: American Psychological Association. TK Logan and her colleagues have written a clear and comprehensive overview of women's experiences with sexual assault, physical assault, stalking, and psychological abuse.

ANSWERS TO THE DEMONSTRATIONS

Demonstration 13.1 (Judgments About Sexual Harassment): Calculate a subtotal by adding together your ratings for items 1, 4, and 6. Then calculate an overall score by subtracting the ratings that you gave for items 2, 3, and 5. If your overall score is negative, you tend to be tolerant of sexual harassment. If your overall score is positive, you are aware that sexual harassment can be a serious problem.

Demonstration 13.2 (Knowledge About Rape): 1. False; 2. True; 3. False; 4. False; 5. True; 6. False; 7. False; 8. True; 9. False; 10. False.

ANSWERS TO THE TRUE-FALSE STATEMENTS

1. False (pp. 423–424); 2. False (p. 426); 3. True (p. 427); 4. True (p. 431); 5. True (p. 435); 6. True (p. 431); 7. False (p. 438); 8. True (p. 446); 9. True (p. 450); 10. False (p. 453).

14 | WOMEN AND OLDER ADULTHOOD

True or False?

_____ 1. Because most researchers are middle aged or older, journals publish much more research on this period than on childhood and adolescence combined.

_____ 2. People are consistently more negative when they are judging elderly women than when they are judging elderly men.

_____ 3. Current research shows that young people in Japan and South Korea believe that elderly people are pleasant, but not very smart.

_____ 4. Women typically have fewer retirement problems than men do.

_____ 5. Young men earn significantly more than young women; however, the incomes for retired men and women are roughly equal.

_____ 6. Hormone replacement therapy is currently recommended for most women who have reached menopause.

_____ 7. Women who have reached menopause frequently report psychological symptoms such as depression and irritability. According to the most recent research, biological factors are primarily responsible for these problems.

_____ 8. Most women experience moderate depression when their children move away from home.

_____ 9. Elderly European American women are more likely than Asian American and Native American grandmothers to live with younger family members.

_____ 10. Older women often experience health, financial, and social problems. However, most of them are reasonably satisfied with their lives.

Consider these comments from two women in their middle years:

> My attitude toward aging has changed over the years. My youngest daughter was born when I was 42. She sees me as young, and I feel relatively young at 58. I can't believe that I thought my mother was old when she turned 38 and I was the same age my daughter is now. My sense of the lifespan has increased, with an extended adulthood of active years and old age beginning around 80 or 85.

> I want to use my time well and live in a way that is true to my values. Some women face this question in college. For me, I just wanted to get married and have children. What do I want to do now? I want to feel I am leaving a legacy. It hit me full force at mid-life. (Boston Women's Health Book Collective, 2005, pp. 527–528)

In this chapter, we will explore the experiences of women in midlife and old age, and we will see many examples of the energy and sense of purpose revealed in these two quotations. Throughout this textbook, we have emphasized the contrast between people's stereotypes about women and the reality of women's lives. This contrast is also obvious when we examine the lives of older women. We seldom see media coverage of this group. (More evidence of our theme of invisible women!)

No clear-cut age spans define middle age and old age. However, one fairly standard guideline is that middle age begins at about 40 and that old age begins at about 60 or 65 (Etaugh & Bridges, 2006; Lachman, 2004).

For many years, psychological research has ignored older people, especially older women, consistent with our invisibility theme (Canetto, 2001a; Lachman,

2004). Feminist research has also paid little attention to older women (Calasanti & Slevin, 2001; S. Greene, 2003); articles about women over 40 seldom appear in prominent journals such as *Psychology of Women Quarterly* and *Sex Roles*. Even the popular "advice books" rarely mention older women (A. R. Hochschild, 2003). This neglect is especially shameful because the average life span for a woman in North America and Europe is around 80 years (Kinsella, 2000). In other words, about half of a woman's life has been largely ignored.

The absence of information is also unfortunate because North America has so many elderly women. In the 2000 Census, the United States had 20.6 million women and 14.4 million men over the age of 65—roughly 43% more women than men (U.S. Census Bureau, 2001). The comparable figures for Canada—in the 2001 Census—were 2.2 million women and 1.7 million men over age 65, or 33% more women than men (Statistics Canada, 2001, 2006). As an increasing number of women live into their 70s, 80s, and older, we need to emphasize the issues of older women.

Both psychology and women's studies now show somewhat more concern about the needs and experiences of older women (Sinnott & Shifren, 2001). For instance, we have already explored research about older women's lives in earlier chapters. Specifically, in Chapter 8, we discussed long-lasting romantic relationships, and in Chapter 9, we looked at sexuality and aging. In Chapter 11, we explored some issues relevant to older women's health, including heart disease, osteoporosis, reproductive system cancer, and breast cancer.

In this chapter, we'll focus on four additional topics: (1) attitudes toward older women, (2) retirement and economic issues, (3) menopause, and (4) social aspects of older women's lives.

ATTITUDES TOWARD OLDER WOMEN

Ageism is a bias based on age, most often a bias against elderly people (Cruikshank, 2003; T. D. Nelson, 2005b; Palmore, 2001). Common examples of ageism include negative emotions, attitudes, myths, stereotypes, and discrimination. Other examples include jokes about elderly people and attempts to avoid interacting with them (Bytheway, 2005; Siegel, 2004; Sneed & Whitbourne, 2005). We already mentioned one example of ageism: that researchers generally avoid studying elderly people. Another example of ageism is that people may speak to elderly people in slow, very simple sentences, as if they are talking to a young child (Hummert et al., 2004). Furthermore, many physicians believe that elderly individuals complain too much about relatively minor medical problems (Jorgensen, 2001; Zebrowitz & Montepare, 2000). Physicians also treat elderly patients with less respect, compared to younger patients (Palmore, 2001; Pasupathi & Löckenhoff, 2002; T. L. Thompson et al., 2004).

Ageism is an ironic bias, because the elderly constitute the only stigmatized social group that we all will join eventually—unless we happen to die early. Furthermore, if our ageism prevents us from interacting with elderly people, we won't realize that many ageist assumptions are not correct (H. Giles & Reid, 2005; Hagestad & Uhlenberg, 2005). Unfortunately, however, ageism is studied much less than either racism or sexism (Hedge et al., 2006; T. D. Nelson, 2005b).

We'll begin this section on attitudes by considering how the media treat older women. Then we'll examine whether women are more likely than men to experience ageism—the double standard of aging. Finally, we'll see that elderly women may be treated more positively in some other cultures.

OLDER WOMEN AND THE MEDIA

Try Demonstration 14.1 to discover how television represents older women. For example, older women are usually missing from the advertisements on television (Kaid & Garner, 2004). When you finally find a TV show that features older women, most of those women will be concerned about cookie recipes or holiday decorations rather than issues of greater significance.

We all know spirited, accomplished older women in real life—women who lead active, purposeful lives consistent with the two quotations at the beginning of this chapter. However, your inspection of television's older women may not reveal many women of that caliber (Bedford, 2003; Cruikshank, 2003; J. D. Robinson et al., 2004). Many of you who are reading this book are older women, and you may have noticed that women like yourself are invisible in the media (Bedford, 2003; Kjaersgaard, 2005; J. D. Robinson et al., 2004). It's possible that older women may be more prominent as the "baby boomer" women reach their mid-60s, but the trends so far are not hopeful.

Older women are also underrepresented in the movies (Markson & Taylor, 1993). For instance, an analysis of the 100 most popular films of 2002 found that only 34% of the major female characters were older than 40, although 54% of the U.S. female population is in this category. Older men are represented more fairly; 45% of the major male characters in these films were older than 40, and 51% of the U.S. male population is in this category (Lauzen & Dozier, 2005).

Demonstration 14.1

OLDER WOMEN ON TELEVISION

Between now and the end of this academic term, keep a written record of how television portrays both middle-aged women and elderly women. Be sure to include several kinds of programs (soap operas, game shows, situation comedies, shows during prime time, and Saturday morning cartoons), as well as advertisements.

Pay attention to the number of older women and what they do. Are they working outside the home? Do they have interests, hobbies, and important concerns, or are they mainly busy being nurturant? Are they portrayed as intelligent or absent minded? Do they enjoy the friendship of other women—the way that real older women do? Do they seem "real," or are they represented in a stereotypical fashion?

A glance through magazines reveals the same message: Older women are essentially invisible (McConatha et al., 1999). In the fashion magazines, older women are featured primarily in advertisements for age-concealing products. These ads are designed to make older women feel especially inadequate (Calasanti & Slevin, 2001; Etaugh & Bridges, 2001). To hide signs of age, the ads say, women should dye their hair and have face-lifts. One surgical procedure removes fat from a woman's thighs or buttocks and injects it into her lips, to restore a youthful fullness. Just imagine: You could be the first on your block to wear your hips on your lips!

This pervasive bias against older women has not been limited to recent decades. Images of evil elderly women have been common throughout Western literature, storytelling, and fairy tales (Mangum, 1999; Rostosky & Travis, 2000). Children dress up as "wicked old witches" for Halloween, but have you ever seen a costume for a wicked old *man*? You've heard many mother-in-law jokes; how about *father*-in-law jokes? We shouldn't be surprised, then, when older women themselves show ageism. Sadly, they are often biased against people their own age (H. Giles & Reid, 2005; B. R. Levy & Banaji, 2002; Whitbourne & Sneed, 2002).

THE DOUBLE STANDARD OF AGING

As we've seen, North Americans typically have negative views about the aging process. Some theorists have proposed that people judge elderly women even more harshly than elderly men, a discrepancy called the **double standard of aging** (Halliwell & Dittmar, 2003; Whitbourne & Skultety, 2006). For example, people tend to think that wrinkles in a man's face reveal character and maturity. However, people often believe that wrinkles in a woman's face send a negative message (Erber, 2005; Etaugh & Bridges, 2006). After all, the ideal woman's face should be unblemished and show no signs of previous experiences or emotions!

Does the research provide evidence for the double standard of aging? This is a difficult question to answer because our stereotypes about older men and women are complicated. As you'll see, these stereotypes depend on the particular attribute we are judging, and how we measure the judgments (Canetto, 2001a; Kite et al., 2005; D. J. Schneider, 2004). Let's consider two areas in which the double standard of aging may operate: (1) personality characteristics and (2) potential as a romantic partner.

PERSONALITY CHARACTERISTICS.   In a classic study, Hummert and her colleagues (1997) demonstrated a double standard of aging about personality characteristics. These researchers assembled photographs of men and women representing different age groups. Let's consider specifically the part of this study in which the photographs being judged (the targets) had neutral facial expressions and were of people in either their 60s or their 70s. The participants in this study included men and women whose ages ranged from 18 through 96. They were asked to place each photograph next to one of six cards that described either a

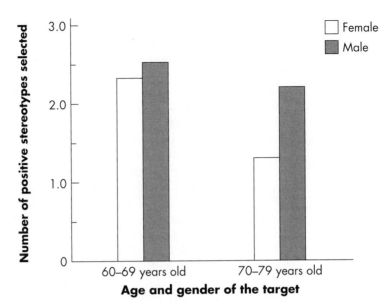

FIGURE 14.1 | AVERAGE NUMBER OF POSITIVE STEREOTYPES SELECTED, AS A FUNCTION OF TARGET AGE AND TARGET GENDER. (NOTE: MAXIMUM POSITIVE SCORE = 3.0.)

Source: Based on Hummert et al. (1997).

positive stereotype (e.g., a person who was lively, sociable, and interesting) or a negative stereotype (e.g., a person who was depressed, afraid, and lonely).

Figure 14.1 shows the average number of positive stereotypes that the participants selected. (The participants' age did not have a major impact on judgments, so Figure 14.1 combines the judgments of all participants.) As you can see, people selected far fewer positive stereotypes for the older group of women than for all of the other three groups.

A recent, large-scale meta-analysis by Mary Kite and her colleagues (2005) shows evidence for a double standard of aging in some characteristics, but not in others. If a double standard of aging exists, then people should evaluate an old woman much more negatively than a young woman; at the same time, they should evaluate an old man only slightly more negatively than a young man. In other words, the "drop" should be larger for female targets than for male targets. Kite and her coauthors found that people did demonstrate a larger drop for female targets in two conditions: (1) when the people rated the target males and females on characteristics such as generosity or friendliness and (2) when the people rated how willing they would be to interact with the target males and females.

However, Kite and her colleagues found some surprising results when people rated the target males and females on intelligence, memory skills, and other characteristics related to competence. Specifically, the drop was larger for male targets than for female targets. In other words, people rated old men as being much less competent than young men; in contrast, they rated old women and young women about the same. We have seen throughout this book that people often undervalue women's competence. Should we be pleased that people think that women do not become even *less* competent as they grow older?

We've looked at attitudes toward other people. How do women visualize themselves during the aging process? Quirouette and Pushkar (1999) studied Canadian college-educated women between the ages of 45 and 65. They found that most women were optimistic and confident about their own future aging. The women anticipated stability rather than change during their aging. People often believe that negative stereotypes apply to the other people in a particular group, but not to themselves (Kopera-Frye et al., 2003).

POTENTIAL AS A ROMANTIC PARTNER. Mary Kite and her colleagues (2005) suggested that the double standard of aging would be especially likely to operate when people judge whether males and females are physically attractive. However, there were not enough formal studies to allow a meta-analysis about attractiveness. One study reported that older women were much more critical than older men about how their aging bodies looked (Halliwell & Dittmar, 2003).

Furthermore, as we saw on page 462, older men are more likely than elderly women to appear in films, often as the romantic lead. In contrast, older women rarely appear in these romantic relationships. For example, the day before I proofread this section, I saw a preview for the film *Venus,* starring 74-year-old Peter O'Toole, whose character is enchanted by a younger woman, played by 24-year-old Jodie Whitaker. According to other research, people often think that a marriage is not likely to succeed when a wife is much older than the husband (G. Cowan, 1984).

Lesbians also report that people react negatively when one partner is much older than the other. A 41-year-old woman wrote:

> I set about telling my friends that I am a lesbian and, at the same time, that I love a 63-year-old woman. The questions, stated or implied: Am I looking for a mother? Is she looking for some security in her old age? Is lesbian love, then, really asexual? (Macdonald & Rich, 2001, p. 11)

The double standard of aging also applies to sexuality because aging women are often dismissed as being undesirable sex partners (Blieszner, 1998; R. H. Jacobs, 1997). As we noted in Chapter 9, people admire an older man's interest in sexuality, but they condemn the same interest shown by an older woman. Older women therefore face a particular disadvantage with respect to sexuality. Not only are they considered to look sexually unattractive, but they are also expected to show minimal interest in sexuality.

In this discussion, we've seen that older women are downgraded when people judge how pleasant someone is and whether they would enjoy interacting with this person. However, older men are downgraded in judgments about competence. When we consider physical attractiveness and romantic potential, the older women are again downgraded. Notice that the double standard of aging is, in fact, a variant of Theme 2 of this book: People often react differently to women than they do to men. Furthermore, the differential treatment may increase as men and women grow older.

CROSS-CULTURAL VIEWS OF OLDER WOMEN

In this book, we have often focused on women in North America. However, when we explore other cultures, we sometimes find useful alternative models for viewing older women. In many of these cultures, a woman's power within the family increases as she grows older (Uba, 1994). For example, in some subcultures in African countries such as Nigeria and Kenya, elderly women are quite powerful (Calasanti & Slevin, 2001).

These positive attitudes in other cultures could have important implications for cognitive functioning. In one study, for example, elderly women showed little memory decline in China, a culture that had positive attitudes toward elderly people at the time the study was conducted (B. R. Levy & Langer, 1994). In contrast, suppose that a culture does not expect elderly women to be very intelligent. These expectations may indirectly encourage elderly women to perform less well on a variety of cognitive tasks (Gilleard & Higgs, 2000).

Unfortunately, modernization can bring about a change for the worse. More recent research has been conducted in Hong Kong, Japan, and South Korea. These three East Asian countries have traditionally emphasized respect for elderly people. Surprisingly, Cuddy and her coauthors (2005) recently found that young people in these countries judged their elders to be warm and good natured, but not very competent or intelligent. However, the research did not investigate whether the elderly people actually did show cognitive deficits. It also did not examine whether young people demonstrated a double standard of aging, with a greater decline for older women than for older men.

Section Summary

Attitudes Toward Older Women

1. Ageism is a bias against people, based on their age; it is primarily directed toward elderly people.

2. The media under-represent and misrepresent elderly women—for example, in the movies and in magazines.

3. The double standard of aging proposes that people judge older women more harshly than they do older men. The evidence supports this double standard in some areas, such as judgments about the person's pleasantness, but not in judgments about competence.

4. The double standard of aging applies when people assess physical attractiveness; an older man is considered more appropriate as a romantic partner, compared to an older woman.

5. Cross-cultural ideas about aging seem to be in transition. In some cultures outside North America, older women's power increases as they grow older. However, in some Asian countries, elderly people (both males and females) are considered to be warm, but not very competent.

OLDER WOMEN, RETIREMENT, AND FINANCIAL PROBLEMS

Think about the topic of women and retirement for a moment. Have you ever read a short story or a book about a woman retiring from her job? Have you seen many television shows or movies on this issue? Women are missing from the popular lore about retirement—and from the research (Canetto, 2003; Moen & Roehling, 2005; Whitbourne & Skultety, 2006). For example, an article in a Canadian publication is titled "Working Past Age 65"; however, the study included only males (M. Walsh, 1999). Once again, we have evidence for the relative invisibility of women.

However, the invisibility of retired women may change now that so many women work outside the home. For example, about 65% of U.S. women between the ages of 45 and 64 are currently employed (Bureau of Labor Statistics, 2004c). The media typically lag behind reality, but maybe we'll soon see a movie that includes a retirement party for a woman! Let's first consider several components of retirement, and then we'll focus on the economic issues that older women face.

PLANNING FOR RETIREMENT

Women retire for a number of reasons, such as personal health problems and the appeal of free time (Etaugh & Bridges, 2006; Price & Joo, 2005). Many women retire early to take care of relatives with health problems (Kim & Moen, 2001b; Whitbourne & Skultety, 2006).

One worrisome gender difference is that women are less likely than men to seek information about retirement benefits before they retire (Dailey, 1998; Kim & Moen, 2001a, 2001b). An important reason is that many married women assume that their husbands will be responsible for financial planning (Onyx & Benton, 1999). This avoidance may be a major problem because, as we'll soon see, women receive much lower retirement benefits than men do.

ADJUSTING TO RETIREMENT

Consistent with Theme 4 of this book, women differ widely in their reactions to retirement (Bauer-Maglin & Radosh, 2003b). Many women welcome retirement as an opportunity to relax, pursue new interests, do volunteer work, focus on social-justice issues, and enjoy interactions with friends. However, most of the research suggests that women may experience more retirement problems than men. Women may also need more time to adapt to retirement (Kim & Moen, 2001a, 2001b; Price & Joo, 2005). They may need time to feel comfortable simply enjoying projects, without feeling guilty about being "selfish" (S. B. Levine, 2005). However, Reitzes and Mutran (2004) found no gender differences in adjustment to retirement. Researchers will need to identify factors that help both men and women enjoy their retirement.

One reason for gender differences in adjusting to retirement is that many women have lower incomes, so they often have financial problems (Calasanti & Slevin, 2001). Another reason is that retired women perform more housework than their retired husbands (Bernard & Phillipson, 2004; Charles & Carstensen, 2002; Szinovacz, 2000), and few women are inspired by housework. As one woman commented, "When a married couple retire, the women seem to spend most of the time doing housework etc., whereas men *do* retire" (Skucha & Bernard, 2000, p. 32).

When professional women retire, they frequently report that they miss their professional identity (Bauer-Maglin & Radosh, 2003b; Whitbourne & Skultety, 2006). Barbara Rubin had been a successful college professor in New York City. She reports on her emotions during her first year of retirement:

> Cut loose from an identity that been carefully crafted and hard won, I became shaky as I suddenly questioned who I was now. Would I ever do anything of real importance again, anything as compelling as what I had already done? I went to a Manhattan party just around that time, and the host introduced me to another guest . . . "She used to be a chair of women's studies." (B. Rubin, 2003, p. 190)

As you can imagine, a woman's adjustment during retirement depends on her reasons for retirement. If a woman retires because she wants more time for herself and her leisure interests, she will probably adjust well to retirement. In contrast, if a woman retires because she needs to care for a sick relative, she will probably not enjoy her retirement (Bauer-Maglin & Radosh, 2003a; V. E. Richardson, 1999). Significant life events, such as divorce or the death of family members, also influence a woman's adjustment to retirement. However, when married couples have been retired for at least 2 years, both women and men are usually happier with their lives and their marriages, compared with couples who have not yet retired (Kim & Moen, 2001a; Moen et al., 2001).

We still have many unanswered questions about women and retirement. For example, how can we encourage women to learn more about their retirement benefits? What successful strategies do married women use to negotiate a more equal sharing of housework during retirement? How can women best maintain their social connections from work? And what kinds of activities are most likely to help women feel more satisfied with retirement?

FINANCIAL PROBLEMS

Many elderly women in the United States face economic difficulties. For U.S. women over the age of 65, the average annual income is about $15,300, compared to $28,400 for men. U.S. women also receive lower Social Security benefits than men do (Hartmann & Lee, 2003). Economic problems are even more widespread for women of color. For example, more than half of Black and Latina elderly women are living in poverty (Canetto, 2001a; Cox, 2001; Markham, 2006). Meanwhile, the poverty rate for Canadian women over the age of 65 has decreased in recent decades; only 9% are currently in the low-income category (Statistics Canada, 2006).

The other major source of income for elderly women is private pension plans. These are also based on earned income, and most employed women do not have jobs with pension plans. In the United States, only 30% of women over 65 and 47% of men over 65 have a pension plan (Hartmann & Lee, 2003). African American and Latina women are especially unlikely to have a pension plan (Canetto, 2001a; Older Women's League, 2006a). However, current data for Canada show no gender differences; a pension plan covers 39% of employed women and 40% of employed men (Statistics Canada, 2006).

Silvia Canetto (2003) comments that "poverty in late adulthood reflects the accumulation of a lifetime of disadvantages for women" (p. 59). Here are some other reasons that women have fewer financial resources than men during old age (Bedford, 2003; Cruikshank, 2003; Markham, 2006; Moen & Roehling, 2005; Older Women's League, 2006a, 2006b):

1. Employed women receive lower salaries than men. For example, in Canada, employed women aged 55 to 64 earn salaries that are about half of the salaries earned by men in this age range (Statistics Canada, 2006). In the United States, the wage gap means that women's cumulative, lifetime earnings are an average of $250,000 less than men's (Butler, 2002). Furthermore, many middle-aged women have unexpected layoffs—without a source of income (Moen & Roehling, 2005).
2. Women are not compensated for their unpaid work in the home.
3. Many women are displaced homemakers who worked in the home and then became divorced or widowed; as a result, they have limited financial resources. For widows, the husband's health-care expenses may have depleted the family finances. Furthermore, widows also lose the health-care benefits available from their husband's job.
4. Women live longer, so their annual income from savings is much lower than men's annual income from savings. Furthermore, women's savings must be stretched across a larger number of post-retirement years.
5. As we saw in Chapter 11, women are more likely to have chronic illnesses, and the expense of treatment and medications further decreases their usable income.

Naturally, we need to remind ourselves about individual differences. Many elderly women's lives are altered by poverty. Many low-income women cannot afford to retire (Hedge et al., 2006). In contrast, some women are relatively well-off financially. As the fourth section of this chapter shows, many elderly women lead lives that are satisfying and emotionally rich.

Section Summary

Older Women, Retirement, and Financial Problems

1. The issue of women's retirement is relatively invisible in both the media and the psychological research.

2. Women are less likely than men to seek information about retirement benefits.

3. Although individual differences are large, women are likely to experience more adjustment problems in retirement than men do, especially if they face financial difficulties.

4. Many elderly women in the United States live in poverty; they are likely to have lower incomes than men because of such factors as lower salaries when they were employed, lower retirement benefits, unpaid work in the home, and chronic illness.

MENOPAUSE

So far, our study of older adulthood has examined two topics that are central to older women: (1) how other people react to older women and represent them in the media and (2) how older women experience retirement and economic issues. Let's turn our attention to menopause, a topic that has definitely generated more media coverage than either of those two topics. As we'll see, most older women do not consider the experience of menopause centrally important in their lives.

As women grow older, their ovaries gradually produce less estrogen and progesterone, so that women no longer menstruate on a regular basis (Baram, 2005; Kurpius & Nicpon, 2003). A woman enters **menopause** when she has stopped having menstrual periods for 12 months. Most women experience menopause between the ages of 45 and 55, with 51 being the most common age (Dell, 2005; Derry, 2004).

Let's consider four components of menopause. We'll begin with the physical symptoms and next discuss why hormone replacement therapy is no longer widely recommended. We'll then consider people's attitudes toward menopause, ending with a discussion of women's psychological reactions to menopause.

PHYSICAL CHANGES DURING MENOPAUSE

Several common physical symptoms accompany menopause. The most common symptom is the **hot flash**, a sensation of heat coming from within the body. Heavy perspiration may accompany hot flashes, which can sometimes disrupt sleep (Lachman, 2004; Stanton et al., 2002). However, the frequency and the intensity of hot flashes decrease over time (Boston Women's Health Book Collective, 2005; Derry, 2004; Sommer, 2001).

Other physical changes during menopause may include osteoporosis (which we discussed in Chapter 11), decreased vaginal secretions, thinning of the vaginal tissues, headaches, urinary symptoms, and fatigue (Dell, 2005; Sommer, 2001; Stanton et al., 2002). This list of physical symptoms sounds frightening, but few women experience all of them. Throughout this book, we have emphasized individual differences in gynecological issues such as menarche, menstrual pain, premenstrual syndrome, pregnancy, and childbirth. Women's reactions to the physical changes of menopause show similar variation (Crooks & Baur, 2005; Derry, 2004; Stanton et al., 2002), providing additional evidence for Theme 4 of this book.

CURRENT STATUS OF HORMONE REPLACEMENT THERAPY

Between about 1990 and 2001, health-care providers often recommended that women should take hormones during and after menopause (Lachman, 2004). **Hormone replacement therapy** is a term that usually refers to a combination of estrogen and progestin. Hormone replacement therapy relieves some of the physical symptoms of menopause, such as hot flashes. At that time, the research also seemed to show that hormones offered additional health benefits, such as reducing the risk of heart disease.

However, people concerned about women's health were waiting to hear the results of several long-term research projects. One of the largest of these projects is the Women's Health Initiative study, which included more than 16,000 women. In this carefully designed study, half of the women were given hormone replacement therapy. The other half were in the control group; they were given a placebo, a pill with no active ingredients.

In May 2002, the Women's Health Initiative researchers suddenly halted the study—more than 3 years before the scheduled completion date. After examining the results, the researchers discovered that the estrogen-progestin combination did not prevent heart disease. In fact, it slightly increased the risk of heart attacks, strokes, and blood clots. It also slightly increased the risk of breast cancer. The combination did reduce the risk of hip fractures and of cancers of the colon and rectum, but not enough to offset the increase in the other risks (Cheung, 2005; Grodstein et al., 2003; Writing Group for the Women's Health Initiative Investigators, 2002). The Women's Health Initiative authors recommended that women should stop taking hormone-replacement medication. Other research confirmed that hormone replacement therapy had no beneficial effect on other measures, such as physical pain, sleep disturbances, and reported mental health (Hays et al., 2003).

Naturally, this discovery about hormone replacement therapy left millions of North American women angry and puzzled (S. B. Levine, 2005; Seaman, 2003; Solomon & Dluhy, 2003). Why hadn't earlier researchers conducted the appropriate studies? Why hadn't the drug companies discovered the potentially harmful effects of this hormone combination? At present, health-care professionals usually do not recommend hormone replacement therapy. Instead, they encourage women to eat nutritious food and exercise appropriately. In addition, we have all learned an important message: Be cautious about the claims that drug companies make (Naughton et al., 2005; Seaman, 2003).

ATTITUDES TOWARD MENOPAUSE

You can assess your friends' attitudes toward menopause by trying Demonstration 14.2. Menopause is no longer a taboo subject, but my students in their 20s report that they rarely discuss menopause with their friends. Furthermore, many women who are experiencing menopause say that they do not have detailed information about menopause. Some also report that they do not even discuss menopause with their friends (Koch & Mansfield, 2004).

Unfortunately, the medical literature has a long history of representing menopause negatively—as if menopause were a chronic illness (Derry, 2002, 2004; Dillaway, 2005; M. M. Gergen & Gergen, 2006; S. Greene, 2003; Rostosky & Travis, 2000). Self-help books and other popular media echo this negative view of menopause. These sources suggest that a woman who is experiencing menopause is plagued by wildly fluctuating hormones, which force her to be grouchy, highly anxious, and depressed (e.g., Futterman & Jones, 1998). One examination of the popular print media revealed 350 negative descriptions and only 27 positive descriptions of menopausal symptoms (Gannon, 1999).

Another problem is that the media often provide worst-case scenarios, which contribute to the public's negative attitudes toward menopause. The media also perpetuate another related myth: that menopausal women are no longer interested in sexual activity. In Chapter 9, though, we noted that women who have sexual partners typically remain sexually active during old age.

Demonstration 14.2

ATTITUDES TOWARD MENOPAUSE

For this demonstration, you will need at least six friends to participate in a brief study on what people of all ages think about typical people during middle age. Test at least two people in each of the three conditions.

Tell the people in the first group, "Please list items that you associate with men in the age range of 45 to 55 years. You can list words that describe their personality, appearance, attitudes, interests, emotions, and behaviors." After a couple of minutes, tell them to go back over those items and give a rating to indicate how positive or negative each characteristic is. Instruct them to use a rating scale where 1 is very negative, 3 is neutral, and 5 is very positive.

Repeat these instructions with people in two additional groups. For the second group, substitute the phrase "women in the age range of 45 to 55 years." For the third group, substitute the phrase "menopausal women in the age range of 45 to 55 years."

After you have tested everyone, calculate an "average rating" for each of the three middle-aged groups. Do your three groups differ?

Source: Based on Marcus-Newhall et al. (2001, p. 704).

Given the negative representation of menopause in both medicine and the media, you won't be surprised to learn that the general public has similar negative attitudes. For example, Amy Marcus-Newhall and her colleagues (2001) asked people to list words that they would associate with each of three middle-aged groups of people. (Demonstration 14.2 is based on this study.) Then people evaluated each term on a rating scale. Attitudes toward 45- to 55-year-old menopausal women were significantly more negative than attitudes toward both 45- to 55-year-old women (with no mention of menopause) and 45- to 55-year-old men. For example, they believed that menopausal women would be significantly less likely than members of the other two groups to have hobbies or to look attractive and significantly more likely to express negative emotions. In Demonstration 14.2, do your friends show this same trend?

PSYCHOLOGICAL REACTIONS TO MENOPAUSE

At the beginning of this chapter, we emphasized that attitudes toward elderly women are often negative; they do not accurately describe the characteristics of real-world elderly women. Similarly, we find that attitudes toward menopause do not accurately describe women's actual experiences during menopause (Hvas, 2001; Stanton et al., 2002). Some women report psychological symptoms such as depression, irritability, and mood swings. However, we have no evidence that normal menopause—by itself—causes these symptoms (Sommer, 2001; Stanton et al., 2002).

In this chapter, we have already pointed out a number of depressing factors in the lives of older women, including attitudes toward older women and women's economic status. Women also experience health problems, divorce, and death of relatives and friends. All these stressful factors are more important than menopause itself in determining the psychological status of middle-aged women (Avis, 2003; Glazer et al., 2002; Sommer 2001).

Most women do not report depression or other negative psychological reactions to menopause (Avis et al., 2004; G. Robinson, 2002; Sommer et al., 1999). For example, a 50-year-old woman provides her perspective on menopause: "I was well into my menopause before I realized what was happening. My symptoms were so minor and rather vague. I didn't understand all the hype about symptoms" (L. L. Alexander et al., 2001, p. 398). Some are relieved that they no longer need to be worried about becoming pregnant. Other women regard menopause as a life event that encourages them to evaluate their lives and decide whether they want to change directions (Rich & Mervyn, 1999; Zerbe, 1999).

As Figure 14.2 shows, the group of women who are *least negative* about menopause are those who have already experienced it (Gannon & Ekstrom, 1993). For example, Lotte Hvas (2001) asked Danish women to describe their experiences with menopause. About half described at least one positive component. For instance, a 51-year-old woman said:

> Physically I have obtained a great strength passing the menopause—my sexual life has become more fun—I know for sure what I want—I look forward to becoming a

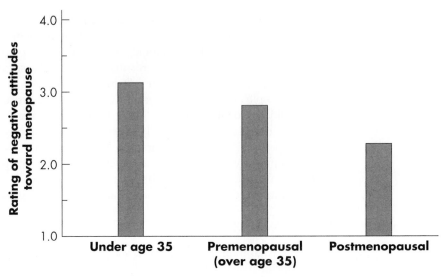

FIGURE 14.2 | NEGATIVE ATTITUDE TOWARD MENOPAUSE, AS
A FUNCTION OF AGE AND MENOPAUSAL EXPERIENCE.
(NOTE: 1 = NEUTRAL; 5 = MOST NEGATIVE.)

Source: From Gannon, L., & Ekstrom, B. (1993). Attitudes toward menopause. The influence of sociocultural paradigms. *Psychology of Women Quarterly, 17,* 275–288 (Figure 1, p. 283).

grandmother soon, I am about to change my job, and I look forward to it. (Hvas, 2001, p. 14)

In general, however, both the medical world and the media ignore the potentially positive aspects of menopause (Sherwin, 2001).

Some research explores how women of color experience menopause. One study reported that African American women were more likely than European American women to believe that menstruation is a normal part of life (Sampselle et al., 2002). In a large-scale study, Barbara Sommer and her colleagues (1999) analyzed telephone interviews that had been conducted with more than 16,000 middle-aged women throughout the United States. Ethnic group differences were small but statistically significant. African American women had the most positive attitudes; European American and Latina women were intermediate; and Asian American women were least positive. Studies have also shown that other factors may influence attitudes toward menopause among women of color. For instance, immigrant Korean and Filipina women report that menopause is a relatively minor problem compared to the significant challenges these women face in adjusting to a new culture (J. A. Berg & Lipson, 1999; Im & Meleis, 2000).

Women from Greece, southern Mexico, and several other cultures outside North America seem to have relatively positive views, especially if older women are valued in the culture (S. Greene, 2003; G. Robinson, 2002). For example, Lamb (2000) studied women in a town in the West Bengal region of

India. Young women and older women uniformly described menopause in positive terms because menopause meant that they were free of the hassles of menstruation and that they could participate in religious ceremonies that are forbidden to menstruating women. Alternative viewpoints such as this one help us to understand how each culture constructs menopause according to its own values. Multicultural and cross-cultural perspectives also provide us with some positive alternatives.

Section Summary

Menopause

1. Menopause is the cessation of menstrual periods; common physical symptoms of menopause include hot flashes, osteoporosis, genital changes, headaches, and fatigue.

2. Hormone replacement therapy is no longer recommended for women who have reached menopause.

3. Both medicine and the media have represented menopause negatively, and the general public has negative reactions toward the phrase "menopausal women."

4. Contrary to folklore, menopause does not cause psychological symptoms such as depression and irritability. Many women have some positive reactions to menopause. Small ethnic-group differences have been reported in the United States, and women in other parts of the world may have relatively positive reactions to menopause.

SOCIAL RELATIONSHIPS IN OLDER WOMEN'S LIVES

In this chapter, we have considered how society views older women, as well as women's experiences as they pass through menopause and retire from the workforce. Now let's examine the changing social world of older women. How do their family relationships evolve as they grow older? How do women respond to the death of a spouse or other romantic partner? Do women of color and European American women have similar experiences? How happy are women with their lives—and how do they alter their lives if they are not satisfied? Throughout this section, you will see substantial evidence for our theme of individual differences (Kjaersgaard, 2005).

FAMILY RELATIONSHIPS

In Chapter 8, on love relationships, we explored one family role that is important for many women: being a wife. In that chapter, we examined some characteristics of happy, long-term relationships. We also looked at lesbian and bisexual relationships, which are central in the lives of many women. Let's now explore other important family roles for many older women—their roles as mothers, daughters, and grandmothers.

OLDER WOMEN AS MOTHERS.   Much of the earlier research and theory on middle-aged women focused on the **empty nest**, or the period after children are no longer living at home. Notice that the name *empty nest* implies that a woman's identity focuses completely on being a mother. Years ago, researchers were eager to demonstrate that mothers felt depressed when children left home.

In reality, however, the research reveals the same individual differences that our other discussions of women's lives have uncovered (Theme 4). In general, though, the current research confirms that the empty nest does not cause depression (Canetto, 2003; Hunter et al., 2002). In fact, middle-aged mothers whose children have left home tend to be as happy as or even slightly happier than middle-aged mothers who have at least one child at home (Antonucci et al., 2001; Calasanti & Slevin, 2001; Johnston-Robledo, 2000). Keep in mind, too, that most mothers still feel deeply connected with their children, even when those children no longer live at home (Pruchno & Rosenbaum, 2003).

My students who are in their early 20s are often dismayed to learn that their mothers may be somewhat happier after the children leave home. Please do not conclude that women are overjoyed with their children's departure. Mothers may indeed be saddened. However, serious depression is rare. Instead, mothers learn to reshape their lives around new interests and activities as their daughters and sons move into adulthood (Johnston-Robledo, 2000).

OLDER WOMEN AS DAUGHTERS.   We usually think of adult women's roles as mothers and grandmothers. However, adult women are often daughters, as well. Most of the research on the daughter role focuses on adult women who take care of elderly parents. Many women now spend more years caring for their parents than caring for their children (Crose, 2003). The term **sandwich generation** refers to middle-aged people, especially women, who find themselves responsible for both their dependent children and their aging parents (Boston Women's Health Book Collective, 2005). Most researchers estimate that daughters are about three times as likely as sons to become caretakers for an elderly parent who is in poor health (Cruikshank, 2003; Hunter et al., 2002; Mosher & Danoff-Burg, 2004). Because women spend much more time on these tasks than men do, taking care of elderly parents is really a women's issue.

Many of the resources on women's caregiving roles emphasize that the tasks are unpleasant and burdensome for middle-aged daughters. In fact, caregiving is often stressful, and it can have negative effects on people's physical and mental health (E. M. Brody, 2004; Miller-Day, 2004; Vitaliano et al., 2003). However, recent studies have found that many daughters willingly accept this responsibility, especially because they feel that their parents had raised them with so much love and generosity (Martire & Stephens, 2003; Musil et al., 2005; Whitbourne, 2005). They also feel satisfied that they can provide their parents with good care (Fingerman, 2003; Hunter et al, 2002; Menzies, 2005).

For instance, a colleague described how she commuted 800 miles each way to care for her severely ill mother—while working toward tenure at her university. Indeed, she had experienced incredible strain. On one occasion, in the intensive care unit, she held her mother's hand with her right hand as her mother fought pneumonia. Simultaneously, with her left hand, this woman typed a psychology exam that was later faxed to a colleague teaching the course for her. The additional responsibilities did have an impact on her academic career. However, as she wrote:

> I considered myself blessed to have been able to give so much to my mother and to provide her hospice care in her home. She died in my arms. Yes it was stressful. Yes it was difficult. And, yes, I had these positive feelings—as well as negative feelings—at the time I was doing this. But I have no regrets and would do it again without thinking about it. (L. Skinner, personal communication, 1999)

A small number of researchers have begun to explore other aspects of the relationship between grown children and their parents—beyond the caretaking role (Fingerman, 2001, 2003; Hunter et al., 2002). Unfortunately, however, the media generally ignore the social interactions between middle-aged people and their parents. Aside from an occasional brief reference, how often have you seen or read about a relationship between an adult woman and her mother in which they were interacting as adults?

OLDER WOMEN AS GRANDMOTHERS. According to one of the traditional stereotypes, grandmothers are jolly white-haired old ladies who bestow cookies and affection on their grandchildren. According to another stereotype, grandmothers are fussy, frail, and helpless (Denmark, 2002; L. Morgan & Kunkel, 2001; P. K. Smith & Drew, 2002). Neither of these stereotypes captures the wide variety of capabilities, interests, and personality characteristics that are typical of real grandmothers (Barer, 2001).

Most women are grandmothers for about one-third of their lives (P. K. Smith & Drew, 2002). Compared to grandfathers, grandmothers are typically more involved with their grandchildren (P. K. Smith & Drew, 2002). However, once again, we have relatively little recent research on this role.

How do grandmothers interact with their grandchildren? In terms of activities, they are likely to babysit and take grandchildren on trips. When grandmothers visit, they often play games, read books, share family history, and enjoy conversations.

Grandmothers are also likely to impart advice that emphasizes moral values and social responsibility (Erber, 2005; Fingerman, 2003; P. K. Smith & Drew, 2002). For instance, a White grandmother in Quebec was friendly with an Ethiopian family, and she brought her grandson along to this family's birthday celebration. Later, the grandson remarked that he had never before met any Ethiopian people. As the grandmother emphasized, "I think it's important that whatever I do as a grandmother, I'm also teaching my grandchildren. I believe very much that what you do is reflected back" (Pushkar et al., 2003, p. 258).

However, our theme of individual differences is evident in patterns of grandmothering. Some women argue that good grandparents should not interfere with their grandchildren's upbringing, but others feel it is their duty to advise (Erber, 2005; Whitbourne, 2005). In Black and Native American families, grandmothers may be expected to play an especially important role in supporting and advising their grandchildren (P. K. Smith & Drew, 2002; Trotman & Brody, 2002).

I am writing this section several days after my husband and I traveled to Boston to celebrate the second birthday of our grandson, Jacob Matlin-Heiger. (See photograph on page 322.) It's difficult to capture the combination of joy and amazement that we feel when interacting with Jake. It's also difficult to describe the admiration we feel for our daughter and our son-in-law, when we see how competently and lovingly they are raising our grandson! According to the research, grandmothers consistently report that being a grandparent is much more relaxing than being a parent. After all, grandmothers do not need to be responsible for rearing a child on a daily basis. As one grandmother said, "I don't have to be on the front lines anymore, I can just watch the show" (Miller-Day, 2004, p. 81).

WIDOWHOOD AND THE DEATH OF LIFE PARTNERS

For married women, the death of a spouse is typically one of the most traumatic and stressful events of their lives (Carr & Ha, 2006). Women are more likely to become widows than men are to become widowers. Several factors explain this discrepancy. For example, women live longer, they typically marry men older than themselves, and they are less likely to remarry (Canetto, 2001a; Carr & Ha, 2006; Freund & Riediger, 2003). As a result, the U.S. census shows 4.1 times as many widows as widowers (U.S. Census Bureau, 2005). The ratio in other regions of the world is even more extreme. For instance, Africa has about seven times as many widows as widowers (United Nations, 2000).

When a woman's husband dies, she faces the pain, grief, and mourning that accompany bereavement. She may feel emotionally exhausted and physically weakened, especially if she was an active caregiver during her husband's final weeks (Christakis & Allison, 2006; H. E. Edwards & Noller, 2002; Pruchno & Rosenbaum, 2003). Loneliness is one of the major problems for widows (Bedford & Blieszner, 2000; P. Chambers, 2000). Widows also report that they often feel awkward in social situations where most people are with a spouse.

Most of the recent gender comparisons in bereavement patterns show that men are more likely than women to experience depression (Canetto, 2001a; Charles & Carstensen, 2002; Pruchno & Rosenbaum, 2003). However, when a spouse dies, both women and men are likely to experience loneliness, grief, stress, and health problems. Adjustment to widowhood is especially difficult when people have been happily married, with little interpersonal conflict (Pruchno & Rosenbaum, 2003).

We know relatively little about the grieving process for lesbian partners. After all, many lesbians found their life partners during an era when most people condemned same-gender relationships (D'Augelli et al., 2001; Deevey, 2000; Whipple, 2006). Furthermore, elderly lesbian women of color are especially invisible (R. L. Hall & Fine, 2005).

Consider the situation of Marilyn, whose partner, Cheryl, had recently died. Marilyn described her dilemma:

> I am a widow. The law does not say so. My tax form does not say so. Neither do any of the countless forms that I fill out that include marital status say so. But every time I check off the box that says single, I want to scream and white it out and write "widow." But I am a lesbian who has lost her female partner, so in most places I am not accorded the status of widow. . . . It does not seem to matter that we lived in a monogamous, loving relationship for thirty-one years, or that we coparented three wonderful children. (Whipple, 2006, p. 129)

Unfortunately, our culture's heterosexism is likely to deny lesbians the kind of social support that is typically offered to women whose husbands have died. For instance, one woman teaching in a small rural school was afraid she would lose her job if she revealed her grief after the death of her partner (Deevey, 2000). They had spent years concealing their romantic relationship, and now she could not publicly express her sorrow.

We find enormous individual differences in bereavement, as in all important transitions in women's lives (Siegel, 2004; Stroebe et al., 2005). Many women are deeply depressed, long after the death of a romantic partner. In fact, a widow who does not remarry may not regain her sense of well-being until 8 or more years after her husband's death (Lucas et al., 2003; Whitbourne, 2005).

However, some women discover a hidden strength that aids their recovery. For example, a 48-year-old woman wrote:

> I think that when you lose a loved one, it's a rebirth for yourself. You can't always dwell on the loss of the loved one. You have to look forward to what you are going to do with your life now. . . . Every day's a little learning experience for myself, of doing new things and learning new things as a single person. (Nolen-Hoeksema & Larson, 1999, p. 149)

OLDER WOMEN OF COLOR

In discussing elderly women of color, we need to emphasize the substantial individual differences within each ethnic group (Iwamasa & Sorocco, 2002). We also need to realize the potential challenges of conducting research about this topic. For example, Delores Mullings (2004) is a young Caribbean Canadian who wanted to learn more about elderly women who shared her ethnic background. She describes numerous ways in which she was able to convey her genuine respect for the participants in her study, including her choice of clothing, specific choice of words, and conversational patterns.

We noted earlier in the chapter that Black and Latina elderly women are much more likely than European American elderly women to live in poverty

(Canetto, 2001a; Cox, 2001; Markham, 2006). Consequently, many elderly women of color face a daily struggle in paying for housing, health care, transportation, and even enough food to eat. However, older women of color also benefit from an advantage: They are more likely than European American women to have an extended family living nearby who can provide assistance and support (Armstrong, 2001; Saperstein, 2002; Trotman, 2002).

Elderly Black women are represented by two opposing stereotypes (Ralston, 1997; Trotman, 2002). One portrays them as victims of poverty and urban decay. In contrast, the other stereotype portrays them as superhuman individuals who surmount obstacles through hard work and a good heart. Neither portrayal captures the complexity of their actual lives.

In general, elderly Black women are likely to be active in selected community organizations such as a church (Armstrong, 2001; Conway-Turner, 1999). In addition, Black women are often closely involved in the lives of their grandchildren (Conway-Turner, 1999; McWright, 2002; P. K. Smith & Drew, 2002). These women give their grandchildren social support, monitor their activities, discipline them, and encourage them to achieve. However, many Black grandmothers report resentment about becoming the primary caretaker for grandchildren, especially if they only recently finished rearing their own children (Barer, 2001; Calasanti & Slevin, 2001; Harm, 2001).

We have relatively little research about Latinas (Du Bois et al., 2001). As with Black grandmothers, Latina grandmothers are treated with respect, and they typically enjoy their social role. However, they often describe the role as "confining" or "limiting," especially if they must take on child-care responsibilities (Facio, 1997; Harm, 2001). Elderly Puerto Rican women living in the United States are expected to provide help to children and grandchildren. Furthermore, elderly women are expected to seek help from younger relatives when they need it (Sánchez, 2001; Sánchez-Ayéndez, 1993).

When we look at elderly Asian American women, we see additional evidence of diversity within ethnic groups. For example, an elderly woman from India may be a retired physician. In contrast, relatively few elderly women from Laos have completed high school (Kagawa-Singer et al., 1997). However, elderly Asians generally are more likely than European Americans to live with their children (Armstrong, 2001; Conway-Turner, 1999; Saperstein, 2002). Furthermore, Asian Americans are usually more likely to respect elderly people. Researchers have not yet determined whether this respect translates into greater life satisfaction for Asian American elders (Iwamasa & Sorocco, 2002).

Elderly Native American and First Nation women are the least visible group in the psychology research (Polacca, 2001). About half of elderly Native American women live in cities; little is known about these women (Armstrong, 2001). The remaining half live in rural areas or on reservations, where they typically assume the roles of grandmother, caregiver, educator, and wisdom keeper (Conway-Turner, 1999; Polacca, 2001).

A study of Apache grandmothers living on a reservation in Arizona emphasizes the strong bond between grandmothers and their grandchildren

(Bahr, 1994). Apache children are more likely than European American children to live with their grandparents because parents often leave the reservation to seek employment in an urban setting. Most grandmothers in this study reported that they felt great satisfaction in caring for their grandchildren. These grandmothers are expected to be wise, energetic, and resourceful, especially in transmitting their cultural heritage to their grandchildren. In turn, young Native Americans are more likely than young European Americans to believe that they have a responsibility to take care of elderly relatives (Gardiner et al., 1998; Polacca, 2001).

Throughout this chapter, we have discussed the invisibility of older women. Older women of color are even less visible. Psychologists may glance briefly at elderly women of color, but we typically lack the crucial information for a clear picture of their lives and experiences.

SATISFACTION WITH LIFE

If you browse through some of the topics discussed in this book, you'll see that many older women have every right to be unhappy. In Chapter 11, we examined physical problems such as breast cancer and osteoporosis, which are relatively common among older women. In the current chapter, we have seen that women may be unhappy about retiring. Many worry about the health of their parents. Many will mourn the loss of a spouse or a life partner.

Many older women, especially women of color, are likely to face economic crises. Even women who do not have any of these problems are likely to experience negative reactions from others because they live in a culture that rejects older women's wrinkles and other signs of aging.

In reality, however, most middle-aged and elderly women are reasonably satisfied with their lives (Bourque et al., 2005; Freund & Riediger, 2003; Miner-Rubino et al., 2004; Whitbourne & Sneed, 2002). For example, Neill and Kahn (1999) found that elderly widows gave themselves an average rating of 19 on a life satisfaction scale where the most negative score was 0 and the most positive was 26. Furthermore, older women are actually less likely than younger women to be depressed (D. G. Myers, 2000). This research demonstrates the **paradox of well-being;** many older women report high life satisfaction, despite the objective difficulties they encounter (Kahana et al., 2005; K. S. Lee, 2004; Whitbourne, 2005).

Several factors help explain why most older women are reasonably happy. Specifically, they have learned how to cope effectively with negative emotions and how to spend time on activities they enjoy. They have also adjusted their goals so that they are more realistic. In addition, they can maintain a positive view of themselves, even when they encounter disappointments (Hunter et al., 2002; Magai, 2001; Whitbourne & Sneed, 2002).

A relatively new focus in research about elderly people is called "successful aging." Although definitions vary, **successful aging** means that a person maximizes gains and minimizes losses. For example, an elderly woman could demonstrate successful aging if: (1) She is satisfied with various aspects of her life, such as her family and friends; (2) She is optimistic, and she believes she is achieving her personal goals; (3) She is healthy, and she is cognitively competent; and (4) She is satisfied with her income and living conditions (Freund & Riediger, 2003; Whitbourne, 2005).

Throughout this book, we have emphasized the theme of individual variation. Women also vary in the ways they achieve happiness. They do not share a ready-made blueprint for happiness (Charles & Pasupathi, 2003; S. B. Levine, 2005). One woman might find happiness through her husband and children, whereas another might be equally happy with a less traditional lifestyle.

REWRITING OUR LIFE STORIES

Many young women think they know exactly where their lives are heading, and many women's lives do reveal a pattern of continuity and predictability. However, many women find that their lives take an unexpected route (Plunkett, 2001). Most middle-aged women welcome new challenges and are more confident than they were in earlier years (S. B. Levine, 2005; A. J. Stewart et al., 2001). Furthermore, middle-aged women often report that the women's movement had helped them feel more powerful and self-confident (S. B. Levine, 2005; A. M. Young et al., 2001).

Yes, some middle-aged women say that—several years earlier—they had regrets about their life path. However, if they make life changes, and they rewrite their life stories, they are typically more satisfied than those who continued to live with their regrets (S. B. Levine, 2005; A. J. Stewart & Vandewater, 1999). For example, at the age of 46, Linda N. Edelstein (1999) faced the possibility of cancer. Fortunately, the tumor turned out to be benign. She reported that the incident forced her to question what she really wanted and how she should pursue these dreams. As she wrote, "The sadness and hopelessness some women experience in the middle years does not come from trying and failing, but from not trying" (p. 195). Elderly women have rewritten their lives by developing greater appreciation for their loved ones and developing new interests (K. J. Gergen & Gergen, 2004).

We need to emphasize, however, that older women in the United States would be more likely to create positive, productive life stories if our society—especially our government—truly valued these women. In a country of such enormous wealth, none of these women should have to struggle to obtain adequate food, housing, and health care. For the last demonstration of this chapter, try Demonstration 14.3, when you have a convenient opportunity.

FINAL WORDS

To conclude this chapter, I asked a 69-year-old friend to reflect about her life and about old age. At the age of 58, Anne Hardy and her husband, Duane, decided to leave their comfortable community in Rochester, New York, to

Demonstration 14.3

The instructions for this demonstration are more open ended than for the previous demonstrations. Think of a woman you know fairly well who is at least 40 years old. Ask if you might interview her at a convenient time.

Before the interview, select some of this demonstration's sample questions, keeping in mind that a few questions may be too personal. Also, construct several other questions based on the information in this chapter. Before you begin the interview, be sure to emphasize that she can choose not to answer any question you ask.

Sample Questions

1. What was the happiest time in your life?
2. When you were 20, did you think that your life would take you along the pathway you have been going?
3. Is there anything you would have done differently if you had the chance to relive part of your life?
4. Has your self-confidence changed since you were 20 or 30 years old?
5. If you were 20 years old, living in today's world, what kind of choices would you make?
6. (If relevant) When your children left home, what kinds of emotional reactions did you have?
7. (If relevant) When you retired from your job, what kinds of emotional reactions did you have?
8. Do you feel that you are still searching for a sense of who you are?
9. Do you feel that people treat you differently because of your age and your gender?
10. Is there a question about your life that I somehow didn't ask—one that is personally interesting to you?

Sources: Questions based on A. J. Stewart and Vandewater (1999) and A. J. Stewart et al. (2001).

work in the South for several organizations that are concerned with civil rights and social justice. She wrote about this period in her life:

> When our children were through college and on their own, our feeling was that it was time to close out the marketplace phase of our lives. We never had the empty-nest feeling. It was, instead, a kind of liberation, a time to move into a new phase. Just as marriage had been a new phase, followed by parenthood, this was another.
>
> The caring, the sharing of concerns, the readiness to be of help to each other when necessary, would continue with our children, unchanged by the fact that we were no longer living under one roof, but we were ready to move on, just as they were. We had both done a great deal of volunteer work in our free time for many years, and now we had the opportunity to do it full-time. Our needs are modest, we were able to accept subsistence salaries until we were able to "retire" on Social

Security, at which time we continued to work full-time but no longer drew salaries.

. . . I am very conscious that my life hasn't been "typical," if there is such a thing. I've had many advantages denied to others. We have had fairly low income at times but were never really poor and certainly never hungry; my health has, for the most part, been good; we have loving, caring children; and best of all, I've had, in my husband, a superb companion and best friend. With today's economic stresses and disrupted families, I doubt it's a norm.

After 10 years of work in the South, Anne and her husband retired and moved back north. Anne continued to work for organizations such as the Women's International League for Peace and Freedom and the U.S.-China People's Friendship Association. She commented on this transition:

"Retirement" has many advantages. It's possible to be involved in many activities, yet not be pressured by them. We set our own schedules. We're free of regimentation. If something interesting to do comes up, we can do that and shift other commitments around. It's a more flexible, less rigid, less scheduled life.

At the age of 69, I still don't feel "old," although chronologically, I'm not "young." I think one ages—given reasonable health—as one has been gradually aging in all the years before, very much depending on the quality of life one has built. My interests haven't changed, except that we have the added joy of six grandchildren in our lives. Elderly people are as diverse as young people. Differences between them remain; previous likes and dislikes remain, for the most part. I am still me, "old" or not, though I feel that I have become more understanding, less judgmental, more open to new experiences, still trying to grow as a person.

We have begun to experience the loss of relatives and friends, and chronic and serious illnesses are beginning to appear among our associates. It's sad, of course, but it has the positive side of drawing us closer to those of our families and friends who are still in our lives, makes us more loving, more willing to overlook small irritants, more giving. . . .

There are serious concerns and hopes about the future, naturally, both in regard to personal matters such as health and loss of close ones, and in regard to national and international events. . . . I have lost much of my sense that we can influence the course of events; I have increasingly stronger conviction that we are in the hands of multinationals and conglomerates, of Eisenhower's "military-industrial complex." That feeling can be an immobilizing one. But to do nothing is to go along with what's happening. I know it's a cliché, but the future is *now*. This is the only world any of us has, and if we don't like it, or if we are worried about the direction it's going, we have to work to change it. "This is the way it is" is something we can't settle for. We have to work toward being able to say, "That is the way it *was*, and we have helped to improve it." I console myself a bit with the recollection that 40 years ago, when we debated whether we should bring children into the world, I had the same concerns—and we're all still here!

A Fundamentalist relative asked me recently what I felt about eternity. I answered that for me eternity is being created daily in what I do, how I live vis-à-vis other human beings, what kinds of values I gave and continue to give our children so that they in turn would have good values to pass on to their world and their children.

Section Summary

Social Relationships in Older Women's Lives

1. Some women experience the empty-nest effect, but research shows that most women are relatively happy after their children leave home.

2. During middle age, daughters are more likely than sons to become caregivers for elderly parents. Research emphasizes the negative aspects of this caregiver role, but many women identify positive aspects.

3. Women differ widely in their grandmothering styles. Many grandmothers believe that they should convey moral values and social responsibility to their grandchildren.

4. Most married women find that the death of a spouse is traumatic, and loneliness is a frequent problem. When lesbians lose a life partner, they may have the added burden of needing to conceal their grief.

5. Older women of color are especially likely to experience poverty, yet they are more likely than older European American women to have the support of an extended family.

6. Elderly Black women are likely to be active in community organizations, and many help to rear their grandchildren. Elderly Latinas are expected to help with children and grandchildren and to seek help when they need it. Elderly Asian American women and Native American women often live with their extended family. Elderly Native American women are expected to share their cultural heritage with their grandchildren.

7. Despite many problems, middle-aged and elderly women are typically just as satisfied with their lives as younger women are; this phenomenon is called ''the paradox of well-being.''

8. Many women rethink their lives during middle age or later, and they make choices that take them in new directions.

CHAPTER REVIEW QUESTIONS

1. One theme of this book is that women tend to be relatively invisible. Discuss how this tendency is especially true for older women, pointing out how older women have not received enough attention in the following areas: (a) representation in the media, (b) research on retirement, and (c) the lives of elderly women of color. Then add to the list any other areas of older women's lives that seem important and were not covered in this chapter.

2. What is the double standard of aging? When does it seem most likely to operate, and when does it not apply? What other aspects—not mentioned in this chapter—might be affected by the double standard of aging?

3. From your knowledge about retirement, describe a woman who is likely to adjust well to retirement. Then describe a woman who is likely to adjust poorly to retirement.

4. Describe the economic situation of elderly women, and list factors that help to explain

the gender differences in income for elderly men and women.

5. Think about several women you know who have retired from their paid employment. How do their lives match the information on retirement that this chapter discussed, with respect to the timing of their retirement, their financial resources during later adulthood, and their adjustment to retirement?

6. What are some of the physical symptoms of menopause? Imagine that a middle-aged friend is now experiencing menopause. What information would you tell her about hormone replacement therapy?

7. What psychological reactions do women have to menopause? How do the attitudes of premenopausal women compare with women's actual experiences?

8. Research in the psychology of women often focuses too heavily on the experiences of European American middle-class women. What did you learn in this chapter about the lives of elderly women of color, economically disadvantaged women, and women in other cultures?

9. The theme of individual differences has been prominent throughout this book. However, some researchers argue that individual differences increase during our lives. Look at the topics outlined on page 459, and describe the nature of those individual differences, where relevant.

10. In this chapter, we have discussed many legitimate reasons why older women might be dissatisfied with their lives. List as many of these as you can. Then suggest why the paradox of well-being applies to many older women.

KEY TERMS

*ageism (461)

double standard of aging (463)

*menopause (470)

*hot flash (470)

*hormone replacement therapy (471)

*empty nest (476)

*sandwich generation (476)

paradox of well-being (481)

successful aging (481)

 Note: The terms asterisked in the Key Terms section serve as good search terms for InfoTrac College Edition. Go to http://infotrac.thomsonlearning.com and try these added search terms.

RECOMMENDED READINGS

Chrisler, J. C. (Ed.). (2004). *From menarche to menopause: The female body in feminist therapy.* New York: Haworth. Several current resources focus on menopause, but Chrisler's book provides the most informative feminist framework, with chapters on menstruation and pregnancy, as well as menopause.

Nelson, T. D. (Ed.). (2005). Ageism. *Journal of Social Issues, 61*(2). This special issue of the respected periodical, *Journal of Social Issues,* examines age biases, including general attitudes toward elderly adults, ageism in other countries, and reducing

ageism. Most of the research does not examine whether ageism differs for males and females, so this volume is useful if you are searching for interesting research topics that could be related to gender.

Nussbaum, J. F., & Coupland, J. (Eds.). (2004). *Handbook of communication and aging research* (2nd ed.). Mahwah, NJ: Erlbaum. Here is a wonderful resource for information about stereotypes about aging, the portrayal of elderly people in the media, and the nature of social and family relationships in later life.

Whitbourne, S. K. (2005). *Adult development and aging: Biopsychosocial perspectives* (2nd ed.). Hoboken, NJ: Wiley. I recommend this book for anyone who wants a good general perspective on aging processes. Whitbourne includes chapters on such topics as research methods, cognitive processes, retirement, social relationships, and successful aging.

ANSWERS TO THE TRUE-FALSE STATEMENTS

1. False (pp. 460–461); 2. False (pp. 464–465); 3. True (p. 466); 4. False (p. 467); 5. False (pp. 468–469); 6. False (p. 471); 7. False (p. 473); 8. False (p. 476); 9. False (pp. 480–481); 10. True (p. 485).

© Getty Images

15 | MOVING ONWARD . . .

True or False?

_____ 1. Despite progress in women's education, men still earn about 70% of all Ph.D. degrees in the United States.

_____ 2. When psychological research looks at women of color, the normative European-American female group often serves as the standard of comparison.

_____ 3. When women from some ethnic groups become feminist activists, the men in their ethnic community often tell them that this activism is a threat to ethnic unity.

_____ 4. Chicana feminism has been active in the United States since the early 1970s.

_____ 5. One branch of the men's movement, called the "profeminists," argues that rigid gender roles can harm men as well as women.

_____ 6. One of the basic beliefs of the Promise Keepers—and others who support the religious approach to the men's movement—is that men must take back their roles as family leaders and women should be followers.

_____ 7. According to qualitative research, students say that their women's studies courses have increased their feminist identity; however, quantitative research shows that women's studies courses do not have a significant effect.

_____ 8. The first wave of the North American feminist movement began in the 1920s, as a result of women winning the right to vote.

_____ 9. The number of feminist groups in North America has actually decreased during the past decade.

_____ 10. By the year 2005, women had been heads of state in only 12 countries, and women's studies courses were taught only in North America and Europe.

You have now read 14 chapters about the lives of females, from their prenatal development through old age. As you try to gain a perspective on all the diverse statistics, research studies, theories, and personal testimonies, you may focus on one central question: Have women's lives improved in recent years? To answer this question, let's consider some representative information—both uplifting and depressing—on the lives of women in the current era:

- Women now receive 45% of all Ph.D. degrees in the United States ("The Nation: Students," 2005).
- In Multan, Pakistan, a tribal council was distressed that a young boy had been walking with a woman from a higher-caste family. To punish the boy's "crime," the council ordered that his older *sister*, Mukhtaran Bibi, be sentenced to gang rape. Four men raped her repeatedly. Tradition demanded that she commit suicide. However, she accepted the $8,300 awarded to her by the government and used the money to found a school for girls. The Canadian government, the readers of the *New York Times*, and other donors have provided funds that she plans to use for a library, a playground, and a women's fund-raising project (Kristof, 2005; Moreau & Hussain, 2005).
- The United Nations Convention on the Elimination of All Forms of Discrimination Against Women (CEDAW) has been ratified by more than 170 countries throughout the world. The signers include Iraq and Afghanistan—two countries not known for policies consistent with

feminism. The CEDAW legislation condemns female genital mutilation, selling women for prostitution, domestic abuse, and other actions that harm women. However, several countries have refused to sign the document, including Somalia, Sudan, Oman, Brunei, and . . . the United States (Quindlen, 2005b).

As these examples suggest, women's lives have improved considerably in some areas, yet the progress is often slow. Let's begin this chapter by discussing the status of the discipline we call the psychology of women. Then we'll examine how women of color view feminism. Our third section explores several different components of the men's movement. The final section looks at current trends in the women's movement, in both North America and other regions of the world.

THE FUTURE OF THE DISCIPLINE OF THE PSYCHOLOGY OF WOMEN

As we noted in Chapter 1, the discipline of the psychology of women is relatively young. Most college courses with that title were offered for the first time in the 1970s or 1980s. People who teach courses in the psychology of women or the psychology of gender often emphasize the strong connection we immediately felt with this emerging discipline (e.g., Baker, 2006; Deaux, 2001; Hyde, 2001). For example, Letitia Anne Peplau said, "Feminist perspectives helped me understand my own life experiences and relationships in new and more insightful ways. . . . Feminist activism sought to improve the lives of women and to work toward a more just society that places a high value on women as well as men" (Peplau, 1994, p. 44).

Hundreds of professors throughout North America share this passion for teaching and studying the psychology of women. Two topics related to the future of our discipline are (1) the increasing number of women entering psychology and (2) the issue of developing a more inclusive psychology of women.

THE INCREASING NUMBER OF WOMEN IN PSYCHOLOGY

Between 1920 and 1974, women earned only 23% of all psychology Ph.D. degrees in the United States (Baker, 2006). Fortunately, the picture has changed. Now they earn 69% of these degrees (The Nation: Students, 2005). Furthermore, women constitute 70% of the full-time students in psychology Ph.D. programs in Canada (Boatswain et al., 2001). The current gender ratio for psychology faculty members still favors males, but it will approach equality as the current female graduate school students become faculty members.

The increasing number of women in psychology does not necessarily *guarantee* a strong feminist discipline. As we have seen throughout this book, women and men often hold similar stereotypes about gender. However, the increasing number of women entering psychology has certainly contributed to the growing support for feminist theory and research.

DEVELOPING A MORE INCLUSIVE PSYCHOLOGY OF WOMEN

In constructing the new discipline of psychology of women, feminists hoped to create a new perspective that values women's and men's lives equally. An ongoing problem, however, has been that the psychology of women has typically focused on educated, heterosexual, non-disabled, middle-class European American females (Enns, 2004a; Olkin, 2006; J. D. Yoder & Kahn, 1993). After all, the psychologists—as well as the college women whom they typically study—are most likely to be educated, heterosexual, non-disabled, middle-class European American women (Enns, 2004a).

In recent years, many scholars have moved away from the traditional population of European American females to examine other populations (e.g., Baca Zinn & Dill, 2005; Blea, 2003; K. R. King, 2003). However, much of the current research on women of color, lesbian women, or lower-class women is limited to a comparison between the normative group and the "nonstandard" group. This group-comparisons approach often keeps European American women at the center. Every other group is then a "special case," located on the periphery (Morawski & Bayer, 1995; J. D. Yoder & Kahn, 1993).

Another problem with a group-comparisons approach is that psychologists often select topics for research in which the ethnic group that is not European American is suspected to be deficient. For example, when I was searching for studies on Native Americans and Canadian Aboriginals, I kept finding research on alcoholism and suicide. Why couldn't I find a similar abundance of research about other topics concerning this ethnic group, such as the experiences of lesbian and bisexual women or their reactions to becoming a mother?

Unfortunately, too, psychologists seldom explore areas in which people of color successfully negotiate a problem. We could all learn from research in Chapter 14, which noted that older Black women are likely to be active in community organizations. How do these organizations provide support networks that may assist older, low-income women from other ethnic backgrounds?

In summary, the psychology of women must not repeat the errors made by earlier generations of psychologists when they ignored women. Consistent with Theme 4, we need to value the diversity of females included within the category "women." In the next section, we'll focus on a related topic: How women of color respond to the feminist movement.

Section Summary

The Future of the Discipline of the Psychology of Women

1. The psychology of women is a relatively new discipline; people in this area are committed to its continued growth.

2. In psychology, the percentage of Ph.D. degrees that women earn has been increasing markedly; however, not all female psychologists have feminist perspectives. Still, this trend encourages teaching and research about feminism.

3. The discipline needs to emphasize the diversity of backgrounds that women represent, rather than centering on educated, heterosexual, non-disabled, middle-class European American females.

WOMEN OF COLOR AND THE FEMINIST MOVEMENT

Throughout this book, we have seen that women from different ethnic groups may have diverse experiences. Similarly, Black women, Latina women, and Asian women may differ in their perspectives on feminism. They also may report that they feel left out of "mainstream" White feminism (Enns, 2004a).

BLACK FEMINISTS

A Black feminist scholar, bell hooks, recalls giving a lecture in which she described how feminism had changed her life. A Black female student then rose to give an impassioned speech against feminism. The student said that feminism addressed the needs of White women only, with whom she had nothing in common (hooks, 1994).

Many Black women do not feel connected with feminism. Some Black women report that their experiences are too different from the experiences of White women, who are more economically privileged (Cole & Guy-Sheftall, 2003; G. C. N. Hall & Barongan, 2001; Roth, 2004). Black women also complain that they feel no connection with racist White women (hooks, 2001; Roth, 2004). In addition, Black women may be reluctant to criticize Black men, who already experience negative reactions from White individuals (S. A. Jackson, 1998; Rosen, 2000). Furthermore, Black men may argue that feminism draws Black women away from reducing racism, a goal that the Black men perceive to be more important (Cole & Guy-Sheftall, 2006).

Some Black women engage in feminist activities, but they do not label themselves feminists (J. James, 1999; Roth, 2004). For instance, S. A. Jackson (1998) interviewed Black women who were active in a variety of organizations in which Black women held leadership roles. One woman saw herself as a feminist, which she defined as someone who "works on issues to promote the interests of women" (p. 41). However, most of the other participants in this study avoided calling themselves feminists. Many participants were also unclear about the definition of the term, or they had mixed feelings about feminism. As you can imagine, many women from other ethnic groups also share these perspectives.

LATINA/O FEMINISTS

Most U.S. students learn something about Black history and the civil rights movement in high school. However, unless you live in the western United States, you are less likely to know about the Chicana/o movement, which addresses the concerns of Mexican Americans. Chicana feminism has a longer history than most people would guess. In 1971, for example, Chicana feminists organized a national conference in Houston, Texas (Roth, 2004).

When women began to participate in the Chicana/o movement, they started questioning their traditional roles. They also protested that this movement ignored women's issues (Blea, 2003; Enns, 2004a; Saldívar-Hull, 2000). In addition, these women acknowledged that Chicana feminism would need to address both race and class, in addition to gender (Moraga, 1993; Roth, 2004).

Chicano males have often misinterpreted the Chicana feminist movement as a threat to the political unity of the Chicana/o movement. In fact, Chicano male activists may label these women *vendidas,* or "sellouts." They might also accuse Chicana feminists of "acting like White women" (Kafka, 2000; E. Martínez, 1995; Roth, 2004). However, many college courses in Chicana/o studies now acknowledge the important contributions of Chicana women (Blea, 1997; Saldívar-Hull, 2000).

ASIAN AMERICAN FEMINISTS

Asian American women face different challenges in identifying with the feminist movement. In general, Asian cultures require women to be relatively passive, invisible, and supportive of men (Chu, 2004; Root, 1995). Amita Handa (2003) describes the difficulties of growing up as a teenager in Toronto, with parents who had emigrated from the Punjabi region of India. She sensed that she "did not fit into any expectations about Western teenagers or good South Asian girls" (p. 109).

Asian women may prefer to achieve social change by using indirect methods rather than more confrontational approaches (Ang, 2001). When Asian American women do express feminist perspectives, community members are likely to criticize them. These critics accuse them of diluting the resources in the Asian American community and destroying the working relationships between Asian women and men (Chow, 1991).

Furthermore, many women with an Asian background are not familiar with the feminist movement. This issue is especially likely if they recently immigrated to North America (G. C. N. Hall & Barongan, 2001; J. Lee, 2001). Pramila Aggarwal (1990) described how she discovered a way to discuss feminist issues with Indian immigrant women in Canada. Aggarwal, a bilingual student, had been hired to teach English to Punjabi women who were working in a garment factory in Toronto. During these English classes, Aggarwal discovered that the women were interested in women's issues, such as the division of labor in the home and sexual harassment in the workplace. From this experience, she concluded that feminist organizing requires being sensitive to the specific needs of women, rather than imposing one's own personal viewpoint.

Some regions in the United States and Canada have had a substantial Asian population for many decades. As a result, feminism may be more visible in these communities. During the 1970s, for example, universities such as UC Berkeley, UCLA, and San Francisco State began to offer courses about Asian American women (Chu, 2004). College students who complete these courses are likely to acquire a sophisticated perspective on both feminism and racism.

In summary, women of color may identify feminist issues in their lives. However, they are often reluctant to label themselves feminists. They may find it difficult to become feminist activists because activism is not consistent with their culture or because the males in their culture might believe that feminism threatens the efforts to unify their ethnic group. In addition, they may feel that feminist groups that are organized by European Americans may not be sensitive to the concerns of women of color.

Fortunately, however, the situation is gradually changing, and women from every ethnic group are now writing about how feminism can transform the lives of women of color (Enns, 2004a; Kirk & Okazawa-Rey, 2001). In the words of Black feminists Johnetta Betsch Cole and Beverly Guy-Sheftall (2003), "We believe it is possible to free ourselves as a community from the traps of sexism and heterosexism even as we continue our struggle against the ever present threats of racial inequality and poverty" (p. 70).

At the same time, feminists from all ethnic backgrounds acknowledge that contemporary feminism must extend beyond gender issues. Claire Kirch, who works with a feminist publisher, addresses this perspective:

> Feminism today is about social justice. Not justice just for women, but for all people. It is many voices saying one thing: Peace on earth, economic justice now, and social justice for all. It is about a living wage, national health care, the love of oneself as a political act, and the promotion of ecological justice. (cited in Braun, 2003, p. 24)

Section Summary

Women of Color and the Feminist Movement

1. Many Black women do not experience a connection with feminism because their lives are too different from the lives of European American women and because they are reluctant to criticize Black men.

2. Similarly, Chicano males may accuse feminists of undermining the Chicana/o movement. College courses on Chicana issues now acknowledge the contributions of Chicanas.

3. Asian American women may find that feminist activism is not consistent with the traditional role of women in Asian cultures; critics may accuse Asian feminists of undermining the unity in their community.

4. An increasing number of women of color are writing about feminism; they emphasize that feminism is an important component of social justice.

THE MEN'S MOVEMENT

Beginning in the 1970s, some men began examining the masculine gender role and its implications for men's lives (Kilmartin, 2007; Smiler, 2004). These investigations inspired a new academic field, called men's studies. **Men's studies** is a collection of scholarly activities, such as teaching courses and conducting research, that focus on men's lives. Men's studies often emphasizes gender-role socialization, gender-role conflict, the sexism problem, and ethnic diversity (Blazina, 2003; A. J. Lott, 2003; Richmond & Levant, 2003).

Men's studies also explores areas in which men's behaviors are maladaptive. For example, as we saw in Chapters 11 and 12, men are less likely than women to seek help for health and psychological problems (Addis & Mahalik, 2003; Greer, 2005; Rochlen et al., 2006; D. R. Williams, 2003). Men of color may be especially reluctant to seek help (A. J. Lott, 2003; Smiler, 2004). Several resources present more details on men's studies (e.g., Berila et al., 2005; Blazina, 2003; G. R. Brooks, 2003; Hammond & Mattis, 2005; Kersting, 2005; Kilmartin, 2007; Kimmel, 2004).

Just as there is no unitary women's movement, we also find no unitary, single-focus men's movement (Kilmartin, 2007). Three strands within the men's movement are commonly mentioned: (1) the profeminists, (2) the mythopoetic movement, and (3) the religiously oriented approach. Students who are learning about the psychology of women need to know that some men's groups serve as allies, whereas others may be antagonists.

PROFEMINIST APPROACHES

The **profeminists** want to eliminate the destructive aspects of gender, such as gender stereotypes, gender inequalities, and gender-related violence (Kilmartin, 2007). The profeminist movement is the strand of the men's movement that grew out of the feminist movement. Profeminists believe that strict gender roles can hurt both men and women (Blazina, 2003). They also oppose the sexual exploitation of women (Goldrick-Jones, 2002). A resource compiled by Goldrick-Jones (2002) lists 25 profeminist organizations, mostly in Canada and the United States. Most people who teach men's studies in colleges and universities would probably call themselves profeminists (Rhode, 1997).

At the national level, the largest profeminist organization is the National Organization of Men Against Sexism (NOMAS), which was formed during the early 1970s. Within psychology, the most visible profeminist group is called the Society for the Psychological Study of Men and Masculinity (SPSMM, Division 51 of the American Psychological Association). According to its mission statement, this organization:

- Promotes the critical study of how gender shapes and constricts men's lives.
- Is committed to an enhancement of men's capacity to experience their full human potential.

Demonstration 15.1

IDENTIFYING ALLIES

As we note in the text, allies are people who provide support to groups other than their own group. Begin this demonstration by thinking of several males you know personally who are likely to provide support to females. (If you are male, you may be able to include yourself in this list.)

Write down each man's name and then list some specific things that this individual did to support girls and women. Then repeat this exercise by thinking about White people who are likely to provide support to people of color; identify their specific contributions. Continue this process with several other social groups that frequently experience biased treatment (e.g., gays and lesbians, immigrants, people with disabilities).

- Endeavors to erode constraining definitions of masculinity that historically have inhibited men's development, limited their capacity to form meaningful relationships, and contributed to the oppression of other people.
- Acknowledges its historical debt to feminist-inspired scholarship on gender, and commits itself to the support of groups such as women, gays, lesbians, and people of color that have been uniquely oppressed by the gender/class/race system.
- Contends vigorously that the empowerment of all persons beyond narrow and restrictive gender-role definitions leads to the highest level of functioning in individual women and men, to the healthiest interactions between the genders, and to the richest relationships between them. (SPSSM, 2006)

As individuals, profeminist men can serve as **allies**, people who provide support to groups other than their own (Kilmartin, 2007; Roades & Mio, 2000). Try Demonstration 15.1 to explore this concept in more detail.

Profeminist men can also work together to organize public actions. For example, the White Ribbon Campaign (2006) began when men in Canada began wearing white ribbons after the murder of 14 women at École Polytechnique in Montreal in 1989.[1] White Ribbon Campaign groups continue to examine issues related to male violence (Goldrick-Jones, 2002). At the University of Michigan, for instance, men handed out white ribbons, organized a teach-in on sexual assault, and held a vigil to raise awareness about violence against women (K. Schwartz, 2006).

MYTHOPOETIC APPROACHES

Whereas the profeminist men focus on how traditional gender roles hurt both men and women, the mythopoetic men focus on how these gender roles hurt themselves. Men who favor the **mythopoetic approaches** believe that modern men should use myths and poetry to develop their own spiritual growth

---

[1]In 1989, a man named Marc Lepin entered a classroom in the engineering school at École Polytechnique, in Montreal, Canada. He forced the female students to line up along a wall. Shouting "You are all feminists," he shot them all. He then tracked down other women in the building, killing a total of 14 women.

(Blazina, 2003; Kimmel, 2004; Sweet, 2000). To achieve this growth, men join all-male gatherings, often in a wilderness setting. Their goal is for the men to work through their psychological difficulties, focus on male role models, and work toward a mature form of masculinity. In general, the men who adopt the mythopoetic approach believe that profeminist men focus too much on women's issues, instead of their own gender (Kilmartin, 2007).

Many men in the mythopoetic movement express somewhat feminist views, with an emphasis on gender justice (Barton, 2000; Goldrick-Jones, 2002). However, profeminists point out that the majority of the men at these all-male mythopoetic gatherings are middle-class, middle-aged European American heterosexual men. This group represents the most powerful cohort in North America; compared to most other men, they have greater economic resources and have benefited more than any other group in our society (Kilmartin, 2007; S. R. Wilson & Mankowski, 2000).

RELIGIOUS APPROACHES

The religiously oriented approaches to the men's movement have become more visible in recent years. The **religious approaches** argue that men should take back their roles as head of the household so that they can become leaders in their family, church, and community (Blazina, 2003; Levant, 2001; Metzger, 2002). As a result, women should accept the role of being followers. If these basic principles don't sound alarming, try replacing the sexism with racist equivalents: "Whites should take back their roles as masters, and Blacks should accept the role of being slaves."

Among the religious approaches, the most visible is the Promise Keepers (Kilmartin, 2007; Metzger, 2002; Van Leeuwen, 2002). There huge rallies usually take place in football stadiums, and the messages are strongly traditional. Men are told to be assertive about taking back their natural role, and they are encouraged to invite male friends to attend future rallies. Promise Keeper websites list branches in U.S. cities such as Kansas City, Dallas, Colorado Springs, and Atlanta, as well as in Canada and New Zealand. The Promise Keeper rallies emphasize essentialism—that men and women are different because women were created for men (Kilmartin, 2007).

The Promise Keepers and other religiously based forms of the men's movement may voice some admirable statements, such as racial reconciliation and encouraging men to become more actively involved in nurturing their children (L. B. Silverstein et al., 1999; Van Leeuwen, 2002). However, we must carefully examine their principles because these groups typically want to reduce the rights of women.

How do college students react to these different men's groups? Rickabaugh (1994) asked undergraduates at a California university to read descriptions of several men, each representing a different strand of the men's movement. Both men and women gave the highest rating to the profeminist man. They saw the profeminist man as both nurturant and competent—a finding that should be encouraging to profeminist male students who are reading this book.

Section Summary

The Men's Movement	1. Men's studies includes scholarly activities, such as teaching courses and conducting research that focuses on men's lives and the problems they encounter.
	2. Three major strands within the men's movement are (a) the profeminists, who believe that gender roles hurt both men and women, (b) the mythopoetic approach, which focuses on men's spiritual growth, and (c) the religious approach, such as the Promise Keepers.

CURRENT TRENDS IN FEMINISM

Is feminism thriving, approximately one decade into the twenty-first century? What about issues important to women? Let's consider four perspectives on these questions: (1) Women's studies courses, (2) the women's movement in North America, (3) the women's movement at the international level, and (4) how you can contribute to the well-being of girls and women.

WOMEN'S STUDIES COURSES

Thousands of women's studies courses are offered at colleges and universities throughout North America. The National Women's Studies Association currently estimates that U.S. colleges and universities have about 1,000 women's studies programs (L. Younger, personal communication, 2006). Women's studies is now a well-established field, especially because it enrolls more college students than any other interdisciplinary field (Buhle, 2000; Maynard, 2005; S. M. Shaw & Lee, 2001). Furthermore, numerous women's studies courses are available at the graduate level, and 10 U.S. universities offer a Ph.D. degree in women's studies (Banerji, 2006; O. C. Smith, 2006).

Students often comment that they gain a new perspective from women's studies courses (Dodwell, 2003; Musil, 2000b). In these courses, students learn to appreciate the connections between the scholarly resources and their personal experiences (Enns & Forrest, 2005). As one woman reported, women's studies courses generate "learning that does more than fill your brain. It fills your body, it fills your heart, and it makes you grow" (Musil, 2000b, p. 2124).

Women of color sometimes comment that their women's studies courses help them understand both gender and ethnicity issues. For example, a Chicana student from Wisconsin commented on her women's studies course:

> I am a Chicana; not only must I deal with racism but I must also live in a sexist world. I come from a family with strong conservative views compared to other families in the U.S. . . . . Machismo is very prominent and sometimes cannot be seen but it is there. I never really thought about important feminist issues in high school.

But I always knew that women were oppressed in our society. I saw it in my own home. It was not until I broke away from home that I began to think about my identity. I must say that my first real exposure to feminist ideas was when I left home for college. It is here where I am learning and trying to understand feminist ideas. (Rhoades, 1999, p. 68)

Research using quantitative methods confirms that these courses have a significant impact on students' lives. For instance, women enrolled in women's studies courses are significantly more likely than similar women enrolled in other courses to develop a more nontraditional attitude toward gender roles. They are also more likely to develop a strong feminist identity after taking the course (K. L. Harris et al., 1999; Malkin & Stake, 2004; Stake & Hoffmann, 2001). Other research shows that women and men are equally likely to benefit from these women's studies courses (Stake & Malkin, 2003). Also, women's studies courses are more likely than other courses to encourage activism related to women's issues (Stake & Hoffmann, 2001). In addition, these courses enhance self-confidence and a sense of control over one's life (Malkin & Stake, 2004; Stake & Hoffmann, 2000). Finally, students emphasize that their women's studies courses encourage critical thinking (Sinacore & Boatwright, 2005; Stake & Hoffmann, 2000).

Michelle Fine is an especially creative feminist psychologist. She and her colleagues have documented the impact of women's studies in an unusual setting: Bedford Women's Prison, a maximum-security prison located in New York State (M. Fine, 2001; M. Fine & Torre, 2001; M. Fine et al., 2001). As part of an educational program, the women read novels by Alice Walker and discussed postmodern philosophy. Even the correction officers were astonished at the transformation. As one officer reported, "Before, at night, they would fight or bite each other. Now they are reading!" (M. Fine, 2001). Furthermore, after release from prison, those women who had participated in the educational program were only 24% as likely to be imprisoned for new crimes, compared to non-participants.

In summary, college students report that their women's studies courses are thought provoking and informative. These courses also change students' attitudes, activism, self-confidence, and critical-thinking ability. In a prison setting, women's studies courses have the potential to completely change women's lives.

THE WOMEN'S MOVEMENT IN NORTH AMERICA

The anti-slavery movement of the 1830s inspired the first wave of the feminist movement in North America. Women such as Susan B. Anthony and Elizabeth Cady Stanton created strategies for political organizing, and they saw clear links between freedom for slaves and freedom for women (Enns, 2004a; Kravetz & Marecek, 2001). However, their concerns were not answered for almost a century. For instance, U.S. women did not win the right to vote until August 26, 1920, with the passage of the Nineteenth Amendment to the U.S. Constitution.

The current women's movement emerged from the attempts to resolve important social problems during the 1960s. Women were active in the civil rights movement and in protesting the war in Vietnam. As in the previous century, this focus on issues of social justice made women in the United States and Canada more aware that they were second-class citizens (Rebick, 2005; Tobias, 1997). The National Organization for Women (NOW) was founded in 1966, and it remains one of the most important women's rights organizations in the United States. In Canada, the National Action Committee on the Status of Women (NAC) was founded in 1972. NAC includes more than 700 member groups, and it addresses issues such as women's shelters, immigrant women, lesbian groups, and student issues (National Action Committee, 2006; Rebick, 2005).

The scope of current feminist organizations is astonishing. Some groups, such as NOW, have a general focus that addresses issues such as violence against women, reproductive rights, and workplace issues. Other groups emphasize more specific issues. For example, Emily's List is an organization that raises money to help elect feminist women to the U.S. Congress and other important leadership positions (S. M. Evans, 2003).

Other North American feminist groups focus on the abuse of women, anti-militarism, women's health, reproductive rights, women's spirituality, welfare issues, urban schools, women of color, older women, lesbian and bisexual concerns, immigration issues, anti-poverty issues, or community problems (S. M. Evans, 2003; Freedman, 2002; Kravetz & Marecek, 2001). Some groups emphasize **ecofeminism**, an approach that opposes the way that humans destroy other animals and natural resources. Also, feminist communities have created a variety of feminist-run organizations. These include feminist therapy groups, feminist bookstores, theater groups, vacation resorts, and music festivals. Feminism is clearly not "dead," despite the misinformed claims of the media (Pozner, 2003).

Critics of the women's movement argue that feminism specifies a rigid set of regulations. However, there is no single, unified version of feminism (S. M. Evans, 2003; Felski, 2003; Jervis, 2004/2005). For example, feminists disagree among themselves about many important issues. Some of these issues include whether women should be encouraged to join the military, whether pornography should be regulated, and whether gender differences are large or small (R. C. Barnett & Rivers, 2004; W. S. Rogers & Rogers, 2001). Feminist principles argue that we should respect women and their life choices. We should also examine the social forces influencing these choices (Pollitt & Baumgardner, 2003; Stange, 2002).

Critics of the women's movement also argue that women and men are now being treated equally, and feminists should just stop whining. A stream of anti-feminist messages from the media has created a backlash within the general population in both the United States and Canada (S. M. Evans, 2003). For example, the right-wing televangelist Pat Robertson has said, "Feminists encourage women to leave their husbands, kill their children, practice witch-craft, become lesbians, and destroy capitalism" (cited in Baumgardner

Demonstration 15.2

DIVERSITY OF
VIEWS ABOUT
FEMINISM

At the top of several pieces of paper, write these instructions: "Please define feminism in your own words, and describe how feminism is relevant or irrelevant in your life." Distribute one page to each of several friends, and ask them to provide a written reply. (You may wish to specify that they can omit their names from the sheets or use other precautions so that their replies are anonymous.) Among those who have positive views of feminism, can you identify a variety of perspectives? (Check pp. 6–7 to remind yourself about various kinds of feminism.) Among those with negative views, can you think about why the media would have influenced their perspectives?

& Richards, 2000, p. 61). Unfortunately, this backlash undercuts the genuine progress that the women's movement has made in recent years. This misinformation about feminism also affects many people who respect women and believe that women and men should be socially, economically, and legally equal. Specifically, these people try to distance themselves from the feminist label by saying, "I'm not a feminist, but . . ." (A. N. Zucker, 2004). Try Demonstration 15.2 to identify how several of your friends feel about feminism.

In summary, the North American feminist movement has grown and diversified considerably in recent decades, despite the attacks from critics. Fortunately, too, feminists in the United States and Canada now emphasize a global approach: Women face discrimination in every country, and we must work to change this problem.

THE WOMEN'S MOVEMENT WORLDWIDE

In New Zealand, women won the right to vote in 1893. Australia, Canada, and many European countries followed within the next three decades. However, women living in Kuwait were not granted the right to vote until 2005. Women have been heads of state in more than 30 countries—among them, India, Haiti, Nicaragua, Bolivia, Turkey, Iceland, Great Britain, and Canada—but not the United States. Furthermore, women hold more than one-third of the seats in the national legislature, in only six countries. All six of these countries are in northern Europe (Sapiro, 2003). In summary, women are a long way from equality when we consider official positions within national governments.

In some cases, a remarkable person can have an important effect on the lives of females. For example, in 2003 an Iranian woman named Shrin Ebadi won the Nobel Peace Prize for her work in support of the rights of women and children (Denmark, 2004).

Women's grassroots activism has had impressive consequences in countries outside North America. Consider the Mothers of the Plaza de Mayo, a group of women whose children "disappeared" during the military dictatorship in Argentina between 1976 and 1983. More than 30,000 people were killed during that era. Many of them were young people who were secretly murdered because they had opposed the government. The government had forbidden all public demonstrations, yet these mothers risked their lives by gathering at the Plaza de Mayo in Buenos Aires every Thursday, holding large photos of their missing children. Their bravery ultimately helped end that terrifying regime, and it helped women in countries such as El Salvador and Guatemala to become activists (Brabeck & Rogers, 2000).

This mothers' group in Argentina inspired a group of Mexican American women who called themselves "Mothers of East Los Angeles." These U.S. women successfully blocked the construction of a hazardous-waste incinerator that was planned within their community (Pardo, 2005). Notice, then, that political strategies often spread from developing countries to North America, rather than only in the reverse direction (Brownhill & Turner, 2003; Mendez, 2005).

Throughout the world, groups of women are working to improve women's lives. We now have rich resources describing women's global activism (e.g., Chesler, 2006; Essed et al., 2005; Grewal & Kaplan, 2002; Maynard, 2005; Mendez, 2005; Mohanty, 2003; Naples & Desai, 2002). Women's studies courses are now being taught in countries such as India, Japan, Korea, Thailand, Croatia, Latvia, Turkey, Ghana, and Brazil (Bonder, 2000; Howe, 2001b; Kuninobu, 2000; Musil, 2000a; L. White, 2001).

A superb group called The Global Fund for Women (2006) provides small grants for projects developed by women in countries throughout the world. By 2006, the Fund had donated more than $53 million to more than 3,200 groups in 160 countries.

Here are four representative examples from a recent list of the Fund's projects:

- In Lomé, Togo, a country in Africa, for a group that trains women in basic literacy and also helps these women understand their human rights.
- In Gaza, Palestine, for a group of women who are working to improve the sanitation system in refugee camps.
- In Santiago, Chile, to educate the public about domestic violence.
- In Jakarta, Indonesia, to increase public awareness about how women are treated violently by the national police.

Women in developing countries share many of the same perspectives and concerns that women in North America and Europe express. However, women in these countries must also overcome basic survival problems. Some of the subtler points of North American feminism may seem irrelevant to a woman in India who knows that she must give her son more food than her daughter so that he can grow strong. These points may also seem irrelevant for a woman in Burma who must work under harsh conditions for much less than $1 a day, making sneakers for a prestigious American company.

In recent years, women and men in wealthy countries have begun to realize an important issue: People in the rest of the world are suffering intensely in order to make North American lives more comfortable or more entertaining (Mendez, 2005). In Chapter 7, we considered the exploitation of women who work in sweatshops. A more terrifying form of exploitation is called *trafficking,* or the sale of human beings for illegal purposes. More than 50,000 women and children each year are smuggled into the United States and Canada. These individuals were kidnapped or sold from their homes in Asian, Latin America, and Eastern Europe. They are shipped—much like shoes or shirts—to North America, where they can generate money for other people, by working as prostitutes (Poulin, 2003; Seager, 2003). This international women's issue is nowhere near a solution (Trépanier, 2003).

Helping to Change the Future: Becoming an Activist

So far, in this section on some hopeful trends in women's issues, we have examined women's studies courses, the women's movement in North America, and the women's movement worldwide. In most psychology courses, students remain passive as they read about the future of a discipline. This time it's different: *You* can be part of the solution—if you're not already involved— rather than assuming that someone else will do the work. For example, at Bennett College in North Carolina, a group of Black women decided to develop an educational program to celebrate National American Indian Heritage Month (Malveaux, 2006). Here are just a few of many other options:

- Subscribe to a feminist magazine, such as *Ms. Magazine* or *Canadian Woman Studies/Les cahiers de la femme*. It will inform you about political activities that you may want to support, and the articles will keep you thinking about feminist issues.
- Visit a website on feminist activism such as http://www.feminist.com/ activism/ and find a topic that matches your interests. Then speak out and become involved!
- Talk with friends and relatives about feminist issues. In our everyday conversations, we need to make many decisions. If someone makes a sexist or a racist remark, we can take a small activist step by deciding not to join in the laughter. Even better, we can respond with a comment such as, "That's not funny."
- Serve as a mentor to a girl or a younger woman. For example, a student in my psychology of women class traveled with her mother, her aunt, and her 10-year-old cousin to the Women's Rights Museum in Seneca Falls, New York—the site of first-wave feminists' early activism. Her cousin was both impressed to learn about the early history of the women's movement and outraged to learn that women still earn much less than men (K. DePorter, personal communication, 2002). Some students choose to work on more formal projects—for example, organizing a 6-week program for teenagers about gender issues (E. C. Rose, 2002).
- Give gifts that provide information about girls and women. For instance, send a gift subscription to *New Moon* to any girl between the ages of 9 and 12 (see pp. 101–102). Buy the book *33 Things Every Girl Should Know about Women's History* (Bolden, 2002) for anyone older than about 10, including yourself!

- Help fight negative representations of women. When you see an offensive advertisement, for example, find the company's address through the Internet. Then write the company to express your dissatisfaction. Also, when you see a positive ad, send a compliment to the company.
- Be a "critical consumer" when you read or listen to reports about women in the media. Review the research biases in Figure 1.3, and ask yourself whether the conclusions in the report seem justified. If you'd like to express your discontent—or possibly your approval!—call in to a radio show or write a letter to the editor of a newspaper or magazine. Remember: You now have more information about women's lives than most other individuals in your community, so you can inform other people about these perspectives.
- Join a women's group on campus or in your community—or help to start one. Work with the group to make certain that diversity issues are an integral part of your mission. An important feminist book called *Our Bodies, Ourselves* provides some excellent suggestions about organizing for social change (Boston Women's Health Book Collective, 2005).

Remember: No one individual can attack all the problems that women face. Also, change does not happen overnight (Baumgardner & Richards, 2000; Naples, 2002). Celebrate the small victories, and share these victories with other people. Also, keep in mind a bumper sticker that quotes advice from anthropologist Margaret Mead: "Never doubt that a small group of thoughtful, committed citizens can change the world; indeed it's the only thing that ever has."

Section Summary

Current Trends in Feminism

1. According to qualitative and quantitative research, women's studies courses can change people's attitudes, self-confidence, and critical-thinking skills; they can also change women's lives.

2. The first wave of the feminist movement in North America arose out of the anti-slavery movement and eventually led to the passage of the Nineteenth Amendment to the U.S. Constitution.

3. The current feminist movement arose out of the civil rights movement and the anti-war movement; feminist groups in the current era have addressed numerous different issues concerned with women.

4. Women hold relatively few national leadership positions throughout the world; grassroots women's organizations have achieved many victories, but important problems are still widespread.

5. Students can improve women's lives by methods such as talking about gender discrimination, mentoring a younger female, and working with women's organizations.

CHAPTER REVIEW QUESTIONS

1. What are the trends with respect to the gender ratio in psychology? What is the current gender ratio for psychology faculty and psychology majors at your own college or university? Why might the changing gender ratio help the women's movement, and why might it be less effective than expected?

2. People concerned about the psychology of women have emphasized that the discipline should include more information about women of color. Describe two problems that can arise when researchers use traditional approaches to study people of color.

3. In one section of this chapter, we focused on women of color and feminism, and we mentioned that most students have little exposure to research on ethnic groups other than Blacks. Before you took any courses on the psychology of women (or the psychology of gender), what kind of information did you learn in high school or college about ethnicity? What have you learned outside class in the popular media? Did this information focus more on men or women?

4. Why do women of color face special challenges in identifying with the feminist movement? Why would men of color oppose women from their ethnic group who want to be active feminists?

5. Describe the three basic strands within the men's movement. Which would be likely to support the growth of the women's movement? Which would oppose it? Which might consider it irrelevant? Do you see any evidence of the men's movement in your community or in your academic institution?

6. Briefly trace the history of the women's movement in North America. What issues were important to the early activists? Then comment on the women's movement worldwide. What kinds of concerns have been addressed?

7. In several parts of this chapter, we examined attitudes toward feminist issues. Why do you think that people in North America and throughout the world are reluctant to call themselves feminists?

8. Identify an issue related to women and girls that is especially important to you. If you wanted to increase people's awareness about this issue, what strategies could you adopt from the section on becoming an activist?

(These final two questions require you to review the entire textbook.)

9. In this chapter, we focused on the current trends with respect to women and gender. To help yourself review this book, go back through the 15 chapters. Note which specific developments are moving in a positive direction and which are moving in a negative direction.

10. You will need to set aside several hours for this final task: On separate pieces of paper, list each of the four themes of this book. Then skim through each of the 15 chapters and note any mention of the themes on the appropriate piece of paper. (You can determine whether your lists are complete by checking the entries for Themes 1, 2, 3, and 4 in the subject index.) After you have completed that task, try to synthesize the material within each of the four themes.

KEY TERMS

*men's studies (495)

profeminists (495)

*allies (496)

mythopoetic approach (496)

*religious approach (497)

*ecofeminism (500)

 Note: The terms asterisked in the Key Terms section serve as good search terms for InfoTrac College Edition. Go to http://infotrac.thomsonlearning.com and try these added search terms.

RECOMMENDED READINGS

Baca Zinn, M., Hondagneu-Sotelo, P., & Messner, M. A. (Eds.). (2005). *Gender through the prism of difference* (3rd ed.). New York: Oxford University Press. This feminist-studies textbook focuses on topics such as families, gender in the workplace, and education; at the same time, it focuses on how ethnicity affects gender roles.

Dicker, R., & Piepmeier, A. (Eds.). (2003). *Catching a wave: Reclaiming feminism for the 21st century*. Boston: Northeastern University Press. Here's an interesting book that focuses on the diversity of perspectives within current feminism. The authors of the 16 chapters analyze the media, the feminist movement in the present decade, and creative new directions that feminists can pursue.

Enns, C. Z., & Sinacore, A. L. (Eds.). (2005). *Teaching and social justice: Integrating multicultural and feminist theories in the classroom*. Washington, DC: American Psychological Association. Here is an excellent resource that illustrates how feminist theory can be applied to the college classroom, while emphasizing multicultural approaches.

Kilmartin, C. (2007). *The masculine self* (3rd ed.). Cornwall-on-Hudson, NY: Sloan Publishing. I recommend this excellent textbook, which provides a concise, profeminist summary of the research on the psychology of men. Kilmartin's description of the various groups within the men's movement is especially useful.

ANSWERS TO THE TRUE-FALSE STATEMENTS

1. False (p. 489); 2. True (p. 491); 3. True (pp. 492–493); 4. True (p. 493); 5. True (p. 495); 6. True (p. 497); 7. False (pp. 498–499); 8. False (p. 499); 9. False (p. 500); 10. False (p. 501).

REFERENCES

Abbey, A. (2002). Alcohol-related sexual assault: A common problem among college students. *Journal of Studies on Alcohol, 14*(Suppl.), 118–128.

Abbey, A., & McAuslan, P. (2004). A longitudinal examination of male college students' perpetration of sexual assault. *Journal of Consulting and Clinical Psychology, 72*, 747–756.

Abbey, A., Zawacki, T., & McAuslan, P. (2000). Alcohol's effects on sexual perception. *Journal of Studies on Alcohol, 61*, 688–697.

Abbey, A., et al. (2001). Attitudinal, experiential, and situational predictors of sexual assault perpetration. *Journal of Interpersonal Violence, 16*, 784–807.

Abbey, A., et al. (2002). Alcohol-involved rapes: Are they more violent? *Psychology of Women Quarterly, 26*, 99–109.

Abele, A. E. (2000). A dual-impact model of gender and career-related processes. In T. Eckes & H. M. Traytner (Eds.), *The developmental social psychology of gender* (pp. 361–388). Mahwah, NJ: Erlbaum.

Aboud, F. E., & Fenwick, V. (1999). Exploring and evaluating school-based interventions to reduce prejudice. *Journal of Social Issues, 55*, 767–786.

Adair, L. S., & Gordon-Larsen, P. (2001). Maturational timing and overweight prevalence in U.S. adolescent girls. *American Journal of Public Health, 91*, 642–644.

Adair, V. C., & Dahlberg, S. L. (Eds.). (2003). *Reclaiming class: Women, poverty, and the promise of higher education in America*. Philadelphia: Temple University Press.

Adams, A. (1995). Maternal bonds: Recent literature on mothering. *Signs, 20*, 414–427.

Adams, K. L., & Ware, N. C. (2000). Sexism and the English language: The linguistic implications of being a woman. In A. Minas (Ed.), *Gender basics* (pp. 70–78). Belmont, CA: Wadsworth/Thomson Learning.

Adams, S., Juebli, J., Boyle, P. A., & Fivush, R. (1995). Gender differences in parent-child conversations about past emotions: A longitudinal investigation. *Sex Roles, 33*, 309–323.

Adams-Curtis, L. E., & Forbes, G. B. (2004). College women's experiences of sexual coercion. *Trauma, Violence, & Abuse, 5*, 91–122.

Addis, M. E., & Mahalik, J. R. (2003). Men, masculinity, and the contexts of help seeking. *American Psychologist, 58*, 5–14.

Adler, N. E., & Conner Snibbe, A. (2003). The role of psychosocial processes in explaining the gradient between socioeconomic status and health. *Current Directions in Psychological Science, 12*, 119–123.

Adler, N. E., Ozer, E. J., & Tschann, J. (2003). Abortion among adolescents. *American Psychologist, 58*, 211–217.

Adler, N. E., & Smith, L. B. (1998). Abortion. In E. A. Blechman & K. D. Brownell (Eds.), *Behavioral medicine and women: A comprehensive handbook* (pp. 510–514). New York: Guilford.

Agars, M. D. (2004). Reconsidering the impact of gender stereotypes on the advancement of women in organizations. *Psychology of Women Quarterly, 28,* 103–111.

Agathangelou, A. M. (2000, Winter). Nationalist narratives and (dis)-appearing women. *Canadian Woman Studies/Les cahiers de la femme, 19,* 12–27.

Aggarwal, P. (1990). English classes for immigrant women: A feminist organizing tool. *Fireweed, 30,* 95–100.

Agras, W. S., & Apple, R. F. (2002). Understanding and treating eating disorders. In F. K. Kaslow (Ed.), *Comprehensive handbook of psychotherapy: Cognitive-behavioral approaches* (Vol. 2, pp. 189–212). New York: Wiley.

Aiken, L. S., Gerend, M. A., & Jackson, K. M. (2001). Subjective risk and health protective behavior: Cancer screening and cancer prevention. In A. Baum, T. A. Revenson, & J. E. Singer (Eds.), *Handbook of health psychology* (pp. 727–746). Mahwah, NJ: Erlbaum.

Alan Guttmacher Institute. (2001). *Can more progress be made? Teenage sexual and reproductive behavior in developed countries: Executive summary.* New York: Author.

Alan Guttmacher Institute. (2004). *U.S. teenage pregnancy statistics: Overall trends, trends by race and ethnicity and state-by-state information.* New York: Author.

Alan Guttmacher Institute. (2005). *Get "in the know": 20 Questions about pregnancy, contraception and abortion.* Retrieved July 11, 2005 from http://www.guttmacher.org/in-the-know/index

Alden, P. B. (2000). Crossing the moon. In R. Ratner (Ed.), *Bearing life: Women's writings on childlessness* (pp. 106–111). New York: Feminist Press.

Alexander, L. L., LaRosa, J. H., & Bader, H. (2001). *New dimensions in women's health* (2nd ed.). Boston: Jones and Bartlett.

Alexander, L. L., LaRosa, J. H., Bader, H., & Garfield, S. (2004). *New dimensions in women's health* (3rd ed.). Sudbury, MA: Jones and Bartlett.

Alexander, S. H. (1999). Messages to women on love and marriage from women's magazines. In M. Meyers (Ed.), *Mediated women: Representations in popular culture* (pp. 25–37). Cresskill, NJ: Hampton Press.

Algoe, S. B., Buswell, B. N., & DeLamater, J. D. (2000). Gender and job status as contextual cues for the interpretation of facial expression of emotion. *Sex Roles, 42,* 183–208.

Ali, A., & Toner, B. B. (2001). Emotional abuse of women. In J. Worell (Ed.), *Encyclopedia of women and gender* (pp. 379–390). San Diego: Academic Press.

Allen, K. R. (1994). Feminist reflections on lifelong single women. In D. L. Sollie & L. A. Leslie (Eds.), *Gender, families, and close relationships: Feminist research journeys* (pp. 97–119). Thousand Oaks, CA: Sage.

Allen, M., & Burrell, N. A. (2002). Sexual orientation of the parent: The impact on the child. In M. Allen, R. W. Preiss, B. M. Gayle, & N. A. Burrell (Eds.), *Interpersonal communication research: Advances through meta-analysis* (pp. 125–143). Mahwah, NJ: Erlbaum.

Allen, M., Emmers-Summer, T. M., & Crowell, T. L. (2002). Couples negotiating safer sex behaviors: A meta-analysis of the impact of conversation and gender. In M. Allen, R. W. Preiss, B. M. Gayle, & N. A. Burrell (Eds.), *Interpersonal communication research: Advances through meta-analysis* (pp. 263–279). Mahwah, NJ: Erlbaum.

Allgeier, E. R., & Allgeier, A. R. (2000). *Sexual interactions* (5th ed.). Boston: Houghton Mifflin.

Amato, P. R., Johnson, D. R., Booth, A., & Roers, S. J. (2003). Continuity and change in marital quality between 1980 and 2000. *Journal of Marriage and Family, 65,* 1–22.

Ambady, N., Shih, M., Kim, A., & Pittinsky, T. L. (2001). Stereotype susceptibility in children: Effects of identity activation on quantitative performance. *Psychological Science, 12,* 385–390.

American Academy of Pediatrics. (2001). WIC Program. *Pediatrics, 108,* 1216–1217.

American Academy of Pediatrics. (2002a). Coparent or second-parent adoption by same-sex parents. *Pediatrics, 109,* 339–340.

American Academy of Pediatrics. (2002b). Technical report: Coparent or second-parent adoption by same-sex parents. *Pediatrics, 109,* 341–344.

American Cancer Society. (2003). *Breast cancer: Early detection.* Retrieved January 7, 2003, from http://documents.cancer.org/6114.00

American Cancer Society. (2005). *Cancer facts and figures now available.* Retrieved October 1, 2005 from American Cancer Society http://www.cancer.org/docroot/NWS/content/NWS_1_1x_Cancer_Facts_and_Figures_Now_Available .asp

American Institutes for Research. (1998). *Gender gaps: Where schools still fail our children.* Washington, DC: American Association of University Women Educational Foundation.

American Medical Association. (2005). *Women in U.S. medical schools.* Retrieved April 22, 2005, from http://www.ama assn.org/ama/pub/category/print/.12914.html

American Psychiatric Association. (2000). *Diagnostic and statistical manual of mental disorders* (DSM-IV-TR; 4th ed.). Washington, DC: American Psychiatric Press.

American Psychological Association. (1990). Ethical principles of psychologists. *American Psychologist, 45,* 390–395.

American Psychological Association. (2001). *Publication manual of the American Psychological Association* (5th ed.). Washington, DC: Author.

American Psychological Association. (2003). Guidelines on multicultural education, training, research, practice, and organizational change for psychologists. *American Psychologist, 58,* 377–402.

American Psychological Association (2004). *Resolution on sexual orientation and marriage.* Retrieved June 8, 2005, from www.apa.org/releases/gaymarriage_reso.pdf

Amiri, R., Hunt, S., & Sova, J. (2004). Transition within tradition: Women's participating in restoring Afghanistan. *Sex Roles, 51,* 283–291.

Anastasopoulos, V., & Desmarais, S. (2000). *Deciding whether to self-label as a feminist: Examining the effects of attitudes.* Paper presented at the annual convention of the Canadian Psychological Association.

Andersen, B. L., & Farrar, W. B. (2001). Breast disorders and breast cancer. In N. L. Stotland & D. E. Stewart (Eds.), *Psychological aspects of women's health care* (2nd ed., pp. 457–475). Washington, DC: American Psychiatric Press.

Anderson, B. (2003). Just another job? The commodification of domestic labor. In B. Ehrenreich & A. R. Hochschild (Eds.), *Global woman* (pp. 104–114). New York: Metropolitan Books.

Anderson, C. A., & Bushman, B. J. (2002). Human aggression, *Annual Review of Psychology, 53,* 27–51.

Anderson, D. A., & Hamilton, M. (2005). Gender role stereotyping of parents in children's picture books: The invisible father. *Sex Roles, 52,* 145–151.

Anderson, K. J., & Leaper, C. (1998). Meta-analyses of gender effects on conversational interruption: Who, what, when, where, and how. *Sex Roles, 39,* 225–252.

Anderson, L. A., & Whiston, S. C. (2005). Sexual assault education programs: A meta-analytic examination of their effectiveness. *Psychology of Women Quarterly, 29,* 374–388.

Anderson, P. B., & Struckman-Johnson, C. (Eds.). (1998). *Sexually aggressive women: Current perspectives and controversies.* New York: Guilford.

Anderson, S. E., Dallal, G. E., & Must, A. (2003). Relative weight and race influence average age at menarche: Results from two nationally representative surveys of US girls studied 25 years apart. *Pediatrics, 111,* 844–850.

Anderson, V., Simpson-Taylor, D., & Herrmann, D. J. (2004). Gender, age, and rape-supportive rules. *Sex Roles, 50,* 77–90.

Anderson, W. (2001, Spring). International news: Pakistani women victims of abuse. *International Psychology Reporter,* pp. 9–18.

Andreasen, N. C., & Black, D. W. (2001). *Introductory textbook of psychiatry* (3rd ed.). Washington, DC: American Psychiatric Publishing.

Ang, I. (2001). I'm a feminist but . . . "Other" women and postnational feminism. In K. Bhavnani (Ed.), *Feminism and "race"* (pp. 394–409). Oxford, England: Oxford University Press.

Anthis, K. S. (2002). The role of sexist discrimination in adult women's identity development. *Sex Roles, 47,* 477–484.

Antill, J. K., Goodnow, J. J., Russell, G., & Cotton, S. (1996). The influence of parents and family context on children's involvement in household tasks. *Sex Roles, 34,* 215–236.

Antonucci, T. C., Akiyama, H., & Merline, A. (2001). Dynamics of social relationships in midlife. In M. E. Lachman (Ed.), *Handbook of midlife development* (pp. 571–598). New York: Wiley.

Aponte, J. F. (2004). The role of culture in the treatment of culturally diverse populations. In U. P. Gielen, J. M. Fish, & J. G. Draguns (Eds.), *Handbook of culture, therapy, and healing* (pp. 103–120). Mahwah, NJ: Erlbaum.

Apparala, M. L., Reifman, A., & Munsch, J. (2003). Cross-national comparison of attitudes toward fathers' and mothers' participation in household tasks and childcare. *Sex Roles, 48,* 189–203.

Arbuckle, J., & Williams, B. D. (2003). Students' perceptions of expressiveness: Age and gender effects on teacher evaluations. *Sex Roles, 49,* 507–516.

Archer, J. (2004). Sex differences in aggression in real–world settings: A meta-analytic review. *Review of General Psychology, 8,* 291–322.

Archer, J., & Coyne, S. M. (2005). An integrated review of indirect, relational, and social aggression. *Personality and Social Psychology Review, 9,* 212–230.

Archer, J., & Lloyd, B. (2002). *Sex and gender* (2nd ed.). New York: Cambridge University Press.

Arias, E., MacDorman, M. F., Strobino, D. M., & Guyer, B. (2003). Annual summary of vital statistics—2002. *Pediatrics, 112,* 1215–1230.

Aries, E. (1996). *Men and women in interaction: Reconsidering the differences.* New York: Oxford University Press.

Aries, E. (1998). Gender differences in interaction. In D. J. Canary & K. Dindia (Eds.), *Sex differences and similarities in communication* (pp. 65–81). Mahwah, NJ: Erlbaum.

Arima, A. N. (2003). Gender stereotypes in Japanese television advertisements. *Sex Roles, 49,* 81–90.

Armstrong, M. J. (2001). Ethnic minority women as they age. In J. D. Garner & S. O. Mercer (Eds.), *Women as they age* (2nd ed., pp. 97–111). New York: Haworth.

Arnett, J. L., Nicholson, I. R., & Breault, L. (2004). Psychology's role in health in Canada: Reactions to Romanow and Marchildon. *Canadian Psychology/Psychologie canadienne, 45,* 228–232.

Arnold, K. D., Noble, K. D., & Subotnik, R. F. (1996). Perspectives on female talent development. In K. D. Arnold, K. D. Noble, & R. F. Subotnik (Eds.), *Remarkable women: Perspectives on female talent development* (pp. 1–19). Cresskill, NJ: Hampton Press.

Arredondo, P. (2004). Psychotherapy with Chicanas. In R. J. Valásquez, L. M. Arellano, & B. W. McNeill (Eds.), *The handbook of Chicana/o psychology and mental health* (pp. 231–250). Mahwah, NJ: Erlbaum.

Asch, A. (2004). Critical race theory, feminism, and disability. In B. G. Smith & B. Hutchison (Eds.), *Gendering disability* (pp. 9–44). New Brunswick, NJ: Rutgers University Press.

Asch, A., & Fine, M. (1992). Beyond pedestals: Revisiting the lives of women with disabilities. In M. Fine (Ed.), *Disruptive voices: The possibilities of feminist research* (pp. 139–171). Ann Arbor: University of Michigan Press.

Asch, A., & McCarthy, H. (2003). Infusing disability issues into the psychology curriculum. In P. Bronstein & K. Quina (Eds.), *Teaching gender and multicultural awareness* (2nd ed., pp. 253–269). Washington, DC: American Psychological Association.

Asch, A., Perkins, T. S., Fine, M., & Rousso, H. (2001). Disabilities and women: Deconstructing myths and reconstructing realities. In J. Worell (Ed.), *Encyclopedia of women and gender* (pp. 345–354). San Diego: Academic Press.

Asch-Goodkin, J. (1994, April). Women in pediatrics. *Contemporary Pediatrics,* pp. 54–67.

Ashkinaze, C. (2005, Summer). A matter of opinion. *Ms. Magazine,* p. 17.

Astin, H. S., & Lindholm, J. A. (2001). Academic aspirations and degree attainment of women. In J. Worell (Ed.), *Encyclopedia of women and gender* (pp. 15–27). San Diego: Academic Press.

Athenstaedt, U., Haas, E., & Schwab, S. (2004). Gender role self-concept and gender-typed communication behavior in mixed-sex and same-sex dyads. *Sex Roles, 50,* 37–52.

Atwater, L. E., Carey, J. A., & Waldman, D. A. (2001). Gender and discipline in the workplace: Wait until your father gets home. *Journal of Management, 27,* 537–561.

Atwater, L. E., et al. (2004). Men's and women's perceptions of the gender typing of management subroles. *Sex Roles, 50,* 191–199.

Aubeeluck, A., & Maguire, M. (2002). The Menstrual Joy Questionnaire items alone can positively prime reporting of menstrual attitudes and symptoms. *Psychology of Women Quarterly, 26,* 160–162.

Aubrey, J. S. (2004). Sex and punishment: An examination of sexual consequences and the sexual double standard in teen programming. *Sex Roles, 50,* 505–514.

Auster, C. J., & Ohm, S. C. (2000). Masculinity and femininity in contemporary American society: A reevaluation using the Bem Sex-Role Inventory. *Sex Roles, 43,* 499–528.

AVERT. (2005, July 26). *Canada HIV & AIDS statistics summary.* Retrieved September 4, 2005 from http:www.avert.org/canstatg.htm

Avis, N. E. (2003). Depression during the menopausal transition. *Psychology of Women Quarterly, 27,* 91–100.

Avis, N. E., et al. (2004). Quality of life in diverse groups of midlife women: Assessing the influence of menopause, health status and psychosocial and demographic factors. *Quality of Life Research, 13,* 933–946.

Baber, K. M. (2000). Women's sexualities. In M. Biaggio & M. Hersen (Eds.), *Issues in the psychology of women* (pp. 145–171). New York: Kluwer Academic/Plenum.

Baca Zinn, M., & Dill, B. T. (2005). Theorizing difference from multiracial feminism. In M. Baca Zinn, P. Hondagneu-Sotelo, & M. A. Messner (Eds.), *Gender through the prism of difference* (3rd ed., pp. 19–25). New York: Oxford University Press.

Baca Zinn, M., & Eitzen, D. S. (2002). *Diversity in families* (6th ed.). Boston: Allyn & Bacon.

Baca Zinn, M., Hondagneu-Sotelo, P., & Messner, M. A. (2001). Gender through the prism of difference. In M. L. Anderson & P. H. Collins (Eds.), *Race, class, and gender* (4th ed., pp. 168–176). Belmont, CA: Wadsworth.

Baca Zinn, M., Hondagneu-Sotelo, P., & Messner, M. A. (Eds.). (2005).

Gender through the prism of difference (3rd ed.). New York: Oxford University Press.

Baca Zinn, M., & Wells, B. (2000). Diversity within Latino families: New lessons for family social science. In D. H. Demo, K. R. Allen, & M. A. Fine (Eds.), *Handbook of family diversity* (pp. 252–273). New York: Oxford University Press.

Bachand, L. L., & Caron, S. L. (2001). Ties that bind: A qualitative study of happy long-term marriages. *Contemporary Family Therapy, 23,* 105–121.

Bachar, K., & Koss, M. (2001). Rape. In J. Worell (Ed.), *Encyclopedia of women and gender* (pp. 893–903). San Diego: Academic Press.

Backus, V. P. (2002). Psychiatric aspects of breast cancer. *Harvard Review of Psychiatry, 10,* 307–314.

Baer, J. (1999). Gender differences. In M. A. Runco & S. R. Pritzker (Eds.), *Encyclopedia of creativity* (Vol. 1, pp. 753–758). San Diego: Academic Press.

Bahr, K. S. (1994). The strengths of Apache grandmothers: Observations on commitment, culture, and caretaking. *Journal of Comparative Family Studies, 25,* 233–248.

Bailey, D. S. (2004, February). Number of psychology PhDs declining. *Monitor on Psychology,* pp. 18–19.

Bailey, J. M., Dunne, M. P., & Martin, N. G. (2000). Genetic and environmental influences on sexual orientation and its correlates in an Australian twin sample. *Journal of Personality and Social Psychology, 78,* 524–536.

Bailey, J. M., Pillard, R. C., Neale, M. C., & Agyei, Y. (1993). Heritable factors influence sexual orientation in women. *Archives of General Psychiatry, 50,* 217–223.

Bains, A. (1998, February). Thirty-eight cents a shirt. *Toronto Life,* pp. 41–50.

Baird-Windle, P., & Bader, E. J. (2001). *Targets of hatred: Anti-abortion terrorism.* New York: Palgrave.

Baker, C. N. (2005). Images of women's sexuality in advertisements: A content analysis of

Black- and White-oriented women's and men's magazines. *Sex Roles, 52,* 13–27.

Baker, N. L. (2006). Feminist psychology in the service of women: Staying engaged without getting married. *Psychology of Women Quarterly, 30,* 1–14.

Baker, T. B., Brandon, T. H., & Chassin, L. (2004). Motivational influences on cigarette smoking. *Annual Review of Psychology, 55,* 463–491.

Baldwin, J., & DeSouza, E. (2001). *Modelo de María* and machismo: The social construction of gender in Brazil. *Revisto Interamericana de Psicología/Interamerican Journal of Psychology, 35,* 9–29.

Ballou, M., & Brown, L. S. (Eds.). (2002). *Rethinking mental health and disorder: Feminist perspectives.* New York: Guilford.

Bancroft, J., Loftus, J., & Long, J. S. (2003). Distress about sex: A national survey of women in heterosexual relationships. *Archives of Sexual Behavior, 32,* 193–208.

Bandura, A., & Bussey, K. (2004). On broadening the cognitive, motivational, and sociostructural scope of theorizing about gender development and functioning. *Psychological Bulletin, 130,* 691–701.

Banerji, S. (2006, May 4). Manning the ship. *Diverse Education,* pp. 27–28.

Banks, C., & Arnold, P. (2001). Opinions towards sexual partners with a large age difference. *Marriage and Family Review, 33,* 5–17.

Banks, M. E., & Kaschak, E. (Eds.). (2003). *Women with visible and invisible disabilities.* New York: Haworth.

Bao, X. (2003). Sweatshops in Sunset Park. In D. E. Bender & R. A. Greenwald (Eds.), *Sweatshop USA: The American sweatshop in historical and global perspective* (pp. 117–139). New York: Routledge.

Baram, D. A. (2005). Physiology and symptoms of menopause. In D. E. Stewart (Ed.), *Menopause: A mental health practitioner's guide* (pp. 15–32). Washington, DC: American Psychiatric Press.

Barbee, A. P., et al. (1993). Effects of gender role expectations on the social support process. *Journal of Social Issues, 49,* 175–190.

Barber, B. L., & Eccles, J. S. (2003). The joy of romance: Healthy adolescent relationships as an educational agenda. In P. Florsheim (Ed.), *Adolescent romantic relations and sexual behavior* (pp. 355–370). Mahwah, NJ: Erlbaum.

Barber, J. S., Axinn, W. G., & Thornton, A. (1999). Unwanted childbearing, health, and mother-child relationships. *Journal of Health and Social Behavior, 40,* 231–257.

Barer, B. M. (2001). The "grands and greats" of very old black grandmothers. *Journal of Aging Studies, 15,* 1–11.

Bargad, A., & Hyde, J. S. (1991). A study of feminist identity development in women. *Psychology of Women Quarterly, 15,* 181–201.

Barker, G., Knaul, F., Cassaniga, N., & Schrader, A. (2000). *Urban girls: Empowerment in especially difficult circumstances.* London: Intermediate Technology Publications.

Barlow, D. H., & Durand, V. M. (2005). *Abnormal psychology* (4th ed.). Belmont, CA: Thomson Wadsworth.

Barnett, O., Miller-Perrin, C. L., & Perrin, R. D. (2005). *Family violence across the lifespan* (2nd ed.). Thousand Oaks, CA: Sage.

Barnett, R. C. (1997). How paradigms shape the stories we tell: Paradigm shifts in gender and health. *Journal of Social Issues, 53,* 351–368.

Barnett, R. C. (2001). Work-family balance. In J. Worell (Ed.), *Encyclopedia of women and gender* (pp. 1181–1190). San Diego: Academic Press.

Barnett, R. C. (2004). Preface: Women and work: Where are we, where did we come from, and where are we going. *Journal of Social Issues, 60,* 667–674.

Barnett, R. C., & Hyde, J. S. (2001). Women, men, work, and family: An expansionist theory. *American Psychologist, 56,* 781–796.

Barnett, R. C., & Rivers, C. (1996). *She works, he works.* San Francisco: Harper.

Barnett, R. C., & Rivers, C. (2004). *Same difference: How gender myths are hurting our relationships, our children, and our jobs.* New York: Basic Books.

Barone, D. F., Maddux, J. E., & Snyder, C. R. (1997). *Social cognitive psychology: History and current domains.* New York: Plenum.

Barstow, A. L. (2001). *War's dirty secret: Rape, prostitution, and other crimes against women.* New York: Women's Ink.

Bartell, R. (2005, Winter). Abstinence-only-until-marriage programs. *Informed Choice,* p. 1.

Bartlett, S. J., et al. (2004). Maternal depressive symptoms and adherence to therapy in inner-city children with asthma. *Pediatrics, 113,* 229–237.

Barton, E. R. (2000). Parallels between mythopoetic men's work/men's peer mutual support group and selected feminist theories. In E. R. Barton (Ed.), *Mythopoetic perspectives of men's healing work* (pp. 3–20). Westport, CT: Bergin & Garvey.

Bartsch, R. A., Burnett, T., Diller, T. R., & Rankin Williams, E. (2000). Gender representation in television commercials: Updating an update. *Sex Roles, 43,* 735–743.

Basow, S. A. (2001). Androcentrism. In J. Worell (Ed.), *Encyclopedia of women and gender* (pp. 125–135). San Diego: Academic Press.

Basow, S. A. (2004). Gender dynamics in the classroom. In J. C. Chrisler, C. Golden, & P. D. Rozee (Eds.), *Lectures on the psychology of women* (3rd ed., pp. 45–55). Boston: McGraw-Hill.

Basow, S. A., & Johnson, K. (2000). Predictors of homophobia in female college students. *Sex Roles, 42,* 391–404.

Basow, S. A., & Rubin, L. R. (1999). Gender influences on adolescent development. In N. G. Johnson, M. C. Roberts, & J. Worell (Eds.), *Beyond appearance: A new look at adolescent girls* (pp. 25–52). Washington, DC: American Psychological Association.

Basson, R. (2006). Sexual desire and arousal disorders in women.

New England Journal of Medicine, 354, 1497–1506.

Bate, B., & Bowker, J. (1997). *Communication and the sexes* (2nd ed.). Prospect Heights, IL: Wavelength Press.

Bates, M. (2005, September 9). Tenured and battered. *Chronicle of Higher Education,* C1, C4.

Bauer, A. M. (2001). "Tell them we're girls": The invisibility of girls with disabilities. In P. O'Reilly, E. M. Penn, & K. deMarrais (Eds.), *Educating young adolescent girls* (pp. 29–45). Mahwah, NJ: Erlbaum.

Bauer, C. C., & Baltes, B. B. (2002). Reducing the effects of gender stereotypes on performance evaluations. *Sex Roles, 47,* 465–476.

Bauer-Maglin, N., & Radosh, A. (2003a). Introduction. In N. Bauer-Maglin & A. Radosh (Eds.), *Women confronting retirement: A nontraditional guide* (pp. 1–30). New Brunswick, NJ: Rutgers University Press.

Bauer-Maglin, N., & Radosh, A. (Eds.). (2003b). *Women confronting retirement: A nontraditional guide.* New Brunswick, NJ: Rutgers University Press.

Baumeister, R. F. (2000). Gender differences in erotic plasticity: The female sex drive as socially flexible and responsive. *Psychological Bulletin, 126,* 347–374.

Baumeister, R. F., Catanese, K. R., & Wallace, H. M. (2002). Conquest by force: A narcissistic reactance theory of rape and sexual coercion. *Review of General Psychology, 6,* 92–135.

Baumeister, R. F., & Twenge, J. M. (2002). Cultural suppression of female sexuality. *Review of General Psychology, 6,* 166–203.

Baumgardner, J., & Richards, A. (2000). *Manifesta: Young women, feminism, and the future.* New York: Farrar, Straus and Giroux.

Bay-Cheng, L. Y., Zucker, A. N., Stewart, A. J., & Pomerleau, C. S. (2002). Linking femininity, weight concern, and mental health among Latina, Black, and White women. *Psychology of Women Quarterly, 26,* 36–45.

Beach, S. (2001, August/September). Census takers. *Ms. Magazine,* p. 30.

Beall, A. E. (1993). A social constructionist view of gender. In A. E. Beall & R. J. Sternberg (Eds.), *The psychology of gender* (2nd ed., pp. 127–147). New York: Guilford.

Beall, A. E., Eagly, A. H., & Sternberg, R. J. (2004). Introduction. In A. H. Eagly, A. E. Beall, & R. J. Sternberg (Eds.), *The psychology of gender* (2nd ed., pp. 1–8). New York: Guilford.

Beals, K. P., Impett, E. A., & Peplau, L. A. (2002). Lesbians in love: Why some relationships endure and others end. *Journal of Lesbian Studies, 6,* 53–64.

Beals, K. P., & Peplau, L. A. (2005). Identity support, identity devaluation, and well-being among lesbians. *Psychology of Women Quarterly, 29,* 140–148.

Beaton, A. M., & Tougas, F. (1997). The representation of women in management: The more, the merrier? *Personality and Social Psychology Bulletin, 23,* 773–782.

Beatty, L. A., Wetherington, C. L., Jones, D. J., & Roman, A. B. (2006). Substance use and abuse by girls and women. In J. Worell & C. D. Goodheart (Eds.), *Handbook of girls' and women's psychological health: Gender and well-being across the life span* (pp. 113–121). New York: Oxford University Press.

Beatty, L. A., Wheeler, D., & Gaiter, J. (2004). HIV prevention research for African Americans: Current and future directions. *Journal of Black Psychology, 30,* 40–58.

Beatty, W. W., & Bruellman, J. A. (1987). Absence of gender differences in memory for map learning. *Bulletin of the Psychonomic Society, 25,* 238–239.

Becker, E., Rankin, E., & Rickel, A. U. (1998). *High-risk sexual behavior: Interventions with vulnerable populations.* New York: Plenum.

Becker, S. W., & Eagly, A. H. (2004). The heroism of women and men. *American Psychologist, 59,* 163–178.

Beckman, L. J. (2006). Women's reproductive health: Issues, findings, and controversies. In J. Worell & C. D. Goodheart (Eds.), *Handbook of girls' and women's psychological health: Gender and well-being across the life span* (pp. 330–338). New York: Oxford University Press.

Beckman, L. J., & Harvey, S. M. (Eds.). (2005). Current reproductive technologies: Psychological, ethical, cultural and political considerations [Special issue]. *Journal of Social Issues, 61*(1).

Beckman, L. J., Harvey, S. M., Satre, S. J., & Walker, M. A. (1999). Cultural beliefs about social influence strategies of Mexican immigrant women and their heterosexual partners. *Sex Roles, 40,* 871–892.

Bedford, V. H. (2003). Men and women in old age: Incorporating aging into psychology of gender courses. In S. K. Whitbourne & J. Cavanaugh (Eds.), *Integrating aging topics into psychology: A practical guide for teaching undergraduates* (pp. 159–172). Washington, DC: American Psychological Association.

Bedford, V. H., & Blieszner, R. (2000). Older adults and their families. In D. H. Demo, K. R. Allen, & M. A. Fine (Eds.), *Handbook of family diversity* (pp. 216–232). New York: Oxford University Press.

Bélanger, A., et al. (2002). Gender differences in disability-free life expectancy for selected risk factors and chronic conditions in Canada. In S. B. Laditka (Ed.), *Health expectations for older women: International perspectives* (pp. 61–83). Binghamton, NY: Haworth.

Belansky, E. S., & Boggiano, A. K. (1994). Predicting helping behaviors: The role of gender and instrumental/expressive self-schemata. *Sex Roles, 30,* 647–661.

Belansky, E. S., Clements, P., & Eccles, J. S. (1992, March). *Adolescence: A crossroads for gender-role transcendence or gender-role intensification.* Paper presented at the Meeting of the Society for Research on Adolescence, Washington, DC.

Bell, A. R. (1990). Separate people: Speaking of Creek men and women. *American Anthropologist, 92,* 332–345.

Bell, L. C. (2004). Psychoanalytic theories of gender. In A. H. Eagly, A. E. Beall, & R. J. Sternberg (Eds.), *The psychology of gender* (2nd ed., pp. 145–168). New York: Guilford.

Bell, N. J., O'Neal, K. K., Feng, D., & Schoenrock, C. J. (1999). Gender and sexual risk. *Sex Roles, 41,* 313–332.

Bellamy, C. (2000). *The state of the world's children 2000.* New York: United Nations Children's Fund.

Belle, D. (2004). Poor women in a wealthy nation. In J. C. Chrisler, C. Golden, & P. D. Rozee (Eds.), *Lectures on the psychology of women* (3rd ed., pp. 28–43). Boston: McGraw-Hill.

Belle, D., & Dodson, L. (2006). Poor women and girls in a wealthy nation. In J. Worell & C. D. Goodheart (Eds.), *Handbook of girls' and women's psychological health: Gender and well-being across the life span* (pp. 122–126). New York: Oxford University Press.

Belle, D., & Doucet, J. (2003). Poverty, inequality, and discrimination as sources of depression among U.S. women. *Psychology of Women Quarterly, 27,* 101–113.

Bellinger, D. C., & Gleason, J. B. (1982). Sex differences in parental directives to young children. *Sex Roles, 8,* 1123–1139.

Bem, S. L. (1974). The measurement of psychological androgyny. *Journal of Consulting and Clinical Psychology, 42,* 155–162.

Bem, S. L. (1977). On the utility of alternative procedures for assessing psychological androgyny. *Journal of Consulting and Clinical Psychology, 45,* 196–205.

Bem, S. L. (1981). Gender schema theory: A cognitive account of sex typing. *Psychological Review, 88,* 354–364.

Bem, S. L. (1983). Gender schema theory and its implications for child development: Raising gender aschematic children in a gender-schematic society. *Signs, 8,* 598–616.

Bem, S. L. (1993). *The lenses of gender: Transforming the debate on sexual inequality.* New Haven, CT: Yale University Press.

Bem, S. L. (1998). *An unconventional family.* New Haven, CT: Yale University Press.

Bem, S. L. (2004). Transforming the debate on sexual inequality. In C. Chrisler, C. Golden, & P. D. Rozee (Eds.), *Lectures on the psychology of women* (3rd ed., pp. 3–15). New York: McGraw-Hill.

Bemak, F., & Chung, E. C., (2004). Culturally oriented psychotherapy with refugees. In U. P. Gielen, J. M. Fish, & J. G. Draguns (Eds.), *Handbook of culture, therapy, and healing* (pp. 121–132). Mahwah, NJ: Erlbaum.

Bender, D. E., & Greenwald, R. A. (2003a). Introduction: Sweatshop USA: The American sweatshop in global and historical perspective. In D. E. Bender & R. A. Greenwald (Eds.), *Sweatshop USA: The American sweatshop in historical and global perspective* (pp. 1–16). New York: Routledge.

Bender, D. E., & Greenwald, R. A. (Eds.). (2003b). *Sweatshop USA: The American sweatshop in historical and global perspective.* New York: Routledge.

Beneke, T. (1997). Men on rape. In M. Baca Zinn, P. Hondagneu-Sotelo, & M. A. Messner (Eds.), *Through the prism of difference: Readings on sex and gender* (pp. 130–135). Boston: Allyn & Bacon.

Benjamin, L. T., Jr., & Shields, S. A. (1990). Foreword. In H. L. Hollingworth, *Leta Stetter Hollingworth: A biography* (pp. ix–xviii). Bolton, MA: Anker Publishing.

Bennett, P. (2004). Psychological interventions in patients with chronic illness. In A. Kaptein & J. Weinman (Eds.), *Health psychology* (pp. 337–357). Malden, MA: Blackwell.

Benokraitis, N. V. (1998). Working in the ivory basement: Subtle sex discrimination in higher education. In L. H. Collins, J. C. Chrisler, & K. Quina (Eds.), *Career strategies for women in academe: Arming Athena* (pp. 3–43). Thousand Oaks, CA: Sage.

Benrud, L. M., & Reddy, D. M. (1998). Differential explanations of illness in women and men. *Sex Roles, 38,* 375–386.

Berenson, C. (2002). What's in a name? Bisexual women define their terms. *Journal of Bisexuality, 2,* 9–21.

Berg, F. M. (1999). Health risks associated with weight loss and obesity treatment programs. *Journal of Social Issues, 55,* 277–297.

Berg, F. M. (2000). *Women afraid to eat: Breaking free in today's weight obsessed world.* Hettinger, ND: Healthy Weight Network.

Berg, J. A., & Lipson, J. G. (1999). Information sources, menopause beliefs, and health complaints of midlife Filipinas. *Health Care for Women International, 20,* 81–92.

Berg, J. H., Stephen, W. G., & Dodson, M. (1981). Attributional modesty in women. *Psychology of Women Quarterly, 5,* 711–727.

Berger, R. (2004). *Immigrant women tell their stories.* New York: Haworth.

Bergevin, T. A., Bukowski, W. M., & Karavasilis, L. (2003). Childhood sexual abuse and pubertal timing: Implications for long-term psychosocial adjustment. In C. Hayward (Ed.), *Gender differences at puberty* (pp. 187–216). New York: Cambridge University Press.

Bergman, B. (2003). The validation of the women workplace culture questionnaire: Gender-related stress and health for Swedish working women. *Sex Roles, 49,* 287–297.

Bergman, B., Ahmad, F., & Stewart, D. E. (2003). Physician health, stress and gender at a university hospital. *Journal of Psychosomatic Research, 54,* 171–178.

Bergman, B., & Hallberg, L. R.-M. (2002). Women in a male-dominated industry: Factor analysis of a women workplace culture questionnaire based on a grounded theory model. *Sex Roles, 46,* 311–322.

Bergmann, B. R. (2003). The economic risks of being a housewife. In E. Mutari & D. M. Figart (Eds.), *Women and the economy* (pp. 101–107). Armonk, NY: M. E. Sharpe.

Bergum, V. (1997). *A child on her mind: The experience of becoming a mother.* Westport, CT: Bergin & Garvey.

Berila, B., et al. (2005). His story/her story: A dialogue about including men and masculinities in the women's studies curriculum. *Feminist Teacher, 16,* 34–52.

Berkman, B. (2004). Celebrating the many roles of women. In L. Flanders (Ed.), *The W effect* (pp. 185–187). New York: Feminist Press.

Berkowitz, C. D. (2005). Recognizing and responding to domestic violence. *Pediatric Annals, 34,* 395–401.

Berman, P. W. (1980). Are women more responsive than men to the young? A review of developmental and situational variables. *Psychological Bulletin, 88,* 668–695.

Bernal, G., Trimble, J. E., Burlew, A. K., & Leong, F. T. L. (Eds.). (2003). *Handbook of racial and ethnic minority psychology.* Thousand Oaks, CA: Sage.

Bernard, M., & Phillipson, C. (2004). Retirement and leisure. In J. F. Nussbaum & J. Coupland (Eds.), *Handbook of communication and aging research* (2nd ed., pp. 353–381). Mahwah, NJ: Erlbaum.

Bersoff, D. N. (2003). *Ethical conflicts in psychology.* Washington, DC: American Psychological Association.

Best, D. L., & Thomas, J. J. (2004). Cultural diversity and cross-cultural perspectives. In A. H. Eagly, A. E. Beall, & R. J. Sternberg (Eds.), *The psychology of gender* (2nd ed., pp. 296–327). New York: Guilford.

Bettencourt, B. A., & Miller, N. (1996). Gender differences in aggression as a function of provocation: A meta-analysis. *Psychological Bulletin, 119,* 422–447.

Betz, N. E. (1994). Basic issues and concepts in career counseling for women. In W. B. Walsh & S. H. Osipow (Eds.), *Career counseling for women* (pp. 1–41). Hillsdale, NJ: Erlbaum.

Betz, N. E. (2006). Women's career development. In J. Worell & C. D. Goodheart (Eds.), *Handbook of girls' and women's psychological health: Gender and well-being across the life span* (pp. 312–320). New York: Oxford University Press.

Beumont, P. J. V. (2002). Clinical presentation of anorexia nervosa and bulimia nervosa. In C. G. Fairburn & K. D. Brownell (Eds.), *Eating disorders and obesity: A comprehensive handbook* (2nd ed., pp. 162–170). New York: Guilford.

Beyer, C. E., et al. (1996). Gender representation in illustrations, text, and topic areas in sexuality education curricula. *Journal of School Health, 66,* 361–364.

Beyer, S. (1998). Gender differences in self-perception and negative recall biases. *Sex Roles, 38,* 103–133.

Beyer, S. (1998/1999). Gender differences in causal attribution by college students of performance on course examinations. *Current Psychology: Developmental, Learning, Personality, Social, 17,* 346–358.

Beyer, S. (1999a). The accuracy of academic gender stereotypes. *Sex Roles, 40,* 787–813.

Beyer, S. (1999b). Gender differences in the accuracy of grade expectancies and evaluation. *Sex Roles, 41,* 279–296.

Beyer, S., & Bowden, E. M. (1997). Gender differences in self-perceptions: Convergent evidence from three measures of accuracy and bias. *Personality and Social Psychology Bulletin, 23,* 157–172.

Biehl, M., et al. (1997). Matsumoto's and Ekman's Japanese and Caucasian Facial Expressions of Emotion (JACFEE): Reliability data and cross-national differences. *Journal of Nonverbal Behavior, 21,* 3–21.

Biernat, M., Crosby, F. J., & Williams, J. C. (Eds.). (2004). The

maternal wall: Research and policy perspectives on discrimination against mothers [Special issue]. *Journal of Social Issues, 60*(4).

Bigler, R. S. (1995). The role of classification skill in moderating environmental influences on children's gender stereotyping: A study of the functional use of gender in the classroom. *Child Development, 66,* 1072–1087.

Bigler, R. S. (1999a). Psychological interventions designed to counter sexism in children: Empirical limitations and theoretical foundations. In W. B. Swann Jr., J. H. Langlois, & L. A. Gilbert (Eds.), *Sexism and stereotypes in modern society* (pp. 129–151). Washington, DC: American Psychological Association.

Bigler, R. S. (1999b). The use of multicultural curricula and materials to counter racism in children. *Journal of Social Issues, 55,* 687–705.

Bilbao, J. A. (2003, June). *Maquilas* are like aspirin: Temporary pain relief but no cure. *Envío,* pp. 11–16.

Binder, R. (2001). Changing a culture: Sexual assault prevention in the fraternity and sorority community. In A. J. Ottens & K. Hotelling (Eds.), *Sexual violence on campus: Policies, programs, and perspectives* (pp. 120–140). New York: Springer.

Birchard, K. (2004, January 9). Canada's billion-dollar controversy. *Chronicle of Higher Education,* pp. A38–A39.

Birchard, K. (2006, January 13). Native suspicion. *Chronicle of Higher Education,* pp. A46–A49.

Bird, C. E. (1999). Gender, household labor, and psychological distress: The impact of the amount and division of housework. *Journal of Health and Social Behavior, 40,* 32–45.

Bird, S. E. (1999). Tales of difference: Representations of American Indian women in popular film and television. In M. Meyers (Ed.), *Mediated women: Representations in popular culture* (pp. 91–109). Cresskill, NJ: Hampton Press.

Birns, B. (1999). Battered wives: Causes, effects, and social change. In C. Forden, A. E. Hunter, & B. Birns (Eds.), *Readings in the psychology of women: Dimensions of the female experience* (pp. 280–288). Boston: Allyn & Bacon.

Black, L., & Jackson, V. (2005). Families of African origin. In M. McGoldrick, J. Giordano, & N. Garcia-Preto (Eds.), *Ethnicity and family therapy* (3rd ed., pp. 77–86). New York: Guilford.

Blair, I. V. (2001). Implicit stereotypes and prejudice. In G. B. Moskowitz (Ed.), *Cognitive social psychology* (pp. 359–374). Mahwah, NJ: Erlbaum.

Blake, D. R., Weber, B. M., & Fletcher, K. E. (2004). Adolescent and young adult women's misunderstanding of the term *Pap smear. Archives of Pediatrics and Adolescent Medicine, 158,* 966–970.

Blakemore, J. E. O. (1998). The influence of gender and parental attitudes on preschool children's interest in babies: Observations in natural settings. *Sex Roles, 38,* 73–94.

Blakemore, J. E. O. (2003). Children's beliefs about violating gender norms: Boys shouldn't look like girls, and girls shouldn't act like boys. *Sex Roles, 48,* 411–419.

Blalock, A. C., & Campos, P. E. (2003). Human immunodeficiency virus and acquired immune deficiency syndrome. In L. M. Cohen, D. E. McChargue, & F. L. Collins, Jr. (Eds.), *The health psychology handbook* (pp. 383–396). Thousand Oaks, CA: Sage.

Blank, R., & Slipp, S. (1994). *Voices of diversity: Real people talk about problems and solutions in a workplace where everyone is not alike.* New York: American Management Association.

Blau, G., & Tatum, D. (2000). Correlates of perceived gender discrimination for female versus male medical technologists. *Sex Roles, 43,* 105–118.

Blayo, C., & Blayo, Y. (2003). The social pressure to abort. In A. M.

Basu (Ed.), *The sociocultural and political aspects of abortion: Global perspectives* (pp. 237–247). Westport, CT: Praeger.

Blazina, C. (2003). *The cultural myth of masculinity.* Westport, CT: Praeger.

Blea, I. (1997). *U.S. Chicanas and Latinas within a global context.* Westport, CT: Praeger.

Blea, I. (2003). *The feminization of racism: Promoting world peace in America.* Westport, CT: Praeger.

Blieszner, R. (1998). *Feminist perspectives on old women's lives and ageism in society.* Paper presented at Virginia Polytechnic Institute, Blacksburg.

Blizzard, R. M. (2002). Intersex issues: A series of continuing conundrums. *Pediatrics, 110,* 616–621.

Blum, L. M. (1999). *At the breast.* Boston: Beacon Press.

Blum, R. W., & Nelson-Mmari, K. (2004). Adolescent health from an international perspective. In R. M. Lerner & L. Steinberg (Eds.), *Handbook of adolescent psychology* (2nd ed., pp. 553–586). Hoboken, NJ: Wiley.

Blume, S. B. (1998, March). Alcoholism in women. *Harvard Mental Health Letter,* pp. 5–7.

Boatswain, S., et al. (2001). Canadian feminist psychology: Where are we now? *Canadian Psychology/Psychologie canadienne, 42,* 276–285.

Bobo, M., Hildreth, B. L., & Durodoye, B. (1998). Changing patterns in career choices among African-American, Hispanic, and Anglo children. *Professional School Counseling, 1,* 37–42.

Bociurkiw, M. (2005, Winter/Spring). It's not about the sex. *Canadian Woman Studies/Les cahiers de la femme,* pp. 15–21.

Bohan, J. S. (1996). *Psychology and sexual orientation: Coming to terms.* New York: Routledge.

Bohan, J. S. (2002). Sex differences and/in the self: Classic themes, feminist variations, postmodern challenges. *Psychology of Women Quarterly, 26,* 74–88.

Bolden, T. (2002). *33 things every girl should know about women's history.* New York: Crown.

Bombardieri, M. (2005, January 17). Summers' remarks on women

draw fire. *The Boston Globe,* pp. A1, B6.

Bonder, G. (2000). Women's studies: Central and South America. In C. Kramarae & D. Spender (Eds.), *Routledge international encyclopedia of women* (Vol. 4, pp. 2081–2084). New York: Routledge.

Bondurant, B., & Donat, P. L. N. (1999). Perceptions of women's sexual interest and acquaintance rape. *Psychology of Women Quarterly, 23,* 691–705.

Bonebright, T. L., Thompson, J. L., & Leger, D. W. (1996). Gender stereotypes in the expression and perception of vocal affect. *Sex Roles, 34,* 429–445.

Bontempo, D. E., & D'Augelli, A. R. (2002). Effects of at-school victimization and sexual orientation on lesbian, gay, or bisexual youths' health risk behavior. *Journal of Adolescent Health, 30,* 364–374.

Boot, T. (1999). Black or African American: What's in a name? In Y. Alaniz & N. Wong (Eds.), *Voices of color* (pp. 69–72). Seattle: Red Letter Press.

Borchelt, G. (2005). Sexual violence against women in war and armed conflict. In A. Barnes (Ed.), *The handbook of women, psychology, and the law* (pp. 293–327). San Francisco: Jossey-Bass.

Bordo, S. (1998, May 1). Sexual harassment is about bullying, not sex. *Chronicle of Higher Education,* p. B6.

Boris, E. (2003, July). Caring for the caretakers. *Women's Review of Books, 20,* p. 21.

Bornstein, R. F. (2001). The impending death of psychoanalysis. *Psychoanalytic Psychology, 18,* 3–20.

Borrayo, E. A. (2004). Where's Maria? A video to increase awareness about breast cancer and mammography screening among low-literacy Latinas. *Preventive Medicine, 39,* 99–110.

Borrayo, E. A., Guarnaccia, C. A., & Mahoney, M. J. (2001). Prediction of breast cancer screening behavior among older women of Mexican descent: Applicability of theoretical models. *Revista Internacional de Psicología Clínica y de la Salud/International Journal of Clinical and Health Psychology, 1,* 73–90.

Borrayo, E. A., & Jenkins, S. R. (2001). Feeling indecent: Breast cancer screening resistance of Mexican-descent women. *Journal of Health Psychology, 6,* 537–550.

Borrayo, E. A., & Jenkins, S. R. (2003). Feeling frugal: Socioeconomic status, acculturation, and cultural health beliefs among women of Mexican descent. *Cultural Diversity and Ethnic Minority Psychology, 9,* 197–206.

Borrayo, E. A., Thomas, J. J., & Lawsin, C. (2004). Cervical cancer screening among Latinas: The importance of referral and participation in parallel cancer screening behaviors. *Women & Health, 39,* 13–29.

Bosacki, S. L., & Moore, C. (2004). Preschoolers' understanding of simple and complex emotions: Links with gender and language. *Sex Roles, 50,* 659–675.

Bosco, A., Longoni, A. M., & Vecchi, T. (2004). Gender effects in spatial orientation: Cognitive profiles and mental strategies. *Applied Cognitive Psychology, 18,* 519–532.

Boston, L. B., Chambers, S., Canetto, S. S., & Slinkard, B. (2001, August). *That kind of woman: Stereotypical representations in computer magazine advertising.* Paper presented at the annual meeting of the American Psychological Association, San Francisco.

Boston Women's Health Book Collective. (2005). *Our bodies, our selves* (4th ed.). New York: Touchstone.

Botta, R. A. (2003). For your health? The relationship between magazine reading and adolescents' body image and eating disturbances. *Sex Roles, 48,* 389–399.

Bourque, P., Pushkar, D., Bonneville, L., & Béland, F. (2005). Contextual effects on life satisfaction of older men and women. *Canadian Journal on Aging/La Revue canadienne du viellissement, 24,* 31–44.

Bowen, D. J., Tomoyasu, N., & Cauce, A. M. (1999). The triple

threat: A discussion of gender, class, and race differences in weight. In L. A. Peplau et al. (Eds.), *Gender, culture, and ethnicity: Current research about women and men* (pp. 291–306). Mountain View, CA: Mayfield.

Bowleg, L. (1999). "When I look at you, I don't see race" and other diverse tales from the introduction to women's studies classroom. In B. S. Winkler & C. DiPalma (Eds.), *Teaching introduction to women's studies: Expectations and strategies* (pp. 111–122). Westport, CT: Bergin & Garvey.

Bowleg, L., Lucas, K. J., & Tschann, J. M. (2004). "The ball was always in his court": An exploratory analysis of relational scripts, sexual scripts, and condom use among African American women. *Psychology of Women Quarterly, 28,* 70–82.

Boyatzis, C. J., & Eades, J. (1999). Gender differences in preschoolers' and kindergartners' artistic production and preference. *Sex Roles, 41,* 627–638.

Brabeck, M. M. (1996). The moral self, values, and circles of belonging. In K. F. Wyche & F. J. Crosby (Eds.), *Women's ethnicities: Journeys through psychology* (pp. 145–165). Boulder, CO: Westview Press.

Brabeck, M. M., & Brabeck, K. M. (2006). Women and relationships. In J. Worell & C. D. Goodheart (Eds.), *Handbook of girls' and women's psychological health: Gender and well-being across the life span* (pp. 208–217). New York: Oxford University Press.

Brabeck, M. M., & Rogers, L. (2000). Human rights as a moral issue: Lessons for moral educators from human rights work. *Journal of Moral Education, 29,* 167–182.

Brabeck, M. M., & Satiani, A. (2001). Feminist ethics and moral psychology. In J. Worell (Ed.), *Encyclopedia of women and gender* (pp. 439–446). San Diego: Academic Press.

Brabeck, M. M., & Shore, E. L. (2002). Gender differences in intellectual and moral develop-

ment? The evidence that refutes the claim. In J. Demick & C. Andreoletti (Eds.), *Handbook of adult development* (pp. 351–368). New York: Plenum.

Brabeck, M. M., & Ting, K. (2000). Feminist ethics: Lenses for examining ethical psychological practice. In M. M. Brabeck (Ed.), *Practicing feminist ethics in psychology* (pp. 17–35). Washington, DC: American Psychological Association.

Bradbury, T., Rogge, R., & Lawrence, E. (2001). Reconsidering the role of conflict in marriage. In A. Booth, A. C. Crouter, & M. Clements (Eds.), *Couples in conflict* (pp. 59–81). Mahwah, NJ: Erlbaum.

Brady, K. L., & Eisler, R. M. (1995). Gender bias in the college classroom: A critical review of the literature and implications for future research. *Journal of Research and Development in Education, 29,* 9–19.

Brady, K. L., & Eisler, R. M. (1999). Sex and gender in the college classroom: A quantitative analysis of faculty-student interactions and perceptions. *Journal of Educational Psychology, 91,* 127–145.

Bragger, J. D., Kutcher, E., Morgan, J., & Firth, P. (2002). The effects of the structured interview on reducing biases against pregnant job applicants. *Sex Roles, 46,* 215–226.

Brain responses vary by sexual orientation, new research shows. (2005, May 10). *Wall Street Journal,* p. D4.

Brainerd, C. J., & Reyna, V. F. (2005). *The science of false memory.* New York: Oxford University Press.

Braithwaite, D. O., & Thompson, T. L. (2000). *Handbook of communication and people with disabilities.* Mahwah, NJ: Erlbaum.

Brannon, L. & Feist, J. (2004). *Health psychology: An introduction to behavior and health* (5th ed.). Belmont, CA: Thomson Wadsworth.

Brant, C. R., Mynatt, C. R., & Doherty, M. E. (1999). Judgments about sexism: A policy capturing approach. *Sex Roles, 41,* 347–374.

Braun, N. (2003, Mid-Winter). The new culture: Today's feminist presses embody activism and critical thinking. *ForeWord Magazine*, pp. 24–27.

Brehm, S. S., Kassin, S., & Fein, S. (2005). *Social psychology* (6th ed.). Boston: Houghton Mifflin.

Brehm, S. S., Miller, R. S., Perlman, D., & Campbell, S. M. (2002). *Intimate relationships* (3rd ed.). Boston: McGraw-Hill.

Brescoll, V., & LaFrance, M. (2004). The correlates and consequences of newspaper reports of research on sex differences. *Psychological Science, 15*, 515–520.

Bretl, D. J., & Cantor, J. (1988). The portrayal of men and women in U.S. television commercials: A recent content analysis and trends over 15 years. *Sex Roles, 18*, 595–609.

Bridge, M. J. (1994). *Arriving on the scene: Women's growing presence in the news.* New York: Women, Men and Media.

Bridges, J. S. (1993). Pink or blue: Gender-stereotypic perceptions of infants as conveyed by birth congratulations cards. *Psychology of Women Quarterly, 17,* 193–205.

Bridges, J. S., & Etaugh, C. (1995). College students' perceptions of mothers: Effects of maternal employment-childrearing pattern and motive for employment. *Sex Roles, 32,* 735–751.

Bridges, J. S., & Etaugh, C. (1996). Black and White college women's maternal employment outcome expectations and their desired timing of maternal employment. *Sex Roles, 35,* 543–562.

Briere, J., & Lanktree, C. (1983). Sex-role related effects of sex bias in language. *Sex Roles, 9,* 625–632.

Briton, N. J., & Hall, J. A. (1995). Beliefs about female and male nonverbal communication. *Sex Roles, 32,* 79–90.

Brockwood, K. J., Hammer, L. B., Neal, M. B., & Colton, C. L. (2001). Effects of accommodations made at home and at work on wives' and husbands' family and job satisfaction. *Journal of Feminist Family Therapy, 13,* 41–64.

Broderick, P. C., & Korteland, C. (2002). Coping style and depression in early adolescence: Relationships to gender, gender roles, and implicit beliefs. *Sex Roles, 46,* 201–213.

Brody, E. M. (2004). *Women in the middle: Their parent-care years* (2nd ed.). New York: Springer.

Brody, L. R. (1999). *Gender, emotion, and the family.* Cambridge, MA: Harvard University Press.

Brody, L. R., & Hall, J. A. (2000). Gender, emotion, and expression. In M. Lewis & J. M. Haviland-Jones (Eds.), *Handbook of emotions* (2nd ed., pp. 338–349). New York: Guilford Press.

Bronstein, P. A. (2006). The family environment: Where gender role socialization begins. In J. Worell & C. D. Goodheart (Eds.), *Handbook of girls' and women's psychological health: Gender and well-being across the life span* (pp. 262–271). New York: Oxford University Press.

Bronstein, P. A., Briones, M., Brooks, T., & Cowan, B. (1996). Gender and family factors as predictors of late adolescent emotional expressiveness and adjustment: A longitudinal study. *Sex Roles, 34,* 739–765.

Bronstein, P. A., & Farnsworth, L. (1998). Gender differences in faculty experiences of interpersonal climate and processes for advancement. *Research in Higher Education, 39,* 557–572.

Brooks, B. L., Mintz, A. R., Dobson, K. S. (2004). Diversity training in Canadian predoctoral clinical psychology internships: A survey of directors of internship training. *Canadian Psychology/ Psychologie canadienne, 45,* 308–312.

Brooks, C. I. (1987). Superiority of women in statistics achievement. *Teaching of Psychology, 14,* 45.

Brooks, G. R. (1997). The centerfold syndrome. In R. F. Levant & G. R. Brooks (Eds.), *Men and sex: New psychological perspectives* (pp. 28–57). New York: Wiley.

Brooks, G. R. (2003). Helping men embrace equality. In L. B. Silverstein & T. J. Goodrich (Eds.), *Feminist family therapy: Empowerment in social context* (pp. 163–176). Washington, DC: American Psychological Association.

Brooks-Gunn, J., Han, W., & Waldfogel, J. (2002). Maternal employment and child cognitive outcomes in the first three years of life: The NICHD Study of Early Child Care. *Child Development, 73,* 1052–1072.

Brown, B. B. (2004). Adolescents' relationships with peers. In R. M. Lerner & L. Steinberg (Eds.), *Handbook of adolescent psychology* (2nd ed., pp. 363–394). Hoboken, NJ: Wiley.

Brown, B. B., Dolcini, M. M., & Leventhal, A. (1997). Transformations in peer relationships at adolescence: Implications for health-related behavior. In J. Schulenberg, J. L. Maggs, & K. Hurrelmann (Eds.), *Health risks and developmental transitions during adolescence* (pp. 161–189). New York: Cambridge University Press.

Brown, D. R., & Gary, L. E. (1985). Social support network differentials among married and nonmarried Black females. *Psychology of Women Quarterly, 9,* 229–241.

Brown, D. R., Keith, V. M., Jackson, J. S., & Gary, L. E. (2003). (Dis)respected and (dis)regarded: Experiences of racism and psychological distress. In D. R. Brown & V. M. Keith (Eds.), *In and out of our right minds: The mental health of African American women* (pp. 85–98). New York: Columbia University Press.

Brown, J. D., Steele, J. R., & Walsh-Childers, K. (Eds.). (2002). *Sexual teens, sexual media: Investigating media's influence on adolescent sexuality.* Mahwah, NJ: Erlbaum.

Brown, J. D., et al. (2006). Sexy media matter: Exposure to sexual content in music, movies, television, and magazines predicts Black and White adolescents' sexual behavior. *Pediatrics, 117,* 1018–1027.

Brown, L. M. (1998). *Raising their voices: The politics of girls' anger.* Cambridge, MA: Harvard University Press.

Brown, L. M., Way, N., & Duff, J. L. (1999). The others in my I: Adolescent girls' friendships and peer relations. In N. G. Johnson, M. C. Roberts, & J. Worell (Eds.), *Beyond appearance: A new look at adolescent girls* (pp. 205–225). Washington, DC: American Psychological Association.

Brown, L. S. (2000). Dangerousness, impotence, silence, and invisibility: Heterosexism in the construction of women's sexuality. In C. B. Travis & J. W. White (Eds.), *Sexuality, society, and feminism* (pp. 273–297). Washington, DC: American Psychological Association.

Brown, L. S. (2004). Memories of childhood abuse: Recovered, discovered, and otherwise. In B. J. Cling (Ed.), *Sexualized violence against women and children* (pp. 188–211). New York: Guilford.

Brown, N. M., & Amatea, E. S. (2000). *Love and intimate relationships: Journeys of the heart*. Philadelphia: Brunner/Mazel.

Brown, S. S., & Eisenberg, L. (1995). *The best intentions: Unintended pregnancy and the well-being of children and families*. Washington, DC: National Academy Press.

Browne, B. A. (1997). Gender and beliefs about work force discrimination in the United States and Australia. *Journal of Social Psychology, 137*, 107–116.

Brownell, K. D. (2005). Introduction. In K. D. Brownell, R. M. Puhl, M. B. Schwartz, & L. Rudd (Eds.), *Weight bias: Nature, consequences, and remedies* (pp. 1–11). New York: Guilford.

Brownhill, L. S., & Turner, T. E. (2003, Fall/Winter). Mau Mau women rise again: The reassertion of commoning in twenty-first century Kenya. *Canadian Woman Studies/Les cahiers de la femme, 23*, 168–176.

Brownlow, S., Jacobi, T., & Rogers, M. (2000). Science anxiety as a function of gender and experience. *Sex Roles, 42*, 119–131.

Brownlow, S., McPheron, T. K., & Acks, C. N. (2003). Science background and spatial abilities in men and women. *Journal of Science Education and Technology, 12*, 371–380.

Brownlow, S., & Miderski, C. A. (2002). How gender and college chemistry experience influence mental rotation ability. *Themes in Education, 3*, 133–140.

Brownlow, S., Rosamond, J. A., & Parker, J. A. (2003). Gender-linked linguistic behavior in television interviews. *Sex Roles, 49*, 121–132.

Brownlow, S., Smith, T. J., & Ellis, B. R. (2002). How interest in science negatively influences perceptions of women. *Journal of Science Education and Technology, 11*, 135–144.

Brownlow, S., Whitener, R., & Rupert, J. M. (1998). "I'll take gender differences for $1000!": Domain-specific intellectual success on "Jeopardy." *Sex Roles, 38*, 269–285.

Brueggemann, B. J. (2002). An enabling pedagogy. In S. L. Snyder, B. J. Brueggemann, & R. Garland-Thomson (Eds.), *Disability studies: Enabling the humanities* (pp. 317–336). New York: Modern Language Association of America.

Brush, L. D. (1998). Gender, work, who cares?! Production, reproduction, industrialization, and business as usual. In M. M. Ferree, J. Lorber, & B. B. Hess (Eds.), *Revisioning gender* (pp. 161–189). Thousand Oaks, CA: Sage.

Bryant, A. N. (2003). Changes in attitudes toward women's roles: Predicting gender-role traditionalism among college students. *Sex Roles, 48*, 131–142.

Bub, K. L., & McCartney, K. (2004). On childcare as a support for maternal employment wages and hours. *Journal of Social Issues, 60*, 819–824.

Bucy, E. P., & Newhagen, J. E. (Eds.). (2004). *Media access: Social and psychological dimensions of new technology use*. Mahwah, NJ: Erlbaum.

Buhle, J. (2000). Introduction. In F. Howe (Ed.), *Testimony from thirty founding mothers* (pp. xv–xxvi). New York: Feminist Press.

Bullock, H. E., Wyche, K. F., & Williams, W. R. (2001). Media images of the poor. *Journal of Social Issues, 57*, 229–246.

Bureau of Labor Statistics. (2004a). *Highlights of women's earnings in 2003*. Washington, DC: U.S. Department of Labor.

Bureau of Labor Statistics. (2004b, September 14). *Time use survey*. Retrieved May 3, 2005, from http:www.bls.gov/tus/

Bureau of Labor Statistics. (2004c). *Women in the labor force: A databook*. Washington, DC: U.S. Department of Labor.

Burgess, E. O. (2004). Sexuality in midlife and later life couples. In J. H. Harvey, A. Wenzel, & S. Sprecher (Eds.), *The handbook of sexuality in close relationships* (pp. 437–454). Mahwah, NJ: Erlbaum.

Burk, M. (2004, July 12). Wal-Mart's woman troubles. *Liberal Opinion Week*, p. 24.

Burk, M. (2005, Summer). Power plays: Six ways the male corporate elite keeps women out. *Ms. Magazine*, pp. 61–63.

Burke, R. J. (1999). Workaholism in organizations: Gender differences. *Sex Roles, 41*, 333–345.

Burlingame-Lee, L. J., & Canetto, S. S. (2005). Narratives of gender in computer advertisements. In E. Cole & J. Henderson Daniel (Eds.), *Media, women, and girls: Implications for feminist psychology* (pp. 85–99). Washington, DC: American Psychological Association.

Burn, S. M. (1996). *The social psychology of gender*. New York: McGraw-Hill.

Burn, S. M., Aboud, R., & Moyles, C. (2000). The relationship between gender, social identity, and support for feminism. *Sex Roles, 42*, 1081–1089.

Burn, S. M., & Ward, Z. A. (2005). Men's conformity to traditional masculinity and relationship satisfaction. *Psychology of Men and Masculinity, 6*, 254–263.

Burns, L. H. (2001). Gynecologic oncology. In N. L. Stotland & D. E. Stewart (Eds.), *Psychological aspects of women's health care* (pp. 307–329). Washington, DC: American Psychiatric Press.

Bursik, K. (1991a). Adaptation to divorce and ego development in adult women. *Journal of Personality and Social Psychology, 60,* 300–306.

Bursik, K. (1991b). Correlations of women's adjustment during the separation and divorce process. *Journal of Divorce and Remarriage, 14,* 137–162.

Bursik, K. (2000, August). *Gender, gender role, and ego level: Individual differences in feminism.* Paper presented at the annual convention of the American Psychological Association, Washington, DC.

Buss, D. M. (1995). Psychological sex differences: Origins through sexual selection. *American Psychologist, 50,* 164–168.

Buss, D. M. (1998). The psychology of human mate selection: Exploring the complexity of the strategic repertoire. In C. Crawford & D. L. Krebs (Eds.), *Handbook of evolutionary psychology: Ideas, issues, and applications* (pp. 405–429). Mahwah, NJ: Erlbaum.

Buss, D. M. (2000). *The dangerous passion: Why jealousy is as necessary as love and sex.* New York: Free Press.

Bussey, K., & Bandura, A. (1999). Social cognitive theory of gender development and differentiation. *Psychological Review, 106,* 676–713.

Bussey, K., & Bandura, A. (2004). Social cognitive theory of gender development and functioning. In A. H. Eagly, A. E. Beall, & R. J. Sternberg (Eds.). *The psychology of gender* (2nd ed., pp. 92–120). New York: Guilford.

Butler, A. (2002). *The state of older women in America.* Washington, DC: Older Women's League.

Buttner, E. H., & McEnally, M. (1996). The interactive effect of influence tactic, applicant gender, and type of job on hiring recommendations. *Sex Roles, 34,* 581–591.

Byers, E. S., & Demmons, S. (1999). Sexual satisfaction and sexual self-disclosure within dating relationships. *Journal of Sex Research, 36,* 180–189.

Bylsma, W. H., & Major, B. (1992). Two routes to eliminating gender differences in personal entitlement: Social comparisons and performance evaluations. *Psychology of Women Quarterly, 16,* 193–200.

Byrne, A., & Carr, D. (2005). Caught in the cultural lag: The stigma of singlehood. *Psychological Inquiry, 16,* 84–141.

Byrnes, J. P. (2004). Gender differences in math: Cognitive processes in an expanded framework. In A. M. Gallagher & J. C. Kaufman (Eds.), *Gender differences in mathematics: An integrative psychological approach* (pp. 73–98). New York: Cambridge University Press.

By the numbers. (2006, January 12). *Diverse Education,* p. 36.

Bytheway, B. (2005). Ageism and age categorization. *Journal of Social Issues, 61,* 361–374.

Cachelin, F. M., Veisel, C., Barzegarnazari, E., & Striegel-Moore, R. H. (2000). Disordered eating, acculturation, and treatment-seeking in a community sample of Hispanic, Asian, Black, and White women. *Psychology of Women Quarterly, 24,* 244–253.

Cadinu, M., Maass, A., Rosabianca, A., & Kiesner, J. (2005). Why do women underperform under stereotype threat? Evidence for the role of negative thinking. *Psychological Science, 16,* 572–578.

Cahan, S., & Ganor, Y. (1995). Cognitive gender differences among Israeli children. *Sex Roles, 32,* 469–484.

Calasanti, T. M., & Slevin, K. F. (2001). *Gender, social inequalities, and aging.* Walnut Creek, CA: AltaMira Press.

Caldera, Y. M., & Sciaraffa, M. A. (1998). Parent-toddler play with feminine toys: Are all dolls the same? *Sex Roles, 39,* 657–668.

Caldwell, J. C., & Caldwell, P. (2003). Introduction: Induced abortion in a changing world. In A. M. Basu (Ed.), *The sociocultural and political aspects of abortion: Global perspectives* (pp. 1–13). Westport, CT: Praeger.

Callan, J. E. (2001). Gender development: Psychoanalytic perspectives. In J. Worell (Ed.), *Encyclopedia of women and gender* (pp. 523–536). San Diego: Academic Press.

Callen, J., & Pinelli, J. (2004). Incidence and duration of breast-feeding for term infants in Canada, United States, Europe, and Australia: A literature review. *Birth, 31,* 285–292.

Calogero, R. M., Davis, W. N., & Thompson, J. K. (2005). The role of self-objectification in the experience of women with eating disorders. *Sex Roles, 52,* 43–50.

Cameron, D., McAlinden, F., & O'Leary, K. (1993). Lakoff in context: The social and linguistic functions of tag questions. In S. Jackson (Ed.), *Women's studies: Essential readings* (pp. 421–426). New York: New York University Press.

Cameron, L. D., & Ross-Morris, R. (2004). Illness-related cognition and behaviour. In A. Kaptein & J. Weinman (Eds.), *Health psychology* (pp. 84–110). Malden, MA: Blackwell.

Campbell, A. (2002). *A mind of her own: The evolutionary psychology of women.* New York: Oxford University Press.

Campbell, C. R., & Henry, J. W. (1999). Gender differences in self-attributions: Relationship of gender to attributional consistency, style, and expectations for performance in a college course. *Sex Roles, 41,* 95–104.

Campbell, R., & Raja, S. (2005). The sexual assault and secondary victimization of female veterans: Help-seeking experiences with military and civilian social systems. *Psychology of Women Quarterly, 29,* 97–106.

Campenni, C. E. (1999). Gender stereotyping of children's toys: A comparison of parents and non-parents. *Sex Roles, 40,* 121–138.

Canadian Cancer Society. (2005a). *Breast cancer stats.* Retrieved September 13, 2005 from http://www.cancer.ca/ccs/internet/standard/0,3182,3172_14435__langId-en,00.html

Canadian Cancer Society (2005b). *Tobacco statistics in Canada.* Retrieved October 1, http://www.cancer.ca/ccs/internet/standard/0,3182,3172_13163_langId-en,00.html

Canadian Institute for Health Information. (2004, September). *Giving birth in Canada: A regional profile.* Retrieved October 26, 2004 from http://www.cihi.ca

Canetto, S. S. (2001a). Older adult women: Issues, resources, and challenges. In R. K. Unger (Ed.), *Handbook of the psychology of women and gender* (pp. 183–197). New York: Wiley.

Canetto, S. S. (2001b). Suicidal behavior in girls. In M. Forman-Brunell (Ed.), *Girlhood in America: An encyclopedia* (pp. 616–621). Santa Barbara, CA: ABC-CLIO.

Canetto, S. S. (2003). Older adulthood. In L. Slater, J. H. Daniel, & A. E. Banks (Eds.), *The complete guide to mental health for women* (pp. 56–64). Boston: Beacon Press.

Canetto, S. S., Timpson, W. M., Borrayo, E. A., & Yang, R. K. (2003). Teaching about human diversity: Lessons learned and recommendations. In W. M. Timpson, S. S. Canetto, E. A. Borrayo, & R. Yang (Eds.), *Teaching diversity: Challenges and complexities, identities and integrity* (pp. 189–205). Madison, WI: Atwood.

Cann, A. (1993). Evaluative expectations and the gender schema: Is failed inconsistency better? *Sex Roles, 28,* 667–678.

Canterbury, R. J. (2002). Alcohol and other substance abuse. In S. C. Kornstein & A. H. Clayton (Eds.), *Women's mental health* (pp. 222–243). New York: Guilford.

Caplan, J. B., & Caplan, P. J. (2004). The perseverative search for sex differences in mathematics ability. In A. M. Gallagher & J. C. Kaufman (Eds.), *Gender differences in mathematics: An integrative psychological approach* (pp. 25–47). New York: Cambridge University Press.

Caplan, P. J. (1998). Mother-blaming. In M. Ladd Taylor & L. Umansky (Eds.), *"Bad" mothers: The politics of blame in twentieth-century America* (pp. 127–144). New York: New York University Press.

Caplan, P. J. (2000). *The new don't blame mother: Mending the mother-daughter relationship.* New York: Routledge.

Caplan, P. J. (2001). Motherhood: Its changing face. In J. Worell (Ed.), *Encyclopedia of women and gender* (pp. 783–794). San Diego: Academic Press.

Caplan, P. J. (2004). The debate about PMDD and Serafem: Suggestions for therapists. *Women and Therapy, 55,* 55–67.

Caplan, P. J., & Caplan, J. B. (1999). *Thinking critically about research on sex and gender* (2nd ed.). New York: Longman.

Caplan, P. J., & Cosgrove, L. (Eds.). (2004a). *Bias in psychiatric diagnosis.* Lanham, MD: Jason Aronson.

Caplan, P. J., & Cosgrove, L. (2004b). Is this really necessary? In P. J. Caplan & L. Cosgrove (Eds.), *Bias in psychiatric diagnosis* (pp. xix–xxxiii). Lanham, MD: Jason Aronson.

Carli, L. L. (1990). Gender, language, and influence. *Journal of Personality and Social Psychology, 59,* 941–951.

Carli, L. L. (1999). Gender, interpersonal power, and social influence. *Journal of Social Issues, 55,* 81–99.

Carli, L. L. (2001). Gender and social influence. *Journal of Social Issues, 57,* 725–741.

Carli, L. L., & Bukatko, D. (2000). Gender, communication and social influence: A developmental perspective. In T. Eckes & H. M. Trautner (Eds.), *The developmental social psychology of gender* (pp. 295–331). Mahwah, NJ: Erlbaum.

Carli, L. L., & Eagly, A. H. (2002). Gender effects on social influence and emergent leadership. In G. N. Powell (Ed.), *Handbook of gender and work* (3rd ed., pp. 203–222). Thousand Oaks, CA: Sage.

Carli, L. L., LaFleur, S. J., & Loeber, C. C. (1995). Nonverbal behavior, gender, and influence. *Journal of Personality and Social Psychology, 68,* 1030–1041.

Carlo, G., Raffaeli, M., Laible, D. J., & Meyer, K. A. (1999). Why are girls less physically aggressive than boys? Personality and parenting mediators of physical aggression. *Sex Roles, 40,* 711–729.

Carmichael, M. (2004, January 26). No girls please. *Newsweek,* p. 50.

Carothers, B. J., & Allen, J. B. (1999). Relationships of employment status, gender role, insult, and gender with use of influence tactics. *Sex Roles, 41,* 375–387.

Carpenter, L. M. (1998). From girls into women: Scripts for sexuality and romance in *Seventeen* magazine. *Journal of Sex Research, 35,* 158–168.

Carr, D., & Ha, J. (2006). Bereavement. In J. Worell & C. D. Goodheart (Eds.), *Handbook of girls' and women's psychological health: Gender and well-being across the life span* (pp. 397–405). New York: Oxford University Press.

Carroll, J. L. (2005). *Sexuality now: Embracing diversity.* Belmont, CA: Wadsworth.

Carver, P. R., Yunger, J. L., & Perry, D. G. (2003). Gender identity and adjustment in middle childhood. *Sex Roles, 49,* 95–109.

Casey, T. (1998). *Pride and joy: The lives and passions of women without children.* Hillsboro, OR: Beyond Words Publishing.

Cassell, J., & Jenkins, H. (Eds.). (1998). *From Barbie to Mortal Kombat: Gender and computer games.* Cambridge, MA: MIT Press.

Castañeda, D. (2000a). The close relationship context and HIV/AIDS risk reduction among Mexican Americans. *Sex Roles, 42,* 551–580.

Castañeda, D. (2000b). Gender issues among Latinas. In J. C. Chrisler, C. Golden, & P. D. Rozee (Eds.), *Lectures on the psychology of women* (2nd ed., pp. 192–207). Boston: McGraw-Hill.

Castañeda, D. (2004). Gender issues among Latinas. In J. C. Chrisler, C. Golden, & P. D. Rozee (Eds.), *Lectures on the psychology of women* (3rd ed., pp. 202–218). New York: McGraw-Hill.

Castañeda, D., & Burns-Glover, A. (2004). Gender, sexuality, and intimate relationships. In M. A. Paludi (Ed.), *Praeger guide to the psychology of gender* (pp. 69–90). Westport, CT: Praeger.

Castañeda, D. M., & Collins, B. E. (1998). The effects of gender, ethnicity, and a close relationship theme on perceptions of persons introducing a condom. *Sex Roles, 39,* 369–390.

Ceballo, R. (1999). "The only Black woman walking the face of the earth who cannot have a baby?" In M. Romero & A. Stewart (Eds.), *Women's untold stories: Outside the master narrative.* New York: Routledge.

Ceballo, R., Lansford, J. E., Abbey, A., & Stewart, A. J. (2004). Gaining a child: Comparing the experiences of biological parents, adoptive parents, and stepparents. *Family Relations, 53,* 38–48.

Centers for Disease Control. (2002, September 23). *HIV/AIDS Surveillance Report 13.* Retrieved January 8, 2003, from http://www.cdc.gov/hiv/stats/hasrlink.htm

Centers for Disease Control. (2004a). Surveillance summaries, May 21, 2004. *Morbidity and Mortality Weekly Report, 53* (No. SS-2).

Centers for Disease Control. (2004b). *Women and tobacco fact sheet.* Retrieved October 1, 2005 from http://www.cdc.gov/tobacco/factsheets/WomenTobacco_Factsheet.htm

Centers for Disease Control and Prevention. (2005). *HIV/AIDS Surveillance Report 17.* Rockville, MD: Author.

Cervantes, J. M., & Sweatt, L. I. (2004). Family therapy with Chicana/os. In R. J. Velásquez, L. M. Arellano, & B. W. McNeill (Eds.), *The handbook of Chicana/o psychology and mental health* (pp. 285–322). Mahwah, NJ: Erlbaum.

Challenging cases: Family. Benefits of a doula present at the birth of a child. (2004). *Pediatrics, 114,* 1488–1491.

Chalmers, B. (2002). How often must we ask for sensitive care before

we get it? (2002). *Birth, 29,* 79–82.

Chambers, P. (2000). Widowhood in later life. In M. Bernard, J. Phillips, L. Machin, & V. H. Davies (Eds.), *Women ageing: Changing identities, challenging myths* (pp. 127–147). London: Routledge.

Chambers, W. (2005). *Educating MENA: The benefits of female education and how it can be improved in the Middle East.* Unpublished paper, University of Georgia, Athens, GA.

Chan, C. S. (1997). Don't ask, don't tell, don't know: The formation of a homosexual identity and sexual expression among Asian American lesbians. In B. Greene (Ed.), *Ethnic and cultural diversity among lesbians and gay men* (pp. 240–248). Thousand Oaks, CA: Sage.

Chan, C. S. (2003). Psychological issues of Asian Americans. In P. Bronstein & K. Quina (Eds.), *Teaching gender and multicultural awareness* (pp. 179–193). Washington, DC: American Psychological Association.

Chan, C. S. (2004). Asian American women and adolescent girls: Sexuality and sexual expression. In J. C. Chrisler, C. Golden, & P. D. Rozee (Eds.), *Lectures on the psychology of women* (3rd ed., pp. 158–169). New York: McGraw-Hill.

Chance, C., & Fiese, B. H. (1999). Gender-stereotyped lessons about emotion in family narratives. *Narrative Inquiry, 9,* 243–255.

Chand, A. E. (2002). *The influence of national culture on self-objectification and body shame.* Unpublished master's thesis, New School University, New York.

Chang, C., & Hitchon, J. C. B. (2004). When does gender count? Further insights into gender schematic processing of female candidates' political advertisements. *Sex Roles, 51,* 197–208.

Charles, S. T., & Carstensen, L. L. (2002). Marriage in old age. In M. Yalom & L. L. Carstensen (Eds.), *Inside the American couple* (pp. 236–254). Berkeley: University of California Press.

Charles, S. T., & Pasupathi, M. (2003). Age-related patterns of variability in self-descriptions: Implications for everyday affect experience. *Psychology and Aging, 18,* 524–536.

Chase, C., & Hegarty, P. (2000). Intersex activism, feminism and psychology: Opening a dialogue on theory, research and clinical practice. *Feminism & Psychology, 10,* 117–132.

Chatterjee, C. (2004, July 6). *Senate votes to confirm controversial judicial nominee.* Retrieved August 2, 2004, from http://www.truthout.org/docs

Chesler, P. (1976). *Women, money, and power.* New York: Bantam Books.

Chesler, P. (2006, February 24). The failure of feminism. *Chronicle of Higher Education,* p. B12.

Cheung, A. M. (2005). Medical aspects of perimenopause and menopause. In D. E. Stewart (Ed.), *Menopause: A mental health practitioner's guide* (pp. 105–142.). Washington, DC: American Psychiatric Press.

Chew, L. (2005, April). Breaking the wave of silence: How women are regrouping in the aftermath of the tsunami. *Raising Our Voices,* pp. 1–11.

Chin, J. L. (2004). 2003 Division 35 Presidential address: Feminist leadership: Feminist visions and diverse voices. *Psychology of Women Quarterly, 28,* 1–8.

Chinn, S. E. (2004). Feeling her way: Audre Lorde and the power of touch. In B. G. Smith & B. Hutchison (Eds.), *Gendering disability* (pp. 192–215). New Brunswick, NJ: Rutgers University Press.

Chipman, S. F. (2004). Research on the women and mathematics issue: A personal case history. In A. M. Gallagher & J. C. Kaufman (Eds.), *Gender differences in mathematics: An integrative psychological approach* (pp. 1–24). New York: Cambridge University Press.

Chodorow, N. J. (1994). *Femininities, masculinities, sexualities: Freud and beyond.* Lexington: University Press of Kentucky.

Chodorow, N. J. (1999). *The power of feelings: Personal meaning in psychoanalysis, gender, and culture*. New Haven, CT: Yale University Press.

Chodorow, N. J. (2000). The psychodynamics of the family. In S. Saguaro (Ed.), *Psychoanalysis and woman: A reader* (pp. 108–127). New York: New York University Press.

Choo, P., Levine, T., & Hatfield, E. (1996). Gender, love schemas, and reactions to romantic break-ups. *Journal of Social Behavior and Personality, 11*, 143–160.

Chow, E. N. (1991). The development of feminist consciousness among Asian American women. In J. Lorber & S. A. Farrell (Eds.), *The social construction of gender* (pp. 255–268). Newbury Park, CA: Sage.

Chrisler, J. C. (2001). Gendered bodies and physical health. In R. K. Unger (Ed.), *Handbook of the psychology of women and gender* (pp. 289–301). New York: Wiley.

Chrisler, J. C. (2002). Hormone hostages: The cultural legacy of PMS as a legal defense. In L. H. Collins, J. C. Chrisler, & M. R. Dunlap (Eds.), *Charting a new course for feminist psychology*. Westport, CT: Praeger.

Chrisler, J. C. (Ed.). (2004a). *From menarche to menopause: The female body in feminist therapy*. New York: Haworth.

Chrisler, J. C. (2004b). PMS as a culture-bound syndrome. In J. C. Chrisler, C. Golden, & P. D. Rozee (Eds.), *Lectures on the psychology of women* (3rd ed., pp. 110–127). Boston: McGraw-Hill.

Chrisler, J. C., & Caplan, P. (2002). The strange case of Dr. Jekyll and Ms. Hyde: How PMS became a cultural phenomenon and a psychiatric disorder. *Annual Review of Sex Research, 13*, 274–306.

Chrisler, J. C., Golden, C., & Rozee, P. D. (Eds.). (2004). *Lectures on the psychology of women* (3rd ed.). Boston: McGraw-Hill.

Chrisler, J. C., Johnston, I. K., Champagne, N. M., & Preston, K. E. (1994). Menstrual joy: The construct and its consequences. *Psychology of Women Quarterly, 18*, 375–387.

Chrisler, J. C., & Levy, K. B. (1990). The media construct a menstrual monster: A content analysis of PMS articles in the popular press. *Women and Health, 16*, 89–104.

Chrisler, J. C., & Smith, C. A. (2004). Feminism and psychology. In M. A. Paludi (Ed.), *Praeger guide to the psychology of gender* (pp. 271–291). Westport, CT: Praeger.

Christakis, N. A., & Allison, P. D. (2006). Mortality after the hospitalization of a spouse. *New England Journal of Medicine, 354*, 719–730.

Christensen, A., & Heavey, C. L. (1999). Intervention for couples. *Annual Review of Psychology, 50*, 165–190.

Christensen, A., & Jacobson, N. S. (2000). *Reconcilable differences*. New York: Guilford.

Christopher, F. S., & Kisler, T. S. (2004). Sexual aggression in romantic relationships. In J. H. Harvey, A. Wenzel, & S. Sprecher (Eds.), *The handbook of sexuality in close relationships* (pp. 287–209). Mahwah, NJ: Erlbaum.

Christopher, F. S., & Lloyd, S. A. (2000). Physical and sexual aggression in relationships. In C. Hendrick & S. S. Hendrick (Eds.), *Close relationships* (pp. 331–356). Thousand Oaks, CA: Sage.

Chu, J. (2004). Asian American women's studies courses. In L. T. Võ et al. (Eds.), *Asian American women: The Frontiers reader* (pp. 201–213). Lincoln: University of Nebraska Press.

Chumlea, W. C., et al. (2003). Age at menarche and racial comparisons in US girls. *Pediatrics, 111*, 110–113.

Ciambrone, D. (2003). *Women's experiences with HIV/AIDS: Mending fractured selves*. Binghamton, NY: Haworth.

Cisneros, S. (2001). Only daughter. In S. M. Shaw & J. Lee (Eds.), *Women's voices, feminist visions* (pp. 301–303). Mountain View, CA: Mayfield.

Clark, J., & Zehr, D. (1993). Other women can: Discrepant performance predictions for self and same-sex other. *Journal of College Student Development, 34*, 31–35.

Clark, M. S., & Graham, S. M. (2005). Do researchers neglect singles? Can we do better? *Psychological Inquiry, 16*, 131–136.

Clark, R., Guilmain, J., Saucier, P. K., & Tavarez, J. (2003). Two steps forward, one step back: The presence of female characters and gender stereotyping in award-winning picture books between the 1930s and the 1960s. *Sex Roles, 49*, 439–449.

Clark, R., Lennon, R., & Morris, L. (1993). Of Caldecotts and Kings: Gendered images in recent American children's books by Black and non-Black illustrators. *Gender and Society, 7*, 227–245.

Clark, R. A. (1993). Men's and women's self-confidence in persuasive, comforting, and justificatory communicative tasks. *Sex Roles, 28*, 553–567.

Clark, R. A. (1998). A comparison of topics and objectives in a cross section of young men's and women's everyday conversations. In D. J. Canary & K. Dindia (Eds.), *Sex differences and similarities in communication* (pp. 303–319). Mahwah, NJ: Erlbaum.

Clarren, R. (2005, Summer). The green motel. *Ms. Magazine*, pp. 41–45.

Cleveland, J. N., Stockdale, M., & Murphy, K. R. (2000). *Women and men in organizations*. Mahwah, NJ: Erlbaum.

Clinchy, B. M., & Norem, J. K. (Eds.). (1998). *The gender and psychology reader*. New York: New York University Press.

Cling, B. J. (2004). Rape and rape trauma syndrome. In B. J. Cling (Ed.), *Sexualized violence against women and children* (pp. 13–40). New York: Guilford.

Coates, T. J., & Szekeres, G. (2004). A plan for the next generation of HIV prevention research: Seven key policy investigative challenges. *American Psychologist, 59*, 747–757.

Cobb, R. J., Davila, J., & Bradbury, T. N. (2001). Attachment security and marital satisfaction: The role of positive perceptions and social support. *Personality and Social Psychology Bulletin, 27,* 1131–1143.

Cocco, M. (2004, May 4). Scandal shows women acting like men. *Liberal Opinion Week,* p. 20.

Coffin, F. (1997). Drywall rocker and taper. In M. Martin (Ed.), *Hard-hatted women: Life on the job* (pp. 63–70). Seattle: Seal Press.

Cogan, J. C., & Ernsberger, P. (1999). Dieting, weight, and health: Reconceptualizing research and policy. *Journal of Social Issues, 55,* 187–205.

Cohen, J., et al. (1996). *Girls in the middle: Working to succeed in school.* Washington, DC: American Association of University Women.

Cohen, L. M., et al. (2003). The etiology and treatment of nicotine dependence. In L. M. Cohen, D. E. McChargue, & F. L. Collins, Jr. (Eds.), *The health psychology handbook* (pp. 101–124). Thousand Oaks, CA: Sage.

Colapinto, J. (2000). *As nature made him: The boy who was raised as a girl.* New York: HarperCollins.

Cole, J. B., & Guy-Sheftall, B. (2003). *Gender talk: The struggle for women's equality in African American communities.* New York: Ballantine Books.

Colen, S. (1997). "With respect and feelings": Voices of West Indian child care and domestic workers in New York City. In M. Crawford & R. Unger (Eds.), *In our own words: Readings on the psychology of women and gender* (pp. 199–218). New York: McGraw-Hill.

Collaer, M. L., & Hines, M. (1995). Human behavioral sex differences: A role for gonadal hormones during early development? *Psychological Bulletin, 118,* 55–107.

Colley, A., et al. (2002). Gender-linked differences in everyday memory performance: Effort makes the difference. *Sex Roles, 47,* 577–582.

Collins, L. H. (2002a). Alcohol and drug addiction in women. In M. Ballou & L. S. Brown (Eds.), *Rethinking mental health and disorders* (pp. 208–230). New York: Guilford.

Collins, L. H. (2002b). Charting a new course in feminist psychology. In L. H. Collins, M. R. Dunlap, & J. C. Chrisler (Eds.), *Charting a new course for feminist psychology* (pp. 139–166). Westport, CT: Praeger.

Collins, P. H. (1990). *Black feminist thought: Knowledge, consciousness, and the politics of empowerment.* Boston: Unwin Hyman.

Collins, P. H. (1991). The meaning of motherhood in Black culture and Black mother-daughter relationships. In P. Bell-Scott et al. (Eds.), *Double stitch: Black women write about mothers and daughters* (pp. 42–60). Boston: Beacon Press.

Collins, P. H. (1994). Shifting the center: Race, class, and feminist theorizing about motherhood. In D. Bassin, M. Honey, & M. M. Kaplan (Eds.), *Representations of motherhood* (pp. 56–74). New Haven, CT: Yale University Press.

Collins, W. A., & Laursen, B. (2004). Parent-adolescent relationships and influences. In R. M. Lerner & L. Steinberg (Eds.), *Handbook of adolescent psychology* (2nd ed., pp. 331–361). Hoboken, NJ: Wiley.

Collins, W. A., & Sroufe, L. A. (1999). Capacity for intimate relationships: A developmental construction. In W. Furman, B. B. Brown, & C. Feiring (Eds.), *The development of romantic relationships in adolescence* (pp. 125–147). New York: Cambridge University Press.

Collison, M. N.-K. (2000, February 3). The "other Asians." *Black Issues in Higher Education,* pp. 20–24.

Coltrane, S. (1998). *Gender and families.* Thousand Oaks, CA: Pine Forge Press.

Coltrane, S., & Adams, M. (1997). Children and gender. In T. Arendell (Ed.), *Parenting: Contemporary issues and challenges.* Newbury Park, CA: Sage.

Coltrane, S., & Adams, M. (2001a). Men, women, and housework. In D. Vannoy (Ed.), *Gender mosaics: Social perspectives* (pp. 145–154). New York: Roxbury.

Coltrane, S., & Adams, M. (2001b). Men's family work: Child-centered fathering and the sharing of domestic labor. In R. Hertz & N. L. Marshall (Eds.), *Working families: The transformation of the American home* (pp. 72–99). Berkeley: University of California Press.

Coltrane, S., & Messineo, M. (2000). The perpetuation of subtle prejudice: Race and gender imagery in 1990s television advertising. *Sex Roles, 42,* 363–389.

Comas-Díaz, L. (2000). An ethnopolitical approach to working with people of color. *American Psychologist, 55,* 1319–1325.

Comas-Díaz, L., & Greene, B. (1994). Women of color with professional status. In L. Comas-Díaz & B. Greene (Eds.), *Women of color: Integrating ethnic and gender identities in psychotherapy* (pp. 347–388). New York: Guilford.

Commonwealth Secretariat and Maritime Centre of Excellence for Women's Health. (2002). *Gender mainstreaming in HIV/AIDS.* London: Commonwealth Secretariat.

Compas, B. E., & Luecken, L. (2002). Psychological adjustment to breast cancer. *Current Directions in Psychological Science, 11,* 111–114.

Compian, L., & Hayward, C. (2003). Gender differences in opposite sex relationships: Interactions with puberty. In C. Hayward (Ed.), *Gender differences at puberty* (pp. 77–92). New York: Cambridge University Press.

Condon, J. T., & Corkindale, C. (1997). The correlates of antenatal attachment in pregnant women. *British Journal of Medical Psychology, 70,* 359–372.

Condry, J. C., & Condry, S. (1976). Sex differences: A study of the eye of the beholder. *Child Development, 47,* 812–819.

Conger, R. D., Lorenz, F. O., & Wickrama, K. A. S. (Eds.). (2004). *Continuity and change in family relations: Theory, methods, and empirical findings.* Mahwah, NJ: Erlbaum.

Conley, F. K. (1998). *Walking out on the boys.* New York: Farrar, Straus & Giroux.

Conrad, S., & Milburn, M. (2001). *Sexual intelligence*. New York: Crown.

Conway, M., Wood, W., Dugas, M., & Pushkar, D. (2003). Are women perceived as engaging in more maladaptive worry than men? A status interpretation. *Sex Roles, 49*, 2–10.

Conway-Turner, K. (1999). Older women of color: A feminist exploration of the intersections of personal, familial, and community life. In J. D. Garner (Ed.), *Fundamentals of feminist gerontology* (pp. 115–130). New York: Haworth.

Cook, J. A. (2003). Depression, disability, and rehabilitation services for women. *Psychology of Women Quarterly, 27*, 121–129.

Coontz, S. (1997). *The way we really are: Coming to terms with America's changing families.* New York: Basic Books.

Coontz, S. (2005, May 6). The new fragility of marriage, for better or for worse. *Chronicle of Higher Education*, B7–B9.

Cooper, J., & Weaver, K. D. (2003). *Gender and computers: Understanding the digital divide*. Mahwah, NJ: Erlbaum.

Cooper, M. (2003). *The psychology of bulimia nervosa*. Oxford, England: Oxford University Press.

Cope-Farrar, K. M., & Kunkel, D. (2002). Sexual messages in teens' favorite prime-time television programs. In J. D. Brown, J. R. Steele, & K. Walsh-Childers (Eds.), *Sexual teens, sexual media: Investigating media's influence on adolescent sexuality* (pp. 59–78). Mahwah, NJ: Erlbaum.

Corcoran, C. B., & Mahlstedt, D. (1999). Preventing sexual assault on campus: A feminist perspective. In C. Forden, A. E. Hunter, & B. Birns (Eds.), *Readings in the psychology of women* (pp. 289–299). Boston: Allyn & Bacon.

Corcoran, C. B., & Parker, J. A. (2004). *Powerpuff Girls*: Fighting evil gender messages or postmodern paradox? In J. L. Chin (Ed.), *The psychology of prejudice and discrimination* (Vol. 3,

pp. 27–59). Westport, CT: Praeger.

Corcoran, C. B., & Thompson, A. R. (2004). "What's race got to do, got to do with it?" Denial of racism on predominantly White college campuses. In J. L. Chin (Ed.), *The psychology of prejudice and discrimination* (Vol. 1, pp. 137–176). Westport, CT: Praeger.

Cortés, C. E. (1997). Chicanas in film: History of an image. In C. E. Rodríguez (Ed.), *Latin looks: Images of Latinas and Latinos in the U.S. media* (pp. 121–141). Boulder, CO: Westview Press.

Cortese, A. J. (1999). *Provocateur: Images of women and minorities in advertising*. Oxford, England: Rowman & Littlefield.

Coryat, K. M. (2006). *Visibility of women in video news broadcasts*. Unpublished manuscript, SUNY Geneseo.

Cosgrove, L., & Caplan, P. J. (2004). Medicalizing menstrual distress. In P. J. Caplan & L. Cosgrove (Eds.), *Bias in psychiatric diagnosis* (pp. 221–230). Lanham, MD: Jason Aronson.

Cosgrove, L., & Riddle, B. (2001a). *Constructions of femininity and experiences of menstrual distress.* Paper presented at the Society for Menstrual Cycle Research, Avon, CT.

Cosgrove, L., & Riddle, B. (2001b, August). *Libidinal and bleeding bodies: Deconstructing menstrual cycle research.* Paper presented at the annual meeting of the American Psychological Association, San Francisco.

Costello, C. B., & Stone, A. J. (2001). *The American woman 2001–2002*. New York: Norton.

Costos, D., Ackerman, R., & Paradis, L. (2002). Recollections of menarche: Communication between mothers and daughters regarding menstruation. *Sex Roles, 46*, 49–5.

Cota, A. A., Reid, A., & Dion, K. L. (1991). Construct validity of a diagnostic ratio measure of gender stereotypes. *Sex Roles, 25*, 225–235.

Cowan, C. P., & Cowan, P. A. (1992). *When partners become parents:*

The big life change for couples. New York: Basic Books.

Cowan, G. (1984). The double standard in age discrepant relationships. *Sex Roles, 11*, 17–24.

Cowan, G. (2002). Content analysis of visual materials. In M. W. Wiederman & B. E. Whitley, Jr. (Eds.), *Handbook for conducting research on human sexuality* (pp. 345–368). Mahwah, NJ: Erlbaum.

Cowan, G., & Hoffman, C. D. (1986). Gender stereotyping in young children: Evidence to support a concept-learning approach. *Sex Roles, 14*, 11–22.

Cowan, G., & Khatchadourian, D. (2003). Empathy, ways of knowing, and interdependence as mediators of gender differences in attitudes toward hate speech and freedom of speech. *Psychology of Women Quarterly, 27*, 300–308.

Cowley, G. (2004, July 19). Medicine without doctors. *Newsweek*, pp. 44–48.

Cowley, G., & Kalb, C. (2005, August 22). The deadliest cancer. *Newsweek*, pp. 42–49.

Cox, M. (2001, February/March). Zero balance. *Ms. Magazine*, pp. 56–59.

Crabb, P. B., & Bielawski, D. (1994). The social representation of material culture and gender in children's books. *Sex Roles, 30*, 69–79.

Craighead, W. E., Hart, A. B., Craighead, L. W., & Ilardi, S. S. (2002). Psychosocial treatments for major depressive disorder. In P. E. Nathan & J. Gorman (Eds.), *A guide to treatments that work* (2nd ed., pp. 245–261). New York: Oxford University Press.

Cramer, K. M., Million, E., & Perreault, L. A. (2002). Perceptions of musicians: Gender stereotypes and social role theory. *Psychology of Music, 30*, 164–174.

Crandall, C. S., & Eshleman, A. (2003). A justification-suppression model of the expression and experience of prejudice. *Psychological Bulletin, 129*, 414–446.

Crandall, C. S., Tsang, J., Goldman, S., & Pennington, J. T. (1999).

Newsworthy moral dilemmas: Justice, caring, and gender. *Sex Roles, 40,* 187–209.

Crawford, D., & Ostrove, J. M. (2003). Representation of disability and the interpersonal relationships of women with disabilities. In M. E. Banks & E. Kaschak (Eds.), *Women with visible and invisible disabilities* (pp. 179–194). New York: Haworth.

Crawford, M. (1995). *Talking difference: On gender and language.* Thousand Oaks, CA: Sage.

Crawford, M. (2001). Gender and language. In R. K. Unger (Ed.), *Handbook of the psychology of women and gender* (pp. 228–244). New York: Wiley.

Crawford, M., & Chaffin, R. (1997). The meanings of difference: Cognition in social and cultural context. In P. J. Caplan, M. Crawford, J. S. Hyde, & J. T. E. Richardson (Eds.), *Gender differences in human cognition* (pp. 81–130). New York: Oxford University Press.

Crawford, M., & MacLeod, M. (1990). Gender in the college classroom: An assessment of the "chilly climate" for women. *Sex Roles, 23,* 101–122.

Crick, N. R., Casas, J. F., & Nelson, D. A. (2002). Toward a more comprehensive understanding of peer maltreatment: Studies of relational victimization. *Current Directions in Psychological Science, 11,* 98–101.

Crick, N. R., Grotpeter, J. K., & Bigbee, M. A. (2002). Relationally and physically aggressive children's intent attributions and feelings of distress for relational and instrumental peer provocations. *Child Development, 73,* 1134–1142.

Crick, N. R., & Nelson, D. A. (2002). Relational and physical victimization within friendships: Nobody told me there'd be friends like these. *Journal of Abnormal Child Psychology, 30,* 599–607.

Crick, N. R., & Rose, A. J. (2000). Toward a gender-balanced approach to the study of social-emotional development: A look at relational aggression. In P. M.

Miller & E. K. Scholnick (Eds.), *Toward a feminist developmental psychology* (pp. 153–168). New York: Routledge.

Crick, N. R., & Zahn-Waxler, C. (2003). The development of psychopathology in females and males: Current progress and future challenges. *Development and Psychopathology, 15,* 719–742.

Crick, N. R., et al. (2004). Relational aggression in early childhood. In M. Putallaz & K. L. Bierman (Eds.), *Aggression, antisocial behavior, and violence among girls* (pp. 71–89). New York: Guilford.

Crimmins, E. M., Kim, J. K., & Hagedorn, A. (2002). Life with and without disease: Women experience more of both. In S. B. Laditka (Ed.), *Health expectations for older women: International perspectives* (pp. 47–59). Binghamton, NY: Haworth.

Crocker, J., & Park, L. E. (2004a). The costly pursuit of self-esteem. *Psychological Bulletin, 130,* 292–414.

Crocker, J., & Park, L. E. (2004b). Reaping the benefits of pursuing self-esteem without the costs? *Psychological Bulletin, 130,* 430–434.

Crockett, L. J., Raffaeli, M., & Moilanen, K. (2002). Adolescent sexuality: Behavior and meaning. In G. R. Adams & M. Berzonsky (Eds.), *Blackwell handbook of adolescence.* Oxford, England: Blackwell.

Croll, E. (2000). *Endangered daughters: Discrimination and development in Asia.* New York: Routledge.

Crombie, G., et al. (2005). Predictors of young adolescents' math grades and course enrollment intentions: Gender similarities and differences. *Sex Roles, 52,* 351–367.

Crooks, R., & Baur, K. (2005). *Our sexuality* (9th ed.). Belmont, CA: Wadsworth.

Crosby, F. J., & Clayton, S. (2001). Affirmative action: Psychological contributions to policy. *Analysis of Social Issues and Public Policy, 1,* 71–87.

Crosby, F. J., Iyer, A., Clayton, S., & Downing, R. A. (2003). Affirmative action: Psychological data and the policy debates. *American Psychologist, 58,* 93–115.

Crosby, F. J., & Sabattini, L. (2006). Family and work balance. In J. Worell & C. D. Goodheart (Eds.), *Handbook of girls' and women's psychological health: Gender and well-being across the life span* (pp. 350–358). New York: Oxford University Press.

Crose, R. (2003). Teaching the psychology of later life. In P. Bronstein & K. Quina (Eds.), *Teaching gender and multicultural awareness* (pp. 271–283). Washington, DC: American Psychological Association.

Cross, S. E. (2001). Training the scientists and engineers of tomorrow: A person-situation approach. *Journal of Applied Social Psychology, 31,* 296–323.

Cross, S. E., & Vick, N. V. (2001). The interdependent self-construal and social support: The case of persistence in engineering. *Personality and Social Psychology Bulletin, 27,* 820–832.

Crowley, K., Callanan, M. A., Tenenbaum, H. R., & Allen, E. (2001). Parents explain more often to boys than to girls during shared scientific thinking. *Psychological Science, 12,* 258–261.

Cruikshank, M. (2003). *Learning to be old: Gender, culture, and aging.* Lanham, MD: Rowman & Littlefield.

Csoboth, C. T. (2003). Women's health issues. In L. M. Cohen, D. E. McChargue, & F. L. Collins, Jr. (Eds.), *The health psychology handbook* (pp. 469–484). Thousand Oaks, CA: Sage.

Cuddy, A. J. C., & Fiske, S. T. (2004). When professionals become mothers, warmth doesn't cut the ice. *Journal of Social Issues, 60,* 701–718.

Cuddy, A. J. C., Norton, M. I., & Fiske, S. T. (2005). This old stereotype: The pervasiveness and persistence of the elderly stereotype. *Journal of Social Issues, 61,* 267–285.

Cull, P. (1997). Carpenter. In M. Martin (Ed.), *Hard-Hatted women: Life on the job* (pp. 45–54). Seattle: Seal Press.

Cushner, K. (2003). *Human diversity in action*. Boston: McGraw-Hill.

Cusk, R. (2002). *A life's work: On becoming a mother*. New York: Picador.

Cutrona, C. E., Russell, D. W., & Gardner, K. A. (2005). The relationship enhancement mode of social support. In T. A. Revenson, K. Kayser, & Bodenmann, G. (2005). *Couples coping with stress* (pp. 73–95). Washington, DC: American Psychological Association.

Dabul, A. J., & Russo, N. F. (1998). Rethinking psychological theory to encompass issues of gender and ethnicity: Focus on achievement. In B. M. Clinchy (Ed.), *The gender and psychology reader* (pp. 754–768). New York: New York University Press.

D'Adesky, A. (2004). *Moving mountains: The race to treat global AIDS*. New York: Verso.

Dahlberg, K., Berg, M., & Lundgren, I. (1999). Commentary: Studying maternal experiences of childbirth. *Birth, 26*, 215–225.

Dailey, N. (1998). *When baby boom women retire*. Westport, CT: Praeger.

Daly, F. Y. (2001). Perspectives of Native American women on race and gender. In G. Kirk & M. Okazawa-Rey (Eds.), *Women's lives: Multicultural perspectives* (2nd ed., pp. 60–68). Mountain View, CA: Mayfield.

Daniluk, J. C., & Towill, K. (2001). Sexuality education: What is it, who gets it, and does it work? In J. Worell (Ed.), *Encyclopedia of women and gender* (pp. 1023–1031). San Diego: Academic Press.

Dannenbring, D., Stevens, M. J., & House, A. E. (1997). Predictors of childbirth pain and maternal satisfaction. *Journal of Behavioral Medicine, 20*, 127–142.

Daseler, R. (2000). Asian Americans battle "model minority" stereotype. In A. Minas (Ed.), *Gender basics* (2nd ed., pp. 45–49). Belmont, CA: Wadsworth.

Das Gupta, M. (2003, Spring/Summer). The neoliberal state and the domestic workers' movement in New York City. *Canadian Woman Studies/Les cahiers de la femme*, pp. 78–85.

Daubman, K. A., Heatherington, L., & Ahn, A. (1992). Gender and the self-presentation of academic achievement. *Sex Roles, 27*, 187–204.

D'Augelli, A. R. (2002). Mental health problems among lesbian, gay, and bisexual youths ages 14 to 21. *Clinical Child Psychology and Psychiatry, 7*, 1359–1045.

D'Augelli, A. R. (2003). Lesbian and bisexual female youths aged 14 to 21: Developmental challenges and victimization experiences. *Journal of Lesbian Studies, 7*, 9–29.

D'Augelli, A. R., Grossman, A. H., Hershberger, S. L., & O'Connell, T. S. (2001). Aspects of mental health among older lesbian, gay, and bisexual adults. *Aging & Mental Health, 5*, 149–158.

D'Augelli, A. R., Pilkington, N. W., & Hershberger, S. L. (2002). Incidence and mental health impact of sexual orientation victimization of lesbian, gay, and bisexual youths in high school. *School Psychology Quarterly, 17*, 148–167.

Davey, F. H. (1998). Young women's expected and preferred patterns of employment and child care. *Sex Roles, 38*, 95–102.

David, H. P., Dytrych, Z., & Matejcek, Z. (2003). Born unwanted: Observations from the Prague study. *American Psychologist, 58*, 224–229.

David, H. P., Dytrych, Z., Matejek, Z., & Schüler, V. (Eds.). (1988). *Born unwanted: Developmental effects of denied abortion*. New York: Springer.

David, H. P., & Lee, E. (2001). Abortion and its health effects. In J. Worell (Ed.), *Encyclopedia of women and gender* (pp. 1–14). San Diego, CA: Academic Press.

David, H. P., & Russo, N. F. (2003). Psychology, population, and reproductive behavior. *American Psychologist, 58*, 193–196.

Davies, C. (2002). When is a map not a map? Task and language in spatial interpretation with digital map displays. *Applied Cognitive Psychology, 16*, 273–285.

Davies, P. G., & Spencer, S. J. (2004). The gender-gap artifact: Women's underperformance in quantitative domains through the lens of stereotype threat. In A. M. Gallagher & J. C. Kaufman (Eds.), *Gender differences in mathematics: An integrative psychological approach* (pp. 172–188). New York: Cambridge University Press.

Davis, K. C., George, W. H., & Norris, J. (2004). Women's responses to unwanted sexual advances: The role of alcohol and inhibition conflict. *Psychology of Women Quarterly, 22*, 333–334.

Davison, K. K., & Birch, L. L. (2001). Weight status, parent reaction, and self-concept in five-year-old girls. *Pediatrics, 107*, 46–53.

Davison, K. K., Susman, E. J., & Birch, L. L. (2003). Percent body fat at age 5 predicts earlier pubertal development among girls at age 9. *Pediatrics, 111*, 815–821.

Davison, T. F., & McCabe, M. P. (2005). Relationship between men's and women's body image and their psychological, social, and sexual functioning. *Sex Roles, 52*, 463–475.

Dayhoff, S. A. (1983). Sexist language and person perceptions: Evaluation of candidates from newspaper articles. *Sex Roles, 9*, 543–555.

Dean-Jones, L. A. (1994). *Women's bodies in classical Greek science*. New York: Oxford University Press.

Deaux, K. (1979). Self-evaluation of male and female managers. *Sex Roles, 5*, 571–580.

Deaux, K. (1995). How basic can you be? The evolution of research on gender stereotypes. *Journal of Social Issues, 51*, 11–20.

Deaux, K. (1999). An overview of research on gender: Four themes from 3 decades. In W. B. Swann, Jr., J. H. Langlois, & L. A. Gilbert (Eds.), *Sexism and stereotypes in modern society: The gender science of Janet Taylor Spence* (pp. 11–33). Washington, DC: American Psychological Association.

Deaux, K. (2001). Autobiographical perspectives. In A. N. O'Connell (Ed.), *Models of achievement: Reflections of eminent women in psychology* (Vol. 3, pp. 202–218). Mahwah, NJ: Erlbaum.

de Beauvoir, S. (1961). *The second sex.* New York: Bantam Books.

Debold, E., Brown, L. M., Weseen, S., & Brookins, G. K. (1999). Cultivating hardiness zones for adolescent girls: A reconceptualization of resilience in relationships with caring adults. In N. Johnson, M. C. Roberts, & J. Worell (Eds.), *Beyond appearance: A new look at adolescent girls* (pp. 181–204). Washington, DC: American Psychological Association.

Deevey, S. (2000). Cultural variation in lesbian bereavement experiences in Ohio. *Journal of the Gay and Lesbian Medical Association, 4*, 9–17.

DeFour, D. C., David, G., Diaz, F. J., & Thompkins, S. (2003). The interface of race, sex, sexual orientation, and ethnicity in understanding sexual harassment. In M. A. Paludi & C. A. Paludi (Eds.), *Academic and workplace sexual harassment* (pp. 31–45). Westport, CT: Praeger.

DeFrain, J., & Olson, D. H. (1999). Contemporary family patterns and relationships. In M. Sussman, S. K. Steinmetz, & G. W. Peterson (Eds.), *Handbook of marriage and the family* (2nd ed., pp. 309–326). New York: Plenum.

de Guzman, M. R. T., et al. (2004). Gender and age differences in Brazilian children's friendship nominations and peer sociometric ratings. *Sex Roles, 51*, 217–225.

DeHart, G. B., Sroufe, L. A., & Cooper, R. G. (2004). *Child development: Its nature and course* (5th ed.). New York: McGraw-Hill.

De Judicibus, M., & McCabe, M. P. (2001). Blaming the target of sexual harassment: Impact of gender role, sexist attitudes, and work role. *Sex Roles, 44*, 401–417.

DeKeseredy, W. S., & Schwartz, M. D. (1998). *Woman abuse on campus: Results from the Canadian National Survey.* Thousand Oaks, CA: Sage.

DeKeseredy, W. S., & Schwartz, M. D. (2002). The incidence and prevalence of woman abuse in Canadian courtship. In K. M. J. McKenna & J. Larkin (Eds.), *Violence against women: New Canadian perspectives* (pp. 93–122). Toronto, ON: Inanna Publications and Education.

DeLamater, J., & Hyde, J. S. (2004). Conceptual and theoretical issues in studying sexuality in close relationships. In J. H. Harvey, A. Wenzel, & S. Sprecher (Eds.), *The handbook of sexuality in close relationships* (pp. 7–30). Mahwah, NJ: Erlbaum.

Delaney, C. (2000). Making babies in a Turkish village. In J. DeLoache & A. Gottlieb (Eds.), *A world of babies: Imagined childcare guides for seven societies* (pp. 117–144). New York: Cambridge University Press.

Delaney, J., Lupton, M. J., & Toth, E. (1988). *The curse: A cultural history of menstruation* (2nd ed.). Urbana: University of Illinois Press.

De las Fuentes, C., Barón, A., Jr., & Vásquez, M. J. T. (2003). Teaching Latino psychology. In P. Bronstein & K. Quina (Eds.), *Teaching gender and multicultural awareness* (pp. 207–220). Washington, DC: American Psychological Association.

De las Fuentes, C., & Vasquez, M. J. T. (1999). Immigrant adolescent girls of color: Facing American challenges. In N. G. Johnson, M. C. Roberts, & J. Worell (Eds.), *Beyond appearance: A new look at adolescent girls* (pp. 131–150). Washington, DC: American Psychological Association.

De Lisi, R., & McGillicuddy-De Lisi, A. (2002). Sex differences in mathematical abilities and achievement. In A. McGillicuddy-De Lisi & R. De Lisi (Eds.), *Biology, society, and be-*

havior: The development of sex differences in cognition (pp. 155–181). Westport, CT: Ablex Publishing.

Delk, J. L., Madden, R. B., Livingston, M., & Ryan, T. T. (1986). Adult perceptions of the infant as a function of gender labeling and observer gender. *Sex Roles, 15*, 527–534.

Dell, D. L. (2005). Gynecologic aspects of perimenopause and menopause. In D. E. Stewart (Ed.), *Menopause: A mental health practitioner's guide* (pp. 143–164). Washington, DC: American Psychiatric Press.

Dell, D. L., Chen, H., Ahmad, F., & Stewart, D. E. (2000). Knowledge about human papillomavirus among adolescents. *Obstetrics and Gynecology, 96*, 653–656.

Dello Stritto, M. E., & Guzmán, B. L. (2001, Spring). Media images of female sexuality: The impact on women's psychological health. *Community Psychologist*, p. 30.

DeLoache, J., & Gottlieb, A. (Eds.). (2000). *A world of babies.* New York: Cambridge University Press.

Demarest, J., & Glinos, F. (1992). Gender and sex role differences in young adult reactions towards "newborns" in a pretend situation. *Psychological Reports, 71*, 727–737.

Denham, S. A. (1998). *Emotional development in young children.* New York: Guilford.

Denmark, F. L. (2002, March). *Myths of aging.* Paper presented at the annual convention of the Southeastern Psychological Association.

Denmark, F. L. (2004). Looking ahead: Concluding remarks. *Sex Roles, 51*, 367–369.

Denner, J., & Griffin, A. (2003). The role of gender in enhancing program strategies for healthy youth development. In F. Villarruel, D. F. Perkins, L. M. Borden, & J. G. Keith (Eds.), *Community youth development* (pp. 118–144). Thousand Oaks, CA: Sage.

Dennerstein, L., Alexander, J. L., & Kotz, K. (2003). The menopause and sexual functioning: A review of the population-based studies. *Annual Review of Sex Research, 14,* 64–82.

Dennis, C. (2002). Breastfeeding support: Maternal and volunteer perceptions from a randomized controlled trial. *Birth, 29,* 169–176.

Denton, T. C. (1990). Bonding and supportive relationships among black professional women: Rituals of restoration. *Journal of Organizational Behavior, 11,* 447–457.

DePaulo, B. M. (2006). *Singled out: How singles are stereotyped, stigmatized, and ignored, and still live happily ever after.* New York: St. Martin's Press.

DePaulo, B. M., & Morris, W. L. (2005). Singles in society and in science. *Psychological Inquiry, 16,* 57–83.

DePaulo, J. R., Jr., & Horvitz, L. A. (2002). *Understanding depression.* New York: Wiley.

Deprez, L. S., Butler, S. S., & Smith, R. J. (2004). Securing higher education for women on welfare in Maine. In V. Polakow, S. S. Butler, L. S. Deprez, & P. Kahn (Eds.), *Shut out: Low income mothers and higher education in post-welfare America* (pp. 217–236). Albany, NY: State University of New York Press.

De Puy, C., & Dovitch, D. (1997). *The healing choice: Your guide to emotional recovery after an abortion.* New York: Simon & Schuster.

Derlega, V., Winstead, B. A., Oldfield, E. C., & Barbee, A. P. (2003). Close relationships and social support in coping with HIV: A test of sensitive interaction systems theory. *AIDS and Behavior, 7,* 119–129.

Derry, P. S. (2002). What do we mean by "The biology of menopause"? *Sex Roles, 46,* 13–23.

Derry, P. S. (2004). Coping with distress during perimenopause. In J. C. Chrisler (Ed.), *From menarche to menopause: The female body in feminist therapy* (pp. 165–177). New York: Haworth.

Desmarais, S., & Curtis, J. (1997a). Gender and perceived pay entitlement: Testing for effects of experience with income. *Journal of Personality and Social Psychology, 72,* 141–150.

Desmarais, S., & Curtis, J. (1997b). Gender differences in pay histories and views on pay entitlement among university students. *Sex Roles, 37,* 623–642.

Desmarais, S., & Curtis, J. (2001). Gender and perceived income entitlement among full-time workers: Analysis for Canadian national samples, 1984 and 1994. *Basic and Applied Social Psychology, 23,* 157–168.

DeSouza, E., & Fansler, A. G. (2003). Contrapower sexual harassment: A survey of students and faculty members. *Sex Roles, 48,* 529–542.

des Rivieres-Pigeon, C., Saurel-Cubizolles, M., & Lelong, N. (2004). Considering a simple strategy for detection of women at risk of psychological distress after childbirth. *Birth, 31,* 34–42.

Desrochers, S. (1995). What types of men are most attractive and most repulsive to women? *Sex Roles, 32,* 375–391.

Deutsch, F. M. (1999). *Halving it all: How equally shared parenting works.* Cambridge, MA: Harvard University Press.

Deutsch, F. M. (2001). Equally shared parenting. *Current Directions in Psychological Science, 10,* 25–28.

Deutsch, F. M., Roksa, J., & Meeske, C. (2003). How gender counts when couples count their money. *Sex Roles, 48,* 291–304.

Deutsch, F. M., & Saxon, S. E. (1998a). The double standard of praise and criticism for mothers and fathers. *Psychology of Women Quarterly, 22,* 665–683.

Deutsch, F. M., & Saxon, S. E. (1998b). Traditional ideologies, nontraditional lives. *Sex Roles, 38,* 331–362.

Deutsch, F. M., Servis, L. J., & Payne, J. D. (2001). Paternal participation in child care and its effects on children's self-esteem and attitudes toward gendered roles. *Journal of Family Issues, 22,* 1000–1024.

Deveny, K. (2003, June 30). We're not in the mood. *Newsweek,* pp. 40–46.

De Wolff, A. (2000, Fall). The face of globalization: Women working poor in Canada. *Canadian Woman Studies/Les cahiers de la femme,* pp. 54–59.

DeZolt, D. M., & Hull, S. H. (2001). Classroom and school climate. In J. Worell (Ed.), *Encyclopedia of women and gender* (pp. 257–264). San Diego: Academic Press.

Dhruvarajan, V. (1992). Conjugal power among first generation Hindu Asian Indians in a Canadian city. *International Journal of Sociology of the Family, 22,* 1–33.

Diamond, L. M. (2000). Sexual identity, attractions, and behavior among young sexual-minority women over a 2-year period. *Developmental Psychology, 36,* 241–250.

Diamond, L. M. (2002). What we got wrong about sexual identity development: Unexpected findings from a longitudinal study of young women. In A. Omoto & H. Kurtzman (Eds.), *Recent research on sexual orientation.* Washington, DC: American Psychological Association.

Diamond, L. M. (2003a). Love matters: Romantic relationships among sexual-minority adolescents. In P. Florsheim (Ed.), *Adolescent romantic relations and sexual behavior* (pp. 85–107). Mahwah, NJ: Erlbaum.

Diamond, L. M. (2003b). Was it a phase? Young women's relinquishment of lesbian/bisexual identities over a 5-year period. *Journal of Personality and Social Psychology, 84,* 352–364.

Diamond, L. M. (2003c). What does sexual orientation orient? A biobehavioral model distinguishing romantic love and sexual desire. *Psychological Review, 110,* 173–192.

Diamond, L. M. (2004). Emerging perspectives on distinctions between romantic love and sexual desire. *Current Directions in Psychological Science, 13,* 116–119.

Diamond, L. M. (2005). A new view of lesbian subtypes: Stable versus fluid identity trajectories over an 8-year period. *Psychology of Women Quarterly, 29,* 119–128.

Diamond, L. M., & Dubé, E. M. (2002). Friendship and attachment among heterosexual and sexual-minority youths: Does the gender of your friend matter? *Journal of Youth and Adolescence, 31,* 155–166.

Diamond, L. M., Savin-Williams, R. C., & Dubé, E. M. (1999). Sex, dating, passionate friendships, and romance: Intimate peer relations among lesbian, gay, and bisexual adolescents. In W. Furman, C. Feiring, & B. B. Brown (Eds.), *Contemporary perspectives on adolescent romantic relationships.* New York: Oxford University Press.

Diamond, M. (1996). Prenatal predisposition and the clinical management of some pediatric conditions. *Journal of Sex and Marital Therapy, 22,* 139–147.

Diamond, M., & Sigmundson, H. K. (1999). Sex reassignment at birth. In S. J. Ceci & S. M. Williams (Eds.), *The nature-nurture debate* (pp. 57–75). Malden, MA: Blackwell.

Di Caccavo, A., & Reid, F. (1998). The influence of attitudes toward male and female patients on treatment decisions in general practice. *Sex Roles, 38,* 613–629.

Dicker, R., & Piepmeier, A. (Eds.). (2003). *Catching a wave: Reclaiming feminism for the 21st century.* Boston: Northeastern University Press.

Diekman, A. B., McDonald, M., & Gardner, W. L. (2000). Love means never having to be careful: The relationship between reading romance novels and safe sex behavior. *Psychology of Women Quarterly, 24,* 179–188.

Diekman, A. B., & Murnen, S. K. (2004). Learning to be little women and little men: The inequitable gender equality of nonsexist children's literature. *Sex Roles, 50,* 373–385.

Dietz, T. L. (1998). An examination of violence and gender role portrayals in video games: Implications for gender socialization and aggressive behavior. *Sex Roles, 38,* 425–442.

Diggs, R. C., & Socha, T. (2004). Communication, families, and exploring the boundaries of cultural diversity. In A. L. Vangelisti (Ed.), *Handbook of family communication* (pp. 249–266). Mahwah, NJ: Erlbaum.

Dill, K. E., Gentile, D. A., Richter, W. A., & Dill, J. C. (2005). Violence, sex, race, and age in popular video games: A content analysis. In E. Cole & J. H. Daniel (Eds.), *Featuring females: Feminist analyses of media* (pp. 115–130). Washington, DC: American Psychological Association.

Dillaway, H. E. (2005). (Un)changing menopausal bodies: How women think and act in the face of a reproductive transition and gendered beauty ideals. *Sex Roles, 53,* 1–17.

Dillon, K. (2000). Sizing myself up: Tales of a plus-size model. In O. Edut (Ed.), *Body outlaws: Young women write about body image and identity* (pp. 232–239). Seattle: Seal Press.

Dindia, K. (2002). Self-disclosure research: Knowledge through meta-analysis. In M. Allen, R. W. Preiss, B. M. Gayle, & N. A. Burrell (Eds.), *Interpersonal communication research: Advances through meta-analysis* (pp. 169–185). Mahwah, NJ: Erlbaum.

Dindia, K., & Allen, M. (1992). Sex differences in self-disclosure: A meta-analysis. *Psychological Bulletin, 112,* 106–124.

Dingfelder, S. F. (2004, February). Programmed for psychopathology? *Monitor on Psychology,* p. 56.

Dion, K. K., & Dion, K. L. (2001a). Gender and cultural adaptation in immigrant families. *Journal of Social Issues, 57,* 511–521.

Dion, K. K., & Dion, K. L. (2001b). Gender and relationships. In R. K. Unger (Ed.), *Handbook of the psychology of women and gender* (pp. 256–271). New York: Wiley.

Dion, K. K., & Dion, K. L. (2004). Gender, immigrant generation, and ethnocultural identity. *Sex Roles, 50,* 347–355.

Dion, K. L. (2003). Prejudice, racism, and discrimination. In I. B. Weiner (Ed.), *Handbook of psychology* (Vol. 6, pp. 507–536). Hoboken, NJ: Wiley.

Dion, K. L., & Dion, K. K. (1993). Gender and ethnocultural comparisons in styles of love. *Psychology of Women Quarterly, 17,* 463–473.

Dion, K. L., & Giordano, C. (1990). Ethnicity and sex as correlates of depression symptoms in a Canadian university sample. *International Journal of Social Psychiatry, 36,* 30–41.

DiPietro, J. A. (2004). The role of prenatal maternal stress in child development. *Current Directions in Psychological Science, 13,* 71–74.

Dittman, M. (2004, January). Weighing in on fat bias. *Monitor on Psychology,* pp. 60–61.

Do women make better leaders? (2004, July). *Harvard Mental Health Letter,* p. 7.

Dobbert, D. L. (2004). *Halting the sexual predators among us.* Westport, CT: Praeger.

Doctors Without Borders. (2005). *Treating people in danger (brochure).* Merrifield, VA: Author.

Dodd, E. H., Giuliano, T. A., Boutell, J. M., & Moran, B. A. (2001). Respected or rejected: Perceptions of women who confront sexist remarks. *Sex Roles, 45,* 567–577.

Dodgen, C. E. (2005). *Nicotine dependence.* Washington, DC: American Psychological Association.

Dodson, J. E. (1997). Conceptualizations of African American families. In H. P. McAdoo (Ed.), *Black families* (3rd ed., pp. 67–82). Thousand Oaks, CA: Sage.

Dodwell, K. (2003). Marketing and teaching a women's literature course to culturally conservative students. *Feminist Teacher, 14,* 234–247.

Doll, L. S., Koenig, L. J., & Purcell, D. W. (2004). Child sexual abuse and adult sexual risk: Where are we now? In L. J. Koenig, L. S. Doll, A. O'Leary, & W. Pequegnat (Eds.), *From child sexual abuse to adult sexual risk:*

Trauma, revictimization, and intervention (pp. 3–10). Washington, DC: American Psychological Association.

Donaghue, N., & Fallon, B. J. (2003). Gender-role self-stereotyping and the relationship between equity and satisfaction in close relationships. *Sex Roles, 48,* 217–230.

Donovan, P. (2000, March). Game designed with girls in mind. *UUP Voice,* p. 11.

Dookie, I. J. (2004). Canada. In K. Malley-Morrison (Ed.), *International perspectives on family violence and abuse* (pp. 431–449). Mahwah, NJ: Erlbaum.

Dotson, L. A. Stinson, J., & Christian, L. (2003). "People tell me I can't have sex": Women with disabilities share their personal perspective on health care, sexuality, and reproductive rights. In M. E. Banks & E. Kaschak (Eds.), *Women with visible and invisible disabilities* (pp. 195–209). New York: Haworth.

Douglas, E. (2001, July/August). HIV/AIDS: A new report from CDC, the response from Congress, and psychology's role in the solution. *Psychological Science Agenda,* p. 12.

Douglas, S. J., & Micahels, M. W. (2004). *The mommy myth: The idealization of motherhood and how it has undermined women.* New York: Free Press.

Dowdall, J. (2003, June 20). Gender and the administrative search. *Chronicle of Higher Education,* p. C3.

Dowling, C. (2000). *The frailty myth: Women approaching physical equality.* New York: Random House.

Downs, D. A., & Fisher, J. (2005). Battered woman syndrome: Tool of justice or false hope in self-defense cases? In D. R. Loseke, R. J. Gelles, & M. M. Cavanaugh (Eds.), *Current controversies on family violence* (2nd ed., pp. 241–255). Thousand Oaks, CA: Sage.

Doyle, J. A. (1995). *The male experience* (3rd ed.). Madison, WI: Brown & Benchmark.

Drolet, M. (2001). *The persistent gap: New evidence on the Canadian gender gap* (Catalogue # 11F0019MPE No. 157). Ottawa: Business and Labour Market Analysis Division.

Dryden, C. (1999). *Being married, doing gender.* London: Routledge.

Dubé, E. M., Savin-Williams, R. C., & Diamond, L. M. (2001). Intimacy development, gender, and ethnicity among sexual-minority youths. In A. R. D'Augelli & C. J. Patterson (Eds.), *Lesbian, gay, and bisexual identities and youth* (pp. 129–152). New York: Oxford University Press.

Dube, K. (2004, June 18). What feminism means to today's undergraduates. *Chronicle of Higher Education,* p. B5.

Du Bois, B. C., Yavno, C. H., & Stanford, E. P. (2001). Care options for older Mexican Americans: Issues affecting health and long-term care services needs. In L. K. Olson (Ed.), *Age through ethnic lenses: Caring for the elderly in a multicultural society* (pp. 71–85). Lanham, MD: Rowman & Littlefield.

Duck, S., & Wright, P. H. (1993). Reexamining gender differences in same-gender friendships: A close look at two kinds of data. *Sex Roles, 28,* 709–727.

Dudley, C., O'Sullivan, L. F., & Moreau, D. (2002). Does familiarity breed complacency? HIV knowledge, personal contact, and sexual risk behavior of psychiatrically referred Latino adolescent girls. *Hispanic Journal of Behavioral Sciences, 24,* 353–368.

Duffy, J., Wareham, S., & Walsh, M. (2004). Psychological consequences for high school students of having been sexually harassed. *Sex Roles, 50,* 811–821.

Duffy, J., Warren, K., & Walsh, M. (2001). Classroom interactions: Gender of teacher, gender of student, and classroom subject. *Sex Roles, 45,* 579–593.

Duncan, K. A. (2004). *Healing from the trauma of childhood sexual abuse.* Westport, CT: Praeger.

Dunivin, D. L. (2006). Psychopharmacotherapy and women: Issues for consideration. In J. Worell & C. D. Goodheart (Eds.), *Handbook of girls' and women's psychological health: Gender and well-being across the life span* (pp. 447–454). New York: Oxford University Press.

Dunne, M. P. (2002). Sampling considerations. In M. W. Wiederman & B. E. Whitley, Jr. (Eds.), *Handbook for conducting research on human sexuality* (pp. 85–112). Mahwah, NJ: Erlbaum.

Dunning, D., & Sherman, D. A. (1997). Stereotypes and tacit inference. *Journal of Personality and Social Psychology, 73,* 459–471.

Duong, T. C. (2004). My multiple identity disorder. In K. K. Kumashiro (Ed.), *Restoried selves: Autobiographies of queer Asian/Pacific American activists* (pp. 47–52). New York: Harrington Park Press.

Durkin, K., & Nugent, B. (1998). Kindergarten children's gender-role expectations for television actors. *Sex Roles, 38,* 387–402.

Dworkin, T. M. (2002). Personal relationships and the right to privacy. In L. Diamant & J. A. Lee (Eds.), *The psychology of sex, gender, and jobs* (pp. 295–307). Westport, CT: Praeger.

Dziech, B. W. (2003). Sexual harassment on college campuses. In M. A. Paludi & C. A. Paludi (Eds.), *Academic and workplace sexual harassment* (pp. 147–171). Westport, CT: Praeger.

Eagly, A. H. (2001). Social role theory of sex differences and similarities. In J. Worell (Ed.), *Encyclopedia of women and gender* (pp. 1069–1078). San Diego: Academic Press.

Eagly, A. H. (2003). The rise of female leaders. *Zeitschrift für Socialpsychologie, 34,* 123–132.

Eagly, A. H. (2004). Prejudice: Toward a more inclusive understanding. In A. H. Eagly, R. M. Baron, & V. L. Hamilton (Eds.), *The social psychology of group identity and social conflict* (pp. 45–64). Washington, DC: American Psychological Association.

Eagly, A. H., Beale, A. E., & Sternberg, R. J. (Eds.). (2004). *The psychology of gender* (2nd ed.). New York: Guilford.

Eagly, A. H., & Carli, L. L. (2003). The female leadership advantage: An evaluation of the evidence. *The Leadership Quarterly, 14,* 807–834.

Eagly, A. H., & Crowley, M. (1986). Gender and helping behavior: A meta-analytic review of the social psychological literature. *Psychological Bulletin, 100,* 283–308.

Eagly, A. H., & Johannesen-Schmidt, M. C. (2001). The leadership styles of women and men. *Journal of Social Issues, 57,* 781–797.

Eagly, A. H., Johannesen-Schmidt, M. C., & van Engen, M. L. (2003). Transformational, transactional, and laissez-faire leadership styles: A meta-analysis comparing women and men. *Psychological Bulletin, 129,* 569–591.

Eagly, A. H., & Karau, S. J. (2002). Role congruity theory of prejudice toward female leaders. *Psychological Review, 109,* 573–598.

Eagly, A. H., Makhijani, M. G., & Klonsky, B. G. (1992). Gender and the evaluation of leaders: A meta-analysis. *Psychological Bulletin, 111,* 3–22.

Eagly, A. H., & Mladinic, A. (1994). Are people prejudiced against women? Some answers from research on attitudes, gender stereotypes, and judgments of competence. In W. Stroebe & M. Hewstone (Eds.), *European review of social psychology.* New York: Wiley.

Eagly, A. H., Mladinic, A., & Otto, S. (1991). Are women evaluated more favorably than men? An analysis of attitudes, beliefs, and emotions. *Psychology of Women Quarterly, 15,* 203–216.

Eagly, A. H., & Wood, W. (1991). Explaining sex differences in social behavior: A meta-analytic perspective. *Personality and Social Psychology Bulletin, 17,* 306–315.

Eagly, A. H., & Wood, W. (1999). The origins of sex differences in human behavior: Evolved dispositions versus social roles. *American Psychologist, 54,* 408–423.

Eagly, A. H., Wood, W., & Diekman, A. (2000). Social role theory of sex differences and similarities: A current appraisal. In T. Eckes & H. M. Trautner (Eds.), *The devel-* *opmental social psychology of gender.* Mahwah, NJ: Erlbaum.

Easton, D., O'Sullivan, L. F., & Parker, R. G. (2002). Sexualities and sexual health/Lessons from history: Emergence of sexuality as a sexual health and political issue. In D. Miller & J. Green (Eds.), *The psychology of sexual health* (pp. 53–67). Malden, MA: Blackwell.

Eberhardt, J. L., & Fiske, S. T. (1998). Affirmative action in theory and practice: Issues of power, ambiguity, and gender versus race. In D. L. Anselmi & A. L. Law (Eds.), *Questions of gender: Perspectives and paradoxes* (pp. 629–641). New York: McGraw-Hill.

Eccles, J. S. (1987). Gender roles and women's achievement-related decisions. *Psychology of Women Quarterly, 11,* 135–172.

Eccles, J. S. (1994). Understanding women's educational and occupational choices. *Psychology of Women Quarterly, 18,* 585–609.

Eccles, J. S. (1997). User-friendly science and mathematics: Can it interest girls and minorities in breaking through the middle school wall? In D. Johnson (Ed.), *Minorities and girls in school: Effects on achievement and performance* (pp. 65–104). Thousand Oaks, CA: Sage.

Eccles, J. S. (2001). Achievement. In J. Worell (Ed.), *Encyclopedia of women and gender* (pp. 43–53). San Diego: Academic Press.

Eccles, J. S. (2004). Schools, academic motivation, and stage-environment fit. In R. M. Lerner & L. Steinberg (Eds.), *Handbook of adolescent psychology* (2nd ed., pp. 125–153). Hoboken, NJ: Wiley.

Eccles, J. S., Jacobs, J. E., & Harold, R. D. (1990). Gender-role stereotypes, expectancy effects, and parents' socialization of gender differences. *Journal of Social Issues, 46,* 183–201.

Eccles, J. S., Wigfield, A., & Byrnes, J. (2003). Cognitive development in adolescence. In I. B. Weiner (Ed.), *Handbook of psychology* (Vol. 6, pp. 325–350). Hoboken, NJ: Wiley.

Eccles, J. S., et al. (2000). Gender-roles socialization in the family: A longitudinal approach. In T. Eckes & H. M. Trautner (Eds.), *The developmental social psychology of gender* (pp. 333–360). Mahwah, NJ: Erlbaum.

Eckert, P., & McConnell-Ginet, S. (2003). *Language and gender.* New York: Cambridge University Press.

Eckes, T., & Trautner, H. M. (Eds.). (2000a). *The developmental social psychology of gender.* Mahwah, NJ: Erlbaum.

Eckes, T., & Trautner, H. M. (2000b). Developmental social psychology of gender: An integrative framework. In T. Eckes & H. M. Trautner (Eds.), *The developmental social psychology of gender* (pp. 3–32). Mahwah, NJ: Erlbaum.

Edelstein, L. N. (1999). *The art of midlife.* Westport, CT: Bergin & Garve.

Edwards, C. P., Knoche, L., & Kumuru, A. (2001). Play patterns and gender. In J. Worell (Ed.), *Encyclopedia of women and gender.* San Diego: Academic Press.

Edwards, H. E., & Noller, P. (2002). Care giving and its influence on marital interactions between older spouses. In P. Noller & J. A. Feeney (Eds.), *Understanding marriage* (pp. 437–462). New York: Cambridge University Press.

Edwards, N., & Sim-Jones, N. (1998). Smoking and smoking relapse during pregnancy and postpartum: Results of a qualitative study. *Birth, 25,* 94–100.

Edwards, R., & Hamilton, M. A. (2004). You need to understand my gender role: An empirical test of Tannen's model of gender and communication. *Sex Roles, 50,* 491–504.

Edwards, T. M. (2000, August 28). Flying solo. *Time,* pp. 47–53.

Ehrenreich, B. (2001). *Nickel and dimed: On (not) getting by in America.* New York: Metropolitan Books.

Eisenberg, N., Fabes, R., & Shea, C. (1989). Gender differences in empathy and prosocial moral reasoning: Empirical investigations. In M. M. Brabeck (Ed.), *Who cares? Theory, research,* and educational implications of the ethic of care (pp. 127–143). New York: Praeger.

Eisenberg, N., & Lennon, R. (1983). Sex differences in empathy and related capacities. *Psychological Bulletin, 94,* 100–131.

Eisenberg, N., Martin, C. L., & Fabes, R. A. (1996). Gender development and gender effects. In D. C. Berliner & R. C. Calfee (Eds.), *Handbook of educational psychology* (pp. 358–396). New York: Macmillan.

Eisenberg, S. (1998). *We'll call you if we need you: Experiences of women working construction.* Ithaca, NY: Cornell University Press.

Eisenstat, S. A., & Bancroft, L. (1999). Domestic violence. *New England Journal of Medicine, 341,* 886–892.

El-Bushra, J. (2000). Rethinking gender and development practice for the twenty-first century. In C. Sweetman (Ed.), *Gender in the 21st century* (pp. 55–62). Oxford, England: Oxfam.

Eliason, M. J. (1995). Accounts of sexual identity formation in heterosexual students. *Sex Roles, 32,* 821–834.

Ellis, B. J. (2004). Timing of pubertal maturation in girls: An integrated life history approach. *Psychological Bulletin, 130,* 920–958.

Ellison, C. R. (2001). A research inquiry into some American women's sexual concerns and problems. In E. Kaschak & L. Tiefer (Eds.), *A new view of women's sexual problems* (pp. 147–159). New York: Haworth.

Ellsberg, M., et al. (1998). *¿Cómo atender a las mujeres que viven situaciones de violencia doméstica? [How to attend to women who live in violent domestic situations.]* Managua, Nicaragua: Arco Producciones.

El-Safty, M. (2004). Women in Egypt: Islamic rights versus cultural practice. *Sex Roles, 51,* 273–281.

Else-Quest, N. M., Hyde, J. S., & Clark, R. (2003). Breastfeeding, bonding, and the mother-infant relationship. *Merrill-Palmer Quarterly, 49,* 495–517.

Elson, J. (2004). *Am I still a woman? Hysterectomy and gender iden-*

tity. Philadelphia: Temple University Press.

Emmers-Sommer, T. M., et al. (2005). The impact of film manipulation on men's and women's attitudes toward women and film editing. *Sex Roles, 52,* 683–695.

Englander, A. (1997). *Dear Diary, I'm pregnant.* Toronto: Annick Press.

Enns, C. Z. (2004a). *Feminist theories and feminist psychotherapies* (2nd ed.). New York: Haworth.

Enns, C. Z. (2004b). The politics and psychology of false memory syndrome. In J. C. Chrisler, C. Golden, & P. D. Rozee (Eds.), *Lectures on the psychology of women* (3rd ed., pp. 357–373). New York: McGraw-Hill.

Enns, C. Z., & Forrest, L. M. (2005). Toward defining and integrating multicultural and feminist pedagogy. In C. Z. Enns & A. L. Sinacore (Eds.), *Teaching and social justice: Integrating multicultural and feminist theories in the classroom* (pp. 3–23). Washington, DC: American Psychological Association.

Enns, C. Z., & Sinacore, A. L. (2001). Feminist theories. In J. Worell (Ed.), *Encyclopedia of women and gender* (pp. 469–480). San Diego: Academic Press.

Enns, C. Z., & Sinacore, A. L. (Eds.). (2005). *Teaching and social justice: Integrating multicultural and feminist theories in the classroom.* Washington, DC: American Psychological Association.

Enright, E. (2004, July/August). A house divided. *AARP Magazine,* pp. 62–65.

Erber, J. T. (2005). *Aging & older adulthood.* Belmont, CA: Thomson/Wadsworth.

Erblich, J., & Earleywine, M. (2003). Alcohol problems. In L. M. Cohen, D. E. McChargue, & F. L. Collins, Jr. (Eds.), *The health psychology handbook* (pp. 79–100). Thousand Oaks, CA: Sage.

Erchick, D. B. (2001). Developing mathematical voice: Women reflecting on the adolescent years. In P. O'Reilly, E. M. Penn, & K. deMarrais (Eds.), *Educating young adolescent girls.* Mahwah, NJ: Erlbaum.

Erchull, M. J., Chrisler, J. C., Gorman, J. A., & Johnston-Robledo,

I. (2002). Education and advertising: A content analysis of commercially produced booklets about menstruation. *Journal of Early Adolescence, 22,* 455–474.

Erel, O., Oberman, Y., & Yirmiya, N. (2000). Maternal versus nonmaternal care and seven domains of children's development. *Psychological Bulletin, 126,* 727–747.

Erkut, S., Marx, F., & Fields, J. P. (2001). A delicate balance: How teachers can support middle school girls' confidence and competence. In P. O'Reilly, E. M. Penn, & K. deMarrais (Eds.), *Educating young adolescent girls* (pp. 83–101). Mahwah, NJ: Erlbaum.

Erler, M. C., & Kowaleski, M. (Eds.). (2003). *Gendering the master narrative: Women and power in the Middle Ages.* Ithaca, NY: Cornell University Press.

Ernsberger, P., & Koletsky, R. J. (1999). Biomedical rationale for a wellness approach to obesity: An alternative to a focus on weight loss. *Journal of Social Issues, 55,* 221–260.

Escobar-Chaves, S. L., et al. (2005). Impact of the media on adolescent sexual attitudes and behaviors. *Pediatrics, 116* (Suppl.), 297–326.

Espín, O. M. (1999). *Women crossing boundaries: A psychology of immigration and transformations of sexuality.* New York: Routledge.

Espinosa, P. (1997, October 3). The rich tapestry of Hispanic America is virtually invisible on commercial TV. *Chronicle of Higher Education,* p. B7.

Essed, P., Goldberg, D. T., & Kobayashi, A. (2005). *A companion to gender studies.* Malden, MA: Blackwell.

Esterberg, K. G. (1996). Gay cultures, gay communities: The social organization of lesbians, gay men, and bisexuals. In R. C. Savin-Williams & K. Cohen (Eds.), *The lives of lesbians, gays, and bisexuals: Children to adults* (pp. 375–392). Fort Worth, TX: Harcourt Brace.

Etaugh, C. A. (1993). Maternal employment: Effects on children. In J. Frankel (Ed.), *Employed mothers and the family context* (pp. 68–88). New York: Springer.

Etaugh, C. A., & Bridges, J. S. (2001). Midlife transitions. In J. Worell (Ed.), *Encyclopedia of women and aging* (pp. 759–769). San Diego: Academic Press.

Etaugh, C. A., & Bridges, J. S. (2006). Midlife transitions. In J. Worell & C. D. Goodheart (Eds.), *Handbook of girls' and women's psychological health: Gender and well-being across the life span* (pp. 359–367). New York: Oxford University Press.

Etaugh, C. A., & Hoehn, S. (1995). Perceiving women: Effects of marital, parental, and occupational sex-typing variables. *Perceptual and Motor Skills, 80,* 320–322.

Etaugh, C. A., & Liss, M. B. (1992). Home, school, and playroom: Training grounds for adult gender roles. *Sex Roles, 26,* 129–147.

Etson, T. D. (2003, December 18). Sharing the responsibility: Increasing Black male student enrollment. *Black Issues in Higher Education,* p. 124.

Etzkowitz, H., Kemelgor, C., & Uzzi, B. (2000). *Athena unbound: The advancement of women in science and technology.* New York: Cambridge University Press.

Evans, E. M., Schweingruber, H., & Stevenson, H. W. (2002). Gender differences in interest and knowledge acquisition: The United States, Taiwan, and Japan. *Sex Roles, 47,* 153–167.

Evans, L., & Davies, K. (2000). No sissy boys here: A content analysis of the representation of masculinity in elementary school reading textbooks. *Sex Roles, 42,* 255–270.

Evans, S. M. (2003). *Tidal wave: How women changed America at century's end.* New York: Free Press.

Evelyn, J. (2000, August 3). Double standard reform. *Black Issues in Higher Education,* p. 6.

Ex, C. T. G. M., & Janssens, J. M. A. M. (1998). Maternal influences on daughters' gender role attitudes. *Sex Roles, 38,* 171–186.

Ex, C. T. G. M., & Janssens, J. M. A. M. (2000). Young females'

images of motherhood. *Sex Roles, 43,* 865–890.

Fabes, R. A., & Martin, C. L. (2000). *Exploring child development: Transactions and transformations.* Boston: Allyn & Bacon.

Fabes, R. A., Martin, C. L., & Hanish, L. D. (2003). Young children's play qualities in same-, other-, and mixed-sex peer groups. *Child Development, 74,* 921–932.

Facio, E. (1997). Chicanas and aging: Toward definitions of womanhood. In J. M. Coyle (Ed.), *Handbook on women and aging* (pp. 335–350). Westport, CT: Greenwood Press.

Fagot, B. I. (1978). The influence of sex of child on parental reactions to toddler children. *Child Development, 49,* 459–465.

Fagot, B. I. (1995). Psychological and cognitive determinants of early gender-role development. *Annual Review of Sex Research, 6,* 1–31.

Fagot, B. I., Rodgers, C. S., & Leinbach, M. D. (2000). Theories of gender socialization. In T. Eckes & H. M. Trautner (Eds.), *The developmental social psychology of gender* (pp. 65–89). Mahwah, NJ: Erlbaum.

Family Planning Advocates of New York State. (2005). *Funding for reproductive health care.* Retrieved July 14, 2005, from www.fpaofnys.org/publications/fact_sheets.html

Farber, N. (2003). *Adolescent pregnancy: Policy and prevention services.* New York: Springer.

Farberman, R. (2004, October). Council actions include gay-marriage resolution. *Monitor on Psychology,* p. 24.

Fassinger, R. E. (2002). Hitting the ceiling: Gendered barriers to occupational entry, advancement, and achievement. In L. Diamant & J. A. Lee (Eds.), *The psychology of sex, gender, and jobs* (pp. 21–45). Westport, CT: Praeger.

Fausto-Sterling, A. (1985). *Myths of gender: Biological theories about women and men.* New York: Basic Books.

Fausto-Sterling, A. (2000). *Sexing the body: Gender politics and the construction of sexuality.* New York: Basic Books.

Fausto-Sterling, A. (2005). The bare bones of sex: Part 1—Sex and gender. *Signs, 30,* 1492–1517.

Favreau, O. E. (1993). Do the N's justify the means? Null hypothesis testing applied to sex and other differences. *Canadian Psychology/Psychologie canadienne, 34,* 64–78.

Favreau, O. E. (1997). Sex and gender comparisons: Does null hypothesis testing create a false dichotomy? *Feminism and Psychology, 7,* 63–81.

Favreau, O. E., & Everett, J. C. (1996). A tale of two tails. *American Psychologist, 51,* 268–269.

Fazio, R. H., & Olson, M. A. (2003). Implicit measures in social cognition research: Their meaning and use. *Annual Review of Psychology, 54,* 297–327.

Fears, D. (2003, September 1–7). The power of a label. *The Washington Post National Weekly Edition,* p. 29.

Fechner, P. Y. (2003). The biology of puberty: New developments in sex differences. In C. Hayward (Ed.), *Gender differences at puberty* (pp. 17–28). New York: Cambridge University Press.

Federman, D. D. (2004). Three facets of sexual differentiation. *New England Journal of Medicine, 350,* 323–324.

Federman, D. D. (2006). The biology of human sex differences. *New England Journal of Medicine, 354,* 1507–1514.

Feeney, J. A., Hohaus, L., Noller, P., & Alexander, R. P. (2001). *Becoming parents: Exploring the bonds between mothers, fathers, and their infants.* New York: Cambridge University Press.

Fehr, B. (2004). Intimacy expectation in same-sex friendships: A prototype interaction-pattern model. *Journal of Personality and Social Psychology, 86,* 265–285.

Feingold, A. (1988). Cognitive gender differences are disappearing. *American Psychologist, 43,* 95–103.

Feingold, A. (1994). Gender differences in personality: A meta-analysis. *Psychological Bulletin, 116,* 429–456.

Feiring, C. (1996). Concepts of romance in 15-year-old adolescents.

Journal of Research on Adolescents, 6, 181–200.

Feiring, C. (1998). Gender identity and the development of romantic relationships in adolescence. In W. Furman, B. B. Brown, & C. Feiring (Eds.), *Contemporary perspectives in adolescent romantic relationships.* Cambridge, England: Cambridge University Press.

Feiring, C. (1999a). Gender identity and the development of romantic relationships in adolescence. In W. Furman, B. B. Brown, & C. Feiring (Eds.), *The development of romantic relationships in adolescence* (pp. 211–232). New York: Cambridge University Press.

Feiring, C. (1999b). Other-sex friendship networks and the development of romantic relationships in adolescence. *Journal of Youth and Adolescence, 28,* 495–512.

Feldt, G. (2002). *Behind every choice is a story.* Denton, TX: University of North Texas Press.

Felski, R. (2003, July 25). Feminist criticism: More than one voice. *Chronicle of Higher Education,* p. B11.

Felson, R. B. (2002). *Violence and gender reexamined.* Washington, DC: American Psychological Association.

Ferguson, S. J. (2000). Challenging traditional marriage: Never married Chinese American and Japanese American women. *Gender and Society, 14,* 136–159.

Fiala, S. E., Giuliano, T. A., Remlinger, N. M., & Braithwaite, L. C. (1999). Lending a helping hand: The effects of gender stereotypes and gender on the likelihood of helping. *Journal of Applied Social Psychology, 29,* 2164–2176.

Field, H. L., & Brackin, R. (2002). Neurological disorders of increased prevalence in women: Migraine, multiple sclerosis, and Alzheimer's disease. In S. C. Kornstein & A. H. Clayton (Eds.), *Women's mental health* (pp. 467–480). New York: Guilford.

Field, T. (1998). Maternal cocaine use and fetal development. In E. A. Blechman & K. D. Brownell (Eds.), *Behavioral medicine and women: A comprehensive handbook* (pp. 27–30). New York: Guilford.

Fields, C. D. (2002, January 31). Sexual responsibility on campus. *Black Issues in Higher Education,* pp. 18–24.

Fiese, B. H., & Skillman, G. (2000). Gender differences in family stories: Moderating influence of parent gender role and child gender. *Sex Roles, 43,* 267–283.

Figert, A. E. (1996). *Women and the ownership of PMS: The structuring of a psychiatric disorder.* New York: Aldine de Gruyter.

Fikkan, J., & Rothblum, E. (2005). Weight bias in employment. In K. D. Brownell, R. M. Puhl, M. B. Schwartz, & L. Rudd (Eds.), *Weight bias: Nature, consequences, and remedies* (pp. 15–28). New York: Guilford.

Fincham, F. D. (2004). Communication in marriage. In A. L. Vangelisti (Ed.), *Handbook of family communication* (pp. 83–103). Mahwah, NJ: Erlbaum.

Fincham, F. D., & Beach, S. R. H. (1999). Conflict in marriage: Implications for working with couples. *Annual Review of Psychology, 50,* 47–77.

Fine, M. (1997). Coping with rape: Critical perspectives on consciousness. In M. Crawford & R. Unger (Ed.), *In our own words: Readings on the psychology of women and gender* (pp. 152–164). New York: McGraw-Hill.

Fine, M. (2001, August). *The presence of an absence.* Paper presented at the annual convention of the American Psychological Association, San Francisco.

Fine, M., & Burns, A. (2003). Class notes: Toward a critical psychology of class and schooling. *Journal of Social Issues, 59,* 841–860.

Fine, M., & Carney, S. (2001). Women, gender, and the law: Toward a feminist rethinking of responsibility. In R. K. Unger (Ed.), *Handbook of the psychology of women and gender* (pp. 388–409). New York: Wiley.

Fine, M., Roberts, R., & Weis, L. (2000). Refusing the betrayal: Latinas redefining gender, sexuality, culture and resistance. *Review of Education/Psychology/Cultural Studies, 22,* 87–119.

Fine, M., & Torre, M. E. (2001). Remembering exclusions: Participatory action research in public institutions. *Qualitative Research in Psychology, 1,* 15–37.

Fine, M., et al. (2001). *Changing minds: The impact of college in a maximum security prison.* New York: The Graduate School and University Center, City University of New York.

Fine, M. A. (2000). Divorce and single parenting. In C. Hendrick & S. S. Hendrick (Eds.), *Close relationships* (pp. 138–152). Thousand Oaks, CA: Sage.

Fingerhut, A. W., Peplau, L. A., & Ghavami, N. (2005). A dual-identity framework for understanding lesbian experience. *Psychology of Women Quarterly, 29,* 129–139.

Fingerman, K. L. (2001). *Aging mothers and their adult daughters: A study in mixed emotions.* New York: Springer.

Fingerman, K. L. (2003). *Mothers and their adult daughters: Mixed emotions, enduring bonds.* New York: Springer.

Finlay, B., & Love, G. D. (1998). Gender differences in reasoning about military intervention. *Psychology of Women Quarterly, 22,* 481–485.

Finnie, R., Lascelles, E., & Sweetman, A. (2005). *Who goes? The direct and indirect impact of family background on access to postsecondary education.* (Catalogue # 11F0019MIE no. 237). Ottawa: Statistics Canada.

Firestone, J. M., & Harris, R. J. (2003). Personal responses to structural problems: Organizational climate and sexual harassment in the U.S. military, 1988 and 1995. *Gender, Work, and Organization, 10,* 42–64.

Fischer, A. H., & van Vianen, A. E. M. (2005). Corporate masculinity. In P. Essed, D. T. Goldberg, & A. Kobayashi (Eds.), *A companion to gender studies* (pp. 342–354). Malden, MA: Blackwell.

Fischhoff, B. (1992). Giving advice: Decision theory perspectives on sexual assault. *American Psychologist, 47,* 577–588.

Fisher, C. B. (2003). *Decoding the ethics code: A practical guide for psychologists.* Thousand Oaks, CA: Sage.

Fisher-Thompson, D., & Burke, T. A. (1998). Experimenter influences and children's cross-gender behavior. *Sex Roles, 39,* 669–684.

Fiske, S. T. (1993). Social cognition and social perception. *Annual Review of Psychology, 44,* 155–194.

Fiske, S. T. (2004). *Social beings: A core motives approach to social psychology.* Hoboken, NJ: Wiley.

Fiske, S. T., Cuddy, A. J. C., Glick, P., & Xu, J. (2002). A model of (often mixed) stereotype content: Competence and warmth respectively follow from perceived status and competition. *Journal of Personality and Social Psychology, 82,* 878–902.

Fiske, S. T., & Stevens, L. E. (1993). What's so special about sex? Gender stereotyping and discrimination. In S. Oskamp & M. Costanzo (Eds.), *Gender issues in contemporary society* (pp. 173–196). Newbury Park, CA: Sage.

Fiske, S. T., et al. (1991). Social science research on trial: Use of sex stereotyping research in *Price Waterhouse* v. *Hopkins. American Psychologist, 46,* 1049–1060.

Fiske, S. T., et al. (1993). Accuracy and objectivity on behalf of the APA. *American Psychologist, 48,* 55–56.

Fitch, R. H., Cowell, P. E., & Denenberg, V. H. (1998). The female phenotype: Nature's default? *Developmental Neuropsychology, 14,* 213–231.

Fitzgerald, L. F., Collinsworth, L. L., & Harned, M. S. (2001). Sexual harassment. In J. Worell (Ed.), *Encyclopedia of women and gender* (pp. 991–1004). San Diego: Academic Press.

Fivush, R. (1989). Exploring sex differences in the emotional content of mother-child conversations about the past. *Sex Roles, 20,* 675–691.

Fivush, R., Brotman, M. A., Buckner, J. P., & Goodman, S. H. (2000). Gender differences in parent-child emotion narratives. *Sex Roles, 42,* 233–253.

Fivush, R., & Buckner, J. P. (2000). Gender, sadness, and depression: The development of emotional focus through gendered discourse. In A. H. Fischer (Ed.), *Gender and emotion: Social psychological perspectives* (pp. 232–253). Cambridge, England: Cambridge University Press.

Fivush, R., & Nelson, K. (2004). Culture and language in the emergence of autobiographical memory. *Psychological Science, 15,* 573–577.

Flanders, L. (1997). *Real majority, media minority.* Monroe, ME: Common Courage Press.

Flannagan, D., & Perese, S. (1998). Emotional references in mother-daughter and mother-son dyads' conversations about school. *Sex Roles, 39,* 353–367.

Fletcher, G. (2002). *The new science of intimate relationships.* Malden, MA: Blackwell.

Fletcher, T. D., & Major, D. A. (2004). Medical students' motivations to volunteer: An examination of the nature of gender differences. *Sex Roles, 51,* 109–114.

Flores, L. Y., & O'Brien, K. M. (2002). The career development of Mexican American adolescent women: A test of social cognitive career theory. *Journal of Counseling Psychology, 49,* 14–27.

Flores-Ortiz, Y. (1998). Voices from the couch: The co-creation of a Chicana psychology. In C. Trujillo (Ed.), *Living Chicana theory* (pp. 102–122). Berkeley, CA: Third Woman Press.

Flores-Ortiz, Y. (2004). Domestic violence in Chicana/o families. In R. J. Velásquez, L. M. Arellano, & B. W. McNeill (Eds.), *The handbook of Chicana/o psychology and mental health* (pp. 267–284). Mahwah, NJ: Erlbaum.

Florsheim, P. (Ed.). (2003). Adolescent romantic and sexual behavior: What we know and where we go from here. In P. Florsheim (Ed.), *Adolescent romantic relations and sexual behavior: Theory, research, and practical implications* (pp. 371–385). Mahwah, NJ: Erlbaum.

Florsheim, P., Moore, D., & Edgington, C. (2003). Romantic relations among adolescent parents. In P. Florsheim (Ed.), *Adolescent romantic relations and sexual behavior* (pp. 297–322). Mahwah, NJ: Erlbaum.

Foels, R., & Tomcho, T. J. (2005). Gender, interdependent self-construals, and collective self-esteem: Women and men are mostly the same. *Self and Identity, 4,* 213–225.

Foertsch, J., & Gernsbacher, M. A. (1997). In search of gender neutrality: Is singular they a cognitively efficient substitute for generic he? *Psychological Science, 8,* 106–111.

Fogg, P. (2003, April 18). The gap that won't go away. *Chronicle of Higher Education,* pp. A12–A18.

Fogg, P. (2005, April 29). Don't stand so close to me. *Chronicle of Higher Education,* pp. A10–A12.

Foley, S., Kope, S. A., & Sugrue, D. P. (2002). *Sex matters for women: A complete guide to taking care of your sexual self.* New York: Guilford.

Fonn, S. (2003). Not only what you do, but how you do it: Working with health care practitioners on gender equality. In L. Manderson (Ed.), *Teaching gender, teaching women's health* (pp. 105–120). Binghamton, NY: Haworth.

Fontes, L. A. (2001). The new view and Latina sexualities: *¡Pero no soy una máchina!* In E. Kaschak & L. Tiefer (Eds.), *A new view of women's sexual problems* (pp. 33–37). New York: Haworth.

Foote, W. E., & Goodman-Delahunty, J. (2005). *Evaluating sexual harassment: Psychological, social, and legal considerations in forensic examinations.* Washington, DC: American Psychological Association.

Forbes, G. B., Adams-Curtis, L. E., White, K. B., & Holmgren, K. M. (2003). The role of hostile and benevolent sexism in women's and men's perceptions of the menstruating woman. *Psychology of Women Quarterly, 27,* 58–63.

Forbes, G. B., Doroszewicz, K., Card, K., & Adams-Curtis, L. (2004). Association of the thin body ideal, ambivalent sexism, and self-esteem with body acceptance and the preferred body size of college women in Poland and the United States. *Sex Roles, 50,* 331–345.

Ford, T. (1999). *Becoming multicultural: Personal and social construction through critical teaching.* New York: Falmer Press.

Fort, D. C. (Ed.). (2005a). *A hand up: Women mentoring women in science* (2nd ed.). Washington, DC: The Association for Women in Science.

Fort, D. C. (2005b). The consensus. In D. C. Fort (Ed.), *A hand up: Women mentoring women in science* (2nd ed., pp. 155–198). Washington, DC: The Association for Women in Science.

Foster, D. (2005, Winter/Spring). Why do children do so well in lesbian households? Research on lesbian parenting. *Canadian Woman Studies/Les cahier de la femme, 24,* 50–56.

Fouts, B., & Knapp, J. (2001). A sexual assault education and risk reduction workshop for college freshmen. In A. J. Ottens & K. Hotelling (Eds.), *Sexual violence on campus: Policies, programs, and perspectives* (pp. 98–119). New York: Springer.

Fouts, G., & Burggraf, K. (1999). Television situation comedies: Female body images and verbal reinforcements. *Sex Roles, 40,* 473–481.

Fox, R. C. (1996). Bisexuality in perspective: A review of theory and research. In B. A. Firestein (Ed.), *Bisexuality: The psychology and politics of an invisible minority* (pp. 3–50). Thousand Oaks, CA: Sage.

Fox, R. C. (1997). Understanding bisexuality. *Society for the Psychological Study of Men and Masculinity Bulletin, 2*(4), 13–14.

Fox, R. F. (2000). *Harvesting minds: How TV commercials control kids.* Westport, CT: Praeger.

Frank, E., Brogan, D., & Schiffman, M. (1998). Prevalence and correlates of harassment among U.S. women physicians. *Archives of Internal Medicine, 158,* 352–358.

Frankowski, B. L. (2004). Sexual orientation and adolescents. *Pediatrics, 113,* 1827–1832.

Franzoi, S. L., & Chang, Z. (2002). The body esteem of Hmong and Caucasian young adults. *Psychology of Women Quarterly, 26,* 89–91.

Fraser, L. (1997, July/August). Fear of fat: Why images of overweight women are taboo. *Extra!,* pp. 22–23.

Freedman, E. B. (2002). *No turning back: The history of feminism and the future of women.* New York: Ballantine.

French, M. (1992). *The war against women.* New York: Summit Books.

Freund, A. M., & Riediger, M. (2003). Successful aging. In R. M. Lerner, M. A. Easterbrooks, & J. Mistry (Eds.), *Handbook of psychology* (Vol. 6, pp. 601–628). New York: Wiley.

Frey, C., & Hoppe-Graff, S. (1994). Serious and playful aggression in Brazilian girls and boys. *Sex Roles, 30,* 249–268.

Freyd, J. J., et al. (2005). The science of child sexual abuse. *Science, 308,* 501.

Friedman, H. S., et al. (1995). Psychosocial and behavioral predictors of longevity. *American Psychologist, 50,* 69–78.

Frieze, I. H. (2005). *Hurting the one you love: Violence in relationships.* Belmont, CA: Thomson Wadsworth.

Frieze, I. H., et al. (2003). Gender-role attitudes in university students in the United States, Slovenia, and Croatia. *Psychology of Women Quarterly, 27,* 256–261.

Frigoletto, F. D., Jr., et al. (1995). A clinical trial of active management of labor. *New England Journal of Medicine, 333,* 745–750.

Frodi, A., & Ahnlund, K. (1995). *Gender differences in the vulnerability to depression.* Paper presented at the annual convention of the Eastern Psychological Association, Boston.

Frodi, A., Macaulay, J., & Thome, P. R. (1977). Are women always less aggressive than men? A review of the experimental litera-

ture. *Psychological Bulletin, 84,* 634–660.

Frost, J., & McKelvie, S. (2004). Self-esteem and body satisfaction in male and female elementary school, high school, and university students. *Sex Roles, 51,* 45–54.

Frost, J. A., et al. (1999). Language processing is strongly left lateralized in both sexes: Evidence from functional MRO. *Brain, 122,* 199–208.

Fuligni, A. S., & Brooks-Gunn, J. (2002). Meeting the challenges of new parenthood: Responsibilities, advice, and perceptions? In N. Halfon, K. T. McLearn, & M. A. Schuster (Eds.), *Child rearing in America: Challenges facing parents with young children* (pp. 83–116). New York: Cambridge University Press.

Funderburk, J. R. (2001). Group counseling for survivors of sexual assault. In A. J. Ottens & K. Hotelling (Eds.), *Sexual violence on campus: Policies, programs, and perspectives* (pp. 254–282). New York: Springer.

Funk, J. B., & Buchman, D. D. (1996). Children's perceptions of gender differences in social approval for playing electronic games. *Sex Roles, 35,* 219–231.

Furman, W., & Shaffer, L. (2003). The role of romantic relationships in adolescent development. In P. Florsheim (Ed.), *Adolescent romantic relations and sexual behavior* (pp. 1–22). Mahwah, NJ: Erlbaum.

Furnham, A. (2000). Parents' estimates of their own and their children's multiple intelligences. *British Journal of Developmental Psychology, 18,* 583–594.

Furnham, A., & Mak, T. (1999). Sex-role stereotyping in television commercials: A review and comparison of fourteen studies done on five continents over 25 years. *Sex Roles, 41,* 413–437.

Furnham, A., Mak, T., & Tanidjojo, L. (2000). An Asian perspective on the portrayal of men and women in television advertisements: Studies from Hong Kong and Indonesian television. *Journal of Applied Social Psychology, 30,* 2341–2364.

Furnham, A., Rakow, T., Sarmany-Schuller, I., & De Fruyt, F. (1999). European differences in self-perceived multiple intelligences. *European Psychologist, 4*, 131–138.

Furnham, A., & Skae, E. (1997). Changes in the stereotypical portrayal of men and women in British television advertisements. *European Psychologist, 2*, 44–51.

Furnham, A., & Thomson, L. (1999). Gender role stereotyping in advertisements on two British radio stations. *Sex Roles, 40*, 153–165.

Furr, S. R. (2002). Men and women in cross-gender careers. In L. Diamant & J. A. Lee (Eds.), *The psychology of sex, gender, and jobs* (pp. 47–68). Westport, CT: Praeger.

Furumoto, L. (1996, August). *Reflections on gender and the character of American psychology.* Paper presented at the annual convention of the American Psychological Association, Toronto, Canada.

Furumoto, L. (2003). Beyond great men and great ideas: History of psychology in sociocultural context. In P. Bronstein & K. Quina (Eds.), *Teaching gender and multicultural awareness* (pp. 113–124). Washington, DC: American Psychological Association.

Futterman, L. A., & Jones, J. E. (1998). *The PMS and perimenopause sourcebook.* Los Angeles: Lowell House.

Gadsden, V. L. (1999). Black families in intergenerational and cultural perspective. In M. E. Lamb (Ed.), *Parenting and child development in "nontraditional" families* (pp. 221–246). Mahwah, NJ: Erlbaum.

Gager, C. T., McLanahan, S. S., & Glei, D. A. (2002). Preparing for parenthood: Who's ready, who's not? In N. Halfon, K. T. McLearn, & M. A. Schuster (Eds.), *Child rearing in America: Challenges facing parents with young children* (pp. 50–80). New York: Cambridge University Press.

Gahagan, J., & Loppie, C. (2001, Summer/Fall). Counting pills or counting on pills? What HIV+ women have to say about anti-retroviral therapy. *Canadian Woman Studies/Les cahiers de la femme, 21*, 118–123.

Gaines, S. O., Jr., & Brennan, K. A. (2001). Establishing and maintaining satisfaction in multicultural relationships. In J. Harvey & A. Wenzel (Eds.), *Close romantic relationships: Maintenance and enhancement* (pp. 237–253). Mahwah, NJ: Erlbaum.

Galambos, N. L. (2004). Gender and gender role development in adolescence. In R. M. Lerner & L. Steinberg (Eds.), *Handbook of adolescent psychology* (2nd ed., pp. 233–262). Hoboken, NJ: Wiley.

Galea, L. A. M., & Kimura, D. (1993). Sex differences in route-learning. *Personality and Individual Differences, 14*, 53–65.

Galician, M. (2004). *Sex, love, and romance in the mass media.* Mahwah, NJ: Erlbaum.

Galinsky, E., & Bond, J. T. (1996). Work and family: The experiences of mothers and fathers in the U.S. labor force. In C. Costello & B. K. Krimgold (Eds.), *The American woman, 1996–97: Women and work.* New York: W. W. Norton.

Gallagher, A. M., & Kaufman, J. C. (Eds.). (2004a). *Gender differences in mathematics: An integrative psychological approach.* New York: Cambridge University Press.

Gallagher, A. M., & Kaufman, J. C. (2004b). Gender differences in mathematics: What we know and what we need to know. In A. M. Gallagher & J. C. Kaufman (Eds.), *Gender differences in mathematics: An integrative psychological approach* (pp. 316–331). New York: Cambridge University Press.

Gallo, L. C., & Matthews, K. A. (2003). Understanding the association between socioeconomic status and physical health: Do negative emotions play a role? *Psychological Bulletin, 129*, 10–51.

Gan, S. C., et al. (2000). Treatment of acute myocardial infarction and 30-day mortality among women and men. *New England Journal of Medicine, 343*, 8–15.

Ganahl, D. J., Prinsen, T. J., & Netzley, S. B. (2003). A content analysis of prime time commercials: A contextual framework of gender representation. *Sex Roles, 49*, 545–551.

Gannon, L. R. (1999). *Women and aging: Transcending the myths.* New York: Routledge.

Gannon, L., & Ekstrom, B. (1993). Attitudes toward menopause. The influence of sociocultural paradigms. *Psychology of Women Quarterly, 17*, 275–288.

Ganong, L. H., & Coleman, M. (1995). The content of mother stereotypes. *Sex Roles, 32*, 495–512.

Ganong, L. H., & Coleman, M. (1999). *Changing families, changing responsibilities: Family obligations following divorce and remarriage.* Mahwah, NJ: Erlbaum.

Gapinski, K. D., Brownell, K. D., & LaFrance, M. (2003). Body objectification and "fat talk": Effects on emotion, motivation, and cognitive performance. *Sex Roles, 48*, 377–388.

García-Moreno, C., & Türmen, T. (1995). International perspectives on women's reproductive health. *Science, 269*, 790–792.

Garcia-Preto, N. (2005). Puerto Rican families. In M. McGoldrick, J. Giordano, & N. Garcia-Preto (Eds.), *Ethnicity and family therapy* (3rd ed., pp. 242–255). New York: Guilford.

Gardiner, H. W., Mutter, J. D., & Kosmitzki, C. (1998). *Lives across cultures: Cross-cultural human development.* Boston: Allyn & Bacon.

Gardner, M. (2006, January/February). The memory wars. *Skeptical Inquirer,* pp. 28–31.

Gardner, W. L., & Gabriel, S. (2004). Gender differences in relational and collective interdependence. In A. H. Eagly, A. E. Beall, & R. J. Sternberg (Eds.), *The psychology of gender* (2nd ed., pp. 169–191). New York: Guilford.

Garfinkel, P. E. (2002). Classification and diagnosis of eating disorders. In C. G. Fairburn & K. D. Brownell (Eds.), *Eating disorders and obesity: A comprehensive handbook* (2nd ed., pp. 155–161). New York: Guilford.

Garland-Thomson, R. (2004). Integrating disability, transforming feminist theory. In B. G. Smith & B. Hutchison (Eds.), *Gendering disability* (pp. 73–103). New Brunswick, NJ: Rutgers University Press.

Garner, P. W., & Estep, K. M. (2001). Empathy and emotional expressivity. In J. Worell (Ed.), *Encyclopedia of women and gender* (pp. 391–402). San Diego: Academic Press.

Garnets, L. D. (2004a). Life as a lesbian: What does gender have to do with it? In J. C. Chrisler, C. Golden, & P. D. Rozee (Eds.), *Lectures on the psychology of women* (3rd ed., pp. 171–186). New York: Boston.

Garnets, L. D. (2004b, August). Pride and prejudice: Gay marriage. *SPSSI Newsletter*, p. 8.

Garrod, A., Smulyan, L., Powers, S., & Kilkenny, R. (1992). *Adolescent portraits*. Boston: Allyn & Bacon.

Garst, J., & Bodenhausen, G. V. (1997). Advertising's effects on men's gender role attitudes. *Sex Roles, 36*, 551–572.

Gaspar de Alba, A. (1993). Tortillerismo: Work by Chicana lesbians. *Signs, 18*, 956–963.

Gastil, J. (1990). Generic pronouns and sexist language: The oxymoronic character of masculine generics. *Sex Roles, 23*, 629–643.

Gavey, N. (2005). *Just sex? The cultural scaffolding of rape*. New York: Routledge.

Geary, D. C. (1998). *Male, female: The evolution of human sex differences*. Washington, DC: American Psychological Association.

Geiger, T. C., Zimmer-Gembeck, M., & Crick, N. R. (2004). The science of relational aggression: Can we guide intervention? In M. M. Moretti, C. L. Odgers, & M. A. Jackson (Eds.), *Girls and aggression: Contributing factors and intervention principles* (pp. 27–40). New York: Kluwer Academic/Plenum.

Gelles, R. J., & Cavanaugh, M. M. (2005). Association is not causation. In D. R. Loseke, R. J. Gelles, & M. M. Cavanaugh (Eds.), *Current controversies on family violence* (2nd ed., pp. 175–189). Thousand Oaks, CA: Sage.

Gender affects educational learning styles, researchers confirm. (1995, October). *Women in Higher Education*, p. 7.

George, D., Carroll, P., Kersnick, R., & Calderon, K. (1998). Gender-related patterns of helping among friends. *Psychology of Women Quarterly, 22*, 685–704.

George, W. H., & Martínez, L. J. (2002). Victim blaming in rape: Effects of victim and perpetrator race, type of rape, and participant racism. *Psychology of Women Quarterly, 26*, 110–119.

Gerber, G. L. (2001). *Women and men police officers: Status, gender, and personality*. Westport, CT: Praeger.

Gerbner, G. (1997). Gender and age in prime-time television. In S. Kirschner & D. A. Kirschner (Eds.), *Perspectives on psychology and the media* (pp. 69–94). Washington, DC: American Psychological Association.

Gergen, K. J., & Gergen, M. M. (2004). *Social construction: Entering the dialogue*. Chagrin Falls, OH: Taos Institute Publications.

Gergen, M. M. (2001). Social constructionist theory. In J. Worell (Ed.), *Encyclopedia of women and gender* (pp. 1043–1058). San Diego: Academic Press.

Gergen, M. M., & Gergen, K. J. (2006). Positive aging: Reconstructing the life course. In J. Worell & C. D. Goodheart (Eds.), *Handbook of girls' and women's psychological health: Gender and well-being across the life span* (pp. 416–424). New York: Oxford University Press.

Gernsbacher, M. A., & Kaschak, M. P. (2003). Neuroimaging studies of language production and comprehension. *Annual Review of Psychology, 54*, 91–114.

Gianakos, I. (2001). Predictors of career decision-making self-efficacy. *Journal of Career Assessment, 9*, 101–114.

Gibbon, M. (1999). *Feminist perspectives on language*. London: Longman.

Gibbons, J. L. (2000). Gender development in crosscultural perspective. In T. Eckes & H. M. Trautner (Eds.), *The developmental social psychology of gender* (pp. 389–415). Mahwah, NJ: Erlbaum.

Gibbons, J. L., Brusi-Figueroa, R., & Fisher, S. L. (1997). Gender-related ideals of Puerto Rican adolescents: Gender and school context. *Journal of Early Adolescence, 17*, 349–370.

Gibbons, J. L., Stiles, D. A., & Shkodriani, G. M. (1991). Adolescents' attitudes toward family and gender roles: An international comparison. *Sex Roles, 25*, 625–643.

Gilbert, L. A., Bravo, M. J., & Kearny, L. K. (2004). Partnering with teachers to educate girls in the new computer age. *Journal of Women and Minorities in Science and Engineering, 10*, 1–24.

Gilbert, L. A., & Kearney, L. K. (2006). The psychotherapeutic relationship as a positive and powerful resource for girls and women. In J. Worell & C. D. Goodheart (Eds.), *Handbook of girls' and women's psychological health: Gender and well-being across the life span* (pp. 229–238). New York: Oxford University Press.

Gilbert, L. A., & Rader, J. (2001). Counseling and psychotherapy: Gender, race/ethnicity, and sexuality. In J. Worell (Ed.), *Encyclopedia of women and gender* (pp. 265–277). San Diego: Academic Press.

Gilbert, L. A., & Scher, M. (1999). *Gender and sex in counseling and psychotherapy*. Boston: Allyn & Bacon.

Giles, D. (2003). *Media psychology*. Mahwah, NJ: Erlbaum.

Giles, H., & Reid, S. A. (2005). Ageism across the lifespan: Towards a self-categorization model of ageing. *Journal of Social Issues, 61*, 389–404.

Gilleard, C., & Higgs, P. (2000). *Cultures of ageing: Self, citizen, and the body*. Harlow, England: Prentice Hall.

Gilligan, C. (1982). *In a different voice*. Cambridge, MA: Harvard University Press.

Ginorio, A. B., Gutièrrez, L., Cauce, A. M., & Acosta, M. (1995). Psychological issues for Latinas. In H. Landrine (Ed.), *Bringing cultural diversity to feminist psychology: Theory, research, and practice* (pp. 241–263). Washington, DC: American Psychological Association.

Giordano, F. (2001). Helping cohabiting college students manage angry feelings to prevent relationship violence. In A. J. Ottens & K. Hotelling (Eds.), *Sexual violence on campus* (pp. 162–189). New York: Springer.

Girgus, J. S., & Nolen-Hoeksema, S. (2006). Cognition and depression. In C. L. M. Keyes & S. H. Goodman (Eds.), *Women and depression: A handbook for the social, behavioral, and biomedical sciences* (pp. 147–175). New York: Cambridge University Press.

Gitlin, M. J. (2002). Pharmacological treatment of depression. In I. H. Gotlib & C. L. Hammen (Eds.), *Handbook of depression* (pp. 360–382). New York: Guilford.

Gjerdingen, D. W., & Center, B. A. (2005). First-time parents' postpartum changes in employment, childcare, and housework responsibilities. *Social Science Research, 34*, 103–116.

Glazer, G., et al. (2002). The Ohio Midlife Women's Study. *Health Care for Women International, 23*, 612–630.

Gleeson, K., & Frith, H. (2004). Pretty in pink: Young women presenting mature sexual identities. In A. Harris (Ed.), *All about the girl: Culture, power, and identity* (pp. 103–113). New York: Routledge.

Gleiser, M. (1998). The glass wall. In A. M. Pattatucci (Ed.), *Women in science* (pp. 204–218). Thousand Oaks, CA: Sage.

Glenn, D. (2004, April 30). A dangerous surplus of sons? *Chronicle of Higher Education*, pp. A14–A16, A-18.

Glick, P. (1991). Trait-based and sex-based discrimination in occupational prestige, occupational salary, and hiring. *Sex Roles, 25*, 351–378.

Glick, P., & Fiske, S. T. (1996). The Ambivalent Sexism Inventory: Differentiating hostile and benevolent sexism. *Journal of Personality and Social Psychology, 70*, 491–512.

Glick, P., & Fiske, S. T. (2001a). An ambivalent alliance: Hostile and benevolent sexism as complementary justifications for gender inequality. *American Psychologist, 56*, 109–118.

Glick, P., & Fiske, S. T. (2001b). Ambivalent sexism. *Advances in Experimental Social Psychology, 33*, 115–188.

Glick, P., Wilk, K., & Perreault, M. (1995). Images of occupations: Components of gender and status in occupational stereotypes. *Sex Roles, 32*, 565–582.

Glick, P., et al. (2000). Beyond prejudice as simple antipathy: Hostile and benevolent sexism across cultures. *Journal of Personality and Social Psychology, 79*, 763–775.

Glick, P., et al. (2004). Bad but bold: Ambivalent attitudes toward men predict gender inequality in 16 nations. *Journal of Personality and Social Psychology, 86*, 713–728.

Global Health Facts. (2006). *AIDS deaths (adults and children): Global data, 2006.* Retrieved December 13, 2006, from http://www.globalhealthfacts.org/topic.jsp?l=7

Gluckman, R., Hartmann, B., & Shariatmadar, A. (2004, September). Pro-*whose*-life? Ten reasons why militarism is bad for your health. *Women's Review of Books*, pp. 12–13.

Go, M., Dunnigan, T., & Schuchman, K. M. (2004). Bias in counseling Hmong clients with limited English proficiency. In J. L. Chin (Ed.), *The psychology of prejudice and discrimination* (Vol. 2, pp. 109–136). Westport, CT: Praeger.

Gold, A. G. (2001). New light in new times? Women's songs on schooling girls in rural Rajasthan. *Manushi, 123*, 27–35.

Goldberg, P. A. (1968). Are women prejudiced against women? *Transaction, 5*, 28–30.

Golden, C. (1996). What's in a name? Sexual self-identification among women. In R. C. Savin-Williams & K. M. Cohen (Eds.), *The lives of lesbians, gays, and bisexuals* (pp. 229–249). Fort Worth, TX: Harcourt Brace.

Golden, C. (2004). The intersexed and the transgendered: Rethinking sex/gender. In J. C. Chrisler, C. Golden, & P. D. Rozee (Eds.), *Lectures on the psychology of women* (3rd ed., pp. 29–43). New York: McGraw-Hill.

Goldenberg, J. L., & Roberts, T. (2004). The beast within the beauty. In J. Greenberg, S. L. Koole, & T. Pyszczynski (Eds.), *Handbook of experimental existential psychology* (pp. 71–85). New York: Guilford.

Goldenberg, R. L., & Culhane, J. R. (2005). Editorial: Prepregnancy health status and the risk of preterm delivery. *Archives of Pediatric and Adolescent Medicine, 159*, 89–90.

Goldfarb, P. (2005). Intimacy and injury: Legal interventions for battered women. In A. Barnes (Ed.), *The handbook of women, psychology, and the law* (pp. 212–264). San Francisco: Jossey-Bass.

Goldrick-Jones, A. (2002). *Men who believe in feminism.* Westport, CT: Praeger.

Goldstein, L. A. (2001, Fall). "And you can quote me on that." *Michigan Today*, pp. 10–11.

Golombok, S., & Fivush, R. (1994). *Gender development.* New York: Cambridge University Press.

Golombok, S., & Hines, M. (2002). Sex differences in social behavior. In P. K. Smith & C. H. Hart (Eds.), *Blackwell handbook of childhood social development* (pp. 117–136). Malden, MA: Blackwell.

Golombok, S., et al. (2003). Children with lesbian parents: A community study. *Developmental Psychology, 39*, 20–33.

Golub, S. (1992). *Periods: From menarche to menopause.* Newbury Park, CA: Sage.

González, F. J. (2001). *HIV and depression.* San Francisco: UCSF AIDS Health Project.

Gonzalez, P. M., Blanton, H., & Williams, K. J. (2002). The effects of stereotype threat and double-minority status on the test performance of Latino women. *Personality and Social Psychology Bulletin, 28,* 659–670.

Good, C., Aronson, J., & Inzlicht, M. (2003). Improving adolescents' standardized test performance: An intervention to reduce the effects of stereotype threat. *Applied Developmental Psychology, 24,* 645–662.

Gooden, A. M., & Gooden, M. A. (2001). Gender representation in notable children's picture books: 1995–1999. *Sex Roles, 45,* 89–101.

Goodman, G. S. (2005). Wailing babies in her wake. *American Psychologist 60,* 872–881.

Goodman, G. S., et al. (2003). A prospective study of memory for child sexual abuse. *Psychological Science, 14,* 113–118.

Goodrich, T. J. (2003). A feminist family therapist's work is never done. In L. B. Silverstein & T. J. Goodrich (Eds.), *Feminist family therapy: Empowerment in social context* (pp. 3–15). Washington, DC: American Psychological Association.

Gordon, R. A. (2000). *Eating disorders* (2nd ed.). Oxford, England: Blackwell.

Gorlick, C. A. (1995). Divorce: Options available, constraints forced, pathways taken. In N. Mandell & A. Duffy (Eds.), *Canadian families: Diversity, conflict, and change* (pp. 211–234). Toronto: Harcourt Brace Canada.

Gorney, C. (1998). *Articles of faith: A frontline history of the abortion wars.* New York: Simon & Schuster.

Gotay, C. C., Muraoka, M., & Holup, J. (2001). Cultural aspects of cancer prevention and control. In S. S. Kazarian & D. R. Evans (Eds.), *Handbook of cultural health psychology* (pp. 163–193). San Diego, CA: Academic Press.

Gottheil, M., Steinberg, R., & Granger, L. (1999). An exploration of clinicians' diagnostic approaches to premenstrual symptomatology. *Canadian Journal of Behavioural Sciences, 31,* 254–262.

Graber, J. A., & Brooks-Gunn, J. (1999). "Sometimes I think that you don't like me": How mothers and daughters negotiate the transition into adolescence. In M. J. Cox & J. Brooks-Gunn (Eds.), *Conflict and cohesion in families: Causes and consequences* (pp. 207–242). Mahwah, NJ: Erlbaum.

Grady-Weliky, T. A. (2003). Premenstrual dysphoric disorder. *New England Journal of Medicine, 348,* 433–438.

Graham, S. (1997). "Most of the subjects were White and middle class": Trends in published research on African Americans in selected APA journals. In L. A. Peplau & S. E. Taylor (Eds.), *Sociocultural perspectives in social psychology: Current readings* (pp. 52–71). Upper Saddle River, NJ: Prentice Hall.

Grant, L. (1994). Helpers, enforcers, and go-betweens: Black females in elementary school classrooms. In M. Baca Zinn & B. T. Dill (Eds.), *Women of color in U.S. society* (pp. 43–63). Philadelphia: Temple University Press.

Grassia, T. (2005, September). Heterosexual black women and teens: The face of the U.S. AIDS epidemic. *Infectious Diseases in Children,* pp. 67–68.

Gray, J. (1992). *Men are from Mars, women are from Venus.* New York: HarperCollins.

Grayson, D. A. (2001). Squeaky wheel versus invisibility: Gender bias in teacher-student interactions. In H. Rousso & M. L. Wehmeyer (Eds.), *Double jeopardy: Addressing gender equity in special education* (pp. 155–183). Albany, NJ: SUNY Press.

Green, B. L., & Kenrick, D. T. (1994). The attractiveness of gender-typed traits at different relationship levels: Androgynous characteristics may be desirable after all. *Personality and Social Psychology Bulletin, 20,* 244–253.

Greenberg, B. S., & Worrell, T. R. (2005). The portrayal of weight in the media and its social impact. In K. D. Brownell, R. M. Puhl, M. B. Schwartz, & L. Rudd (Eds.), *Weight bias: Nature, consequences, and remedies* (pp. 42–53). New York: Guilford.

Greenberg, B. S., et al. (2003). Portrayals of overweight and obese individuals on commercial television. *American Journal of Public Health, 93,* 1342–1348.

Greene, B. (2000a). African American lesbian and bisexual women. *Journal of Social Issues, 56,* 239–249.

Greene, B. (2000b). African American lesbian and bisexual women in feminist-psychodynamic psychotherapies. In L. C. Jackson & B. Greene (Eds.), *Psychotherapy with African American women* (pp. 82–125). New York: Guilford.

Greene, K. (2004). The politics of birth. *AWP Newsletter,* pp. 6, 18.

Greene, S. (2003). *The psychological development of girls and women: Rethinking change in time.* New York: Routledge.

Greenhaus, J. H., & Parasuraman, S. (2002). The allocation of time to work and family roles. In D. L. Nelson & R. J. Burke (Eds.), *Gender, work stress, and health* (pp. 115–128). Washington, DC: American Psychological Association.

Greenwald, A. G., McGee, D. E., & Schwartz, J. L. K. (1998). Measuring individual differences in implicit cognition: The Implicit Association Test. *Journal of Personality and Social Psychology, 74,* 1464–1480.

Greenwald, A. G., & Nosek, B. A. (2001). Health of the Implicit Association Test at age 3. *Zeitschrift für Experimentelle Psychologie, 48,* 85–93.

Greenwood, D. N., & Pietromonaco, P. R. (2004). The interplay among attachment orientation, idealized media images of women, and body dissatisfaction: A social psychological analysis. In L. J. Shurm (Ed.), *The psychology of entertainment media* (pp. 291–308). Mahwah, NJ: Erlbaum.

Greer, M. (2005, June). "Keeping them hooked in." *Monitor on Psychology,* pp. 60–62.

Grewal, I., & Kaplan, C. (2002). *An introduction to women's studies.* Boston: McGraw-Hill.

Grieco, H. (1999, Fall). Media institute sets sights on feminist network. *National NOW Times,* p. 3.

Grilo, C. M. (2002). Binge eating disorder. In C. G. Fairburn & K. D. Brownell (Eds.), *Eating disorders and obesity: A comprehensive handbook* (2nd ed., pp. 178–182). New York: Guilford.

Grodstein, F., Clarkson, T. B., & Manson, J. E. (2003). Understanding the divergent data on postmenopausal therapy. *New England Journal of Medicine, 348,* 645–650.

Grolnick, W. S., Gurland, S. T., Jacob, K. F., & Decourcey, W. (2002). The development of self-determination in middle childhood and adolescence. In A. Wigfield & J. S. Eccles (Eds.), *Development of achievement motivation* (pp. 147–171). San Diego, CA: Academic Press.

Grote, N. K., & Frieze, I. H. (1994). The measurement of friendship-based love in intimate relationships. *Personal Relationships, 1,* 275–300.

Gruber, S. (1999). "I, a Mestiza, continually walk out of one culture into another": Alba's story. In K. Blair & P. Takayoshi (Eds.), *Feminist cyberspaces: Mapping gendered academic spaces* (pp. 105–132). Stamford, CT: Ablex.

Grusec, J. E., & Lytton, H. (1988). *Social development.* New York: Springer.

Guisinger, S. (2003). Adapted to flee famine: Adding an evolutionary perspective on anorexia nervosa. *Psychological Review, 110,* 745–761.

Gunning, I. R. (2002). Female genital surgeries: Eradication measures at the Western local level—a cautionary tale. In S. M. James & C. C. Robertson (Eds.), *Genital cutting and transnational sisterhood* (pp. 114–125). Urbana: University of Illinois Press.

Gunter, B., Harrison, J., & Wykes, M. (2003). *Violence on television: Distribution, form, context, and themes.* Mahwah, NJ: Erlbaum.

Gunter, B., & McAleer, J. (1997). *Children and television* (2nd ed.). London: Routledge.

Gupta, S. R. (1999). Forged by fire: Indian-American women reflect on their marriages, divorces, and on rebuilding lives. In S. R. Gupta (Ed.), *Emerging voices: South Asian American women redefine self, family, and community* (pp. 193–221). Walnut Creek, CA: AltaMira Press.

Gur, R. C., et al. (1999). Sex differences in brain gray and white matter in healthy young adults: Correlations with cognitive performance. *Journal of Neuroscience, 19,* 4065–4072.

Gurung, R. A. R. (2006). *Health psychology: A cultural approach.* Belmont, CA: Wadsworth.

Gutek, B. A. (2001). Working environments. In J. Worell (Ed.), *Encyclopedia of women and gender* (pp. 1191–1204). San Diego: Academic Press.

Gutek, B. A., Murphy, R. O., & Douma, B. (2004). A review and critique of the sexual experiences questionnaire (SEQ). *Law and Human Behavior, 28,* 457–482.

Guthrie, R. V. (1998). *Even the rat was white: A historical view of psychology* (2nd ed.). Boston: Allyn & Bacon.

Haas, J. S., et al. (2005). Prepregnancy health status and the risk of preterm delivery. *Archives of Pediatric and Adolescent Medicine, 159,* 58–63.

Haddock, G., & Zanna, M. P. (1994). Preferring "housewives" to "feminists": Categorization and the favorability of attitudes toward women. *Psychology of Women Quarterly, 18,* 25–52.

Hafter, D. M. (1979). An overview of women's history. In M. Richmond-Abbott (Ed.), *The American woman* (pp. 1–27). New York: Holt, Rinehart & Winston.

Hagestad, G. O., & Uhlenberg, P. (2005). The social separation of old and young: A root of ageism. *Journal of Social Issues, 61,* 343–360.

Hahn, C. (2004, April). Virgin territory. *Ms. Magazine,* 54–56.

Haley, H. (2001, June). *Crisscrossing gender lines and color lines: A test of the subordinate male target hypothesis.* Paper presented at the meeting of the American Psychological Society, Toronto, Ontario.

Haley-Banez, L., & Garrett, J. (2002). *Lesbians in committed relationships: Extraordinary couples, ordinary lives.* Binghamton, NY: Haworth.

Hall, G. C. N. (2002). Culture-specific ecological models of Asian American violence. In G. C. N. Hall & S. Okazaki (Eds.), *Asian American psychology* (pp. 153–170). Washington, DC: American Psychological Association.

Hall, G. C. N., & Barongan, C. (2002). *Multicultural psychology.* Upper Saddle River, NJ: Prentice Hall.

Hall, G. S. (1906). The question of coeducation. *Munsey's Magazine,* 588–592.

Hall, J. A. (1984). *Nonverbal sex differences: Communication accuracy and expressive style.* Baltimore: Johns Hopkins University Press.

Hall, J. A. (1987). On explaining gender differences: The case of nonverbal communication. In P. Shaver & C. Hendrick (Eds.), *Sex and gender* (pp. 177–200). Newbury Park, CA: Sage.

Hall, J. A. (1998). How big are nonverbal sex differences? The case of smiling and sensitivity to nonverbal cues. In D. J. Canary & K. Dindia (Eds.), *Sex differences and similarities in communication* (pp. 155–177). Mahwah, NJ: Erlbaum.

Hall, J. A., & Carter, J. D. (1999). Gender-stereotype accuracy as an individual difference. *Journal of Personality and Social Psychology, 77,* 350–359.

Hall, J. A., Carter, J. D., & Horgan, T. G. (2000). Gender differences in nonverbal communication of emotion. In A. H. Fischer (Ed.), *Gender and emotion: Social psychological perspectives* (pp. 97–117). New York: Cambridge University Press.

Hall, J. A., & Halberstadt, A. G. (1986). Smiling and gazing. In J. S. Hyde & M. C. Linn (Eds.), *The psychology of gender: Advances through meta-analysis* (pp. 136–158). Baltimore: Johns Hopkins University Press.

Hall, J. A., & Halberstadt, A. G. (1997). Subordination and nonverbal sensitivity: A hypothesis in search of support. In M. R. Walsh (Ed.), *Women, men, and gender: Ongoing debates* (pp. 120–133). New Haven, CT: Yale University Press.

Hall, J. A., Smith LeBeau, L., Gordon Reinoso, J. G., & Thayer, F. (2001). Status, gender, and non-verbal behavior in candid and posed photographs: A study of conversations between university employees. *Sex Roles, 44,* 677–692.

Hall, R. L. (2004). Sweating it out. In J. C. Chrisler, C. Golden, & P. D. Rozee (Eds.), *Lectures on the psychology of women* (3rd ed., pp. 56–74). Boston: McGraw-Hill.

Hall, R. L., & Fine, M. (2005). The stories we tell: The lives and friendship of two older Black lesbians. *Psychology of Women Quarterly, 29,* 177–187.

Hall, R. L., & Greene, B. (2002). Not any one thing: The complex legacy of social class on African American lesbian relationships. *Journal of Lesbian Studies, 6,* 65–74.

Hall, R. L., & Greene, B. (2003). Contemporary African American families. In L. B. Silverstein & T. J. Goodrich (Eds.), *Feminist family therapy: Empowerment in social context* (pp. 107–120). Washington, DC: American Psychological Association.

Hall, R. M., & Sandler, B. R. (1982). *The classroom climate: A chilly one for women?* Project on the Status and Education of Women. Washington, DC: Association of American Colleges.

Halliwell, E., & Dittmar, H. (2003). A qualitative investigation of women's and men's body image concerns and their attitudes toward aging. *Sex Roles, 49,* 675–684.

Halpern, C. T. (2003). Biological influences on adolescent romantic and sexual behavior. In P. Florsheim (Ed.), *Adolescent romantic relations and sexual behavior* (pp. 57–84). Mahwah, NJ: Erlbaum.

Halpern, D. F. (1985). The influence of sex-role stereotypes on prose recall. *Sex Roles, 12,* 363–375.

Halpern, D. F. (1997). Sex differences in intelligence: Implications for education. *American Psychologist, 52,* 1091–1102.

Halpern, D. F. (2000). *Sex differences in cognitive abilities* (3rd ed.). Mahwah, NJ: Erlbaum.

Halpern, D. F. (2001). Sex difference research: Cognitive abilities. In J. Worell (Ed.), *The encyclopedia of women and gender* (pp. 963–971). San Diego: Academic Press.

Halpern, D. F. (2004a). A cognitive-process taxonomy for sex differences in cognitive abilities. *Current Directions in Psychological Science, 13,* 135–139.

Halpern, D. F. (2004b, February). I dare you to try this at home (or at work). *Monitor on Psychology,* p. 5.

Halpern, D. F. (2006). Girls and academic success: Changing patterns of academic achievement. In J. Worell & C. D. Goodheart (Eds.), *Handbook of girls' and women's psychological health: Gender and well-being across the life span* (pp. 272–282). New York: Oxford University Press.

Halpern, D. F., & Collaer, M. L. (2005). Sex differences in visuospatial abilities: More than meets the eye. In A. Miyake & P. Shaw (Eds.), *The Cambridge handbook of visuospatial thinking.* New York: Cambridge University Press.

Halpern, D. F., & Ikier, S. (2002). Causes, correlates, and caveats: Understanding the development of sex differences in cognition. In A. McGillicuddy-De Lisi & R. De Lisi (Eds.), *Biology, society, and behavior: The development of sex differences in cognition* (pp. 3–19). Westport, CT: Ablex Publishing.

Halpern, D. F., & Tan, U. (2001). Stereotypes and steroids: Using a psychobiosocial model to understand cognitive sex differences. *Brain and Cognition, 45,* 392–414.

Halpern, D. F., Wai, J., & Saw, A. (2004). A psychobiosocial model: Why females are sometimes greater than and sometimes less than males in math achievement. In A. M. Gallagher & J. C.

Kaufman (Eds.), *Gender differences in mathematics: An integrative psychological approach* (pp. 48–72). New York: Cambridge University Press.

Hambright, M. K., & Decker, J. D. (2002). The unprotected: The sexual harassment of lesbians and gays. In L. Diamant & J. A. Lee (Eds.), *The psychology of sex, gender, and jobs* (pp. 121–140). Westport, CT: Praeger.

Hamby, S. L., & Koss, M. P. (2003). Shades of gray: A qualitative study of terms used in the measurement of sexual victimization. *Psychology of Women Quarterly, 27,* 243–255.

Hamilton, J. A., & Russo, N. F. (2006). Women and depression: Research, theory, and social policy. In C. L. M. Keyes & S. H. Goodman (Eds.), *Women and depression: A handbook for the social, behavioral, and biomedical sciences* (pp. 479–522). New York: Cambridge University Press.

Hamilton, M. C. (1991). Masculine bias in the attribution of personhood: People = male, male = people. *Psychology of Women Quarterly, 15,* 393–402.

Hamilton, M. C. (2001). Sex-related difference research: Personality. In J. Worell (Ed.), *Encyclopedia of women and gender* (pp. 973–981). San Diego: Academic Press.

Hamilton, M. C., Anderson, D., Broaddus, M., & Young, K. (2006). Gender stereotyping and under-representation of female characters in 200 popular children's picture books: A 21st century update. *Sex Roles,* in press.

Hammond, W. P., & Mattis, J. S. (2005). Being a man about it: Manhood meaning among African American men. *Psychology of Men & Masculinity, 6,* 114–126.

Hamon, R. R., & Ingoldsby, B. B. (Eds.). (2003). *Mate selection across cultures.* Thousand Oaks, CA: Sage.

Hampson, E., & Moffat, S. D. (2004). The psychobiology of gender: Cognitive effects of reproductive hormones in the adult nervous system. In A. H. Eagly, A. E.

Beall, & R. J. Sternberg (Eds.), *The psychology of gender* (2nd ed., pp. 38–64). New York: Guilford.

Handa, A. (2003). *Of silk saris and mini-skirts: South Asian girls walk the tightrope of culture.* Toronto: Women's Press.

Hans, A. (2004). Escaping conflict: Afghan women in transit. In W. Giles & J. Hyndman (Eds.), *Sites of violence: Gender and conflict zones* (pp. 232–248). Berkeley: University of California Press.

Hansen, S. (2002). Cardiovascular disease. In S. G. Kornstein & A. H. Clayton (Eds.), *Women's mental health* (pp. 422–436). New York: Guilford.

Hanson, S. L., & Johnson, E. P. (2000). Expecting the unexpected: A comparative study of African American women's experiences in science during the high school years. *Journal of Women and Minorities in Science and Engineering, 6,* 265–294.

Hardie, E. A. (1997). Prevalence and predictors of cyclic and noncyclic affective change. *Psychology of Women Quarterly, 21,* 299–314.

Hare-Mustin, R. T., & Marecek, J. (1994). Asking the right questions: Feminist psychology and sex differences. *Feminism and Psychology, 4,* 531–537.

Harm, N. J. (2001). Grandmothers raising grandchildren: Parenting the second time around. In J. D. Garner & S. O. Mercer (Eds.), *Women as they age* (2nd ed., pp. 131–146). New York: Haworth.

Harper, M., & Schoeman, W. J. (2003). Influences of gender as a basic-level category in person perception on the gender belief system. *Sex Roles, 49,* 517–526.

Harris, K. L., Melaas, K., & Rodacker, E. (1999). The impact of women's studies courses on college students in the 1990s. *Sex Roles, 40,* 969–977.

Harris, M. B., & Miller, K. C. (2000). Gender and perceptions of danger. *Sex Roles, 43,* 843–863.

Harris, M. G. (1994). Cholas, Mexican-American girls, and gangs. *Sex Roles, 30,* 289–301.

Harris, R. J., & Firestone, J. M. (1998). Changes in predictors of gender role ideologies among women: A multivariate analysis. *Sex Roles, 38,* 239–252.

Hartmann, H., & Lee, S. (2003, April). *Social security: The largest source of income for both women and men in retirement* (Briefing Paper #D455). Washington, DC: Institute for Women's Policy Research.

Hartup, W. W. (1999). Foreword. In W. Furman, B. B. Brown, & C. Feiring (Eds.), *The development of romantic relationships in adolescence* (pp. xi–xv). New York: Cambridge University Press.

Harvey, J. A., & Hansen, C. E. (1999). Gender role of male therapists in both professional and personal life. *Sex Roles, 41,* 105–113.

Harvey, J. H., & Weber, A. L. (2002). *Odyssey of the heart: Close relationships in the 21st century* (2nd ed.). Mahwah, NJ: Erlbaum.

Harvey, P. D. (2000). *Let every child be wanted.* Westport, CT: Auburn House.

Harville, M. L., & Rienzi, B. M. (2000). Equal worth and gracious submission: Judeo-Christian attitudes toward employed women. *Psychology of Women Quarterly, 24,* 145–147.

Harway, M. (2003). Assessment of domestic violence. In L. B. Silverstein & T. J. Goodrich (Eds.), *Feminist family therapy: Empowerment in social context* (pp. 319–331). Washington, DC: American Psychological Association.

Harwood, R., et al. (2002). Parenting among Latino families in the U.S. In M. H. Bornstein (Ed.), *Handbook of parenting* (2nd ed., Vol. 4, pp. 21–46). Mahwah, NJ: Erlbaum.

Hase, M. (2001). Student resistance and nationalism in the classroom: Some reflections on globalizing the curriculum. *Feminist Teacher, 13,* 90–107.

Haskell, M. (1997). *Holding my own in no man's land: Women and men and film and feminists.* New York: Oxford University Press.

Hatcher, R. A., et al. (2004). *Contraceptive technology* (18th rev. ed.). New York: Ardent Media.

Hatfield, E., & Rapson, R. L. (1993). *Love, sex, and intimacy: Their psychology, biology, and history.* New York: HarperCollins.

Hatfield, E., & Rapson, R. L. (1996). *Love and sex: Cross-cultural perspectives.* Boston: Allyn & Bacon.

Hatfield, E., & Sprecher, S. (1995). Men's and women's preferences in marital partners in the United States, Russia, and Japan. *Journal of Cross-Cultural Psychology, 26,* 728–750.

Haugen, E. N., Schmutzer, P. A., & Wenzel, A. (2004). Sexuality and the partner relationship during pregnancy and the postpartum period. In J. H. Harvey, A. Wenzel, & S. Sprecher (Eds.), *The handbook of sexuality in close relationships* (pp. 411–435). Mahwah, NJ: Erlbaum.

Hawkes, E. (2003, Fall). What Wal-Mart women want. *Ms. Magazine,* pp. 52–55.

Hawkins, B. D. (1994, November 3). An evening with Gwendolyn Brooks. *Black Issues in Higher Education,* pp. 16–21.

Hawkins, B. D. (2005, January 27). Cultural attitudes and body dissatisfaction. *Black Issues in Higher Education,* p. 27.

Hawkins, J. W., & Aber, C. S. (1993). Women in advertisements in medical journals. *Sex Roles, 28,* 233–242.

Hawkins, S. R., Miller, S. P., & Steiner, H. (2003). Aggression, psychopathology, and delinquency: Influences of gender and maturation—where did all the good girls go? In C. Hayward (Ed.), *Gender differences at puberty* (pp. 93–110). New York: Cambridge University Press.

Hay, D. F., et al. (2003). Pathways to violence in the children of mothers who were depressed postpartum. *Developmental Psychology, 39,* 1083–1094.

Hays, J., et al. (2003). Effects of estrogen plus progestin on health-related quality of life. *New England Journal of Medicine, 348,* 1839–1854.

Hayward, C. (2003). Methodological concerns in puberty-related research. In C. Hayward (Ed.), *Gender differences at puberty* (pp. 1–14). New York: Cambridge University Press.

Hearn, K. D., O'Sullivan, L. F., & Dudley, C. D. (2003). Assessing reliability of early adolescent girls' reports of romantic and sexual behavior. *Archives of Sexual Behavior, 32,* 513–521.

Heatherington, L., Burns, A. B., & Gustafson, T. B. (1998). When another stumbles: Gender and self-presentation to vulnerable others. *Sex Roles, 38,* 889–913.

Heatherington, L., et al. (1993). Two investigations of "female modesty" in achievement situations. *Sex Roles, 29,* 739–754.

Hebl, M. R., Kazama, S. M., Singletary, S. L., & Glick, P. (2006). *Hostile and benevolent discrimination toward pregnant women: Complementary interpersonal punishments and rewards that maintain traditional roles.* Unpublished manuscript, Rice University.

Hecht, M. A., & LaFrance, M. (1998). License or obligation to smile: The effect of power and sex on amount and type of smiling. *Personality and Social Psychology Bulletin, 24,* 1332–1342.

Heck, K. E., Schoendorf, K. C., Chávez, G. F., & Braverman, P. (2003). Does postpartum length of stay affect breastfeeding duration? A population-based study. *Birth, 30,* 153–159.

Heckert, T. M., et al. (2002). Gender differences in anticipated salary: Role of salary estimates for others, job characteristics, career paths, and job inputs. *Sex Roles, 47,* 139–151.

Hedge, J. W., Borman, W. C., & Lammlein, S. E. (2006). *The aging workforce.* Washington, DC: American Psychological Association.

Hedges, L., & Nowell, A. (1995). Sex differences in mental test scores, variability, and numbers of high-scoring individuals. *Science, 269,* 41–45.

Hedley, M. (2002a). The geometry of gendered conflict in popular film: 1986–2000. *Sex Roles, 47,* 201–217.

Hedley, M. (2002b). Gendered conflict resolution in popular film: Epiphanies of female deference. *The Journal of American and Contemporary Cultures, 25,* 363–374.

Heilman, M. E. (2001). Description and prescription: How gender stereotypes prevent women's ascent up the organizational ladder. *Journal of Social Issues, 57,* 657–674.

Heilman, M. E., Wallen, A. S., Fuchs, D., & Tamkins, M. M. (2004). Penalties for success: Reactions to women who succeed at male gender-typed tasks. *Journal of Applied Psychology, 89,* 416–427.

Heiman, J. R. (2000). Orgasmic disorders in women. In S. R. Leiblum & R. C. Rosen (Eds.), *Principles and practice of sex therapy* (3rd ed., pp. 118–153). New York: Guilford.

Helgeson, V. S., & Fritz, H. L. (1998). Distinctions of unmitigated communion from communion: Self-neglect and overinvolvement with others. *Personality and Social Psychology Review, 75,* 121–140.

Hellenga, K., Aber, M. S., & Rhodes, J. E. (2002). African American adolescent mothers' vocational aspiration-expectation gap: Individual, social and environmental influences. *Psychology of Women Quarterly, 26,* 200–212.

Helstrom, A. W., Coffey, C., & Jorgannathan, P. (1998). Asian-American women's health. In A. Blechman & K. D. Brownell (Eds.), *Behavioral medicine and women: A comprehensive handbook* (pp. 826–832). New York: Guilford.

Helwig, A. A. (1998). Gender-role stereotyping: Testing theory with a longitudinal sample. *Sex Roles, 38,* 403–423.

Henderson-King, D., Henderson-King, E., & Hoffman, L. (2001). Media images and women's self-evaluations: Social context and importance of attractiveness as moderators. *Personality and Social Psychology Bulletin, 27,* 1407–1416.

Henderson-King, D., & Zhermer, N. (2003). Feminist consciousness among Russians and Americans. *Sex Roles, 48,* 143–155.

Hendrick, C., & Hendrick, S. (1996). Gender and the experience of heterosexual love. In J. T. Wood (Ed.), *Gendered relationships* (pp. 131–148). Mountain View, CA: Mayfield.

Hendrick, S. S. (2006). Love, intimacy, and partners. In J. Worell & C. D. Goodheart (Eds.), *Handbook of girls' and women's psychological health: Gender and well-being across the life span* (pp. 321–329). New York: Oxford University Press.

Henley, N. M. (1985). Psychology and gender. *Signs, 11,* 101–119.

Henley, N. M., et al. (1998). Developing a scale to measure the diversity of feminist attitudes. *Psychology of Women Quarterly, 22,* 317–348.

Henningsen, D. D. (2004). Flirting with meaning: An examination of miscommunication in flirting interactions. *Sex Roles, 50,* 481–489.

Henrie, R. L., Aron, R. H., Nelson, B. D., & Poole, D. A. (1997). Gender-related knowledge variations within geography. *Sex Roles, 36,* 605–623.

Henschke, C. I., & Miettinen, O. S. (2004). Women's susceptibility to tobacco carcinogens. *Lung Cancer, 43,* 1–5.

Herbert, S. E. (1996). Lesbian sexuality. In R. P. Cabaj & T. S. Stein (Eds.), *Textbook of homosexuality and mental health* (pp. 723–742). Washington, DC: American Psychiatric Press.

Herbert, S. E., & Bachanas, P. (2002). HIV/AIDS. In S. G. Kornstein & A. H. Clayton (Eds.), *Women's mental health* (pp. 452–466). New York: Guilford.

Herdt, G. (2001). Social change, sexual diversity, and tolerance for bisexuality in the United States. In A. R. D'Augelli & C. J. Patterson (Eds.), *Lesbian, gay, and bisexual identities and youth* (pp. 267–283). New York: Oxford University Press.

Herek, G. M. (1996). Why tell if you're not asked? Self-disclosure, intergroup contact, and heterosexuals' attitudes toward lesbians and gay men. In G. M.

Herek, J. B. Jobe, & R. M. Carney (Eds.), *Out in force: Sexual orientation and the military* (pp. 197–225). Chicago: University of Chicago Press.

Herek, G. M. (2000). The psychology of sexual prejudice. *Current Directions in Psychological Science, 9,* 19–22.

Herek, G. M. (2002a). Gender gaps in public opinion about lesbians and gay men. *Public Opinion Quarterly, 66,* 40–66.

Herek, G. M. (2002b). Heterosexuals' attitudes toward bisexual men and women in the United States. *The Journal of Sex Research, 38,* 264–272.

Herek, G. M. (2004). Beyond "homophobia": Thinking about sexual prejudice and stigma in the twenty-first century. *Sexuality Research & Social Policy, 1,* 6–24.

Herek, G. M., Cogan, J. C., & Gillis, J. R. (2002). Victim experiences in hate crimes based on sexual orientation. *Journal of Social Issues, 38,* 319–339.

Herek, G. M., Gillis, J. R., & Cogan, J. C. (1999). Psychological sequelae of hate-crime victimization among lesbian, gay, and bisexual adults. *Journal of Consulting and Clinical Psychology, 67,* 945–951.

Herek, G. M., Gillis, J. R., Cogan, J. C., & Glunt, E. K. (1997). Hate crime victimization among lesbian, gay, and bisexual adults: Prevalence, psychological correlates, and methodological issues. *Journal of Interpersonal Violence, 12,* 195–215.

Herlitz, A., Airaksinen, E., & Nordström, E. (1999). Sex differences in episodic memory: The impact of verbal and visuospatial ability. *Neuropsychology, 13,* 590–597.

Herlitz, A., Nilsson, L., & Bäckman, L. (1997). Gender differences in episodic memory. *Memory and Cognition, 25,* 801–811.

Herlitz, A., & Yonker, J. E. (2002). Sex differences in episodic memory: The influence of intelligence. *Journal of Clinical and Experimental Neuropsychology, 24,* 107–114.

Herrera, V. M., et al. (2006). Survivors of male violence: Research and training initiative to facilitate recovery from depression and posttraumatic stress disorder. In J. Worell & C. D. Goodheart (Eds.), *Handbook of girls' and women's psychological health: Gender and well-being across the life span* (pp. 455–466). New York: Oxford University Press.

Herrmann, D. J., Crawford, M., & Holdsworth, M. (1992). Gender-linked differences in everyday memory performance. *British Journal of Psychology, 83,* 221–231.

Hershberger, S. L. (2001). Biological factors in the development of sexual orientation. In A. R. D'Augelli & C. J. Patterson (Eds.), *Lesbian, gay, and bisexual identities and youth* (pp. 27–51). New York: Oxford University Press.

Hesse-Biber, S., & Carter, G. L. (2000). *Working women in America: Split dreams.* New York: Oxford University Press.

Hettema, J., Steele, J., & Miller, W. R. (2005). Motivational interviewing. *Annual Review of Clinical Psychology, 1,* 91–111.

Hewitt, E. C., & Moore, L. D. (2002). The role of lay theories of the etiologies of homosexuality in attitudes towards lesbians and gay men. *Journal of Lesbian Studies, 6,* 59–72.

Hewstone, M., Rubin, M., & Willis, H. (2002). Intergroup bias. *Annual Review of Psychology, 53,* 575–604.

Heyman, G. D. (2001). Children's interpretation of ambiguous behavior: Evidence for a "boys are bad" bias. *Social Development, 10,* 230–247.

Hickman, S. E., & Muehlenhard, C. L. (1997). College women's fears and precautionary behaviors relating to acquaintance rape and stranger rape. *Psychology of Women Quarterly, 21,* 527–547.

Hickman, S. E., & Muehlenhard, C. L. (1999). "By the semi-mystical appearance of a condom": How young women and men communicate sexual consent in heterosexual situations. *Journal of Sex Research, 36,* 258–272.

Higgins, L. T., Zheng, M., Liu, Y., & Sun, C. H. (2002). Attitudes to marriage and sexual behaviors: A survey of gender and culture differences in China and United Kingdom. *Sex Roles, 46,* 75–89.

Hill, S. A. (2002). Teaching and doing gender in African American families. *Sex Roles, 47,* 493–506.

Hillard, P. J. A., & Kahn, J. A. (2005). Understanding and preventing human papillomavirus infection during adolescence and young adulthood. *Journal of Adolescent Health, 37,* S1–S2.

Hilton, J. L., & von Hippel, W. (1996). Stereotypes. *Annual Review of Psychology, 47,* 237–271.

Hines, D. A., & Malley-Morrison, K. (2005). *Family violence in the United States: Defining, understanding, and combating abuse.* Thousand Oaks, CA: Sage.

Hines, M. (2004). *Brain gender.* New York: Oxford University.

Hines, P. M., & Boyd-Franklin, N. (2005). African American families. In M. McGoldrick, J. Giordano, & N. Garcia-Preto (Eds.), *Ethnicity and family therapy* (3rd ed., pp. 87–100). New York: Guilford.

Ho, C. K. (1997). An analysis of domestic violence in Asian American communities: A multicultural approach to counseling. In K. P. Monteiro (Ed.), *Ethnicity and psychology* (pp. 138–152). Dubuque, IA: Kendall/Hunt.

Hochschild, A. R. (2003). *The commercialization of intimate life.* Berkeley: University of California Press.

Hochschild, J. L. (2003). Social class in public schools. *Journal of Social Issues, 59,* 821–840.

Hodges, L. (2000, June 1). Any complaints, students? Go and tell the Queen. *The Independent,* pp. 2–3.

Hoff, T., & Greene, L. (2000). *Sex education in America.* Menlo Park, CA: Henry J. Kaiser Family Foundation.

Hoffman, L. W. (2000). Maternal employment: Effects of social context. In R. D. Taylor and M. C. Wang (Eds.), *Resilience across contexts: Family, work, culture, and community* (pp. 147–176). Mahwah, NJ: Erlbaum.

Hoffman, L. W., & Kloska, D. D. (1995). Parents' gender-based attitudes toward marital roles and child rearing: Development and validation of new measures. *Sex Roles, 32,* 273–295.

Hoffman, L. W., & Youngblade, L. M. (1999). *Mothers at work: Effects on children's well-being.* New York: Cambridge University Press.

Hoffmann, M. L., Powlishta, K. K., & White, K. J. (2004). An examination of gender differences in adolescent adjustment: The effect of competence on gender role differences in symptoms of psychopathology. *Sex Roles, 50,* 795–810.

Hoffnung, M. (1992). *What's a mother to do? Conversations on work and family.* Pasadena, CA: Trilogy.

Hoffnung, M. (1993). *College women's expectations for work and family.* Poster presented at the annual meeting of the Association for Women in Psychology, Atlanta, GA.

Hoffnung, M. (1995). Motherhood: Contemporary conflict for women. In J. Freeman (Ed.), *Women: A feminist perspective* (pp. 162–181). Mountain View, CA: Mayfield.

Hoffnung, M. (1999, Spring). Women's changing attitudes toward work and family: College to five years after. *Women and Work, 1,* 27–39.

Hoffnung, M. (2000, March). *Motherhood and career: Changes in college women's thoughts over time.* Paper presented at the annual meeting of the Eastern Psychological Association, Baltimore.

Hoffnung, M. (2003). Studying women's lives: College to seven years after. In E. S. Adler & R. Clark (Eds.), *How it's done: An invitation to social research* (pp. 74–78). Pacific Grove, CA: Wadsworth.

Hoffnung, M. (2004). Wanting it all: Career, marriage, and motherhood during college-educated women's 20's. *Sex Roles, 50,* 711–723.

Hofschire, L. J., & Greenberg, B. S. (2002). Media's impact on adolescents' body dissatisfaction. In J. D. Brown, J. R. Steele, & K. Walsh-Childers (Eds.), *Sexual teens, sexual media: Investigating media's influence on adolescent sexuality* (pp. 125–149). Mahwah, NJ: Erlbaum.

Hogue, M., & Yoder, J. D. (2003). The role of status in producing depressed entitlement in women's and men's pay allocations. *Psychology of Women Quarterly, 27,* 330–337.

Holland, D. C., & Eisenhart, M. A. (1990). *Educated in romance: Women, achievement, and college culture.* Chicago: University of Chicago Press.

Holliday, B. G., & Holmes, A. L. (2003). A tale of challenge and change: A history and chronology of ethnic minorities in psychology in the United States. In G. Bernal, J. E. Trimble, A. K. Burley, & F. T. L. Leong (Eds.), *Handbook of racial and ethnic minority psychology* (pp. 15–64). Thousand Oaks, CA: Sage.

Hollingworth, L. S. (1914). Functional periodicity: An experimental study of mental and motor abilities of women during menstruation (Contributions to *Education* No. 69, pp. v–14, 86–101). New York: Teachers College, Columbia University.

Hollon, S. D., & DeRubeis, R. J. (2004). Effectiveness of treatment for depression. In R. L. Leahy (Ed.), *Contemporary cognitive therapy* (pp. 45–61). New York: Guilford.

Holmes, J. (1998). Women's talk: The question of sociolinguistic universals. In J. Coates (Ed.), *Language and gender: A reader* (pp. 461–483). Malden, MA: Blackwell.

Hom, A. Y. (2003). Stories from the homefront: Perspectives of Asian-American parents with lesbian daughters and gay sons. In L. D. Garnets & D. C. Kimmel (Eds.), *Psychological perspectives on lesbian, gay, and bisexual experiences* (2nd ed., pp. 549–570). New York: Columbia University Press.

Hood, A. (1995). It's a wonderful divorce. In P. Kaganoff & S. Spano (Eds.), *Women and divorce* (pp. 119–133). New York: Harcourt Brace.

hooks, b. (1994, July 13). Black students who reject feminism. *Chronicle of Higher Education,* p. A44.

hooks, b. (2000a). *Feminism is for everybody: Passionate politics.* Cambridge, MA: South End Press.

hooks, b. (2000b, November 17). Learning in the shadow of race and class. *Chronicle of Higher Education,* pp. B14–B15.

hooks, b. (2001). Revolutionary feminism: An antiracist agenda. In S. M. Shaw & J. Lee (Eds.), *Women's voices, feminist visions* (pp. 33–36). Mountain View, CA: Mayfield.

Hoover, E. (2004, October 15). Bates calls its SAT-optional policy a boon. *Chronicle of Higher Education,* pp. A32–A33.

Horgan, D. (1983). The pregnant woman's place and where to find it. *Sex Roles, 9,* 333–339.

Horgan, J. (2004, November 26). Do our genes influence behavior? Why we want to think they do. *Chronicle of Higher Education,* pp. B12–B13.

Horner, M. S. (1968). *Sex differences in achievement motivation and performance in competitive and noncompetitive situations.* Unpublished doctoral dissertation, University of Michigan, Ann Arbor.

Horner, M. S. (1978). The measurement and behavioral implications of fear of success in women. In J. W. Atkinson & J. O. Raynor (Eds.), *Personality, motivation, and achievement* (pp. 41–70). Washington, DC: Hemisphere.

Horowitz, L. M. (2004). *Interpersonal foundations of psychopathology.* Washington, DC: American Psychological Association.

Horvath, M., & Ryan, A. M. (2003). Antecedents and potential moderators of the relationship between attitudes and hiring discrimination on the basis of sexual orientation. *Sex Roles, 48,* 115–130.

Houseman, B. L. (2003). *Mother's milk: Breastfeeding controversies in American culture.* New York: Routledge.

Houts, A. C. (2002). Discovery, invention, and the expansion of the modern Diagnostic and Statistical Manuals of Mental Disorders. In L. E. Beutler & M. L. Malik (Eds.), *Rethinking the DSM: A psychological perspective* (pp. 17–65). Washington, DC: American Psychological Association.

Howard, J. A., & Hollander, J. (1997). *Gendered situations, gendered selves.* Thousand Oaks, CA: Sage.

Howe, F. (2001a). *The politics of women's studies: Testimony from thirty founding mothers.* New York: Feminist Press.

Howe, F. (2001b). "Promises to keep": Trends in women's studies worldwide. In S. Ruth (Ed.), *Issues in feminism* (5th ed.). Mountain View, CA: Mayfield.

Howell-White, S. (1999). *Birth alternatives: How women select childbirth care.* Westport, CT: Greenwood Press.

Hoyert, D. L., Daniel, I., & Tully, P. (2000). Maternal mortality, United States and Canada, 1982–1997. *Birth, 27,* 4–11.

Hoynes, W. (1999, September/October). The cost of survival. *Extra!,* pp. 11–23.

Hu, F. B., et al. (2004). Adiposity as compared with physical activity in predicting mortality among women. *New England Journal of Medicine, 351,* 2694–2704.

Hudson, V. M., & den Boer, A. M. (2004). *Bare branches: Security implications of Asia's surplus male population.* Cambridge, MA: MIT Press.

Huggler, J. (November 2006). Women's lives "no better" in new Afghanistan. *The Independent UK.* Retrieved November 15, 2006 from http://www.truthout.org/issues_06/110106WB.shtml

Hughes, F. M., & Seta, C. E. (2003). Gender stereotypes: Children's perceptions of future compensatory behavior following violations of gender roles. *Sex Roles, 49,* 685–691.

Hughes, T. L., Matthews, A. K., Razzano, L., & Aranda, F. (2003). Psychological distress in African American lesbian and heterosexual women. In T. L. Hughes, C. Smith, & A. Dan

(Eds.), *Mental health issues for sexual minority women: Redefining women's mental health* (pp. 51–68). New York: Haworth.

Human Rights Campaign Foundation/Urban Institute. (2003, June 13). *United States: Long form census data.* Retrieved July 25, 2005 from http://www.hrc.org/Template.cfm?Section=Search&Template=/ContentManagement/ContentDisplay.cfm&ContentID=18757

Humes, C. W., Szymanski, E. M., & Hohenshil, T. H. (1995). Roles of counseling in enabling persons with disabilities. In R. R. Atkinson & G. Hackett (Eds.), *Counseling diverse populations* (pp. 155–166). Madison, WI: Brown & Benchmark.

Hummert, M. L., Garstka, T. A., Ryan, E. B., & Bonnesen, J. L. (2004). The role of age stereotypes in interpersonal communication. In J. F. Nussbaum & J. Coupland (Eds.), *Handbook of communication and aging research* (2nd ed., pp. 91–114). Mahwah, NJ: Erlbaum.

Hummert, M. L., Garstka, T. A., & Shaner, J. L. (1997). Stereotyping of older adults: The role of target facial cues and perceiver characteristics. *Psychology and Aging, 12,* 107–114.

Hung, S., Morrison, D. R., Whittington, L. A., & Fein, S. B. (2002). Prepartum work, job characteristics, and risk of cesarean delivery. *Birth, 29,* 10–17.

Huntemann, N., & Morgan, M. (2001). Mass media and identity development. In D. G. Singer & J. L. Singer (Eds.), *Handbook on children and the media* (pp. 309–322). Thousand Oaks, CA: Sage.

Hunter College Women's Studies Collective. (1995). *Women's realities, women's choices* (2nd ed.). New York: Oxford University Press.

Hunter, S., Sundel, S. S., & Sundel, M. (2002). *Women at midlife.* Washington, DC: National Association of Social Workers.

Hurtado, A. (2003). *Voicing Chicana feminisms: Young women speak out on sexuality and identity.* New York: New York University Press.

Hurtz, W., & Durkin, K. (1997). Gender role stereotyping in Australian radio commercials. *Sex Roles, 36,* 103–114.

Husten, C. G. (1998). Cigarette smoking. In E. A. Blechman & K. D. Brownell (Eds.), *Behavioral medicine and women: A comprehensive handbook* (pp. 425–430). New York: Guilford.

Huston, T. L., & Holmes, E. K. (2004). Becoming parents. In A. L. Vangelisti (Ed.), *Handbook of family communication* (pp. 105–133). Mahwah, NJ: Erlbaum.

Huston, T. L., & Melz, H. (2004). The case for (promoting) marriage: The devil is in the details. *Journal of Marriage and Family, 66,* 943–958.

Huttenlocher, J., et al. (1991). Early vocabulary growth: Relation to language input and gender. *Developmental Psychology, 27,* 236–248.

Hvas, L. (2001). Positive aspects of menopause: A qualitative study. *Maturitas, 39,* 11–17.

Hyde, J. S. (1981). How large are cognitive gender differences? A meta-analysis using w^2 and d. *American Psychologist, 36,* 892–901.

Hyde, J. S. (1996a). Gender and cognition: A commentary on current research. *Learning and Individual Differences, 8,* 33–38.

Hyde, J. S. (1996b). Where are the gender differences? Where are the gender similarities? In D. M. Buss & N. M. Malamuth (Eds.), *Sex, power, conflict: Evolutionary and feminist perspectives* (pp. 107–118). New York: Oxford University Press.

Hyde, J. S. (2001). Autobiographical perspectives. In A. N. O'Connell (Ed.), *Models of achievement: Reflections of eminent women in psychology* (Vol. 3, pp. 308–327). Mahwah, NJ: Erlbaum.

Hyde, J. S. (2002). Another good evolution story [Review of the book *The dangerous passion: Why jealousy is as necessary as love and sex*], *Psychology of Women Quarterly, 26,* 170.

Hyde, J. S. (2005a). The gender similarities hypothesis. *American Psychologist, 60,* 581–592.

Hyde, J. S. (2005b). The genetics of sexual orientation. In J. S. Hyde (Ed.), *Biological substrates of human sexuality* (pp. 9–20). Washington, DC: American Psychological Association.

Hyde, J. S., & DeLamater, J. (2000). Sexuality during pregnancy and the year postpartum. In C. B. Travis & J. W. White (Eds.), *Sexuality, society, and feminism* (pp. 167–180). Washington, DC: American Psychological Association.

Hyde, J. S., & DeLamater, J. D. (2003). *Understanding human sexuality* (8th ed.). New York: McGraw-Hill.

Hyde, J. S., & DeLamater, J. D. (2006). *Understanding human sexuality* (9th ed.). New York: McGraw-Hill.

Hyde, J. S., Fennema, E., Ryan, M., Frost, L. A., & Hopp, C. (1990). Gender comparisons of mathematics attitudes and affect: A meta-analysis. *Psychology of Women Quarterly, 14,* 299–324.

Hyde, J. S., & Jaffee, S. R. (2000). Becoming a heterosexual adult: The experiences of young women. *Journal of Social Issues, 56,* 283–296.

Hyde, J. S., & Kling, K. C. (2001). Women, motivation, and achievement. *Psychology of Women Quarterly, 25,* 364–378.

Hyde, J. S., & Linn, M. C. (1988). Gender differences in verbal ability: A meta-analysis. *Psychological Bulletin, 104,* 53–69.

Hyde, J. S., & Mezulis, A. H. (2001). Gender difference research. In J. Worell (Ed.), *Encyclopedia of women and gender* (pp. 551–559). San Diego: Academic Press.

Hyde, J. S., & Oliver, M. B. (2000). Gender differences in sexuality: Results from meta-analysis. In C. B. Travis & J. W. White (Eds.), *Sexuality, society, and feminism* (pp. 57–77). Washington, DC: American Psychological Association.

Hyde, J. S., & Plant, E. A. (1995). Magnitude of psychological gender differences: Another side to the story. *American Psychologist, 50,* 159–161.

Hyman, I. E., Jr., Husband, T. H., & Billings, F. J. (1995). False mem-

ories of childhood experiences. *Applied Cognitive Psychology, 9,* 181–197.

Hynie, M., Lydon, J. E., & Taradash, A. (1997). Commitment, intimacy, and women's perceptions of premarital sex and contraceptive readiness. *Psychology of Women Quarterly, 21,* 447–464.

Ickovics, J. R., Thayaparan, B., & Ethier, K. A. (2001). Women and AIDS: A contextual analysis. In A. Baum, T. A. Revenson, & J. E. Singer (Eds.), *Handbook of health psychology* (pp. 817–840). Mahwah, NJ: Erlbaum.

Idle, T., Wood, E., & Desmarais, S. (1993). Gender role socialization in toy play situations: Mothers and fathers with their sons and daughters. *Sex Roles, 28,* 679–691.

Im, E., & Meleis, A. I. (2000). Meanings of menopause to Korean immigrant women. *Western Journal of Nursing Research, 22,* 84–102.

Impett, E. A., & Peplau, L. A. (2002). Why some women consent to unwanted sex with a dating partner: Insights from attachment theory. *Psychology of Women Quarterly, 26,* 360–370.

Impett, E. A., & Peplau, L. A. (2003). Sexual compliance: Gender, motivational, and relationship perspectives. *Journal of Sex Research, 40,* 87–100.

Impett, E. A., & Peplau, L. A. (2005). Comparing the experiences of women and men in intimate relationships. In A. Vangelisti & D. Perlman (Eds.), *The Cambridge handbook of personal relationships.* New York: Cambridge University Press.

India Abroad. (2005, May 20). *Matrimonial Bride.* Retrieved May 26, 2005, from http://www.indiaabroad.com/CLASSIFIED/current-listing/2910.shtml

Ineichen, B., Pierce, M., & Lawrenson, R. (1997). Teenage mothers as breastfeeders: Attitudes and behavior. *Journal of Adolescence, 20,* 505–509.

Ivins, M. (1997, September 27). Teen mothers lack good role models. *Liberal Opinion Week,* p. 12.

Iwamasa, G. Y., & Sorocco, K. H. (2002). Aging and Asian Americans: Developing culturally appropriate research methodology. In G. C. N. Hall & S. Okazaki (Eds.), *Asian American psychology* (pp. 105–130). Washington, DC: American Psychological Association.

Jack, D. C. (1999). *Behind the mask: Destruction and creativity in women's aggression.* Cambridge, MA: Harvard University Press.

Jack, D. C. (2003). The anger of hope and the anger of despair. In M. Stoppard & L. M. McMullen (Eds.), *Situating sadness: Women and depression in social context* (pp. 62–87). New York: New York University Press.

Jacklin, C. N., & Maccoby, E. E. (1983). Issues of gender differentiation. In M. D. Levine, W. B. Carey, A. C. Crocker, & R. T. Gross (Eds.), *Developmental behavioral pediatrics* (pp. 175–184). Philadelphia: Saunders.

Jackson, A. P., Brooks-Gunn, J., Huang, C., & Glassman, M. (2000). Single mothers in low-wage jobs: Financial strain, parenting, and preschoolers' outcomes. *Child Development, 71,* 1409–1423.

Jackson, L. A., Fleury, R. E., & Lewandowski, D. A. (1996). Feminism: Definitions, support, and correlates of support among female and male college students. *Sex Roles, 34,* 687–693.

Jackson, S. A. (1998). "Something about the word": African American women and feminism. In K. M. Blee (Ed.), *No middle ground: Women and radical protest* (pp. 38–50). New York: New York University Press.

Jackson, V. (2005). Robbing Peter to pay Paul. In M. P. Mirkin, K. L. Suyemoto, & B. F. Okun (Eds.), *Psychotherapy with women: Exploring diverse contexts and identities* (pp. 237–253). New York: Guilford.

Jacobi, C., Hayward, C., et al. (2004). Coming to terms with risk factors for eating disorders: Application of risk terminology and suggestions for a general taxonomy. *Psychological Bulletin, 130,* 19–65.

Jacobi, C., Paul, T., et al. (2004). Specificity of self-concept disturbances in eating disorders. *International Journal of Eating Disorders, 35,* 204–210.

Jacobs, J. E., et al. (2002). Changes in children's self-competence and values: Gender and domain differences across grades one through twelve. *Child Development, 73,* 509–527.

Jacobs, J. E., et al. (2004). "I can, but I don't want to." In A. M. Gallagher & J. C. Kaufman (Eds.), *Gender differences in mathematics: An integrative psychological approach* (pp. 246–263). New York: Cambridge University Press.

Jacobs, R. H. (1997). *Be an outrageous older woman.* New York: HarperCollins.

Jacobson, N. S., & Gottman, J. M. (1998). *When men batter women.* New York: Simon & Schuster.

Jadack, R. A. (2001). Sexually transmitted infections and their consequences. In J. Worell (Ed.), *Encyclopedia of women and gender* (pp. 1033–1041). San Diego: Academic Press.

Jaffee, S., & Hyde, J. S. (2000). Gender differences in moral orientation: A meta-analysis. *Psychological Bulletin, 126,* 703–726.

Jaffee, S., et al. (1999). The view from down here: Feminist graduate students consider innovative methodologies. *Psychology of Women Quarterly, 23,* 423–430.

James, E. M. (1994, August). *Helen Thompson Woolley: Forgotten pioneer of the psychology of women.* Paper presented at the annual convention of the American Psychological Association, Los Angeles, CA.

James, J. (1999). *Shadowboxing: Representations of Black feminist politics.* New York: St. Martin's Press.

James, J. B. (1997). What are the social issues involved in focusing on difference in the study of gender? *Journal of Social Issues, 53,* 213–232.

James, S. M., & Robertson, C. C. (2002). Introduction: Reimagining transnational sisterhood. In S. M. James & C. C. Robertson (Eds.), *Genital cutting and transnational sisterhood* (pp. 5–15). Urbana: University of Illinois Press.

Janz, T. A., & Pyke, S. W. (2000). A scale to assess student perceptions of academic climates. *Canadian Journal of Higher Education, 30,* 89–122.

Jay, T. (2000). *Why we curse.* Philadelphia: John Benjamins.

Jayakody, R., & Cabrera, N. (2002). What are the choices for low-income families?: Cohabitation, marriage, and remaining single. In A. Booth & A. C. Crouter (Eds.), *Just living together* (pp. 85–95). Mahwah, NJ: Erlbaum.

Jenkins, S. R. (2000). Introduction to the special issue: Defining gender, relationships, and power. *Sex Roles, 42,* 467–493.

Jennings, J., Geis, L., & Brown, V. (1980). Influence of television commercials on women's self-confidence and independent judgments. *Journal of Personality and Social Psychology, 38,* 203–210.

Jensen-Campbell, L. A., Graziano, W. G., & West, S. G. (1995). Dominance, prosocial orientation, and female preferences: Do nice guys really finish last? *Journal of Personality and Social Psychology, 68,* 427–440.

Jensvold, M. E., & Dan, C. E. (2001). Psychological aspects of the menstrual cycle. In N. L. Stotland & D. E. Stewart (Eds.), *Psychological aspects of women's health care* (pp. 177–203). Washington, DC: American Psychiatric Press.

Jernigan, D. H., Ostroff, J., Ross, C., & O'Hara, J. A. (2004). Sex differences in adolescent exposure to alcohol advertising in magazines. *Archives of Pediatric and Adolescent Medicine, 158,* 629–634.

Jerome, R., & Meadows, B. (2003, November 17). Uncommon valor. *People,* pp. 86–94.

Jersild, D. (2002, May 31). Alcohol in the vulnerable lives of college women. *Chronicle of Higher Education,* pp. B10–B11.

Jervis, L. (2004/2005). The end of feminism's third wave. *Ms. Magazine,* pp. 56–58.

Jipguep, M.-C., Sanders-Phillips, K., & Cotton, L. (2004). Another look at HIV in African American women: The impact of psychosocial and contextual factors. *Journal of Black Psychology, 30,* 366–385.

Jiwani, Y. (2000, Fall). The 1999 general social survey on spousal violence: An analysis. *Canadian Woman Studies/Les cahiers de la femme, 20,* 34–40.

Johannesen-Schmidt, M. C., & Eagly, A. H. (2002). Another look at sex differences in preferred mate characteristics: The effects of endorsing the traditional female gender role. *Psychology of Women Quarterly, 26,* 322–328.

Johnson, A. G. (2001). *Privilege, power, and differences.* Mountain View, CA: Mayfield.

Johnson, B. E., Kuck, D. L., & Schander, P. R. (1997). Rape myth acceptance and sociodemographic characteristics: A multidimensional analysis. *Sex Roles, 36,* 693–707.

Johnson, B. T., et al. (2003). Interventions to reduce sexual risk for the human immunodeficiency virus in adolescents, 1985–2000. *Archives of Pediatric and Adolescent Medicine, 157,* 381–388.

Johnson, C. A. (2005). Personal reflections on bias, stigma, discrimination, and obesity. In K. D. Brownell, R. M. Puhl, M. B. Schwartz, & L. Rudd (Eds.), *Weight bias: Nature, consequences, and remedies* (pp. 175–191). New York: Guilford.

Johnson, D., & Piore, A. (2004, October 18). Home in two worlds. *Newsweek,* pp. 52–54.

Johnson, L. B. (1997). Three decades of Black family empirical research: Challenges for the 21st century. In H. P. McAdoo (Ed.), *Black families* (3rd ed., pp. 94–113). Thousand Oaks, CA: Sage.

Johnson, M., & Helgeson, V. S. (2002). Sex differences in response to evaluative feedback: A field study. *Psychology of Women Quarterly, 26,* 242–251.

Johnson, M. E., & Dowling-Guyer, S. (1996). Effects of inclusive vs. exclusive language on evaluations of the counselor. *Sex Roles, 34,* 407–418.

Johnson, N. G. (2001, October). Changing outcomes in women's health. *APA Monitor,* p. 5.

Johnson, N. G. (2004). Introduction: Psychology and health—taking the initiative to bring it together. In R. H. Rozensky, N. G. Johnson, C. D. Goodheart, & W. R. Hammond (Eds.), *Psychology builds a healthy world* (pp. 3–31). Washington, DC: American Psychological Association.

Johnson, S. M., & O'Connor, E. (2001). *For lesbian parents: Your guide to helping your family grow up happy, healthy, and proud.* New York: Guilford.

Johnson, S. M., & O'Connor, E. (2002). *The gay baby boom: The psychology of gay parenthood.* New York: New York University Press.

Johnston, D. D., & Swanson, D. H. (2002, November). *Defining mother: The experience of mothering ideologies by work status.* Paper presented at the annual meeting of the National Communication Association, New Orleans.

Johnston, D. D., & Swanson, D. H. (2003a). Invisible mothers: A content analysis of motherhood ideologies and myths in magazines. *Sex Roles, 49,* 21–33.

Johnston, D. D., & Swanson, D. H. (2003b). Undermining mothers: A content analysis of the representation of mothers in magazines. *Mass Communication & Society, 6,* 243–265.

Johnston, D. D., & Swanson, D. H. (2004). Moms hating moms: The internalization of mother war rhetoric. *Sex Roles, 51,* 497–509.

Johnston, D. D., & Swanson, D. H. (2006). *Cognitive acrobatics in the construction of mother identity.* Unpublished manuscript, Hope College.

Johnston-Robledo, I. (2000). From postpartum depression to the empty nest syndrome: The motherhood mystique revisited. In J. C. Chrisler, C. Golden, & P. D. Rozee (Eds.), *Lectures on the psychology of women* (2nd ed., pp. 128–147). Boston: McGraw-Hill.

Johnston-Robledo, I., & Barnack, J. (2004). Psychological issues in childbirth: Potential roles for psychotherapists. *Women & Therapy, 27,* 133–150.

Join the global effort to end poverty and promote development. (2005, Summer). *MADRE,* pp. 7–10.

Jones, J., Doss, B. D., & Christensen, A. (2001). Integrative behavioral couple therapy. In J. Harvey & A. Wenzel (Eds.), *Close romantic relationships: Maintenance and enhancement* (pp. 321–344). Mahwah, NJ: Erlbaum.

Jones, S. (2003). Identities of race, class, and gender inside and outside the math classroom: A girls' math club as a hybrid possibility. *Feminist Teacher, 14,* 220–233.

Jordan, J. V. (1997). The relational model is a source of empowerment for women. In M. R. Walsh (Ed.), *Women, men, and gender: Ongoing debates* (pp. 373–379). New Haven, CT: Yale University Press.

Jordan, J. V. (2000). The role of mutual empathy in relational/cultural therapy. *Journal of Clinical Psychology, 56,* 1005–1016.

Jorgensen, L. A. B. (2001). Public policy effects on the health care of older women: Who is in charge? In J. D. G. Garner & S. O. Mercer (Eds.), *Women as they age* (2nd ed., pp. 195–214). New York: Haworth.

Jowett, M. (2004). "I don't see feminists as you see feminists": Young women negotiating feminism in contemporary Britain. In A. Harris (Ed.), *All about the girl* (pp. 91–100). New York: Routledge.

Joyner, K., & Laumann, E. O. (2002). Teenage sex and the sexual revolution. In E. O. Laumann & R. T. Michael (Eds.), *Sex, love, and health in America* (pp. 41–71). Chicago: University of Chicago Press.

Jussim, L., et al. (2000). Stigma and self-fulfilling prophecies. In T. F. Heatherton, R. E. Kleck, M. R. Hebl, & J. G. Hull (Eds.), *The social psychology of stigma* (pp. 374–418). New York: Guilford.

Kaelin, C. (2005, April). When a breast cancer expert gets breast cancer. *Harvard Women's Health Watch,* pp. 4–6.

Kafka, P. (2000). *(Out)classed women: Contemporary Chicana writers on inequitable gendered power relations.* Westport, CT: Greenwood Press.

Kaganoff, P., & Spano, S. (Eds.). (1995). *Women and divorce.* New York: Harcourt Brace.

Kagawa-Singer, M., Hikoyeda, N., & Tanjasiri, S. P. (1997). Aging, chronic conditions, and physical disabilities in Asian and Pacific Islander Americans. In K. S. Markides & M. R. Miranda (Eds.), *Minorities, aging, and health* (pp. 149–180). Thousand Oaks, CA: Sage.

Kahana, E., et al. (2005). Successful aging in the face of chronic disease. In M. L. Wykle, P. J. Whitehouse, & D. L. Morris (Eds.), *Successful aging through the life span* (pp. 101–123). New York: Springer.

Kahn, A. S. (2004). 2003 Carolyn Sherif Award Address: What college women do and do not experience as rape. *Psychology of Women Quarterly, 28,* 9–15.

Kahn, A. S., & Andreoli Mathie, V. (2000). Understanding the unacknowledged rape victim. In C. B. Travis & J. W. White (Eds.), *Sexuality, society, and feminism* (pp. 377–403). Washington, DC: American Psychological Association.

Kahn, A. S., & Yoder, J. D. (1989). The psychology of women and conservatism. *Psychology of Women Quarterly, 13,* 417–432.

Kahn, A. S., et al. (2003). Calling it rape: Differences in experiences of women who do or do not label their sexual assault as rape. *Psychology of Women Quarterly, 27,* 233–242.

Kahn, P., Butler, S. S., Deprez, L. S., & Polakow, V. (2004). Introduction. In V. Polakow, S. S. Butler, L. S. Deprez, & P. Kahn (Eds.), *Shut out: Low income mothers and higher education in post-welfare America* (pp. 1–19). Albany, NY: State University of New York Press.

Kahn, P., & Polakow, V. (2004). "That's not how I want to live": Student mothers fight to stay in school under Michigan's welfare-to-work regime. In

V. Polakow, S. S. Butler, L. S. Deprez, & P. Kahn (Eds.), *Shut out: Low income mothers and higher education in post-welfare America* (pp. 75–96). Albany, NY: State University of New York Press.

Kahne, H. (2004). Low-wage single-mother families in this jobless recovery: Can improved social policies help? *Analysis of Social Issues and Public Policy, 4,* 47–68.

Kaid, L. L., & Garner, J. (2004). The portrayal of older adults in political advertising. Media usage patterns and portrayals of seniors. In J. F. Nussbaum & J. Coupland (Eds.), *Handbook of communication and aging research* (2nd ed., pp. 407–421). Mahwah, NJ: Erlbaum.

Kail, R. V., Jr., Carter, P., & Pellegrino, J. (1979). The locus of sex differences in spatial ability. *Perception and Psychophysics, 26,* 182–186.

Kaiser Family Foundation. (2003). *National survey of adolescents and young adults: Sexual knowledge, attitudes, and experiences.* Menlo Park, CA: Author.

Kalev, H. D. (2004). Cultural rights or human rights: The case of female genital mutilation. *Sex Roles, 31,* 339–348.

Kalichman, S. C. (2003). *The inside story on AIDS.* Washington, DC: American Psychological Association.

Kalick, S. M., Zebrowitz, L. A., Langlois, J. H., & Johnson, R. M. (1998). Does human face attractiveness honestly advertise health? *Psychological Science, 9,* 8–13.

Kalodner, C. R. (2003). *Too fat or too thin? A reference guide to eating disorders.* Westport, CT: Greenwood.

Kamen, P. (2000). *Her way: Young women remake the sexual revolution.* New York: New York University Press.

Kantrowitz, B. (2004, January 26). One, two, three or more? *Newsweek,* pp. 52–53.

Kantrowitz, B., & Springen, K. (2004, August 9). What dreams are made of. *Newsweek,* pp. 40–47.

Kaplan, H. S. (1995). *The sexual desire disorders: Dysfunctional regulation of sexual motivation.* Philadelphia, PA: Brunner/Mazel.

Kaplan, J., & Aronson, D. (1994, Spring). The numbers gap. *Teaching Tolerance,* pp. 21–27.

Kaplan, P. S., Bachorowski, J., Smoski, M. J., & Hudenko, W. J. (2002). Infants of depressed mothers, although competent learners, fail to learn in response to their own mothers' infant-directed speech. *Psychological Science, 13,* 268–271.

Karney, B. R., & Bradbury, T. M. (2004). Trajectories of change during the early years of marriage. In R. D. Conger, F. O. Lorenz, & K. A. S. Wickrama (Eds.), *Continuity and change in family relationships* (pp. 65–96). Mahwah, NJ: Erlbaum.

Karney, B. R., McNulty, J. K., & Frye, N. E. (2001). A social-cognitive perspective on the maintenance and deterioration of relationship satisfaction. In J. Harvey & A. Wenzel (Eds.), *Close romantic relationships: Maintenance and enhancement* (pp. 195–214). Mahwah, NJ: Erlbaum.

Karniol, R., Gabay, R., Ochion, Y., & Harari, Y. (1998). Is gender or gender-role orientation a better predictor of empathy in adolescence? *Sex Roles, 39,* 45–59.

Karniol, R., Grosz, E., & Schorr, I. (2003). Caring, gender role orientation, and volunteering. *Sex Roles, 49,* 11–19.

Karraker, K. H., Vogel, D. A., & Lake, M. A. (1995). Parents' gender-stereotyped perceptions of newborns: The eye of the beholder revisited. *Sex Roles, 33,* 687–701.

Kaschak, E., & Tiefer, L. (Eds.). (2001). *A new view of women's sexual problems.* New York: Haworth.

Kasser, T., & Sharma, Y. S. (1999). Reproductive freedom, educational equality, and females' preferences for resource-acquisition characteristics in mates. *Psychological Science, 10,* 374–377.

Kastberg, S. M., & Miller, D. G. (1996). Of blue collars and ivory towers: Women from blue-collar backgrounds in higher education. In K. Arnold, K. D. Noble, & R. F. Subotnik (Eds.), *Remarkable women: Perspectives on female talent development* (pp. 49–67). Creskill, NJ: Hampton Press.

Kato, N. R. (1999). Asian Americans defy "model minority" myth. In Y. Alaniz & N. Wong (Eds.), *Voices of color* (pp. 150–153). Seattle: Red Letter Press.

Katon, W. J., & Ludman, E. J. (2003). Improving services for women with depression in primary care settings. *Psychology of Women Quarterly, 27,* 114–120.

Katz, J., Carino, A., & Hilton, A. (2002). Perceived verbal conflict behaviors associated with physical aggression and sexual coercion in dating relationships: A gender-sensitive analysis. *Violence and Victims, 17,* 93–109.

Katz, J., Kuffel, S. W., & Coblentz, A. (2002). Are there gender differences in sustaining dating violence? An examination of frequency, severity, and relationship satisfaction. *Journal of Family Violence, 17,* 247–271.

Katz, P. A. (1987). Variations in family constellation: Effects on gender schemata. In L. S. Liben & M. L. Signorella (Eds.), *Children's gender schemata* (pp. 39–56). San Francisco: Jossey-Bass.

Katz, P. A. (1996). Raising feminists. *Psychology of Women Quarterly, 20,* 323–340.

Katz, P. A. (2003). Racists or tolerant multiculturalists? How do they begin? *American Psychologist, 58,* 897–909.

Katz, P. A., Boggiano, A., & Silvern, L. (1993). Theories of female personality. In F. L. Denmark & M. A. Paludi (Eds.), *Psychology of women: A handbook of issues and theories* (pp. 247–280). Westport, CT: Greenwood Press.

Katz, P. A., & Kofkin, J. A. (1997). Race, gender, and young children. In S. Luthar, J. A. Baruck, D. Cicchetti, & J. Weisz (Eds.), *Developmental psychopathology: Perspectives on adjustment, risk, and disorder* (pp. 51–74). New York: Cambridge University Press.

Kaufman, G. (1999). The portrayal of men's family roles in television commercials. *Sex Roles, 41,* 439–458.

Keel, P. K., & Klump, K. L. (2003). Are eating disorders culture-bound syndromes? Implications for conceptualizing their etiology. *Psychological Bulletin, 129*, 747–769.

Keel, P. K., et al. (2001). Relationship between depression and body dissatisfaction in women diagnosed with bulimia nervosa. *International Journal of Eating Disorders, 30*, 48–56.

Keel, P. K., et al. (2003). Predictors of mortality in eating disorders. *Archives of General Psychiatry, 60*, 179–183.

Keitel, M. A., & Kopala, M. (2000). *Counseling women with breast cancer*. Thousand Oaks, CA: Sage.

Kelly, J. R., & Hutson-Comeaux, S. L. (2000). The appropriateness of emotional expression in women and men: The double-bind of emotion. *Journal of Social Behavior and Personality, 15*, 515–528.

Kendall-Tackett, K. A. (2005). *Depression in new mothers: Causes, consequences, and treatment alternatives*. New York: Haworth.

Kennedy, M. A., & Gorzalka, B. B. (2002). Asian and non-Asian attitudes toward rape, sexual harassment, and sexuality. *Sex Roles, 46*, 227–238.

Kennedy, M. A., Parhar, K. K., Samra, J., & Gorzalka, B. (2005). Suicide ideation in different generations of immigrants. *Canadian Journal of Psychiatry, 50*, 353–356.

Kennedy, M. A., Templeton, L., Gandhi, A., & Gorzalka, B. B. (2004). Asian body image satisfaction: Ethnic and gender differences across Chinese, Indo-Asian and European descent students. *Eating Disorders: The Journal of Treatment and Prevention, 12*, 321–336.

Kerpelman, J. L., & Schvaneveldt, P. L. (1999). Young adults' anticipated identity importance of career, marital, and parental roles: Comparisons of men and women with different role balance orientations. *Sex Roles, 41*, 189–217.

Kersting, K. (2005, June). Men and depression: Battling stigma through public education. *Monitor on Psychology*, pp. 66–68.

Kessler, R. C. (2006). The epidemiology of depression among women. In C. L. M. Keyes & S. H. Goodman (Eds.), *Women and depression: A handbook for the social, behavioral, and biomedical sciences* (pp. 22–37). New York: Cambridge University Press.

Kessler, R. C., et al. (2005). Prevalence and treatment of mental disorders, 1990–2003. *New England Journal of Medicine, 352*, 2515–2523.

Kessler, S. J. (1998). *Lessons from the intersexed*. Piscataway, NJ: Rutgers University Press.

Ketenjian, T. (1999a). Interview of Alice Wolfson. In G. Null & B. Seaman (Eds.), *For women only: Your guide to health empowerment* (pp. 1495–1499). New York: Seven Stories Press.

Ketenjian, T. (1999b). Interview of Patsy Mink. In G. Null & B. Seaman (Eds.), *For women only: Your guide to health empowerment* (pp. 1042–1045). New York: Seven Stories Press.

Ketz, K., & Israel, T. (2002). The relationship between women's sexual identity and perceived wellness. *Journal of Bisexuality, 2*, 227–242.

Kiernan, K. (2002). Cohabitation in western Europe: Trends, issues, and implications. Cohabitation in contemporary North America. In A. Booth & A. C. Crouter (Eds.), *Just living together* (pp. 3–31). Mahwah, NJ: Erlbaum.

Kilbey, M. M., & Burgermeister, D. (2001). Substance abuse. In J. Worell (Ed.), *Encyclopedia of women and gender* (pp. 1113–1127). San Diego: Academic Press.

Kilbourne, J. (1999). *Deadly persuasion*. New York: Free Press.

Kilbourne, J. (2003). Advertising and disconnection. In T. Reichert & J. Lambiase (Eds.), *Sex in advertising* (pp. 173–180). Mahwah, NJ: Erlbaum.

Kilmartin, C. T. (2007). *The masculine self* (3rd ed.). Cornwall-on-Hudson, NY: Sloan Publishing.

Kim, J. E., & Moen, P. (2001a). Is retirement good or bad for subjective well-being? *Current Directions in Psychological Science, 10*, 83–86.

Kim, J. E., & Moen, P. (2001b). Moving into retirement: Preparation and transitions in late midlife. In M. E. Lachman (Ed.), *Handbook of midlife development* (pp. 487–527). New York: Wiley.

Kim, J. L., & Ward, L. M. (2004). Pleasure reading: Associations between young women's sexual attitudes and their reading of contemporary women's magazines. *Psychology of Women Quarterly, 28*, 48–58.

Kimball, M. M. (1989). A new perspective on women's math achievement. *Psychological Bulletin, 105*, 198–214.

Kimball, M. M. (1995). *Feminist visions of gender similarities and differences*. Binghamton, NY: Haworth.

Kimball, M. M. (2003). Feminists rethink gender. In D. B. Hill & M. J. Kral (Eds.), *About psychology: Essays at the crossroads of history, theory, and philosophy* (pp. 127–146). Albany, NY: State University of New York Press.

Kimmel, M. S. (2004). *The gendered society* (2nd ed.). New York: Oxford University Press.

Kimura, D. (1987). Are men's and women's brains really different? *Canadian Psychology/Psychologie canadienne, 28*, 133–147.

Kimura, D. (1992, September). Sex differences in the brain. *Scientific American, 267*, 118–125.

King, G. A., Brown, E. G., & Smith, L. K. (2003a). Introduction: An invitation to learn from the turning points of people with disabilities. In G. A. King, E. G. Brown, & L. K. Smith, *Resilience: Learning from people with disabilities and the turning points in their lives* (pp. 1–6). Westport, CT: Praeger.

King, G. A., Brown, E. G., & Smith, L. K. (Eds.). (2003b). *Resilience: Learning from people with disabilities and the turning points in their lives*. Westport, CT: Praeger.

King, K. R. (2003). Do you see what I see? Effects of group consciousness on African American women's attributions to prejudice. *Psychology of Women Quarterly, 27*, 17–30.

King, Y. (1997). The other body: Reflections on difference, disability, and identity politics. In M. Crawford & R. Unger (Eds.), *In our own words: Readings on the psychology of women and gender* (pp. 107–111). New York: McGraw-Hill.

Kingsberg, S. (2002). The impact of aging of sexual function in women and their partners. *Archives of Sexual Behavior, 33,* 431–437.

Kinsella, K. (2000). Demographic dimensions of global aging. *Journal of Family Issues, 21,* 541–558.

Kirk, G., & Okazawa-Rey, M. (2001). *Women's lives: Multicultural perspectives* (2nd ed.). Mountain View, CA: Mayfield.

Kisber, S. (2001, Spring). Reflections on my experience as a disabled feminist psychologist. *Association for Women in Psychology Newsletter,* pp. 4–5.

Kishwar, M. (1999). *Off the beaten track: Rethinking gender justice for Indian women.* New Delhi: Oxford University Press.

Kissling, E. A. (2002). On the rag on screen: Menarche in film and television. *Sex Roles 46,* 5–12.

Kissling, E. A. (2003). Menstrual taboo. In J. J. Ponzetti, Jr. (Ed.), *International encyclopedia of marriage and family* (2nd ed., Vol. 3, pp. 1123–1126). New York: Macmillan Reference USA.

Kissling, E. A. (2005). *Capitalizing on the curse: The business of menstruation.* Boulder, CO: Lynne Rienner Publishers.

Kite, M. E. (1994). When perceptions meet reality: Individual differences in reactions to lesbians and gay men. In B. Greene & G. M. Herek (Eds.), *Contemporary perspectives on gay and lesbian psychology* (pp. 25–53). Newbury Park, CA: Sage.

Kite, M. E., & Branscombe, N. R. (1998). *Evaluation of subtypes of women and men.* Unpublished manuscript.

Kite, M. E., & Deaux, K. (1986). Attitudes toward homosexuality: Assessment and behavioral consequences. *Basic and Applied Social Psychology, 7,* 137–162.

Kite, M. E., Stockdale, G. D., Whitley, B. E., Jr., & Johnson, B. T. (2005). Attitudes toward younger and older adults: An updated meta-analytic review. *Journal of Social Issues, 61,* 241–266.

Kite, M. E., & Whitley, B. E., Jr. (1998). Do heterosexual women and men differ in their attitudes toward homosexuality? A conceptual and methodological analysis. In G. M. Herek (Ed.), *Stigma, prejudice, and violence against lesbians and gay men.* Thousand Oaks, CA: Sage.

Kite, M. E., & Whitley, B. E., Jr. (2002). Do heterosexual women and men differ in their attitudes toward homosexuality? A conceptual and methodological analysis. In L. D. Garnets & D. C. Kimmel (Eds.), *Psychological perspectives on lesbian, gay, and bisexual experiences* (2nd ed., pp. 165–187). New York: Columbia University Press.

Kite, M. E., et al. (2001). Women psychologists in academe: Mixed progress, unwarranted complacency. *American Psychologist, 56,* 1080–1098.

Kitzinger, C., & Wilkinson, S. (1997). Transitions from heterosexuality to lesbianism: The discursive production of lesbian identities. In M. R. Walsh (Ed.), *Women, men, and gender: Ongoing debates* (pp. 188–203). New Haven, CT: Yale University Press.

Kitzinger, S. (1995). *Ourselves as mothers: The universal experience of motherhood.* Reading, MA: Addison Wesley.

Kitzmann, K. M., & Gaylord, N. K. (2001). Divorce and child custody. In J. Worell (Ed.), *Encyclopedia of women and gender* (pp. 355–367). San Diego: Academic Press.

Kjaersgaard, K. (2005). Aging to perfection or perfectly aged? The image of women growing older on television. In E. Cole & J. H. Daniel (Eds.), *Featuring females: Feminist analyses of media* (pp. 199–210). Washington, DC: American Psychological Association.

Klaus, M. H., Kennell, J. H., & Klaus, P. H. (2002). *The doula book: How a trained labor companion can help you have a shorter, easier, and healthier birth* (2nd ed.). Cambridge, MA: Perseus Publishing.

Klebanoff, M. A., Shiono, P. H., & Rhoads, G. G. (1990). Outcomes of pregnancy in a national sample of resident physicians. *New England Journal of Medicine, 323,* 1040–1045.

Klebanov, P. K., & Jemmott, J. B., III. (1992). Effects of expectations and bodily sensations on self-reports of premenstrual symptoms. *Psychology of Women Quarterly, 16,* 289–310.

Kleege, G. (2002). Disabled students come out: Questions without answers. In S. L. Snyder, B. J. Brueggemann, & R. Garland-Thomson (Eds.), *Disability studies: Enabling the humanities* (pp. 308–316). New York: Modern Language Association of America.

Klein, A. G. (2002). *A forgotten voice: A biography of Leta Stetter Hollingworth.* Scottsdale, AZ: Great Potential Press.

Klein, E., Campbell, J., Soler, E., & Ghez, M. (1997). *Ending domestic violence: Changing public perceptions/Halting the epidemic.* Thousand Oaks, CA: Sage.

Klein, K. J. K., & Hodges, S. D. (2001). Gender differences, motivation, and empathic accuracy: When it pays to understand. *Personality and Social Psychology Bulletin, 27,* 720–730.

Klein, M. C. (2004). Quick fix culture: The cesarean-section-on-demand debate. *Birth, 31,* 161–164.

Klein, M. H., Hyde, J. S., Essex, M. J., & Clark, R. (1998). Maternity leave, role quality, work involvement, and mental health one year after delivery. *Psychology of Women Quarterly, 22,* 239–266.

Kling, K. C., & Hyde, J. S. (2001). Self-esteem. In J. Worell (Ed.), *Encyclopedia of women and gender.* San Diego: Academic Press.

Kling, K. C., Hyde, J. S., Showers, C., & Buswell, B. (1999). Gender differences in self-esteem: A meta-analysis. *Psychological Bulletin, 125,* 470–500.

Klinger, R. L. (1996). Lesbian couples. In R. P. Cabaj & T. S. Stein (Eds.), *Textbook of homosexuality and mental health* (pp. 339–352). Washington, DC: American Psychiatric Press.

Klonis, S., Endo, J., Cosby, F., & Worell, J. (1997). Feminism as life raft. *Psychology of Women Quarterly, 21,* 333–345.

Klonoff, E. A., & Landrine, H. (1997). *Preventing misdiagnosis of women: A guide to physical disorders that have psychiatric symptoms.* Thousand Oaks, CA: Sage.

Klonoff, E. A., Landrine, H., & Campbell, R. (2000). Sexist discrimination may account for well-known gender differences in psychiatric symptoms. *Psychology of Women Quarterly, 24,* 93–99.

Knight, G. P., Fabes, R. A., & Higgins, D. A. (1996). Concerns about drawing causal inferences from meta-analyses: An example in the study of gender differences in aggression. *Psychological Bulletin, 119,* 410–421.

Knight, J. L., & Giuliano, T. A. (2001). He's a Laker; she's a "looker": The consequences of gender-stereotypical portrayals of male and female athletes by the print media. *Sex Roles, 45,* 217–229.

Knight, M. (2004, Winter). Black self-employed women in the twenty-first century: A critical approach. *Canadian Woman Studies/Les cahiers de la femme,* pp. 104–110.

Koch, P. B., & Mansfield, P. K. (2004). Facing the unknown: Social support during the menopausal transition. In J. C. Chrisler (Ed.), *From menarche to menopause: The female body in feminist therapy* (pp. 179–194). New York: Haworth.

Kohlberg, L. (1966). A cognitive-developmental analysis of children's sex-role concepts and attitudes. In E. E. Maccoby (Ed.), *The development of sex differences* (pp. 82–173). Stanford, CA: Stanford University Press.

Kohlberg, L. (1981). *The philosophy of moral development: Essays on moral development* (Vols. 1 & 2). San Francisco: Harper & Row.

Kohlberg, L. (1984). *Essays on moral development* (Vol. 2). *The psychology of moral development.* San Francisco: Freeman.

Konrad, A. M., & Linnehan, F. (1999). Affirmative action: History, effects, and attitudes. In G. N. Powell (Ed.), *Handbook of gender and work* (pp. 429–452). Thousand Oaks, CA: Sage.

Kopera-Frye, K., Wiscott, R., Blevins, D., & Begovic, A. (2003). Incorporating aging into undergraduate social psychology courses. In S. K. Whitbourne & J. Cavanaugh (Eds.), *Integrating aging topics in psychology: A practical guide for teaching undergraduates* (pp. 107–122). Washington, DC: American Psychological Association.

Kornstein, S. G., & Wojcik, B. A. (2002). Depression. In S. G. Kornstein & A. H. Clayton (Eds.), *Women's mental health: A comprehensive textbook* (pp. 147–165). New York: Guilford.

Korol, C. T., & Craig, K. D. (2001). Pain from the perspectives of health psychology and culture. In S. S. Kazarian & D. R. Evans (Eds.), *Handbook of cultural health psychology* (pp. 241–265). San Diego: Academic Press.

Koski, L. R., & Shaver, P. R. (1997). Attachment and relationship satisfaction across the lifespan. In R. J. Sternberg & M. Hojjat (Eds.), *Satisfaction in close relationships* (pp. 26–55). New York: Guilford.

Koss, M. P. (2003). Evolutionary models of why men rape: Acknowledging the complexities. In C. B. Travis (Ed.), *Evolution, gender, and rape* (pp. 191–205). Cambridge, MA: MIT Press.

Koss, M. P., Ingram, M., & Pepper, S. L. (2001). Male partner violence: Relevance to health care providers. In A. Baum, T. A. Revenson, & J. E. Singer (Eds.), *Handbook of health psychology* (pp. 541–557). Mahwah, NJ: Erlbaum.

Koss, M. P., et al. (2003). Depression and PTSD in survivors of male violence: Research and training initiatives to facilitate recovery. *Psychology of Women Quarterly, 27,* 130–142.

Kossek, E. E., Meece, D., Barratt, M. E., & Prince, B. E. (2005). U.S. Latino migrant farm workers: Managing acculturative stress and conserving work-family resources. In S. A. Y. Poelmans (Ed.), *Work and family: An international research perspective* (pp. 47–70). Mahwah, NJ: Erlbaum.

Kowalski, R. (2000). Including gender, race, and ethnicity in psychology content courses. *Teaching of Psychology, 27,* 18–24.

Kozak, L. J., & Weeks, J. D. (2002). U.S. trends in obstetric procedures, 1999–2000. *Birth, 29,* 153–156.

Krahé, B., Bieneck, S., & Möller, I. (2005). Understanding gender and intimate partner violence from an international perspective. *Sex Roles, 52,* 807–827.

Kravetz, D., & Marecek, J. (2001). The feminist movement. In J. Worell (Ed.), *Encyclopedia of women and gender* (pp. 457–468). San Diego: Academic Press.

Kreipe, R. E., & Birndorf, S. A. (2000). Eating disorders in adolescents and young adults. *Medical Clinics of North America, 84,* 1027–1049.

Kreston, R. (2003). Disability as part of the diversity curriculum. In W. M. Timpson, S. S. Canetto, E. Barrayo, & R. Yang (Eds.), *Teaching diversity* (pp. 169–187). Madison, WI: Atwood.

Krishman, A., & Sweeney, C. J. (1998). Gender differences in fear of success imagery and other achievement-related background variables among medical students. *Sex Roles, 39,* 299–310.

Kristof, N. D. (1996, December 9). Wife-beating still common practice in much of Korea. *San Jose Mercury News,* p. 17A.

Kristof, N. D. (2004, February 23). Afghan women still in chains, the U.S. looks away. *Liberal Opinion Week,* p. 26.

Kristof, N. D. (2005, November 23). The Rosa Parks for the 21st century. *Liberal Opinion Week,* p. 30.

Kruse, L., Denk, C. E., Feldman-Winter, L., & Rotondo, F. M. (2005). Comparing sociodemographic and hospital influences on breastfeeding initiation. *Birth, 32,* 81–85.

Kuck, V. J., Marzabadi, C. H., Nolan, S. A., & Buckner, J. P. (2004). Analysis by gender of the doctoral and postdoctoral institutions of faculty members at the top-fifty ranked chemistry departments. *Journal of Chemical Education, 81,* 356–363.

Kuffel, S. W., & Katz, J. (2002). Preventing physical, psychological, and sexual aggression in college dating relationships. *The Journal of Primary Prevention, 22,* 361–374.

Kunda, Z. (1999). *Social cognition: Making sense of people.* Cambridge, MA: MIT Press.

Kunda, Z., & Sherman-Williams, B. (1993). Stereotypes and the construal of individuating information. *Personality and Social Psychology Bulletin, 19,* 90–99.

Kundanis, R. M. (2003). *Children, teens, families, and mass media.* Mahwah, NJ: Erlbaum.

Kuninobu, J. (2000). Women's studies: East Asia. In C. Kramarae & D. Spender (Eds.), *Routledge international encyclopedia of women* (Vol. 4, pp. 2008–2092). New York: Routledge.

Kunkel, A. W., & Burleson, B. R. (1998). Social support and the emotional lives of men and women: An assessment of the different cultures perspective. In D. J. Canary & K. Dindia (Eds.), *Sex differences and similarities in communication* (pp. 101–125). Mahwah, NJ: Erlbaum.

Kurdek, L. A. (1991). The dissolution of gay and lesbian couples. *Journal of Social and Personal Relationships, 8,* 265–278.

Kurdek, L. A. (1995a). Assessing multiple determinants of relationship commitment in cohabiting gay, cohabiting lesbian, dating heterosexual, and married heterosexual couples. *Family Relations, 44,* 261–266.

Kurdek, L. A. (1995b). Developmental changes in relationship quality in gay and lesbian cohabiting couples. *Developmental Psychology, 31,* 86–94.

Kurdek, L. A. (1998). Relational outcomes and their predictors: Longitudinal evidence from heterosexual married, gay cohabiting, and lesbian cohabiting couples. *Journal of Marriage and the Family, 60,* 553–568.

Kurdek, L. A. (2004). Are gay and lesbian cohabiting couples *really* different from heterosexual married couples? *Journal of Marriage & Family, 66,* 880–900.

Kurdek, L. A. (2005). Gender and marital satisfaction early in marriage: A growth curve approach. *Journal of Marriage and Family, 67,* 68–84.

Kurpius, S. E. R., & Nicpon, M. F. (2003). Menopause and the lives of midlife women. In M. Kopala & M. A. Keitel (Eds.), *Handbook of counseling women* (pp. 269–276). Thousand Oaks, CA: Sage.

Kurth, S. B., Spiller, B. B., & Travis, C. B. (2000). Consent, power, and sexual scripts: Deconstructing sexual harassment. In C. B. Travis & J. W. White (Eds.), *Sexuality, society, and feminism* (pp. 323–354). Washington, DC: American Psychological Association.

Kusnir, D. (2005). Salvadoran families. In M. McGoldrick, J. Giordano, & N. Garcia-Preto (Eds.), *Ethnicity and family therapy* (3rd ed., pp. 256–265). New York: Guilford.

Kwa, L. (1994). Adolescent females' perceptions of competence: What is defined as healthy and achieving. In J. Gallivan, S. D. Crozier, & V. M. Lalande (Eds.), *Women, girls, and achievement* (pp. 121–132). North York, Canada: Captus University Publications.

Lachman, M. E. (2004). Development in midlife. *Annual Review of Psychology, 55,* 305–351.

Laflamme, D., Pomerleau, A., & Malcuit, G. (2002). A comparison of fathers' and mothers' involvement in childcare and stimulation behaviors during free-play with their infants at 9 and 15 months. *Sex Roles, 47,* 507–518.

LaFrance, M., Hecht, M. A., & Paluck, E. L. (2003). The contingent smile: A meta-analysis of sex differences in smiling. *Psychological Bulletin, 129,* 305–334.

LaFrance, M., & Henley, N. M. (1997). On oppressing hypotheses: Or, differences in nonverbal sensitivity revisited. In M. R. Walsh (Ed.), *Women, men, and gender: Ongoing debates* (pp. 104–119). New Haven, CT: Yale University Press.

LaFrance, M., Paluck, E. L., & Brescoll, V. (2004). Sex changes: A current perspective on the psychology of gender. In A. H. Eagly, A. E. Beall, & R. J. Sternberg (Eds.), *The psychology of gender* (2nd ed., pp. 328–344). New York: Guilford.

La Greca, A. M., Mackay, E. R., & Miller, K. B. (2006). The interplay of physical and psychosocial development. In J. Worell & C. D. Goodheart (Eds.), *Handbook of girls' and women's psychological health: Gender and well-being across the life span* (pp. 252–261). New York: Oxford University Press.

Lakoff, R. T. (1990). *Talking power: The politics of language in our lives.* New York: Basic Books.

Lalumiere, M., Harris., G. T., Quinsey, V. L., & Rice, M. E. (2005). *The causes of rape: Understanding individual differences in male propensity for sexual aggression.* Washington, DC: American Psychological Association.

Lamb, S. (2000). *White saris and sweet mangoes: Aging, gender, and body in North India.* Berkeley: University of California Press.

Lambdin, J. R., et al. (2003). The Animal = Male hypothesis: Children's and adults' beliefs about the sex of non-sex-specific stuffed animals. *Sex Roles, 48,* 471–482.

Lambert, A. J., & Raichle, K. (2000). The role of political ideology in mediating judgments of blame in rape victims and their assailants: A test of the just world, personal responsibility, and legitimization hypothesis. *Personality and Social Psychology Bulletin, 26,* 853–863.

Lambert, J. C. (2000, May 2). Self-made? Male myth. *City Newspaper,* p. 6.

Lambert, T. A., Kahn, A. S., & Apple, K. J. (2003). Pluralistic ignorance and hooking up. *The Journal of Sex Research, 40,* 129–133.

Lambiase, J. J. (2003). Sex—online and in internet advertising. In T. Reichert & J. Lambiase (Eds.), *Sex in advertising: Perspectives on the erotic appeal* (pp. 247–269). Mahwah, NJ: Erlbaum.

Lamke, L. K., Sollie, D. L., Durbin, R. G., & Fitzpatrick, J. A. (1994). Masculinity, femininity, and relationship satisfaction: The mediating role of interpersonal competence. *Journal of Social and Personal Relationships, 11,* 535–554.

Lance, L. M. (1998). Gender differences in heterosexual dating: A content analysis of personal ads. *Journal of Men's Studies, 6,* 297–305.

Landrine, H., & Klonoff, E. A. (1997). *Discrimination against women: Prevalence, consequences, remedies.* Thousand Oaks, CA: Sage.

Landrine, H., & Klonoff, E. A. (2001). Health and health care: How gender makes women sick. In J. Worell (Ed.), *Encyclopedia of women and gender* (pp. 577–592). San Diego: Academic Press.

Landry, B. (2000). *Black working wives.* Berkeley: University of California Press.

Langlois, J. H., et al. (2000). Maxims or myths of beauty? A meta-analytic and theoretical review. *Psychological Bulletin, 126,* 390–423.

Lapointe, V., & Marcotte, D. (2000). Gender-typed characteristics and coping strategies of depressed adolescents. *European Review of Applied Psychology, 50,* 451–460.

Larson, M. S. (2003). Gender, race, and aggression in television commercials that feature children. *Sex Roles, 48,* 67–75.

Larson, R. W., Clore, G. L., & Wood, G. A. (1999). The emotions of romantic relationships: Do they wreak havoc on adolescents? In W. Furman, B. D. Brown, & C. Feiring (Eds.), *The development of romantic relationships in adolescence.* New York: Cambridge University Press.

Larsson, M., Lövdén, M., & Lars-Göran, N. (2003). Sex differences in recollective experience for olfactory and verbal information. *Acta Psychologica, 112,* 89–103.

Latifa. (2001). *My forbidden face: Growing up under the Taliban: A young woman's story.* New York: Hyperion.

Latner, J. D., & Schwartz, M. B. (2005). Weight bias in a child's world. In K. D. Brownell, R. M. Puhl, M. B. Schwartz, & L. Rudd (Eds.), *Weight bias: Nature, consequences, and remedies* (pp. 54–67). New York: Guilford.

Laumann, E. O., Gagnon, J. H., Michael, R. T., & Michaels, S. (1994). *The social organization of sexuality: Sexual practices in the United States.* Chicago: University of Chicago Press.

Laumann, E. O., Paik, A., & Rosen, R. C. (2002). Sexual dysfunction in the United States: Prevalence and predictors. In E. O. Laumann & R. T. Michael (Eds.), *Sex, love, and health in America* (pp. 352–376). Chicago: University of Chicago Press.

Lauzen, M. M., & Dozier, D. M. (2002). You look mahvelous: An examination of gender and appearance comments in the 1999–2000 prime-time season. *Sex Roles, 46,* 2002.

Lauzen, M. M., & Dozier, D. M. (2005). Maintaining the double standard: Portrayals of age and gender in popular films. *Sex Roles, 52,* 437–446.

Lavender, T., & Walkinshaw, S. A. (1998). Can midwives reduce postpartum psychological morbidity? A randomized trial. *Birth, 25,* 215–219.

Lawrence, R. A. (1998). Breastfeeding. In E. A. Blechman & K. D. Brownell (Eds.), *Behavioral medicine and women: A comprehensive handbook* (pp. 495–500). New York: Guilford.

Lawrence, R. A., & Lawrence, R. M. (1998). *Breastfeeding: A guide for the medical profession.* St. Louis, MO: Mosby.

Lawton, C. A. (1996). Strategies for indoor wayfinding: The role of orientation. *Journal of Environmental Psychology, 16,* 137–145.

Lawton, C. A., Charleston, S. I., & Zieles, A. S. (1996). Individual and gender-related differences in indoor wayfinding. *Environment and Behavior, 28,* 204–219.

Lawton, C. A., & Kallai, J. (2002). Gender differences in wayfinding strategies and anxiety about wayfinding: A cross-cultural comparison. *Sex Roles, 47,* 389–401.

Lawton, C. A., & Morrin, K. A. (1999). Gender differences in pointing accuracy in computer-simulated 3D mazes. *Sex Roles, 40,* 73–92.

Leaper, C. (2000). The social construction and socialization of gender during development. In P. H. Miller & E. K. Scholnick (Eds.), *Toward a feminist developmental psychology* (pp. 129–152). New York: Routledge.

Leaper, C. (2002). Parenting girls and boys. In M. H. Bornstein (Ed.), *Handbook of parenting* (Vol. 1). Mahwah, NJ: Erlbaum.

Leaper, C., Anderson, K. J., & Sanders, P. (1998). Moderators of gender effects on parents' talk to their children: A meta-analysis. *Developmental Psychology, 34,* 3–27.

Le Bourdais, C., & Juby, H. (2002). The impact of cohabitation on the family life course in contemporary North America: Insights from across the border. Cohabitation in contemporary North America. In A. Booth & A. C. Crouter (Eds.), *Just living together* (pp. 107–118). Mahwah, NJ: Erlbaum.

Lederman, R. P. (1996). *Psychosocial adaptation in pregnancy* (2nd ed.). New York: Springer.

Lee, E. (2003). *Abortion, motherhood, and mental health.* New York: Aldine de Gruyter.

Lee, E., & Mock, M. R, (2005a). Asian families: An overview. In M. McGoldrick, J. Giordano, & N. Garcia-Preto (Eds.), *Ethnicity and family therapy* (3rd ed., pp. 269–289). New York: Guilford.

Lee, E., & Mock, M. R, (2005b). Chinese families. In M. McGoldrick, J. Giordano, & N. Garcia-Preto (Eds.), *Ethnicity and family therapy* (3rd ed., pp. 302–318). New York: Guilford.

Lee, J. (2001). Beyond bean counting. In S. M. Shaw & J. Lee (Eds.),

Women's voices, feminist visions (pp. 36–39). Mountain View, CA: Mayfield.

Lee, K. S. (2004). The effects of social activism on the occupational experience, locus of control, and well-being of Black midlife women. *Journal of Black Psychology, 30,* 386–405.

Lee, S. (2002). Health and sickness: The meaning of menstruation and premenstrual syndrome in women's lives. *Sex Roles, 46,* 25–35.

Lee, W. M. L. (1999). *An introduction to multicultural counseling.* Philadelphia: Taylor & Francis.

Lee, Y. G., & Bhargava, V. (2004). Leisure time: Do married and single individuals spend it differently? *Family and Consumer Sciences Research Journal, 32,* 254–274.

Leeds-Hurwitz, W. (2002). *Wedding as text: Communicating cultural identities through ritual.* Mahwah, NJ: Erlbaum.

LeEspiritu, Y. (2001). Ideological racism and cultural resistance. In M. L. Anderson & P. H. Collins (Eds.), *Race, class, and gender* (4th ed., pp. 191–201). Belmont, CA: Wadsworth.

Leiblum, S. R., & Segraves, R. T. (2000). Sex therapy with aging adults. In S. R. Leiblum & R. C. Rosen (Eds.), *Principles and practice of sex therapy* (3rd ed., pp. 423–448). New York: Guilford.

Leifer, M. (1980). *Psychological effects of motherhood.* New York: Praeger.

Lennon, M. C. (2006). Women, work, and depression. In C. L. M. Keyes & S. H. Goodman (Eds.), *Women and depression: A handbook for the social, behavioral, and biomedical sciences* (pp. 309–327). New York: Cambridge University Press.

Leonard, D. K., & Jiang, J. (1999). Gender bias and the college predictions of the SAT's: A cry of despair. *Research in Higher Education, 40,* 375–407.

Lepowsky, M. (1998). Women, men, and aggression in an egalitarian society. In D. L. Anselmi & A. L. Law (Eds.), *Questions of gender* (pp. 170–179). New York: McGraw-Hill.

Lerner, H. (1989). *Women in therapy.* New York: Harper & Row.

Lerner, R. M., & Steinberg, L. (Eds.). (2004). *Handbook of adolescent psychology* (2nd. ed.). Hoboken, NJ: Wiley.

Lesbian, gay, bisexual, and transgendered youth issues. (2001, April/May). *Siecus Report Supplement, 29,* pp. 1–5.

Levant, R. F. (2001). Men and masculinity. In J. Worell (Ed.), *Encyclopedia of women and gender* (pp. 717–727). San Diego: Academic Press.

Levant, R. F., & Majors, R. G. (1997). Masculinity ideology among African American and European American college women and men. *Journal of Gender, Culture, and Health, 2,* 33–43.

Levant, R. F., Majors, R. G., & Kelley, M. L. (1998). Masculinity ideology among young African American and European American women and men in different regions of the United States. *Cultural Diversity and Mental Health, 4,* 227–236.

LeVay, S. (1996). *The use and abuse of research into homosexuality.* Cambridge, MA: MIT Press.

Levenson, R. W., Carstensen, L. L., & Gottman, J. M. (1994). The influence of age and gender on affect, physiology, and their interrelations: A study of long-term marriages. *Journal of Personality and Social Psychology, 67,* 56–68.

Levering, M. (1994). Women, the state, and religion today in the People's Republic of China. In A. Sharma (Ed.), *Today's woman in world religions* (pp. 171–224). Albany, NY: State University of New York Press.

Levesque, M. J., & Lowe, C. A. (1999). Face-ism as a determinant of interpersonal perceptions: The influence of context on facial prominence effects. *Sex Roles, 41,* 241–259.

Levesque, R. J. R. (2001). *Culture and family violence.* Washington, DC: American Psychological Association.

Levine, F., & Le De Simone, L. (1991). The effects of experimenter gender on pain report in male and female subjects. *Pain, 44,* 69–72.

Levine, S. B. (2005). *Inventing the rest of our lives: Women in second adulthood.* New York: Viking.

Levstik, L. S. (2001). Daily acts of ordinary courage: Gender-equitable practice in the social studies classroom. In P. O'Reilly, E. M. Penn, & K. deMarrais (Eds.), *Educating young adolescent girls* (pp. 189–211). Mahwah, NJ: Erlbaum.

Levy, B. R., & Banaji, M. R. (2002). Implicit ageism. In T. Nelson (Ed.), *Ageism: Stereotyping and prejudice against older persons* (pp. 49–75). Cambridge, MA: MIT Press.

Levy, B. R., & Langer, E. (1994). Aging free from negative stereotypes: Successful memory in China and among the American deaf. *Journal of Personality and Social Psychology, 66,* 989–997.

Levy, G. D., Sadovsky, A. L., & Troseth, G. L. (2000). Aspects of young children's perceptions of gender-type occupations. *Sex Roles, 42,* 993–1006.

Lewin, C., & Herlitz, A. (2002). Sex differences in face recognition—women's faces make the difference. *Brain and Cognition, 50,* 121–128.

Lewis, C., Crawford, J., & Sygall, S. (2002). *Loud, proud and passionate.* New York: Women, Ink.

Lewis, C., Scully, D., & Condor, S. (1992). Sex stereotyping of infants: A re-examination. *Journal of Reproductive and Infant Psychology, 10,* 53–63.

Lewis, J. M., Wallerstein, J. S., & Johnson-Reitz, L. (2004). Communication in divorced and single-parent families. In A. L. Vangelisti (Ed.), *Handbook of family communication* (pp. 197–214). Mahwah, NJ: Erlbaum.

Lewis, K. G., & Moon, S. (1997). Always single and single again women: A qualitative study. *Journal of Marital and Family Therapy, 23,* 115–134.

Lex, B. W. (2000). Gender and cultural influences on substance abuse. In R. M. Eisler & M. Hersen (Eds.), *Handbook of gender, culture, and health* (pp. 255–297). Mahwah, NJ: Erlbaum.

Leyendecker, B., & Lamb, M. E. (1999). Latino families. In M. E. Lamb (Ed.), *Parenting and child development in "nontraditional" families* (pp. 247–262). Mahwah, NJ: Erlbaum.

Li, A. K. F., & Adamson, G. (1995). Motivational patterns related to gifted students' learning of mathematics, science, and English: An examination of gender differences. *Journal for the Education of the Gifted, 18,* 284–297.

Li, R., & Grummer-Strawn, L. (2002). Racial and ethnic disparities in breastfeeding among United States infants: Third national health and nutrition examination survey, 1988–1994. *Birth, 29,* 251–257.

Liben, L. S., & Bigler, R. S. (2002). The developmental course of gender differentiation. *Monographs of the Society for Research in Child Development, 67* (2, Serial No. 269).

Liben, L. S., Bigler, R. S., & Krogh, H. R. (2002). Language at work: Children's gendered interpretations of occupational titles. *Child Development, 73,* 810–828.

Lieu, N. T. (2004). Remembering "the Nation" through pageantry. In L. T. Võ et al. (Eds.), *Asian American women: The Frontiers reader.* Lincoln: University of Nebraska Press.

Lightdale, J. R., & Prentice, D. A. (1994). Rethinking sex differences in aggression: Aggressive behavior in the absence of social roles. *Personality and Social Psychology Bulletin, 20,* 34–44.

Lim, I.-S. (1997). Korean immigrant women's challenge to gender inequality at home: The interplay of economic resources, gender, and family. *Gender and Society, 11,* 31–51.

Lin, C. A. (1998). Uses of sex appeal in prime-time television commercials. *Sex Roles, 38,* 461–475.

Lindsey, L. L. (1996). Full-time homemaker as unpaid laborer. In P. J. Dubeck & K. Borman (Eds.), *Women and work: A handbook* (pp. 98–99). New York: Garland Press.

Linn, M. C., & Kessel, C. (1995, April). *Participation in mathematics courses and careers: Climate, grades, and entrance examination scores.* Paper presented at the annual meeting of the American Educational Research Association, San Francisco.

Lips, H. M. (2001). Power: Social and interpersonal aspects. In J. Worell (Ed.), *Encyclopedia of women and gender* (pp. 847–858). San Diego: Academic Press.

Lips, H. M. (2003). The gender pay gap: Concrete indicator of women's progress toward equality. *Analyses of Social Issues and Public Policy, 3,* 87–109.

Lips, H. M. (2004). The gender gap in possible selves: Divergence of academic self-views among high school and university students. *Sex Roles, 50,* 357–371.

Lipson, J. (2003, Fall/Winter). A fervent desire to learn. *Outlook,* pp. 10–14.

Liss, M., Hoffner, C., & Crawford, M. (2000). What do feminists believe? *Psychology of Women Quarterly, 24,* 279–284.

Liss, M., O'Connor, C., Morosky, E., & Crawford, M. (2001). What makes a feminist? Predictors and correlates of feminist social identity in college women. *Psychology of Women Quarterly, 25,* 124–133.

Litt, I. F. (1997). *Taking our pulse: The health of America's women.* Stanford, CA: Stanford University Press.

Livingston, M. (1999). How to think about women's health. In C. Forden, A. E. Hunter, & B. Birns (Eds.), *Readings in the psychology of women: Dimensions of the female experience* (pp. 244–253). Boston: Allyn & Bacon.

Lloyd, S. A., & Emery, B. C. (2000). *The dark side of courtship: Physical and sexual aggression.* Thousand Oaks, CA: Sage.

Lobel, T. E., et al. (2000). Gender schema and social judgments: A developmental study of children from Hong Kong. *Sex Roles, 43,* 19–42.

Locke, L. M., & Richman, C. L. (1999). Attitudes toward domestic violence: Race and gender issues. *Sex Roles, 40,* 227–247.

Locklin, M. P., & Naber, S. J. (1993). Does breastfeeding empower women? Insights from a select group of educated, low-income, minority women. *Birth, 20,* 30–35.

Loeb, S., Fuller, B., Kagan, S. L., & Carrol, B. (2004). Child care in poor communities: Early learning effects of type, quality, and stability. *Child Development, 75,* 47–65.

Loftus, E. F. (1997, September). Creating false memories. *Scientific American,* pp. 71–75.

Loftus, E. F. (2004, February). Evidently enough. *American Psychological Society Newsletter,* p. 8.

Loftus, E. F., & Guyer, M. J. (2002a, May/June). Who abused Jane Doe? (Part 1). *Skeptical Inquirer,* pp. 24–32.

Loftus, E. F., & Guyer, M. J. (2002b, July/August). Who abused Jane Doe? (Part 2). *Skeptical Inquirer,* pp. 37–40.

Logan, TK, Cole, J., & Leukefeld, C. (2002). Women, sex, and HIV: Social and contextual factors, meta-analysis of published interventions, and implications for practice and research. *Psychological Bulletin, 128,* 851–885.

Logan, TK, Walker, R., Jordan, C. E., & Leukefeld, C. G. (2006). *Women and victimization: Contributing factors, interventions, and implications.* Washington, DC: American Psychological Association.

Lonner, W. J. (2003). Teaching cross-cultural psychology. In P. Bronstein & K. Quina (Eds.), *Teaching gender and multicultural awareness* (pp. 169–179). Washington, DC: American Psychological Association.

LoPiccolo, J. (2002). Integrative sex therapy: A postmodern model. In J. Lebow (Ed.), *Comprehensive handbook of psychotherapy* (Vol. 4). New York: Wiley.

Loppie, C., & Gahagan, J. (2001, Summer/Fall). Stacked against us: HIV/AIDS statistics and women. *Canadian Woman Studies/ Les cahiers de la femme, 21,* 6–9.

Lorber, J. (1994). *Paradoxes of gender.* New Haven, CT: Yale University Press.

Lorde, A. (2001). Age, race, class, and sex: Women redefining difference. In M. L. Anderson &

P. H. Collins (Eds.), *Race, class, and gender* (4th ed., pp. 177–184). Belmont, CA: Wadsworth.

Loring-Meier, S., & Halpern, D. F. (1999). Sex differences in visuospatial working memory: Components of cognitive processing. *Psychonomic Bulletin and Review, 6,* 464–471.

Loseke, D. R., & Kurz, D. (2005). Men's violence toward women is the serious social problem. In D. R. Loseke, R. J. Gelles, & M. M. Cavanaugh (Eds.), *Current controversies on family violence* (2nd ed., pp. 79–95). Thousand Oaks, CA: Sage.

Lott, A. J. (2003). A course on men and masculinity. In P. Bronstein & K. Quina (Eds.), *Teaching gender and multicultural awareness* (pp. 299–312). Washington, DC: American Psychological Association.

Lott, B. (1987). Sexist discrimination as distancing behavior: I. A laboratory demonstration. *Psychology of Women Quarterly, 11,* 47–58.

Lott, B. (1996). Politics or science? The question of gender sameness/difference. *American Psychologist, 51,* 155–156.

Lott, B. (2000). Global connections: The significance of women's poverty. In J. C. Chrisler, C. Golden, & Rozee, P. D. (Eds.), *Lectures on the psychology of women* (2nd ed., pp. 27–36). Boston: McGraw-Hill.

Lott, B. (2002). Cognitive and behavioral distancing from the poor. *American Psychologist, 57,* 100–110.

Lott, B. (2003). Recognizing and welcoming the standpoint of low-income parents in the public schools. *Journal of Educational and Psychological Consultation, 14,* 91–104.

Lott, B., & Maluso, D. (1993). The social learning of gender. In A. E. Beall & R. J. Sternberg (Eds.), *The psychology of gender* (pp. 99–123). New York: Guilford.

Lott, B., & Maluso, D. (1995). Introduction: Framing the questions. In B. Lott & D. Maluso (Eds.), *The social psychology of interpersonal discrimination* (pp. 1–11). New York: Guilford.

Lott, B., & Maluso, D. (2001). Gender development: Social learning. In J. Worell (Ed.), *Encyclopedia of women and gender* (pp. 537–549). San Diego: Academic Press.

Lott, B., & Saxon, S. (2002). The influence of ethnicity, social class, and context on judgments about U.S. women. *Journal of Social Psychology, 142,* 481–499.

Lubinski, D., et al. (2001). Men and women at promise for scientific excellence: Similarity not dissimilarity. *Psychological Science, 12,* 309–317.

Lucas, R. E., Clark, A. E., Georgellis, Y., & Diener, E. (2003). Reexamining adaptation and the set point model of happiness: Reactions to changes in marital status. *Journal of Personality and Social Psychology, 84,* 527–539.

Luker, K. (1996). *Dubious conceptions: The politics of teenage pregnancy.* Cambridge, MA: Harvard University Press.

Lundeberg, M. A., Fox, P. W., Brown, A. C., & Elbedour, S. (2000). Cultural influences on confidence: Country and gender. *Journal of Educational Psychology, 92,* 152–159.

Lundberg-Love, P., & Marmion, S. (2003). Sexual harassment in the private sector. In M. A. Paludi & C. A. Paludi (Eds.), *Academic and workplace sexual harassment* (pp. 77–101). Westport, CT: Praeger.

Lykes, M. B., & Qin, D. (2001). Individualism and collectivism. In J. Worell (Ed.), *Encyclopedia of women and gender* (pp. 625–643). San Diego: Academic Press.

Lyness, K. S., & Judiesch, M. K. (1999). Are women more likely to be hired or promoted into management positions? *Journal of Vocational Behavior, 53,* 158–17.

Lyness, K. S., & Thompson, D. E. (1997). Above the glass ceiling? A comparison of matched samples of female and male executives. *Journal of Applied Psychology, 82,* 359–375.

Lyness, K. S., & Thompson, D. E. (2000). Climbing the corporate ladder: Do female and male executives follow the same route? *Journal of Applied Psychology, 85,* 86–101.

Lynn, S. J., Loftus, E. F., Lilienfeld, S. O., & Lock, T. (2003, July/August). Memory recovery techniques in psychotherapy. *Skeptical Inquirer,* pp. 40–46.

Lyons, N. P. (1990). Listening to voices we have not heard. In C. Gilligan, N. P. Lyons, & T. J. Hanmer (Eds.), *Making connections* (pp. 30–72). Cambridge, MA: Harvard University Press.

Lytton, H., & Romney, D. M. (1991). Parents' differential socialization of boys and girls: A meta-analysis. *Psychological Bulletin, 109,* 267–296.

Macalister, H. E. (2003). In defense of ambiguity: Understanding bisexuality's invisibility through cognitive psychology. *Journal of Bisexuality, 3,* 23–32.

Maccoby, E. E. (1998). *The two sexes: Growing up apart, coming together.* Cambridge, MA: Harvard University Press.

Maccoby, E. E. (2002). Gender and group process: A developmental perspective. *Current Directions in Psychological Science, 11,* 54–58.

Maccoby, E. E., & Jacklin, C. N. (1974). *The psychology of sex differences.* Stanford, CA: Stanford University Press.

MacDermid, S. M., Leslie, L. A., & Bissonette, L. (2001). Walking the walk: Insights from research on helping clients navigate work and family. *Journal of Feminist Therapy, 13,* 21–40.

Macdonald, B., & Rich, C. (2001). *Look me in the eye: Old women, aging, and ageism* (Expanded ed.). Denver, CO: Spinsters Ink.

MacGeorge, E. L. (2003). Gender differences in attributions and emotions in helping contexts. *Sex Roles, 48,* 175–182.

MacGeorge, E. L., Gillihan, S. J., Samter, W., & Clark, R. A. (2003). Skill deficit or differential motivation? *Communication Research, 30,* 273–303.

MacGeorge, E. L., et al. (2004). The myth of gender cultures: Similarities outweigh differences in men's and women's provision of and responses to supportive communication. *Sex Roles, 50,* 143–175.

MacKay, N. J., & Covell, K. (1997). The impact of women in advertisements on attitudes toward women. *Sex Roles, 36*, 573–583.

Mackey, R. A., Diemer, M. A., & O'Brien, B. A. (2000). Psychological intimacy in the lasting relationships of heterosexual and same-gender couples. *Sex Roles, 43*, 201–227.

Mackie, M. (1991). *Gender relations in Canada: Further explorations.* Toronto: Butterworths.

MacKinnon, E., Brown, E. G., Polgar, J. M., & Havens, L. (2003). "Choral music" for community change. In G. A. King, E. G. Brown, & L. K. Smith (Eds.), *Resilience: Learning from people with disabilities and the turning points in their lives* (pp. 129–151). Westport, CT: Praeger.

MacLaughlin, D. T., & Donahoe, P. K. (2004). Sex determination and differentiation. *New England Journal of Medicine, 350*, 367–378.

Macrae, C. N., & Bodenhausen, G. V. (2000). Social cognition: Thinking categorically about others. *Annual Review of Psychology, 51*, 93–120.

Madden, M. E., & Hyde, J. S. (1998). Integrating gender and ethnicity into psychology courses. *Psychology of Women Quarterly, 22*, 1–12.

Madi, B. C., Sandall, J., Bennett, R., & MacLeod, C. (1999). Effects of female relative support in labor: A randomized controlled trial. *Birth, 26*, 4–8.

Madsen, S. S. (2003). From welfare to academe. In V. C. Adair & S. L. Dahlberg (Eds.), *Reclaiming class: Women, poverty, and the promise of higher education in America* (pp. 139–156). Philadelphia, PA: Temple University Press.

Magai, C. (2001). Emotions over the life span. In J. E. Birren & K. W. Schaie (Eds.), *Handbook of the psychology of aging* (5th ed., pp. 399–426). San Diego: Academic Press.

Mahaffy, K. A., & Ward, S. K. (2002). The gendering of adolescents' childbearing and educational plans: Reciprocal effects and the influence of social context. *Sex Roles, 46*, 403–417.

Mahalik, J. R., Van Ormer, E. A., & Simi, N. L. (2000). Ethical issues in using self-disclosure in femin-

ist therapy. In M. M. Brabeck (Ed.), *Practicing feminist ethics in psychology* (pp. 189–201). Washington, DC: American Psychological Association.

Mahay, J., Laumann, E. O., & Michaels, S. (2002). Race, gender, and class in sexual scripts. In E. O. Laumann & R. T. Michael (Eds.), *Sex, love, and health in America* (pp. 197–238). Chicago: University of Chicago Press.

Maher, F. A., & Ward, J. V. (2002). *Gender and teaching.* Mahwah, NJ: Erlbaum.

Major, B., Barr, L., Zubek, J., & Babey, S. H. (1999). Gender and self-esteem: A meta-analysis. In W. B. Swann, Jr., J. H. Langlois, & L. A. Gilbert (Eds.), *Sexism and stereotypes in modern society* (pp. 223–253). Washington, DC: American Psychological Association.

Major, B., et al. (1998). Personal resilience, cognitive appraisals, and coping: An integrative model of adjustment to abortion. *Journal of Personality and Social Psychology, 74*, 735–752.

Malamuth, N. M. (1998). The confluence model as an organizing framework for research on sexually aggressive men: Risk moderators, imagined aggression, and pornography consumption. In R. G. Geen & E. Donnerstein (Eds.), *Human aggression: Theories, research, and implications for social policy* (pp. 229–245). San Diego: Academic Press.

Malanchuk, O., & Eccles, J. S. (2006). Self-esteem. In J. Worell & C. D. Goodheart (Eds.), *Handbook of girls' and women's psychological health: Gender and well-being across the life span* (pp. 149–156). New York: Oxford University Press.

Malkin, C., & Stake, J. E. (2004). Changes in attitudes and self-confidence in the women's and gender studies classroom: The role of teacher alliance and student cohesion. *Sex Roles, 50*, 455–468.

Malley-Morrison, K. (2004). *International perspectives on family violence and abuse.* Mahwah, NJ: Erlbaum.

Malveaux, J. (2006, January 12). Dimensions of diversity: When

you teach, you learn. *Diverse Education*, p. 39.

Manderson, L. (Ed.). (2003a). *Teaching gender, teaching women's health: Case studies in medical and health science education.* Binghamton, NY: Haworth.

Manderson, L. (2003b). Teaching gender, teaching women's health: Introduction. In L. Manderson (Ed.), *Teaching gender, teaching women's health* (pp. 1–9). Binghamton, NY: Haworth.

Mangum, T. (1999). Little women: The aging female character in nineteenth-century British children's literature. In K. Woodward (Ed.), *Figuring age: Women, bodies, generations* (pp. 59–87). Bloomington: Indiana University Press.

Mann, J. J. (2005). The medical management of depression. *New England Journal of Medicine, 353*, 1819–1834.

Mansfield, P. K., Koch, P. B., & Voda, A. M. (1998). Qualities midlife women desire in their sexual relationships and their changing sexual response. *Psychology of Women Quarterly, 22*, 285–303.

Mantsios, G. (2001). Media magic: Making class invisible. In M. L. Andersen & P. H. Collins (Eds.), *Race, class, and gender* (pp. 333–341). Belmont, CA: Wadsworth.

Marchell, T., & Cummings, N. (2001). Alcohol and sexual violence among college students. In A. J. Ottens & K. Hotelling (Eds.), *Sexual violence on campus* (pp. 30–52). New York: Springer.

Marcus-Newhall, A., Thompson, S., & Thomas, C. (2001). Examining a gender stereotype: Menopausal women. *Journal of Applied Social Psychology, 31*, 698–719.

Marecek, J. (2001a). After the facts: Psychology and the study of gender. *Canadian Psychology/Psychologie canadienne, 42*, 254–267.

Marecek, J. (2001b). Disorderly constructs: Feminist frameworks for clinical psychology. In R. K. Unger (Ed.), *Handbook of women and gender* (pp. 303–329). New York: Wiley.

Marecek, J. (2006). Social suffering, gender, and women's depression.

In C. L. M. Keyes & S. H. Goodman (Eds.), *Women and depression: A handbook for the social, behavioral, and biomedical sciences* (pp. 283–308). New York: Cambridge University Press.

Marecek, J., Crawford, M., & Popp, D. (2004). On the construction of gender, sex, and sexualities. In A. H. Eagly, A. E. Beall, & R. J. Sternberg (Eds.), *The psychology of gender* (2nd ed., pp. 192–216). New York: Guilford.

Marecek, J., et al. (2003). Psychology of women and gender. In I. B. Weiner (Ed.), *Handbook of psychology* (Vol. 1, pp. 249–268). Hoboken, NJ: Wiley.

MariAnna, C. J. (2002). *Abortion: A collective story.* Westport, CT: Praeger.

Marin, A. J., & Russo, N. F. (1999). Feminist perspectives on male violence against women. In M. Harway & J. M. O'Neil (Eds.), *What causes men's violence against women?* (pp. 18–35). Thousand Oaks, CA: Sage.

Marín, B. V. (2003). Challenges of HIV prevention in diverse communities. In G. Bernal, J. E. Trimble, A. K. Burlew, & F. T. L. Leong (Eds.), *Handbook of racial and ethnic minority psychology* (pp. 608–620). Thousand Oaks, CA: Sage.

Marine, S. (2004, November 26). Waking up from the nightmare of rape. *Chronicle of Higher Education,* p. B5.

Markey, C. N. (2004). Culture and the development of eating disorders: A tripartite model. *Eating Disorders, 12,* 139–156.

Markham, B. (2006). Older women and security. In J. Worell & C. D. Goodheart (Eds.), *Handbook of girls' and women's psychological health: Gender and well-being across the life span* (pp. 388–396). New York: Oxford University Press.

Marks, M. J., & Fraley, R. C. (2005). The sexual double standard: Fact or fiction? *Sex Roles, 52,* 175–186.

Marks, N. F. (1996). Flying solo at midlife: Gender, marital status, and psychological well-being. *Journal of Marriage and the Family, 58,* 917–932.

Markson, E. W., & Taylor, C. A. (1993). Real versus reel world: Older women and the Academy Awards. *Women and Therapy, 14,* 157–172.

Marleau, J. D., & Saucier, J.-F. (2002). Preference for a first-born boy in Western societies. *Journal of Biosocial Science, 34,* 13–27.

Marshall, N. L. (2004). The quality of early child care and children's development. *Current Directions in Psychological Science, 13,* 165–168.

Martell, C. R., Safren, S. A., & Prince, S. E. (2004). *Cognitive-behavioral therapies with lesbian, gay, and bisexual clients.* New York: Guilford.

Martell, R. F. (1991). Sex bias at work: The effects of attentional and memory demands on performance ratings of men and women. *Journal of Applied Social Psychology, 21,* 1939–1960.

Martell, R. F. (1996). What mediates gender bias in work behavior ratings? *Sex Roles, 35,* 153–169.

Martin, C. L. (1987). A ratio measure of sex stereotyping. *Journal of Personality and Social Psychology, 52,* 489–499.

Martin, C. L., & Dinella, L. M. (2001). Gender development: Gender schema theory. In J. Worell (Ed.), *Encyclopedia of women and gender* (pp. 507–521). San Diego: Academic Press.

Martin, C. L., & Fabes, R. A. (2001). The stability and consequences of young children's same-sex peer interactions. *Developmental Psychology, 37,* 431–446.

Martin, C. L., & Halverson, C. (1981). A schematic processing model of sex typing and stereotyping in children. *Child Development, 52,* 1119–1134.

Martin, C. L., & Ruble, D. (2004). Children's search for gender cues. *Current Directions in Psychological Science, 13,* 67–70.

Martin, C. L., Ruble, D. N., & Szkrybalo, J. (2002). Cognitive theories of early gender development. *Psychological Bulletin, 128,* 903–933.

Martin, C. L., Ruble, D. N., & Szkrybalo, J. (2004). Recognizing the centrality of gender

identity and stereotype knowledge in gender development and moving toward theoretical integration. *Psychological Bulletin, 130,* 702–710.

Martin, E. (2001). The egg and the sperm: How science has constructed a romance based on stereotypical male-female roles. In S. Ruth (Ed.), *Issues in feminism* (5th ed., pp. 473–482). Mountain View, CA: Mayfield.

Martin, P. Y., & Collinson, D. L. (1998). Gender and sexuality in organizations. In M. M. Ferree, J. Lorber, & B. B. Hess (Eds.), *Revisioning gender* (pp. 285–310). Thousand Oaks, CA: Sage.

Martin, R., & Suls, J. (2003). How gender stereotypes influence self-regulation of cardiac health care-seeking and adaptation. In L. D. Cameron & H. Leventhal (Eds.), *The self-regulation of health and illness behaviour* (pp. 220–241). New York: Routledge.

Martin, S. F. (2004). *Refugee women* (2nd ed.). Lanham, MD: Lexington.

Martínez, E. (1995). In pursuit of Latina liberation. *Signs: Journal of Women in Culture and Society, 20,* 1019–1028.

Martínez, R., Johnston-Robledo, I., Ulsh, H. M., & Chrisler, J. C. (2000). Singing "the baby blues": A content analysis of popular press articles about postpartum affective disturbances. *Women and Health, 31,* 37–56.

Martire, L. M., & Stephens, M. A. P. (2003). Juggling parent care and employment responsibilities: The dilemmas of adult daughter caregivers in the workforce. *Sex Roles, 48,* 167–173.

Martire, L. M., Stephens, M. A. P., & Townsend, A. L. (2000). Centrality of women's multiple roles: Beneficial and detrimental consequences for psychological well-being. *Psychology and Aging, 15,* 148–156.

Marton, K. (2004, May 10). A worldwide gender gap. *Newsweek,* p. 94.

Martz, D. J. F., & Saraurer, D. B. (2002). Domestic violence and the experiences of rural women in East Central Saskatchewan. In K. M. J. McKenna & J. Larkin

(Eds.), *Violence against women: New Canadian perspectives* (pp. 163–196). Toronto, ON: Inanna Publications and Education.

Marx, D. M., & Roman, J. S. (2002). Female role models: Protecting women's math test performance. *Personality and Social Psychology Bulletin, 28,* 1183–1193.

Mason, A., et al. (2004). Prejudice toward people with disabilities. In J. L. Chin (Ed.), *The psychology of prejudice and discrimination* (Vol. 4, pp. 51–93). Westport, CT: Praeger.

Masser, B. M., & Abrams, D. (2004). Reinforcing the glass ceiling: The consequences of hostile sexism for female managerial candidates. *Sex Roles, 51,* 609–615.

Massoth, N. A. (1997). Editorial: It's not comical. *Society for the Psychological Study of Men and Masculinity Bulletin, 3*(1), 2.

Masters, W. H., & Johnson, V. E. (1966). *Human sexual response.* Boston: Little, Brown.

Masters, W. H., & Johnson, V. E. (1970). *Human sexual inadequacy.* Boston: Little, Brown.

Mathur, A. K., Reichle, J., Strawn, J., & Wiseley, C. (2004). Credentials count: How California's community colleges help parents move from welfare to self-sufficiency. In V. Polakow, S. S. Butler, L. S. Deprez, & P. Kahn (Eds.), *Shut out: Low income mothers and higher education in post-welfare America* (pp 149–170). Albany, NY: State University of New York Press.

Maticka-Tyndale, E., Herold, E. S., & Mewhinney, D. (1998). Casual sex on spring break: Intentions and behaviors of Canadian students. *Journal of Sex Research, 35,* 254–264.

Maticka-Tyndale, E., McKay, A., & Barrett, M. (2001, November). *Teenage sexual and reproductive behavior in developed countries: Country report for Canada.* New York: Alan Guttmacher Institute.

Matlin, M. W. (2000). *The psychology of women* (4th ed.). Fort Worth, TX: Harcourt College.

Matlin, M. W. (2003). From menarche to menopause: Misconceptions about women's reproductive lives. *Psychology Science, 45,* 106–122.

Matlin, M. W. (2005). *Cognition* (6th ed.). Hoboken, NJ: Wiley.

Matsakis, A. (2003). *The rape recovery handbook: Step-by-step help for survivors of sexual assault.* Oakland, CA: New Harbinger.

Matsumoto, D., & Juang, L. (2004). *Culture and psychology* (3rd ed.). Belmont, CA: Wadsworth.

Maushart, S. (1999). *The mask of motherhood.* New York: New Press.

Mauthner, N. S. (2002). *The darkest days of my life: Stories of postpartum depression.* Cambridge, MA: Harvard University Press.

Maynard, M. (2005). Women's studies. In P. Essed, D. T. Goldberg, & A. Kobayashi (Eds.), *A companion to gender studies* (pp. 29–39). Malden, MA: Blackwell.

Mazer, D. B., & Percival, E. F. (1989). Students' experiences of sexual harassment at a small university. *Sex Roles, 20,* 1–22.

McAdoo, H. P. (2002). African American parenting. In M. H. Bornstein (Ed.), *Handbook of parenting* (2nd ed., Vol. 4, pp. 47–58). Mahwah, NJ: Erlbaum.

McAdoo, J. L. (1993). Decision making and marital satisfaction in African American families. In H. P. McAdoo (Ed.), *Family ethnicity: Strength in diversity* (pp. 109–119). Newbury Park, CA: Sage.

McCallum, M., & Lauzon, A. (2005, Summer/Fall). If there's no mark, there's no crime. *Canadian Woman Studies/Les cahiers de la femme,* pp. 130–135.

McCarthy, P., & Loren, J. A. (1997). *Breast cancer? Let me check my schedule!* Boulder, CO: Westview Press.

McClure, E. B. (2000). A meta-analytic review of sex differences in facial expression processing and their development in infants, children, and adolescence. *Psychological Bulletin, 126,* 424–453.

McConatha, J. T., Schnell, F., & McKenna, A. (1999). Descriptions of older adults as depicted in magazine advertisements. *Psychological Reports, 85,* 1051–1056.

McCormick, N. B. (1994). *Sexual salvation: Affirming women's sexual rights and pleasures.* Westport, CT: Praeger.

McCreary, D. R., & Sadava, S. W. (2001). Gender differences in relationships among perceived attractiveness, life satisfaction, and health in adults as a function of Body Mass Index and perceived weight. *Psychology of Men and Masculinity, 2,* 108–116.

McCreight, B. S. (2005). Perinatal grief and emotional labour: A study of nurses' experiences in gynae wards. *International Journal of Nursing Studies, 42,* 439–448.

McDougall, J., DeWit, D. J., & Ebanks, C. E. (1999). Parental preferences for sex of children in Canada. *Sex Roles, 41,* 615–626.

McGann, V. L., & Steil, J. M. (2006). The sense of entitlement: Implications for gender equity and psychological well-being. In J. Worell & C. D. Goodheart (Eds.), *Handbook of girls' and women's psychological health: Gender and well-being across the life span* (pp. 175–182). New York: Oxford University Press.

McGoldrick, M., Giordano, J., & Garcia-Preto, N. (Eds.). (2005a). *Ethnicity and family therapy* (3rd ed.). New York: Guilford.

McGoldrick, M., Giordano, J., & Garcia-Preto, N. (2005b). Overview: Ethnicity and family therapy. In M. McGoldrick, J. Giordano, & N. Garcia-Preto (Eds.), *Ethnicity and family therapy* (3rd ed., pp. 1–40). New York: Guilford.

McGuinness, C. (1998). Cognition. In K. Trew & J. Kremer (Eds.), *Gender and psychology* (pp. 66–81). London: Arnold Publishers.

McHale, S. M., Dariotis, J., & Kauh, T. J. (2002). Social development and social relationships in middle childhood. In I. B. Weiner (Ed.), *Handbook of psychology* (Vol. 6, pp. 241–265). Hoboken, NJ: Wiley.

McHugh, M. C. (2005). Understanding gender and intimate partner abuse. *Sex Roles, 52,* 717–724.

McHugh, M. C., & Bartoszek, T. A. R. (2000). Intimate violence. In M. Biaggio & M. Hersen (Eds.), *Issues in the psychology of women* (pp. 115–142). New York: Kluwer Academic/Plenum.

McHugh, M. C., & Cosgrove, L. (1998). Research for women: Feminist methods. In D. M. Ashcraft (Ed.), *Women's work: A survey of scholarship by and about women* (pp. 19–43). New York: Haworth.

McIntosh, P. (2001). White privilege and male privilege. In S. M. Shaw & J. Lee (Eds.), *Women's voices, feminist visions* (pp. 78–86). Mountain View, CA: Mayfield.

McKenry, P. C., & McKelvey, M. W. (2003). The psychosocial well-being of Black and White mothers following marital dissolution: A brief report of a follow-up study. *Psychology of Women Quarterly, 27,* 31–36.

McKenzie-Pollock, L. (2005). Cambodian families. In M. McGoldrick, J. Giordano, & N. Garcia-Preto (Eds.), *Ethnicity and family therapy* (3rd ed., pp. 290–301). New York: Guilford.

McLeod, B. A. (2003, Fall/Winter). First Nations women and sustainability on the Canadian prairies. *Canadian Woman Studies/Les cahiers de la femme,* pp. 47–54.

McMahon, M. (1995). *Engendering motherhood: Identity and self-transformation in women's lives.* New York: Guilford.

McMullen, L. N. (2003). "Depressed" women's constructions of the deficient self. In J. M. Stoppard & L. M. McMullen (Eds.), *Situating sadness: Women and depression in social context* (pp. 17–38). New York: New York University Press.

McNair, L. D., & Prather, C. M. (2004). African American women and AIDS: Factors influencing risk and reaction to HIV disease. *Journal of Black Psychology, 30,* 106–123.

McNally, R. J. (2003a). Progress and controversy in the study of post-traumatic stress disorder. *Annual Review of Psychology, 54,* 229–252.

McNally, R. J. (2003b). *Remembering trauma.* Cambridge, MA: Harvard University Press.

McSweeney, S. (2004). Depression in women. In P. J. Caplan & L. Cosgrove (Eds.). *Bias in psychiatric diagnosis* (pp. 183–188). Lanham, MD: Jason Aronson.

McWright, L. (2002). African American grandmothers' and grandfathers' influence in the value socialization of grandchildren. In H. P. McAdoo (Ed.), *Black children* (2nd ed., pp. 27–44). Thousand Oaks, CA: Sage.

Medland, S. E., Geffen, G., & McFarland, K. (2002). Lateralization of speech production using verbal/manual dual tasks: Meta-analysis of sex differences and practice effects. *Neuropsychologia, 40,* 1233–1239.

Mednick, M. T., & Thomas, V. (1993). Women and the psychology of achievement: A view from the eighties. In F. L. Denmark & M. A. Paludi (Eds.), *Psychology of women: A handbook of issues and theories* (pp. 585–626). Westport, CT: Greenwood Press.

Medora, N. P. (2003). Mate selection in contemporary India. In R. R. Hamon & B. B. Ingoldsby (Eds.), *Mate selection across cultures* (pp. 209–230). Thousand Oaks, CA: Sage.

Meece, J. L., & Scantlebury, K. (2006). Gender and schooling: Progress and persistent barriers. In J. Worell & C. D. Goodheart (Eds.), *Handbook of girls' and women's psychological health: Gender and well-being across the life span* (pp. 283–291). New York: Oxford University Press.

Megan, C. E. (2000, November). Childless by choice. *Ms. Magazine,* pp. 43–46.

Meinz, E. J., & Salthouse, T. A. (1998). Is age kinder to females than to males? *Psychonomic Bulletin and Review, 5,* 56–70.

Melender, H. (2002). Experiences of fears associated with pregnancy and childbirth: A study of 329 pregnant women. *Birth, 29,* 101–111.

Mendelsohn, K. D. et al. (1994). Sex and gender bias in anatomy and physical diagnosis text illustrations. *Journal of the American Medical Association, 272,* 1267–1270.

Mendelson, T., & Muñoz, R. F. (2006). Prevention of depression in women. In C. L. M. Keyes & S. H. Goodman (Eds.), *Women and depression: A handbook for the social, behavioral, and bio-*

medical sciences (pp. 450–478). New York: Cambridge University Press.

Mendez, J. B. (2005). *From the revolution to the maquiladoras: Gender, labor, and globalization in Nicaragua.* Durham, NC: Duke University Press.

Menzies, C. H. (2005, Winter). Caregiving and being in touch: Lessons from my 85-year-old mum and me. *Canadian Woman Studies/Les cahiers de la femme, 24,* pp. 122–126.

Merin, Y. (2002). *Equality for same sex couples: The legal recognition of gay partnerships in Europe and the United States.* Chicago: University of Chicago Press.

Merline, A. C., et al. (2004). Substance use among adults 35 years of age: Prevalence, adulthood predictors, and impact of adolescent substance use. *American Journal of Public Health, 94,* 96–102.

Merritt, R. D., & Kok, C. J. (1995). Attribution of gender to a gender- unspecified individual: An evaluation of the people = male hypothesis. *Sex Roles, 33,* 145–157.

Merskin, D. (1999). Adolescence, advertising, and the ideology of menstruation. *Sex Roles, 40,* 941–957.

Metzger, T. (2002, June 19–25). The cross and the Y chromosome: Promise Keepers storm Rochester. *City Newspaper,* pp. 10–12.

Meyer, C. L., & Oberman, M. (2001). *Mothers who kill their children.* New York: New York University Press.

Meyer, I. L. (2003). Prejudice, social stress, and mental health in lesbian, gay, and bisexual populations: Conceptual issues and research evidence. *Psychological Bulletin, 129,* 674–697.

Meyerowitz, B. E., & Weidner, G. (1998). Section editors' overview. In E. A. Blechman & K. D. Brownell (Eds.), *Behavioral medicine and women: A comprehensive handbook* (pp. 537–545). New York: Guilford.

Mezulis, A. H., Abramson, L. Y., Hyde, J. S., & Hankin, B. L. (2004). Is there a universal positivity bias in attributions? A meta-analytic review of individual, developmental, and cultural differences in the self-serving attributional bias. *Psychological Bulletin, 139,* 711–747.

Michel, D. M., & Willard, S. G. (2003). *When dieting becomes dangerous.* New Haven, CT: Yale University Press.

Mighty, E. J. (2004). Working with abuse: Workplace responses to family violence. In M. L. Stirling, C. A. Cameron, N. Nason-Clark, & B. Miedema (Eds.), *Partnering for change* (pp. 111–132). Toronto: University of Toronto Press.

Milar, K. S. (2000). The first generation of women psychologists and the psychology of women. *American Psychologist, 55,* 616–619.

Milburn, S. S., Carney, D. R., & Ramirez, A. M. (2001). Even in modern media, the picture is still the same: A content analysis of clipart images. *Sex Roles, 44,* 277–294.

Milhausen, R. R., & Herold, E. S. (1999). Does the sexual double standard exist? Perceptions of university women. *Journal of Sex Research, 36,* 361–368.

Milkie, M. A., Bianchi, S. M., Mattingly, M. J., & Robinson, J. P. (2002). Gendered division of childrearing: Ideals, realities, and the relationship to parental well-being. *Sex Roles, 47,* 21–38.

Millard, J. E., & Grant, P. R. (2001). *Stereotypes of women in magazines: Content analysis of advertisements and fashion photographs.* Paper presented at the annual meeting of the Canadian Psychological Association, St. Foy, Quebec, Canada.

Miller, C. F., Trautner, H. M., & Ruble, D. N. (2006). The role of gender stereotypes in children's preferences and behavior. In L. Balter & C. S. Tamis-LeMonda (Eds.), *Child psychology: A handbook of contemporary issues* (2nd ed.). New York: Psychology Press.

Miller, D. T., Taylor, B., & Buck, M. L. (1991). Gender gaps: Who needs to be explained? *Journal of Personality and Social Psychology, 61,* 5–12.

Miller, E. J., Smith, J. E., & Trembath, D. L. (2000). The "skinny" on body size requests in personal ads. *Sex Roles, 43,* 129–141.

Miller, J., & Chamberlin, M. (2000). Women are teachers, men are professors: A study of student perceptions. *Teaching Sociology, 28,* 283–298.

Miller, K. E., & Rasco, L. M. (2004a). An ecological framework for addressing the mental health needs of refugee communities. In K. E. Miller & L. M. Rasco (Eds.), *The mental health of refugees: Ecological approaches to healing and adaptation* (pp. 1–64). Mahwah, NJ: Erlbaum.

Miller, K. E., & Rasco, L. M. (2004b). *The mental health of refugees: Ecological approaches to healing and adaptation.* Mahwah, NJ: Erlbaum.

Miller, L. C., Putcha-Bhagavatula, A., & Pedersen, W. C. (2002). Men's and women's mating preferences: Distinct evolutionary mechanisms. *Current Directions in Psychological Science, 11,* 88–93.

Miller, L. J. (2001). Psychiatric disorders during pregnancy. In N. L. Stotland & D. E. Stewart (Eds.), *Psychological aspects of women's health care* (2nd ed., pp. 51–66). Washington, DC: American Psychiatric Press.

Miller, L. J. (2002). Postpartum depression. *JAMA, 287,* 762–765.

Miller-Day, M. A. (2004). *Communication among grandmothers, mothers, and adult daughters.* Mahwah, NJ: Erlbaum.

Miller-Johnson, S., Moore, B. L., Underwood, M. K., & Coie, J. D. (2005). African-American girls and physical aggression: Does stability of childhood aggression predict later negative outcomes? In D. J. Pepler, K. C. Madsen, C. Webster, & K. S. Levene (Eds.), *The development and treatment of girlhood aggression* (pp. 75–101). Mahwah, NJ: Erlbaum.

Mills, J. (1984). Self-posed behavior of females and males in photographs. *Sex Roles, 10,* 633–637.

Mills, R. S. L., Pedersen, J., & Grusec, J. E. (1989). Sex differences in reasoning and emotion about

altruism. *Sex Roles, 20,* 603–621.

Mills, S. (2003). *Gender and politeness.* New York: Cambridge University Press.

Min, P. G. (1993). Korean immigrants' marital patterns and marital adjustment. In H. P. McAdoo (Ed.), *Family ethnicity: Strength in diversity* (pp. 287–299). Newbury Park, CA: Sage.

Miner-Rubino, K., Winter, D. G., & Stewart, A. J. (2004). Gender, social class, and the subjective experience of aging: Self-perceived personality change from early adulthood to late midlife. *Personality and Social Psychology Bulletin, 30,* 1599–1610.

Minton, H. L. (2000). Psychology and gender at the turn of the century. *American Psychologist, 55,* 613–615.

Mischel, W. (1966). A social-learning view of sex differences in behavior. In E. Maccoby (Ed.), *The development of sex differences* (pp. 56–81). Stanford, CA: Stanford University Press.

Mishel, L., Bernstein, J., & Allegretto, S. (2004). *The state of working America 2004/2005.* Ithaca, NY: Cornell University Press.

Moen, P., Kim, J. E., & Hofmeister, H. (2001). Couples' work/retirement transitions, gender, and marital quality. *Social Psychology Quarterly, 64,* 55–71.

Moen, P., & Roehling, P. (2005). *The career mystique: Cracks in the American dream.* Lanham, MD: Rowman & Littlefield.

Mohanty, C. T. (2003). *Feminism without borders.* Durham, NC: Duke University Press.

Monsour, M. (1992). Meanings of intimacy in cross- and same-sex friendships. *Journal of Social and Personal Relationships, 9,* 277–295.

Monsour, M. (2002). *Women and men as friends.* Mahwah, NJ: Erlbaum.

Monteith, M. J., & Voils, C. I. (2001). Exerting control over prejudiced responses. In G. B. Moskowitz (Ed.), *Cognitive social psychology* (pp. 375–388). Mahwah, NJ: Erlbaum.

Moore, F., & Keel, P. K. (2003). Influence of sexual orientation and age on disordered eating attitudes and behaviors in women. *International Journal of Eating Disorders, 34,* 370–374.

Mor, N., & Winquist, J. (2002). Self-focused attention and negative affect: A meta-analysis. *Psychological Bulletin, 128,* 638–662.

Moraga, C. (1993). Women's subordination through the lens of sex/gender, sexuality, class, and race: Multicultural feminism. In A. M. Jaggar & P. S. Rothenberg (Eds.), *Feminist frameworks: Alternative theoretical accounts of the relations between women and men* (3rd ed., pp. 203–212). New York: McGraw-Hill.

Morawski, J. G. (1994). *Sex matters? The unending search for a valid psychology of sex differences.* Paper presented at the annual meeting of the History of Science Society, New Orleans, LA.

Morawski, J. G., & Agronick, G. (1991). A restive legacy: The history of feminist work in experimental and cognitive psychology. *Psychology of Women Quarterly, 15,* 567–579.

Morawski, J. G., & Bayer, B. M. (1995). Stirring trouble and making theory. In H. Landrine (Ed.), *Bringing cultural diversity to feminist psychology: Theory, research, and practice* (pp. 113–137). Washington, DC: American Psychological Association.

Moreau, R., & Hussain, Z. (2005, March 28). "I decided to fight back." *Newsweek,* p. 36.

Morgan, B. L. (1998). A three-generational study of tomboy behavior. *Sex Roles, 39,* 787–800.

Morgan, L., & Kunkel, S. (2001). *Aging: The social context* (2nd ed.). Thousand Oaks, CA: Pine Forge Press.

Morling, B., Kitayama, S., & Miyamoto, Y. (2003). American and Japanese women use different coping strategies during normal pregnancy. *Personality and Social Psychology Bulletin, 29,* 1533–1546.

Morokoff, P. J. (1998). Sexual functioning. In E. A. Blechman & K. D. Brownell (Eds.), *Behavioral medicine and women: A comprehensive handbook* (pp. 440–446). New York: Guilford.

Morokoff, P. J. (2000). A cultural context for sexual assertiveness in women. In C. B. Travis & J. W. White (Eds.), *Sexuality, society, and feminism* (pp. 299–319). Washington, DC: American Psychological Association.

Morokoff, P. J., et al. (1997). Sexual Assertiveness Scale for women: Development and validation. *Journal of Personality and Social Psychology, 73,* 790–804.

Morris, J. F. (2000, August). *Lesbian women of color in communities: Social activities and mental health services.* Paper presented at the annual convention of the American Psychological Association, Washington, DC.

Morris, J. F., & Hart, S. (2003). Defending claims about mental health. In M. R. Stevenson & J. C. Cogan (Eds.), *Everyday activism: A handbook for lesbian, gay, and bisexual people and their allies* (pp. 57–78). New York: Routledge.

Morris, J. F., Waldo, C. R., & Rothblum, E. D. (2001). A model of predictors and outcomes of outness among lesbian and bisexual women. *American Journal of Orthopsychiatry, 71,* 61–71.

Morris, L. A. (1997). *The male heterosexual.* Thousand Oaks, CA: Sage.

Morrison, D. (1987). *Being pregnant: Conversations with women.* Vancouver, Canada: New Star.

Morrison, M. M., & Shaffer, D. R. (2003). Gender-role congruence and self-referencing as determinants of advertising effectiveness. *Sex Roles, 49,* 265–275.

Morrongiello, B. A., & Hogg, K. (2004). Mothers' reactions to children misbehaving in ways that can lead to injury. *Sex Roles, 50,* 103–118.

Moscicki, A. B. (2005). Impact of HPV infection in adolescent populations. *Journal of Adolescent Health, 37,* S3–S9.

Mosher, C. E. (2002). Impact of gender and problem severity upon intervention selection. *Sex Roles, 46,* 113–119.

Mosher, C. E., & Danoff-Burg, S. (2004). Effects of gender and employment status on support provided to caregivers. *Sex Roles, 51,* 589–595.

Mosher, C. E., & Danoff-Burg, S. (2005). Agentic and communal personality traits: Relations to attitudes toward sex and sexual experiences. *Sex Roles, 52,* 121–129.

Moskowitz, G. B. (Ed.). (2001). *Cognitive social psychology.* Mahwah, NJ: Erlbaum.

Mozurkewich, E. L., et al. (2000). Working conditions and adverse pregnancy outcome: A meta-analysis. *Obstetrics and Gynecology, 95,* 623–635.

Mueller, K. A., & Yoder, J. D. (1997). Gendered norms for family size, employment, and occupation: Are there personal costs for violating them? *Sex Roles, 36,* 207–220.

Mueller, K. A., & Yoder, J. D. (1999). Stigmatization of non-normative family size status. *Sex Roles, 41,* 901–919.

Mulac, A., Bradac, J. J., & Gibbons, P. (2001). Empirical support for the gender-as-culture hypothesis. *Human Communication Research, 27,* 121–152.

Mullings, D. V. (2004, Winter). Situating older Caribbean Canadian women in feminist research: A reflection. *Canadian Woman Studies/Les cahiers de la femme, 23,* pp. 134–139.

Murkoff, H., Eisenberg, A., & Hathaway, S. (2002). *What to expect when you're expecting.* New York: Workman.

Murphy, C. P. (2003). *Lavinia Fontana: A painter and her patrons in sixteenth-century Bologna.* New Haven, CT: Yale University Press.

Murphy, E. F. (2005). *Getting even: Why women get not paid like men—and what to do about it.* New York: Simon & Schuster.

Murphy, E. M. (2003). Being born female is dangerous for your health. *American Psychologist, 58,* 205–210.

Murray, S. L., Meinholdt, C., & Bergmann, L. S. (1999). Addressing gender issues in the engineering classroom. *Feminist Teacher, 12,* 169–183.

Musil, C. M. (2000a). Women's studies: Overview. In C. Kramarae

& D. Spender (Eds.), *Routledge international encyclopedia of women* (Vol. 4, pp. 2061–2068). New York: Routledge.

Musil, C. M. (2000b). Women's studies: United States. In C. Kramarae & D. Spender (Eds.), *Routledge international encyclopedia of women* (Vol. 4, pp. 2121–2125). New York: Routledge.

Musil, C. M., Warner, C. B., Stoller, E. P., & Andersson, T. E. (2005). Women and intergenerational caregiving in families: Structures, ethnicity, and building family ties. In M. L. Wykle, P. J. Whitehouse, & D. L. Morris (Eds.), *Successful aging through the life span* (pp. 143–158). New York: Springer.

Mwangi, M. W. (1996). Gender roles portrayed in Kenyan television commercials. *Sex Roles, 34,* 205–214.

Myers, A. M., & Rothblum, E. D. (2004). Coping with prejudice and discrimination based on weight. In J. L. Chin (Ed.), *The psychology of prejudice and discrimination* (Vol. 4, pp. 111–134). Westport, CT: Praeger.

Myers, D. G. (2000). *The American paradox.* New Haven, CT: Yale University Press.

Nabors, N. & Pettee, M. F. (2003). Womanist therapy with African American women with disabilities. In M. E. Banks & E. Kaschak (Eds.), *Women with visible and invisible disabilities* (pp. 331–341). New York: Haworth.

Naidoo, J. C. (1999). The experience of contrasting subjective cultures: The case of South Asian women in Canada. In J. Adamopoulos & Y. Kashima (Eds.), *Social and cultural context* (pp. 125–137). Thousand Oaks, CA: Sage.

Naidoo, J. C. (2000). The problem of Canada in the new millennium: Sociopsychological challenges for visible minority women. *Psychologia, 8,* 1–19.

Naples, N. A. (2002). Teaching community action in the introductory women's studies classroom. In N. A. Naples & K. Bojar (Eds.), *Teaching feminist activism: Strategies from the field* (pp. 71–94). New York: Routledge.

Naples, N. A., & Desai, M. (Eds.). (2002). *Women's activism and globalization: Linking local struggles and transnational politics.* New York: Routledge.

Narter, D. B. (2006). The development of prejudice in children. In B. E. Whitley, Jr., & M. E. Kite (Eds.), *The psychology of prejudice and discrimination* (pp. 260–299). Belmont, CA: Wadsworth.

National Action Committee on the Status of Women. (2006). *About NAC.* Retrieved June 19, 2006, from http://www.nac-cc/about/about_e.htm

National Center for Education Statistics. (2004). *Highlights from the Trends in International Mathematics and Science Study (TIMSS) 2003.* Washington, DC: U.S. Department of Education.

National Committee on Pay Equity. (2005). *Equal pay day—Tuesday, April 19, 2005.* Retrieved April 22, 2005, from http://www.pay-equity.org/

National Institute of Mental Health. (2001). *Eating disorders: Facts about eating disorders and the search for solutions.* Bethesda, MD: Author.

National Priorities Project. (2007). *Cost of war.* Retrieved January 25, 2007, from http://costofwar.com/index.html

Naughton, M. J., Jones, A. S., & Shumaker, S. A. (2005). When practices, promises, profits, and policies outpace hard evidence: The post-menopausal hormone debate. *Journal of Social Issues, 61,* 159–179.

Navarro, M. (2004, September 19). When gender isn't a given. *New York Times,* pp. 9–1, 9–6.

Nayak, M. B., Byrne, C. A., Martin, M. K., & Abraham, A. G. (2003). Attitudes toward violence against women: A cross-nation study. *Sex Roles, 49,* 333–342.

Neft, N., & Levine, A. D. (1997). *Where women stand: An international report on the status of women in 140 countries.* New York: Random House.

Neill, C. M., & Kahn, A. S. (1999). The role of personal spirituality and religious social activity on the life satisfaction of older widowed women. *Sex Roles, 40,* 319–329.

Nelson, A. (2000). The pink dragon is female: Halloween costumes and gender markers. *Psychology of Women Quarterly, 24,* 137–144.

Nelson, A. L., & Marshall, J. R. (2004). Impaired fertility. In R. A. Hatcher et al. (Eds.), *Contraceptive technology* (18th ed., pp. 651–671). New York: Ardent Media.

Nelson, D. L., & Burke, R. J. (2002). A framework for examining gender, work stress, and health. In D. L. Nelson & R. J. Burke (Eds.), *Gender, work stress, and health* (pp. 3–14). Washington, DC: American Psychological Association.

Nelson, T. D. (Ed.). (2005a). Ageism [Special issue]. *Journal of Social Issues, 61*(2).

Nelson, T. D. (2005b). Ageism: Prejudice against our feared future self. *Journal of Social Issues, 61,* 207–221.

Nelson, T. S. (2002). *For love of country: Confronting rape and sexual harassment in the U.S. military.* New York: Haworth.

Nencel, L. (2005). Heterosexuality. In P. Essed, D. T. Goldberg, & A. Kobayashi (Eds.), *A companion to gender studies* (pp. 132–142). Malden, MA: Blackwell.

Ness, I. (2003). Globalization and worker organization in New York City's garment industry. In D. E. Bender & R. A. Greenwald (Eds.), *Sweatshop USA: The American sweatshop in historical and global perspective* (pp. 169–182). New York: Routledge.

Ness, R. B., et al. (1999). Cocaine and tobacco use and the risk of spontaneous abortion. *New England Journal of Medicine, 340,* 333–339.

Neto, F., & Pinto, I. (1998). Gender stereotypes in Portuguese television advertisements. *Sex Roles, 39,* 153–164.

Neumark-Sztainer, D., & Eisenberg, M. (2005). Weight bias in a teen's world. In K. D. Brownell, R. M. Puhl, M. B. Schwartz, & L. Rudd (Eds.), *Weight bias: Nature, consequences, and remedies* (pp. 68–79). New York: Guilford.

Nevill, D. D., & Calvert, P. D. (1996). Career assessment and the salience inventory. *Journal of Career Assessment, 4*, 399–412.

New CDC data show high rates of chlamydia in young people in the U.S. (2005, September). *Infectious Diseases in Children*, p. 66.

Newcombe, N. S., Mathason, L., & Terlecki, M. (2002). Maximization of spatial competence: More important than finding the cause of sex differences. In A. McGillicuddy-De Lisi & R. De Lisi (Eds.), *Biology, society, and behavior: The development of sex differences in cognition* (pp. 183–206). Westport, CT: Ablex Publishing.

New England tribal college would be the first to serve Eastern tribes. (2004, December 16). *Black Issues in Higher Education*, p. 20.

Newland, M. C., & Rasmussen, E. B. (2003). Behavior in adulthood and during aging is affected by contaminant exposure in utero. *Current Directions in Psychological Science, 12*, 212–217.

Newtson, R. L., & Keith, P. M. (1997). Single women in later life. In J. M. Coyle (Ed.), *Handbook on women and aging* (pp. 385–399). Westport, CT: Greenwood Press.

Ngai, P. (2005). *Made in China: Women factory workers in a global workplace*. Durham, NC: Duke University Press.

NICHD Early Child Care Research Network. (1999). Contexts of development and developmental outcomes over the first seven years of life. In J. Brooks-Gunn & J. Berlin (Eds.), *Young children's education, health, and development: Profile and synthesis project report*. Washington, DC: Department of Education.

NICHD Early Child Care Research Network. (2001). Nonmaternal care and family factors in early development. *Applied Developmental Psychology, 22*, 457–492.

NICHD Early Child Care Research Network. (2002). Child-care structure → process → outcome: Direct and indirect effects of child-care quality on young children's development. *Psychological Science, 13*, 199–206.

NICHD Early Child Care Research Network. (2004). Type of child care and children's development at 54 months. *Early Childhood Research Quarterly, 19*, 203–230.

Nichols, M. (2000). Therapy with sexual minorities. In S. R. Leiblum & R. C. Rosen (Eds.), *Principles and practice of sex therapy* (3rd ed., pp. 335–367). New York: Guilford.

Nichols, S. L., & Good, T. L. (2004). *America's teenagers—myths and realities*. Mahwah, NJ: Erlbaum.

Nicotera, A. M. (1997). *The mate relationship: Cross-cultural applications of a rules theory*. Albany, NY: State University of New York Press.

Niedźwieńska, A. (2003). Gender differences in vivid memories. *Sex Roles, 49*, 321–331.

Nielsen, L. B. (2002). Subtle, pervasive, harmful: Racist and sexist remarks as hate speech. *Journal of Social Issues, 58*, 265–280.

Niemann, Y. F., et al. (1994). Use of free responses and cluster analysis to determine stereotypes of eight groups. *Personality and Social Psychology Bulletin, 20*, 379–390.

Nikolic-Ristanovic, V. (2000, Winter). Victimization by war rape. *Canadian Woman Studies/Les cahiers de la femme, 19*, 28–35.

Noar, S. M., Zimmerman, R. S., & Atwood, K. A. (2004). Safer sex and sexually transmitted infections from a relationship perspective. In J. H. Harvey, A. Wenzel, & S. Sprecher (Eds.), *The handbook of sexuality in close relationships* (pp. 519–544). Mahwah, NJ: Erlbaum.

Nolen-Hoeksema, S. (1990). *Sex differences in depression*. Stanford, CA: Stanford University Press.

Nolen-Hoeksema, S. (2001). Gender differences in depression. *Current Directions in Psychological Science, 10*, 173–176.

Nolen-Hoeksema, S. (2002). Gender differences in depression. In I. H. Gotlib & C. L. Hammen (Eds.), *Handbook of depression* (pp. 492–509). New York: Guilford.

Nolen-Hoeksema, S. (2003). *Women who think too much: How to break free of overthinking and reclaim your life*. New York: Holt.

Nolen-Hoeksema, S., & Jackson, B. (2001). Mediators of the gender difference in rumination. *Psychology of Women Quarterly, 25*, 37–47.

Nolen-Hoeksema, S., & Larson, J. (1999). *Coping with loss*. Mahwah, NJ: Erlbaum.

Nolen-Hoeksema, S., Larson, J., & Grayson, C. (1999). Explaining the gender difference in depressive symptoms. *Journal of Personality and Social Psychology, 77*, 1061–1072.

Noller, P., & Feeney, J. A. (2002). Communication, relationship concerns, and satisfaction in early marriage. In A. L. Vangelisti, H. T. Reis, & M. A. Fitzpatrick (Eds.), *Stability and change in relationships* (pp. 129–155). New York: Cambridge.

Noor, N. M. (1996). Some demographic, personality, and role variables as correlates of women's well-being. *Sex Roles, 34*, 603–620.

Noor, N. M. (1999). Roles and women's well-being: Some preliminary findings from Malaysia. *Sex Roles, 41*, 123–145.

Nordvik, H., & Amponsah, B. (1998). Gender differences in spatial activity among university students in an egalitarian educational system. *Sex Roles, 38*, 1009–1023.

Norton, S. (2002). Women exposed: Sexual harassment and female vulnerability. In L. Diamant & J. A. Lee (Eds.), *The psychology of sex, gender, and jobs* (pp. 83–101). Westport, CT: Praeger.

Nosek, B. A., Banaji, M. R., & Greenwald, A. G. (2002). Math = male, me = female, therefore math ≠ me. *Journal of Personality and Social Psychology, 83*, 44–59.

Nour, N. M. (2005). Female genital cutting is both a health and human rights issue. In Boston Women's Health Book Collective (Eds.), *Our bodies, ourselves* (pp. 644–655). New York: Touchstone.

Novack, L. L., & Novack, D. R. (1996). Being female in the

eighties and nineties: Conflicts between new opportunities and traditional expectations among White, middle class, heterosexual college women. *Sex Roles, 35,* 57–77.

Nussbaum, J. F., & Coupland, J. (Eds.). (2004). *Handbook of communication and aging research* (2nd ed.). Mahwah, NJ: Erlbaum.

Nussbaum, M. (2000, September 8). Globalization debate ignores the education of women. *Chronicle of Higher Education,* pp. B16–B17.

Nyanzi, S., Nyanzi, B., & Kalina, B. (2004). Contemporary myths, sexuality misconceptions, information sources, and risk perceptions of Bodabodamen in Southwest Uganda. *Sex Roles, 52,* 111–119.

Nydegger, R. (2004). Gender and mental health: Incidence and treatment issues. In M. A. Paludi (Ed.), *Praeger guide to the psychology of gender* (pp. 93–116). Westport, CT: Praeger.

Obama, B., & Brownback, S. (2006, January 11). Policy adrift on Darfur. *Liberal Opinion Week,* p. 31.

O'Brien, M., et al. (2000). Gender-role cognition in three-year-old boys and girls. *Sex Roles, 42,* 1007–1025.

Ocampo, C., et al. (2003). Diversity research in *Teaching of Psychology:* Summary and agenda. *Teaching of Psychology, 30,* 5–18.

Ochman, J. M. (1996). The effects of nongender-role stereotyped, same-sex role models in storybooks on the self-esteem of children in grade three. *Sex Roles, 35,* 711–735.

O'Connell, A. N. (2001). *Models of achievement: Reflections of eminent women in psychology* (Vol. 3). Mahwah, NJ: Erlbaum.

Oerton, S. (1998). Reclaiming the "housewife"? Lesbians and household work. In G. A. Dunne (Ed.), *Living "difference": Lesbian perspectives on work and family life* (pp. 69–83). New York: Haworth.

Offman, A., & Kleinplatz, P. J. (2004, Spring). Does PMDD belong in the DSM? Challenging the med-

icalization of women's bodies. *Canadian Journal of Human Sexuality, 13,* 17–27.

Offman, A., & Matheson, K. (2004). The sexual self-perceptions of young women experiencing abuse in dating relationships. *Sex Roles, 51,* 551–560.

Oggins, J., Veroff, J., & Leber, D. (1993). Perceptions of marital interaction among Black and White newlyweds. *Journal of Personality and Social Psychology, 65,* 494–511.

O'Hara, M. W., & Stuart, S. (1999). Pregnancy and postpartum. In R. G. Robinson & W. R. Yates (Eds.), *Psychiatric treatment of the medically ill* (pp. 253–277). New York: Marcel Dekker.

Oksman, J. C. (2002). *An analysis of the portrayal of menstruation in menstrual product advertisements.* Unpublished manuscript, SUNY Geneseo.

Olafson, E. (2004). Child sexual abuse. In B. J. Cling (Ed.), *Sexualized violence against women and children* (pp. 151–187). New York: Guilford.

Oldenburg, B., & Burton, N. W. (2004). Primary prevention. In A. Kaptein & J. Weinman (Eds.), *Health psychology* (pp. 305–336). Malden, MA: Blackwell.

Older Women's League. (2006a). *Older women and poverty.* Retrieved March 7, 2006 from http://www.owl-national.org/poverty.html

Older Women's League. (2006b). *Women and retirement income.* Retrieved March 7, 2006 from http://www.owl-retirementincome.html

O'Leary, K. D., & Maiuro, R. D. (Eds.). (2001). *Psychological abuse in violent domestic relations.* New York: Springer.

O'Leary, V. E., & Bhaju, J. (2006). Resilience and empowerment. In J. Worell & C. D. Goodheart (Eds.), *Handbook of girls' and women's psychological health: Gender and well-being across the life span* (pp. 157–165). New York: Oxford University Press.

Olio, K. A. (2004). The truth about "false memory syndrome." In P. J. Caplan & L. Cosgrove (Eds.), *Bias in psychiatric diagnosis*

(pp. 163–169). Lanham, MD: Jason Aronson.

Oliver, M. B., & Hyde, J. S. (1993). Gender differences in sexuality: A meta-analysis. *Psychological Bulletin, 114,* 29–51.

Olkin, R. (2004). Women with disabilities. In J. C. Chrisler, C. Golden, & P. D. Rozee (Eds.), *Lectures on the psychology of women* (3rd ed., pp. 144–157). Boston: McGraw-Hill.

Olkin, R. (2006). Physical or systemic disabilities. In J. Worell & C. D. Goodheart (Eds.), *Handbook of girls' and women's psychological health: Gender and well-being across the life span* (pp. 94–102). New York: Oxford University Press.

Olkin, R., & Pledger, C. (2003). Can disability studies and psychology join hands? *American Psychologist, 58,* 296–304.

O'Neill, S. K. (2003). African American women and eating disturbances: A meta-analysis. *Journal of Black Psychology, 29,* 3–16.

Online. (2004, September 17). *Chronicle of Higher Education,* p. A29.

Onyx, J., & Benton, P. (1999). What does retirement mean for women? In J. Onyx, R. Leonard, & R. Reed (Eds.), *Revisioning aging: Empowering of older women* (pp. 93–108). New York: Peter Lang.

Orazio and Artemisia Gentileschi: Father and daughter painters in Baroque Italy. (2002, April–June). *Saint Louis Art Museum Magazine,* pp. 4–7.

O'Reilly, P., Penn, E. M., & deMarrais, K. (Eds.). (2001). *Educating young adolescent girls.* Mahwah, NJ: Erlbaum.

Orozco, A. E. (1999). Mexican blood runs through my veins. In D. L. Galindo & M. D. Gonzales (Eds.), *Speaking Chicana: Voice, power, and identity* (pp. 106–120). Tucson: University of Arizona Press.

Osland, J. A., Fitch, M., & Willis, E. E. (1996). Likelihood to rape in college males. *Sex Roles, 35,* 171–183.

Osman, S. L. (2004). Victim resistance: Theory and data on understanding perceptions of sexual harassment. *Sex Roles, 50,* 267–275.

Ostenson, R. S. (2004). Who's in and who's out: The results of oppression. In J. C. Chrisler, C. Golden, & P. D. Rozee (Eds.), *Lectures on the psychology of women* (3rd ed., pp. 16–26). New York: McGraw-Hill.

Ostrov, J. M., et al. (2004). An observational study of delivered and received aggression, gender, and social-psychological adjustment in preschool: "This white crayon doesn't work . . ." *Early Childhood Research Quarterly, 19,* 355–371.

Ostrove, J. M., & Cole, E. R. (2003). Privileging class: Toward a critical psychology of social class in the context of education. *Journal of Social Issues, 59,* 677–692.

O'Sullivan, L. F., & Gaines, M. E. (1998). Decision-making in college students' heterosexual dating relationship: Ambivalence about engaging in sexual activity. *Journal of Social and Personal Relationships, 15,* 347–363.

O'Sullivan, L. F., Graber, J. A., & Brooks-Gunn, J. (2001). Adolescent gender development. In J. Worell (Ed.), *Encyclopedia of women and gender* (pp. 55–67). San Diego: Academic Press.

O'Sullivan, L. F., McCrudden, M. C., & Tolman. D. L. (2006). To your sexual health! Incorporating sexuality into the health perspective. In J. Worell & C. D. Goodheart (Eds.), *Handbook of girls' and women's psychological health: Gender and well-being across the life span* (pp. 192–207). New York: Oxford University Press.

O'Sullivan, L. F., & Meyer-Bahlburg, H. F. L. (2003). African-American and Latina inner-city girls' reports of romantic and sexual development. *Journal of Social and Personal Relationships, 20,* 221–238.

O'Sullivan, L. F., Meyer-Bahlburg, H. F. L., & Watkins, B. X. (2001). Mother-daughter communication about sex among urban African American and Latino families. *Journal of Adolescent Research, 16,* 269–292.

Oswald, D. L., & Harvey, R. D. (2003). A Q-methodological study of women's subjective perspectives on mathematics. *Sex Roles, 49,* 133–142.

Owens, R. E., Jr. (1998). *Queer kids: The challenges and promise for lesbian, gay, and bisexual youth.* Binghamton, NY: Haworth.

Ozer, E. J., & Weiss, D. S. (2004). Who develops posttraumatic stress disorder. *Current Directions in Psychological Science, 13,* 169–172.

Padavic, I., & Reskin, B. (2002). *Women and men at work* (2nd ed.). Thousand Oaks, CA: Pine Forge Press.

Paik, H. (2001). The history of children's use of electronic media. In D. G. Singer & J. L. Singer (Eds.), *Handbook on children and the media* (pp. 7–27). Thousand Oaks, CA: Sage.

Pajares, F., Miller, M. D., & Johnson, M. J. (1999). Gender differences in writing self-beliefs of elementary school students. *Journal of Educational Psychology, 91,* 50–61.

Pallier, G. (2003). Gender differences in the self-assessment of accuracy on cognitive tasks. *Sex Roles, 48.* 265–276.

Palmore, E. (2001). The ageism survey: First findings. *The Gerontologist, 41,* 572–575.

Paludi, C. A., Jr., & Paludi, M. A. (2003). Developing and enforcing effective policies, procedures, and training programs for educational institutions and businesses. In M. A. Paludi & C. A. Paludi (Eds.), *Academic and workplace sexual harassment* (pp. 175–198). Westport, CT: Praeger.

Paludi, M. A. (2004). Sexual harassment of college students: Cultural similarities and differences. In J. C. Chrisler, C. Golden, & P. D. Rozee (Eds.), *Lectures on the psychology of women* (3rd ed., pp. 332–355). New York: McGraw-Hill.

Pappas, G., Queen, S., Hadden, W., & Fisher, G. (1993). The increasing disparity in mortality between socioeconomic groups in the United States, 1960 and 1986. *New England Journal of Medicine, 329,* 103–109.

Pardo, M. (2005). Mexican American women, grassroots community activists: "Mothers of East Los Angeles." In M. Baca Zinn, P. Hondagneu-Sotelo, & M. A. Messner (Eds.), *Gender through the prism of difference* (3rd ed., pp. 541–546). New York: Oxford University Press.

Park, J., & Liao, T. F. (2000). The effect of multiple roles of South Korean married women professors: Role changes and the factors which influence potential role gratification and strain. *Sex Roles, 43,* 571–591.

Parke, R. D. (2004). Development in the family. *Annual Review of Psychology, 55,* 365–399.

Parks, J. B., & Roberton, M. A. (1998a). Contemporary arguments against nonsexist language: Blaubergs (1980) revisited. *Sex Roles, 39,* 445–461.

Parks, J. B., & Roberton, M. A. (1998b). Influence of age, gender, and context on attitudes toward sexist/nonsexist language: Is sport a special case? *Sex Roles, 38,* 477–494.

Parks, J. B., & Roberton, M. A. (2000). Development and validation of an instrument to measure attitudes toward sexist/nonsexist language. *Sex Roles, 42,* 415–438.

Parrot, A. (1996). Sexually assertive communication training. In T. L. Jackson (Ed.), *Acquaintance rape: Assessment, treatment, and prevention* (pp. 215–242). Sarasota, FL: Professional Resource Press.

Parrot, A. (1999). *Coping with date and acquaintance rape.* New York: Rosen Publishing Group.

Pascarella, E. T., et al. (1997). Women's perceptions of a "chilly climate" and their cognitive outcomes during the first year of college. *Journal of College Student Development, 38,* 109–124.

Pasch, L. (2001). Confronting fertility problems: Current research and future challenges. In A. Baum, T. A. Revenson, & J. E. Singer (Eds.), *Handbook of health psychology* (pp. 559–570). Mahwah, NJ: Erlbaum.

Pasupathi, M. (2002). Arranged marriages. In Y. Yalom & L. L. Carstensen (Eds.), *Rethinking the couple: Some feminist answers* (pp. 211–235). Berkeley: University of California Press.

Pasupathi, M., & Löckenhoff, C. E. (2002). Ageist behavior. In T. D. Nelson (Eds.), *Ageism: Stereotyping and prejudice against older persons* (pp. 201–246). Cambridge, MA: MIT Press.

Pattatucci, A. M., & Hamer, D. H. (1995). Development and familiality of sexual orientation in females. *Behavior Genetics, 25,* 407–420.

Patterson, C. J. (1995). Sexual orientation and human development: An overview. *Developmental Psychology, 31,* 3–11.

Patterson, C. J. (2003). Children of lesbian and gay parents. In L. D. Garnets & D. C. Kimmel (Eds.), *Psychological perspectives on lesbian, gay, and bisexual experiences* (2nd ed., pp. 497–548). New York: Columbia University Press.

Patterson, C. J., & Chan, R. W. (1999). Families headed by lesbian and gay parents. In M. E. Lamb (Ed.), *Parenting and development in "nontraditional" families* (pp. 191–221). Mahwah, NJ: Erlbaum.

Patterson, M. L., & Werker, J. F. (2002). Infants' ability to match dynamic phonetic and gender information in the face and voice. *Journal of Experimental Child Psychology, 81,* 93–115.

Pauwels, A. (1998). *Women changing language.* London: Longman.

Payne, K. E. (2001). *Different but equal: Communication between the sexes.* Westport, CT: Praeger.

Pedersen, W. C., Miller, L. C., Putvha-Bhagavatula, & Yang, Y. (2002). Evolved sex differences in the number of partners desired? *Psychological Science, 13,* 157–161.

Pediatrician testifies on impact of sexuality in media. (2001, October). *American Academy of Pediatrics News,* p. 141.

Peirce, K. (1990). A feminist theoretical perspective on the socialization of teenage girls through *Seventeen* magazine. *Sex Roles, 23,* 491–500.

Peltola, P., Milkie, M. A., & Presser, S. (2004). The "feminist" mystique: Feminist identity in three generations of women. *Gender & Society, 18,* 1–23.

Peña, M. (1998). Class, gender, and machismo: The "treacherous-woman" folklore of Mexican male workers. In M. S. Kimmel & M. A. Messner (Eds.), *Men's lives* (4th ed., pp. 273–284). Boston: Allyn & Bacon.

Pennebaker, J. W., Mehl, M. R., & Niederhoffer, K. G. (2003). Psychological aspects of natural language use: Our words, our selves. *Annual Review of Psychology, 54,* 547–577.

Peplau, L. A. (1983). Roles and gender. In H. H. Kelley et al. (Eds.), *Close relationships* (pp. 220–264). San Francisco: Freeman.

Peplau, L. A. (1994). Men and women in love. In D. L. Sollie & L. A. Leslie (Eds.), *Gender, families, and close relationships: Feminist research journeys* (pp. 19–49). Thousand Oaks, CA: Sage.

Peplau, L. A. (2001). Rethinking women's sexual orientation: An interdisciplinary, relationship-focused approach. *Personal Relationships, 8,* 1–19.

Peplau, L. A. (2003). Human sexuality: How do men and women differ? *Current Directions in Psychological Science, 12,* 37–40.

Peplau, L. A., & Beals, K. P. (2001). Lesbians, gay men, and bisexuals in relationships. In J. Worell (Ed.), *Encyclopedia of women and gender* (pp. 657–666). San Diego: Academic Press.

Peplau, L. A., & Beals, K. P. (2004). The family lives of lesbians and gay men. In A. L. Vangelisti (Ed.), *Handbook of family communication* (pp. 233–248). Mahwah, NJ: Erlbaum.

Peplau, L. A., Cochran, S. D., & Mays, V. M. (1997). A national survey of the intimate relationships of African-American lesbians and gay men. In B. Greene (Ed.), *Ethnic and cultural diversity among lesbians and gay men* (pp. 11–38). Thousand Oaks, CA: Sage.

Peplau, L. A., & Fingerhut, A. (2004). The paradox of the lesbian worker. *Journal of Social Issues, 60,* 719–735.

Peplau, L. A., & Garnets, L. D. (2000). A new paradigm for

understanding women's sexuality and sexual orientation. *Journal of Social Issues, 56,* 329–350.

Peplau, L. A., & Spalding, L. R. (2000). The close relationships of lesbians, gay men, and bisexuals. In C. Hendrick & S. S. Hendrick (Eds.), *Close relationships* (pp. 111–123). Thousand Oaks, CA: Sage.

Peplau, L. A., Veniegas, R. C., & Campbell, S. M. (1996). Gay and lesbian relationships. In R. C. Savin-Williams & K. Cohen (Eds.), *The lives of lesbians, gays, and bisexuals: Children to adults* (pp. 250–273). Fort Worth, TX: Harcourt Brace.

Peplau, L. A., Veniegas, R. C., Taylor, P. L., & DeBro, S. C. (1999). Sociocultural perspectives on the lives of women and men. In L. A. Peplau et al. (Eds.), *Gender, culture, and ethnicity: Current research about women and men* (pp. 23–37). Mountain View, CA: Mayfield.

Pérez-Stable, E. J., & Nápoles-Springer, A. M. (2001). Physical health status of Latinos in the United States. In A. G. López & E. Carrillo (Eds.), *The Latino psychiatric patient* (pp. 19–36). Washington, DC: American Psychiatric Publishing.

Perloff, R. M. (2001). *Persuading people to have safer sex: Applications of social science to the AIDS crisis.* Mahwah, NJ: Erlbaum.

Perry-Jenkins, M., Pierce, C. P., & Goldberg, A. E. (2004). Discourse on diapers and dirty laundry: Family communication about child care and housework. In A. L. Vangelisti (Ed.), *Handbook of family communication* (pp. 541–561). Mahwah, NJ: Erlbaum.

Perse, E. M. (2001). *Media effects and society.* Mahwah, NJ: Erlbaum.

Peterkin, A., & Risdon, C. (2003). *Caring for lesbian and gay people: A clinical guide.* Toronto: University of Toronto Press.

Peterson, J. (2003). The challenge of comparable worth. In E. Mutari & D. M. Figart (Eds.), *Women and the economy* (pp. 277–283). Armonk, NY: M. E. Sharpe.

Peterson, Z. D., & Muehlenhard, C. L. (2004). Was it rape? The function of women's rape myth acceptance and definitions of sex in labeling their own experiences. *Sex Roles, 51,* 129–144.

Pezdek, K. (2001). A cognitive analysis of the role of suggestibility in explaining memories for abuse. In J. J. Freyd & A. P. DePrince (Eds.), *Trauma and cognitive science: A meeting of minds, science, and human experience* (pp. 73–85). New York: Haworth.

Philbin, M., Meier, E., Hoffman, S., & Boverie, P. (1995). A survey of gender and learning styles. *Sex Roles, 32,* 485–494.

Philipp, D. A., & Carr, M. L. (2001). Normal and medically complicated pregnancies. In N. L. Stotland & D. E. Stewart (Eds.), *Psychological aspects of women's health care: The interface between psychiatry and obstetrics and gynecology* (2nd ed., pp. 13–32). Washington, DC: American Psychiatric Publishing.

Phillips, C. R. (2000, Summer). Supportive language in family-centered maternity care. *Advances in Family-Centered Care,* pp. 16–18.

Phillips, L. (1998). *The girls report.* New York: National Council for Research on Women.

Phizacklea, A. (2001). Women, migration, and the state. In K. Bhavnani (Ed.), *Feminism and "race"* (pp. 319–330). New York: Oxford University Press.

Physicians for Human Rights. (1998). *The Taliban's war on women: A health and human rights crisis in Afghanistan.* Boston: Author.

Pickup, F. (2001). *Ending violence against women: A challenge for development and humanitarian work.* Oxford, England: Oxfam.

Pierce, R. L., & Kite, M. E. (1999). Creating expectations in adolescent girls. In S. N. Davis, M. Crawford, & J. Sebrechts (Eds.), *Coming into her own: Educational success in girls and women* (pp. 175–192). San Francisco: Jossey-Bass.

Pierce, W. D., Sydie, R. A., Stratkotter, R., & Krull, C. (2003). Social concepts and judgments: A semantic differential analysis of the concepts *feminist, man,* and *woman. Psychology of Women Quarterly, 27,* 338–346.

Pilkington, N. W., & D'Augelli, A. R. (1995). Victimization of lesbian, gay, and bisexual youth in community settings. *Journal of Community Psychology, 23,* 34–56.

Pincus, J. (2000). Childbirth advice literature as it relates to two childbearing ideologies. *Birth, 27,* 209–213.

Pipher, M. (1994). *Reviving Ophelia: Saving the selves of adolescent girls.* New York: Ballantine.

Piran, N. (2001). Eating disorders and disordered eating. In J. Worell (Ed.), *Encyclopedia of women and gender* (pp. 369–378). San Diego: Academic Press.

Piran, N., & Ross, E. (2006). From girlhood to womanhood: Multiple transitions in context. In J. Worell & C. D. Goodheart (Eds.), *Handbook of girls' and women's psychological health: Gender and well-being across the life span* (pp. 301–310). New York: Oxford University Press.

Plant, E. A., Hyde, J. S., Keltner, D., & Devine, P. G. (2000). The gender stereotyping of emotions. *Psychology of Women Quarterly, 24,* 81–92.

Plant, E. A., Kling, K. C., & Smith, G. L. (2004). The influence of gender and social role on the interpretation of facial expressions. *Sex Roles, 51,* 187–196.

Pleck, J. H., & Masciadrelli, B. P. (2004). Paternal involvement in U.S. residential fathers: Levels, sources, and consequences. In M. E. Lamb (Ed.), *The role of the father in child development* (4th ed., 222–271). New York: Wiley.

Plunkett, M. (2001). Serendipity and agency in narratives of transition: Young adult women and their careers. In D. P. McAdams, R. Josselson, & A. Lieblich (Eds.), *Turns in the road: Narrative studies of lives in transition* (pp. 151–175). Washington, DC: American Psychological Association.

Poelmans, S. A. Y. (Ed.). (2005). *Work and family: An international research perspective.* Mahwah, NJ: Erlbaum.

Pogrebin, L. C. (1997, September/October). Endless love. *Ms. Magazine,* pp. 36–37.

Polacca, M. (2001). American Indian and Alaska Native elderly. In L. K. Olson (Ed.), *Age through ethnic lenses: Caring for the elderly in a multicultural society* (pp. 112–122). Lanham, MD: Rowman & Littlefield.

Polakow, V., Butler, S. S., Deprez, L. S., & Kahn, P. (Eds.). (2003). *Shut out: Low income mothers and higher education in post-welfare America.* Albany, NY: State University of New York Press.

Polce-Lynch, M., et al. (1998). Gender and age patterns in emotional expression, body image, and self-esteem: A qualitative analysis. *Sex Roles, 38,* 1025–1048.

Poling, J. N., Grundy, C., & Min, H. (2002). Men helping men to become pro-feminist. In J. N. Poling & C. C. Neuger (Eds.), *Men's work in preventing violence against women* (pp. 107–122). New York: Haworth.

Polivy, J., & Herman, C. P. (2002). Experimental studies of dieting. In C. G. Fairburn & K. D. Brownell (Eds.), *Eating disorders and obesity: A comprehensive handbook* (2nd ed., pp. 84–87). New York: Guilford.

Polivy, J., & McFarlane, T. L. (1998). Dieting, exercise, and body weight. In E. A. Blechman & K. D. Brownell (Eds.), *Behavioral medicine and women: A comprehensive handbook* (pp. 369–373). New York: Guilford.

Pollack, W. (1998). *Real boys.* New York: Random House.

Pollitt, K. (2004). U.S. feminism lite: Claiming independence, asserting personal choice. In L. Flanders (Ed.), *The W effect: Bush's war on women* (pp. 280–284). New York: Feminist Press.

Pollitt, K., & Baumgardner, J. (2003). Afterword. In R. Dicker & A. Piepmeier (Eds.), *Catching a wave: Reclaiming feminism for the 21st century* (pp. 309–319). Boston: Northeastern University.

Pomerantz, E. M., & Ruble, D. N. (1998). The role of maternal control in the development of sex differences in child self-evaluative factors. *Child Development, 69,* 458–478.

Pomerleau, A., Bolduc, D., Malcuit, G., & Cossette, L. (1990). Pink or blue: Environmental gender stereotypes in the first two years of life. *Sex Roles, 22,* 359–367.

Pomerleau, C. S., Zucker, A. N., & Stewart, A. J. (2001). Characterizing concerns about postcessation weight gain: Results from a national survey of women smokers. *Nicotine and Tobacco Research, 3,* 51–60.

Pomfret, J. (2001, June 3). China's boy boom tied to ultrasound machines. *Dallas Morning News,* p. 31A.

Pope, K. (2001). Sex between therapists and clients. In J. Worell (Ed.), *Encyclopedia of women and gender* (pp. 955–962). San Diego: Academic Press.

Popenoe, D. (2004). Without a piece of paper [Review of the book *Just living together: Implications of cohabitation on families, children, and social policy*]. *Contemporary Psychology, 49,* 240–241.

Popenoe, D., & Whitehead, B. D. (2002). *The state of our unions.* Piscataway, NJ: National Marriage Project.

Popp, D., et al. (2003). Gender, race, and speech style stereotypes. *Sex Roles, 48,* 317–325.

Poran, M. A. (2002). Denying diversity: Perceptions of beauty and social comparison processes among Latina, Black, and White women. *Sex Roles, 47,* 65–81.

Porzelius, L. K. (2000). Physical health issues for women. In M. Biaggio & M. Hersen (Eds.), *Issues in the psychology of women* (pp. 229–249). New York: Plenum.

Poulin, R. (2003, Spring/Summer). Globalization and the sex trade: Trafficking and the commodification of women and children. *Canadian Woman Studies/Les cahiers de la femme, 22,* 38–43.

Powell, G. N., & Graves, L. M. (2003). *Women and men in management* (3rd ed.). Thousand Oaks, CA: Sage.

Powers, P. S. (2002). Eating disorders. In S. G. Kornstein & A. H. Clayton (Eds.), *Women's mental health: A comprehensive textbook* (pp. 244–262). New York: Guilford.

Powlishta, K. K. (1995). Intergroup processes in childhood: Social categorization and sex role development. *Developmental Psychology, 31,* 781–788.

Powlishta, K. K. (2000). The effect of target age on the activation of gender stereotypes. *Sex Roles, 42,* 271–282.

Powlishta, K. K., et al. (2001). From infancy through middle childhood: The role of cognitive and social factors in becoming gendered. In R. K. Unger (Ed.), *Handbook of the psychology of women and gender* (pp. 116–132). New York: Wiley.

Pozner, J. L. (2001, March/April). Cosmetic coverage. *Extra!,* pp. 8–10.

Pozner, J. L. (2003). The "big lie": False feminist death syndrome, profit, and the media. In R. Dicker & A. Piepmeier (Eds.), *Catching a wave: Reclaiming feminism for the 21st century* (pp. 21–56). Boston: Northeastern University.

Prager, K. J., & Roberts, L. J. (2004). Deep intimate connection: Self and intimacy in couple relationships. In D. J. Mashek & A. Aron (Eds.), *Handbook of closeness and intimacy* (pp. 43–60). Mahwah, NJ: Erlbaum.

Preston, A. E. (2004). *Leaving science.* New York: Russell Sage Foundation.

Prezbindowski, K. S., & Prezbindowski, A. K. (2001). Educating young adolescent girls about lesbian, bisexual, and gay issues. In P. O'Reilly, E. M. Penn, & K. deMarrais (Eds.), *Educating young adolescent girls* (pp. 47–80). Mahwah, NJ: Erlbaum.

Price, C. A., & Joo, E. (2005). Exploring the relationship between marital status and women's retirement satisfaction. *International Journal of Aging and Human Development, 61,* 37–55.

Price, J. M., & Pecjak, V. (2003). Obesity and stigma: Important issues in women's health. *Psychology Science, 45,* 6–42.

Prince, C. J. (2004). Media myths: The truth about the opt-out hype. *NAFE Magazine,* pp. 14–17.

Princess or prisoner? (2004, June 7). *People,* p. 72.

Pruchno, R., & Rosenbaum, J. (2003). Social relationships in adulthood and old age. In R. M. Lerner, M. Ann Easterbrooks, & J. Mistry (Eds.), *Handbook of psychology* (Vol. 6, pp. 487–508). New York: Wiley.

Pryzgoda, J., & Chrisler, J. C. (2000). Definitions of gender and sex: The subtleties of meaning. *Sex Roles, 43,* 553–569.

Pulera, D. (2002). *Visible differences: Why race will matter to Americans in the twenty-first century.* New York: Continuum.

Pulford, B. D., & Colman, A. M. (1997). Overconfidence: Feedback and item difficulty effects. *Personality and Individual Differences, 23,* 125–133.

Pushkar, D., et al. (2003). Emergent values and the experience of aging. *Journal of Adult Development, 10,* 249–259.

Pyke, S. W. (1998, June). *The inferior sex: Psychology's construction of gender.* Paper presented at the annual convention of the Canadian Psychological Association, Edmonton, Canada.

Pyke, S. W. (2001). Feminist psychology in Canada: Early days. *Canadian Psychology/Psychologie canadienne, 42,* 268–275.

Quart, A. (2003). *Branded: The buying and selling of teenagers.* New York: Perseus.

Quatman, T., & Watson, C. M. (2001). Gender differences in adolescent self-esteem: An exploration of domains. *Journal of Genetic Psychology, 162,* 93–117.

Quick, B. (2000). *Under her wing: The mentors who changed our lives.* Oakland, CA: New Harbinger.

Quindlen, A. (2001a, July 2). Playing God on no sleep. *Newsweek,* p. 6.

Quindlen, A. (2001b, December 17). The terrorists here at home. *Newsweek,* p. 78.

Quindlen, A. (2005a, February 21). The good enough mother. *Newsweek,* pp. 50–51.

Quindlen, A. (2005b, March 21). We're missing some senators. *Newsweek,* p. 70.

Quirouette, C. C., & Pushkar, D. (1999). Views of future aging among middle-aged university educated women. *Canadian Journal on Aging, 18,* 236–258.

Raag, T. (1999). Influences of social expectations of gender, gender stereotypes, and situational constraints on children's toy choices. *Sex Roles, 41*, 809–831.

Rabinowitz, F. E., & Cochran, S. V. (2002). *Deepening psychotherapy with men.* Washington, DC: American Psychological Association.

Rabuzzi, K. A. (1994). *Mother with child.* Bloomington: Indiana University Press.

Raffaelli, M. (2005). Adolescent dating experiences described by Latino college students. *Journal of Adolescence, 28*, 559–572.

Raffaelli, M., & Green, S. (2003). Parent-adolescent communication about sex: Retrospective reports by Latino college students. *Journal of Marriage and Family, 65*, 474–481.

Raffaelli, M., & Ontai, L. L. (2004). Gender socialization in Latino/a families: Results from two retrospective studies. *Sex Roles, 50*, 287–299.

Ragan, J. M. (1982). Gender displays in portrait photographs. *Sex Roles, 8*, 33–43.

Raisz, L. G. (2005). Screening for osteoporosis. *New England Journal of Medicine, 353*, 164–171.

Raitt, F. E., & Zeedyk, S. (2000). *The implicit relation of psychology and law: Women and syndrome evidence.* London: Routledge.

Rajvanshi, D. (2005, May/June). Sorry state of women's health. *Manushi,* Issue 148.

Ralston, P. A. (1997). Midlife and older Black women. In J. M. Coyle (Ed.), *Handbook on women and aging* (pp. 273–289). Westport, CT: Greenwood Press.

Ramsey, J. L., & Langlois, J. H. (2002). Effects of the "beauty is good" stereotype on children's information processing. *Journal of Experimental Child Psychology, 81*, 320–340.

Rand, C. S. W., & Resnick, J. L. (2000). The "good enough" body size as judged by people of varying age and weight. *Obesity Research, 8*, 309–316.

Rand, C. S. W., & Wright, B. A. (2000). Continuity and change in the evaluation of ideal and acceptable body sizes across a wide age span. *International Journal of Eating Disorders, 28*, 90–100.

Range, L. M. (2006). Women and suicide. In J. Worell & C. D. Goodheart (Eds.), *Handbook of girls' and women's psychological health: Gender and well-being across the life span* (pp. 129–136). New York: Oxford University Press.

Rapoza, K. A. (2004). The United States. In K. Malley-Morrison (Ed.), *International perspectives on family violence and abuse* (pp. 451–470). Mahwah, NJ: Erlbaum.

Rastogi, M., & Wieling, E. (Eds.). (2005). *Voices of color: First-person accounts of ethnic minority therapists.* Thousand Oaks, CA: Sage.

Ratner, L. (2004). Failing low income students: Education and training in the age of reform. In V. Polakow, S. S. Butler, L. S. Deprez, & P. Kahn (Eds.), *Shut out: Low income mothers and higher education in post-welfare America* (pp. 45–74). Albany: State University of New York Press.

Räty, H. (2003). At the threshold of school: Parental assessments of the competencies of their preschool-aged children. *Journal of Applied Social Psychology, 33*, 1862–1877.

Räty, H., Kasanen, K., Kiiskinen, J., & Nykky, M. (2004). Learning intelligence—Children's choices of the best pupils in the mother tongue and mathematics. *Social Behavior and Personality, 32*, 303–312.

Räty, H., Vänskä, J., Kasanen, K., & Kärkkäinen, R. (2002). Parents' explanations of their child's performance in mathematics and reading. *Sex Roles, 46*, 115–122.

Rebick, J. (2005). *Ten thousand roses: The making of a feminist revolution.* Toronto: Penguin Canada.

Reese, L. A., & Lindenberg, K. E. (1999). *Implementing sexual harassment policy.* Thousand Oaks, CA: Sage.

Regan, P. C., & Berscheid, E. (1997). Gender differences in characteristics desired in a potential sexual and marriage partner. *Journal of Psychology and Human Sexuality, 9*, 25–37.

Regan, P. C., et al. (2000). Partner preferences: What characteristics do men and women desire in their short-term sexual and long-term romantic partners? *Journal of Psychology and Human Sexuality, 12*, 1–21.

Reid, A., & Purcell, N. (2004). Pathways to feminist identification. *Sex Roles, 50*, 759–769.

Reid, P. T. (2000). Foreword. In L. C. Jackson & B. Greene (Eds.), *Psychotherapy with African American women* (pp. xiii–xv). New York: Guilford.

Reid, P. T., & Bing, V. M. (2000). Sexual roles of girls and women: An ethnocultural lifespan perspective. In C. B. Travis & J. W. White (Eds.), *Sexuality, society, and feminism* (pp. 141–166). Washington, DC: American Psychological Association.

Reid, P. T., & Kelly, E. (1994). Research on women of color: From ignorance to awareness. *Psychology of Women Quarterly, 18*, 477–486.

Reid, P. T., & Zalk, S. R. (2001). Academic environments: Gender and ethnicity in U.S. higher education. In J. Worell (Ed.), *Encyclopedia of women and gender* (pp. 29–42). San Diego: Academic Press.

Reis, S. M. (1998). *Work left undone: Choices and compromises of talented females.* Mansfield Center, CT: Creative Learning Press.

Reis, S. M., Callahan, C. M., & Goldsmith, D. (1996). Attitudes of adolescent gifted girls and boys toward education, achievement, and the future. In K. Arnold, K. D. Noble, & R. F. Subotnik (Eds.), *Remarkable women: Perspectives on female talent development* (pp. 209–224). Cresskill, NJ: Hampton Press.

Reiser, C. (2001). *Reflections on anger: Women and men in a changing society.* Westport, CT: Praeger.

Reitzes, D. C., & Mutran, E. J. (2004). The transition to retirement: Stages and factors that influence retirement adjustment. *International Journal of Aging and Human Development, 59*, 63–84.

Remafedi, G., et al. (1998). The relationship between suicide risk and sexual orientation: Results of a population-based study. *American Journal of Public Health, 88,* 57–60.

Rensenbrink, C. W. (2001). *All in our places: Feminist challenges in elementary school classrooms.* Lanham, MD: Rowman & Littlefield.

Revenson, T. A. (2001). Chronic illness adjustment. In J. Worell (Ed.), *Encyclopedia of women and gender* (pp. 245–255). San Diego: Academic Press.

Rheingold, A. A., Acierno, R., & Resnick, H. S. (2004). Trauma, posttraumatic stress disorder, and health risk behaviors. In P. P. Schnurr & B. L. Green (Eds.), *Trauma and health: Physical health consequences of exposure to extreme stress* (pp. 217–243). Washington, DC: American Psychological Association.

Rhoades, K. A. (1999). Border zones: Identification, resistance, and transgressive teaching in introductory women's studies courses. In B. S. Winkler & C. DiPalma (Eds.), *Teaching introduction to women's studies* (pp. 61–71). Westport, CT: Bergin & Garvey.

Rhode, D. L. (1997). *Speaking of sex: The denial of gender inequality.* Cambridge, MA: Harvard University Press.

Ricciardelli, L. A., & McCabe, M. P. (2004). A biopsychosocial model of disordered eating and the pursuit of muscularity in adolescent boys. *Psychological Bulletin, 130,* 179–205.

Rice, J. K. (2001a, Summer). Cross-cultural perspectives: Global divorce and the feminization of poverty. *International Psychology Reporter,* pp. 14–16.

Rice, J. K. (2001b). Family roles and patterns, contemporary trends. In J. Worell (Ed.), *Encyclopedia of women and gender* (pp. 411–423). San Diego: Academic Press.

Rice, J. K., & Else-Quest, N. (2006). The mixed messages of motherhood. In J. Worell & C. Goodheart (Eds.), *Handbook of girls' and women's psychological health: Gender and well-being across the life span* (pp. 339–349). New York: Oxford University Press.

Rich, P., & Mervyn, F. (1999). *The healing journey through menopause.* New York: Wiley.

Richardson, H. R. L., Beazley, R. P., Delaney, M. E., & Langille, D. B. (1997). Factors influencing condom use among students attending high school in Nova Scotia. *Canadian Journal of Human Sexuality, 6,* 185–197.

Richardson, J. T. E. (1997a). Conclusions from the study of gender differences in cognition. In P. J. Caplan, M. Crawford, J. S. Hyde, & J. T. E. Richardson (Eds.), *Gender differences in human cognition* (pp. 131–169). New York: Oxford University Press.

Richardson, J. T. E. (1997b). Introduction to the study of gender differences in cognition. In P. J. Caplan, M. Crawford, J. S. Hyde, & J. T. E. Richardson (Eds.), *Gender differences in human cognition* (pp. 3–29). New York: Oxford University Press.

Richardson, V. E. (1999). Women and retirement. In J. D. Garner (Ed.), *Fundamentals of feminist gerontology* (pp. 49–66). New York: Haworth.

Richeson, J. A., & Ambady, N. (2001). Who's in charge? Effects of situational roles on automatic gender bias. *Sex Roles, 44,* 493–512.

Richman, E. L., & Shaffer, D. R. (2000). "If you let me play sports": How might sport participation influence the self-esteem of adolescent females? *Psychology of Women Quarterly, 24,* 189–199.

Richmond, K., & Levant, R. (2003). Clinical application of the gender role strain paradigm: Group treatment for adolescent boys. *Journal of Clinical Psychology/In Session, 59,* 1237–1245.

Rickabaugh, C. A. (1994). Just who is this guy, anyway? Stereotypes of the men's movement. *Sex Roles, 30,* 459–470.

Rickert, V. I., Wiemann, C. M., Vaughan, R. D., & White, J. W. (2004). Rates and risk factors for sexual violence among an ethnically diverse sample of adolescents. *Archives of Pediatric and Adolescent Medicine, 158,* 1132–1139.

Ridgeway, C. L., & Bourg, C. (2004). Gender as status: An expectation states theory approach. In A. H. Eagly, A. E. Beall, & R. J. Sternberg (Eds.), *The psychology of gender* (2nd ed., pp. 217–241). New York: Guilford.

Ridgeway, C. L., & Correll, S. J. (2004). Motherhood as a status characteristic. *Journal of Social Issues, 60,* 683–700.

Ridker, P. M., et al. (2005). A randomized trial of low-dose aspirin in the primary prevention of cardiovascular disease in women. *New England Journal of Medicine, 352,* 1293–1304.

Riger, S., & Galligan, P. (1980). Women in management: An exploration of competing paradigms. *American Psychologist, 35,* 902–910.

Riger, S., Staggs, S. L., & Schewe, P. (2004). Intimate partner violence as an obstacle to employment among mothers affected by welfare reform. *Journal of Social Issues, 60,* 801–818.

Riggs, J. M. (2001). *Who's going to care for the children? College students' expectations for future employment and family roles.* Paper presented at the annual meeting of the Eastern Psychological Association.

Rimer, B. K., McBride, C., & Crump, C. (2001). Women's health promotion. In A. Baum, T. A. Revenson, & J. E. Singer (Eds.), *Handbook of health psychology* (pp. 519–539). Mahwah, NJ: Erlbaum.

Rinfret-Raynor, M., & Cantin, S. (1997). Feminist therapy for battered women. In G. K. Kantor & J. L. Jasinski (Eds.), *Out of the darkness: Contemporary perspectives on family violence* (pp. 219–234). Thousand Oaks, CA: Sage.

Rist, R. C. (2000). Author's introduction: The enduring dilemmas of class and color in American education. *Harvard Educational Review, 70,* 257–265.

Ristock, J. L. (2002). *No more secrets: Violence in lesbian relationships.* New York: Routledge.

Ritter, D. (2004). Gender role orientation and performance on stereotypically feminine and masculine cognitive tasks. *Sex Roles, 50,* 583–591.

Rivero, A. J., Kaminski, P. L., & York, C. D. (2004, August). *Sex and gender differences in actual and perceived leader effectiveness: Self- and subordinate views.* Paper presented at the annual convention of the American Psychological Association, Honolulu, HI.

Roach, R. (2001, May 10). Where are the Black men on campus? *Black Issues in Higher Education,* 18–20.

Roades, L. A., & Mio, L. A. (2000). Allies: How they are created and what are their experiences. In J. S. Mio & G. I. Awakuni (Eds.), *Resistance to multiculturalism: Issues and interventions* (pp. 63–82). Philadelphia: Brunner/Mazel.

Robb-Nicholson, C. (2004, September). Screening for ovarian cancer. *Harvard Women's Health Watch,* p. 5.

Robert, M., & Chevrier, E. (2003). Does men's advantage in mental rotation persist when real three-dimensional objects are either felt or seen? *Memory & Cognition, 31,* 1136–1145.

Roberts, D. F., Henriksen, L., & Foehr, U. G. (2004). Adolescents and media. In R. M. Lerner & L. Steinberg (Eds.), *Handbook of adolescent psychology* (2nd ed., pp. 487–521). Hoboken, NJ: Wiley.

Roberts, M. C., et al. (2004). Family health through injury and violence prevention at home. In R. H. Rozensky, N. G. Johnson, C. D. Goodheart, & W. R. Hammond (Eds.), *Psychology builds a healthy world* (pp. 77–104). Washington, DC: American Psychological Association.

Roberts, T. (1991). Gender and the influence of evaluations on self-assessments in achievement settings. *Psychological Bulletin, 109,* 297–308.

Roberts, T., & Gettman, J. Y. (2004). Mere exposure: Gender differences in the negative effects of priming a state of self-objectification. *Sex Roles, 51,* 17–27.

Roberts, T., Goldenberg, J. L., Power, C., & Pyszczynski, T. (2002). "Feminine protection": The effects of menstruation on attitudes toward women. *Psychology of Women Quarterly, 26,* 131–139.

Roberts, T., & Nolen-Hoeksema, S. (1989). Sex differences in reactions to evaluative feedback. *Sex Roles, 21,* 725–747.

Roberts, T., & Nolen-Hoeksema, S. (1994). Gender comparisons in responsiveness to others' evaluations in achievement settings. *Psychology of Women Quarterly, 18,* 221–240.

Roberts, T., & Waters, P. L. (2004). Self-objectification and that "not so fresh feeling": Feminist therapeutic interventions for health female embodiment. *Women and Therapy, 27,* 5–21.

Robertson, K., O'Connor, V., Hegarty, K., & Gunn, J. (2003). Women teaching women's health. In L. Manderson (Ed.), *Teaching gender, teaching women's health* (pp. 49–65). Binghamton, NY: Haworth.

Robin, L., & Hamner, K. (2000). Bisexuality: Identities and community. In V. A. Wall & N. J. Evans (Eds.), *Toward acceptance: Sexual orientation issues on campus* (pp. 245–259). Lanham, MD: American College Personnel Association.

Robinson, D. (2001). Differences in occupational earnings by sex. In M. F. Loutfi (Ed.), *Women, gender, and work* (pp. 157–188). Geneva, Switzerland: International Labour Organization.

Robinson, G. (2002). Cross-cultural perspectives on menopause. In A. E. Hunter & C. Forden (Eds.), *Readings in the psychology of gender* (pp. 140–149). Boston: Allyn & Bacon.

Robinson, G. E., & Stewart, D. S. (2001). Postpartum disorders. In N. L. Stotland & D. E. Stewart (Eds.), *Psychological aspects of women's health care* (pp. 117–139). Washington, DC: American Psychiatric Press.

Robinson, J. D., Skill, T., & Turner, J. W. (2004). Media usage patterns and portrayals of seniors. In J. F. Nussbaum & J. Coupland (Eds.), *Handbook of communication and aging research* (2nd ed., pp. 423–446). Mahwah, NJ: Erlbaum.

Robinson, M. D., & Johnson, J. T. (1997). Is it emotion or is it stress? Gender stereotypes and the perception of subjective experience. *Sex Roles, 36,* 235–258.

Robinson-Walker, C. (1999). *Women and leadership in health care.* San Francisco: Jossey-Bass.

Rochlen, A. B., McKelley, R. A., & Pituch, K. A. (2006). A preliminary examination of the "real men, real depression" campaign. *Psychology of Men & Masculinity, 7,* 1–13.

Rodríguez, C. E. (1997). Promoting analytical and critical viewing. In C. E. Rodríguez (Ed.), *Latin looks: Images of Latinas and Latinos in the U.S. media* (pp. 240–253). Boulder, CO: Westview Press.

Rogers, L. (2001). *Sexing the brain.* New York: Columbia University Press.

Rogers, N., & Henrich, J. (2003). Teaching women's health into the 21st century. In L. Manderson (Ed.), *Teaching gender, teaching women's health* (pp. 11–21). Binghamton, NY: Haworth.

Rogers, S. J. (1996). Mothers' work hours and marital quality: Variations by family structure and family size. *Journal of Marriage and the Family, 58,* 606–617.

Rogers, S. J., & DeBoer, D. D. (2001). Changes in wives' income: Effects on marital happiness, psychological well-being, and the risk of divorce. *Journal of Marriage and Family, 63,* 458–472.

Rogers, T. B., Kuiper, N. A., & Kirker, W. S. (1977). Self-reference and the encoding of personal information. *Journal of Personality and Social Psychology, 35,* 677–688.

Rogers, T. L., Emanuel, K., & Bradford, J. (2003). Sexual minorities seeking services: A retrospective study of the mental health concerns of lesbian and bisexual women. *Journal of Lesbian Studies, 7,* 127–146.

Rogers, W. S., & Rogers, R. S. (2001). *The psychology of gender and sexuality.* Buckingham, England: Open University Press.

Romaine, S. (1999). *Communicating gender.* Mahwah, NJ: Erlbaum.

Romanow, R. J., & Marchildon, G. P. (2003). Psychological services and the future of health care in Canada. *Canadian Psychology/Psychologie canadienne, 44,* 283–295.

Romo-Carmona, M. (1995). Lesbian Latinas: Organizational efforts to end oppression. *Journal of Gay and Lesbian Social Services, 3,* 85–93.

Roos, P. A., & Gatta, M. L. (1999). The gender gap in earnings: Trends, explanations, and prospects. In G. N. Powell (Ed.), *Handbook of gender and work* (pp. 95–123). Thousand Oaks, CA: Sage.

Root, M. P. P. (1995). The psychology of Asian American women. In H. Landrine (Ed.), *Bringing cultural diversity to feminist psychology: Theory, research, and practice* (pp. 265–301). Washington, DC: American Psychological Association.

Root, M. P. P. (2005). Filipino families. In M. McGoldrick, J. Giordano, & N. Garcia-Preto (Eds.), *Ethnicity and family therapy* (3rd ed., pp. 269–289). New York: Guilford.

Roschelle, A. R. (1998). Gender, family structure, and social structure. In M. M. Ferree, J. Lorber, & B. B. Hess (Eds.), *Revisioning gender* (pp. 311–340). Thousand Oaks, CA: Sage.

Rose, A. J., Swenson, L. P., & Waller, E. M. (2004). Overt and relational aggression and perceived popularity: Developmental differences in concurrent and prospective relations, *Developmental Psychology, 40,* 378–387.

Rose, E. C. (2002). Activism and the women's studies curriculum. In N. A. Naples & K. Bojar (Eds.), *Teaching feminist activism: Strategies from the field* (pp. 108–120). New York: Routledge.

Rose, S. (2000). Heterosexism and the study of women's romantic and friend relationships. *Journal of Social Issues, 56,* 315–328.

Rose, S., & Hall, R. (2005). Innovations in lesbian research [Special section]. *Psychology of Women Quarterly, 29* (2), 119–187.

Rose, T. (2003). *Longing to tell: Black women talk about sexuality and intimacy.* New York: Farrar, Straus & Giroux.

Rosen, R. (2000). *The world split open: How the modern women's movement changed America.* New York: Viking.

Rosenbaum, M. E., & Roos, G. M. (2000). Women's experiences of breast cancer. In A. S. Kasper & S. J. Ferguson (Eds.), *Breast cancer: Society shapes an epidemic* (pp. 153–181). New York: St. Martin's.

Rosenthal, R. (1993). Interpersonal expectations: Some antecedents and some consequences. In P. D. Blank (Ed.), *Interpersonal expectations: Theory, research, and applications* (pp. 3–24). New York: Cambridge University Press.

Rosin, H. M., & Korabik, K. (2002). Do family-friendly policies fulfill their promise? An investigation of their impact on work-family conflict and work and personal outcomes. In D. L. Nelson & R. J. Burke (Eds.), *Gender, work stress, and health* (pp. 211–226). Washington, DC: American Psychological Association.

Ross, M. J. (2003). *Success factors of young African American women at a historically black college.* Westport, CT; Praeger.

Rostosky, S. S., & Travis, C. B. (2000). Menopause and sexuality: Ageism and sexism unite. In C. B. Travis & J. W. White (Eds.), *Sexuality, society, and feminism* (pp. 181–209). Washington, DC: American Psychological Association.

Rostosky, S. S., Welsh, D. P., Kawaguchi, M. C., & Galliher, R. V. (1999). Commitment and sexual behaviors in adolescent dating relationships. In J. M. Adams & W. H. Jones (Eds.), *Handbook of interpersonal commitment and relationship stability* (pp. 323–338). New York: Kluwer Academic/Plenum.

Roter, D. L., & Hall, J. A. (1997). Gender differences in patient-physician communication. In S. J. Gallant, G. P. Keita, & R. Royak-Schaler (Eds.), *Health care for women* (pp. 57–71). Washington, DC: American Psychological Association.

Roth, B. (2004). *Separate roads to feminism: Black, Chicana, and White feminist movements in America's Second Wave.* New York: Cambridge University Press.

Rothblum, E. D. (2000). Sexual orientation and sex in women's lives: Conceptual and methodological issues. *Journal of Social Issues, 56,* 193–204.

Rothblum, E. D. (2002). Gay and lesbian body images. In T. F. Cash & T. Pruzinsky (Eds.), *Body images: A handbook of theory, research, and clinical practice.* New York: Guilford.

Rothblum, E. D., & Factor, R. (2001). Lesbians and their sisters as a control group. *Psychological Science, 12,* 63–69.

Rotheram-Borus, M. J., Dopkins, S., Sabate, N., & Lightfoot, M. (1996). Personal and ethnic identity, values, and self-esteem among Black and Latino adolescent girls. In B. J. R. Leadbeater & N. Way (Eds.), *Urban girls: Resisting stereotypes, creating identities* (pp. 35–52). New York: New York University Press.

Rousar, E. E., III, & Aron, A. (1990, July). *Valuing, altruism, and the concept of love.* Paper presented at the Fifth International conference on Personal Relationships, Oxford, England.

Rouse, L. P. (2002). *Marital and sexual lifestyles in the United States.* Binghamton, NY: Haworth.

Rowe-Murray, H. J., & Fisher, J. R. W. (2002). Baby-friendly hospital practices: Cesarean section is a persistent barrier to early initiation of breastfeeding. *Birth, 29,* 124–131.

Rozee, P. D. (2004). Women's fear of rape: Cause, consequences, and coping. In J. C. Chrisler, C. Golden, & P. D. Rozee (Eds.), *Lectures on the psychology of women* (3rd ed., pp. 277–291). New York: McGraw-Hill.

Rozee, P. D. (2005). Rape resistance: Successes and challenges. In A. Barnes (Ed.), *The handbook of women, psychology, and the law* (pp. 265–279). San Francisco: Jossey-Bass.

Rozee, P. D., Golden, C., & Chrisler, J. C. (2004). Introduction. In

J. C. Chrisler, C. Golden, & P. D. Rozee (Eds.), *Lectures on the psychology of women* (3rd ed., pp. xi–xvii). New York: McGraw-Hill.

Rubin, B. (2003). Every day a Sunday? Reflections on a first year of retirement. In N. Bauer-Maglin & A. Radosh (Eds.), *Women confronting retirement: A nontraditional guide* (pp. 187–200). New Brunswick, NJ: Rutgers University Press.

Rubin, D. C., Schulkind, M. D., & Rabhal, T. A. (1999). A study of gender differences in autobiographical memory: Broken down by age and sex. *Journal of Adult development, 6,* 61–71.

Rubin, D. L., & Greene, K. (1994). The suppressed voice hypothesis in women's writing: Effects of revision on gender-typical style. In D. L. Rubin (Ed.), *Composing social identity in written language* (pp. 133–149). Hillsdale, NJ: Erlbaum.

Ruble, D. N., & Martin, C. L. (1998). Gender development. In W. Damon (Series Ed.) & N. Eisenberg (Vol. Ed.), *Handbook of child psychology: Vol. 4. Social, emotional, and personality development* (pp. 933–1016). New York: Wiley.

Ruble, D. N., et al. (2004). The development of a sense of "we": The emergence and implications of children's collective identity. In M. Bennett & F. Sani (Eds.), *The development of the social self* (pp. 29–76). New York: Psychology Press.

Rudman, L. A. (1998). Self-promotion as a risk factor for women: The costs and benefits of counterstereotypical impression management. *Journal of Personality and Social Psychology, 74,* 629–645.

Rudman, L. A., & Glick, P. (1999). Feminized management and backlash toward agentic women: The hidden costs to women of a kinder, gentler image of middle managers. *Journal of Personality and Social Psychology, 77,* 1004–1010.

Runions, D. (1996). HIV/AIDS: A personal perspective. In L. D. Long & E. M. Ankrah (Eds.), *Women's experiences with HIV/AIDS* (pp. 56–72). New York: Columbia University Press.

Runkle, S. (2004). Manufactured beauties: India's integration into the global beauty industry. *Manushi,* Issue 143, pp. 14–24.

Runté, M. (1998). Women with disabilities: Alone on the playground. *Canadian Women Studies/Les cahiers de la femme, 18,* 101–105.

Rupp, R. E., Stanberry, L. R., & Rosenthal, S. L. (2005). Vaccines for sexually transmitted infections. *Pediatric Annals, 34,* 818–824.

Ruscio, J., Whitney, D. M., & Amabile, T. M. (1998). Looking inside the fishbowl of creativity: Verbal and behavioral predictors of creative performance. *Creativity Research Journal, 11,* 243–263.

Russell, B. L., & Trigg, K. Y. (2004). Tolerance of sexual harassment: An examination of gender differences, ambivalent sexism, social dominance, and gender roles. *Sex Roles, 50,* 565–573.

Russell-Brown, K. (2004). *Underground codes: Race, crime and related fires.* New York: New York University Press.

Russo, N. F. (1999). Putting the *APA Publication Manual* in context. *Psychology of Women Quarterly, 23,* 399–402.

Russo, N. F. (2004). Understanding emotional responses after abortion. In J. C. Chrisler, C. Golden, & P. D. Rozee (Eds.), *Lectures on the psychology of women* (3rd ed., pp. 129–143). Boston: McGraw-Hill.

Russo, N. F., Kelly, R. M., & Deacon, M. (1991). Gender and success-related attributions: Beyond individualistic conceptions of achievement. *Sex Roles, 25,* 331–350.

Rust, P. C. (1996). Monogamy and polyamory: Relationship issues for bisexuals. In B. A. Firestein (Ed.), *Bisexuality: The psychology and politics of an invisible minority* (pp. 127–148). Thousand Oaks, CA: Sage.

Rust, P. C. (2000). Bisexuality: A contemporary paradox for women. *Journal of Social Issues, 56,* 205–221.

Ruth, S. (2001). *Issues in feminism: An introduction to women's studies* (5th ed.). Mountain View, CA: Mayfield.

Sabattini, L., & Leaper, C. (2004). The relation between mothers' and fathers' parenting styles and their division of labor in the home: Young adults' retrospective reports. *Sex Roles, 50,* 217–225.

Sadker, M., & Sadker, D. (1994). *Failing at fairness: How America's schools cheat girls.* New York: Scribner's.

Sáez-Santiago, E., & Bernal, G. (2003). Depression in ethnic minorities. In G. Bernal, J. E. Trimble, A. K. Burlew, & F. T. L. Leong (Eds.), *Handbook of racial and ethnic minority psychology* (pp. 406–428). Thousand Oaks CA: Sage.

Saguaro, S. (Ed.). (2000). *Psychoanalysis and woman: A reader.* New York: New York University Press.

Saldívar-Hull, S. (2000). *Feminism on the border.* Berkeley: University of California Press.

Salinas, M. F. (2003). *The politics of stereotype: Psychology and affirmative action.* Westport, CT: Praeger.

Saluja, G., et al. (2004). Prevalence of and risk factors for depressive symptoms among young adolescents. *Archives of Pediatric and Adolescent Medicine, 158,* 760–765.

Sampselle, C. M., et al. (2002). Midlife development and menopause in African American and Caucasian women. *Health Care for Women International, 23,* 351–363.

Sánchez, C. D. (2001). Puerto Rican elderly. In L. K. Olson (Ed.), *Age through ethnic lenses: Caring for the elderly in a multicultural society* (pp. 86–94). Lanham, MD: Rowman & Littlefield.

Sánchez-Ayéndez, M. (1993). Puerto Rican elderly women: Shared meanings and informal supportive networks. In L. Richardson & V. Taylor (Eds.), *Feminist frontiers III* (pp. 270–278). New York: McGraw-Hill.

Sanday, P. R. (2003). Rape-free versus rape-prone: How culture makes a difference. In C. B. Travis

(Ed.), *Evolution, gender, and rape* (pp. 337–361). Cambridge, MA: MIT Press.

Sanderson, C. A., Darley, J. M., & Messinger, C. S. (2002). "I'm not as thin as you think I am": The development and consequences of feeling discrepant from the thinness norm. *Personality and Social Psychology Bulletin, 28,* 172–183.

Sandnabba, N. K., & Ahlberg, C. (1999). Parents' attitudes and expectations about children's crossgender behavior. *Sex Roles, 40,* 249–263.

Sanz de Acedo Lizarraga, M. L., & García Ganuza, J. M. (2003). Improvement of mental rotation in girls and boys. *Sex Roles, 49,* 277–286.

Saperstein, A. R. (2002). Racial & ethnic diversity. In E. M. Brody (Ed.), *Women in the middle* (2nd ed., pp. 274–286). New York: Springer.

Sapiro, V. (2003). Theorizing gender in political psychology research. In D. O. Sears, L. Huddy, & R. Jervis (Eds.), *Oxford handbook of political psychology* (pp. 601–634). New York: Oxford University Press.

Sarafino, E. P. (2006). *Health psychology: Biopsychosocial interactions* (5th ed.). Hoboken, NJ: Wiley.

Saris, R. N., & Johnston-Robledo, I. (2000). Poor women are still shut out of mainstream psychology. *Psychology of Women Quarterly, 24,* 233–235.

Saucier, D. M., et al. (2002). Are sex differences in navigation caused by sexually dimorphic strategies or by differences in the ability to use the strategies? *Behavioral Neuroscience, 116,* 403–410.

Saules, K. K., et al. (2004). Relationship of onset of cigarette smoking during college to alcohol use, dieting concerns, and depressed mood. *Addictive Behaviors, 29,* 893–899.

Savic, I., Berglund, H., & Lindström, P. (2005). Brain response to putative pheromones in homosexual men. *Proceedings of the National Academy of Sciences of the United States of America, 102,* 7356–7361.

Savin-Williams, R. C. (1998). The disclosure to families of same-sex attractions by lesbian, gay, and bisexual youths. *Journal of Research on Adolescence, 8,* 49–68.

Savin-Williams, R. C. (2001). *Mom, Dad, I'm gay. How families negotiate coming out.* Washington, DC: American Psychological Association.

Savin-Williams, R. C., & Dubè, E. M. (1998). Parental reactions to their child's disclosure of a gay/lesbian identity. *Family Relations, 47,* 7–13.

Savin-Williams, R. C., & Esterberg, K. G. (2000). Lesbian, gay, and bisexual families. In D. H. Demo, K. R. Allen, & M. A. Fine (Eds.), *Handbook of family diversity* (pp. 197–215). New York: Oxford University Press.

Sawyer, D. F. (1996). *Women and religion in the first Christian centuries.* London: Routledge.

Sax, L. J., Bryant, A. N., & Gilmartin, S. K. (2002, November). *A longitudinal investigation of emotional health among male and female first-year college students.* Paper presented at the Annual Meeting of the Association for the Study of Higher Education, Sacramento, CA.

Sax, L. L., & Bryant, A. N. (2002). Undergraduates in science. In A. M. Martínez Alemán & K. A. Renn (Eds.), *Women in higher education: An encyclopedia.* Santa Barbara, CA: ABC-CLIO.

Sax, L. L., & Bryant, A. N. (2003, November). *The impact of college on sex-atypical career choices of men and women.* Paper presented at the annual meeting of the Association for the Study of Higher Education, Portland, OR.

Saywell, C. (2000). Sexualized illness: The newsworthy body in media representations of breast cancer. In L. K. Potts (Ed.), *Ideologies of breast cancer* (pp. 37–62). New York: St. Martin's Press.

Scali, R. M., & Brownlow, S. (2001). Impact of instructional manipulation and stereotype activation on sex differences in spatial task performance. *Psi Chi Journal of Undergraduate Research, 6,* 3–13.

Scali, R. M., Brownlow, S., & Hicks, J. L. (2000). Gender differences in spatial task performance as a function of speed or accuracy orientation. *Sex Roles, 43,* 359–376.

Scarborough, E. (1992). Women in the American Psychological Association. In R. B. Evans, V. S. Sexton, & T. C. Cadwallader (Eds.), *100 years: The American Psychological Association, a historical perspective* (pp. 303–325). Washington, DC: American Psychological Association.

Scarborough, E., & Furumoto, L. (1987). *Untold lives: The first generation of American women psychologists.* New York: Columbia University Press.

Scarr, S. (1997). Rules of evidence: A larger context for the statistical debate. *Psychological Science, 8,* 16–17.

Schaalma, H. P., Abraham, C., Gillmore, M. R., & Kok, G. (2004). Sex education as health promotion: What does it take? *Archives of Sexual Behavior, 33,* 259–269.

Schacter, D. L., Koutstaal, W., & Norman, K. A. (1999). Can cognitive neuroscience illuminate the nature of traumatic childhood memories? In L. M. Williams & V. L. Banyard (Eds.), *Trauma and memory* (pp. 257–269). Thousand Oaks, CA: Sage.

Schafer, E., Vogel, M. K., Veigas, S., & Hausafus, C. (1998). Volunteer peer counselors increase breastfeeding duration among rural low-income women. *Birth, 25,* 101–106.

Schaller, M., & Conway, L. G., III. (2001). From cognition to culture: The origins of stereotypes that really matter. In G. B. Moskowitz (Ed.), *Cognitive social psychology* (pp. 163–176). Mahwah, NJ: Erlbaum.

Scharrer, E. (1998, December). *Men, muscles, machismo, and the media.* Paper presented at the Department of Communication Research Colloquium, SUNY Geneseo.

Schein, V. E. (2001). A global look at psychological barriers to women's progress in management. *Journal of Social Issues, 57,* 675–688.

Schellenberg, E. G., Hirt, J., & Sears, A. (1999). Attitudes toward homosexuals among students at a Canadian university. *Sex Roles, 40,* 139–152.

Scher, C. D., Segal, Z. V., & Ingram, R. E. (2004). Beck's theory of depression. In R. L. Leahy (Ed.), *Contemporary cognitive therapy* (pp. 27–44). New York: Guilford.

Schiffman, M., & Castle, P. E. (2005). The promise of global cervical-cancer prevention. *New England Journal of Medicine, 353,* 2101–2104.

Schindehette, S., Stockton, P., & Duffy, T. (2004, May 31). Here come the brides. *People,* pp. 77–78.

Schlenker, J. A., Caron, S. L., & Halteman, W. A. (1998). A feminist analysis of *Seventeen* magazine: Content analysis from 1945 to 1995. *Sex Roles, 38,* 135–149.

Schmader, T. (2002). Gender identification moderates stereotype threat effects on women's math performance. *Journal of Experimental Social Psychology, 38,* 194–201.

Schmid Mast, M. (2004). Men are hierarchical, women are egalitarian: An implicit gender stereotype. *Swiss Journal of Psychology, 63,* 107–111.

Schmidt, U. (2002). Risk factors for eating disorders. In C. G. Fairburn & K. D. Brownell (Eds.), *Eating disorders and obesity: A comprehensive handbook* (2nd ed., pp. 247–250). New York: Guilford.

Schmitt, M. T., Branscombe, N. R., Kobrynowicz, D., & Owen, S. (2002). Perceiving discrimination against one's gender group has different implications for well-being in women and men. *Personality and Social Psychology Bulletin, 28,* 197–210.

Schmitz, S. (1999). Gender differences in acquisition of environmental knowledge related to wayfinding behavior, spatial anxiety, and self-estimated environmental competencies. *Sex Roles, 41,* 71–93.

Schnarch, D. (2000). Desire problems: A systematic perspective. In S. R. Leiblum & R. C. Rosen (Eds.), *Principles and practice of sex therapy* (3rd ed., pp. 17–56). New York: Guilford.

Schneider, D. J. (2004). *The psychology of stereotyping.* New York: Guilford.

Schneider, M. S. (2001). Toward a reconceptualization of the coming-out process for adolescent females. In A. R. D'Augelli & C. J. Patterson (Eds.), *Lesbian, gay, and bisexual identities and youth* (pp. 71–96). New York: Oxford University Press.

Schnurr, P. P., & Green, B. L. (2004). Understanding relationships among trauma, posttraumatic stress disorder, and health outcomes. In P. P. Schnurr & B. L. Green (Eds.), *Trauma and health: Physical health consequences of exposure to extreme stress* (pp. 247–275). Washington, DC: American Psychological Association.

Schuklenk, U., Stein, E., Kerin, J., & Byne, W. (2002). The ethics of genetic research on sexual orientation. In I. Grewal & C. Kaplan (Eds.), *An introduction to women's studies* (pp. 48–52). Boston: McGraw-Hill.

Schur, L. (2004). Is there still a "double handicap"? Economic, social, and political disparities experienced by women with disabilities. In B. G. Smith & B. Hutchison (Eds.), *Gendering disability* (pp. 253–271). New Brunswick, NJ: Rutgers University Press.

Schwartz, K. (2006). *Ribbon campaign condemns violent acts against women.* Retrieved April 27, 2006 from http://www.michigandaily.com/

Schwartz, M. D., & DeKeseredy, W. S. (1997). *Sexual assault on the college campus: The role of male peer support.* Thousand Oaks, CA: Sage.

Schwartz, P. (1994). *Peer marriage: How love between equals really works.* New York: Free Press.

Schwartz, P. (2000). *Everything you know about love and sex is wrong.* New York: G. P. Putnam's Sons.

Schwartz, P., & Rutter, V. (1998). *The gender of sexuality.* Thousand Oaks, CA: Pine Forge Press.

Scott, B. A. (2004). Women and pornography: What we don't know can hurt us. In J. C. Chrisler, C. Golden, & P. D. Rozee (Eds.), *Lectures on the psychology of women* (3rd ed., pp. 292–309). New York: McGraw-Hill.

Scott, J. A., Shaker, I., & Reid, M. (2004). Parental attitudes toward breastfeeding: Their association with feeding outcome at hospital discharge. *Birth, 31,* 125–131.

Sczesny, S. (2003). A closer look beneath the surface: Various facets of the think-manager-think-male stereotype. *Sex Roles, 49,* 353–363.

Seager, J. (2003). *The Penguin atlas of women in the world.* New York: Penguin.

Seaman, B. (2003). *The greatest experiment ever performed on women: Exploding the estrogen myth.* New York: Hyperion.

Sechzer, J. A. (2004). "Islam and woman: Where tradition meets modernity": History and interpretations of Islamic women's status. *Sex Roles, 51,* 263–272.

Sered, S. S. (1998). Woman as symbol and women as agents: Gendered religious discourses and practices. In M. M. Ferree, J. Lorber, & B. H. Hess (Eds.), *Revisioning gender* (pp. 193–221). Thousand Oaks, CA: Sage.

Shanahan, J., & Morgan, M. (1999). *Television and its viewers.* New York: Cambridge University Press.

Shandler, S. (1999). *Ophelia speaks.* New York: HarperCollins.

Shapiro, A. F., Gottman, J. M., & Carrére, S. (2000). The baby and the marriage: Identifying factors that buffer against decline in marital satisfaction after the first baby arrives. *Journal of Family Psychology, 14,* 59–70.

Sharps, M. J., Price, J. L., & Williams, J. K. (1994). Spatial cognition and gender: Instructional and stimulus influences on mental image rotation performance. *Psychology of Women Quarterly, 18,* 413–425.

Shatzberg, A. F., Cole, J. O., & DeBattista, C. (2003). *Manual of clinical psychopharmacology* (4th ed.). Washington, DC: American Psychiatric Publishing.

Shaw, S. M., & Lee, J. (2001). *Women's voices, feminist visions.* Mountain View, CA: Mayfield.

Shaywitz, B. A., et al. (1995). Sex differences in the functional organization of the brain for language. *Nature, 373,* 607–609.

Shaywitz, S. E., Shaywitz, B. A., Fletcher, J. M., & Escobar, M. D. (1990). Prevalence of reading disability in boys and girls. *Journal of the American Medical Association, 264,* 998–1002.

Sheldon, J. P. (2004). Gender stereotypes in educational software for young children. *Sex Roles, 51,* 433–444.

Shellenbarger, T., & Lucas, D. (1997). An examination of nursing students' perception of classroom climate. In American Association of University Women (Ed.), *Gender and race on the campus and in the school: Beyond affirmative action* (pp. 151–159). Washington, DC: Author.

Sher, K. L., Grekin, E. R., & Williams, N. A. (2005). The development of alcohol use disorders. *Annual Review of Clinical Psychology, 1,* 493–523.

Sherman, J. W. (2001). The dynamic relationship between stereotype efficiency and mental representation. In G. B. Moskowitz (Ed.), *Cognitive social psychology* (pp. 177–190). Mahwah, NJ: Erlbaum.

Sherwin, B. B. (2001). Menopause: Myths and realities. In N. Stotland & D. E. Stewart (Eds.), *Psychological aspects of women's health care* (2nd ed., pp. 241–259). Washington, DC: American Psychiatric Press.

Shibusawa, R. (2005). Japanese families. In M. McGoldrick, J. Giordano, & N. Garcia-Preto (Eds.), *Ethnicity and family therapy* (3rd ed., pp. 339–348). New York: Guilford.

Shields, S. A. (1975). Functionalism, Darwinism, and the psychology of women: A study in social myth. *American Psychologist, 30,* 739–754.

Shields, S. A. (2002). *Speaking from the heart: Gender and the social meaning of emotion.* New York: Cambridge University Press.

Shields, S. A. (2005). The politics of emotion in everyday life: "Appropriate" emotion and claims on identity. *Review of General Psychology, 9,* 3–15.

Shifren, J., & Ferrari, N. A. (2004, May 10). A better sex life. *Newsweek,* pp. 86–89.

Shih, M., Pittinksy, T. L., & Ambady, N. (1999). Stereotype susceptibility: Identity salience and shifts in quantitative performance. *Psychological Science, 10,* 80–83.

Shimp, L., & Chartier, B. (1998, June). *Unacknowledged rape and sexual assault in a sample of university women.* Paper presented at the annual convention of the Canadian Psychological Association, Edmonton, Alberta.

Ship, S. J., & Norton, L. (2001, Summer/Fall). HIV/AIDS and Aboriginal women in Canada. *Canadian Woman Studies/Les cahiers de la femme, 21,* 25–31.

Shulman, J. L., & Horne, S. G. (2003). The use of self-pleasure: Masturbation and body image among African American and European American women. *Psychology of Women Quarterly, 27,* 262–269.

Shupe, E. J., et al. (2002). The incidence and outcomes of sexual harassment among Hispanic and non-Hispanic white women: A comparison across levels of cultural affiliation. *Psychology of Women Quarterly, 26,* 298–308.

Sidorowicz, L. S., & Lunney, G. S. (1980). Baby X revisited. *Sex Roles, 6,* 67–73.

Siegel, R. J. (2004). Ageism in psychiatric diagnosis. In P. J. Caplan & L. Cosgrove (Eds.), *Bias in psychiatric diagnosis* (pp. 89–97). Lanham, MD: Jason Aronson.

Siegel, R. J., Choldin, S., & Orost, J. H. (1995). The impact of three patriarchal religions on women. In J. C. Chrisler & A. H. Hemstreet (Eds.), *Variation on a theme: Diversity and the psychology of women* (pp. 107–144). Albany, NY: State University of New York Press.

Sieverding, J. A., Adler, N., With, S., & Ellen, J. (2005). The influence of parental monitoring on adolescent sexual initiation. *Archives of Pediatrics and Adolescent Medicine, 159,* 724–729.

Sigal, J. J., Perry, J. C., Rossignol, M., & Ouimet, M. C. (2003). Unwanted infants: Psychological and physical consequences of inadequate orphanage care 50 years later. *American Journal of Orthopsychiatry, 73,* 3–12.

Sigal, J., et al. (2005). Cross-cultural reactions to academic sexual harassment: Effects of individualist vs. collectivist culture and gender of participants. *Sex Roles, 52,* 201–215.

Sigmon, S. T., Dorhofer, D. M., et al. (2000). Psychophysiological, somatic, and affective changes across the menstrual cycle in women with panic disorder. *Journal of Consulting and Clinical Psychology, 68,* 425–431.

Sigmon, S. T., Rohan, K. J., et al. (2000). Menstrual reactivity: The role of gender-specificity, anxiety sensitivity, and somatic concerns in self-reported menstrual distress. *Sex Roles, 43,* 143–161.

Sigmon, S. T., Whitcomb-Smith, S. R., Rohanh, K. J., & Kendrew, J. J. (2004). The role of anxiety level, coping styles, and cycle phase in menstrual distress. *Anxiety Disorders, 18,* 177–191.

Signorielli, N., & Lears, M. (1992). Children, television, and conceptions about chores: Attitudes and behaviors. *Sex Roles, 27,* 157–170.

Silverstein, L. B., Auerbach, C. F., Grieco, L., & Dunkel, F. (1999). Do Promise Keepers dream of feminist sheep? *Sex Roles, 40,* 665–688.

Silverstein, L. B., & Goodrich, T. J. (2003). (Eds.). *Feminist family therapy: Empowerment in social context.* Washington, DC: American Psychological Association.

Simon, R. J., & Altstein, H. (2003). *Global perspectives on social issues: Marriage and divorce.* Lanham, MD: Lexington.

Simonson, K., & Subich, L. M. (1999). Rape perceptions as a function of gender-role traditionality and victim-perpetrator association. *Sex Roles, 40,* 617–634.

Sinacore, A. L., & Boatwright, K. J. (2005). The feminist classroom: Feminist strategies and student responses. In C. Z. Enns & A. L. Sinacore (Eds.), *Teaching and* social justice: Integrating multi-cultural and feminist theories in the classroom (pp. 109–124). Washington, DC: American Psychological Association.

Sincharoen, S., & Crosby, F. J. (2001). Affirmative action. In J. Worell (Ed.), Encyclopedia of women and gender (pp. 69–79). San Diego: Academic Press.

Singer, D. G., & Singer, J. L. (2001). Introduction: Why a handbook on children and the media? In D. G. Singer & J. L. Singer (Eds.), Handbook on children and the media (pp. xi–xvii). Thousand Oaks, CA: Sage.

Singh, S., & Darroch, J. E. (2000). Adolescent pregnancy and child-bearing: Levels and trends in developed countries. Family Planning Perspectives, 32, 14–23.

Singh, S., Henshaw, S. K., & Brentsen, K. (2003). Abortion: a world-wide overview. In A. M. Basu (Ed.), The sociocultural and political aspects of abortion: Global perspectives (pp. 15–47). Westport, CT: Praeger.

Singley, B. (2004, June). The old wink-and-nod. Women's Review of Books, pp. 13–14.

Sinnott, J. D., & Shifren, K. (2001). Gender and aging: Gender differences and gender roles. In J. E. Birren & K. W. Schaie (Eds.), Handbook of the psychology of aging (pp. 454–476). San Diego: Academic Press.

Sivers, H., Schooler, J., & Freyd, J. J. (2002). Recovered memories. In V. S. Ramachandran (Ed.), Encyclopedia of the human brain (Vol. 4, pp. 169–184). New York: Elsevier.

Skaalvik, S., & Skaalvik, E. M. (2004). Gender differences in math and verbal self-concept, performance expectations, and motivation. Sex Roles, 50, 241–252.

Skevington, S. M. (2004). Pain and symptom perception. In A. Kaptein & J. Weinman (Eds.), Health psychology (pp. 182–206). Malden, MA: Blackwell.

Skoe, E. E. A., et al. (2002). The influences of sex and gender-role identity on moral cognition and prosocial personality traits. Sex Roles, 46, 295–309.

Skrypnek, B. J., & Snyder, M. (1982). On the self-perpetuating nature of stereotypes about women and men. Journal of Experimental Social Psychology, 18, 277–291.

Skucha, J., & Bernard, M. (2000). "Women's work" and the transition to retirement. In M. Bernard, J. Phillips, L. Machin, & V. H. Davies (Eds.), Women ageing: Changing identities, challenging myths (pp. 23–39). London: Routledge.

Slater, L., Henderson-Daniel, J., & Banks, A. E. (Eds.). (2003). The complete guide to mental health for women. Boston: Beacon Press.

Slipp, S. (1993). The Freudian mystique: Freud, women, and feminism. New York: New York University Press.

Slusser, W. M., & Lange, L. (2002). Breastfeeding in the United States today: Are families prepared? In N. Halfon, K. T. McLearn, & M. A. Schuster (Eds.), Child rearing in America: Challenges facing parents with young children (pp. 178–216). New York: Cambridge University Press.

Smetana, J. G. (1996, August). Autonomy and authority in adolescent-parent relationships. Paper presented at the International Society for the Study of Behavioral Development Conference, Quebec City, Canada.

Smetana, J. G., Daddis, C., & Chuang, S. S. (2003). "Clean your room!" A longitudinal investigation of adolescent-parent conflict and conflict resolution in middle-class African American families. Journal of Adolescent Research, 18, 631–650.

Smetana, J. G., Metzger, A., & Campione-Barr, N. (2004). African American late adolescents' relationships with parents: Development transitions and longitudinal patterns. Child Development, 75, 1–16.

Smiler, A. P. (2004). Thirty years after the discovery of gender: Psychological concepts and measures of masculinity. Sex Roles, 50, 15–26.

Smith, B. G. (2004). Introduction. In B. G. Smith & B. Hutchison (Eds.), Gendering disability (pp. 1–7). New Brunswick, NJ: Rutgers University Press.

Smith, B. G., & Hutchison, B. (Eds.). (2004). Gendering disability. New Brunswick, NJ: Rutgers University Press.

Smith, C. A. (2004). Women, weight, and body image. In J. C. Chrisler, P. Rozee, & C. Golden (Eds.), Lectures on the psychology of women (3rd ed., pp. 77–93). New York: McGraw-Hill.

Smith, C. A., & Stillman, S. (2002). What do women want? The effects of gender and sexual orientation on the desirability of physical attributes in the personal ads of women. Sex Roles, 46, 337–342.

Smith, C. J., Noll, J. A., & Bryant, J. B. (1999). The effect of social context on gender self-concept. Sex Roles, 40, 499–512.

Smith, G. J. (1985). Facial and full-length ratings of attractiveness related to the social interactions of young children. Sex Roles, 12, 287–293.

Smith, J. L. (2004). Understanding the process of stereotype threat: A review of mediational variables and new performance goal directions. Educational Psychology Review, 16, 177–206.

Smith, J. L., Morgan, C. L., & White, P. H. (2005). Investigating a measure of computer technology domain identification: A tool for understanding gender differences and stereotypes. Educational and Psychological Measurement, 65, 336–355.

Smith, J. L., & White, P. H. (2002). An examination of implicitly activated, explicitly activated, and nullified stereotypes on mathematical performance: It's not just a woman's issue. Sex Role, 47, 179–191.

Smith, L. (2005). Psychotherapy, classism, and the poor: Conspicuous by their absence. American Psychologist, 60, 687–696.

Smith, O. C. (2006). Guide to graduate work in women's and gender studies (4th ed.). College Park, MD: National Women's Studies Association.

Smith, P. K., & Drew, L. M. (2002). Grandparenthood. In M. H. Bornstein (Ed.), Handbook of parenting (2nd ed., Vol. 3, pp. 141–172). Mahwah, NJ: Erlbaum.

Smith, S. D. (2004). Sexually under-represented youth: Understanding gay, lesbian, bisexual, transgendered, and questioning (GLBT-Q) youth. In J. L. Chin (Ed.), *The psychology of prejudice and discrimination* (Vol. 3, pp. 151–199). Westport, CT: Praeger.

Smith, S. E., & Huston, T. L. (2004). How and why marriages change over time: Shifting patterns of companionship. In R. D. Conger, F. O. Lorenz, & K. A. S. Wickrama (Eds.), *Continuity and change in family relationships* (pp. 145–180). Mahwah, NJ: Erlbaum.

Smith, T. J., Ellis, B. R., & Brownlow, S. (2001, March). *Does science interest negatively influence perceptions of women?* Paper presented at the annual meeting of the Southeastern Psychological Association, Atlanta, GA.

Smock, P. J., & Gupta, S. (2002). Cohabitation in contemporary North America. In A. Booth & A. C. Crouter (Eds.), *Just living together* (pp. 53–84). Mahwah, NJ: Erlbaum.

Smolak, L. (2006). Body image. In J. Worell & C. D. Goodheart (Eds.), *Handbook of girls' and women's psychological health: Gender and well-being across the life span* (pp. 69–76). New York: Oxford University Press.

Smolak, L., & Levine, M. P. (2001). Body image in children. In J. K. Thompson & L. Smolak (Eds.), *Body image, eating disorders, and obesity in youth* (pp. 41–66). Washington, DC: American Psychological Association.

Smolak, L., & Striegel-Moore, R. H. (2001). Body-image concerns. In J. Worell (Ed.), *Encyclopedia of women and gender* (pp. 201–210). San Diego: Academic Press.

Sneed, J. R., & Whitbourne, S. K. (2005). Models of the aging self. *Journal of Social Issues, 61,* 375–388.

Snowden, L. R., & Yamada, A. (2005). Cultural differences in access to care. *Annual Review of Clinical Psychology, 1,* 143–166.

Snyder, S. L., Brueggemann, B. J., & Garland-Thomson, R. (Eds.). (2002). *Disability studies.* New York: Modern Language Association of America.

Society for the Psychological Study of Men and Masculinity (2006). *Mission statement.* Retrieved April 27, 2006 from http://www.apa.org/divisions/div51/

Society for Women's Health Research. (2006). *Homepage.* Retrieved June 22, 2006 from http://www.womenshealthresearch.org/site/PageServer

Soet, J. E., Brack, G. A., & Dilorio, C. (2003). Prevalence and predictors of women's experience of psychological trauma during childbirth. *Birth, 30,* 36–46.

Sohn, A. (2005, January 3). Obstacle course. *New York Magazine,* p. 58.

Sohn, D. (1982). Sex differences in achievement self-attributions: An effect-size analysis. *Sex Roles, 8,* 345–357.

Solheim, B. O. (2000). *On top of the world: Women's political leadership in Scandinavia and beyond.* Westport, CT: Greenwood Press.

Solomon, C. G., & Dluhy, R. G. (2003). Rethinking postmenopausal hormone therapy. *New England Journal of Medicine, 348,* 579–580.

Sommer, B. (2001). Menopause. In J. Worell (Ed.), *Encyclopedia of women and gender* (pp. 729–738). San Diego: Academic Press.

Sommer, B., et al. (1999). Attitudes toward menopause and aging across ethnic/racial groups. *Psychosomatic Medicine, 61,* 868–875.

Sommers-Flanagan, J., & Sommers-Flanagan, R. (2003). *Clinical interviewing* (3rd ed.). New York: Wiley.

Song, H. (2001). The mother-daughter relationship as a resource for Korean women's career aspirations. *Sex Roles, 44,* 79–97.

Spelke, E. S. (2005). Sex differences in intrinsic aptitude for mathematics and science? A critical review. *American Psychologist, 60,* 950–958.

Spencer, J. M., Zimet, G. G., Aalsma, M. C., & Orr, D. P. (2002). Self-esteem as a predictor of initiation of coitus in early adolescents. *Pediatrics, 109,* 581–584.

Spiegel, A. (2005, January 3). The dictionary of disorder. *New Yorker,* pp. 56–63.

Spira, J. L., & Reed, G. M. (2003). *Group psychotherapy for women with breast cancer.* Washington, DC: American Psychological Association.

Spotlight on Canada. (2000, Summer). *Advances in Family-Centered Care, 6,* 26–29.

Sprecher, S., & Sedikides, C. (1993). Gender differences in perceptions of emotionality: The case of close heterosexual relationships. *Sex Roles, 28,* 511–530.

Sprecher, S., Sullivan, Q., & Hatfield, E. (1994). Mate selection preferences: Gender differences examined in a national sample. *Journal of Personality and Social Psychology, 66,* 1074–1080.

Springen, K. (2004, May 10). Women, cigarettes and death. *Newsweek,* p. 69.

Springen, K., & Kantrowitz, B. (2004, May 10). Alcohol's deadly triple threat. *Newsweek,* pp. 90–92.

Sprock, J., & Yoder, C. Y. (1997). Women and depression: An update on the report of the APA Task Force. *Sex Roles, 36,* 269–303.

Sramek, J. J., & Frackiewicz, E. J. (2002). Effect of sex on psychopharmacology of antidepressants. In F. Lewis-Hall, T. S. Williams, J. A. Panetta, & J. M. Herrera (Eds.), *Psychiatric illness in women* (pp. 113–131). Washington, DC: American Psychiatric Publishing.

Stacey, J. (2000). The handbook's tail: Toward revels or a requiem for family diversity? In D. H. Demo, K. R. Allen, & M. A. Fine (Eds.), *Handbook of family diversity* (pp. 424–439). New York: Oxford University Press.

Stacey, J., & Biblarz, T. J. (2001). (How) does the sexual orientation of parents matter? *American Sociological Review, 66,* 159–183.

Stahly, G. B. (2004). Battered women: Why don't they just leave? In J. C. Chrisler, C. Golden, & P. D. Rozee (Eds.), *Lectures on the psychology of women* (3rd ed., pp. 310–330). New York: McGraw-Hill.

Stake, J. E. (1997). Integrating expressiveness and instrumentality in real-life settings: A new perspective on the benefits of androgyny. *Sex Roles, 37,* 541–564.

Stake, J. E. (2000). When situations call for instrumentality and expressiveness: Resource appraisal, coping strategy choice, and adjustment. *Sex Roles, 42,* 865–885.

Stake, J. E. (2003). Understanding male bias against girls and women in science. *Journal of Applied Social Psychology, 33,* 667–682.

Stake, J. E., & Hoffmann, F. L. (2000). Putting feminist pedagogy to the test. *Psychology of Women Quarterly, 24,* 30–38.

Stake, J. E., & Hoffmann, F. L. (2001). Changes in student social attitudes, activism, and personal confidence in higher education: The role of women's studies. *American Educational Research Journal, 38,* 411–436.

Stake, J. E., & Malkin, C. (2003). Students' quality of experience and perceptions of intolerance and bias in the women's and gender studies classroom. *Psychology of Women Quarterly, 27,* 174–185.

Stake, J. E., & Nickens, S. D. (2005). Adolescent girls' and boys' science peer relationships and perceptions of the possible self as scientist. *Sex Roles, 52,* 1–11.

Stange, M. Z. (2002, June 21). The political intolerance of academic feminism. *Chronicle of Higher Education,* p. B16.

Stanton, A. L., & Courtenay, W. (2004). Gender, stress, and health. In R. H. Rozensky, N. G. Johnson, C. D. Goodheart, & W. R. Hammond (Eds.), *Psychology builds a healthy world* (pp. 105–135). Washington, DC: American Psychological Association.

Stanton, A. L., Lobel, M., Sears, S., & DeLuca, R. S. (2002). Psychosocial aspects of selected issues in women's reproductive health: Current status and future directions. *Journal of Consulting and Clinical Psychology, 70,* 751–770.

Starr, T. (1991). *The "natural inferiority" of women: Outrageous pronouncements by misguided males.* New York: Poseidon Press.

Statham, H., Green, J. M., & Kafetsios, K. (1997). Who worries that something might be wrong with the baby? A prospective study of 1072 pregnant women. *Birth, 24,* 223–233.

Statistics Canada. (2000). *Women in Canada 2000: A gender-based statistical report.* Ottawa, Ontario, Canada: Author.

Statistics Canada. (2001). *2001 Census of Canada.* Retrieved March 3, 2006, from http://www12.statcan.ca/english/census/census01/home/index.cfm

Statistics Canada. (2002, July). *Changing conjugal life in Canada.* Ottawa, Ontario, Canada: Author.

Statistics Canada. (2004). *Women in Canada: Work chapter updates 2003* (Catalogue no. 89F0133-XIE). Ottawa, Ontario, Canada: Author.

Statistics Canada. (2005a). *Disability-free life expectancy, by provinces and territories.* Retrieved September 16, 2005, from http://www40.statcan.ca/101/cst01/health38.htm

Statistics Canada (2005b). *Life expectancy at birth, by sex, by provinces.* Retrieved August 31, 2005, from http://www40.statcan.ca/101/cst01/health26.htm

Statistics Canada (2005c). *2001 Census: Standard data products.* Retrieved May 3, 2005, from http://www12.statcan.ca/english/census01/ products/

Statistics Canada. (2006). *Women in Canada: A gender-based statistical report* (5th ed.). Ottawa, Ontario, Canada: Minister of Industry.

Status of Women Canada. (2000). *Statistics on women in Canada throughout the 20th century.* Retrieved January 22, 2002, from http://www.swccfc.gc.ca/whm/whm2000/whmstats-e.html

Steeh, J. (2002, Fall). Female faculty report negative climate in engineering, sciences. *Michigan Today,* p. 10.

Steele, C. M., Spencer, S. J., & Aronson, J. (2002). Contending with group image: The psychology of stereotype and social identity threat. *Advances in Experimental Social Psychology, 34,* 379–440.

Steele, J., & Barling, J. (1996). Influence of maternal gender-role beliefs and role satisfaction on daughters' vocational interests. *Sex Roles, 34,* 637–648.

Steele, J., James, J. B., & Barnett, R. C. (2002). Learning in a man's world: Examining the perceptions of undergraduate women in male-dominated academic areas. *Psychology of Women Quarterly, 26,* 46–50.

Steele, J. R. (2002). Teens and movies: Something to do, plenty to learn. In J. D. Brown, J. R. Steele, & K. Walsh-Childers (Eds.), *Sexual teens, sexual media: Investigating media's influence on adolescent sexuality* (pp. 227–252). Mahwah, NJ: Erlbaum.

Steil, J. M. (1997). *Marital equality: Its relationship to the well-being of husbands and wives.* Thousand Oaks, CA: Sage.

Steil, J. M. (2000). Contemporary marriage: Still an unequal partnership. In C. Hendrick & S. S. Hendrick (Eds.), *Close relationships: A sourcebook* (pp. 125–136). Thousand Oaks, CA: Sage.

Steil, J. M. (2001a). Family forms and member well-being: A research agenda for the decade of behavior. *Psychology of Women Quarterly, 25,* 344–363.

Steil, J. M. (2001b). Marriage: Still "his" and "hers"? In J. Worell (Ed.), *Encyclopedia of women and gender* (pp. 677–686). San Diego: Academic Press.

Steil, J. M., McGann, V. L., & Kahn, A. S. (2001). Entitlement. In J. Worell (Ed.), *Encyclopedia of women and gender* (pp. 403–410). San Diego: Academic Press.

Stein, M. D., et al. (1998). Sexual ethics: Disclosure of HIV-positive status to partners. *Archives of Internal Medicine, 158,* 253–257.

Steinberg, L., & Morris, A. S. (2001). Adolescent development. *Annual Review of Psychology, 52,* 83–110.

Steinpreis, R. H., Anders, K. A., & Ritzke, D. (1999). The impact of gender on the review of the curricula vitae of job applicants and tenure candidates: A national empirical study. *Sex Roles, 41,* 509–528.

Stephenson, J. (2000). *Women's roots: The history of women in Western civilization* (5th ed.). Fullerton, CA: Diemer, Smith Publishing.

Steptoe, A., & Wardle, J. (2004). Health-related behaviour: Prevalence and links with disease. In A. Kaptein & J. Weinman (Eds.), *Health psychology* (pp. 22–51). Malden, MA: Blackwell.

Stern, M., & Karraker, M. K. (1989). Sex stereotyping of infants: A review of gender labeling studies. *Sex Roles, 20*, 501–522.

Sternberg, R. J. (1998). *Cupid's arrow: The course of love through time*. New York: Cambridge University Press.

Stewart, A. J. (1998). Doing personality research: How can feminist theories help? In B. M. Clinchy & J. K. Norem (Eds.), *The gender and psychology reader* (pp. 54–77). New York: New York University Press.

Stewart, A. J., & McDermott, C. (2004). Gender in psychology. *Annual Review of Psychology, 55*, 519–544.

Stewart, A. J., Ostrove, J. M., & Helson, R. (2001). Middle aging in women: Patterns of personality change from the 30s to the 50s. *Journal of Adult Development, 8*, 23–37.

Stewart, A. J., & Vandewater, E. A. (1999). "If I had it to do over again": Midlife review, midcourse corrections, and women's well-being in midlife. *Journal of Personality and Social Psychology, 76*, 270–283.

Stewart, D. E., & Robinson, G. E. (2001). Eating disorders and reproduction. In N. L. Stotland & D. E. Stewart (Eds.), *Psychological aspects of women's health care* (pp. 441–456). Washington, DC: American Psychiatric Press.

Stewart, M. (1998). Gender issues in physics education. *Educational Research, 40*, 283–293.

Stewart, S., & Jambunathan, J. (1996). Hmong women and postpartum depression. *Health Care for Women International, 17*, 319–330.

Stewart, S. H., & Israeli, A. L. (2002). Substance abuse and co-occurring psychiatric disorders in victims of intimate violence. In C. Wekerle & A. Wall (Eds.), *The violence and addiction equation* (pp. 98–

122). New York: Brunner-Routledge.

Stewart, T. L., & Vassar, P. M. (2000). The effect of occupational status cues on memory for male and female targets. *Psychology of Women Quarterly, 24*, 161–169.

Stewart, T. L., Vassar, P. M., Sanchez, D. T., & David, S. E. (2000). Attitude toward women's societal roles moderates the effect of gender cues on target individuation. *Journal of Personality and Social Psychology, 79*, 143–157.

Stice, E. (2002). Risk and maintenance factors for eating pathology: A meta-analytic review. *Psychological Bulletin, 128*, 825–848.

Stice, E. (2003). Puberty and body image. In C. Hayward (Ed.), *Gender differences at puberty* (pp. 61–76). New York: Cambridge University Press.

Stohs, J. H. (2000). Multicultural women's experience of household labor, conflicts, and equity. *Sex Roles, 42*, 339–361.

Stoler, L., Quina, K., DePrince, A. P., & Freyd, J. J. (2001). Recovered memories. In J. Worell (Ed.), *Encyclopedia of women and gender* (pp. 905–917). San Diego: Academic Press.

Stout, K., & Dello Buono, R. A. (1996). Birth control and development in three Latin American countries. In P. J. Dubeck & K. Borman (Eds.), *Women and work: A handbook* (pp. 505–509). New York: Garland.

Straus, M. A. (2005). Women's violence toward men is a serious social problem. In D. R. Loseke, R. J. Gelles, & M. M. Cavanaugh (Eds.), *Current controversies on family violence* (2nd ed., pp. 55–77). Thousand Oaks, CA: Sage.

Strauss, S. (2003). Sexual harassment in K-12. In M. A. Paludi & C. A. Paludi (Eds.), *Academic and workplace sexual harassment* (pp. 175–198). Westport, CT: Praeger.

Street, S., Kimmel, E. B., & Kromrey, J. D. (1995). Revisiting university student gender role perceptions. *Sex Roles, 33*, 183–201.

Streissguth, A. P., et al. (1999). The long-term neurocognitive conse-

quences of prenatal alcohol exposure: A 14-year study. *Psychological Science, 10*, 186–190.

Streit, U., & Tanguay, Y. (1994). Professional achievement, personality characteristics, and professional women's self-esteem. In J. Gallivan, S. D. Crozier, & V. M. Lalande (Eds.), *Women, girls, and achievement* (pp. 63–75). North York, Canada: Captus University Publications.

Striegel-Moore, R. H., et al. (2003). Eating disorders in white and black women. *American Journal of Psychiatry, 160*, 1326–1331.

Strober, M. H. (2003). Rethinking economics through a feminist lens. In E. Mutari & D. M. Figart (Eds.), *Women and the economy* (pp. 5–12). Armonk, NY: M. E. Sharpe.

Stroebe, M., Schut, H., & Stroebe, W. (2005). Attachment in coping with bereavement: A theoretical integration. *Review of General Psychology, 9*, 48–66.

Strouse, J. (1999, August 16). She got game. *New Yorker*, pp. 36–40.

Stumpf, H. (1995). Gender differences in performance on tests of cognitive abilities: Experimental design issues and empirical results. *Learning and Individual Differences, 7*, 275–287.

Stumpf, H., & Stanley, J. C. (1998). Stability and change in gender-related differences on the College Board Advanced Placement and Achievement Tests. *Current Directions in Psychological Science, 7*, 192–196.

Subrahmanyam, K., Greenfield, P. M., Kraut, R., & Gross, E. (2002). The impact of computer use on children's and adolescents' development. In S. L. Calvert, A. B. Jordan, & R. R. Cocking (Eds.), *Children in the digital age: Influence of electronic media on development* (pp. 3–33). Westport, CT: Praeger.

Sue, D. W. (2004). Whiteness and ethnocentric monoculturalism: Making the "invisible" visible. *American Psychologist, 59*, 761–769.

Sue, D. W., & Sue, D. (2003). *Counseling the culturally diverse: Theory and practice* (4th ed.). New York: Wiley.

Sugihara, Y., & Katsurada, E. (1999). Masculinity and femininity in Japanese culture: A pilot study. *Sex Roles, 40,* 635–646.

Sugihara, Y., & Katsurada, E. (2000). Gender-role personality traits in Japanese culture. *Psychology of Women Quarterly, 24,* 309–318.

Sugihara, Y., & Warner, J. A. (1999). Endorsements by Mexican-Americans of the Bem Sex-Role Inventory: Cross-ethnic comparison. *Psychological Reports, 85,* 201–211.

Sullivan, C. M. (2006). Interventions to address intimate partner violence: The current state of the field. In J. R. Lutzker (Ed.), *Preventing violence: Research and evidence-based intervention strategies* (pp. 195–212). Washington, DC: American Psychological Association.

Sullivan, M. (2004). *The family of woman: Lesbian mothers, their children, and the undoing of gender.* Berkeley: University of California Press.

Sullivan, N. (2003). Academic constructions of "White trash," or how to insult poor people without really trying. In V. C. Adair & S. L. Dahlberg (Eds.), *Reclaiming class: Women, poverty, and the promise of higher education in America* (pp. 53–66). Philadelphia: Temple University Press.

Sullivan, P. F. (2002). Course and outcome of anorexia nervosa and bulimia nervosa. In C. G. Fairburn & K. D. Brownell (Eds.), *Eating disorders and obesity: A comprehensive handbook* (2nd ed., pp. 226–230). New York: Guilford.

Summers, L. (2005, January 14). *Remarks at NBER conference on diversifying the science and engineering workforce.* Retrieved June 7, 2006 from http://www.president.harvard.edu/speeches/2005/nber.html

Summers-Effler, E. (2004). Little girls in women's bodies: Social interaction and the strategizing of early breast development. *Sex Roles, 51,* 29–44.

Surra, C. A., Gray, C. R., Cottle, N., & Boettcher, T. M. J. (2004). Research on mate selection and premarital relationships: What do we really know? In A. L. Vangelisti (Ed.), *Handbook of family communication* (pp. 53–82). Mahwah, NJ: Erlbaum.

Susin, L. R. O., et al. (1999). Does parental breastfeeding knowledge increase breastfeeding rates? *Birth, 26,* 149–156.

Susskind, J. E. (2003). Children's perception of gender-based illusory correlations: Enhancing pre-existing relationships between gender and behavior. *Sex Roles, 48,* 483–494.

Sutton, C. T., & Broken Nose, M. A. (2005). American Indian families: An overview. In M. McGoldrick, J. Giordano, & N. Garcia-Preto (Eds.), *Ethnicity and family therapy* (3rd ed., pp. 43–54). New York: Guilford.

Sutton, M. J., Brown, J. D., Wilson, K. M., & Klein, J. D. (2002). Shaking the tree of knowledge for forbidden fruit: Where adolescents learn about sexuality and contraception. In J. D. Brown, J. R. Steele, & K. Walsh-Childers (Eds.), *Sexual teens, sexual media: Investigating media's influence on adolescent sexuality* (pp. 25–55). Mahwah, NJ: Erlbaum.

Swanson, D. H., & Johnston, D. D. (2003). Mothering in the ivy tower: Interviews with academic mothers. *Journal of the Association for Research on Mothering, 5,* 63–75.

Swearingen-Hilker, N., & Yoder, J. D. (2002). Understanding the context of unbalanced domestic contributions: The influence of perceiver's attitudes, target's gender, and presentational format. *Sex Roles, 46,* 91–98.

Sweet, H. (2000). A feminist looks at the men's movement: Search for common ground. In E. R. Barton (Ed.), *Mythopoetic perspectives of men's healing work* (pp. 229–245). Westport, CT: Bergin & Garvey.

Sweetman, C. (1998). Editorial. In C. Sweetman (Ed.), *Gender, education, and training* (pp. 2–8). Oxford, England: Oxfam.

Swim, J. K., Borgida, E., Maruyama, G., & Myers, D. G. (1989). Joan McKay versus John McKay: Do gender stereotypes bias evaluations? *Psychological Bulletin, 105,* 409–429.

Swim, J. K., Hyers, L. L., Cohen, L. L., & Ferguson, M. J. (2001). Everyday sexism: Evidence for its incidence, nature, and psychological impact from three daily diary studies. *Journal of Social Issues, 57,* 31–53.

Swim, J. K., Mallet, R., & Stangor, C. (2004). Understanding subtle sexism: Detection and use of sexist language. *Sex Roles, 51,* 117–128.

Swim, J. K., & Sanna, L. J. (1996). He's skilled, she's lucky: A meta-analysis of observers' attributions for women's and men's successes and failures. *Personality and Social Psychology Bulletin, 22,* 507–551.

Symonds, P. V. (1996). Journey to the land of light: Birth among Hmong women. In P. L. Rice & L. Manderson (Eds.), *Maternity and reproductive health in Asian societies* (pp. 103–123). Amsterdam: Harwood Academic.

Szinovacz, M. E. (2000). Changes in housework after retirement: A panel analysis. *Journal of Marriage and the Family, 62,* 78–92.

Szymanski, D. M. (2003). The feminist supervision scale: Rational/theoretical approach. *Psychology of Women Quarterly, 27,* 221–232.

Szymanski, D. M., Baird, M. K., & Kornman, C. L. (2002). The feminist male therapist: Attitudes anad practices for the 21st century. *Psychology of Men and Masculinity, 3,* 22–27.

Tafoya, N. (2005). Native American women. In M. P. Mirkin, K. L. Suyemoto, & B. F. Okun (Eds.), *Psychotherapy with women: Exploring diverse contexts and identities* (pp. 297–312). New York: Guilford.

Tafoya, N., & Del Vecchio, A. (2005). Back to the future: An examination of the Native American holocaust experience. In M. McGoldrick, J. Giordano, & N. Garcia-Preto (Eds.), *Ethnicity and family therapy* (3rd ed., pp. 55–63). New York: Guilford.

Takagi, D. Y. (2001). Maiden voyage: Excursion into sexuality and identity politics in Asian America. In M. L. Andersen & P. H. Collins (Eds.), *Race, class, and gender* (4th ed.). Belmont, CA: Wadsworth/Thomson.

Tamres, L. K., Janicki, D., & Helgeson, V. S. (2002). Sex differences in coping behavior: A meta-analytic review and an examination of relative coping. *Personality & Social Psychology Review, 6*, 2–30.

Tannen, D. (1994). *Gender and discourse.* New York: Oxford University Press.

Tasker, F. L., & Golombok, S. (1995). Adults raised as children in lesbian families. *American Journal of Orthopsychiatry, 65*, 203–215.

Tasker, F. L., & Golombok, S. (1997). *Growing up in a lesbian family: Effects on child development.* New York: Guilford.

Tassinary, L. G., & Hansen, K. A. (1998). A critical test of the waist-to-hip-ratio hypothesis of female physical attractiveness. *Psychological Science, 9*, 150–155.

Tatum, B. D. (1992, Spring). Talking about race, learning about racism: The application of racial identity development theory in the classroom. *Harvard Educational Review, 62*, 1–24.

Tavris, C. (1992). *The mismeasure of woman.* New York: Simon & Schuster.

Tavris, C., & Wade, C. (1984). *The longest war: Sex differences in perspective* (2nd ed.). New York: Harcourt Brace Jovanovich.

Taylor, J. M., Gilligan, C., & Sullivan, A. M. (1995). *Between voice and silence: Women and girls, race and relationships.* Cambridge, MA: Harvard University Press.

Taylor, L. D. (2005). All for him: Articles about sex in American lad magazines. *Sex Roles, 52*, 153–163.

Taylor, R. L. (2000). Diversity within African American families. In D. H. Demo, K. R. Allen, & M. A. Fine (Eds.), *Handbook of family diversity* (pp. 232–251). New York: Oxford University Press.

Taylor, S. E. (2002). *The tending instinct.* New York: Henry Holt.

Tenenbaum, H. R., & Leaper, C. (1997). Mothers' and fathers' questions to their child in Mexican-descent families: Moderators of cognitive demand during play. *Hispanic Journal of Behavioral Sciences, 19*, 318–332.

Tenenbaum, H. R., & Leaper, C. (2003). Parent-child conversations about science. The socialization of gender inequities. *Developmental Psychology, 39*, 34–47.

Tenure denied. (2005, January). *On Campus*, p. 6.

Tepper, C. A., & Cassidy, K. W. (1999). Gender differences in emotional language in children's picture books. *Sex Roles, 40*, 265–280.

Testa, M., & Livingston, J. A. (1999). Qualitative analysis of women's experiences of sexual aggression: Focus on the role of alcohol. *Psychology of Women Quarterly, 23*, 573–589.

The nation: Faculty and staff. (2006, August 25). *Chronicle of Higher Education* (Almanac Issue, 2006–2007), pp. 23–29.

The nation: Students (2004, August 27). *Chronicle of Higher Education* (Almanac Issue, 2004–2005), pp. 13–22.

The nation: Students (2005, August 26). *Chronicle of Higher Education* (Almanac Issue, 2005–2006), pp. 12–20.

The nation: Students (2006, August 25). *Chronicle of Higher Education* (Almanac Issue, 2006–2007), pp. 14–22.

Thompson, B. (1994). Food, bodies, and growing up female: Childhood lessons about culture, race, and class. In P. Fallon, M. A. Katzman, & S. C. Wooley (Eds.), *Feminist perspectives on eating disorders* (pp. 355–378). New York: Guilford.

Thompson, H. B. (1903). *The mental traits of sex.* Chicago: University of Chicago Press.

Thompson, J. F., Roberts, C. L., Currie, M., & Ellwood, D. A. (2002). Prevalence and persistence of health problems after childbirth: Associations with parity and method of birth. *Birth, 29*, 83–94.

Thompson, J. K., Heinberg, L. J., Altabe, M., & Tantleff-Dunn, S. (1999). *Exacting beauty: Theory, assessment, and treatment of body image disturbance.* Washington, DC: American Psychological Association.

Thompson, T. L., Robinson, J. D., & Beisecker, A. F. (2004). The older patient-physician interaction. In J. F. Nussbaum & J. Coupland (Eds.), *Handbook of communication and aging research* (2nd ed., pp. 451–477). Mahwah, NJ: Erlbaum.

Thompson, T. L., & Zerbinos, E. (1995). Gender roles in animated cartoons: Has the picture changed in 20 years? *Sex Roles, 32*, 651–673.

Thomson, R., Murachver, T., & Green, J. (2001). Where is the gender in gendered language? *Psychological Science, 12*, 171–175.

Thorp, S. R., Krause, E. D., Cukrowicz, K. C., & Lynch, T. R. (2004). Postpartum partner support, demand-withdraw communication, and maternal stress. *Psychology of Women Quarterly, 28*, 362–369.

Thorpe, J. (2005, Winter/Spring). Redrawing national boundaries: Gender, race, class, and same-sex marriage discourse in Canada. *Canadian Woman Studies/ Les cahiers de la femme*, pp. 15–21.

Thorpe, K., Barsky, J., & Boudreau, R. (1998, April). *Women's health: Occupational and life experiences—Women in transition.* Paper presented at the International Research Utilization Conference, Toronto, Canada.

Thrupkaew, N. (1999). Breakthrough against female genital mutilation. In G. Null & B. Seaman (Eds.), *For women only: Your guide to health empowerment* (pp. 1223–1230). New York: Seven Stories Press.

Tiefer, L. (1996). Towards a feminist sex therapy. *Women and Therapy, 19*, 53–64.

Tiefer, L. (2001). A new view of women's sexual problems: Why new? Why now? *Journal of Sex Research, 38*, 89–96.

Tiefer, L. (2004). *Sex is not a natural act and other essays.* Boulder, CO: Westview Press.

Tiefer, L., & Kring, B. (1998). Gender and the organization of sexual behavior. In D. L. Answelmi & A. L. Law (Eds.), *Questions of gender: Perspectives and paradoxes* (pp. 320–328). New York: McGraw-Hill.

Tien, L., & Olson, K. (2003). Confucian past, conflicted present: Working with Asian American families. In L. B. Silverstein & T. J. Goodrich (Eds.), *Feminist family therapy: Empowerment in social context* (pp. 135–145). Washington, DC: American Psychological Association.

Timmerman, L. M. (2002). Comparing the production of power in language on the basis of sex. In M. Allen, R. W. Preiss, B. M. Gayle, & N. A. Burrell (Eds.), *Interpersonal communication research: Advances through meta-analysis* (pp. 73–88). Mahwah, NJ: Erlbaum.

Tjaden, P., & Thoennes, N. (2000). *Extent, nature, and consequences of intimate partner violence: Findings from the National Violence against Women Survey.* Washington, DC: National Institute of Justice.

Tobach, E., & Reed, R. (2003). Understanding rape. In C. B. Travis (Ed.), *Evolution, gender, and rape* (pp. 105–138). Cambridge, MA: MIT Press.

Tobias, S. (1997). *Faces of feminism: An activist's reflections on the women's movement.* Boulder, CO: Westview Press.

Tobin, D. L. (2000). *Coping strategies for bulimia nervosa.* Washington, DC: American Psychological Association.

Todkill, A. M. (2004, April). Me and my uterus [Review of *Am I still a woman? Hysterectomy and gender identity*]. *Women's Review of Books,* pp. 16–17.

Todoroff, M. (1994). Defining "achievement" in the lives of a generation of midlife single mothers. In J. Gallivan, S. D. Crozier, & V. M. Lalande (Eds.), *Women, girls, and achievement* (pp. 96–105). North York, Canada: Captus University Publications.

Toller, P. W., Suter, E. A., & Trautman, T. C. (2004). Gender role identity and attitudes toward feminism. *Sex Roles, 51,* 85–90.

Tolman, D. L. (2002). *Dilemmas of desire: Teenage girls talk about sexuality.* Cambridge, MA: Harvard University Press.

Tolman, D. L., & Diamond, L. (2001a). Desegregating sexuality research: Cultural and biological perspectives on gender and desire. *Annual Review of Sex Research, 12,* 33–74.

Tolman, D. L., & Diamond, L. (2001b). Sexuality and sexual desire. In J. Worell (Ed.), *Encyclopedia of women and gender* (pp. 1005–1021). San Diego: Academic Press.

Tong, R. P. (1998). *Feminist thought* (2nd ed.). Boulder, CO: Westview Press.

Torres, E. E. (2003). *Chicana without apology: The new Chicana cultural studies.* New York: Routledge.

Toubia, N. (1995). Female genital mutilation. In J. Peters & A. Wolper (Eds.), *Women's rights, human rights: International feminist perspectives* (pp. 224–237). New York: Routledge.

Townsend, J. W. (2003). Reproductive behavior in the context of global population. *American Psychologist, 58,* 197–204.

Tracy, A. J., & Erkut, S. (2002). Gender and race patterns in the pathways from sports participation to self-esteem. *Sociological Perspectives, 45,* 445–466.

Tran, C. G., & Des Jardins, K. (2000). Domestic violence in Vietnamese refugee and Korean immigrant communities. In J. L. Chin (Ed.), *Relationships among Asian American women* (pp. 71–96). Washington, DC: American Psychological Association.

Trautner, H. M., & Eckes, T. (2000). Putting gender development into context: Problems and prospects. In T. Eckes & H. M. Trautner (Eds.), *The developmental social psychology of gender* (pp. 419–435). Mahwah, NJ: Erlbaum.

Trautner, H. M., et al. (2005). Rigidity and flexibility of gender stereotypes in childhood: Developmental or differential? *Infant and Child Development, 14,* 365–381.

Travis, C. B. (2005). 2004 Carolyn Sherif award address: Heart disease and gender inequity. *Psychology of Women Quarterly, 29,* 15–23.

Travis, C. B. (2006). Risks to healthy development: The somber planes of life. In J. Worell & C. D. Goodheart (Eds.), *Handbook of girls' and women's psychological health: Gender and well-being across the life span* (pp. 15–24). New York: Oxford University Press.

Travis, C. B., & Compton, J. D. (2001). Feminism and health in the decade of behavior. *Psychology of Women Quarterly, 25,* 312–323.

Travis, C. B., Gressley, D. L., & Crumpler, C. A. (1991). Feminist contributions to health psychology. *Psychology of Women Quarterly, 15,* 557–566.

Travis, C. B., & Meginnis-Payne, K. L. (2001). Beauty politics and patriarchy: The impact on women's lives. In J. Worell (Ed.), *Encyclopedia of women and gender* (pp. 189–200). San Diego: Academic Press.

Treating depression: Update on antidepressants (2004, June). *Harvard Women's Health Watch,* pp. 4–5.

Trépanier, M. (2003, Spring/Summer). Trafficking in women for purposes of sexual exploitation. *Canadian Woman Studies/Les cahiers de la femme, 22,* 48–54.

Trimble, J. E. (2003). Infusing American Indian and Alaska Native topics into the psychology curriculum. In P. Bronstein & K. Quina (Eds.), *Teaching gender and multicultural awareness* (pp. 221–236). Washington, DC: American Psychological Association.

Trotman, F. K. (2002). Old, African American, and female: Political, economic, and historical contexts. In F. K. Trotman & C. M. Brody (Eds.), *Psychotherapy and counseling with older women* (pp. 70–86). New York: Springer.

Trotman, F. K., & Brody, C. M. (2002). Cross-cultural perspectives: Grandmothers. In F. K. Trotman & C. M. Brody (Eds.), *Psychotherapy and counseling with older women* (pp. 41–57). New York: Springer.

Truthout. (2005, May 13). *Developing countries pledge to empower women*. Retrieved May 14, 2005 from http://www.truthout.org/issues_05/051305WA.shtml

Tsai, J. L., Chentsova-Dutton, Y., & Wong, Y. (2002). Why and how researchers should study ethnic identity, acculturation, and cultural orientation. In G. C. N. Hall & S. Okazaki (Eds.), *Asian American psychology* (pp. 41–65). Washington, DC: American Psychological Association.

Tudiver, S., et al. (2002). Remembrance of things past: The legacy of childhood sexual abuse in midlife women. In K. M. J. McKenna & J. Larkin (Eds.), *Violence against women: New Canadian perspectives* (pp. 255–262). Toronto: Inanna Publications.

Turk, C. (2004, April 5). A woman can learn anything a man can. *Newsweek*, p. 12.

Twenge, J. M. (1997). Attitudes toward women, 1970–1995. *Psychology of Women Quarterly, 21*, 35–51.

Twenge, J. M., & Zucker, A. N. (1999). What is a feminist? Evaluations and stereotypes in closed- and open-ended responses. *Psychology of Women Quarterly, 23*, 591–605.

Tyre, P. (2004, April 19). No longer most likely to succeed. *Newsweek*, p. 59.

Uba, L. (1994). *Asian Americans: Personality patterns, identity, and mental health*. New York: Guilford.

Ullman, S. E. (2000). Psychometric characteristics of the social reactions questionnaire: A measure of reactions to sexual assault victims. *Psychology of Women Quarterly, 24*, 257–271.

Ullman, S. E. (2003). Social reactions to child sexual abuse disclosures: A critical review. *Journal of Child Sexual Abuse, 12*, 89–121.

Ullman, S. E. (2004). Sexual assault victimization and suicidal behavior in women: A review of the literature. *Aggression and Violent Behavior, 9*, 331–351.

Ullman, S. E., & Brecklin, L. R. (2003). Sexual assault history and health-related outcomes in a national sample of women. *Psychology of Women Quarterly, 27*, 46–57.

UNAIDS. (2004, December). *AIDS epidemic update*. Geneva, Switzerland: Author.

Underwood, M. K. (2003). *Social aggression among girls*. New York: Guilford.

UNESCO (2007). *UNESCO Institute for Statistics*. Retrieved January 10, 2007, from http://www.uis.unesco.org/ev_en.php?ID= 6116_201&ID2=DO_TOPIC

Unger, R. K. (1997). The three-sided mirror: Feminists looking at psychologists looking at women. In R. Fuller, P. N. Walsh, & P. McGinley (Eds.), *A century of psychology: Progress, paradigms, and prospects for the new millennium* (pp. 16–35). New York: Routledge.

Unger, R. K. (1998). *Resisting gender: Twenty-five years of feminist psychology*. London: Sage.

United Nations. (1995). *The world's women, 1995: Trends and statistics*. New York: Author.

United Nations. (2000). *The world's women 2000: Trends and statistics*. New York: Author.

United Nations. (2005a, February). *Infant mortality rate*. Retrieved July 18, 2005 from http://milleniumindicators.un.org/unsd/mi/mi_series_results

United Nations. (2005b). *World fertility patterns 2004*. New York: Author.

United Nations. (2006). *The world's women 2005: Progress in statistics*. New York: Author.

Uray, N., & Burnaz, S. (2003). An analysis of the portrayal of gender roles in Turkish television advertisements. *Sex Roles, 48*, 77–87.

Urbaniak, G. C., & Kilmann, P. R. (2003). Physical attractiveness and the "nice guy paradox"; Do nice guys really finish last? *Sex Roles, 49*, 413–426.

U.S. Census Bureau. (2001). *Statistical abstract of the United States: 2001* (121st ed.). Washington, DC: Author.

U.S. Census Bureau. (2005). *Statistical abstract of the United States: 2004–2005*. Washington, DC: Author.

U.S. Census Bureau. (2006). *Statistical abstract of the United States: 2005–2006*. Washington, DC: Author.

U.S. Census Bureau. (2007). *Health insurance*. Retrieved January 10, 2007, from http://www.census.gov/hhes/www/hlthins/hlthin05/hlth05asc.html

U.S. General Accounting Office. (2003, October). *Women's earnings: Work patterns partially explain differences between men's and women's earnings*. Washington, DC: Author.

Useem, A. (2005, Summer). Holy radical. *Ms. Magazine*, pp. 27–18.

Valian, V. (1998). *Why so slow?: The advancement of women*. Cambridge, MA: MIT Press.

Van Blyderveen, S., & Wood, J. (2001). *Gender differences in the tendency to generate self-evaluations based on the views of others in the autobiographical memories of events*. Paper presented at the annual convention of the Canadian Psychological Association.

Vance, E. B., & Wagner, N. N. (1977). Written descriptions of orgasm: A study of sex differences. In D. Byrne & L. A. Byrne (Eds.), *Exploring human sexuality* (pp. 201–212). New York: Thomas Y. Crowell.

Van Evra, J. P. (2004). *Television and child development* (3rd ed.). Mahwah, NJ: Erlbaum.

Vangelisti, A. L. (Ed.). (2004). *Handbook of family communication*. Mahwah, NJ: Erlbaum.

Vangelisti, A. L., & Daily, J. A. (1999). Gender differences in standards for romantic relationships: Different cultures or different experiences? In L. A. Peplau, S. C. DeBro, R. C. Veniegas, & P. L. Taylor (Eds.), *Gender, culture, and ethnicity* (pp. 182–199). Mountain View, CA: Mayfield.

Van Leeuwen, M. S. (2002). *My brother's keeper: What the social sciences do (and don't) tell us about masculinity*. Downers Grove, IL: InterVarsity Press.

Van Olphen-Fehr, J. (1998). *Diary of a midwife: The power of positive childbearing*. Westport, CT: Bergin & Garvey.

Van Rooy, D., et al. (2003). A recurrent connectionist model of group biases. *Psychological Review, 110*, 536–563.

Vargas, J. A. G. (1999). Who is the Puerto Rican woman and how is she?: Shall Hollywood respond? In M. Meyers (Ed.), *Mediated woman: Representations in popular culture* (pp. 111–132). Cresskill, NJ: Hampton Press.

Vasquez, M. J. T. (1999, Winter). President's message: Reaffirming affirmative action. *Psychology of Women Newsletter, 26*, 1–4.

Vasquez, M. J. T. (2002). Latinas: Exercise and empowerment from a feminist psychodynamic perspective. In R. L. Hall & C. A. Oglesby (Eds.), *Exercise and sport in feminist therapy* (pp. 23–38). Binghamton, NY: Haworth Press.

Vasquez, M. J. T., & De las Fuentes, C. (1999). American-born Asian, African, Latina, and American Indian adolescent girls: Challenges and strengths. In N. G. Johnson, M. C. Roberts, & J. Worell (Eds.), *Beyond appearance: A new look at adolescent girls* (pp. 151–173). Washington, DC: American Psychological Association.

Vasta, R., Knott, J. A., & Gaze, C. E. (1996). Can spatial training erase the gender differences on the water-level task? *Psychology of Women Quarterly, 20*, 549–567.

Vaughan, K. K., & Fouts, G. T. (2003). Changes in television and magazine exposure and eating disorder symptomatology. *Sex Roles, 49*, 313–320.

Viers, D., & Prouty, A. M. (2001). We've come a long way? An overview of research on dual-career couples' stressors and strengths. *Journal of Feminist Family Therapy, 13*, 169–190.

Vigorito, A. J., & Curry, T. J. (1998). Marketing masculinity: Gender identity and popular magazines. *Sex Roles, 39*, 135–152.

Villani, S. L. (1997). *Motherhood at the crossroads: Meeting the challenge of a changing role.* New York: Plenum.

Vincent, P. C., Peplau, L. A., & Hill, C. T. (1998). A longitudinal application of the theory of reasoned action to women's career behavior. *Journal of Applied Social Psychology, 28*, 761–778.

Vitaliano, P. P., Zhang, J., & Scanlan, J. M. (2003). Is caregiving hazardous to one's physical health? A meta-analysis. *Psychological Bulletin, 129*, 946–972.

Võ, L. T., & Scichitano, M. (2004). Introduction: Reimagining Asian American women's experiences. In L. T. Võ & M. Scichitano (Eds.), *Asian American women: The Frontiers reader.* Lincoln: University of Nebraska Press.

Vohs, K. D., & Baumeister, R. F. (2004). Sexual passion, intimacy, and gender. In D. J. Mashek & A. Aron (Eds.), *Handbook of closeness and intimacy* (pp. 189–199). Mahwah, NJ: Erlbaum.

Vollmann, W. T. (2000, May 15). Letter from Afghanistan: Across the divide. *New Yorker,* pp. 58–73.

Voyer, D., Nolan, C., & Voyer, S. (2000). The relation between experience and spatial performance in men and women. *Sex Roles, 43*, 891–915.

Voyer, D., Voyer, S., & Bryden, M. P. (1995). Magnitude of sex differences in spatial abilities: A meta-analysis and consideration of critical variables. *Psychological Bulletin, 117*, 250–270.

Vreeland, S. (2002). *The passion of Artemesia.* New York: Penguin Putnam.

Wadden, T. A., Brownell, K. D., & Foster, G. D. (2002). Obesity: Responding to the global epidemic. *Journal of Consulting and Clinical Psychology, 70*, 510–525.

Wade, C., & Cirese, S. (1991). *Human sexuality* (2nd ed.). San Diego: Harcourt Brace Jovanovich.

Wade, C., & Tavris, C. (1999). Gender and culture. In L. A. Peplau et al. (Eds.), *Gender, culture, and ethnicity: Current research about women and men* (pp. 15–22). Mountain View, CA: Mayfield.

Wade, T. J., & DiMaria, C. (2003). Weight halo effects: Individual differences in perceived life success as a function of women's race and weight. *Sex Roles, 48*, 461–465.

Wagle, M. (2004, December 20). Abstinence-only: Breeding ignorance. *Liberal Opinion Week,* p. 7.

Wainer, H., & Steinberg, L. S. (1992). Sex differences in performance on the mathematics section of the Scholastic Aptitude Test: A bidirectional validity study. *Harvard Educational Review, 62*, 323–336.

Waldram, J. B. (1997). The aboriginal peoples of Canada: Colonialism and mental health. In I. Al-Issa & M. Tousignant (Eds.), *Ethnicity, immigration, and psychopathology* (pp. 169–187). New York: Plenum.

Walker, A. E. (1998). *The menstrual cycle.* New York: Routledge.

Walker, E. A., Newman, E., & Koss, M. P. (2004). Costs and health care utilization associated with traumatic experiences. In P. P. Schnurr & B. L. Green (Eds.), *Trauma and health: Physical health consequences of exposure to extreme stress* (pp. 43–69). Washington, DC: American Psychological Association.

Walker, L. E. A. (2000). *The battered woman syndrome* (2nd ed.). New York: Springer.

Walker, L. E. A. (2001). Battering in adult relations. In J. Worell (Ed.), *Encyclopedia of women and gender* (pp. 169–188). San Diego: Academic Press.

Walker, R., Turnbull, D., & Wilkinson, C. (2002). Strategies to address global cesarean section rates: A review of the evidence. *Birth, 29*, 28–39.

Walks, M. (2005, February). Womb is womb, but is birth birth? A look at the queer interaction of medical services, social context and identity understandings in Canadian birthing experiences. *Canadian Woman Studies/Les cahiers de la femme,* pp. 68–73.

Wallace, H. (1999). *Family violence: Legal, medical, and social perspectives* (2nd ed.). Boston: Allyn & Bacon.

Walley, C. J. (2002). Searching for "voices": Feminism, anthropology, and the global debate over female genital operations. In S. M. James & C. C. Robertson (Eds.), *Genital cutting and transnational sisterhood* (pp. 17–53). Urbana: University of Illinois Press.

Walsh, M. (1999, Summer). Working past age 65. *Perspectives*, pp. 16–20.

Walsh, M. R. (1977). *Doctors wanted: No women need apply*. New Haven, CT: Yale University Press.

Walsh, M. R. (1987). Introduction. In M. R. Walsh (Ed.), *The psychology of women: Ongoing debates* (pp. 1–15). New Haven, CT: Yale University Press.

Walsh, M. R. (1990). Women in medicine since Flexner. *New York State Journal of Medicine, 90*, 302–308.

Walsh-Childers, K., Gotthoffer, A., & Lepre, C. R. (2002). From "just the facts" to "downright salacious": Teens' and women's magazine coverage of sex and sexual health. In J. D. Brown, J. R. Steele, & K. Walsh-Childers (Eds.), *Sexual teens, sexual media: Investigating media's influence on adolescent sexuality* (pp. 153–171). Mahwah, NJ: Erlbaum.

Walters, K. L., & Simoni, J. M. (1993). Lesbian and gay male group identity attitudes and self-esteem: Implications for counseling. *Journal of Counseling Psychology, 40*, 94–99.

Walton, M. D., et al. (1988). Physical stigma and the pregnancy role: Receiving help from strangers. *Sex Roles, 18*, 323–331.

Wang, S., Chen, C., Chin, C., & Lee, S. (2005). Impact of postpartum depression on the mother-infant couple. *Birth, 32*, 39–44.

Wangu, M. B. (2003). From curiosity to devotion: The many meanings of Kali. *Manushi*, Issue 134, pp. 14–18.

Ward, C. A. (2000). Models and measurements of psychological androgyny: A cross-cultural extension of theory and research. *Sex Roles, 43*, 529–552.

Ward, L. M. (1999). [Review of the book *The two sexes: Growing up apart, coming together.*] *Sex Roles, 40*, 657–659.

Warin, J. (2000). The attainment of self-consistency through gender in young children. *Sex Roles, 42*, 209–230.

Warner, J. (2005, February 21). The myth of the perfect mother. *Newsweek*, pp. 42–47.

Warner, J., Weber, T. R., & Albanes, R. (1999). "Girls are retarded when they're stoned": Marijuana and the construction of gender roles among adolescent females. *Sex Roles, 40*, 25–43.

Warner, L., & Shields, S. A. (2007). The perception of crying in women and men: Angry tears, sad tears, and the "right way" to weep. In U. Hess & P. Philippot (Eds.), *Group dynamics and emotional expression*. New York: Cambridge University Press.

Warren, E., & Tyagi, A. W. (2003). *The two-income trap*. New York: Basic Books.

Warshaw, C. (2001). Women and violence. In N. L. Stotland & D. E. Stewart (Eds.), *Psychological aspects of women's health care* (2nd ed., pp. 477–548). Washington, DC: American Psychiatric Press.

Wasco, S. M., & Campbell, R. (2002). Emotional reactions of rape victim advocates: A multiple case study of anger and fear. *Psychology of Women Quarterly, 26*, 120–130.

Wasserman, E. B. (1994). Personal reflections of an Anglo therapist in Indian country. In J. Adleman & G. Enguídanos (Eds.), *Racism in the lives of women* (pp. 23–32). New York: Haworth.

Waters, M. C. (1996). The intersection of gender, race, and ethnicity in identity development of Caribbean American teens. In B. J. R. Leadbeater & N. Way (Eds.), *Urban girls: Resisting stereotypes, creating identities* (pp. 65–81). New York: New York University Press.

Watrous, A., & Honeychurch, C. (1999). *After the breakup: Women sort through the rubble and rebuild lives of new possibilities*. Oakland, CA: New Harbinger.

Watson, C. M., Quatman, T., & Edler, E. (2002). Career aspirations of adolescent girls: Effects of achievement level, grade, and single-sex school environment. *Sex Roles, 46*, 323–335.

Watson, P. J., Biderman, M. D., & Sawrie, S. M. (1994). Empathy, sex role orientation, and narcissism. *Sex Roles, 30*, 701–723.

Way, N. (1998). *Everyday courage: The lives and stories of urban teenagers*. New York: New York University Press.

Wayne, L. D. (2005, Winter/Spring). Neutral pronouns: A modest proposal whose time has come. *Canadian Woman Studies/Les cahiers de la femme*, pp. 85–99.

Weatherall, A. (2002). *Gender, language, and discourse*. New York: Routledge.

Weaver, G. D. (1998, August). Emotional health of older African American women with breast cancer. Paper presented at the annual convention of the American Psychological Association, San Francisco, CA.

Webster, J., Pritchard, M., Creedy, D., & East, C. (2003). A simplified predictive index for the detection of women at risk for postnatal depression. *Birth, 30*, 101–108.

Webster, J., et al. (2000). Measuring social support in pregnancy: Can it be simple and meaningful? *Birth, 27*, 97–101.

Wechsler, H., et al. (1994). Health and behavioral consequences of binge drinking in college: A national survey of students at 140 campuses. *Journal of the American Medical Association, 272*, 1672–1677.

Weedon, C. (1999). *Feminism, theory, and the politics of difference*. Malden, MA: Blackwell.

Weichold, K., Silbereisen, R. K., & Schmitt-Rodermund, E. (2003). Short-term and long-term consequences of early versus late physical maturation in adolescents. In C. Hayward (Ed.), *Gender differences at puberty* (pp. 241–276). New York: Cambridge University Press.

Weinberg, M. S., Williams, C. J., & Pryor, D. W. (1994). *Dual attraction: Understanding bisexuality*. New York: Oxford University Press.

Weinraub, M., Hill, C., & Hirsh-Pasek, K. (2001). Child care: Options and outcomes. In J. Worell (Ed.), *Encyclopedia of women and gender* (pp. 233–244). San Diego: Academic Press.

Weinstock, J. S. (2003). Lesbian, gay, bisexual, transgender, and intersex issues in the psychology curriculum. In P. Bronstein & K. Quina (Eds.), *Teaching gender and multicultural awareness* (pp. 285–297). Washington, DC: American Psychological Association.

Wekerle, C., & Avgoustis, E. (2003). Child maltreatment, adolescent dating, and adolescent dating violence. In P. Florsheim (Ed.), *Adolescent romantic relations and sexual behavior* (pp. 213–241). Mahwah, NJ: Erlbaum.

Welsh, D. P., Rostosky, S. S., & Kawaguchi, M. C. (2000). A normative perspective of adolescent girls' developing sexuality. In C. B. Tavris & J. W. White (Eds.), *Sexuality, society, and feminism* (pp. 111–166). Washington, DC: American Psychological Association.

Wendell, S. (1997). Toward a feminist theory of disability. In L. J. Davis (Ed.), *The disability studies reader* (pp. 260–278). New York: Routledge.

Wenniger, M. D., & Conroy, M. H. (2001). Gender equity or bust! On the road to campus leadership with women in higher education. San Francisco: Jossey-Bass.

Wertheimer, A. (2003). *Consent to sexual relations.* New York: Cambridge University Press.

West, C., & Zimmerman, D. H. (1998a). Doing gender. In B. M. Clinchy & J. K. Norem (Eds.), *The gender and psychology reader* (pp. 104–124). New York: New York University Press.

West, C., & Zimmerman, D. H. (1998b). Women's place in everyday talk: Reflections on parent-child interaction. In J. Coates (Ed.), *Language and gender: A reader* (pp. 165–175). Malden, MA: Blackwell.

West, C. M. (1998). Lifting the "political gag order": Breaking the silence around partner violence in ethnic minority families. In J. L. Jasinski & L. M. Williams (Eds.), *Partner violence: A comprehensive review of 20 years of research* (pp. 184–209). Thousand Oaks, CA: Sage.

West, C. M. (2000). Developing an "oppositional gaze" toward the images of Black women. In J. C. Chrisler, C. Golden, & P. D. Rozee (Eds.), *Lectures on the psychology of women* (2nd ed., pp. 220–233). Boston: McGraw-Hill.

West, C. M. (Ed.). (2002). *Violence in the lives of Black women: Battered, black, and blue.* New York: Haworth.

West, C. M. (2004). Mammy, Jezebel, and Sapphire. In J. C. Chrisler, C. Golden, & P. D. Rozee (Eds.), *Lectures on the psychology of women* (3rd ed., pp. 237–252). Boston: McGraw-Hill.

West, M., & Fernández, M. (1997). *Reflexion Cristiana: ¿Como ayudar a una mujer maltratada?* [Christian reflection: How to help an abused woman.] Managua, Nicaragua: Red de Mujeres contra la Violencia.

Wester, S. R., Vogel, D. L., Pressly, P. K., & Heesacker, M. (2002). Sex differences in emotion: A critical review of the literature and implications for counseling psychology. *The Counseling Psychologist, 30,* 630–652.

Whatley, M. H., & Henken, E. R. (2000). *Did you hear about the girl who . . . ? Contemporary legends, folklore, and human sexuality.* New York: New York University Press.

Wheelan, S. A., & Verdi, A. F. (1992). Differences in male and female patterns of communication in groups: A methodological artifact? *Sex Roles, 27,* 1–15.

Wheeler, C. (1994, September/October). How much ink do women get? *Executive Female,* p. 51.

Wheeler, J., & George, W. H. (2005). Rape and race: An overview. In K. Barret & W. H. George (Eds.), *Race, culture, psychology, and law* (pp. 391–402). Sage: Thousand Oaks, CA.

Whelehan, P. (2001). Cross-cultural sexual practices. In J. Worell (Ed.), *Encyclopedia of women and gender* (pp. 291–302). San Diego: Academic Press.

Whiffen, V. E. (2001). Depression. In J. Worell (Ed.), *Encyclopedia of women and gender* (pp. 303–314). San Diego: Academic Press.

Whiffen, V. E., & Demidenko, N. (2006). Mood disturbance across the life span. In J. Worell & C. D. Goodheart (Eds.), *Handbook of girls' and women's psychological health: Gender and well-being across the life span* (pp. 51–59). New York: Oxford University Press.

Whipple, V. (2006). *Lesbian widows: Invisible grief.* Binghamton, NY: Haworth.

Whitbourne, S. K. (1998). Identity and adaptation to the aging process. In C. Ryff & V. Marshall (Eds.), *Self and society in aging processes* (pp. 122–149). New York: Springer.

Whitbourne, S. K. (2001). *Adult development and aging: Biopsychosocial perspectives.* New York: Wiley.

Whitbourne, S. K. (2005). *Adult development and aging: Biopsychosocial perspectives* (2nd ed.). Hoboken, NJ: Wiley.

Whitbourne, S. K., & Skultety, K. M. (2006). Aging and identity: How women face later life transitions. In J. Worell & C. D. Goodheart (Eds.), *Handbook of girls' and women's psychological health: Gender and well-being across the life span* (pp. 370–378). New York: Oxford University Press.

Whitbourne, S. K., & Sneed, J. R. (2002). The paradox of well-being, identity processes, and stereotype threat: Ageism and its potential relationship to the self and later life. In T. D. Nelson (Ed.), *Ageism: Stereotyping and prejudice against older persons* (pp. 247–273). Cambridge, MA: MIT Press.

White, J. W. (2001). Aggression and gender. In J. Worell (Ed.), *Encyclopedia of women and gender* (pp. 81–93). San Diego: Academic Press.

White, J. W., Bondurant, B., & Travis, C. B. (2000). Social constructions of sexuality: Unpacking hidden meanings. In C. B. Travis & J. W. White (Eds.), *Sexuality, society, and feminism* (pp. 11–33). Washington, DC: American Psychological Association.

White, J. W., Donat, P. L. N., & Bondurant, B. (2001). A developmental examination of violence against girls and women. In R. K. Unger (Ed.), *Handbook of the psychology of women and gender* (pp. 343–357). New York: Wiley.

White, J. W., & Frabutt, J. M. (2006). Violence against girls and women: An integrative developmental perspective. In J. Worell & C. D. Goodheart (Eds.), *Handbook of girls' and women's psychological health: Gender and well-being across the life span* (pp. 85–93). New York: Oxford University Press.

White, J. W., & Kowalski, R. M. (1994). Reconstructing the myth of the nonaggressive woman: A feminist analysis. *Psychology of Women Quarterly, 18,* 487–508.

White, J. W., & Kowalski, R. M. (1998). Male violence toward women: An integrated perspective. In R. G. Geen & E. Donnerstein (Eds.), *Human aggression: Theories, research, and implications for social policy* (pp. 203–228). San Diego: Academic Press.

White, J. W., & Post, L. A. (2003). Understanding rape: A metatheoretical framework. In C. B. Travis (Ed.), *Evolution, gender, and rape* (pp. 383–411). Cambridge, MA: MIT Press.

White, L. (2001). Japan: Democracy in a Confucian-based society. In L. Walter (Ed.), *Women's rights: A global view* (pp. 141–154). Westport, CT: Greenwood.

White, L., & Rogers, S. J. (2000). Economic circumstances and family outcomes: A review of the 1990s. *Journal of Marriage and the Family, 62,* 1035–1051.

Whitehead, B. D. (2003). *Why there are no good men left: The romantic plight of the new single woman.* New York: Broadway.

White Ribbon Campaign. (2006). *What is the White Ribbon Campaign?* Retrieved April 27 from: http://www.whiteribbon.ca/

Whitley, B. E., Jr., & Ægisdóttir, S. (2000). The gender belief system, authoritarianism, social dominance orientation, and heterosexuals' attitudes toward lesbians and gay men. *Sex Roles, 42,* 947–967.

Whitley, B. E., Jr., & Kite, M. E. (2006). *The psychology of prejudice and discrimination.* Belmont, CA: Wadsworth.

Whitley, B. E., Jr., McHugh, M. C., & Frieze, I. H. (1986). Assessing the theoretical models for sex differences in causal attributions of success and failure. In J. S. Hyde & M. C. Linn (Eds.), *The psychology of gender: Advances through meta-analysis* (pp. 102–135). Baltimore: Johns Hopkins University Press.

Why don't I have a boyfriend? (And how do I get one?). (2001, August). *Twist,* pp. 26–27.

Wickett, M. (2001). Uncovering bias in the classroom: A personal journey. In H. Rousso & M. L. Wehmeyer (Eds.), *Double jeopardy: Addressing gender equity in special education* (pp. 261–268). Albany, NJ: SUNY Press.

Wickrama., K. A., Bryant, C. M., Conger, R. D., & Brennim, J. M. (2004). Change and continuity in marital relationships during the middle years. In R. D. Conger, F. O. Lorenz, & K. A. S. Wickrama (Eds.), *Continuity and change in family relationships* (pp. 123–143). Mahwah, NJ: Erlbaum.

Widaman, K. F., et al. (1992). Differences in adolescents' self-concept as a function of academic level, ethnicity, and gender. *American Journal on Mental Retardation, 96,* 387–404.

Widen, S. C., & Russell, J. A. (2002). Gender and preschoolers' perception of emotion. *Merrill-Palmer Quarterly, 48,* 248–262.

Widmer, E. D., Treas, J., & Newcomb, R. (1998). Attitudes toward nonmarital sex in 24 countries. *Journal of Sex Research, 35,* 349–358.

Wiesner, M. E. (2000). *Women and gender in early modern Europe* (2nd ed.). New York: Cambridge University Press.

Wigfield, A., Battle, A., Keller, L. B., & Eccles, J. S. (2002). Sex differences in motivation, self-concept, career aspiration, and career choice: Implications for cognitive development. In A. McGillicuddy-De Lisi & R. De Lisi (Eds.), *Biology, society, and behavior: The development of sex differences in cognition* (pp. 93–124). Westport, CT: Ablex Publishing.

Wigfield, A., & Eccles, J. S. (Eds.). (2002). *Development of achievement motivation.* San Diego, CA: Academic Press.

Wilbers, J., Bugg, G., Nance, T., & Hamilton, M. C. (2003, November). *Sexism in titles of address: Dr. or professor?* Paper presented at the meeting of the Kentucky Academy of Science, Louisville.

Wiley, A. (2004). Abnormal psychology textbooks exclude feminist criticism of the DSM. In P. J. Caplan & L. Cosgrove (Eds.), *Bias in psychiatric diagnosis* (pp. 41–46). Lanham, MD: Jason Aronson.

Wilfley, D. E., & Rieger, E. (2003). Further perspectives on psychological interventions for eating disorders. In M. Maj, K. Halmi, J. J. López-Ibor, & N. Sartorius (Eds.), *Eating disorders* (pp. 353–357). Hoboken, NJ: Wiley.

Wilhelm, K. (2006). Depression: From nosology to global burden. In C. L. M. Keyes & S. H. Goodman (Eds.), *Women and depression: A handbook for the social, behavioral, and biomedical sciences* (pp. 3–21). New York: Cambridge University Press.

Willemsen, T. M. (1998). Widening the gender gap: Teenage magazines for girls and boys. *Sex Roles, 38,* 851–861.

Williams, A. (2003/2004, Winter). Sima Samar. *Ms. Magazine,* p. 37.

Williams, C. L. (1998). The glass escalator: Hidden advantages for men in the "female" positions. In M. S. Kimmel & M. A. Messner (Eds.), *Men's lives* (4th ed., pp. 285–299). Boston: Allyn & Bacon.

Williams, D. R. (2003). The health of men: Structured inequalities and opportunities. *American Journal of Public Health, 9,* 724–731.

Williams, J. E., & Best, D. L. (1990). *Measuring sex stereotypes: A multinational study* (Rev. ed.). Newbury Park, CA: Sage.

Williams, J. E., Satterwhite, R. C., & Best, D. L. (1999). Pancultural gender stereotypes revisited: The five factor model. *Sex Roles, 40,* 513–525.

Williams, M. J. K. (1999). *Sexual pathways: Adapting to dual sexual attraction.* Westport, CT: Praeger.

Williams, S. L., & Frieze, I. H. (2005). Patterns of violent relationships, psychological distress, and marital satisfaction in a national sample of men and women. *Sex Roles, 52,* 771–784.

Willingham, W. W., & Cole, N. S. (1997). *Gender and fair assessment.* Mahwah, NJ: Erlbaum.

Wilson, C. C., II, & Gutiérrez, F. (1995). *Race, multiculturalism, and the media: From mass to class communication.* Thousand Oaks, CA: Sage.

Wilson, C. T., & Fairburn, C. G. (2002). Treatments for eating disorders. In P. E. Nathan & J. M. Gorman (Eds.), *A guide to treatments that work* (2nd ed., pp. 559–592). New York: Oxford University Press.

Wilson, R. (2003, July 18). Strength in numbers. *Chronicle of Higher Education,* pp. A10–A12.

Wilson, R. (2004, July 2). Students sue professor and U. of Texas in harassment case. *Chronicle of Higher Education,* p. A12.

Wilson, R. (2006, March 3). The power of professors. *Chronicle of Higher Education,* pp. A10–A13.

Wilson, S. R., & Mankowski, E. S. (2000). Beyond the drum: An exploratory study of group processes in a mythopoetic men's group. In E. R. Barton (Ed.), *Mythopoetic perspectives of men's healing work* (pp. 21–45). Westport, CT: Bergin & Garvey.

Wincze, J. P., & Carey, M. P. (2001). *Sexual dysfunction: A guide for assessment and treatment* (2nd ed.). New York: Guilford.

Winer, R. L., et al. (2003). Genital human papillomavirus infection: Incidence and risk factors in a cohort of female university students. *American Journal of Epidemiology, 157,* 218–226.

Winer, R. L., et al. (2006). Condom use and the risk of genital human papillomavirus infection in young women. *New England Journal of Medicine, 354,* 2645–2666.

Winerman, L. (2004, September). Back to her roots. *American Psychologist,* pp. 46–47.

Winerman, L. (2005, June). Helping men to help themselves. *Monitor on Psychology,* pp. 57–68.

Wing, R. R., & Polley, B. A. (2001). Obesity. In A. Baum, T. A. Revenson, & J. E. Singer (Eds.), *Handbook of health psychology* (pp. 263–279). Mahwah, NJ: Erlbaum.

Winstead, B. A., Derlega, V. J., & Rose, S. (1997). *Gender and close relationships.* Thousand Oaks, CA: Sage.

Winstead, B. A., & Griffin, J. L. (2001). Friendship styles. In J. Worell (Ed.), *Encyclopedia of women and gender* (pp. 481–492). San Diego: Academic Press.

Winston, A. S. (Ed.). (2003). *Defining difference: Race and racism in the history of psychology.* Washington, DC: American Psychological Association.

Winter, D. D. (1996). *Ecological psychology: Healing the split between planet and self.* New York: HarperCollins.

Winters, A. M., & Duck, S. (2001). You ****! Swearing as an aversive and a relational activity. In R. M. Kowalski (Ed.), *Behaving badly* (pp. 59–77). Washington, DC: American Psychological Association.

Wise, D., & Stake, J. E. (2002). The moderating roles of personal and social resources on the relationship between dual expectations (for instrumentality and expressiveness) and well-being. *Journal of Social Psychology, 142,* 109–119.

Wise, E. A., et al. (2001). Women's health: A cultural perspective. In S. Kazarian & D. R. Evans (Eds.), *Handbook of cultural health psychology* (pp. 445–467). San Diego: Academic Press.

Wise, P. H. (2002). Prenatal care, delivery, and birth outcomes. In N. Halfon, K. T. McLearn, & M. A. Schuster (Eds.), *Child rearing in America* (pp. 263–292). New York: Cambridge University Press.

Wodak, R. (2005). Discourse. In P. Essed, D. T. Goldberg, & A. Kobayashi (Eds.), *A companion to gender studies* (pp. 519–529). Malden, MA: Blackwell.

Wolf, N. (2001). *Misconceptions.* New York: Doubleday.

Wolk, S. I., & Weissman, M. M. (1995). Women and depression: An update. *Review of Psychiatry, 14,* 227–259.

Women in Action. (2001). Violence against women: An issue of human rights. In S. M. Shaw & J. Lee (Eds.), *Women's voices, feminist visions* (pp. 407–408). Mountain View, CA: Mayfield.

Women's Justice Center. (2005). *Women in policing.* Retrieved April 22, 2005 from http://www.justicewomen.com/pw_law_suit.html

Wood, E., Desmarais, S., & Gugula, S. (2002). The impact of parenting experience on gender stereotyped toy play of children. *Sex Roles, 47,* 39–49.

Wood, M. D., Vinson, D. C., & Sher, K. J. (2001). Alcohol use and misuse. In A. Baum, T. A. Revenson, & J. E. Singer (Eds.), *Handbook of health psychology* (pp. 281–318). Mahwah, NJ: Erlbaum.

Wood, W., Rhodes, N., & Whelan, M. (1989). Sex differences in positive well-being: A consideration of emotional style and marital status. *Psychological Bulletin, 106,* 249–264.

Woodzicka, J. A., & LaFrance, M. (2005). The effects of subtle sexual harassment on women's performance in a job interview. *Sex Roles, 53,* 67–77.

Woollett, A., & Marshall, H. (1997). Discourses of pregnancy and childbirth. In L. Yardley (Ed.), *Material discourses of health and illness* (pp. 176–198). London: Routledge.

Woolley, H. T. (1910). Psychological literature: A review of the recent literature on the psychology of sex. *Psychological Bulletin, 7,* 335–342.

Word, C. H., Zanna, M. P., & Cooper, J. (1974). The nonverbal mediation of self-fulfilling prophecies in interracial interaction. *Journal of Experimental Social Psychology, 10,* 109–120.

Worell, J. (Ed.). (2001). *The encyclopedia of women and gender*

(Vols. 1 and 2). San Diego: Academic Press.

Worell, J., & Goodheart, C. D. (Eds.). (2006). *Handbook of girls' and women's psychological health: Gender and well-being across the life span*. New York: Oxford.

Worell, J., & Johnson, D. (2001). Therapy with women: Feminist frameworks. In R. K. Unger (Ed.), *Handbook of women and gender* (pp. 317–329). New York: Wiley.

Worell, J., & Remer, P. P. (2003). *Feminist perspectives in therapy: Empowering diverse women* (2nd ed.). New York: Wiley.

Workman, J. E., & Freeburg, E. W. (1999). An examination of date rape, victim dress, and perceiver variables within the context of attribution theory. *Sex Roles, 41*, 261–277.

World Health Organization. (2005a). *Cancer: Screening and early detection of cancer*. Retrieved September 14, 2005, from http//www.who.int/cancer/detection/en/

World Health Organization. (2005b). *World health report 2005 statistical annex*. Retrieved September 7, 2005, from http://www.who.int/whr/2005/annex/en/index.html

Wosinska, W., Dabul, A. J., Whetstone-Dion, M. R., & Cialdini, R. B. (1996). Self-presentational responses to success in the organization: The costs and benefits of modesty. *Basic and Applied Social Psychology, 18*, 229–242.

Wright, K. (1997, February). Anticipatory guidance: Developing a healthy sexuality. *Pediatric Annals*, S142–S145.

Wright, P. H. (1998). Toward an expanded orientation to the study of sex differences in friendship. In D. J. Canary & K. Dindia (Eds.), *Sex differences and similarities in communication* (pp. 41–63). Mahwah, NJ: Erlbaum.

Writing Group for the Women's Health Initiative Investigators. (2002). Risks and benefits of estrogen plus progestin in healthy postmenopausal women. *Journal of the American Medical Association, 288*, 321–333.

Wu, T., Mendola, P., & Buck, G. M. (2002). Ethnic differences in the presence of secondary sex characteristics and menarche among US girls: The third national health and nutrition examination survey, 1988–1994. *Pediatrics, 110*, 752–757.

Wuitchik, M., Hesson, K., & Bakal, D. A. (1990). Perinatal predictors of pain and distress during labor. *Birth, 17*, 186–191.

Wyche, K. F. (2001). Sociocultural issues in counseling for women of color. In R. K. Unger (Ed.), *Handbook of the psychology of women and gender* (pp. 330–340). New York: Wiley.

Wymelenberg, S. (2000). *Breast cancer: Strategies for living*. Cambridge, MA: Harvard Health Publications.

Yarkin, K. L., Town, J. P., & Wallston, B. S. (1982). Blacks and women must try harder: Stimulus persons' race and sex attributions of causality. *Personality and Social Psychology Bulletin, 8*, 21–30.

Ybarra, L. (1995). Marital decision-making and the role of machismo in the Chicano family. In A. S. López (Ed.), *Latina issues* (pp. 252–267). New York: Garland.

Yeh, C. J. (1998). Ethnic identity development. In T. M. Singelis (Ed.), *Teaching about culture, ethnicity, and diversity* (pp. 165–173). Thousand Oaks, CA: Sage.

Yllö, K. A. (2005). Through a feminist lens: Gender, diversity and violence: Extending the feminist framework. In D. R. Loseke, R. J. Gelles, & M. M. Cavanaugh (Eds.), *Current controversies on family violence* (2nd ed., pp. 19–34). Thousand Oaks, CA: Sage.

Yoder, J. D. (2000). Women and work. In M. Biaggio & M. Hersen (Eds.), *Issues in the psychology of women* (pp. 71–91). New York: Kluwer Academic/Plenum.

Yoder, J. D. (2001). Military women. In J. Worell (Ed.), *Encyclopedia of women and gender* (pp. 771–782). San Diego: Academic Press.

Yoder, J. D. (2002). 2001 Division 35 presidential address: Context matters: Understanding tokenism processes and their impact on women's work. *Psychology of Women Quarterly, 26*, 1–8.

Yoder, J. D., & Aniakudo, P. (1997). "Outsider within" the firehouse: Subordination and difference in the social interactions of African American women firefighters. *Gender and Society, 11*, 324–341.

Yoder, J. D., & Berendsen, L. L. (2001). "Outsider within" the firehouse: African American and White women firefighters. *Psychology of Women Quarterly, 25*, 27–36.

Yoder, J. D., & Kahn, A. S. (1993). Working toward an inclusive psychology of women. *American Psychologist, 48*, 846–856.

Yoder, J. D., & Kahn, A. S. (2003). Making gender comparisons more meaningful: A call for more attention to social context. *Psychology of Women Quarterly, 27*, 281–290.

Yoder, J. D., & McDonald, T. W. (1998). Measuring sexist discrimination in the workplace: Support for the validity of the schedule of sexist events. *Psychology of Women Quarterly, 22*, 487–491.

Yoder, J. D., Schleicher, T. L., & McDonald, T. W. (1998). Empowering token women leaders: The importance of organizationally legitimated credibility. *Psychology of Women Quarterly, 22*, 209–222.

Young, A. M., Stewart, A. J., & Miner-Rubino, K. (2001). Women's understandings of their own divorces: A developmental perspective. In D. P. McAdams, R. Josselson, & A. Lieblich (Eds.), *Turns in the road: Narrative studies of lives in transition* (pp. 203–226). Washington, DC: American Psychological Association.

Young, D. (2003). Insight-oriented psychotherapy. In L. Slater, J. Henderson Daniel, & A. E. Banks (Eds.), *The complete guide to mental health for women* (pp. 327–332). Boston: Beacon Press.

Young, Diony. (1982). *Changing childbirth: Family birth in the hospital*. Rochester, NY: Childbirth Graphics.

Young, Diony. (1993). Family-centered maternity care. In B. K. Rothman (Ed.), *Encyclopedia of childbearing: Critical perspectives* (pp. 140–141). Phoenix, AZ: Oryx Press.

Young, Diony. (2003). The push against vaginal birth. *Birth, 30,* 149–152.

Young, J., & Bursik, K. (2000). Identity development and life plan maturity: A comparison of women athletes and nonathletes. *Sex Roles, 43,* 241–254.

Young, P. D. (2005). Religion. In P. Essed, D. T. Goldberg, & Audrey Kobayashi (Eds.), *A companion to gender studies* (pp. 509–518). Malden, MA: Blackwell.

Younge, G. (2004, May 18). Gay rights leap forward as Massachusetts becomes the state of wedded bliss. *The Guardian,* pp. 10–11.

Yurek, D., Farrar, W., & Andersen, B. L. (2000). Breast cancer surgery: Comparing surgical groups and determining individual differences in postoperative sexuality and body change stress. *Journal of Counseling and Clinical Psychology, 68,* 697–709.

Zandy, J. (2001). "Women have always sewed": The production of clothing and the work of women. In J. Zandy (Ed.), *What we hold in common: An introduction to working-class studies* (pp. 148–153). New York: Feminist Press.

Zarbatany, L., McDougall, P., & Hymel, S. (2000). Gender-differentiated experiences in the peer culture: Links to intimacy in preadolescence. *Social Development, 9,* 62–79.

Zarembka, J. M. (2003). America's dirty work: Migrant maids and modern-day slavery. In B. Ehrenreich & A. R. Hochschild (Eds.), *Global woman* (pp. 142–153). New York: Metropolitan Books.

Zebrowitz, L. A., & Montepare, J. M. (2000). "Too young, too old": Stigmatizing adolescents and elders. In T. F. Heatherton et al. (Eds.), *The social psychology of stigma* (pp. 334–373). New York: Guilford.

Zemore, S. E., Fiske, S. T., & Kim, H. J. (2000). Gender stereotypes and the dynamics of social interaction. In T. Eckes & H. M. Trautner (Eds.), *The developmental social psychology of gender* (pp. 207–241). Mahwah, NJ: Erlbaum.

Zerbe, K. J. (1999). *Women's mental health in primary care.* Philadelphia: W. B. Saunders.

Zhou, Q., et al. (1999). Severity of nausea and vomiting during pregnancy: What does it predict? *Birth, 26,* 108–114.

Zia, H. (2000). *Asian American dreams.* New York: Farrar, Straus & Giroux.

Zilbergeld, B. (1999). *The new male sexuality* (Rev. ed.). New York: Bantam Books.

Zucker, A. N. (2004). Disavowing social identities: What it means when women say, "I'm not a feminist, but . . ." *Psychology of Women Quarterly, 28,* 423–436.

Zucker, K. J., Wilson-Smith, D. N., Kurita, J. A., & Stern, A. (1995). Children's appraisals of sex-typed behavior in their peers. *Sex Roles, 33,* 703–725.

Zurbriggen, E. L., & Freyd, J. J. (2004). The link between child sexual abuse and risky sexual behavior: The role of dissociative tendencies, information-processing effects, and consensual sex decision mechanisms. In L. J. Koenig, L. S. Doll, A. O'Leary, & W. Pequegnat (Eds.), *From child sexual abuse to adult sexual risk: Trauma, revictimization, and intervention* (pp. 135–157). Washington, DC: American Psychological Association.

NAME INDEX

This index includes names of people, government agencies, and organizations.

Anderson, W., 60
Andreasen, N. C., 400, 413, 414
Andreoli Mathie, V., 432, 433, 434
Ang, I., 493
Aniakudo, P., 224, 233, 424
Anthis, K. S., 59
Anthony, S. B., 499
Antill, J. K., 89
Antonucci, T. C., 476
Aponte, J. F., 409, 412
Apparala, M. L., 239
Apple, R. F., 414
Arbuckle, J., 223
Archer, J., 82, 200, 201, 202
Arias, E., 327
Aries, E., 178, 179, 182
Arima, A. N., 45, 46
Aristotle, 39
Armbrister, K., 54
Armstrong, M. J., 480
Arnett, J. L., 361
Arnold, K. D., 129
Arnold, P., 305
Aron, A., 256
Aronson, D., 130
Arredondo, P., 410
Asch, A., 5, 370, 372
Asch-Goodkin, J., 243
Ashkinaze, C., 45
Association for Women in Psychology, 11, 18
Astin, H. S., 132, 133
Athenstaedt, U., 179, 184, 187, 188
Atwater, L. E., 222, 223
Aubeeluck, A., 120
Aubrey, J. S., 297
Auster, C. J., 70–71
AVERT, 374
Avgoustis, E., 250
Avis, N. E., 473

Baber, K. M., 279, 280, 291, 298, 302, 307, 308
Baca Zinn, M., 7, 250, 264, 265, 267, 268, 284, 285, 411, 491, 506
Bachanas, P., 376
Bachand, L. L., 262
Bachar, K., 430
Backus, V. P., 364, 365, 367
Bader, E. J., 316
Bader, H., 387

Baer, J., 151
Bahr, K. S., 481
Bailey, D. S., 12
Bailey, J. M., 279
Bains, A., 229
Baird-Windle, P., 316
Baker, C. N., 300
Baker, N. L., 490
Baker, T. B., 382
Baldwin, J., 51
Ballou, M., 416
Baltes, B. B., 216
Banaji, M. R., 463
Bancroft, J., 305
Bancroft, L., 454
Bandura, A., 84, 85, 86, 87, 89, 93, 105
Banerji, S., 498
Banks, C., 305
Banks, M. E., 370
Bao, X., 229
Baram, D. A., 470
Barbee, A. P., 189
Barber, B. L., 139, 300
Barber, J. S., 318
Barer, B. M., 477, 480
Bargad, A., 125
Barker, G., 327
Barling, J., 133
Barlow, D. H., 390, 391
Barnack, J., 323, 326, 327, 332
Barnett, O., 430, 439, 440, 444, 447–448, 449, 452, 453, 454
Barnett, R. C., 50, 73, 89, 179, 194, 208, 232, 237, 239, 241, 243, 244, 339, 346, 500
Barone, D. F., 65
Barongan, C., 17, 20, 410, 411, 412, 492, 493
Barstow, A. L., 430
Bartell, R., 299
Bartlett, S. J., 344
Barton, E. R., 497
Bartoszek, T. A. R., 449, 450
Bartsch, R. A., 45, 46
Basow, S. A., 28, 29, 63, 66, 97, 131, 134, 223
Basson, R., 293, 307, 309
Bate, B., 182, 183
Bates, M., 449
Bauer, A. M., 371
Bauer, C. C., 216

Bauer-Maglin, N., 467, 468
Baumeister, R. F., 275, 279, 280, 295, 299, 302, 304, 423
Baumgardner, J., 500, 500–501, 504
Baur, K., 78, 79, 114, 116, 294, 297, 298, 308, 312, 324, 330, 442, 443, 471
Bay-Cheng, L. Y., 403
Bayer, B. M., 491
Beach, S., 81
Beach, S. R. H., 284
Beall, A. E., 7, 34, 77, 110
Beals, K. P., 271, 272, 273, 304, 341, 342
Beaton, A. M., 217
Beatty, L. A., 378, 381, 384, 385
Beatty, W. W., 157
Becker, E., 313
Becker, S. W., 176, 191
Beckman, L. J., 265, 349, 350
Bedford, V. H., 462, 469, 478
Bélanger, A., 382
Belansky, E. S., 133, 197
Bell, A. R., 121
Bell, L. C., 85
Bell, N. J., 313
Bellamy, C., 80, 99
Belle, D., 5, 214, 394
Bellinger, D. C., 91
Bem, D., 92
Bem, S. L., 28, 29, 65, 66, 69, 70, 85, 86, 92, 101, 177
Bemak, F., 410, 411
Bender, D. E., 230, 246
Beneke, T., 435
Benjamin, L. T., Jr., 10
Bennett, P., 367
Benokraitis, N. V., 223
Benrud, L. M., 356
Benton, P., 467
Berendsen, L. L., 234
Berenson, C., 277
Berg, F. M., 398, 403, 404, 405
Berg, J. A., 474
Berg, J. H., 171
Berger, R., 213
Bergevin, T. A., 301
Bergman, B., 232, 243
Bergmann, B. R., 235, 236
Bergum, V., 326, 332, 338
Berila, B., 495

SUBJECT INDEX

For names of both people and organizations, see the Name Index.